The Last Lincolns

THE LAST
LINCOLNS

---

*The Rise and Fall
of a Great American Family*

BY

Charles Lachman

UNION SQUARE PRESS

An imprint of Sterling Publishing Co., Inc.

New York / London
www.sterlingpublishing.com

STERLING and the distinctive Sterling logo
are registered trademarks of Sterling Publishing Co., Inc.

Library of Congress Cataloging-in-Publication Data Available

1   3   5   7   9   10   8   6   4   2

Published by Sterling Publishing Co., Inc.
387 Park Avenue South, New York, NY 10016
© 2008 by Charles Lachman
Distributed in Canada by Sterling Publishing
c/o Canadian Manda Group, 165 Dufferin Street
Toronto, Ontario, Canada M6K 3H6
Distributed in the United Kingdom by GMC Distribution Services
Castle Place, 166 High Street, Lewes, East Sussex, England BN7 1XU
Distributed in Australia by Capricorn Link (Australia) Pty. Ltd.
P.O. Box 704, Windsor, NSW 2756, Australia

Manufactured in the United States of America
All rights reserved

Sterling ISBN 978-1-4027-5890-4

For information about custom editions, special sales, premium and
corporate purchases, please contact Sterling Special Sales
Department at 800-805-5489 or specialsales@sterlingpublishing.com.

·

To my wife,

NANCY GLASS

and our children,

MAX, PAMELA, AND SLOANE.

And to my parents.

Contents

Prologue

THE MAIDS AND housekeepers at the Grand Pacific Hotel in Chicago trod warily in her presence, for Mary Todd Lincoln, the most detested First Lady in American history, was notorious for her short fuse and shrewish ways. But to the surprise of the hotel staff, the stout little woman in black mourning clothes seemed pleasant and undemanding, respectful and cordial to everyone. Mary Lincoln did not merely live in seclusion after the assassination of her husband—she lived utterly alone. And this was true of her three weeks at the Grand Pacific. She ate her meals in her six-dollar-fifty-cent-a-night room on the third floor. Her son, Robert Lincoln, was her only visitor.

One afternoon in early April 1875, the manager of the Grand Pacific, Samuel Turner, was in his office when Mrs. Lincoln came in to see him. A shawl was draped over her head and she was urgent in her insistence on speaking to Turner about some noise she had been hearing on her floor. It was a strange complaint, and Turner agreed to investigate it with Mrs. Lincoln. They went up to her room. Turner listened, but he heard nothing abnormal. Everything seemed fine.

Turner left Mrs. Lincoln and returned to his office. Several minutes later, there was a commotion in the lobby. Turner went out to investigate, and he saw that it was Mrs. Lincoln again. This time she was making a fuss about a man lurking in the hallway that she claimed was intent on molesting her. Skeptical of her story, Turner accompanied her back to the third floor, looked around, and saw no suspicious characters. Mrs. Lincoln became "greatly excited," even inconsolable. She could not be quieted. She was afraid of being left alone that evening and demanded that she share a room with another hotel guest. Despite her usual preference for seclusion, Mary now seemed desperate for companionship—even that of a stranger.

Over the next few weeks, Mrs. Lincoln's odd behavior became even more erratic. She was awake most nights. Hotel employees could hear her pacing across her small room. She told a housekeeper, Maggie Gavin, that she could hear voices in the walls. Mrs. Lincoln called Maggie over to the window and pointed to a plume of smoke billowing from a chimney. The city was burning down, Mrs. Lincoln cried out. It was another Great Chicago Fire! One day Mrs. Lincoln summoned a waiter, John Fitzhenry, to her room. She opened the door for him, and the young man was distressed to find her "casually dressed" in a nightgown and in a state of wild agitation. "I am afraid! I am afraid," she bellowed.

If anyone had taken notice of the calendar, perhaps they would have understood what was triggering Mary Lincoln's peculiar behavior. A tragic anniversary was approaching. Ten years earlier, on Good Friday, April 14, 1865, John Wilkes Booth had fired a bullet into the back of her husband's head.

Of all her suitors in Springfield, Illinois, so many years ago, the luminous southern belle Mary Todd had chosen the most unlikely to be her husband. Now Mary Todd Lincoln begged for death to take her. "How I am to pass through life, without him who loved us so dearly," she wrote a friend. "I long to lay my aching head and sorrowing heart by the side of this dearly loved one. When the summons comes for my departure I will gladly welcome it."

It was early afternoon when Mrs. Lincoln heard the knock. Hotel manager Samuel Turner was at her door. Mary let him in and saw another gentleman standing there. He was Leonard Swett, a prominent Chicago lawyer. It was said of Swett: "Of all living men, Leonard Swett was the one most trusted by Abraham Lincoln." Mrs. Lincoln welcomed Swett into her room. And then he got right to it.

"I have got some bad news for you," he told her. "Mrs. Lincoln, your friends have with great unanimity come to the conclusion that the troubles you have been called to pass through have been too much and produced mental disease."

Mary absorbed the words, and then she asked whether Swett was insinuating that she was crazy.

"Yes," Swett answered. "I regret to say that is what your friends all think."

Mrs. Lincoln responded formally, "I am much obliged to you, but I am abundantly able to take care of myself and I don't need any aid from any such friends."

Swett kept his voice low and steady. In his pocket, he informed Mary Lincoln, was a warrant for her arrest. Two uniformed police officers were waiting in a carriage outside the hotel. If she did not accompany him voluntarily, right now, he would order them to handcuff and seize her by force.

"Where is my son, Robert? I want him to come here." Robert Lincoln was a Chicago lawyer. Mary Lincoln thought that Robert would put an end to this outrage.

Swett looked at Mrs. Lincoln, and it was then that he delivered the news that broke her heart. Robert Lincoln was in a Chicago courtroom, at this very moment, awaiting her arrival.

It was Robert who had sworn out the warrant for his mother's arrest.

I.

First Generation

I

The Prince of Rails

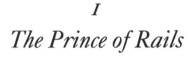

APRIL 14, 1865, dawned brisk and misty when Captain Robert Todd Lincoln awoke in his White House bedroom. His father, President Abraham Lincoln, was already up. On the streets of Washington, even at this early hour, people were hurriedly heading to government offices to start the workday. As this was Good Friday, the church pews were already filling up. Over at the Willard Hotel at Fourteenth and E, General Ulysses S. Grant was getting up, too. Six days earlier, General Robert E. Lee had surrendered at Appomattox. Now General Grant was in the nation's capital to brief the president and take care of War Department business. Captain Lincoln, who served on Grant's staff, had returned with him after a difficult journey from the front lines in Virginia.

The dark clouds of war were passing. Abraham Lincoln's leadership had preserved the Union; slavery was abolished, and now, for the first time since his election in 1860, a certain inner serenity had come to the president. Robert Lincoln found his father in an expansive, even happy mood at breakfast. The president sat at the head of a long table, the First Lady sat on the opposite end, and by her side was Robert's little brother Tad, twelve years old. Robert took a chair next to his mother. Breakfast was light, as was typical among the Lincolns. For the president, it was probably a single egg and one cup of coffee. The president was eager to hear his son's first-hand account of the surrender. He wanted to know his impressions of General Grant and of those momentous last days of battle. Robert presented his father with a spoil of war—a photograph of the defeated General Lee. Mr. Lincoln looked upon the face of this formidable opponent whose generalship had done so much to lengthen the duration of the conflict. He could not help but admire the image.

"It is a good face," the president said. "It is the face of a noble, noble, brave man. I am glad that the war is over at last."

For Mary Todd Lincoln, this was a day of liberation. Now she could at last breathe easily; Robert was home from war uninjured, and they could all turn their attention to the days of peace and prosperity that lay ahead.

"Well, my son," the president said to Robert, "you have returned safely from the front. The war is now closed and we will soon live in peace with the brave men who have been fighting against us. I trust that an era of good feeling has returned and that henceforth we shall live in harmony together." The conversation turned to plans for the evening. The management at Grover's Theater was staging a bombastic, patriotic-themed celebration of victory with songs composed for the occasion. But Mary said she fancied seeing the actress Laura Keene in the comedy *Our American Cousin* at Ford's Theatre. President Lincoln would have preferred to spend a quiet evening at home, but the newspapers were already reporting his expected attendance at Ford's Theatre and he did not want to "disappoint the people" who had bought tickets to the show. Robert was invited but he declined. He had other plans. Plus he was exhausted from his arduous ride to Washington and feeling a little under the weather. Tad complained that nobody was interested in what he wanted to do. It was decided that the little one could see *Aladdin or the Wonderful Lamp* at the National. Yes, that would be perfect for Taddie.

Breakfast was over, and President Lincoln rose from the table and strode back to his office in the southwest corner of the White House. Mrs. Lincoln, Robert, and Tad retired for a chat to the Red Room, on the first floor. At age forty-six, Mary was short and a little round, but still attractive, with rich chestnut hair sharply parted down the middle, blue eyes, and very pale skin. She spoke in the southern accent of her native Kentucky, and she was an incurable flirt. The boys called her "Ma." The president was "Pa," pronounced *Paw*. The Red Room was the Lincolns' favorite in the White House, and they used it as a family parlor. Mary had recently put in an expensive new carpet. The furniture was upholstered with rich crimson satin and gold damask, and in the corner stood a grand piano that Mary's favorite son, Willie, dead now two years, once played.

There were once four Lincoln sons: Robert, the first-born; followed by Edward, who died in 1850 of diphtheria or pulmonary tuberculosis before reaching the age of four; then William; and Tad. Now only Robert and Tad were left. Sitting there in the Red Room, Mary admired her eldest son. He looked so handsome in his captain's uniform. Robert had brown hair, gray eyes, and a round, handsome face. From his father he inherited a manly dimple hewed deep into the chin, but mainly Robert was built like his mother—"short and low," his father once told a friend when Robert was just a toddler. "He is quite smart enough. I sometimes fear he is one of the little rare-ripe sort that are smarter at about five than ever after."

Robert had been born under humble circumstances on August 1, 1843, in the Globe Tavern in Springfield, Illinois, where his parents, too poor yet to afford a home of their own, were living as boarders at the cut-rate price of eight dollars a week, meals and washing included. Four months later, the family moved into a small frame house on South Fourth Street, and the following May, for the sum of twelve hundred dollars, the Lincolns purchased a five-room dwelling at the corner of Eighth and Jackson, close to Lincoln's law offices, and lived there until Lincoln's election.

Mary was a tense, even anxious mother. While a toddler, Robert was playing in the backyard when he climbed into a box filled with lime that was used to sanitize the outdoor privy. Robert grabbed some lime and put a fistful into his mouth. Mary was immobilized with hysteria, screaming, "Bobbie will die!" Fortunately, a neighbor kept her head and quickly washed out the child's mouth.

Abraham and Mary Lincoln were lenient parents. When Robert was disciplined, it was for something serious. It was a chaotic and noisy household, full of great tenderness and loving indulgence. Robert was a solid but not spectacular student, achieving average grades (75 in chemistry, 60 in composition and declamation), but he was ambitious, and in his teenage years became determined to be educated in the East. In August 1859 he set out for Cambridge, Massachusetts, applying in person to Harvard University, already the preeminent college in America.

In his coat pocket he carried a letter of introduction from Stephen A. Douglas, in which the senator from Illinois introduced the young man as the son of his friend Abraham Lincoln. This was generous of Douglas, as it was just a year after the historic Lincoln-Douglas debates. Of course Douglas had defeated Lincoln in the Senate race, so perhaps he could afford to be bighearted. On September 1, Robert took the Harvard entrance examination. He had to translate sentences from English into Latin. Knowledge of Greek was also required, as was geometry, algebra, and basic math. The history portion of the test emphasized ancient times. ("For what do you remember the year 218 B.C.?" The answer was Hannibal crossing the Alps and invading Italy.) Robert failed, and was disconsolate. Apparently, his backwoods education in Springfield wasn't up to Harvard standards.

At least another year of academic polish would be required for him to gain the credentials to become a Harvard freshman. With his parents' approval, Robert enrolled at Phillips Exeter Academy in New Hampshire. In 1859 Exeter had but two instructors and a principal. Tuition was twenty-four dollars a year. In a curious and roundabout way, Robert Lincoln's acceptance at Exeter changed American history. Abraham Lincoln was offered two hundred dollars to lecture in New York City at the Cooper Union, which had been founded by the wealthy industrialist Peter Cooper to offer free education in the arts, architecture, and engineering to the city's poor. Lincoln agreed to deliver the speech because he needed funds to finance his trip to visit Robert in New Hampshire, and New York was more or less on the way. It was also a wonderful opportunity for Lincoln to raise his political profile. Fifteen hundred people gathered in the great hall of the Cooper Union to hear Lincoln's speech on the great issue of the day, in which he urged the nation to "stand by our duty, fearlessly and effectively," and oppose slavery.

The address electrified the crowd, which included the influential newspaper editors Horace Greeley and William Cullen Bryant. One eyewitness wrote, "He was tall, tall—oh, how tall! And so angular and awkward that I had, for an instant, a feeling of pity for so ungainly a man." But once Lincoln started speaking, "his face lighted up as with an inward fire; the whole man was transfigured. I forgot his clothes, his personal appearance and his individual peculiarities. Presently, forgetting myself, I was on my feet like the rest, yelling like a wild Indian, cheering this wonderful man." Lincoln's address was published in several Eastern newspapers and solidified his national reputation. It is an intriguing what-if game to ponder—What if Robert had not attended Exeter and Lincoln had not spoken at the Cooper Union? Could he have ever been nominated, then elected president?

After the speech Lincoln continued on to New Hampshire. He spent the night of February 29, 1860, sleeping in Robert's off-campus room on Pleasant Street in Exeter, sharing the cramped quarters with Robert and his roommate, young George Latham. On Saturday evening, Lincoln was to speak at Phillips Exeter Academy. Local townspeople and most of the student body came to hear him. Lincoln stood to deliver his speech, and the patrician students were shocked at his physical appearance. "Tall, lank, awkward; dressed in a loose, ill-fitting black frock coat, with black trousers, ill fitting and somewhat baggy at the knees." Said one boy, "Isn't it too bad Bob's father is so homely? Don't you feel sorry for him?" And then Lincoln spoke. As at the Cooper Union, the Exeter crowd was won over by the genius of the man. "Not ten minutes had passed before his uncouth appearance was absolutely forgotten by us boys. . . . There was no more pity for our friend Bob."

Ten weeks later, Lincoln won the Republican presidential nomination on the third ballot at the deadlocked convention in Chicago.

It took several hours for the news to reach Exeter. Robert was in a bowling alley when an Exeter student came rushing in grasping a newspaper. "Bob, your father got it!"

"Good," Robert said. "I will have to write home for a check before he spends all of his money in the campaign." It was a pompous crack to make about the triumph of his father's life, but he was a teenager, besotted with the insouciance of youth. Yet in Robert's casual comment, there is evidence of the disdain for life in the public eye that would never leave him.

Presidential elections in the nineteenth century did not involve the children of candidates as they do today, but even so Robert found himself the subject of interest. The American people were getting to know Abraham Lincoln and his family. In 1860, Abraham Lincoln was capitalizing on his humble log-cabin origins and campaigning as the Rail Splitter. Coincidentally, the world's most eligible bachelor was the Prince of Wales, the future King Edward VII. His recent visit to America had been front-page news. To headline writers, the nickname for young Robert Lincoln was irresistible; the Rail Splitter's son was christened the Prince of Rails. When the moniker first cropped up in print, Robert winced and did his best to ignore the hullabaloo of the national political campaign.

The academic year at Exeter had served Robert well; he finally passed the entrance exam for Harvard and gained admission. And like college students everywhere, his world revolved around his own self-importance. The fact that his father was running for president and the Southern states were threatening to secede from the Union upon his election was of less consequence to Robert than passing freshman Latin and Greek. Outside the Lincoln family home in Springfield, on the night of November 6, 1860, an eruption of joy greeted the news of Lincoln's victory. But in Cambridge, Massachusetts, Robert glumly wondered what it all meant for him. In this period, a personality trait became evident that was to trouble Robert for the rest of his life: disdain for the riffraff, an easy irritability. Robert could not let things roll off his back. He bore grudges. And he was getting fed up with all the attention. In December 1860 he wrote derisively to his mother, "Ain't you beginning to get a little tired of this constant uproar?"

In January 1861 Mary went to New York City on a shopping spree. She needed gowns for the inauguration and other social functions. Robert, on winter break, rendezvoused with her in New York. They had not seen each other in eighteen months, and Mary was pleased with this young sophisticate who stood before her. At one of Manhattan's finer haberdasheries, Robert bought a stovepipe hat for the inauguration. He and Mary returned to Springfield together and were met at the railroad station by the president-elect, who had been so anxious to greet the delayed train he had waited at the depot in the snow for three successive nights. When Robert arrived home, his little brothers showered him with affection.

It was only natural that the young ladies of Springfield would fix their gaze on the son of the president-elect, the handsome young buck from Harvard. A dispatch from Springfield by the correspondent for the *New York Herald* read, "'Bob,' the heir apparent to the president-elect, has been the observed of all the observing Springfield girls today." The newspaper complimented Robert for his deportment and Bostonian manners, approvingly noting how it contrasted with the "loose, careless, awkward rigging of his presidential father." The press had sized up the seventeen-year-old and concluded he would make good copy.

The time had come to head to Washington for the inaugural. With alarming talk of assassination in the air, Mr. Lincoln decided it was too dangerous for Mary and the little ones, Willie and Tad, to accompany him. Among them, only Robert was permitted to board the train to the nation's capital. The morning of February 11 was wet and bitter cold as Lincoln bade his neighbors farewell. His trunk, which he had packed himself, was tied with a rope and bore the name tag A. LINCOLN, WHITE HOUSE, WASHINGTON, D.C. There he stood on the observation platform at the rear of the train at the Great Western Railroad Depot in Springfield, gazing out at the crowd of one thousand citizens who had unexpectedly gathered to say good-bye in the rain. The *New York Herald* reported, "His face was pale, and quivered with emotion so deep as to render him almost unable to utter a single word." Lincoln removed his hat and let the rain pour down his face and asked for silence, then spoke from the heart.

My friends—no one, not in my situation, can appreciate my feeling of sadness at this parting. To this place, and the kindness of these people, I owe everything. Here I have lived for a quarter of a century, and have passed from a young man to an old man. . . . I now leave, not knowing when, or whether ever, I may return, with a task before me greater than that which rested upon Washington. . . . I hope in your prayers you will commend me, I bid you an affectionate farewell.

Lincoln's eyes swelled with tears. He disappeared into the car, and the crowd roared three cheers then grew silent as the train slowly pulled out of the station. Lincoln would never see Springfield again.

The president-elect sat alone and depressed in his private car for most of the day, but his spirits lifted when he saw large and friendly crowds lining the railroad tracks. Lincoln settled in for a circuitous twelve-day route to Washington that made no geographical sense but was sound in the realm of political logic. The first stop was Indianapolis. On the train, the president-elect gave Robert the task of holding on to his soft leather briefcase, or gripsack. Unfortunately, Robert took on the assignment with an attitude of undisguised disdain common to teenagers given what they deem a mindless chore. When the train pulled into the next stop, local dignitaries boarded the presidential car to meet Lincoln. Robert was befriended by a collection of lads his age and went off with them for a good time. Just about then his father had an urgent need for the papers in his gripsack and sent an aide to locate his son. Robert was brought back to the train, and his father asked him about the leather case. Robert's response was one of indifference. He informed his father that he believed he had handed the bag to a porter to deliver to the hotel in town where they would be staying that night. Lincoln exploded in anger. The bag, it turned out, contained his inaugural address.

He had written most of it in the back room of his brother-in-law's store in Springfield. It was to be perhaps the most important presidential address ever delivered up to that time, a carefully crafted message of conciliation to the Southern states, drafted to ward off civil war. "I have no purpose, directly or indirectly, to interfere with the institution of slavery in the States where it exists," Lincoln had written. "I believe I have no lawful right to do so and I have no inclination to do so." Although it had not been set in stone and would await the editorial contributions of William H. Seward, among others, it would go down in history as ending with this evocative expression of faith: "I am loath to close. We are not enemies, but friends. We must not be enemies. Though passion may have strained, it must not break our bonds of affection. The mystic chords of memory, stretching from every battlefield and patriot grave, to every living heart and hearth-stone, all over this broad land, will yet they will be, by the better angels of our nature."

It was the language of political poetry, and it was gone. Lincoln was understandably apoplectic. And the manner of Robert's response to the whereabouts of the bag did not improve his mood. Robert, according to one account, answered his father's urgent queries with a "bored and injured virtue." One contemporary witness to Lincoln's fury was his former law partner, Ward Hill Lamon, who was on the train serving as a bodyguard. The barrel-chested Lamon said he had never seen Lincoln "so much annoyed, so much perplexed, and for a time so angry."

"He seldom manifested a spirit of anger toward his children—this was the nearest approach to it that I had ever witnessed," Lamon wrote.

Lincoln enlisted Lamon's assistance in finding the bag, and the two men jumped off the train and went to the hotel. It must have been a comical sight—the lanky president-elect, on his knees, searching through a pile of bags in the lobby. At last, to Lincoln's enormous relief, the missing gripsack was located and the inaugural address retrieved. Thus did Robert Lincoln's career as valet come to an end.

General Winfield "Old Fuss and Feathers" Scott, the first American since George Washington to hold the rank of lieutenant general, was in charge of the president-elect's security. He had determined that the physical presence of Mary Lincoln and the children might actually deter an assassination. Once Mary learned of Scott's perspective, there was no stopping her; against Lincoln's wishes she and the two youngest children were now part of the president-elect's entourage. Mary, Willie, and Tad had joined up with the presidential train.

Robert had several companions his own age on the train, and they were stimulating company. His roommate from Exeter, George Latham, now a student at Yale, was with him. So were Abraham Lincoln's youthful secretaries, John G. Nicolay and John Hay. Elmer Ephraim Ellsworth was also there. Ellsworth studied law in the firm of Lincoln & Herndon in Springfield and was captain of a volunteer military company known as the Zouaves. They wore fezzes and colorful uniforms of red and orange, modeled on those of the French-Algerian Zouaves in the Crimean War. The charismatic Ellsworth was compact at five-foot-six and boyishly charming, with a thicket of curly brown hair and hazel eyes. He was like another son to the Lincolns. Contemporaries describe him as magnetic and chivalrous; Lincoln said of him, "He is the greatest little man I ever met."

Reporters covering the presidential car filed dispatches filled with anecdotal accounts of the impish Lincoln children. After the dry years of the bachelor James Buchanan, the country, in this time of national emergency with the Southern states threatening to secede from the Union, seemed eager to hear about Robert, Willie, and Tad. Tad especially made an impression. According to the *New York Herald*, Tad was a master at pulling off one particular practical joke. He would go up to a spectator waiting to catch a glimpse of Lincoln at a station stop and ask, "Do you want to see Old Abe?" Then he would point to some uncomprehending citizen whom he could pass off as Abraham Lincoln. For Tad and Willie, the trip to Washington was a nonstop carnival of marching bands, big noisy crowds, and patriotic events. A sighting of Mary or the children in the train window would elicit clapping and cheers.

Robert's mood, however, alternated between boredom and bliss. In Cincinnati, a club of young Republicans took him out for drinks and it was dutifully reported the next day that Robert did not suffer from a hangover. But other times he wilted under the glare of the public spotlight. In Indianapolis, Mr. Lincoln gave a speech from a hotel balcony. The crowd wanted more and called for the Prince of Rails to say something, but Robert declined with a dismissive wave of his hand.

The train wound its way through Ohio, Pennsylvania, New York, and New Jersey. During a stop in Philadelphia, word reached Lincoln of a plot to assassinate him in Baltimore, a city of pro-Southern sympathies. Alan Pinkerton, the detective responsible for protecting Lincoln until he reached federal jurisdiction in Washington, advised the president-elect to leave Philadelphia immediately and pass unannounced through Baltimore by night. After some reluctance, Lincoln went along with this plan and secretly boarded the night train to Baltimore, leaving Mary, Robert, Willie, and Tad behind in the presidential car. He even agreed to remove his trademark stovepipe hat and replace it with a soft felt cap, though the six-foot-four Lincoln could hardly be described as traveling incognito. Only Pinkerton, Ward Hill Lamon, and two armed bodyguards traveled with the president-elect.

The train passed Baltimore at 3:30 A.M. and proceeded on to Washington, where, at 6 A.M., the Capitol dome came into view, to the relief of all on board. Lincoln's political enemies later accused him of "creeping" into Washington under cover of night, and Lincoln regretted his decision to follow the advice of his security team. But Mary and the children, on board the train, did have a terrifying encounter when they reached Baltimore. A mob of secessionists boarded and searched every car for the man they called the "black ape," and "that bloody Republican." Fortunately, no one was injured, and a relieved Robert led a chorus of "The Star-Spangled Banner" when the train crossed the Mason-Dixon line. One can only imagine the outcome had Lincoln been on board.

The morning of the inauguration, Lincoln rose before sunrise and reviewed his inaugural address one last time. He and his family were staying in a two-bedroom suite on the second floor of the Willard Hotel. Mary was already awake, having spent a restless night staring out the bedroom window, watching the multitude of people who had come to Washington to witness the historic swearing-in ceremony. Lincoln woke up Robert, Willie, and Tad, and in front of his family read out loud the memorable address that Robert had earlier so carelessly misplaced. Afterward, Lincoln asked for time alone; it seemed somehow appropriate that he should spend these last few moments in solitude.

At noon, President Buchanan arrived at the Willard to escort Lincoln to the Capitol. The two men linked arms, and the Marine band launched into "Hail to the Chief" as the outgoing Democratic president and the incoming Republican climbed into the carriage waiting for them outside the Willard. That day, Washington was a city under virtual martial law. The threat of assassination was real, and troops, cavalry, even sharpshooters on rooftops lined Pennsylvania Avenue and surrounded the Capitol building. As a precaution, General Scott had ordered the construction of a wooden barrier to keep the thirty thousand spectators away from the platform where Lincoln would take the oath of office and give his speech. There had been fifteen swearing-in ceremonies prior to Lincoln's, but this was the first ever for which a physical barrier had been built to separate the president from the people. Given the prospect that Lincoln might be shot at or kidnapped, Mary and the children were advised to stay away, but Mary dismissed the threats, and watched with pride as Chief Justice Roger Taney administered the oath of office.

The Lincolns' new home was 1600 Pennsylvania Avenue. Robert remained there a mere two days. On March 6, the Prince of Rails returned to Harvard. "He is sick of Washington and glad to get back to his college," the *New York Herald* reported.

At the time of Lincoln's inauguration, seven Southern states had already seceded from the Union. A Confederate constitution had been drafted and a provisional president elected. All connections with the federal government in Washington were now severed. On April 12, Confederate batteries opened fire on the Union garrison at Fort Sumter in Charleston Harbor, South Carolina, and the Civil War began. Soon the cry "Forward to Richmond" resounded in the North. The country heeded the call to arms, and at Harvard, sixteen students quit school to join the Union army.

Robert Lincoln was not among them. He had been eager to sign up and do his duty and begged his parents for permission. Privately, Mr. Lincoln agreed that the boy should go to war, but Mary would not have it. She could not bear the thought of losing another son and was unwavering in her determination to keep Robert out of harm's way. "We have lost one son," Mary told her husband, "and his loss is as much as I can bear." During the ensuing four years of war the issue remained a point of contention between Abraham and Mary.

No president could have suffered more internal misery than Lincoln did over the loss of men he sent into combat. A letter of condolence he wrote to Mrs. Lydia Bixby, comforting the Massachusetts mother for the death of five sons in action, attests to his compassion. He tried to make Mary understand the hypocrisy of her position. "The services of every man who loves his country are required in this war," he told her, adding, "You should take a liberal instead of a selfish view of the question, Mother." Mary's favorite half-sister, Emilie Todd Helm, was staying at the White House and overheard one of the frequent arguments the president had started with Mary over the issue of Robert serving in the military. Mary responded in a shaky voice, "I know that Robert's plea to go into the Army is manly and noble and I want him to go, but oh! I am so frightened he may never come back to us."

"Many a poor mother, Mary, has had to make this sacrifice and has given up every son she had—and lost them all," the president said.

"Don't I know that only too well?" Mary responded. "Before this war is ended I may end up like that poor mother."

Emilie Todd Helm was a pretty Southern belle, and she, too, had suffered loss. Her husband, Confederate general Benjamin Hardin Helm, was slain in battle at Chattanooga. Emilie, who lived in Lexington, Kentucky, was issued a special presidential pass allowing her to cross Union lines to attend the funeral, conditional upon her swearing allegiance to the United States government. However, being a proud Southerner, she refused to take the pledge. When Lincoln heard this, he said, "Send her to me." And this was how the wife of a Confederate general had ended up living as a guest of the First Family.

Conversation between the two sisters focused mostly on family matters. They avoided talk of the war. But one night two callers came to visit with Mary—General Dan Sickles, who had lost a leg at Gettysburg, and his friend, Senator Ira Harris of New York. They had heard that a Confederate widow was staying in the White House, and they sought to confirm this extraordinary circumstance for themselves. In the Blue Room, Mary introduced her sister to the two gentlemen, and Emilie gave polite, noncommittal answers to their queries. But the emotions of the time could not keep the exchange civil for long. Senator Harris told Emilie, "Well, we have whipped the rebels at Chattanooga, and I hear, madam, that the scoundrels ran like scared rabbits."

Emilie stiffened. "It was an example, Senator Harris, that you set them at Bull Run and Manassas." Both, of course, had been great victories for the Confederacy, and humiliating defeats for Federal troops.

Mary tried tactfully to change the subject, but Senator Harris turned on her next. "Why isn't Robert in the army? He is old enough and strong enough to serve his country. He should have gone to the front some time ago."

According to Emilie Helm, Mary turned "white as death." As a skilled politician's wife, she understood the need to deflect the controversy. "Robert is making his preparations now to enter the army, Senator Harris. He is not a shirker, as you seem to imply, for he has been anxious to go for a long time. If fault there be, it is mine. I have insisted that he should stay in college a little longer as I think an educated man can serve his country with more intelligent purpose than an ignoramus." Senator Harris was unconvinced. He told Mary, "I have only one son and he is fighting for his country." Then the senator turned to Emilie and, making a low bow, said, "And, madam, if I had twenty sons they should all be fighting the rebels."

"And if I had twenty sons," Emilie retorted, "they should all be opposing yours." After Senator Harris and General Sickles left the White House, Emilie, trembling, ran to her guest room. Mary caught up with her and, through tears and embraces, the two sisters comforted each other.

Robert spent winter and summer breaks at the White House, and his mother also visited him in Boston. But the burdens of the presidency in wartime, plus the physical distance between Boston and Washington, inevitably limited Robert's contact with his father. Robert later said, "Any great intimacy between us became impossible—I scarcely ever had ten minutes quiet talk with him during his presidency, on account of his constant devotion to business." Yet even with the weight of high office, the president always seemed to find time to play with Tad, which perhaps rankled Robert. There was a connection the president had with Tad that he had never had with Robert. Certainly he loved his eldest son, but evidence suggests that he found Robert's personality stiff and boorish.

One anecdote is particularly telling. When Robert was home from Harvard, one night at about 10:00 P.M., he burst into the White House bedroom of John Nicolay, one of the president's secretaries, and, with his face flushed, announced, "Well, I have just had a great row with the President of the United States." His brother Tad had wandered over to the War Department and received a mock officer's commission from Secretary of War Edwin Stanton himself. On the strength of this exalted rank, Tad had returned to the White House and proceeded to dismiss the presidential guards for the night, leaving the White House unprotected in time of war. When Robert heard the story he sought out the president. As he told Nicolay, "Instead of punishing Tad, as I think he ought, he evidently looks upon it as a good joke and won't do anything about it!"

In those college years, Robert and the president exchanged few letters, and most of these dealt with tuition and Robert's allowance. Once Robert asked his father for a political favor, lobbying for the appointment of a candidate for the patronage position of postmaster in Cambridge. Lincoln sent back a scathing letter. "If you do not attend to your studies and let matters such as you write about alone I will take you away from college." Robert learned his lesson, and whenever any friend sought him out for special favors, he would whip out the letter.

Robert was graduated from Harvard in 1864, and it was anticipated that the president would attend the commencement ceremonies. But in addition to prosecuting the war, Lincoln was running for reelection, and he simply could not find the time to get up to Cambridge. Two days before graduation, Robert had the duty of informing the Harvard administration by telegraph, "The president will not be at Commencement." It was a bitter blow to Robert, who, despite an outer shield of superiority, even pomposity, had a sensitive side. Years later it still rankled. "I returned from college in 1864 and one day I saw my father for a few minutes," he wrote. "He said, 'Son, what are you going to do now?' I said, 'As long as you object to my joining the army, I am going back to Harvard to study law.'" The president said, "If you do, you should learn more than I ever did, but you will never have so good a time." Robert admitted, "That is the only advice I had from my father as to my career."

Robert entered Harvard Law School, and soon after, the political damage to the Lincoln administration was becoming intolerable. Letters came to the White House calling Robert Lincoln a coward. Because so many of Robert's relatives on his mother's side were fighting for the Confederacy, there was a suggestion of treason in some of the accusations. Scurrilous and untrue stories circulated, stirred up by Lincoln's political enemies, that Robert had made half a million dollars in wartime speculation. By 1865 the war was drawing to a close, and victory for the Union forces became inevitable. Even Mary, in her borderline hysteria about the security of her eldest son, finally came around. The time had come for Robert to enlist.

On January 19, 1865, President Lincoln wrote a letter to General Grant. First, he asked Grant to read the letter as if it came from a friend, not his commander in chief, and to act accordingly. "My son," the letter began, "now in his twenty-second year, having graduated at Harvard, wishes to see something of the war before it ends. I do not wish to put him in the ranks, nor yet to give him a commission, to which those who have already served long are better entitled and better qualified to hold. Could he, without embarrassment to you, or detriment to the service, go into your Military family with some nominal rank, I, and not the public, furnishing his necessary means?" If the answer was in the negative, Mr. Lincoln assured Grant, "Say so without the least hesitation." Lincoln must have composed the letter with a queasy stomach. There was no question that he was risking political capital in seeking Grant's help.

Grant was a straight shooter, blunt to the point of insolence, but he was also no fool. He did not have to read between the lines to understand what was expected of him. He answered the president with a note—written on the bottom half of Lincoln's own letter. "I will be most happy to have him in my Military family in the manner you propose. The nominal rank given him is immaterial but I would suggest that of Capt. As I have three staff officers now, of considerable service, in no higher grade." It was a good arrangement for Robert: captain in the Union army, on Grant's personal staff. He would be in the thick of history, and probably at no risk to his personal safety. Robert took a leave of absence from law school, and on February 11, 1865, received his military commission.

Just twenty-one days later, Captain Lincoln, in full dress uniform, stood on the platform that had been erected in front of the Capitol building as his father was sworn in for his second term of office. Robert cut a splendid figure in Union blue. His escort for the great event was Mary Harlan, daughter of Senator James Harlan of Iowa. Rain poured down on the assembled crowd, but as President Lincoln turned to deliver his stirring address, the bleakness of the day, as if by a heavenly hand, gave way to sunshine.

"With malice toward none; with charity for all; with firmness in the right, as God gives us the right, let us strive on to finish the work we are in; to bind up the nation's wounds. . . . To do all which may achieve and cherish a just, and a lasting peace, among ourselves, and with all nations." Next to the Gettysburg Address, this came to be considered by many as Lincoln's greatest speech, all delivered in barely seven hundred words of oration. And in the throng of spectators, his black eyes blazing with hate, stood the actor John Wilkes Booth.

The war was drawing to a close. General Lee's Army of Northern Virginia was surrounded. Militarily, his situation was hopeless. On March 20, 1865, Grant invited the president, via War Department telegraph, to visit with him for a personal inspection tour. Remarkable as it may seem today, Lincoln made a family excursion out of the trip, bringing along Mary and Tad for company. The Lincolns boarded the steamboat *River Queen* for the journey down the Potomac River into conquered Confederate territory and the following evening docked at Grant's headquarters at City Point, Virginia. At dawn the next morning, Captain Robert Lincoln arrived on horseback to greet his family. It was a memorable welcome for the young captain; Tad's thrill at seeing his big brother in uniform was boundless. In the distance, cannon fire could be heard, the cloudy sky illuminated with the flash of big guns. This was the bombardment of the city of Petersburg, outside Richmond.

At 8:30 that morning, President Lincoln sent the following telegram to Secretary Stanton at the War Department in Washington: "Robert just now tells me there was a little rumpus up the line this morning, ending about where it began." Finally, Robert was serving his country, and a father's pride was evident in his message. Of course, Robert's function was more public relations than actual combat. His duties consisted primarily of welcoming eminent visitors from Washington and showing them around Grant's headquarters.

Richmond, the capital of the Confederacy, fell on April 3. Six days later, after General Lee found his weakened and exhausted forces checkmated on all fronts, he agreed to concede to Grant's terms of surrender at Appomattox, Virginia. Arrangements were made to meet at the home of Wilmer McLean, a retired colonel who had converted his house into a tavern. Lee arrived first and waited for Grant in the sitting room. Grant came a short time later and told his staff, including Captain Lincoln, to remain outside on the front porch while he spoke with Lee alone. When Grant finally summoned his senior commanders, Robert wisely remained on the front porch. As a junior officer with less than two months' experience in uniform, he evidently knew his place. The other officers entered and found Grant and Lee facing each other in the parlor. The officers arranged themselves against the walls of the room and kept very silent—"very much as people enter a sick-chamber when they expect to find the patient dangerously ill," one witness said later.

The contrast between the two commanders could not have been more stark. Grant, forty-three, was caked with mud after days of hard riding in pursuit of Lee's army, his trousers tucked into his boots and his single-breasted blue flannel coat unbuttoned in front. It was the uniform of a private, the only insignia a pair of shoulder straps that designated his rank of lieutenant general. The vanquished Lee stood six-foot and sat ramrod straight. For this historic occasion he had donned a new uniform and it was buttoned up to the throat. At his side he carried a long sword of exquisite workmanship, the handle studded with jewels. His boots were freshly shined and sparkled with handsome spurs and ornamental stitching. His gray felt hat lay beside him on the marble table, matching the color of his uniform.

As they discussed the surrender, Lee requested that Grant commit the terms to paper. Grant did so and turned the document over to Lee. The pact was made. The two generals shook hands. Negotiations had taken a total of two and a half hours. As Lee waited on the first step of the porch for his horse to be bridled, Grant introduced Abraham Lincoln's son to the Confederate general. Lee looked heartbroken as he mounted his horse. Robert Lincoln stood with the other Union officers and joined

Grant in raising his hat in respectful salute as Lee rode off to inform his army that the war was at an end.

GOOD FRIDAY, APRIL 14, 1865. Breakfast was over, and President Lincoln left his wife and two sons and returned to the business of government. There was an important cabinet meeting at 11:00 A.M. For three hours the president went around the long table soliciting ideas and laying out the foundation of his administration's policy of reconstruction and reconciliation with the South. At 2:20 P.M. Lincoln ate a simple lunch with Mary—probably a biscuit with a glass of milk. Snacking on an apple, he returned to his office at 3:00 P.M. for a meeting with Vice President Andrew Johnson. It was the first time they had seen each other since the inauguration in March—a triumph for Lincoln, and a ruinous embarrassment for the vice president.

Johnson had served as the United States senator from Tennessee, but when his state seceded he had remained in the Senate, which made him a hero in the North and a traitor to his fellow Southerners. In 1864, the Republican Party, seeking to establish its credentials as the party of national reconciliation, nominated Johnson for vice president even though he was a Democrat. The night before the inauguration, as Lincoln put the final touches on his "With Malice Toward None" speech, Johnson was getting drunk. He awoke the next morning with a hangover and a bad case of nerves, which he treated with more whiskey. By the time the inauguration got under way, he was fully intoxicated.

As is tradition, the vice president's address precedes the president's. Johnson took the oath of office and then stood before the assembled crowd of dignitaries and spectators, his face flushed and in obvious distress. They listened in shock as the newly sworn-in vice president delivered his inaugural address with the slurred and belligerent language of a drunkard. Hannibal Hamlin, the outgoing vice president, tugged at Johnson's coattails to urge him to stop. The clerk of the United States Senate, Colonel John Forney, told Johnson to please sit down. Attorney General James Speed held his hands over his eyes in mortification as if he did not want to witness this scene of national disgrace. Characteristically, President Lincoln kept his composure. The First Lady, however, was fit to be tied. At last, Johnson took hold of the Bible with both hands, brought it up to his lips, and said, "I kiss this book in the face of my nation of the United States."

A whispering campaign spread news of the scandal throughout the nation. Johnson was so ashamed he had to leave Washington and hide out at a friend's house in Silver Spring, Maryland, until things settled down. In the Senate, in party caucuses there were private calls for his impeachment, and a resolution was introduced—which everyone knew was aimed at Johnson—to ban the sale of spirits in Capitol building restaurants. Lincoln defended his vice president, but excluded Johnson from all briefings and White House functions. Johnson was not invited to a single cabinet meeting, and sat around Washington waiting for the president to summon him. Finally, that summons arrived. Perhaps it was a premonition that he would not survive his term of office, but Lincoln thought it important that the vice president understand the issues and the administration's policy regarding reconciliation with the South. Lincoln greeted Johnson with a hearty handshake and called him "Andy." No mention was made of inauguration day.

At 5:00 P.M., the president and Mrs. Lincoln went for an afternoon carriage drive. A coachman sat up front; two cavalrymen followed behind. At a trot's pace, the carriage went up G Street and turned down New Jersey Avenue, the president raising his tall silk hat to acknowledge the citizens along the route shouting greetings.

"Dear husband," Mary said, "you almost startle me by your great cheerfulness."

"And well may I feel so. Mother, I consider that this day the war has come to a close." He spoke about the future. After completing his term of office, perhaps they would travel to Europe and then return to Springfield, where he could resume the practice of law. "I never felt so happy in my life," he said.

Dinner was at 6:00 P.M., a cold supper of meat and potatoes. The president sat with his wife and sons. It was the first time the entire family had dinner together in many weeks. Robert was still wondering what to do that night. Tad was all set with the Aladdin show. Lincoln returned to his duties, and was still in the office at 8:05 P.M. when Mary appeared at the door, pulling on her gloves. She wore a pretty bonnet and a low-scooped white dress. "Would you have us be late?" she scolded the president. Tad had already left for the National Theatre, a brisk three-block walk. On the White House front lawn, Mr. and Mrs. Lincoln climbed into the carriage. Lincoln's old friend, Isaac Arnold, a former Illinois congressman, came running up the driveway. He had something urgent to tell the president, but Lincoln sent him away. "Come see me in the morning," he told Arnold. Francis Burns, the coachman, gave the reins a quick flick, and the horses trotted through the White House gates.

Robert decided to spend the evening at home with his closest friend in the White House, John Hay, the president's private secretary. Hay, twenty-six, lived in a corner bedroom on the second floor of the White House—a room he shared with the president's other secretary, John Nicolay. Brilliant, personable, debonair, the Brown University–educated Hay supervised the president's appointment schedule and correspondence. Hay had become almost a surrogate son to Mr. Lincoln, and some historians have even compared their relationship to that of George Washington and Alexander Hamilton. Hay loved the president, affectionately calling Lincoln "the old man" and comparing his wartime leadership to a "backwards Jupiter," wielding the bolts of war and the machinery of government with a bold and steady hand.

The journalist Noah Brooks, a friend of Lincoln's, once wrote, "Nothing is more charming than the story of the relations which existed between these two men, the one in the bloom of youth, the other hastening toward his tragic end." To his credit, Robert was never jealous of his father's fondness for Hay. Robert, too, valued Hay's companionship and sophistication. Hay saw the humor in everything. He also appreciated the ladies, and, when Robert was in town, the two handsome young men cut quite a social path through Washington.

On this evening of Good Friday, John Hay entertained Robert with the latest Washington gossip. They may have studied Spanish together. Undoubtedly, Robert gave Hay his eyewitness account of the surrender at Appomattox. Ninety minutes later, Robert retired to his bedroom. Over at the National Theatre, his brother Tad was sitting in the front row seat, enthralled by the story of Aladdin. Between the second and third acts there was a reading of a new poem, "The Flag of Sumter." Patriotic fervor was sweeping Washington, and Tad was probably thrilled by this tribute to the Union victory. A messenger sent by the White House strode down the aisle and found young Tad and a White House aide in the front row. The messenger whispered something in the aide's ear, and the next thing Tad knew he was being told he had to return to the White House immediately. They arrived at a scene of pandemonium.

At around 10:00 P.M., Thomas Pendel, a Metropolitan police officer assigned to White House guard duty, heard the front doorbell ring. When he opened the door a police sergeant said breathlessly, "Have you heard the news? They have tried to cut the throat of Secretary Seward." Pendel was disbelieving. About half an hour later Pendel observed a crowd running toward the White House. At the head of the mob was Senator Charles Sumner of Massachusetts, coming to inquire whether the rumors about President Lincoln were true. Close behind him was Isaac Newton, the commissioner of agriculture, who confirmed, "They have shot the president." Pendel rushed up the staircase to Robert Lincoln's bedroom, which was positioned directly over the front portico. Robert was now sick in bed, and was about to swallow a teaspoon of medicine when Pendel knocked and opened the door. "Captain, something happened to the president." Robert spilled the medicine onto his night table. "You had better go down to the theater and see what it is," Pendel said.

Robert got out of bed and ordered Pendel to inform John Hay of what he had heard. The guard found Hay in his bedroom. "Captain Lincoln wants to see you at once. The president has been shot." Hay's handsome face turned the color of ash. Intuitively sensing the possibility of a conspiracy, Hay instructed Pendel not to allow anyone into the White House until further notice.

"Very good, Major," Pendel said, addressing Hay by his official military rank. "Nobody shall come in."

A nightmarish scene awaited Robert and Hay as they came downstairs. There was great tumult on the front lawn and wild stories that Secretary of State Seward and the entire cabinet had been murdered. Robert Lincoln and John Hay found a carriage and ordered the driver to take them to Ford's Theatre. They were still disbelieving of the news until they were about a block and a half from the theater, and the carriage tried to turn onto Tenth Street. An enormous crowd was blocking the way and the carriage could go no farther. Now Robert believed that the reports must be true. He and Hay bounded out of the carriage and made their way on foot through the throng until they came to a platoon of Union soldiers standing guard in front of the Petersen House, a private house across the street from the theater, where the mortally wounded president had been taken. The soldiers were under orders not to let anyone pass. Robert told them, "It's my father! My father! I'm Robert Lincoln." The way was cleared.

At the doorstep, as Robert stepped over a pool of blood, his heart sank. Dr. Robert Stone, his father's personal physician, met him inside the house and briefed him on the crisis. He reported that, at twelve minutes after ten, the president had been shot with a single bullet to the brain. There was no hope. Robert convulsed with sobs. Down the narrow corridor he saw a trail of blood, and as he got closer to the bedroom he could hear the death rattle of the president. Robert entered the room and saw his father stretched diagonally across the bed to accommodate his great height. He stood at the head of the bed and looked down at his father's face. A terrible grief overtook him.

Robert found his mother in the parlor. She was in a state of shock and spoke only a few words. Mary was being comforted by two women, the actress Laura Keene and Miss Clara Harris, who with her fiancé Major Henry Rathbone had been sitting in the president's box when the assassin opened fire. "Why did he not shoot me instead of my husband?" Mary cried. "I have tried to be so careful of him, fearing something would happen, and his life seemed to be more precious now than ever." Robert crouched before her and tried to find the right words. He took hold of her hands and said, "Mother, please put your trust in God and all will be well."

Mary insisted on seeing the president: "Take me inside to my husband." She was shown in, but when she looked down at the blood-soaked bed, she screamed and fainted. Robert helped carry her back to the parlor. She begged somebody to find her son Tad. "Bring Tad. He will speak to Tad. He loves him so." Robert must have bristled at this, for even at his father's deathbed he had to be reminded that Tad was the son who had that special attachment with their father.

The Petersen House soon filled up with high-level government officials. Senator Sumner held the president by the hand and sobbed. Surgeon General Joseph Barnes supervised his medical care. Also present were Secretary of the Navy Gideon Welles, Isaac Arnold, and John Hay. Secretary of War Stanton positioned himself in the sitting room and from there began to organize the manhunt for the assassin. At 1:00 A.M. he ordered Attorney General Speed to write a formal letter to Andrew Johnson advising the vice president of Lincoln's death and recommending that he prepare to take over the presidency. Stanton was reviewing the document aloud when he heard a scream—he had not realized that Mary Lincoln had been standing behind him.

"Is he dead?" she cried out. "Oh, is he dead?"

Stanton explained he was just trying to prepare for the possibility, and Mary was escorted back to the parlor. The secretary of war was focusing on his work when he heard another scream coming from the bedroom where

Lincoln lay. He ran inside. Mrs. Lincoln had been caressing the president's face with her cheek when, at that moment, he let forth an "explosive breath." Mary had fainted into the arms of Laura Keene and Clara Harris. Stanton lost his temper. Pointing a finger at the First Lady, he ordered, "Take that woman out, and do not let her in again." Although the stress that the secretary of war was under must have been enormous, his remark was offensive and disrespectful. It foreshadowed Mary Lincoln's treatment by her husband's closest allies in the years to come.

At 2:00 A.M. Andrew Johnson was escorted into the bedroom to see Lincoln. The vice president had not waited for a military escort; he had walked from the Kirkwood House at Twelfth and Pennsylvania Avenue. He stared at Lincoln, spoke not a word, and displayed no visible emotion. Then he spoke a few private words of sympathy to Robert, whispered something in Stanton's ear, and paid his respects to Mary Lincoln.

At some point, Robert heard the name of the suspected assassin, John Wilkes Booth. It must have come as a shock to him for several reasons. Booth was a famous actor, younger brother of Edwin Booth, the most revered Shakespearean player of the age. And Robert had a strange connection to Edwin. The event took place in 1863 or 1864—Robert could not remember the precise year—at a station stop in Jersey City, New Jersey, en route to Washington. Just as the train was starting to move, Robert fell under a crush of passengers into the gap between the train and the platform. All at once somebody seized him by the coat collar and yanked him up. He turned to thank the stranger and saw to his surprise it was the actor Edwin Booth. There was no doubt in Robert's mind that Booth had saved his life, and he thanked him by name. Now Edwin's brother was accused of assassinating the president.

Dawn was approaching. Mary, her dress looking as if it had been dipped in blood, remained in the parlor with Laura Keene and Clara Harris. At 7:00 A.M. the president moaned, and his breathing became swift and shallow. Surgeon General Barnes touched the president's cold skin and knew the time had come. At twenty-two minutes and ten seconds past seven, Abraham Lincoln stopped breathing. The surgeon general peeled an eyelid back and placed his ear to the president's chest to listen for any sign of breath. None came. It was over. Barnes retrieved two silver coins from his vest and placed them on the president's eyes. There was dead silence in the room, broken when Stanton, according to legend, uttered his renowned words, "Now, he belongs to the ages."

Everyone's head bowed in prayer. Then Robert went to inform his mother that her husband had died. When he brought her back for one last look, she flung herself on his body and wept, "Oh my God! I have given my husband to die!" Robert and several of the able-bodied men lifted her from the bed and helped carry her out of the room. A white sheet was pulled over the president's face. Almost immediately, church bells throughout Washington started to toll. Mary was in a state of hysteria. "Oh, why did you not tell me he was dying!" As Mary was escorted out of the Petersen House a steady rain was falling. When she saw Ford's Theatre across the street, she screamed, "That dreadful house! That dreadful house!"

On Pennsylvania Avenue, mourners were already lining up outside the White House. Inside, just as Tad Lincoln was coming down the staircase from the family quarters, Navy Secretary Welles strode in, shaking the rain off his hat. With all the heartbreak at the president's deathbed, the little Lincoln had almost been forgotten. Welles stared at Tad, the son who reminded everyone so much of the now-martyred president.

"Oh, Mr. Welles," young Taddie asked, "who killed my father?"

2

Them Little Devils

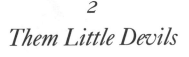

THE MANHUNT WAS on for President Lincoln's assassin. Washington, D.C., was under martial law and in the grip of panic. Boats were banned from the Potomac River, and every bridge and road leading out of the nation's capital was ordered closed. Tad Lincoln, on his way home from the National Theatre, observed the bedlam in the streets and sobbed his heart out. The disconsolate boy, who was taken to a basement entrance on the eastern side of the presidential mansion, ran up the staircase and burst into the main vestibule of the White House. Standing by the window and watching the mob scene outside was White House guard Thomas Pendel, who Tad called "Tom Pen" because he could not pronounce Pendel's last name. Tad burst into tears. "Oh Tom Pen! Tom Pen! They have killed Papa dead. They killed Papa dead." Pendel put his arm around Tad and the twelve-year-old boy buried his face in Pendel's chest. Beside himself with grief, Taddie cried out, "They've killed Papa dead! They've killed Papa dead!"

At midnight, Tad, exhausted from crying, allowed Pendel to take him to bed not in Tad's bedroom but in "Paw's" room, in the southwest corner of the White House. As Pendel pulled down the blanket, Tad undressed and climbed into the president's bed. Pendel tucked Tad in, lay down next to the boy, and put his arm around him. They talked into the night, Pendel's voice soothing and distracting the boy until he fell sleep. Pendel would later say, "That was a sad night for the nation, and to me it was simply awful."

The youngest child of Abraham and Mary Lincoln, Thomas "Tad" Lincoln was born April 4, 1853, surprising his parents, who wanted a girl after the birth of three boys. It was a difficult delivery due to Tad's unusually large head, which resulted in internal injuries to Mary. When Tad was born his brother Robert was nine and Willie just two, and according to family lore, Tad was conceived mere weeks after Willie was weaned so that Willie would have a playmate. The family took to calling baby Thomas Tad, the story goes, because when he was squirming in the bath his outsized head reminded Lincoln of the tadpoles he used to catch as a boy in Kentucky. Lincoln nicknamed him Tadpole, which got shortened to Tad.

Tad was a spirited little fellow who inherited his father's long limbs, dark hair, and murky complexion and his mother's propensity toward explosive fits of temper. Tad was born with a cleft palate, and the resulting speech impediment gave him an appealing but pronounced lisp, so "Pa" became "Paw," and next-door neighbor Mrs. Sprigg became "Mith Spwigg." Willie and Tad were inseparable—not surprising for brothers so close in age—and incorrigible mischief-makers. This special bond created real issues for Robert. Naturally shy, even aloof, Robert resented the way his indulgent parents were raising Willie and Tad. Willie was his mother's pet, the perfect little boy, and Tad the clown prince, able to make his father roar with laughter. This left Robert the odd boy out in the Lincoln family dynamics and may have contributed to the rigidity and uncomfortable reserve that marked his personality.

As inexperienced parents Mary and Abraham had disciplined their firstborn with the occasional whipping, but by the time Willie and Tad came along the Lincolns had softened their approach to parenting. One reason may have been the heartbreaking death of their second-born son, Eddie, at age three. Eddie lingered on his deathbed for an agonizing fifty-two days before he succumbed to what has been suggested was diphtheria, or possibly pulmonary tuberculosis. The births of Willie and Tad brought joy back to the family, and, with their arrival, the Lincolns rejected corporal punishment as a means of discipline. Some of their Springfield neighbors, and Lincoln's law partner William Herndon in particular, thought that Willie and especially Tad regularly deserved a serious whipping. But the Lincolns would not have it. Children, Lincoln believed, should be indulged and happy and unrestrained by what he called "parental tyranny." Love, he said, was the chain that bound a child to his parents.

To Billy Herndon, the Lincoln boys were "them little devils." Herndon was one of those visionaries who saw the greatness in Lincoln early on when it seemed so improbable that he would one day lead the nation. His admiration for Lincoln, however, could not conceal his disdain for the great man's offspring. Admittedly, the pranks the boys pulled off in the Lincoln & Herndon law firm would have tried the patience of most men. On Sundays, when Mrs. Lincoln went to church, Abraham would be left in charge of babysitting responsibilities. On those occasions he would bring Bob, Willie, and Tad to the law office of Lincoln & Herndon, where they would proceed to tear the place apart. While Lincoln buried himself in work, the boys broke pens, spilled ink, overturned important paperwork, and painted the room with ash from the fireplace. Herndon was appalled. He said that he "wanted to wring the necks of these brats and pitch them out the window," but as the junior partner, he kept his mouth shut out of respect for Lincoln. Lincoln, Herndon concluded, "worshipped his children and what they worshipped; he loved what they loved and hated what they hated." But to the aggrieved Herndon, Lincoln was a "fool" to be so tolerant of his children's misbehavior.

Another Lincoln colleague had reason to agree with Herndon's assessment. Judge Samuel H. Treat of the Illinois State Supreme Court truly took pleasure in Lincoln's social company. One early evening Lincoln and the judge were enjoying a game of chess in the judge's chambers when Tad came to fetch Pa home for dinner. This was a regular chore for the Lincoln boys; when suppertime came around, Mary Lincoln would dispatch one of the youngsters to find the notoriously absentminded Mr. Lincoln. On this occasion, Lincoln promised to come right away, and Tad left, mission accomplished. After a while, when Lincoln had still not come home, Mary sent Tad around once more to Judge Treat's office. Again, Lincoln told the boy he was on his way and then went right back to the chess game. On the third try, Tad had had enough and flew into a rage. With a swift kick of his boot he sent the board and chess pieces flying into the air. Judge Treat was spitting mad and expected Lincoln to do his duty as a parent and mete out harsh punishment, but Lincoln remained calm, and as if nothing had happened, took Tad by the hand and said, "Well, Judge, I reckon we'll have to finish this game some other time." Years later, Judge Treat would recount the story to a Lincoln biographer and say, "I can assure you of one thing: if that little rascal been a boy of mine he never would have applied his boots to another chessboard."

Tad was eight years old when Abraham Lincoln became president, but curiously, he still could not manage to dress himself. His mother or father or a nurse had to help him every morning with his buttons and shoelaces. Academically, Tad was impossible. He just could not sit still and focus.

Some historians have suggested that Tad was slightly retarded, but the more probable explanation was hyperactivity and what we now recognize as attention deficit disorder. He needed several more years of maturity to work out in his own head the process of how to learn. This would come later, and Tad would one day show the world what a keen and interesting mind he really had.

Many of the stories about Tad's White House years were recorded by Julia Taft Bayne in her charming little memoir, *Tad Lincoln's Father*. Julia was a bright seventeen-year-old debutante, the daughter of Judge Horatio Taft, who was chief examiner of the United States Patent Office. Julia's father (a distant relative of the Ohio Tafts) had forbidden her to go to the Capitol building on Lincoln's inauguration day for fear of trouble breaking out, so she and her mother watched the inaugural procession from the window inside Woodward's hardware store on Pennsylvania Avenue. Julia was amazed to observe a platoon of sharpshooters march into the store and take positions on the roof with orders to shoot anyone approaching the presidential carriage. The applause was lukewarm, to put it mildly, as the tall, ungainly Lincoln, with President Buchanan sitting next to him, came by, followed closely by cavalry. Julia could hear "ugly murmurs" following the carriage as it passed along Pennsylvania Avenue toward the Capitol. "There goes that Illinois ape," spat a proslavery woman. "The cursed abolitionist. But he will never come back alive."

Julia's surprising friendship with the Lincolns began just a few days after the inauguration. The Taft family lived down the street from the White House, and Mary Lincoln understood that the two youngsters were about the same age as Willie and Tad. She thought they might make good playmates for her boys. On a bright, windy day in March, Julia brought her brothers Horatio Nelson Taft Jr., known as Bud, and Halsey Cook Taft, known as Holly, to the White House. They found Tad and Willie by the goldfish tank in the White House conservatory. In that instant great friendships were born.

Julia's first reaction was "such nice, quiet, shy boys." Willie was the "most lovable boy I ever knew . . . bright, sensible, sweet-tempered and gentle-mannered." Tad, however, had a "fiery temper," and was implacable in his dislikes. Julia also found it difficult to understand Tad at first because of his speech impediment. A few days after this first encounter, Julia was invited to visit with Mary Lincoln in the White House. The First Lady directed Julia to sit with her on a sofa, and the two became acquainted. Mary was being shunned by most of Washington's proslavery social elite, who were of the opinion that the Lincolns were uncouth vagabonds unfit to live in the White House. Even though Julia was just a teenager, it must have been a pleasurable experience for Mary to find somebody to talk to. Julia was showing off her new hat when to her surprise President Lincoln walked in. She instantly jumped to her feet.

"Well, who's this, Mary?" he asked.

"This is Julia Taft, Bud's sister," Mrs. Lincoln answered.

Lincoln, who had great affection for children and was especially charmed by girls, looked down at the young lady from his great height and, to Julia's astonishment, with impressive strength, lifted her by the elbows. The president took an immediate liking to the young lady and pronounced that from then on he would call her "Jewly" or "Flibbertigibbet," a name that came to him out of thin air. At first, Julie was struck by the president's unkempt, even neglected appearance. She wondered how this sad-faced, exhausted fellow could lead the nation in its time of crisis. But like most people who encountered Abraham Lincoln, she very quickly surmised there was something unfathomable about the man. Soon she came to the belief that Lincoln had been sent by divine providence to serve the country in its darkest hour.

Abraham and Mary Lincoln worshipped at the Presbyterian Church on New York Avenue, but it took just a few weeks for mischief makers Tad and Willie to conclude that the Presbyterian Church on Fourth Street was "lots livelier" and much more agreeable to their spiritual needs. The reason was that Bud and Holly went there, with Julia as their sitter. At the Fourth Street church, hatred for the new president was evident even during Sunday services. Many of the worshipers supported the South, and every Sunday when pastor Dr. J. C. Smith offered his traditional prayer for the health of the nation's commander in chief, they would express their contempt for Lincoln. At the mere mention of Lincoln's name, the service would be disrupted by the movement of parishioners getting up from their seats and pew doors slamming shut behind them.

Tad welcomed the weekly drama as a diversion from a long and dull Sunday service; never mind that his father was the target of the protest. The disruptions continued for several Sundays until word got back to the War Department, which assigned a young lieutenant to Fourth Street Presbyterian. The following Sunday, the young officer marched to the front of the church and in crisp military tones informed the parishioners, "It is the order of the Provost Marshal that any one disturbing this service or leaving it before it is out will be arrested and taken to the guardhouse." Tad's reaction was typical—he was upset that order had been restored. He even expressed contempt for the spineless "secesshes"—the closest his speech impediment would allow him to pronounce the word "secessionist."

"If I was a Secesh," Tad boasted, "I wouldn't let him stop me banging pew doors."

"And get put in the guardhouse," the practical, respectful Willie answered.

Tad thought this through. "Well, I guess Pa could get me out," he said.

On May 24, 1861, the day after the state of Virginia voted to secede from the Union and ally itself with the Confederate States of the Deep South, the dashing Colonel Elmer Ellsworth led an invasion of the city of Alexandria, just outside Washington.

Volunteers from a unit of New York City firefighters secured the railroad depot, the telegraph office, General Robert E. Lee's vast estate in Arlington, and other key locations. In downtown Alexandria, Ellsworth saw a Confederate flag flying from atop a hotel. This had particular significance because it could be seen from Washington. Ellsworth ordered a corporal to accompany him, and the two men went to the roof and cut down the flag. As he came down the staircase with the flag bundled in his arms, the owner of the hotel, James Jackson, confronted Ellsworth on the third-floor landing and opened fire with a double-barrel shotgun blast to the chest. Ellsworth died on the spot; the innkeeper was shot in the face and run through with a bayonet by the corporal, who was later awarded the Congressional Medal of Honor.

In the North, Ellsworth became a hero—one of the first casualties of the Civil War—and thousands volunteered to join the Union cause in his honor. The recruiting slogan "Remember Ellsworth" became to the Civil War what "Remember the *Maine*" would later be to the Spanish-American War. In the South, of course, hotelkeeper James Jackson was hailed as a martyr. Songs and poems were written about him, and it was claimed he perished for the cause "amid a pack of wolves."

Lincoln was heartbroken, and ordered Ellsworth's body to lie in state in the East Room. But even on this solemn occasion Tad could not keep out of trouble. With his friend Holly Taft, he hitched himself to the back of

General Winfield Scott's chair. When the 230-pound general, who was too fat to mount a horse, suddenly stood up, he sent the two boys sprawling backward, momentarily interrupting the funeral.

The flag that Ellsworth had hauled down in Alexandria was presented to Mrs. Lincoln as a remembrance of the handsome young officer. Because it was stained with Ellsworth's blood, Mary could not bear to see it, and put it in a bureau drawer. Of course, the resourceful Tad found it one day, and hoisted it up the White House flagpole. Imagine the shock of citizens who looked up that day and saw a bloodstained Confederate flag flying over the White House.

Washington, D.C., was isolated and surrounded by hostile forces. There was real fear of an attack by General Lee's gathering forces in Virginia. Julia Taft said the city "shivered" with rumors of invasion. General Scott deemed Washington so dangerous he recommended that Mary and the children return to Springfield for the duration of Lincoln's term in office, or at least until the national crisis was over.

"Let 'em come," Tad said after Sunday school. "Willie and I are ready for 'em." The Lincoln boys prepared for the defense of the White House by conducting drills with a few condemned rifles and constructing a "fort" on the roof with logs for cannons.

Mary left for New York on a shopping expedition and asked Julia's mother whether Bud and Holly could stay at the White House in her absence to keep Tad and Willie company. Mrs. Taft agreed, with some misgivings. The four lads were already developing a reputation in Washington for unparalleled misbehavior. Several days later, Julia came around with some clean blouses for her brothers. After she got past the sentry, a servant at the front door informed her with a weary smile that the boys were in the attic. Julia went to the attic and opened the door. To her great surprise, two sheets had been pinned together to create a curtain and the room was jammed with soldiers, servants, and gardeners. Tad and the other lads were putting on a circus, charging the spectators five cents each to see the show. Julia went backstage and found Tad struggling to get into his mother's silk evening gown with its expansive décolleté. He was about to blacken his face with shoe polish but Julia took the bottle away.

"Boys, does the president know about this?" she asked.

"Yep," said Tad, always first to come to his own defense. "Paw knows and he doesn't care, neither. He's coming up when those generals go away." Then he asked Julia to sprinkle some of Mrs. Lincoln's "Bloom of Youth" perfume on his head. Just as Tad stepped onstage and started to sing at the top of his lungs the ditty from the 1860 campaign, "Ol' Abe Lincoln Came out of the Wilderness," Julia left. On her way down, she ran into the president's secretary, John Hay, who was striding up to the attic. He seemed upset.

"Have those boys got the president's spectacles?"

"I think they have," Julia said. She had just seen them dangling on the tip of Tad's nose.

Like Billy Herndon, John Hay sometimes seemed to want to wring Tad's little neck. One of Tad's favorite toys was a doll he named Jack that was a replica of a Zouave soldier. Tad tortured the thing and even held a court-martial at which Jack was found guilty of sleeping on duty and sentenced to be shot at sunrise. Julia was there when Tad seized on the idea of a presidential pardon to spare Jack's life. Up the staircase he bounded, followed by Willie, the two Taft boys, and Julia in the rear, calling out, "Don't you dare bother the president." John Hay heard the commotion and rose from his desk outside the president's office in time to block Tad from going in. He told Tad to scat and not waste the president's time. Suddenly, the door opened and there was Abraham Lincoln, a big grin on his long, sad face. "Well, boys," he said, "What's the matter?"

Tad swiveled around Hay and flung himself at his father's legs. "Oh, Paw, we want a pardon for Doll Jack."

"Pardon for Jack, eh," said the president with mock gravity. "You come in here and tell me why you think Jack should have a pardon." Hay stepped aside with a disgusted snort, and the boys tumbled into the president's office. Lincoln sat in his big chair, crossed one long leg over the other, and put the tips of his fingers together judiciously. "State your case, Tad," he said gravely. Apparently, Tad made a good argument because Lincoln pardoned Jack on grounds of double jeopardy (Jack had already been shot by a "firing squad" for desertion and buried in the White House garden). Tad left with an official note signed by the president stating: "The Doll Jack is pardoned by order of the president." It was signed A. Lincoln. Jack's reprieve did not last long. Less than a week later, notwithstanding the pardon, Julia found the doll hanging by his neck from a White House tree.

Lincoln enjoyed rough physical horseplay with his boys. Once, when Julia was engrossed in a book, she heard a terrible racket in the room next door where her brothers were playing with Tad and Willie. She opened the door and was about to tell the boys to keep it down when she saw President Lincoln sprawled on the floor, with the four youngsters pinning him down by his limbs. Willie and Bud had hold of his hands and Tad and Holly were at his legs and feet. The sight distressed Julia, but Lincoln was laughing uproariously. "Julia," called Tad, "come quick and sit on his stomach." Instead she closed the door behind her and left the White House.

Tad once ate all the strawberries set aside for a state dinner. Another time, he was recklessly playing with a ball in the vestibule when, in a "terrifying shattering," he broke a giant mirror. Julia and the others stood there in speechless horror, and all Tad could say was, "Well, it's broken. I don't b'lieve Pa'll care." As usual, it took Willie to set him straight. "It's not Pa's looking glass. It belongs to the United States government." Only when Holly Taft pointed out that by breaking the mirror Tad faced seven years' bad luck did he become concerned. He dashed into the kitchen and returned with a handful of salt, which he quickly flung over his left shoulder.

By the fall of 1861, Mary was determined to give her boys a formal education. She ordered the installation of a desk and blackboard in the state dining room on the first floor of the White House and hired tutors to teach the boys the fundamentals. No tutor lasted very long, mainly because they found Tad incorrigible and impossible to teach. The tutor with the longest tenure was Alexander Williamson, a young Scotsman with a university degree from Edinburgh. Williamson was paid out of government funds, as Mary had secured a place for him at the Treasury Department, where he worked in the mornings; in the afternoons he tutored the boys. To make schooling a little more palatable for Tad and Willie, Mary arranged for the Taft boys to join them (all schools in Washington were closed during the national emergency). Sometimes Julia Taft helped out with the instructions, but her real purpose in going to the White House every day was to find a sanctuary where she could read undisturbed. Her mother did not allow her to read novels, but Julia was clandestinely permitted to use the White House library, and she devoured every book on its shelves.

Understandably, Julia found a natural ally in Abraham Lincoln, whose personal hunger for reading as a youth in Kentucky is now part of American lore. Tad, however, when he found Julia reading a novel, saw an opportunity for mischief. He promptly reported the offense to Mrs. Taft, telling her in his lippy manner, "Julie was reading nobbel books in our house." But Julia would not be deterred. Late one afternoon, the president found her curled up in the window of the sitting room, reading a weighty work. Curious, Lincoln took the book from her hands and leafed through the pages. Then he placed it back in her lap. "Such a big book for little Julie," he said. With a sigh, Lincoln stared out the window, looking across the Potomac River into the rebel state of Virginia where the forces of the Confederacy were gathering. The president almost seemed to forget Julie's presence in the room as he became lost in thought, his hands clasped behind his back, his head lowered, sighing with the heavy burden of war. "He looked so sad and worried that somehow I wanted to comfort him yet knew not how," Julia wrote. "And crying a little, I slipped out in the darkening twilight."

The two older boys, Willie and Bud, were doing well in the improvised White House schoolroom, but Holly and especially Tad, with his learning disabilities and hair-trigger temper, were harder cases to crack. "He had a very bad opinion of books, and no opinion of discipline," John Hay said of Tad. Everyone agreed that Tad was intuitive and naturally bright. He excelled at any subjects dealing with practical matters such as the principles of mechanics (building a kite or a sleigh) and animal behavior, but he could barely read, and his writing was infantile. At this point in time, Abraham Lincoln was surprisingly indifferent to Tad's education. "Let him run," Lincoln would say. "There's time enough yet for him to learn his letters and get pokey."

Tad had a way of taking stock of a new tutor and demolishing him in an instant, but Alexander Williamson stayed longer than most and, despite the grief Tad gave him, actually developed a fondness for the youngster. Williamson also became the custodian of one of the great historic artifacts of the Lincoln administration—the inkwell that the president used to sign the Emancipation Proclamation on New Year's Day, 1863. The way this remarkable item ended up with Williamson was typical of the manner in which Tad's personality affected events at the White House.

As Lincoln picked up the pen to sign the Emancipation Proclamation, he could not keep his hand from trembling, not from any hesitancy he felt about affixing his signature to the momentous political document, but because he had shaken the hands of hundreds of visitors who had come to the White House for New Year's Day celebrations. An unsteady hand could send a signal that he was unsure about the proclamation, when in fact, as he put it, "My whole soul is in it." The president put the pen down and did not pick it up again until he was certain the strength had returned to his hand. Finally, he wrote his name slowly, distinctly, and, when he examined the results, he said, "That will do." The pen was presented to Senator Charles Sumner of Massachusetts, but somehow Tad took possession of the inkwell, which he proudly showed off as the "Emancipation Inkwell" to Williamson, who was justifiably alarmed that in Tad's casual custody it would be lost to history. Williamson sought and obtained the president's approval that he be given the inkwell as a gift. (It was retained by Williamson's descendants until 1995, when it was acquired at auction by the Lincoln Museum.)

In February 1862, with the war news grim and the Union army struggling against the disciplined forces of the Confederacy, Mary Lincoln determined that a party was needed to boost her husband's spirits. Her plan ignited a political firestorm. Several Republican senators questioned the wisdom of throwing a lavish White House function in time of war. Ohio senator Ben Wade, a fervent abolitionist, received one of the coveted invitations for himself and his wife, and went public with the revulsion he felt. "Are the president and Mrs. Lincoln aware that there is a Civil War? If they are not, Mr. and Mrs. Wade are, and for that reason decline to participate in feasting and dancing."

A Philadelphia poet reflected on the uproar with an edgy new work targeting Mary Lincoln that he titled "The Queen Must Dance." Mary Lincoln had excellent political instincts, but in this case her political antennae had failed her. Five hundred invitations were sent out and Mary hired Maillard & Company, New York's most expensive caterer, to supervise the menu and design the presentation, the one thousand dollar costs coming from Lincoln's private funds. The night of the party, Lincoln was standing with his back to a fireplace, his vision fixed on the floor, when he heard a rustling. It was Mary showing off her new gown. It was made of white satin and trimmed with black lace, and it had a daringly low décolletage. He looked at his becoming wife for a few moments. "Whew! Our cat has a long tail tonight," Lincoln said, a gentle jab at the display of so much skin. "Mother, it is my opinion, if some of that tail was nearer the head, it would be in better style."

Ignoring his sly critique, Mary took the president's arm and they went downstairs to the East Room to greet the diplomats, generals, politicians, and leading dignitaries who had started to arrive. Mary made her grand entrance as the Marine band played a lively new piece composed just for the event, "The Mary Lincoln Polka." But just as the president feared, with her appearance came a buzz saw of gossip and disparagement. One U.S. senator remarked that Mrs. Lincoln was putting her "bosom on public display." It reaffirmed for her enemies their contemptuous view of Mary as an uncouth country hick who was unfit to inhabit the White House.

At midnight, the doors to the state dining room were swung open to reveal an amazing buffet dinner of venison, duck, pheasant, turkey, partridge, and ham. The tables were decorated with military-themed confections, including an impressive sugar model of Fort Sumter. The party did not end until daybreak, and the *Washington Star* called it "the most superb affair of its kind ever seen here." Everyone agreed that despite the personal attacks on Mary and the criticism it had generated, the party was a great success, a triumph for Mary Lincoln, as it signaled her formal transformation from frontier wife to important Washington hostess. Unfortunately, though, the Lincolns were in distress. They spent much of the evening upstairs in Willie's bedroom, sitting by his bed, comforting the boy, and nursing him through a high fever. A few days later their worst fears would be affirmed. Their son William Wallace Lincoln was dying.

Robert Lincoln may have been puzzling to his parents, and Tad Lincoln a tiny terror, but Willie was the perfect son, intellectually able and blessed with his father's engaging personality. Willie loved books, and, from the letters he wrote, he appears to have inherited his father's innate gift for language. Like his father, he could not bear to see another human being suffer without trying to help. He also had a kind of poise and simple dignity that reminded everyone of the president. The editor Nathaniel P. Willis, a descendant of Puritans who founded the magazine that is now known as *Town and Country*, met "this little fellow" Willie several times and said he "never failed to seek me out in the crowd, shake hands, and make some pleasant remark; and this in a boy of ten years of age, was, to say the least, endearing to a stranger. His self-possession—aplomb, as the French call it—was extraordinary." Another journalist said Willie had his father's homely face and an interesting glow of intelligence that caused strangers to "speak of him as a fine little fellow."

Academically, Willie was the brightest of the three Lincoln boys and blessed with a future of limitless possibilities, perhaps in politics or as an author, though he sometimes expressed a desire to become a minister because he had a flair for making speeches. Tad saw the Civil War raging around him as an opportunity to play soldier, but Willie had a fuller appreciation for being able to watch history unfold from his front-row seat. He read all the newspapers and kept up with events back home in Springfield.

When a cherished family friend, Colonel Edward D. Baker, was killed in action at the Battle of Ball's Bluff, the Lincolns were bereft. Baker was a sitting United States senator from Oregon who became the only senator in history ever killed in battle. Just the day before his death, Baker, who loved President Lincoln like a brother, paid a courtesy call to the White House.

Afterward, Lincoln and Willie watched from the lawn as Baker mounted his horse and rode off to the front, knowing he was going into battle. Willie was so broken up by Baker's death that he wrote a poem he sent to the Washington *National Republican* newspaper with the cover note: "Dear Sir, I enclose you my first attempt at poetry. Yours truly, William W. Lincoln." After the newspaper editor deemed it "quite credible . . . for one so young," on November 4, 1861, the poem was published. The first two stanzas read:

> *There was no patriot like Baker,*
> *So noble and so true;*
> *He fell as a soldier on the field,*
> *His face to the sky of blue.*
>
> *His voice is silent in the hall,*
> *Which oft his presence grac'd,*
> *No more he'll hear the loud acclaim*
> *Which rang from place to place.*

On February 5, 1862, the night of their mother's contentious ball, Willie and Tad were already seriously ill. Very few guests were aware that the First Lady had been up two straight nights caring for her boys. Willie was the first to fall sick, followed a few days later by Tad. In the beginning, their parents were not overly concerned. Dr. Robert Stone, the dean of Washington's medical community and personal physician to the president, was called in to examine the boys. Dr. Stone told the Lincolns that Willie and Tad had caught common colds and would recover in short order. There was no cause for concern, he said.

Despite the doctor's diagnosis, it quickly became obvious that Willie was gravely ill. Mary wanted to cancel the event, but the invitations had already been sent out, and after consulting again with Dr. Stone, the Lincolns resolved that the party could go on as scheduled. Willie, though, took a sudden turn for the worse, and it became a brutal night for Mary and Abraham. Making cordial small talk with their distinguished guests was a tortuous experience while upstairs in the family quarters their little Willie was so stricken. But amid this personal crisis, the Lincolns tried to be gracious hosts.

One woman in particular received an unusual degree of attention from Lincoln on the reception line. She was Dorothea Dix, superintendent of nurses for the United States Army. "Dragon Dix," as she was called, was a stern and autocratic spinster who accepted into her corps of military nurses only those applicants who were plain looking and older than thirty. Marriage-minded women were rejected as unsuitable. A desperate Lincoln took Miss Dix aside and told her about Willie. Then he asked her to please consider assigning one of her nurses to Willie's care.

Another guest, Kate Chase, the beautiful daughter of Treasury Secretary Salmon Chase, was deemed Washington, D.C.'s most alluring hostess and a bitter rival of Mary Lincoln's, but she put her enmity aside this evening and considerately asked the First Lady about Willie's condition. The boy's illness hovered over the entire evening. Everyone had been expecting to dance to the music of the Marine band, but an announcement was made that dancing was canceled due to an "illness in the house."

Through the long night, the Lincolns kept slipping away to Willie's bedroom to tend to the youngster. As his fever climbed, they would gently stroke his forehead. Robert Lincoln had come home from college to attend the party, and he also helped out, leaving the gathering whenever he could to sit at his little brother's bedside.

Dr. Stone diagnosed Willie with bilious fever, a medical term now deemed archaic that in the 1860s covered several maladies and technically meant the patient was suffering from a disorder of the bile system. But doctors looking at the available information are today unanimous in concluding that Willie probably suffered from typhoid fever, one of history's three "burning fevers," the other two being malaria and yellow fever. Typhoid fever is caused by contaminated food or water and, in Lincoln's time, it killed tens of thousands of people in America every year. Lincoln's archrival, Senator Stephen A. Douglas, the Little Giant, died of typhus in 1861, just one year after Lincoln defeated him for the presidency. General Robert E. Lee's twenty-three-year-old daughter Annie died of the disease in 1862, as did General Stonewall Jackson's parents and daughter. Probably the most famous victim of typhoid fever was Prince Albert of England, the husband of Queen Victoria, in December 1861. It is a curious fact of history that as a mark of mourning for the late Prince Albert, on the night of her White House ball, Mary Lincoln wore flounces of black lace on her white satin gown, not yet knowing that the disease that killed the queen's beloved consort was the same one that would end the life of her son.

At the outbreak of the Civil War, the population of Washington, D.C., was sixty thousand, but this number ballooned to two hundred thousand by 1862. The infusion of soldiers and bureaucrats into what never had been the healthiest of cities generated a public health nightmare. The Army of the Potomac, recruited by the War Department to defend the capital against invasion, camped on the banks of the Potomac River. Not for nothing is typhus sometimes called the "soldier's disease." The medical consensus in Lincoln's time was that rapidly flowing water such as that found in a river was an acceptable place for human waste. In 1862 Washington's raw sewage lines also drained directly into the Potomac River, the source from which the White House drew its water. Whenever the president or family members turned on the faucets in the White House, the water they drank or bathed in was almost certainly contaminated with *Salmonella typhi* bacteria. Only by some miracle did Lincoln himself not succumb to the disease.

Dr. Stone, the physician in charge of Willie's care, was simply not equipped to deal with typhoid. Medical science in those times called for a bizarre and ineffective treatment consisting of beef tea, blackberry cordial, and bland pudding. Dr. Stone also administered quinine, the traditional cure for malaria, a disease that Willie did not have. Willie was prescribed calomel, a toxic, mercury-based chemical used in the 1860s as a diuretic. The overall treatment probably led to his agonizing bouts of diarrhea and vomiting—symptoms not usually associated with typhoid fever—and had the effect of hastening the poor boy's death.

Assisting Dr. Stone was an army nurse sent over by Dorothea Dix, the widow Rebecca Pomroy. The president welcomed her on her arrival at the White House. "I am heartily glad to see you," he said. "You can comfort us and the poor sick boy."

It was a long and tortuous death for Willie. John Hay and John Nicolay could hear the boy screaming in agony from their bedroom. Dr. Stone kept assuring a skeptical Mary that recovery was just around the corner. The news of Willie's illness did not reach the public until the White House made a formal announcement on February 9, four days after the ball. The coverage was low-key and respectful. One newspaper clipping kept by the Lincoln family was headlined SICKNESS IN THE PRESIDENT'S FAMILY, and the article that followed did not even reference Willie by name:

> It was announced yesterday that the usual Saturday receptions at the White House . . . would be omitted on account of the illness of the second son of the president, an interesting lad of about eight years of age [sic], who has been lying dangerously ill of bilious fever

for the last three days. Mrs. Lincoln has not left his bedside since Wednesday night, and fears are entertained for her health. This evening the fever has abated and hopes are entertained for the recovery of the little sufferer.

Bud Taft showed the true steadfastness of a loyal friend and stayed in Willie's room through those bleak days. Many times Bud observed the president enter the room, stand at the bedside staring at his stricken son, and then leave without saying a word. Late one night, the president came in and lovingly stroked Willie's hair. Then he placed his arm across Bud's shoulder.

"You ought to go to bed, Bud," the president said.

"If I go he will call for me," Bud answered.

Another night, the president entered Willie's room and found that an exhausted Bud had fallen asleep in the chair. Tenderly, he lifted Bud into his long arms and carried him to bed.

Some days were better than others. On February 12, the president's birthday, the Lincolns breathed a sigh of relief—Willie appeared to be out of danger. But just five days later, the White House announced that his condition had taken a turn for the worse and he was "hopelessly ill." The next day, the newspapers reported that Willie's recovery was "not expected." In this regard, Willie was following the classic symptoms of typhoid fever— periods of delirium and high fever followed by a slight recovery. On a good day the patient may even seem to be in a state of recuperation, only to have the fever spike the next day.

His doctors did not know it, but Willie's fate had already been sealed. The infection was eroding his intestinal wall from the inside until, in time, it perforated the bowels, spilling bacteria into the abdominal cavity and blood system. He lapsed into a coma on February 18. At noon on February 20, Willie unexpectedly took hold of Bud Taft's hand. He actually seemed to get better, and for a few moments of jubilation everyone in the room thought they were witnessing a miracle. But it was not to be. Willie closed his eyes for the last time at five o'clock. Immediately, the president was summoned. Mary's seamstress, Elizabeth Keckley, helped clean and dress the body. When the president entered, he went to the bed and lifted the sheet from Willie's face. "I never saw a man so bowed down with grief," Mrs. Keckley recalled.

"My poor boy," Lincoln said, "he was too good for this earth. God has called him home. . . . We loved him so. It is hard, hard to have him die."

Lincoln buried his face in his hands and broke down in convulsions of tears. The sight of the president of the United States so racked with grief unnerved Mrs. Keckley and haunted her for the rest of her life.

Lincoln rose unsteadily to his feet and went about the business of informing the people closest to him. He opened the door to his secretary John Nicolay's bedroom. "Well, Nicolay, my boy is gone, he is actually gone." Now he had the hard duty of informing Tad. Lincoln strode into the little one's bedroom, where Tad was still recovering from his own bout with typhoid. Tad was no longer in mortal danger, his body's natural defenses having fought off the infection that killed Willie. Lincoln told Tad that Willie was gone. Tad was inconsolable, his weak, skinny little frame convulsed with sobs. They embraced each other as Lincoln tried to find the words to bring comfort to his grieving youngest son.

There was one more child to console. The president sent word to the Taft household for Bud to come to the White House and see Willie one last time before the body was embalmed. The valiant friend who had spent so many hours patting and caressing Willie through weeks of illness was brought to the White House and taken to Willie's room. But the trauma of seeing Willie's body proved too much for the youngster. He collapsed and had to be carried out. Returned to his house in this abject state, Bud remained in bed for several days, too grief-stricken to move.

Mary Lincoln was so completely overwhelmed with sorrow she stayed in her room for the entire five days that Willie lay in state in the Green Room. The White House was draped in black crepe, and Mrs. Keckley said that every visitor who crossed the threshold of the presidential mansion spoke in the hushed tones of mourning, mindful of the "sweet boy at rest." The day of the funeral, the rosewood and silver casket was transferred to the East Room for the services. The writer and editor Nathaniel Parker Willis came to pay his respects and was permitted a quiet moment with the body an hour before the funeral began. He stood before the coffin for one last look at the boy he called so "bravely and beautifully—himself." With the editor were the nurses who had cared for Willie and the White House servants who had come to love him. Willie's face was ghostly pale, but somehow his bright intelligence still shined through. His eyes were closed, his brown hair was neatly parted, and he was dressed in clothes as if for evening. His hands had been crossed over his chest, and in his little fist he held an exquisite bouquet of flowers.

At just that moment, word came down from the family quarters on the second floor that Mary Lincoln wanted the bouquet preserved for her. Gently the flowers were removed from Willie's hands and presented to his prostrate mother, who was too overwhelmed to attend the funeral. Tad was also still too sick to leave his bed. The coffin was closed and at two o'clock services began. A distinguished group of mourners crowded into the East Room for the touching ceremony, and before long the most powerful men in the nation were weeping tears of grief. The chronically belligerent Major General George McClellan was there, just weeks away from being fired by Lincoln as general-in-chief of the Union army. But on this day his eyes glistened with tears, and he bowed his head in prayer. Even the austere features of Secretary of State Seward and Treasury Secretary Chase seemed to struggle with emotion over the loss of so promising a young life. Nathaniel Willis said a private prayer that God grant Lincoln the strength to carry on with the burden of office in time of war.

Pallbearers lifted the coffin at the end of the service and carried it to a hearse waiting under the White House portico. Behind the coffin followed a line of little mourners, classmates from Willie's Sunday school. Two white horses pulled the hearse onto Pennsylvania Avenue. Two black horses trailed behind, pulling the carriage bearing Lincoln, his son Robert, and two of the president's closest friends in the U.S. Senate, Orville Browning and Lyman Trumbull, both of Illinois. Just a short time before, a violent storm had wreaked havoc on the city. Fallen trees and debris littered the streets, and the wind was still howling as the solemn procession wound its way to Oak Hill Cemetery in Georgetown. Many Washingtonians had hung outdoor funeral wreaths and buntings on their windows and front doors for the president's son. Now these black adornments flew over the city like birds of sorrow, carried by the violent winds.

Arrangements had been made to temporarily place the casket in a vault owned by Lincoln's friend William Thomas Carroll, the clerk of the Supreme Court. The next day Lincoln returned to the vault and opened the coffin to look at his son's corpse. It was understood that Willie would remain there only until Lincoln's term of office came to an end. Then Willie's body would be taken back to Springfield, where he would lay in rest for eternity—under the sod of his own land.

Slowly, Tad Lincoln recovered his health, but life in the White House was not the same. He had lost not just his big brother, whom he idolized, but also his cherished playmate and best buddy. Once his days had been filled with acts of mischief and fun. Now he was alone. Not even his companions Bud and Holly Taft were around to lift his spirits. Mary Lincoln had written an ill-advised letter to Mrs. Taft stating, "Please keep the boys home the day of the funeral; it makes me feel worse to see them." It was a heartless note, and the only charitable explanation is that it was written under a haze of deep anguish. For days after Willie's funeral, the Taft boys waited at home for word from the White House to come comfort Tad. Weeks passed, and Mrs. Taft came to realize that in Mary's irrational state of despair she had banished the Taft boys from the White House. The sight of Willie's two best friends was apparently too much for the First Lady to bear. Bud and Holly were sent north to school, and they never saw Tad again.

Tad's closest companion in this period of recovery was his nurse, Rebecca Pomroy. Mary Lincoln, still barely able to raise herself out of bed, was limited in how supportive she could be. The unremitting flood of tears she shed was actually causing physical damage to her eyes. Although some historians say this story is apocryphal, in her memoirs, Mrs. Keckley claimed that the president became so concerned about his wife's mental health that he took Mary by the arm and gently led her to the window of her bedroom. Solemnly, he pointed to an insane asylum visible in the distance and said, "Mother, do you see that large white building on the hill yonder? Try and control your grief or it will drive you mad and we may have to send you there."

Tad still required round-the-clock care. Sometimes the president would sit up with him through the night. Senator Browning, a dear family friend, also took turns. But most of the duty fell to the compassionate Mrs. Pomroy. Once, Tad could not stop weeping, he missed Willie so. Wailing about his future, he wondered, "Who would ever speak to me any more?" Mrs. Pomroy also offered a kind ear to the president.

"This is the hardest trial of my life," he told her, and Mrs. Pomroy let the president know of the peace she had reached despite the death of her husband and two children. When Lincoln questioned how she could keep her faith in the face of such loss, she said she trusted God but that it had been a long and sorrowful journey. She then reminded the president that he was the subject of Christian prayers around the world. Lincoln thanked Mrs. Pomroy for her counsel and said, "Your experience will help me to bear my afflictions."

A letter Lincoln received from William Florville, a black barber from Springfield who used to cut Willie's and Tad's hair, provided some consolation. "I was surprised about the announcement of the death of your son

Willie," the barber wrote. "I thought him a smart boy for his age, so considerate, so manly. Yet the time comes to all, all must die. Tell Taddy that his and Willie's dog is alive and kicking, doing well. He stays mostly at John E. Rolls with his boys who are about the age now that Tad and Willie were when they left for Washington."

The despair in the White House was so acute that Robert telegraphed relatives in Springfield to enlist the urgent assistance of Mary's sister, Elizabeth Edwards. "Very imploringly" he begged her to come to Washington as soon as she could. Mrs. Edwards arrived in Washington the day after the funeral, on the nine o'clock train. Senator Browning volunteered to pick her up at the railroad station and drove her in his carriage to the White House. On the way over, Browning informed Mrs. Edwards of the alarming family situation. "You have such a power and control, such an influence over Mary," he told her. But the misery Mrs. Edwards found in the White House was even more heartbreaking than she had been led to believe. It was not until ten days after Willie's death that she was able to persuade her sister to finally get out of bed. The outfit Mary chose to wear was one of symbolic magnitude—a heavy black dress over wire hoops, a black widow's cap, and a large black veil. The only touch of color was a thin line of white fabric at the cuffs and neckline. In this mourning dress Mary Lincoln made her first public appearance since Willie's death, at Sunday services at the New York Avenue Presbyterian Church, but as one worshiper said, her costume was so overwhelming "one could scarcely tell she was there." For the rest of her time at the White House Mary refused to enter either the bedroom where Willie lay sick for so many weeks or the Green Room where his body had lain in state.

By March 2 Tad was far enough along that his doctor pronounced him out of danger. After all these weeks of sickness, he barely had the strength to sit up in bed. "Tad is still feeble, can merely walk a few steps at a time," Mrs. Edwards wrote her daughter. "He deeply feels the loss of his loving brother." When the oppressive sense of despair in the White House became intolerable for Mrs. Edwards, she notified the president that she had had enough and was returning to Springfield. Lincoln invited her on an evening walk through Lafayette Park. "He begged me with tears in his eyes to remain longer," she said. But not even the president could persuade his sister-in-law to remain in this bleak house. She left in April.

Lincoln tried to be a good husband and guide Mary through her period of unrelenting mourning. To cheer her up, he bought her a beautiful seed-pearl bracelet and matching necklace from Tiffany & Company in New York. The pieces cost $530, a considerable sum in those days. Meanwhile, Lincoln mourned in his own deep and private way. Every Thursday, the day Willie died, he would lock himself in Willie's bedroom and reflect.

Tad and the president had always shared a special bond of attachment, and they were even closer as a consequence of Willie's death. Tad became a constant presence at Lincoln's side, much to the annoyance of Nicolay and Hay. Even at night, the two were inseparable. Tad and Willie had shared a bedroom, but after Willie's death, Tad could not bear the thought of sleeping alone; in his state of anxiety, the night terrified him. He asked whether he could sleep in the same bed as Pa, and the ever-indulgent Lincoln obliged. Lincoln often worked until midnight, and Tad would stay with him in the office until he fell asleep on the floor beside the president's desk or in front of the fireplace. Lincoln would lovingly hoist the child over his shoulder and carry him down the hallway, ducking under chandeliers and doorways, to the bedroom where he would undress the boy and put him to bed, trying not to wake him up.

Tad became the most famous White House child in U.S. history, a fame not eclipsed until John F. Kennedy's children moved into the White House a hundred years later. Generous folk touched by the death of Willie Lincoln sent Tad letters of encouragement and gifts, even animals, so the little boy who had lost his brother and best friend would not be alone. One citizen who sent Tad two white rabbits received a letter of thanks from President Lincoln, which he signed with his full name instead of his usual A. Lincoln, a rarity that revealed his sentimental state of mind when it came to his children.

A newfound breath of kindness and maturity now marked young Tad. On Easter Sunday, at the traditional egg-rolling contest on the White House lawn, the cook prepared two-dozen dyed eggs for Tad, but he gave a dozen of them to a lame boy named Tommy whose father was a casualty of war. Tad showed his good heart when he brought out a chair for Tommy so he could sit on it to roll the eggs. Then he gave the handicapped boy the thrill of his life when he brought President Lincoln over to shake his hand. One day Tad went out to explore the streets of Washington and returned to the White House with a collection of hungry street urchins whom he insisted the kitchen staff feed. When the cook refused, Tad went right to the president. "Isn't it our kitchen?" he asked. The president ordered the poor children fed.

In this era, the White House was an open house and ordinary citizens could come and request a visit with the president. Usually these petitioners were businessmen seeking a government contract or low-level politicians looking for a patronage appointment. Tad showed contempt for this lot because he saw them as an unnecessary burden on his father. But one day he saw in the mass of people appealing for an audience with the president a woman whose face was streaked with tears. Her downtrodden dress and obvious distress drew Tad's curiosity. He introduced himself to her, and she explained that her son was a soldier and she had received notification that he was seriously ill. She wanted him discharged from the service so she could care for him and nurse him back to health. The story appealed to Tad's big heart. "You tell my father about him," he said, and with that he dashed up the stairs to find Pa. The fact that the president was holding a cabinet meeting did not deter him for a moment. Tad burst into the cabinet room, where no doubt great issues dealing with the Civil War were being debated, and in a flood of words demanded that the president deal with the poor woman right away.

"My son," said the president, "I cannot come now. You see that I am engaged."

"Well, I'll bring the woman up to you," Tad said.

With an indulgent sigh, Lincoln excused himself from the cabinet meeting and followed Tad downstairs, where he was introduced to the astonished woman. The president patiently listened to her story. Then he signed a presidential order authorizing the immediate release of her son from the army and handed it to the grateful mother. When Christmas came around that year, Tad appealed to the president for another favor. A fine-looking turkey had been sent to the White House for holiday dinner and Tad, who had a deep attachment to animals, swiftly adopted him as a pet and gave it his favorite name for playthings, Jack. Tad trained Jack to follow him around the White House lawn, eating out of his hand, evidently not realizing that he was fattening the bird for Christmas dinner. As the holiday approached, once again, Tad burst into the cabinet room in tears. Somebody on the White House kitchen staff had just informed him of Jack's fate. Lincoln tried to reason with the boy. "Jack was sent here to be killed and eaten for this very Christmas."

"I can't help it," Tad wept. "He's a good turkey and I don't want him killed." The president again indulged his son—with what may have been the first presidential pardon of a turkey. Jack's life was spared.

Now and then Tad found a companion his own age to play with, but he never found a friend like Willie or the Taft brothers again. Playing with other children seemed to stir up memories of Willie's death, and he preferred the company of adults. He even mailed Willie's two favorite toy railroad cars to his four-year-old cousin, Edward Lewis Baker Jr., in Springfield, because he could not bear to play with them again.

In winter 1864, Tad's inner turmoil was certainly in evidence when Julia Taft made a surprise return to the White House. Julia was invited to attend one of Mary Lincoln's Saturday afternoon receptions. The First Lady was gracious, seemed delighted to see Julia again after all this time, and asked about her mother and brothers. Perhaps Mary was trying to make amends for banishing the Taft boys from the White House after Willie's death, and this uncomfortable subject was not brought up in the conversation. Then, unexpectedly, Tad entered the reception room. The scene that ensued alarmed everyone present. When Tad saw Julia Taft something in him snapped. He threw himself on the floor and started kicking and screaming. His reaction was almost feral. Julia stood there aghast. Several servants had to lift Tad by the arms and remove him from the room. When things quieted down, Mary said, "You must excuse him, Julia. You know what he remembers."

Writing about the episode some sixty years later, Julia called it "very painful." That day in 1864 was the last time she ever saw Mary or Tad. She never set foot in the White House again.

That same year, in February, the White House stables burned to the ground, and Tad was driven to despair. All his cherished pet goats were killed in the blaze. Worse yet was the death of his beloved pony, which had actually been a birthday gift for Willie. Tad was understandably disconsolate after the disaster, and not even the president could find words to ease his pain. All Lincoln could think of was to immediately replace the goats and pony with new livestock.

Tad was given everything he wanted, and since this was a time of war, most of his requests were military in nature. Not many boys had a father who could deliver such goods. From Rear Admiral John Dahlgren, the head of the navy's ordnance department, President Lincoln requested the procurement of a little gun for Tad "that he could not hurt himself with." The admiral may have gone a little overboard in accommodating his commander in chief by delivering to Tad a miniature brass cannon, a scale model of the famous Boat Howitzer, an artillery piece that was making a major contribution to Union victory. From the secretary of the navy Lincoln requested a navy sword, and from Secretary of War Stanton a set of regimental flags. Very often the president would stride briskly out of the White House, with Tad at his side trying to keep up, and march four blocks down to 1207 New York Avenue, to Stuntz's Fancy Store, a magical little toy shop. The owner, Joseph Stuntz, was a retired French soldier who carved wooden toy soldiers in a tiny back room. Sometimes Lincoln showed up alone at Stuntz's and bought toy soldiers for Tad for Christmas. "I want to give him all the toys I did not have and all the toys I would have given the boy who went away," Lincoln told the master toy maker.

Perhaps no episode came to symbolize their precious relationship more than the day the president took Tad to Richmond, Virginia, the conquered capital of the Confederacy.

Richmond was located 110 miles from Washington, D.C., and like Washington it had experienced a wartime population boom, from 38,000 people in 1861 to 128,000 by 1865. It was now the second-largest city in the South, after New Orleans, and it had become the reigning symbol of the Confederacy. But defending Richmond from the Union army demanded a tremendous expenditure of materiel and men. On April 1, 1865, Union general Philip Sheridan overran Confederate defenses at Five Forks, forcing General Lee to the harsh realization that with federal forces just ten miles away, he could best serve the Confederacy by abandoning its capital and retreating south with his outnumbered forces to fight another day.

To the citizens of Richmond, the first sign of the emergency came on Sunday morning, April 2. President of the Confederacy Jefferson Davis was sitting with his wife in the front-row pew at St. Paul's Church when the church sexton came hurrying up the aisle bearing an important message. Davis opened the telegram and saw that it was a communiqué from Robert E. Lee: "I advise that all preparations be made for leaving Richmond tonight." Keeping his composure, the stiff-backed Davis rose with élan and strode out of the church. Although St. Paul's was packed with the elite of Richmond's citizenry, so graceful was Davis's exit he did not for a moment disrupt the services. But a short time later the church sexton returned and whispered something in the ear of Confederate general Joseph Anderson. The next second General Anderson left the church. Inquiring glances were exchanged among the parishioners. Obviously, something alarming was taking place. When the sexton returned a third and then a fourth time to retrieve an important Confederate leader, panic ensued and the congregation rose en masse and rushed for the doors.

One of those worshipers was Dallas Tucker. In 1865 Tucker was a young boy from a prominent Richmond family. Years later he became an Episcopalian minister, and his memories of the fall of Richmond are among the most vivid eyewitness accounts recorded of those days. Young Tucker followed the crowd out of the church and stood there in bewildered silence, watching as government workers piled documents into huge mounds and set them ablaze in the middle of Grace Street. Official word of the evacuation came at 4:00 P.M., and throughout the feverish afternoon and evening Confederate officials and leading citizens fled the city by any means available—horseback, cart, carriage, skiff, canal barge, and boat. Chaos reigned in Richmond.

Jefferson Davis boarded a train at 11:00 P.M., leaving his wife and children behind. The governor of Virginia fled on horseback. The city council, fearing what would happen if Union soldiers uncovered vast stockpiles of whiskey stored in warehouses around the city, met in emergency session and passed a resolution ordering the destruction of all liquor supplies. Committees of citizens gathered at key points and commandeered every saloon and liquor warehouse. Barrels of alcohol were rolled into the streets, and after the barrelheads were knocked in, the liquor was poured directly into the gutters. Thousands of bottles of whiskey and brandy were smashed.

Inevitably, fleeing Confederate soldiers and the dregs of society were drawn to the spectacle and, as the *Richmond Whig* newspaper reported the next day, "From that moment law and order ceased to exist . . . and a Pandemonium reigned." Whiskey was gulped straight from the gutters; hats and boots were used as bottles and filled with booze. A drunken rampage ensued—not by the Union army, which had not even entered the city proper, but by Richmond's own inebriated citizens and soldiers. A howling mob streamed down Main Street and with the butts of their muskets smashed in plate-glass windows and plundered every store. Jewelry, clothing, shoe, hat, and confectionary stores were particular targets. Mob rule broke out. Young Dallas Tucker saw one of the city's richest men running down Cary Street with a bolt of looted red flannel under his arm. Tucker himself acknowledged many years later that he looted a shoe store and went home with a pair of new boots. Government storehouses filled with bacon, smoked meats, flour, sugar, molasses, coffee, clothes, and boots were ransacked. It was, the Whig newspaper reported, the sacking of the city. But the worst was yet to come.

An immense warehouse filled with tobacco was ordered torched so that it would not fall into Union hands, and then Admiral Raphael Semmes set his fleet of ironclad warships ablaze. The flames engulfed the navy's armory, setting off explosions that blew out every window within a two-mile radius. An estimated one hundred thousand shells exploded in the city over the next four hours. Stiff southerly winds carried the fire to the business district and in quick order all of downtown Richmond was ablaze. By morning, from Seventh to Fifteenth Street, from Main Street to the river—the city's entire business district—turned into a wasteland. The buildings consumed in the conflagration included the Bank of Richmond, Bank of the Commonwealth, Bank of Virginia, the American Hotel, Columbian Hotel, the newspaper offices of the *Richmond Enquirer and Dispatch*, the State Court House, the Confederate Post Office, the War Department—an estimated eight hundred structures in total.

The city of Richmond lay in ruins—not at the Union army's hands, but through the wanton and reckless measures taken by the city's Confederate defenders. The situation was so desperate that the mayor of Richmond, Joseph Mayo, accompanied by his city council and several prominent citizens, rode to the front lines under a white flag of truce and delivered a letter to the commanding general of the Union forces surrounding the city: "The army of the Confederate Government having abandoned the city of Richmond, I respectfully request that you will take possession of it with an organized force, to preserve order, and protect the women and children and property." Monday morning the first advance guards of Union soldiers were seen marching up Main Street. The Confederate Stars and Bars flag was pulled down, and the Stars and Stripes hoisted above the city for the first time in four years.

President Lincoln was on the *River Queen* touring the front lines in Virginia when word came to him that Richmond had fallen. The news electrified the North. Perhaps the only equivalent in U.S. history would come eighty years later with V-E Day and V-J Day. "Glorious news!" Mary Lincoln telegraphed the president. Eager to inspect his prize, Lincoln declared his intentions to enter the city the following day, April 4. Tad was with the president on the *River Queen*, and, as luck would have it, it was also Tad's twelfth birthday. The president, usually so responsive to all of Tad's wishes, was reluctant to take the boy because of the extreme security risk; President Lincoln, with his six-foot-four frame and tall silk hat, would make an easy target for any sniper hiding in Richmond. But Tad begged to go and, of course, Lincoln consented. He just could not say no to the boy.

So on April 4 Lincoln and his son sailed up the James River. Two miles from the city, they could go no farther because of torpedoes floating on the surface, ships gone aground, and other Confederate obstructions that made the river impassable. The torpedoes were so close to the presidential vessel that Tad could reach out his hand and touch them. Lincoln and Tad disembarked and walked the rest of the way. Their only security was a contingent of twelve sailors and marines marching six in front, six in the rear, armed with short carbines. Lincoln and Tad were positioned in the center, Tad's hand being held by William H. Crook, the president's bodyguard, who carried with him a Colt revolver.

For two miles the president, with little Tad trying to keep up, strode uphill toward the city center. And when Abraham Lincoln arrived in Richmond, the reception was momentous. Scores, followed by hundreds, finally thousands of black slaves came out to greet their liberator. "Bless the Lord!" they shouted. "The Great Messiah. Come to free his children from bondage. Glory hallelujah."

"You are free," Lincoln said. "Free as air."

They tried to grab at Lincoln's hand and kiss his boots; they touched his clothes to see if this vision was real. One black man fell to his knees as if Lincoln were king.

"Don't kneel to me," said the president. "That is not right. You must kneel to God only and thank Him for the liberty you will enjoy hereafter."

At one point the president was heard to say, "Thank God I have lived to see this. It seems I have been dreaming a horrid dream for four years and now the nightmare is gone."

The security detachment tightened its circle around Tad and the president, the sailors and marines anxiously looking up at the buildings around them. According to Crook, every window appeared to be jammed with the faces of white citizens, eerily silent and sullen, neither welcoming nor full of hatred. From any window or rooftop a sniper could take a potshot at the commander in chief. Crook glanced at the president and saw that his face was set, a brave man "ready for whatever may come."

Suddenly, to Lincoln's left, the blinds from a window on the second floor partially opened. A man wearing the gray uniform of a Confederate soldier appeared, and he looked as if he was pointing a gun at Lincoln. Crook dropped Tad's hand and stepped in front of the president. "I was sure he meant to shoot," Crook said. But no shots were fired. "It seems to me nothing short of miraculous that some attempt on his life was not made." Fixing their bayonets, the sailors told the crowd to clear the way for the president to pass.

At last, a detachment of cavalry came to the rescue and escorted Lincoln to Capitol Square. Tad looked in wonder at the city. All around him lay still-smoldering ruins. Lincoln was shown the way to the Executive Mansion, which just two days earlier had been the Confederate White House. Now he sat in Jefferson Davis's study and asked for a glass of water. Union soldiers observing the scene erupted into cheers. Major General Godfrey Weitzel, commander of U.S. forces occupying Richmond, asked the president for guidance. How, the general wondered, should the citizenry be treated?

"If I were in your place, I'd let 'em up easy, let 'em up easy," Lincoln said.

Five days later, Robert E. Lee surrendered, as Captain Robert Lincoln stood on that porch in Appomattox. Four days after that, Abraham Lincoln was assassinated.

3
Lady in Black

AFTER THE PRESIDENT was pronounced dead, Mary Lincoln returned to the White House, but she could not bear to enter her bedroom. "Oh, no, not there. Oh, I couldn't go in here." Each room she was shown seemed to be filled with the painful memory of her dead son Willie or her martyred husband. Finally, she stepped into a small spare cubbyhole that President Lincoln sometimes used in the summer because he enjoyed the gentle crosswind. Here Mary was put to bed. Comforting her were two friends, Elizabeth Dixon and Mary Jane Welles, wife of Navy Secretary Gideon Welles.

For the rest of the morning, Mary alternated between fits of screaming hysteria and near catatonia.

At 11:00 A.M., just as Andrew Johnson was being sworn in as the seventeenth president, Mary sent a messenger to find her seamstress, Elizabeth Keckley. "I come from Mrs. Lincoln," the messenger told Mrs. Keckley when she opened her front door. "If you are Mrs. Keckley, come with me immediately to the White House."

Lizzie Keckley hastily put on her shawl and bonnet and was driven by carriage to the White House. On the ride over, it seemed to Lizzie that every house in the city was draped in black. Flags flew at half-mast, and the faces of the pedestrians on the street were grim and solemn. Lizzie, forty-seven, was born a slave in Hillsborough, North Carolina, and was taught the skills of a dressmaker by her mother. She bought her freedom in 1855 with a twelve-thousand-dollar loan from a client, and five years later she moved to Baltimore and started a sewing and etiquette school for young black girls. In 1861, she relocated to Washington, where her talent for sewing made her the most sought-after seamstress in the capital. One of her clients was the wife of Jefferson Davis, then a U.S. senator from Mississippi. She also designed Mary Lincoln's inaugural gown. Lizzie and Mary became close confidantes, drawn together by common sorrow. For Mary it was the death of Willie; for Lizzie, it was the loss of her son George, who was killed in 1861 fighting for the Union army.

When Lizzie arrived at the White House this day she saw that a mass of black people had already gathered on the front lawn. Many were weeping, wondering about the fate of their race now that the man they worshiped as their liberator was gone. Lizzie was shown to Mary's room. The shades were drawn and the room was very dark, but in the meager light she saw Mary in a state of anguish, tossing uneasily on the bed. The only other person present was Mary Jane Welles. Lizzie bowed to the navy secretary's wife, who immediately excused herself and left for home, thankful for the relief after having been up with Mary all night. Lizzie went to Mary's bedside, put her hand on the widow's brow, and realized it was hot with fever.

In a low whisper, Mary moaned, "Why did you not come to me last night, Elizabeth? I sent for you." Apparently, three messengers had been dispatched to find her, but no one had the seamstress's correct address. With that, Mary fell into an exhausted sleep. In this moment of calm, Lizzie went to the guest room on the second floor where President Lincoln's body reposed temporarily. Lizzie trembled as she stepped into the chamber to pay homage to the man she called "the Moses of my people." The room was filled with the shell-shocked members of the president's cabinet and his staff generals. They made space for the former slave, as they knew how highly the Lincolns regarded her, and she was permitted to lift the white cloth that covered the fallen president. Staring into Abraham Lincoln's face, notwithstanding the violent way he was killed, she found "something beautiful" in his expression, something grandly solemn. "There lurked the sweetness and gentleness of childhood, and the stately grandeur of godlike intellect." Mrs. Keckley found her throat tightening. She turned away, her eyes brimming with tears.

When Lizzie returned to Mary's room, she found Robert and Tad at the bedside. Mary had awakened and was in the throes of a paroxysm of grief. Robert was tenderly bending over his mother while little Tad was squatting on the floor at the foot of the bed—"a world of agony on his young face." Mary cried herself into convulsions. She wailed and sobbed and let out almost unearthly shrieks. Mrs. Keckley pressed a cold compress to her brow and tried to calm down the "terrible tornado." Tad's grief was as profound as his mother's, but even he was stricken into silence by his mother's uncontrollable spasms. He threw his arms around Mary's neck and between his own broken sobs said, "Don't, Mama! Don't cry, or you will make me cry, too. You will break my heart." Mary pulled herself together and brought her youngest son into her arms. Somehow she found the strength to bring to Tad a mother's reassurance.

As the eldest son, Robert took on certain burdens that come with the death of the father. His first order of business was to seek the advice of the man he trusted more than any other—Justice David Davis of the United States Supreme Court. Hardly able to keep the pen from shaking, he wrote a telegram to Davis, who was in Chicago: "Please come at once to Washington & take charge of my father's affairs. Answer." Davis replied that he would take on the responsibility. "Many thanks," Robert responded by telegraph. "Please come as soon as possible. R.T. Lincoln." Robert sent another telegram to an uncle he admired, Clark M. Smith, a Springfield merchant who was married to Mary Lincoln's sister Ann. To Smith, who was in New York City on business, Robert telegraphed a single word: "Come."

Workmen were already constructing the wooden platform on which Lincoln's coffin would lie in state in the East Room. It was so huge in scale it became known as the Temple of Death. By Easter Sunday, the sound of construction was driving Mary to the point of madness. To her, each blow of the hammer was like the sound of the shot from John Wilkes Booth's pistol. Mary Jane Welles's son, Edgar, was enlisted to write a note to the work crew supervisor, asking them to be aware of the sensitivities. "Mrs. Lincoln is very much disturbed by noise," he told them. "The other night when putting them up, every plank that dropped gave her a spasm and every nail driven reminded her of a pistol shot." A compromise was reached—the work could go on on the condition that the men muffle the noise level. As quietly as they could, they continued construction.

Mrs. Lincoln's delicate mental health was accommodated in other ways. Monday evening, pallbearers took off their shoes because they did not want to disturb Mary when they lifted the president's coffin from the guest room and carried it to the ornate East Room downstairs where Lincoln would lie in state.

Mary mourned in private. Her only regular visitors were her sons and Lizzie Keckley. The wives of Washington's leading dignitaries called to pay their respects but Mary refused to see any of them; this snub was met with dismay and bitter resentment. It was another mark against Mary Todd Lincoln in a city that had already accused her of Confederate sympathies and coarse behavior. Only a handful of outside visitors got in to see Mary—the abolitionist Senator Charles Sumner of Massachusetts, former Illinois representative Isaac Arnold, and a few select friends: Elizabeth Dixon, Mary Jane Welles, Sally Orne, and Dr. Anson Henry, a physician and friend from Springfield. With all her visitors, Mary would relive the assassination in blood-curdling detail. She seemed completely fixated on the particulars of the assassination.

Mary did not attend her husband's funeral. The explanation was the same given in 1862 when her son Willie died. She was too bereft, too overcome with grief. On Wednesday, six hundred invited guests crowded into the East Room, but Mary remained in her room. They were all there—cabinet officers, leading congressmen, the U.S. Supreme Court justices, and the diplomatic corps. Lincoln's handsome coffin—built at a cost close to two thousand dollars—was made of mahogany and lined with lead. Four silver medallions were set on each side for use as handles for the pallbearers. Lincoln's head rested on a white pillow in the open casket. Standing in a place of honor was the new president of the United States, Andrew Johnson, nervously crossing and uncrossing his hands. Robert and Tad, exhausted, their faces swollen and stained with tears, were positioned at their father's feet. General Grant, a black mourning crepe affixed around his arm, stood at the head of the coffin. Grant could not control his weeping. Later he would say that it was the saddest day of his life. The booming voice of the Reverend Thomas Hall, pastor of the Epiphany Episcopal Church, carried up the staircase and reached Mary's room. "I am the Resurrection and the Life saith the Lord; he that believeth in me, though he were dead, yet shall he live, and whoever liveth and believeth in me shall never die." At that precise moment, timed to coincide with the White House ceremony, Americans gathered in record numbers at churches across the nation to pay their respects to President Lincoln.

When at last the coffin was closed, twelve sergeants carried it out of the White House to a funeral car that bore the president's body up Pennsylvania Avenue to the Capitol building. The day, Wednesday, April 19, was sunny, a perfect spring day in Washington, but the steady roll of drums and dirge of bells that tolled for the dead were a grim reminder of the tragedy that hung over the city. Lincoln's empty boots sat in the stirrups of the riderless horse—a tradition that was followed ninety-eight years later at the funeral of President John F. Kennedy. In slow time, with rhythmic steps, a detachment of black soldiers marched at the head of the procession, followed by regiments of regular troops. Behind these came hundreds of wounded Union soldiers, many in bandages and struggling with crutches. Next came four thousand black Americans, marching forty abreast, in orderly fashion, all wearing white gloves and clasping hands. In the rear of the cortege came heavy artillery. Sixty thousand citizens lined the route. Secretary of State Seward, critically stabbed in the face and throat by one of John Wilkes Booth's coconspirators, watched the procession from his bedroom window.

When the riderless carriage reached the Capitol, the coffin was carried into the rotunda. Every oil painting and statue was draped, except for the portrait of George Washington, adorned for this day only with a simple black sash. There in the rotunda the coffin lay on a wood bier for twenty-four hours as thousands of civilians filed past it for one final gesture of condolence. The next day the coffin was carried to the Washington railroad depot, where it was put on a nine-car funeral train. The route of the train would follow precisely the circuitous journey taken by President-elect Lincoln in 1861, when he left Springfield for the inauguration in Washington. It was a fourteen-day journey back to Springfield that gave the rest of America a chance to bid President Lincoln farewell.

Robert Lincoln decided to stay behind for the time being to take care of Tad and his mother and deal with a hundred details involving his father's estate. But another Lincoln was on board the funeral train. The body of Lincoln's beloved son Willie, dead now three years, was with him. Arrangements were made for Willie's little casket to be removed from its temporary tomb at Oak Hill Cemetery in Georgetown. Now father and son were together again on their last pitiful journey home.

During this time of crisis everyone was impressed with Robert Lincoln. It seemed that dealing with the calamity of his father's assassination had brought out the best in the young man. He was lovingly attentive to his mother and provided a big brother's steady shoulder for Tad. "His manly bearing . . . made me feel that he was a worthy son of a worthy father," said presidential assistant Edward O'Neill. On April 21 Robert resigned his army captain's commission. At some point he also went to Ford's Theatre and conducted a personal inspection of the president's box where his father was shot. There Robert sat and pondered what might have been. If only he had accepted his parents' invitation to go with them to the theater the night of

April 14, how history might have changed. There was a chair in the rear of the box, close to the door by which the assassin Booth had entered. Robert came to believe that because of his position in the presidential party, this is where he would have sat. Perhaps he could have stopped Booth if he had been there. Robert returned several more times to Ford's Theatre, and for the rest of his life he lived with the regret of his decision to stay home the night the president and First Lady went to see *Our American Cousin*.

"Our loss is indeed terrible," Robert wrote to a professor he knew at Harvard. "In all my plans for the future, the chief object I had in view was the approbation of my Father, and now that he is gone and in such a way, I feel utterly without spirit or courage. I know that such a feeling is wrong, and that it is my duty to overcome it. I trust for the sake of my Mother and little brother that I will be able to do so."

Tad Lincoln suffered a double loss—his father was also his best friend. But Tad demonstrated a sensitivity and maturity surprising for a child so coddled and pampered. One night he heard his mother weeping in her room and he went in to soothe her anguish. "Don't cry, Mama; I cannot sleep if you cry! Papa was good and he has gone to heaven. He is happy there. He is with God and my brother Willie. Don't cry, Mama, or I will cry, too." The words had their effect. Mary's tears dried up this evening because she could not bear to be the cause of more misery for Taddie.

Tad knew that time was running out and very soon he and his family would have to leave the White House. His life as the indulged son of the United States president with the entire White House staff at his beck and call was coming to an end. One morning Elizabeth Keckley heard a conversation between Tad and a White House servant who was helping him get dressed. "Pa is dead. I can hardly believe that I shall never see him again. I must learn to take care of myself now." After a moment of thoughtful silence Tad continued. "Yes, Pa is dead, and I am only Tad Lincoln now, little Tad, like other little boys. I am not a president's son now. I won't have many presents any more. Well, I will try and be a good boy, and will hope to go some day to Pa and brother Willie, in heaven." Tad asked his mother to dispense with the services of his nurse. He was determined to become more independent and learn how to dress himself, which at age twelve he was still unable to do.

Though Mary Lincoln was prostrate with grief, her notorious temper still flared on occasion. One particular target of her rage was President Johnson. The day of Abraham Lincoln's death, John Hay advised the family that someone should seek a meeting with Andrew Johnson and work out the details of when Mary and her sons should move out of the White House, which was now rightfully the new president's home. Senator Alexander Ramsey of Minnesota was sent as an emissary to meet with Johnson. Graciously, Johnson agreed there was no hurry. Ramsey reported back to Robert on Easter Sunday. Standing in his father's office, Robert absorbed the news that his family was under no pressure to leave. Johnson seemed to be aware of Mary Lincoln's fragile mental health and was making every effort to be thoughtful to the Lincolns. As he waited for Mary Lincoln to clear out, Andrew Johnson ran the federal government out of a small office set up for him at the Treasury Department. In late April Robert communicated directly with the new president, apologizing with some embarrassment for the continuing delay. Robert acknowledged the "great inconvenience" but added, "My mother is so prostrated that I must beg your indulgence. Mother tells me that she cannot possibly be ready to leave here for 2½ weeks."

But bad blood reigned. Johnson was fully aware of the contempt in which Mary Lincoln held him, stemming from that disastrous performance at Abraham Lincoln's second inaugural when Johnson delivered his address in an obvious state of drunken impairment. The night of the assassination, Johnson had hurried to the Petersen House to see the condition of President Lincoln for himself, and there he paid his respects to Robert and Mary. But privately he was informed that his presence was disturbing the First Lady and he was asked to leave.

Johnson was an honest and honorable man racked by personal demons. He was raised in poverty and never attended school. At age ten he was apprenticed to a tailor. It was his wife who taught him to read and write. Mary Lincoln's treatment of him the night of the assassination was humiliating, and Johnson made the situation worse by never sending her a letter of condolence. Nor did he pay a courtesy call. As the days went by, Mary vented, calling Johnson "wicked" and saying he "behaved in the most brutal way."

At some point, Mary's fury at Johnson entered the realm of irrationality. On April 28 she asked Secretary of War Stanton to visit her at the White House. Robert, who was dealing with most of his mother's correspondence because she was still too physically weak to put pen to paper, wrote Stanton, "Would you, if convenient, be kind enough to call this evening and see Mother?" Stanton's offensive outburst the night of the assassination—when he shouted at Mary Lincoln, "Keep that woman out of here!"—was apparently either forgiven or forgotten. The matter Mary wanted to discuss with Stanton was too pressing, and she considered Stanton to be the only man in government with the authority to deal with her issues. Stanton was shown into Mary Lincoln's room and listened in astonishment as she laid out her theory that Andrew Johnson was involved in the conspiracy to assassinate her husband.

Johnson had been living in a first floor suite at Kirkwood House at Twelfth and Pennsylvania. The morning of the assassination, one of John Wilkes Booth's coconspirators, George Atzerodt, registered for a room at the Kirkwood directly above Johnson's. Atzerodt was given the task of assassinating Johnson, while Booth focused on Lincoln, and another conspirator, Lewis Powell, aka Lewis Paine, dealt with Secretary of State Seward. But the weak link in the chain of conspirators was the German-born Atzerodt, who was a drunk and a dunce. Atzerodt spent Good Friday getting hammered in the hotel bar and feebly pressing the bartender for information about Johnson's security detail and routine. His inquiries were so over the top the bartender became alarmed, but Atzerodt was dismissed as an inebriated idiot.

Later that day, Booth himself appeared at Kirkwood House intending to have a final pep talk with his coconspirator. Booth asked for Atzerodt's room and was told that Atzerodt was out. Then Booth had a diabolical idea. He asked the desk clerk if Vice President Johnson was home. When he was informed Johnson was also out, he requested hotel stationery and penned a note for Johnson: "Don't wish to disturb you. Are you at home? J. Wilkes Booth." He told the desk clerk to leave the note in Johnson's mailbox. Booth's scheme was ingenious. He was quite aware that Atzerodt would probably never carry out his part of the plot. By framing Johnson and making it seem as if the vice president was connected to the assassination of Lincoln, Booth was planting the seed of suspicion about Lincoln's successor.

The day after the assassination, police investigating Booth's associates went to Kirkwood House looking for Atzerodt and found Booth's note addressed to the vice president. It was dismissed as an obvious setup, especially after Atzerodt was arrested five days later and made a full confession, clearing Johnson of any involvement.

But Mary Lincoln had her doubts about Johnson. She presented her hypothesis to Secretary Stanton. "Why was that card of Booth's found in his box—some acquaintance certainly existed. I have been impressed with the harrowing thought that he [Johnson] had an understanding with the conspirators and they knew their man. Did not Booth say there is one thing he would not tell?" Nothing Stanton said would dissuade Mary of her certainty that Johnson was in some way behind the assassination.

On April 25, following a twelve-day pursuit, Union soldiers found John Wilkes Booth hiding in a tobacco barn outside Bowling Green, Virginia. Shot in the neck after refusing to surrender, his last words recorded before dying were, "Tell my mother I died for my country." As his fellow conspirators were rounded up, Mary became convinced that only half the story was getting out. One man in particular felt the sting of her wrath. John F. Parker was one of four Washington City police officers assigned to the White House as President Lincoln's personal bodyguard. On Good Friday, April 14, Parker showed up three hours late for the night shift but arrived in time to accompany Abraham Lincoln and the First Lady to Ford's Theatre.

Parker was thirty-four, the son of a butcher, and lived on L Street with his wife and three children. It is almost impossible to believe that a man with his personnel record would be assigned to protect the president of the United States. Parker joined the metro police force in 1861, and by 1865 he had been brought up on charges of cursing out a grocer, insulting a woman who requested police protection, drinking on duty, firing a pistol through a window, and residing in a whorehouse for five straight weeks. (The prostitutes testified as character witnesses on his behalf at his departmental hearing. He was acquitted.) Twice he was discovered sleeping on duty in a streetcar.

Parker arrived at Ford's Theatre ahead of Lincoln and scouted out the state box. He determined it presented no danger to the president. The Lincoln party arrived at 8:25 P.M. with *Our American Cousin* already in progress. Parker met them outside the theater and led the way inside. On stage, the star of the play, Laura Keene, and the other performers halted production as the president and First Lady, Major Henry Rathbone and his fiancée Clara Harris made their way to the box. The 1,675 people in the audience rose and applauded and the conductor, Professor Withers, lifted his baton and the band played "Hail to the Chief." When Lincoln and his wife settled into their seats, everyone sat and the play resumed.

Parker was supposed to sit on a hardback chair positioned outside the box and stop anyone from accosting the president. But at about 9:00 P.M. he became bored—he could only hear the play and could not see the action on the stage, so he left his post and found a better seat. Even then, evidently, *Our American Cousin* failed to interest Parker, because at intermission he wandered out of the theater, now leaving the president completely unprotected. To make his dereliction of duty even more reprehensible, Parker approached the president's carriage driver on the street and said, "How would you like a little ale?" The two men strolled down to Taltavul's tavern for a drink. As if to further certify Parker's incompetence, John Wilkes Booth walked into the same tavern shortly before 10:00 P.M. and sat at the end of the bar. There Booth fortified himself with whiskey before entering Ford's Theatre and bounding up the stairs to the state box. Booth fully expected to take out the president's guard, but to his amazement all he found was an empty chair—Parker's. There was no one to challenge Booth. He turned the knob and entered, closing the door behind him.

While Parker was having another over at Taltavul's, Booth aimed his derringer and opened fire, forever changing American history. In the chaos of the night, Officer Parker simply disappeared. He showed up at his precinct the next morning at 6:00 A.M., and he had in his custody a prostitute he was acquainted with. Apparently, he was determined to make an arrest—any arrest—to account for his whereabouts. Parker was charged with neglect of duty on May 1. The departmental trial was held two days later. No official transcript of the proceedings survives, and there was no newspaper coverage of the trial. And for some inexplicable reason, the charge was dismissed.

One night, several days after the assassination, Lizzie Keckley was in Mary's room as the widow lay on the bed. A White House servant came in to see whether there was anything Mrs. Lincoln required.

"Who is on watch tonight?" Mary asked the servant. She was told it was John F. Parker. According to Lizzie Keckley, Mary erupted. "What! The man who attended us to the theater on the night my dear, good husband was murdered! He, I believe is one of the murderers. Tell him to come in to me."

It so happened that the Virginia-born Parker was standing behind the half-open door and overheard Mary's accusation. When he entered Mary's room, he was already expecting the worst. She turned on him. "So you are on guard tonight—on guard in the White House after helping to murder the president." Mary had a point. It did seem disgraceful that a guard whose negligence contributed to Lincoln's assassination was still assigned to White House duty.

"Pardon me," Parker answered in a trembling voice, "but I did not help to murder the president. I could never stoop to murder—much less to the murder of so good and great a man as the president."

"But it appears that you did stoop to murder."

"No, no! Don't say that. God knows that I am innocent."

"I don't believe you," Mary told him. "Why were you not at the door to keep the assassin out when he rushed into the box?"

"I did wrong, I admit, and I have bitterly repented it, but I did not help to kill the president. I did not believe that anyone would try to kill so good a man in such a public place and the belief made me careless. I was attracted by the play and did not see the assassin enter the box."

"But you should have seen him," Mary said. "You had no business to be careless. I shall always believe that you are guilty." Parker tried to answer back, but Mary dismissed him with a wave of her hand. "Go now and keep your watch," she told him. Shaken and ashen-faced, Parker left the room. When the door closed behind him, Mary buried her face in her pillow and broke out in sobs. (Parker remained on the metro police force for three more years until he was finally fired in 1868—not for negligence in guarding President Lincoln, but for sleeping on duty. "Parker knew he had failed in duty," said William Crook, Parker's colleague on the metro police force. "He looked like a convicted criminal the next day. He was never the same afterwards." Parker died in 1890 and was buried in an unmarked grave.)

Meanwhile, the funeral train bearing President Lincoln's body crept along at an achingly slow pace. All along the route, ordinary people bowed their heads and saluted the passing of the coffin. In Philadelphia, mourners stood in a three-mile-long line waiting to pay tribute to Lincoln at Independence Hall. One of the mourners was the fifteenth president, James Buchanan. He drove his buggy eighty miles from Lancaster, Pennsylvania, to honor the man who had replaced him in office. The coffin was put on public display to historic crowds in New York City, Albany, Cleveland, Indianapolis, and finally in Chicago. And everywhere along the train route, even in remote prairie country, simple farmers and townspeople bowed their heads in silent tribute to their fallen leader.

Finally, after fourteen days and 1,662 miles, the train reached its ultimate destination, Springfield. At 9:00 A.M. when the train pulled in, there was a dangerous crush of mourners who had gathered at the railroad depot. From the depot, the coffin was transported by hearse to the Illinois capital building, where an estimated seventy-five thousand people—with "the greatest decorum, respect and tenderness"—viewed Lincoln's remains as he lay in state. Hovering over the coffin was a life-size painting of George Washington and a banner with the axiom "Washington the Father, Lincoln the Savior." Already George Washington and Abraham Lincoln were being linked as one in the hearts of Americans.

Dr. O. D. Brown had embalmed Lincoln in Washington, D.C., and on the funeral train the physician examined the body every day and did what he could to retard the process of decomposition. A morbid debate ensued. Some people who viewed the open casket thought the preservation of Lincoln's features remarkable, especially considering the violent nature of his death. Special praise was given to Dr. Brown for his mastery of the embalming process. But others were disappointed. The *New York Evening Post* complained that Lincoln's eyes were sunken, his face discolored, and his lips too tightly compressed. "It is not the genial, kindly face of Abraham Lincoln; it is a ghostly shadow."

Robert Lincoln was in Springfield as the official representative of the Lincoln family. He had left Washington the afternoon of May 1 and arrived there the evening of May 3 on board the Great Western Railroad, traveling with his father's private secretary, John Nicolay. Mary and Tad had remained behind in Washington.

Finally, at 10:00 A.M., the coffin was closed for the last time and placed on a hearse drawn by six magnificent black horses draped in bunting. Directly behind the hearse came two grooms who walked a horse named "Old Bob" once owned by President Lincoln. Next came Robert, and behind him a multitude of ten thousand people on foot. They followed the procession under a clear blue sky to a vault carved into the side of a hill, at the Oak Ridge Cemetery, a piece of pasture just north of the city.

A funeral hymn titled "Rest, Noble Martyr," written for the occasion by the Reverend Dr. Phineas D. Gurley, pastor of the New York Avenue Presbyterian Church in Washington where the Lincolns worshiped, closed the services:

> Rest, noble martyr! Rest in peace
> Who, like thee, fell in Freedom's cause,
> The nation's life to save.
> Thy name shall live while time endures
> And men shall say of thee
> He saved his country from its foes,
> And bade the slave be free.

The *Illinois State Journal* reported that Abraham Lincoln had returned to the bosom of his neighbors and friends who "loved and revered him."

Even the Democratic-leaning *State Register* called it the "saddest, yet the grandest day ever witnessed in Springfield."

The key to the vault was handed over to Robert Lincoln. Robert remained in Springfield for several days at his cousin Elizabeth Grimsley's house, visiting relatives and accepting the condolences of ordinary citizens who came by to pay their respects to the son of Father Abraham. When he returned to Washington the evening of May 8, he went to the White House to check on his mother and brother and give them his account of the funeral. He opened a map of Oak Ridge Cemetery and showed Mary the precise location of the vault. She was pleased to hear that a company of Union soldiers stood guard over the tomb. Oak Ridge was Springfield's most esteemed burial ground, and Mary was very familiar with the property. In 1860, when the Lincolns were still residents of Springfield, Oak Ridge was founded, and overnight became the favored place for internment among Springfield's elite. Her sister Elizabeth Todd Edwards and her cousin John Todd Stuart both owned family plots there. There, she presumed, the body of Abraham Lincoln would rest in peace.

But Robert had the duty of informing his mother that a controversy was brewing in Springfield. Prominent citizens of the city had formed the Lincoln Monument Association, and money was already being collected to purchase a beautiful piece of property in the center of the city where a monument whose spire would tower over every other building in Springfield would be constructed. It would be a proper memorial to Springfield's greatest son, they proposed. Mary listened to Robert's report and erupted. How dare these people! Without even consulting the widow! Mary was rightfully indignant.

The news had one positive impact on Mary—it shocked her out of her dazed state of mourning. In a fury, Mary told Robert to write to the monument association and inform them of the family's objections. Then she wrote her own letter to the governor of Illinois, Richard Oglesby. The letter was written on mourning paper—bordered with a wide black band (for the rest of her life Mary would never again write a letter on anything but mourning paper). She had no issue with the construction of a suitable monument, she told the governor, but it must be placed over her husband's remains in the place of her choosing—Oak Ridge Cemetery—"with the written promise that no other bodies, save the president, his wife, his sons and sons' families shall ever be deposited within the enclosure." In the event the governor and city fathers did not agree immediately, Mary threatened to exercise her widow's prerogative and exhume the body and rebury President Lincoln's remains in a vault beneath the Capitol in Washington. Mary the tornado was back in business.

The news of Mary's objections to the memorial upset the people of Springfield. It was not just an issue of civic pride but also commerce. Six acres in downtown Springfield had already been purchased for the then-considerable sum of $5,300. Real money had been shelled out. But Mary was relentless. Only she, as the widow, could settle on her husband's final resting place.

She even evoked the spirit of Abraham Lincoln himself. Just a few weeks before his assassination, she related in one letter, during their tour of General Grant's headquarters at City Point, Virginia, President Lincoln pointed to a heavenly slip of land along the banks of the James River. She quoted him as saying, "When I am gone, lay my remains in some quiet place like this." Clearly, downtown Springfield was not what the Great One had in mind as his final resting place. Mary was also determined to be buried next to her husband when the day came for her own funeral. For Mary it was a fixation. The entire family—Abraham, Mary, Robert, Eddie, Willie, and Tad—would one day be together again, and this could not be guaranteed if she consented to burial grounds on public property, where ultimate authority would reside with municipal government.

For the good citizens of Springfield, it was a confrontation in which they could not possibly prevail. The contributors to the memorial fund took a big financial hit, and the downtown parcel of land eventually had to be resold at a loss. Mary was victorious, but it came at a price—the alienation of the proud citizens of Springfield. "The people are in a rage about it," wrote one resident in a letter to the editor of the local newspaper. "All the hard stories that ever were told about her are told over again. She has no friends here." However valid her position, Mary had now managed to irritate the populace of yet another capital city.

Mary had a big decision to make: where to start her new life as the widow Mrs. Lincoln. Justice David Davis was now in Washington and, at Robert's request, serving as executor of the Lincoln estate. He urged Mary to go back to Springfield; to Davis, it was the only rational thing to do. An analysis of Abraham Lincoln's assets showed that the president had left an estate valued at eighty thousand dollars in cash, bonds, and securities. Mary would have to live off the meager interest, but if she led a frugal lifestyle, she could just manage. Davis tried to convince her that Springfield made the most sense because she owned her house at Eighth and Jackson free and clear. In this Davis had Robert's full backing. But Mary resisted. Just as she could never again enter her son Willie's bedroom after his death, she could not bear the thought of returning to the house in Springfield that was so full of memories of her great and good husband.

"Elizabeth, I can never go back to Springfield," she told Lizzie Keckley. "No, never, until I go in my shroud to be laid by my dear husband's. Heaven speed that day! I should like to live for my sons, but life is so full of misery that I would rather die." Perhaps Mary also believed that Springfield was too provincial. The storm over Lincoln's burial place in Springfield reinforced Mary's aversion to living there. No, Springfield was out of the question.

So Mary settled on Chicago. She knew the city, and it would be close to Springfield, making it easy for her to visit the graves of her husband and sons.

Mary begged Lizzie to go with her. But the former slave, now Mary Lincoln's closest confidante, was reluctant. "I cannot go west with you, Mrs. Lincoln." One reason was her thriving seamstress business. She explained that she was committed to making a client's wedding trousseau, and it was due in less than a week.

Mary was resolute. "But you must go to Chicago with me, Elizabeth. I cannot do without you. I have determined that you shall go to Chicago with me, and you must go." It was settled. Lizzie could not refuse Abraham Lincoln's widow.

Mary became consumed with the ordeal of collecting and organizing her possessions for this big move. Unfortunately, she seemed to have kept everything she had ever owned. She threw nothing away. Robert was mortified at how long the process was taking. As the liaison between his mother and Andrew Johnson, he knew it would be his burden to explain yet another delay in moving out of the White House. Lizzie Keckley was helping Mary sort out her clothes when Robert suggested speeding the process by burning everything. He was utterly serious.

"What are you going to do with that old dress, Mother?" he pointedly asked.

Mary said dismissively, "Never mind, Robert, I will find a use for it. You do not understand this business."

"What is more, I hope I may never understand it." Robert even expressed the hope that the train carrying Mary's belongings to Chicago would catch fire and "burn all of your old plunder up."

Robert left the room in a huff. "Robert is so impetuous," Mary told Lizzie Keckley. "He never thinks about the future." But even Lizzie Keckley took to calling Mary a "hoarder," and wondered about her judgment. When Lizzie questioned Mary about the wisdom of packing every bonnet she owned, she answered that she might find some use for them. Besides, they were "handy to have about the house."

Oddly, however, Mary did give away many of her late husband's personal effects, partly out of generosity and also out of a desire to break with the past. It was just too painful to be in the presence of so many of articles connected to Abraham Lincoln. Lizzie Keckley was presented with the bloodstained bonnet and cloak Mrs. Lincoln wore the night her husband was assassinated. The seamstress also received Lincoln's comb and brush, the gloves he wore at his second inaugural and a pair of overshoes he relied on when it rained.

Justice moved swiftly in those days, some would argue perhaps too swiftly. The military commission hearing the evidence against Booth's eight accused coconspirators commenced on May 10 on the third floor of the federal penitentiary known as the Old Washington Arsenal. Eight days later, before a packed courtroom, twelve-year-old "Master Tad Lincoln" caused a stir when he strode into the courtroom to observe the trial of the defendants accused of conspiring to murder his father. The trial lasted a total of fifty days. On June 30 the military judges rendered their decision. All eight were found guilty. Lewis Powell, David Herold, George Atzerodt, and Mary Surratt were sentenced to death by hanging. The other defendants, including Dr. Samuel Mudd, received prison terms.

Tension was building between Robert and his mother. It rankled the young Harvard graduate that she treated him like a child and ignored his sensible advice about living in Springfield. It confounded him to see the growing stack of boxes and trunks being filled by Lizzie Keckley at his mother's direction. When packing was finally completed, there were sixty boxes and twenty trunks in total. But as the pile grew, so did a whispering campaign defaming Mary's character.

With Mary secluded and in a permanent state of bereavement in the second-floor living quarters, downstairs, the White House was in chaos. Andrew Johnson was still ensconced at the Treasury Department and, in this power vacuum, anarchy reigned. Honest people who should have known better deemed White House property fair game and made off with the china and silver. Servants and some unscrupulous visitors were mostly to blame. By early May several important pieces of White House crystal and state china with the presidential seal were already up for sale in a Georgetown pawnshop. Somehow, a superb Japanese punch bowl—booty from Commodore Perry's historic opening to Japan—ended up at a saloon on High Street in Baltimore. The White House was being systematically looted.

People started to wonder what Mary Lincoln was really carting off in those boxes and trunks. Did all those possessions really belong to the Lincolns, or were they gifts to the government and thus part of the public treasury? The accusations upset Mary. In her defense, she said she took only simple things that were clearly meant as personal gifts for President Lincoln—a chair built by a Civil War veteran, a country quilt sewn by an elderly woman who revered Abraham Lincoln. These things, Mary said in a letter to a friend, were "more precious than gold to my darling husband." They were of sentimental value only and had no true monetary value, she contended. But it was one more mark against Mary.

Finally, the time came for the Lincolns to leave the White House. Robert called on President Johnson and notified him that in just a few days the White House would be his at last. True to form, Johnson made no effort to inquire about Mrs. Lincoln's well-being.

On May 23, five weeks after the assassination of President Lincoln, his widow and two surviving sons walked out of the White House. Mary looked frail and bent over, dressed head to toe in black. There was no one to see them off, no crowds or friends. The fact that few even seemed to notice her exit must have added to Mary's grief. In her weeks of bereavement Mary had refused to see anyone. Now it was Washington's turn to spurn her. "I go hence, broken hearted, with every hope almost in life—crushed," Mary wrote to a friend.

The Lincolns were taken to the station in a carriage ride so silent it was "almost painful," Lizzie Keckley said. At the railroad depot they boarded a chartered train to Chicago. Accompanying Mary, Robert, and Tad were Lizzie Keckley, Dr. Henry, and two White House guards, Thomas Cross and William Crook.

At dawn the next day, the Stars and Stripes were hoisted up the White House flagpole at full staff for the first time in five weeks. President Johnson, with General Ulysses S. Grant at his side on the reviewing stand, watched in triumph as one hundred and fifty thousand soldiers marched down Pennsylvania Avenue for the grand review of the victorious Armies of the Republic.

Inside the White House, workmen were making last-minute repairs, preparing the executive mansion for the new president. In a second-floor bedroom they found something unexpected—the vast collection of Tad Lincoln's toy soldiers. These were the beautiful, hand-carved figurines Abraham Lincoln had purchased for his son at Stuntz's toy store. They were Tad's favorite playthings, but he had left them behind, probably because he could not bear to see them again. He was no longer the president's son. He was just Tad Lincoln.

4
Chicago

THE JOURNEY FROM Washington to Chicago took fifty-four hours. Mary Lincoln and her sons rode in a private car, but despite this luxury it was a wretched time. Mary wept for most of the seven-hundred-mile trip and suffered excruciating migraines. Other times she was "in a daze," said William Crook, the White House guard assigned to accompany the Lincoln family to Chicago. "It seemed almost a stupor. She hardly spoke. No one could get near enough to her grief to comfort her." Lizzie Keckley, Dr. Anson Henry, and the other White House guard, Thomas Cross, rode with her and did what they could. Robert Lincoln brooded and kept to himself while Tad occupied his time with Crook, who was just twenty-six but reliable and adored by Tad. In the observation car Tad and William Crook watched the passing scenery of a nation that was now at peace. Tad asked many intelligent questions, but other than the boy's enthusiasm for travel and adventure, it was a glum and silent ride. Finally, around noon on May 24, the sad little group reached its destination.

In 1865 Chicago's population was 190,000, ranking it ninth among U.S. cities. It was, according to a European novelist, "one of the most miserable" cities she had ever visited. Another writer declared Chicago "repulsive to every human sense."

Visitors spoke of the city's foul odors, which would have assaulted the Lincolns. Chicago reeked. Even by the appalling hygiene standards of the times, Chicago was notorious for its filth. Homeowners and shopkeepers threw their garbage into open gutters. Heaps of manure littered city streets, even Michigan Avenue. The editor of a local newspaper described the Chicago River as a "mass of blood, grease, and animal entrails." Epidemics of typhoid, cholera, and smallpox were annual events in Chicago; the city's death rate was the highest in the nation. The *Chicago Weekly Democrat* once rhetorically asked, "Why do so many children die in Chicago?" It put forward its own answer: The children were being fed milk that came from cows covered in sores and fed with "whiskey slops." City residents drew their water from Lake Michigan, but this source was suspect. Newts swam in abundance in Lake Michigan, and drinking a glass of water became an experience in queasiness—that "strangely ticklish sensation as a 'finny fellow' wriggled down the throat."

But Chicago was also a robust city, and it was booming. The same historian who called it "repulsive" also acknowledged the city's originality and boldness. "There are no men of leisure in Chicago," he noted. A remarkable collection of entrepreneurs had settled in the city. Marshall Field, Aaron Montgomery Ward, Joseph Medill, Cyrus McCormick, and George Pullman were invigorating Chicago with big ideas, and in the next few years, they would make their mark on the nation.

Then, as now, young people were trying to improve their lot in life. If you looked through the *Chicago Tribune* that month, you would find an ad placed by a "respectable" English girl, just arrived from Canada, looking for work as a chambermaid in a "first-class" home. A young immigrant from Germany was seeking a position in a private household—"upstairs work preferred." Vegetable syrup marketed under the name Cherokee Remedy claimed to cure gonorrhea and urinary tract infections. A one-dollar bottle of Grecian Compound guaranteed the growth of whiskers and mustaches in six weeks on even the smoothest of faces. There was a sale on dentures made of vulcanite rubber at the dental offices of D. M. Towner on Dearborn Street. A ton of ice went for two dollars and a trained pointer dog cost ten dollars.

Just published was a hastily written book on the life and death of John Wilkes Booth, on sale for twenty cents. In May 1865, Abraham Lincoln's enduring legacy in American folklore was already evident in Chicago. A replica of the log cabin in which Lincoln was born was on exhibit at the fairgrounds at Wabash and Randolph streets. There to take questions about the Great One was Dennis Hanks, the son of Lincoln's maternal great-aunt. Hanks, who claimed to have taught young Abe penmanship with a buzzard's quill, bore a startling physical likeness to Abraham Lincoln. This plus Hanks's stovepipe hat, long-legged stride, and Kentuckian country twang completed the eerie portrait of a living reincarnation of the late president.

Without fanfare, Mary Lincoln and her two sons checked into the Tremont House. It must have come as a shock to her how little notice was paid to her presence in the city. When she lived in the White House, every desire was accommodated. When she wanted something, a great fuss was made over getting it done. But here in Chicago she was, according to her biographer Ruth Painter Randall, an ordinary citizen, "a pale, sad little woman in a widow's deep mourning."

In a pitiable letter to Oliver Halstead Jr., a Washington acquaintance, written from her room at Tremont House, Mary wrote of her solitude. "I am alone. . . . [M]y Husband gone from me, the agony is insupportable. I am scarcely able to sit up. . . . My health is so miserable." She added that were it not for her precious boys who still depended on her she would welcome death. "I would pray our Heavenly Father, to remove me from a world, where I have been so bitter a sufferer. To rejoin my Husband, who loved me so devotedly & whom I idolized, would be bliss indeed."

William Crook stayed in Chicago for a week and came by to check on the Lincolns and especially to see how Tad was doing. He found the atmosphere in the rooms depressing and made an effort to take Tad out for a walk. Even Tad, once so full of mischief and high spirits, seemed demoralized. "He was a sad little fellow," Crook said, "and mourned for his father."

Very soon Mary realized that, prestigious and centrally located though it was, Tremont House was just too expensive. She was there only a few days before full-scale panic set in. President Lincoln died without leaving a will, and it would take many months for his assets to be collected and sorted out. In the meantime, Mary was dependent on the largess of David Davis for living expenses. Her stress level was unbearable. She sent Robert to carry out the urgent business of finding a new home. He quickly reported back that he had found a decent place about seven miles south of downtown Chicago, at the Hyde Park House, where the weekly rate for the three Lincolns would run forty dollars.

After just one week, on a Saturday afternoon, the Lincolns checked out of Tremont House and moved into Hyde Park House. Lizzie Keckley helped them settle in. Long before Hyde Park was incorporated into the city of Chicago, it was considered the country, and the Hyde Park House a modest summer resort. On most days the village was a few degrees cooler than downtown Chicago—a noteworthy distinction in the era before the invention of the electric fan. The hotel had been built just a year earlier and served as the village's social hub. The Lincolns were shown to rooms that were very small and, as Lizzie ruefully noted, "plainly furnished." Mary tried to put the best face on it. In her correspondence with Oliver Halstead, she called the Hyde Park House a "beautiful new hotel" with exquisitely clean, even luxurious rooms. Robert had his own room and spent moving day unpacking his books with Lizzie Keckley and arranging them on the shelves. When they were finished, Robert, his arms folded, stared distractedly out the window.

"Mrs. Keckley, how do you like our new quarters?" he asked.

It was plain to Lizzie that Robert was contemplating his great change in fortune and circumstance. She tried to cheer him up, answering brightly, "This is a delightful place, and I think you will pass your time pleasantly."

Robert looked at her quizzically. "You call it a delightful place! Well, perhaps it is. But candidly, I would almost as soon be dead as be compelled to remain three months in this dreary house." Lizzie left Robert to his thoughts and ventured into Mary Lincoln's room. The atmosphere she found there was just as depressing. Mary was in bed, "sobbing as if her heart would break."

"What a dreary place, Lizzie," Mary said. "And to think that I should be compelled to live here because I have not the means to live elsewhere. Ah, what a sad change has come to us all." Only Tad accepted the situation. He seemed to be getting back to his old self. Lizzie called him a child of sunshine. "Nothing seemed to dampen the ardor of his spirits."

The next morning, Sunday, Lizzie woke up and pondered the view of Lake Michigan outside her window. A bright sun made the great lake sparkle. Every now and then a sailboat glided past. The splendid vista made Lizzie wonder how the Lincolns could call Hyde Park bleak. While Robert stayed in his room with his law books, Lizzie tried to talk some sense to Mary. Reach out to people, Lizzie urged. See old friends. It was all right to mourn and remember, but life must go on. Mary would not listen. She was determined to spend the summer in seclusion. Old faces, she said, would only bring back memories she wanted to forget. Meeting new people was out of the question. They could not possibly understand her troubles.

Monday morning, Robert was getting ready to head into the city. Tad really wanted to go with him.

"Ask Mother," Robert said. "I think she will say no."

When Tad sought out Mary she told him, "No, you must stay and keep me company." Mary had other plans for the young one. She informed the boy that he had to start focusing on schoolwork, and the lessons would start right now. Tad threw a fit. "I don't want to get a lesson—I won't get a lesson. I don't want to learn my book. I want to go to town."

Mary looked at him sharply. "I suppose you want to grow up to be a dunce. Hush, Tad, you shall not go to town until you have said a lesson."

Robert tried to calm down his brother. "You must do as Mother tells you. You are getting to be a big boy now and must start to school next fall. You would not like to go to school without knowing how to read."

Caving in, Tad pulled a chair over to his mother while Mary retrieved a book and opened it to page one. It was a basic elementary school primer, filled with simple words and stories. The first word was ape. Next to the word was the illustration of an ape. Mary said, "What does A-P-E spell?"

"Monkey," Tad said straight away.

Mary blinked. "Nonsense! A-P-E does not spell monkey."

"Does spell monkey. Isn't that a monkey?" Tad pointed to the illustration. Obviously, his answer was based on the picture, not his comprehension of the word.

"No, it is not a monkey."

"Not a monkey! What is it then?"

"An ape."

"An ape? 'Taint an ape. Don't I know a monkey when I see it?"

"No, if you say that is a monkey," Mary retorted.

The argument continued until Tad thrust the book into Lizzie Keckley's face. "Isn't this a monkey?" he asked. "And don't A-P-E spell monkey?"

Lizzie burst out in laughter. She could not help herself. At this, Tad took great offense and kept insisting that he was correct. Only when Robert entered the debate and patiently laid out the fundamentals of the word was Tad finally convinced. But he sulked through the rest of the lesson.

So at age twelve, Abraham Lincoln's son still could not read. It was mortifying. Mary must have regretted all those years she and her husband put off Tad's education. For the next few weeks, she labored with Tad on his lessons and reported on the boy's progress to his old Washington, D.C., tutor, Alexander Williamson. Tad, she wrote, was focusing on his studies and applying himself. Two or three times a day she sat with her son as they worked their way through the primer. Tad was "seized with the desire to be able to read & write." It must have pleased Williamson to know that those difficult days in front of the blackboard at the White House were finally paying off. Unfortunately, Mary had to break the news to Williamson in a follow-up letter in August that Tad was reverting to his old habits and not "applying himself as much as he ought." The start of the school year was approaching, and Mary had to settle on a school for Tad. Clearly, the boy would be years behind the other students in basic reading and math aptitude.

The time had also come for Robert to return to his studies in the law. Before receiving his captain's commission, Robert had attended Harvard Law School for four months, intending to return after General Lee's surrender. Of course his father's assassination derailed those plans. Now he had to put his legal studies back on track. Obviously, the name Lincoln carried a lot of weight, and in quick order Robert found work at the prestigious firm of Scammon, McCagg & Fuller on Lake Street in Chicago.

The senior partner was Jonathan Young Scammon, one of the richest men in America. Scammon was born in Maine, studied at what is now Colby College, and became one of the earliest settlers in Chicago, arriving in the city when he was just twenty-three and the population was fifteen hundred. He started the city's first newspaper, the *Chicago Journal*, built the city's first railroad, founded the Marine Bank, and served as president of the Chicago Board of Education. It was also rumored that he was active in the Underground Railroad, the clandestine network that had provided succor and sanctuary to Southern slaves escaping to the Free States and Canada. Scammon stepped up and offered Lincoln's son the opportunity to read the law in his firm. In those days, serving an apprenticeship under the tutelage of a practicing member of the bar was the primary path to a law license. For a mentor, Robert Lincoln could do no better than Jonathan Scammon. He also signed up for law classes at the University of Chicago. (It is now referred to in history books as "Old University of Chicago," to distinguish it from the present institution by that name. It was founded in 1857 by Abraham Lincoln's great rival, Stephen Douglas, and was defunct by 1886.)

Robert became a commuter. Every morning at 8:52 A.M. he caught the Hyde Park Special out of a small depot on Fifty-third Street for the thirty-minute ride to the Water Street stop in Chicago and then made the short walk to the offices of Scammon, McCagg & Fuller.

By now, Lizzie Keckley was anxious to get back to her little dressmaking shop in Washington. Mary Lincoln understood, and perhaps part of her was relieved because she could not afford to pay Lizzie a salary. The former First Lady and the former slave parted company on good terms. Lizzie returned to the capital and sewed dresses for President Johnson's daughters and other leading ladies of Washington society. Later, Congress voted to award her the sum of $210 for her six weeks of service to Mary Lincoln.

Mary was left without adult companionship. Her life was one of seclusion and deep, unrelenting mourning. She spent her days in pitiful isolation, taking long walks along Lake Michigan, "contemplating the waves" and sometimes wishing she could just go under them. Robert purchased a covered buggy and took his mother on rides around the village, the carriage drawn by the horse that was his father's last gift to him. Tad's pony from the White House was also stabled in Hyde Park. Mary continued teaching Tad his lessons and sat at the desk in her room at the Hyde Park House writing long letters to friends back East.

She was a prodigious and erudite letter writer. "She lived in her letters . . . pouring her grief, bitterness and humiliation onto the black-bordered pages, many of them stained with tears," wrote Justin G. Turner and Linda Levitt Turner, editors of the invaluable collection of Mary Todd Lincoln letters. "Her correspondence filled the endless, empty hours during the day when she had nowhere to go, and at night when she could not sleep. . . . In the end letters became her chief contact with that 'outside world,' the inhabitants of which were cheerfully going on with their lives while hers was all but over."

Mary read a half dozen daily Chicago and New York newspapers. From these publications she followed the trial of the conspirators and the blundering administration of Andrew Johnson. Sometimes what she read in the newspapers cut to the bone. On June 14, the *Chicago Journal*—the paper founded by Jonathan Scammon—reported the salacious allegation that when she was First Lady, Mary had once threatened to whip her son Tad for damaging an expensive pair of copper-toed boots. Mary was so upset she clipped the article out of the newspaper and sent it to Alexander Williamson. The article was demonstrably false. For one thing, Mary wrote Williamson, Tad had never had a pair of copper-toed boots. More importantly, she maintained that she had never once whipped Tad. It violated the principles of loving parenting she and President Lincoln held true. "If I have erred, it has been, in being too indulgent."

July came, and Mary was still keeping up the pretense of enjoying Hyde Park. The hotel was filled with summer residents—"some of the very best Chicago people."

"We occupy three very pleasant rooms," she informed Harriet Howe Wilson, wife of Massachusetts senator Henry Wilson, referring to herself, Robert, and Tad. "My son Robert has entered a law office to read & study for the summer." Updating Alexander Williamson, she wrote that Tad continued to be diligent in his studies, "—which with his natural brightness will be half the battle with him. . . . Taddie has a lovely nature & and I have not the least trouble in managing him, he is all love & gentleness."

To these Washington comrades, Mary was cheerful, even optimistic— the brave widow moving on with her life. But in truth she was in deep misery, overwhelmed with money woes and facing a future without a husband. The state of her financial affairs kept her up at night with worry. From her late husband's estate Justice David Davis parceled out the miserly sum of fifteen hundred dollars for Mary to live on for the entire year, her "clerk's salary," as Mary contemptuously called it. Robert and Tad also received the same amount. Mary watched every penny and tried to prod Davis. She told him she wanted a home of her own because she was growing weary of boarding. "It is very unbecoming . . . when it is remembered, from whence we have just come." Mary had to walk a fine line with Davis, who held the power of the purse; her letters to him are both obsequious and proper. But Davis still could not understand why she chose to live in Chicago rather than the house in Springfield that she owned free and clear. To him, it just did not make any sense. He truly believed Mary was irrational on money matters and feared that she would squander the estate if left to her own devices.

Privately, Mary poured out her resentment. Davis, she said, was "intensely selfish." Although he owed his lifelong Supreme Court appointment to President Lincoln, he appeared unmoved by the plight of Lincoln's widow. What other explanation could there be for his indifference? Davis, she complained to her friend Dr. Henry, would "prefer to see us, as we are, without a home, or the prospect of one, rather than have us comfortable." One tense meeting between Mary and Davis took place that summer, when the corpulent judge visited Mary at the Hyde Park Hotel. Davis looked around and said, "I am glad you are so well situated out here."

Mary found Davis's remark typically smug, but she held her tongue and turned the conversation around to her yearning for a house. Perhaps, she suggested, wealthy Republicans could be persuaded to donate a home to the widow of the Great Emancipator. The idea was not entirely preposterous. In that era, war heroes were sometimes bestowed great sums of money through national solicitations. General Grant's thirty-thousand-dollar mortgage on his home in Washington, D.C., had been entirely paid off with donations from a grateful nation. Mary could not comprehend why she was being forgotten: "Roving Generals have elegant mansions showered upon them, and the American people leave the family of the Martyred President to struggle as best they may! Strange justice this."

Davis tried to persuade Mary that she was an unlikely candidate for such a gift—"not the least indication," in his blunt opinion. The pervasive belief in the nation at that time was that Mary Lincoln had been left with substantial assets. President Lincoln's estate was said to total eighty-five thousand dollars, the rough equivalent of one million in modern dollars.

The other issue was Mary Lincoln herself. When she lived in the White House, political enemies had derided "Madame Lincoln" for holding extravagant White House parties in time of war. Her scandalous wardrobe did further damage to her reputation. There was the senator from Oregon who, noting Mary Lincoln's audacious décolletage at a White House reception, ridiculed the First Lady for exhibiting her "milking apparatus to public gaze." Because three of her half-brothers served in the Confederate army, Mary was also unfairly perceived as a Southern sympathizer when in truth she loathed slavery. But Davis did not have to dwell on these particulars. He simply informed Mary that she would have to be "content" and adjust to life as a permanent boarder.

"I board no longer than next spring," Mary responded stiffly. "After that, if we have still to be vagrants, I prefer being so in any state rather than [in Illinois], where every man in the state owes my Husband a deep debt of gratitude."

Taking Mary seriously, Davis asked, "Will you take Robert with you too?"

"Most certainly," Mary answered. "He goes where I do."

Davis's indifference infuriated Mary. She called it "vile" and vented her frustrations to her friend Sally Orne, wife of a wealthy carpet merchant in Philadelphia. Mary said she was "bowed down and heart broken."

"Time does not reconcile me to the loss of the most devoted & loving husband. . . . I long, my kind friend, to lay my aching head & sorrowing heart by the side of this dearly loved one. When the summons comes for my departure, I will gladly welcome it. . . . We are deprived of the comfort of a home, where my poor sadly afflicted sons & myself could quietly indulge our griefs. We are left with only $1,500 a year, each, to live upon . . . and as a matter of course must board, plainly and as genteel as possible, on this sum."

As Mrs. Orne read the letter at her home in Philadelphia, she must surely have been surprised at the strange request that came next. Mary asked Mrs. Orne if she knew anyone who might be interested in buying the elegant white lace dress and matching shawl that she had worn the night of President Lincoln's second inaugural ball. She had "tenderly" folded the gown away after wearing it for just two hours before changing into something less extravagant. Now Mary was offering it for sale—"if I can get $2,500." It was a bargain, Mary assured her friend, pegging the gown's true value at $3,500. In the same letter Mary pitched a second article—sixteen yards of "magnificent" white silk fabric that Mary had intended to make into a dress, for the bargain price of $125.

"You may well be assured only dire necessity, which I have never before known anything about would cause me to write so freely to you," Mary said. "If any of your friends would desire such articles, please advise me—they are rich and beautiful."

Hidden in this pathetic appeal was a very great secret—Mary Lincoln was deeply in debt due to excessive purchases she had made while in the White House. Not even Robert was aware that she owed the mind-blowing sum of twenty thousand dollars. Some of her creditors were threatening to go public; others were sending legal letters menacing Mary with litigation unless she paid in full. Mary was determined to pay off her obligations without letting Robert or Justice Davis know how deeply in the hole she stood. Partly, she was terrified of scandal. But she was also ashamed—she could not abide the idea of Robert discovering how badly she had slipped up. And there was another very practical reason why she fought so hard to keep her debts under wraps. Knowing Justice Davis as she did, Mary believed that he would insist on paying off her creditors out of President Lincoln's estate, thus cutting deeply into the principal and leaving her with diluted assets.

Pondering her options from her desk at the Hyde Park House, Mary began a correspondence with Alexander Williamson, her sons' former tutor, who now labored as a clerk in the U.S. Treasury Department—a patronage job arranged by Mary Lincoln. Her first letters were generous and caring as she brought Williamson up to date on Tad's progress. But within a few weeks, there was an adjustment in tone. Williamson the trusted tutor became Williamson the official representative of Mary Lincoln's financial interests on the East Coast. Williamson was authorized to approach Mary's creditors and negotiate on her behalf, either to reduce or entirely withdraw the debts. She even induced Williamson to work on commission and sell her clothes at night and on weekends. In September she asked Williamson to put President Lincoln's carriage, which she had left behind in Washington, on the market, suggesting the best deal might be made in New York or Philadelphia. "Surely there are persons of means . . . who would purchase it, if for no other reason than it having been the property of my lamented husband." On her own she took care of an outstanding bill from the Washington jeweler Matthew Galt by returning jewelry she had purchased when she was First Lady. The items included two diamond and pearl bracelets each valued at $550, a $440 diamond and pearl ring— "all never worn, scarcely looked at and never shown to anyone"—plus two clocks and a set of eighteen gold-plated spoons.

Mary had no one to blame but herself for the jam she was in. She was a compulsive shopper—she could not help herself. It was said that she purchased a nonsensical eighty-four pairs of gloves in the days leading up to her husband's first inauguration in 1861. In 1865, just a few weeks before the assassination, Mary ordered a 508-piece set of exquisite china from the Philadelphia importer James Kerr. It was an exact replica of the gold-trimmed, official china served during state dinners. The only dissimilarity was the absence of the presidential seal. In its place Mary ordered her china set embossed with her initials, ML. Yet, after the assassination, Mary insisted the delivery date for the china be kept. She actually sent a boorish letter to Kerr complaining about a delay in the shipment. "It will be a great disappointment if you do not soon forward it to me," she told him. When she was in the White House, credit seemed limitless. Who would not want the prestige of doing business with the First Lady of the United States? Now these merchants and clothes makers who had extended her credit were knocking on the widow's door demanding payment.

That summer, an outbreak of scarlet fever struck the Hyde Park House, and Mary sent Tad to live with friends in the country while the epidemic ran its course. In the meantime, she and Robert engaged in a new search for yet another less expensive hotel. Ten weeks after checking into the Hyde Park House, Mary, Robert, and Tad moved into Clifton House in Chicago, at the corner of Wabash Avenue and Madison Street.

Although it was conveniently located in downtown Chicago, not far from the law firm where he was clerking, Robert found Clifton House intolerable. The hotel was filled with transients, questionable Wild West characters, and sketchy fortune hunters. The raucous ambience did not suit Robert's stiff, pompous personality. "I propose on the first of next month to rent a room and begin to live with some degree of comfort—a thing not known to my present quarters," he informed David Davis. Living up to his word, Robert remained at Clifton House until January 1866. That is when he finally escaped his downcast surroundings. Around New Year's Day he received his annual fifteen hundred dollar payment from Abraham Lincoln's estate, doled out by Davis. Not wasting any time, Robert moved out on January 3, 1866, into a place of his own, a two-room flat on Washington Street, above Crosby's Opera House. The Opera House was then just a year old, built by Uranus Crosby, an entrepreneur from Cape Cod who had made a fortune during the Civil War distilling and distributing liquor. Lamenting the state of civilization in his adopted city, Crosby built the magnificent five-story Opera House that very quickly became the cultural heart of Chicago's patrician class.

Moving day was one of conflicting emotions for Robert. At last he was getting out on his own, making a life for himself in a new city. But he was concerned about his little brother, Tad, who was now in the care of their damaged mother, wallowing in unrelenting grief. Hereafter, Robert could only be a part-time influence in Tad's life. Now, after a long day at Scammon, McCagg & Fuller, followed by law classes at the University of Chicago, Robert would return in the evening, done in, to his apartment at Crosby's Opera House. There he would sit at his desk and write heartfelt letters to the beautiful young lady he had left behind in Washington, Mary Harlan.

Robert Todd Lincoln was a lonesome young man deeply in love.

5
The Senator's Daughter

HER NAME WAS Mary Harlan, and she was the daughter of the Republican senator from Iowa, James Harlan. Mary had attended Madame Smith's, the prestigious finishing school at 223 G Street in Washington, where it was said no girl was admitted unless Madame Smith herself knew the student's great-great-grandfather. It was a strict rule that only French was spoken in the school at all times, even in the gymnasium or in casual conversation between students. If Madame Smith or any of the teachers heard a student using a word of English, a mark was recorded next to the girl's name in the headmistress's dreaded black deportment book.

Julia Taft, the sister of the boys befriended by Tad and Willie Lincoln when they moved into the White House, was a classmate of Mary Harlan's at Madame Smith's. Julia could never forget that first day when her parents dropped her off at the school. She was petrified. She knew hardly a word of French when Madame Smith ushered her into the schoolroom and with great ceremony introduced her to the other girls. Julia took a seat, and an instructor came up to her and "reeled off a few yards of French." Julia was mystified. All she could say in response was, "Qu'est ce, que c'est?" to every question. The teacher smiled, quickly made an assessment of Julia's language skills, and sensibly placed the girl in introductory French. In those first few weeks, Julia made herself understood with sign language and a few elementary words of French, but with full immersion at Madame Smith's, Julia was soon communicating with the teaching staff and the other students.

Mary Harlan was a popular student at the school. Music was her favorite subject, and she impressed the other girls with her expertise on the harp. She was a focused and obedient girl. Once, Julia broke the rules and tried to engage Mary in conversation during class. "Taisez-vous," (hush) Mary told her. "Taisez-vous."

The students at Madame Smith's were also taught history, literature, and English. Deportment class at Madame Smith's was a requirement—the girls were instructed in the proper way to stand and sit in a ladylike manner, and how to kick a train out of the way at the completion of a dance and gracefully sweep it under the seat. They were drilled in the court curtsy— "repeated over and over under the critical eye of Madame." Proper behavior on the receiving line was also part of the core curriculum—a necessary business when one realizes that many of the girls were the daughters of diplomats and prominent Washington personalities and were expected to one day take their place as society hostesses.

In 1860, as Abraham Lincoln campaigned for the presidency, Great Britain's Prince of Wales made an unofficial visit to the United States, traveling incognito under the name Lord Renfrew. The girls at Madame Smith's went wild with excitement when it was announced that the Prince of Wales would be inspecting the school. In his day, he was the most socially esteemed young man in the world. Mary Harlan, Julia Taft, and their fellow students assembled in the gymnasium. Madame Smith cautioned the girls not to refer to their visitor as "Your Royal Highness" and in no way suggest that he was Queen Victoria's eldest son. If they made such a gaffe, the headmistress warned, it would be an unforgivable breach of etiquette. The prince was to be addressed merely as "My Lord."

When the Prince of Wales, then only nineteen, entered the gym, the girls kept their composure. He looked them over and made small talk in fluent French. Then, at the prince's request, a game of bowling, or tenpins, was arranged, and three lucky girls were picked to play against him. Julia Taft was one of those chosen, and she actually bowled a strike. The delighted prince bowed before her in tribute, placed his hand over his heart, and rewarded her with a blooming rose in a pot. Later in the week, a grand ball was held in the Prince of Wales's honor. Julia Taft's parents refused to let her attend because she had not yet come out in society. Julia burst into tears, but her mother was adamant and would not yield to Julia's wails. The night of the ball came and Julia remained at home, trying to content herself with the fantasy of dancing and conversing in French with the future king of England. (The Prince of Wales would have a long wait for his throne. Forty-one years later, upon Queen Victoria's death in 1901, he was finally crowned Edward VII.)

The Prince of Wales was an unattainable beau, but Mary Harlan soon enchanted another handsome young bachelor, the "Prince of Rails" himself, Robert Lincoln. Geography and the outbreak of the Civil War made it impossible for the relationship to exceed the realm of flirtation. Robert was away at Harvard, and Mary Harlan also had to leave Washington. Headmistress Smith turned out to be a die-hard secessionist who loathed Abraham Lincoln, and the day came when she abandoned her students and moved to Richmond. A member of her teaching staff took over as headmistress and tried to keep the school running, but after a few weeks the endeavor was abandoned. Madame Smith's French School was closed down, never to reopen.

The daughters of Washington's elite now found themselves without an appropriate school to attend. This, plus the threat of imminent invasion by Southern forces, made Washington an inhospitable place for teenage girls. Julia Taft's parents sent her off to Elmira College in upstate New York, where, Julia admitted, she was a "puzzle to the faculty." She was fluent in French and Spanish—her father had hired a private tutor to teach her Spanish because he believed that no young debutante should come out in Washington society unless she spoke at least two foreign languages. But those years with Madame Smith had left her with no aptitude in math, and in this subject she was placed in a freshman class. Julia was a definitive reflection of the strengths and weaknesses of Madame Smith's nineteenth-century educational values for young women.

Mary Harlan's parents sent her home to Mount Pleasant, Iowa, where for the first year of the Civil War she enrolled as a student at the Iowa Wesleyan College prep school. In 1862 she was admitted into the college as a full-time music student. Tragedy struck the Harlan family that February when Mary's six-year-old sister, Julia Josephine, died of an unknown illness. The Harlan child died the same month as Willie Lincoln, further solidifying the connection between the Lincolns and Harlans. Both families had now experienced the tragic loss of a young one.

Mary Harlan's mother, Ann Eliza Harlan, was a formidable woman. Two months after her young daughter's death, on April 6 and 7, 1862, the Battle of Shiloh was fought in Tennessee. Confederate forces launched a surprise attack on General Grant's bivouacked troops and came close to annihilating the Union army in the West. General P. G. T. Beauregard became so confident after the first day of battle that he sent Jefferson Davis a telegraph declaring, "A complete victory." But the following morning General Grant launched a counterattack, and Confederate forces retreated under the savage assault. Ultimately, it was a victory for the Union, but Grant was vilified for coming within a hair's breath of calamity. Newspapers claimed he had been drunk and criminally negligent in his failure to fortify defense perimeters. Northerners were horrified to read accounts that soldiers had been bayoneted in their tents as they slept. President Lincoln came under intense pressure to fire Grant, but he refused, famously saying, "I can't spare this man; he fights."

Shiloh became the bloodiest battle in United States history up to that time. After just two days of fighting, combined North and South casualties totaled twenty-three thousand men—more than the number of Americans killed, injured, or captured during the Revolutionary War, the War of 1812, and the Mexican-American War combined. One thousand of those killed or wounded came from Iowa. When Ann Harlan read about the terrible loss of life, she boarded a train to St. Louis and then hired a steamboat and loaded it with medicine and supplies. Somehow she managed to steam south on an epic mission of mercy down the Tennessee River, docking at Shiloh. A strongly worded letter from Secretary of War Edwin Stanton was of great assistance in facilitating her passage through Union blockades and patrols. It stated:

> "Mrs. A. E. Harlan of Iowa, wife of the Senator of that State, has permission to pass, with a lady companion, through the lines of the United States forces, to and from Tennessee and wherever sick and wounded soldiers of the United States may be to render them care and attendance."

Horrific scenes awaited Ann Harlan at Shiloh. Thousands of wounded men wandered the battlefield dazed, bloodied, and starving. Mrs. Harlan made it known that she was from Iowa and in quick order some 280 sick and wounded men from her state and neighboring territories made their way to the pier and climbed aboard the Harlan steamboat. Sixty of the soldiers came from Iowa, the rest from Wisconsin and Minnesota. Once it was filled to capacity, the steamboat pulled out of Shiloh and proceeded north, up the Mississippi River. Two weeks later, it reached the town of Keoluk, Iowa, situated in the extreme southeast corner of the state. Seven soldiers died during the voyage; the rest were taken off the ship and either trans-ferred to a hotel in Keoluk that had been converted into a hospital or else permitted to make their own way home for convalescence.

Mary Harlan continued her music studies at Iowa Wesleyan College. Finally, in 1863, with the defeat of General Lee at Gettysburg and the tide of war turning at last, Senator Harlan deemed it safe enough for his daughter to rejoin the family in Washington. For an intellectually gifted young woman like Mary Harlan, Washington had undeniable allure. Mary was seventeen when she returned to Washington, pretty, from the right family, and learned in the social graces. She would be an eyewitness to history during the great national drama in which her father was such an important player. In Mary's set were the daughters and sons of the most powerful people in Washington. It was inevitable that she and Robert Lincoln would meet.

In March 1864, Mary sat next to Robert in the inaugural stands when President Lincoln made his immortal second inaugural address. Two days later she was Robert's escort at the inaugural ball, held in the magnificent marble lobby of the United States Patent Office. Guests started to arrive at 9:00 P.M., and Robert entered arm-in-arm with Mary Harlan. Then, as now, Washington was a city that thrived on gossip, and notice was taken of Mary Harlan in the company of the president's son, who cut such a handsome figure in his captain's uniform.

One week later, Robert was back on duty at General Grant's headquarters at City Point, Virginia. City Point had become a popular tourist attraction for socially and politically connected civilians who desired to see something of the war in its closing days. Robert was assigned to show these digni-taries around. It seemed that he had quite the roving eye. "There have been lots of pretty girls down here lately," he wrote his friend John Hay, the president's secretary. "If you want to do a favor, send some more." In the meantime, Mary Lincoln did everything she could to encourage the rela-tionship between her son and Mary Harlan. When Richmond fell in early April, the First Lady arranged for young Mary to accompany her to the front lines at City Point. Rounding out the First Lady's "charming party" were Mary Harlan's parents, Elizabeth Keckley, a French marquis, and Sen-ator Charles Sumner of Massachusetts. Captain Lincoln took particular pleasure when the presidential party docked at City Point and he undertook the duty of showing his girlfriend around.

Following the assassination, Robert Lincoln bade Mary Harlan a heartfelt farewell when he left Washington and moved to Chicago, in May 1865, with his mother and little brother. Young Mr. Lincoln and Mary Harlan must have wondered what this separation would mean for their future together. Part of Robert's misery those first weeks in Chicago was missing her. Speculation that Robert and Mary were engaged started to appear in the newspapers in the summer of 1865. But their private correspondence indicated nothing so formal as an engagement had been agreed upon.

By fall 1865, Mary was thinking about returning to Iowa and resuming her education at Iowa Wesleyan College. Another young woman who wanted to attend the school was informed there was no room for her—the place was being reserved for Mary Harlan. In a letter to her friend Minnie Chandler, a student at Iowa Wesleyan, Mary worried that she may have fallen behind the others in her studies because she had been out of school for so long. Minnie Chandler dismissed her concerns, telling Mary, "I am so glad you are coming back. I have positively been good-natured all day."

As Mary pondered her return to college, her family's spacious home at 304 H Street was becoming a vital gathering point in Washington society. James Harlan had resigned from the Senate and was now serving as Secretary of the Interior in the cabinet of Andrew Johnson. His new position required him to entertain, although the Harlans, devout Methodists, prohibited both liquor and dancing in their home. It was said that the Harlan parties were marked by "wholesome good cheer" and the "simple application of good taste." On New Year's Eve 1866, the Harlans held an open house at which Secretary Harlan stood at the door and cordially greeted his guests. Later that month, the first important party of the 1866 winter social season was held at the Harlan house. Guests, including nearly every member of Andrew Johnson's cabinet, arrived at 9:00 P.M. and stayed until midnight. "There was a constant ebb and flow of the beauty, bravery, wealth and position that compose the most attractive phase of Washington society."

In the swirl of all this social activity, Mary Harlan attracted the attention of Washington's most eminent and eligible bachelors, especially now that the redoubtable Kate Chase was off the market, having married William Sprague IV, the richest bachelor in America, now a United States senator. Mary had become one of Washington's most prized belles. Robert Lincoln was not her only choice; she was being wooed by several promising young men, including the future governor of Louisiana Henry Clay Warmouth, and Edgar Welles, the son of Navy Secretary Gideon Welles. Mary confided everything to her friend Minnie Chandler in Iowa, but she was careful to write in code in case the letters fell into the wrong hands. In addition to Warmouth and young Welles, there was a man she referred to as "Mr. New Orleans," a gentleman she called "Daddy Henderson," and another suitor by the name of Mr. Denaise. Robert Lincoln was given the code name "Prince Bob." In all, Mary appeared to have five prospective fiancés. As Robert was wallowing in his misery in Chicago, Mary Harlan was having a delightful time in Washington.

It comes then as no surprise that Mary put off her plans to return to Iowa Wesleyan. Instead, she remained in the nation's capital and juggled her suitors there. Even Minnie Chandler was having trouble keeping everyone straight. In July 1866 she wondered in a letter, "How many are you engaged to now? Ten or a dozen?" That summer, a newspaper printed the rumor that Robert and Mary had split up. Minnie said she "didn't believe a word of it," but she also called Mary a "great flirt." It was enough to make Minnie Chandler almost feel pity for the men pursuing Mary Harlan. "I'm glad I'm not a gentleman and one of your lovers," she wrote.

With the war over, it seemed that all of Minnie and Mary's friends were rushing into marriage. Engagements were becoming an "epidemic," Minnie complained, as she bemoaned the dearth of eligible young men in Iowa. She lamented the state of her own love life and even pictured herself and Mary as two old maids sharing a house and knitting in an oversized armchair by a cozy fireplace, "with a dear old cat in their lap."

"How is Bob Lincoln?" Minnie coyly asked in another letter, posted around Christmastime. "I have been asked several times this year if you were engaged to him." Four months later, Minnie sent her "dreadful flirt" of a friend a request for another update on the boyfriend situation because she had heard about "some trouble" in Mary's relationship with Henry Clay Walmouth, who she now called "Judge Walmorth," apparently having forgotten the gentleman's name.

But all this was in the past. There finally came a time when an understanding was reached between Robert Lincoln and Mary Harlan. No formal announcement was made, but the two became a committed couple, and rival suitors drifted away.

As Robert pursued his long-distance romance with Mary from Chicago, Tad struggled with his lessons. He was so far behind in his studies that his mother decided against enrolling him in school in September. Instead Mary privately tutored Tad for another four months before he entered the Brown

School on Warren Street, in January 1866. At age fourteen, for the first time in his life, Tad became an enrolled student. "Taddie is learning to be as diligent in his studies as he used to be at play," Mary Lincoln wrote the artist Francis B. Carpenter. Carpenter was a well-known painter who for six months, in 1864, had lived in the White House where he set up a studio under a lighted chandelier in the state dining room and painted what would become his most famous work, *The First Reading of the Emancipation Proclamation before the Cabinet.*

"He appears to be rapidly making up for the great amount of time he lost," Mary wrote of Taddie. "As you are aware, he was always a marked character." It was a harsh thing to call Tad—a "marked character." Mary adored her son, and it was possible that she wrote the letter after a frustrating day of homeschooling the boy. Just two months later, after his enrollment, she was effusive in her praise of Tad. She said that he was totally focused on his education, did not miss a day of school, and was "much beloved" in his class. His teacher, Mary said, spoke of Tad in the "highest & most affectionate terms."

As Tad settled into school, he proved to have his father's gift of endearing himself to people, and he became interested in hearing anything about his father's life and times. Henry J. Raymond, the founder of the *New York Times,* had just published a history of the Lincoln administration, and Mary borrowed a copy of the book. After reading it she told Robert, "It was the most correct history of his father that had been written." Tad overheard the conversation and spoke up. "Mother, I am going to save all the little money you give me and get one of them," meaning his own copy. Robert looked affectionately at his brother and told the boy not to fret, that he would purchase the book for him.

For the time being, Robert was serving as Tad's legal guardian. Consequently, Mary had to keep an account of all the money she spent on the youngest Lincoln and send it to Robert for his review. A considerable expense went to the care and upkeep of Tad's pony. The animal's shoeing, stabling, and wintering all added up. By February 1866, just a month after he moved into his two-room apartment at the Opera House, Robert had had enough of his administrative burden and, with his mother's consent, requested that Supreme Court Justice Davis take over as Tad's legal guardian.

As the first anniversary of President Lincoln's assassination approached,

Congress voted to pay his widow the sum of $22,025—Lincoln's annual $25,000 salary for the year 1865 minus the six weeks pay that Lincoln had already been issued between the second inauguration and the assassination. It was a bitter pill for Mary to swallow; she believed she was owed $100,000—the entire amount of her husband's salary for the full four-year term of office to which he had been elected, but it was all Congress was willing to authorize. Despite her disappointment, Mary accepted the windfall and started looking for a residence of her own to purchase.

She found a stately house she liked for $30,000, but after several weeks passed without her closing on the deal, the sale fell through. Then Mary fixed her sights on a less expensive house at 375 West Washington Street. The property was valued at $20,000, with $12,000 paid upfront and the remaining $8,000 due two months after the contract was signed. Several weeks of negotiations ensued and the builder came down to $17,000 and actually opened his books to prove to Mary that her house would cost $6,000 less than the other row houses he had built on the block.

Robert tried to talk his mother out of buying the house, and so did David Davis, but Mary would not listen to either of them. She was fed up with her "revolting and offensive" life as a boarder, and, understandably, she wanted to raise Tad in a real family home. On May 22 Mary went to contract. The house was "plain yet elegant," and stood in a middle-class neighborhood on Chicago's West Side, close to Union Park and within walking distance of the Brown School on Warren Avenue where Tad attended classes. Mary and Tad moved into the house in June 1866.

Mary took the money left over from the congressional appropriation and bought a new set of rosewood furniture, the period's most fashionable style. For a time, life returned to normal. Mary went to church at the Third Presbyterian, and Tad attended its Sunday school, as well as Bible studies at the First Baptist Church on Wabash Avenue. At the Brown School, Tad was in a class of thirty boys and girls and became coeditor and copublisher of the school newspaper. It was called the *Brown School Holiday Budget*, and volume 1, no. 1—the first and only issue—came out on Christmas 1866. There was a whimsical article debating the existence of Santa Claus, a holiday weather forecast for Chicago ("exceedingly cold, clear and unpleasant"), and an honor roll of students who had not missed a single day of school that year. Seven children were listed—Tad was not among them. It seems that the boy was susceptible to colds and coughs and stayed home sick several times.

Sometime in 1867 Mary took Tad to a Chicago dentist who fitted the youth with a primitive set of braces to fix his overbite. Tad got up from the dentist's chair wearing a barbaric "spring frame" in his mouth. The science of orthodontics was still in early stages of development; the first paper on orthodontics, written by Dr. Norman Kingsley, had been published in a professional journal just a decade earlier. Although the technique of extracting teeth to improve the alignment of the mouth had been known since ancient times, Dr. Kingsley, a dentist and sculptor, made the important discovery that mild force, at timed intervals, could straighten crooked teeth. But the device in Tad's mouth was pure torture. It also exacerbated his speech impediment and made it difficult for him to be understood by strangers. His fellow students at the Brown School also teased him unmercifully.

"It was annoying Tad very much," Robert wrote David Davis. "He could hardly speak so as to be understood and to keep him from talking in that way for a year I thought, with his present bad habits of speech to be risking so much." Robert took his little brother to another dentist who examined the lad and declared that the spring frame apparatus "was not all necessary." That was the professional opinion Robert was looking for, and the device was extracted from Tad's mouth. Robert then arranged to take Tad to Dr. Amasa McCoy, a well-known orator and professor of elocution and vocal culture, to correct Tad's lisp and work on his pronunciation. "I think he is improving under McCoy's efforts," Robert reported.

The move to West Washington Street turned into a financial disaster for Mary. The house became a money pit and required more work than Mary either had anticipated or could afford. She was faced with yet another looming financial catastrophe. The builder was a man named Cole, and Robert Lincoln came to believe that he was swindling his mother. "I hope you come out of this better than I think you will," Robert told her. "I am surprised that you have allowed Cole to blind you again." Then a smug Robert pronounced himself "done with wasting time" advising his mother on the house when she would not listen to what he believed was his able counsel.

Mary was beside herself with worry about losing her new home. She had to acknowledge that "if I am not assisted I shall have to dispose" of the property. Desperate for cash, she sent out a chain of letters pleading for assistance. The nation's leading philanthropists and wealthiest Republicans received personal appeals from Mary for money, for otherwise, she wrote, she faced a future "without a home, forever a wanderer on the face of the earth."

She hired Alexander Williamson to work on a contingency fee—thirty-five dollars for every one thousand dollars he raised—and directed him to go first to Philadelphia and personally solicit the members of the Union League for money. After all, Lincoln supporters had founded the prestigious club. Then he was told to hit up all the "rich merchants" on Chestnut Street. "Be sharp & find out names," she told Williamson. From Philadelphia, Williamson was ordered to proceed on to New York and visit with William Astor, Cornelius Vanderbilt, and other prominent millionaires. Find "all the rich men," she wrote him. Mary specifically advised Williamson to approach George Peabody, a banker and financier who was considered the leading American philanthropist of the age, having bequeathed eight million dollars to several museums and charities. Peabody lived in London, but Mary heard he was in New York on a visit. Find him, Mary instructed Williamson. "Be sure of this—a rich reward will be yours if successful."

Sometimes Mary's pleas were accompanied by a curious inducement—walking sticks that President Lincoln once used on his strolls around Washington. Attached to the canes came a personal note written by Mary—"a little relic of my Beloved Husband." Shamefully, Mary also mailed out locks of Abraham Lincoln's hair, and was upset to find that she had only a limited supply to distribute to potential contributors. Mary also drafted a fundraising letter that she sent on to Williamson and ordered him to copy it "word for word." Williamson was obliged to sign the letters as "Charles Forsythe," who described himself in the solicitations as a wealthy benefactor—"a warm friend of the Lincolns"—who had already donated considerable funds to Mary Lincoln and was urging other rich Americans to do likewise and give "generously to the widow's needs." But Forsythe was a fiction—a name concocted by Mary apparently because it sounded wealthy and suggested prominence and influence.

Robert was appalled. He took to calling these missives "Mother's begging letters." And David Davis used his connections to sabotage Mary's endeavors by quietly reaching out to friends and spreading the word in friendly newspapers that President Lincoln had provided for his widow and children and that Mary was financially well situated. Through a friend of a friend, Mary heard about Davis's duplicity. Usually obsequious to the man who held the power of the purse, this time, Mary sent Davis a scathing letter, accusing him of telling an acquaintance that she, Mary, had "ample means" at her disposal and that "no assistance was required to enable us to live very comfortably."

Mary told Davis, "I replied to her that there must be some mistake, that it was impossible you could have said this. . . . I assured the lady that I could not realize that you whom my husband so much respected & loved & knew exactly the small & limited state of our finances could have made such an assertion." One can only imagine Davis's fury upon reading Mary's letter. In the end, Mary's ventures raised just ten thousand dollars, and most of the money came from a single sympathetic source, Marshall Owen Roberts, a wealthy capitalist who made a fortune during the Civil War selling steamships to the federal government.

Less than a year after she bought her cherished new house on West Washington Street, Mary and Tad had to move out. She just could not afford the upkeep, although she managed for a time to hang on to owner-ship of the house and make a little money by renting it out. The Lincolns returned to, of all places, Clifton House, where Mary and Tad once again became permanent boarders. Mary could not believe she was back in a place she called "that den of discomfort and dirt."

That summer of 1867, Tad Lincoln, at age fourteen, was summoned to Washington to testify at the trial of a man accused of plotting the assassination of Abraham Lincoln. The defendant was John H. Surratt. His mother, Mary Surratt, ran the eight-room boarding house on H Street in Washington that was the site of meetings between John Wilkes Booth and the other conspirators. John Surratt claimed that he had been in Elmira, New York, on the night of the assassination. He denied any role in the plot but admitted he knew Booth and had been a Confederate spy. Surratt had evaded capture for two years, hiding out in Canada, England, and Italy until November 1866, when he was captured in Alexandria, Egypt, and returned to the United States where, in 1867, he was brought to trial on conspiracy charges.

Tad went by rail to Washington, accompanied by Robert. It was Tad's first time back since he had left the city in the wake of his father's assassination. On the day of his court appearance, Tad's name was called and he strode to the witness stand in the packed courtroom. The once notorious White House mischief-maker made quite an impression. The painter Francis Carpenter had recently published his memoir, *Six Months at the White House with Abraham Lincoln*. It was a bestseller, having sold thirty thousand copies, and the first book to actually detail Tad Lincoln's acts of mischief during his father's administration. Tad was said to be "greatly mortified" by the revelations of his "wayward" White House years. But that was all in the past. Now, as Tad took the witness stand, his demeanor was solemn and respectful, and many in the courtroom remarked about how the lanky teenager bore a strong physical resemblance to his martyred father. Tad was there to testify about a bizarre incident that took place in 1865 at City Point, Virginia, when an intruder boarded the presidential steamship the *River Queen*. Tad was on board the vessel with his father and encountered the intruder, who the government contended was John Surratt.

The federal prosecutor, Edwards Pierrepoint, waited for Tad to settle into the witness chair and then asked his first question. "You are a son of the late President Lincoln?"

Tad answered, "Yes, sir."

"Were you with your father down at City Point in March 1865?"

"Yes, sir."

"Where were you—in a house or on a steamboat?"

"On a steamboat," Tad said.

Pierrepoint asked, "Do you remember anybody coming to the steamer and asking to speak to him?"

"Yes, sir."

"What did the man say?"

Tad testified, "He said he would like to see the president."

Surratt's lawyer, Joseph Bradley, objected to the answer on grounds of hearsay, but he was overruled by Judge David Cartter. The direct examination was allowed to continue, and Pierrepoint asked his next question. "Did he tell you where he came from?"

"Yes. He said from Springfield."

"What further did he say?"

"He said he would like to see the president on particular business."

"State the mode of his saying this," the prosecutor said to Tad. "Whether he urged it."

Tad politely answered, "Yes, sir. He wanted to see him 'real bad.'"

Pierrepoint then asked Tad how many times the man insisted on seeing the president.

"He tried twice, I believe," Tad answered.

"State whether they would allow him to see the president."

"They would not."

"Do you see the man here who tried to see the president?"

The big moment had come. Judge Cartter ordered Surratt to rise at the defense table. Tad stared at the man. Surratt stood five-foot-nine with thinning black hair and a slim build. He had high cheekbones, a narrow chin, and ears that jutted out at the top. Tad pondered the man and at last gave his response. "He looked very much like him."

"Like the prisoner?" Pierrepoint asked.

"Yes, sir."

It was a remarkable performance for Tad in a stressful situation, face-to-face with a man accused of plotting to murder his adored father. Ultimately, however, it became apparent to the jury that Tad could not provide a positive identification of Surratt, beyond a reasonable doubt. Tad left the stand, and the next witness was called. He was Tad's old acquaintance from the White House, the guard William Crook. Crook had remained in contact with Mary and Tad and was even now contemplating moving to Chicago because he had been so taken with the city during his stay there. He had written to Tad to say he was wondering what opportunities might be available in Chicago. Mary Lincoln wrote back saying how delighted everyone in the family would be if Crook made the move. Crook took Tad's place on the witness stand and he was asked about the incident on the *River Queen*. Crook said he was there when a man identifying himself as "Smith" boarded the vessel and requested permission to see the president.

"I told the man that the president was not to be seen," Crook recalled. "The visitor became very much excited. He said that he had rendered Mr. Lincoln valuable services in Illinois during his campaign for the presidency.... He was in trouble; he must see the president. I asked his name. At first he refused to give it, but finally said it was 'Smith' and that he lived near Mr. Lincoln's home in Illinois."

Crook said he went to see Lincoln in his private quarters on board the *River Queen* and informed him that this man Smith was insisting on seeing him. "Mr. Lincoln laughed at first," Crook recalled in his memoirs. The president even cracked a joke about the name Smith being such an obvious alias. Then he became very serious and said, "If what he says is true, I would know him. But I do not. The man is an imposter."

Crook returned to the top deck and confronted Smith, who became "disturbed" at being denied access to the president and then offered Crook a bribe if he would just take him to Lincoln's stateroom. Crook ordered Smith to leave right away and threatened him with arrest if he did not, at which point the man became furious and said, "If Mr. Lincoln does not know me now, he will know me damned soon after he does see me." With that, Smith turned, strode down the gangplank, and disappeared.

The incident was forgotten until Lincoln's assassination, when it took on new significance. Authorities investigating the conspiracy plot determined that Surratt had been in City Point during President Lincoln's excursion. If testimony could establish that a prior attempt had been made to take Lincoln's life, it would prove the conspiracy charge against Surratt.

Like Tad, Crook was asked to identify the defendant. Once again Surratt was ordered to stand at the defense table. Crook studied the man. He was surprised at how sick and emaciated Surratt appeared in court. The intruder on the president's ship was also sunburned, ragged, and looked like a tramp. Yet Crook could not be certain of his identification either.

"I think 'Smith' and Surratt were the same man," Crook later said. "It was impossible for me to be absolutely sure [but] I shall always believe that Surratt was seeking an opportunity to assassinate the President."

After a total of 170 witnesses were heard, the case went to the jury in August 1867, but when the jurors failed to reach a unanimous verdict, a mistrial was declared. The final vote was eight to four in favor of acquittal. Surratt was retried on lesser charges but the court ruled that the statute of limitations had run out, and Surratt was released. John Surratt fared better than his mother Mary, who was forty-two years old when, with her legs chained to a seventy-five-pound iron ball, she was sent to the gallows, in 1865, for her role in the assassination. She was the first woman to be executed by the federal government.

The failure to convict Surratt disappointed Tad and Robert, but the court proceedings did have one interesting consequence. The two Lincoln boys remained in Washington several weeks longer than expected, and Robert took the opportunity to solidify his relationship with Mary Harlan. There was now no question about it: they were going to marry; all that had to be settled was the date. The young lovers had everything going for them—social position, excellent prospects, and true commitment. After so much heartbreak and tragedy, two great political families would be joined in marriage.

But first, Mary Lincoln would devise yet another idea for raising money, and all hell would break loose.

6
Scandal

ROBERT LINCOLN HELD the letter in his hands and wondered what it really meant. The letter came from his late father's law partner of sixteen years, William Herndon, and formally announced Herndon's intention to write and publish a biography of Abraham Lincoln. Now Herndon was making an official request for the cooperation of the Lincoln family. Robert read the letter again.

> "Robt—I want to give a sketch—a short life of your mother in my biography up to her marriage to your father. . . . I wish to do her justice fully—so that the world will understand things better. You understand me. Will she see me."

Robert found the correspondence to be inscrutable. He showed it to his mother. When she read the request from the prickly Herndon, her alarm bells went off; it seemed suspicious that Herndon would be seeking biographical information about Lincoln's widow for a standard work of history. For what purpose then, Mary wondered. In that era, biographies of great men referenced the wife with only the sketchiest of information—birth, date of marriage, number of children, and not much else.

Of course, Mary Lincoln knew Billy Herndon well—they had a long history of enmity that had begun the first day they met, in 1837. Herndon was then nineteen years old, a freshman at Illinois College, and Mary Todd was the enticing Southern belle from Lexington, Kentucky, just arrived in Springfield to live with her married sister Elizabeth Edwards on Aristocracy Hill. Like Herndon, she was nineteen. They were both guests at a ball at the home of a prominent Springfield resident, Colonel Robert Allen. Herndon was introduced to Mary, and asked her to dance. They took to the floor and made small talk. Then Herndon, in an unfortunate breach of good manners, remarked to Mary that she "seemed to glide through the waltz with the ease of a serpent." Taking the simile as an insult, the future Mrs. Abraham Lincoln shot him a poisonous look. "Mr. Herndon, comparison to a serpent is a rather severe irony, especially to a newcomer," Mary declared as she turned on her heel and left the flummoxed Billy Herndon alone on the dance floor. The incident still rankled both parties. Neither could forgive the other.

When Lincoln was courting Mary Todd, Herndon tried to dissuade him from marrying the fiery-tempered belle. Needless to say, Herndon was not invited to their wedding, in 1842, and never once in the twenty-three years of their marriage had he been asked to the Lincoln home for dinner. In 1862, when Herndon visited the White House, Mary was nowhere to be seen. Proud and easy to take offense, Herndon interpreted the affront for what it probably had been, a calculated slight.

The more Mary studied the letter from Herndon, the more convinced she became that something was amiss. Already wary of him because of their thorny history, she also knew of his reputation as a difficult and argumentative drunk. Mary thought the matter through and, even though the letter had been addressed to Robert, decided to answer it herself. First, she effusively acknowledged Abraham Lincoln's great regard for Herndon. (This was the truth. The two lawyers had made a crafty team—Herndon had a true gift for research and organization and almost never left the office, while Lincoln made use of his superlative communication skills and handled most of the high-profile court appearances, traveling the Eighth Judicial Circuit on horseback.) Then Mary expressed bewilderment at what Herndon was really up to with this purported Lincoln biography. In Mary's words: "My sons and myself fail to understand your meaning. Will you please explain." Mary informed Herndon that she would soon be making a private trip to Springfield to visit the tomb of her late husband. She indicated a willingness to sit and chat with Herndon then, as long as the visit was kept confidential. "I have been thinking for some time past that I would like to see you & have a long conversation."

On September 5, 1866, Mary took the train from Chicago to the state capital and checked into the St. Nicholas Hotel, at the corner of Fourth and Jefferson. It was the finest hotel in the city, well regarded for its food and service, and just a short distance from the railroad depot. Herndon arrived at the agreed-upon hour. The two foes had not seen each other since 1861, and neither was aging well. Mary was forty-eight years old but looked a decade older. Herndon was tall and ragged, his teeth stained yellow from tobacco. Mary could see that the hardships of his life and his affection for corn liquor were taking their toll. Herndon sat down at a table, placed some blank paper before him, and got out his pen and inkwell. As he prepared to start his interview, it distressed Mary to realize that Herndon had been drinking. She could smell the liquor on his breath. Understandably, she was reluctant to continue, but after some coaxing by Herndon, she proceeded to relate her life story. Herndon later said that, as Mary began at the beginning, he took these careful notes.

"I was born on the 13th day of December, 1823, in Lexington, Fayette County, Kentucky. Am the daughter of Robert S. and Eliza Todd, maiden name Eliza Parker." Actually, Mary's very first recorded statement was demonstrably false; she was born in 1818. Whether she vainly shaved five years off her age or Herndon just got it wrong is a matter for debate. Herndon did not know shorthand and never claimed his notes constituted a verbatim transcript of the interview. Rather, he maintained, he had recorded "the substance of what she said."

Mary continued. Her husband was the "kindest man and most loving husband and father in the world." Yet he could be a "terribly firm man when he set his foot down. None of us—no man nor woman—could rule him after he had made up his mind. I told him about Seward's intention to rule him. He said: 'I shall rule myself; shall obey my own conscience, and follow God in it.'" He "had a kind of poetry in his nature," and he was not the same man Herndon had known in Springfield. He had grown gloriously in office to meet the challenges of the times. Mary claimed that her husband intended to fire Secretary of State Seward "when peace was declared." And he "hated" Andrew Johnson.

"I often said that God would not let any harm come of my husband. We had passed through five long years—terrible bloody years—unscathed, so that I thought so. So did Mr. Lincoln. He was happy in this idea—was cheerful, almost joyous, as he got gradually to see the end of the war."

Herndon, manipulative and crafty, more partisan lawyer than reliable historian seeking out facts, steered the interview to a discussion of Lincoln's religious beliefs. He wanted to know whether the president had ever joined a church. Mary answered with the truth, that her late husband was not a member of any particular church but he regularly attended services. Perhaps, Herndon suggested, that meant that Lincoln was not a "technical Christian." Mary responded, "Mr. Lincoln had no hope and no faith in the usual acceptance of these words. He was a religious man always as I think and believe. His first thought . . . about this subject was when Willie died—never before. He felt religious more than ever about the time he went to Gettysburg. He was not a technical Christian. He read the Bible a good deal in 1864."

Fifteen minutes into the interview, Mary's cousin John Todd Stuart arrived at the hotel. The time Mary had allotted for Herndon was up, and he was compelled to gather his notes, close his inkwell, and take his leave. In the not-too-distant future, Mary would regret that she had ever agreed to sit down with Billy Herndon.

Herndon's research for his Lincoln biography took him to New Salem, Illinois, and it was the discovery he made on this trip that would soon make him one of the most famous men in America.

The village that Herndon came upon was not the same village that Lincoln had lived in so many years before. For one thing, New Salem had simply ceased to exist. The blacksmith shop, general stores, tavern, shoemaker, carpenter, hatmaker, and tanner were all gone. The twenty-five families that had lived there in Lincoln's time had abandoned the village. But pioneers from the old days were still to be found in Petersburg, the nearest town, about three miles away, and they remembered young Abe Lincoln as an honest and good man who had drifted into New Salem on a flatboat in 1831 and remained there for six years—as a clerk in the general store and a student of the law. It was here in Petersburg that Herndon found an old-timer named Hardin Bale, from whom he first learned of a woman named Ann Rutledge.

Ann Rutledge was the tavern keeper's daughter, a sweet-tempered young woman who stood about five-foot-two and weighed 120 pounds. She'd had auburn hair, blue eyes, and was reputed to be an excellent housekeeper, the most popular girl in New Salem. She was beautiful, considerate, and thoughtful. Her nimble fingers made her "the wonder of the day" when the womenfolk of New Salem gathered for the rites of the quilting bee, a popular nineteenth-century social event at which villagers assembled to gossip and socialize and show off their needlepoint skills. Bale recalled that Lincoln, who boarded at the Rutledge tavern during his first year in New

Salem, started to escort Ann Rutledge to quilting bees, and on one occasion flouted etiquette by insisting that he sit beside her while she did her needlework. "She had a heart as gentle and kind as an angel, and full of love and sympathy," another old-timer, L. M. Greene, told Herndon. "She was amiable and of exquisite beauty, and her intellect was quick, deep, and philosophic as well as brilliant. . . . She was a woman worthy of Lincoln's love."

During the unusually hot and rainy summer of 1835, when Lincoln was twenty-six and serving his first term of elected political office as a member of the Illinois State Assembly, Ann Rutledge came down with "brain fever," a nineteenth-century term that probably meant meningitis or encephalitis or one of the other potentially fatal mosquito-borne diseases. Lincoln was there at her deathbed. The door was closed behind them and what words and vows were exchanged in the room remains unknown. A few days later, Ann lapsed into a coma and died, leaving Lincoln in the throes of grief and depression. He was so bereft that his friends feared he would take his own life, and felt compelled to keep watch over him. Herndon also found an elderly woman who quoted Lincoln as having said to her of Ann Rutledge's grave, "My heart lies buried there."

It was sensational stuff, just the groundbreaking material Herndon was seeking for his Lincoln biography. It revealed that before Abraham Lincoln had ever met Mary Todd, the future president had asked another woman to marry him, Ann Rutledge, and Herndon came to believe that she had been the true love of Lincoln's life. To Herndon, it explained much of what made Lincoln the man he was—melancholic, dispirited, even doomed. Lincoln's profound silences and despondency were now more understandable—he was remembering Ann Rutledge.

Herndon dug further. He learned that the story of Ann Rutledge had been previously published in 1862 in the local newspaper in Menard County, Illinois. At the height of the Civil War the *Menard Axis* reported the unflattering and salacious story that President Lincoln in his youth had been a "love-sick swain," in love with Ann Rutledge, and like a thief in the night he had stolen Ann Rutledge from another man, her fiancé, John McNamar. The author of the article was the newspaper's editor, John Hill, a Democrat who detested Lincoln's policies. John Hill wrote in the *Axis*, "Disease came upon this lovely beauty, and she sickened and died . . . and this was more than [Lincoln] could bear. He saw her to her grave, and as the cold clods fell upon the coffin, he sincerely wished that he too had been enclosed within it. Melancholy came upon him; he was changed and sad. His friends detected strange conduct. . . . They placed him under guard for fear of his commiting [sic] suicide."

The big-city newspapers failed to pick up the story, probably because the *Menard Axis* was such an obscure publication that the information never went beyond the county's borders. But somebody gave Herndon the clipping. Here it was in black and white, even if the article's author had had an obvious political ax to grind.

Herndon worked a full year and then some to flesh out the information about Ann Rutledge. Back at his law office, he corresponded with people from isolated farms or secluded country towns who had known Lincoln back when. As letters and statements from these faraway places came into his office, Herndon analyzed and filed them into what he called the "Lincoln Record," which he expected to one day turn into his full-scale Lincoln book. Herndon hired a clerk to copy every document by hand, and then had a bookbinder in Springfield bind the collection in the finest leather. It totaled three volumes.

In November 1866, about two months after his meeting with Mary Lincoln at the St. Nicholas Hotel, Herndon returned to New Salem on horseback and found that Ann Rutledge's former fiancé, John McNamar, was still living on a farm in Menard County. Herndon rode out to the farmhouse and saw McNamar standing at an open window. Fearlessly approaching, Herndon introduced himself and cut to the chase with his first question: "Did you know Miss Rutledge?" McNamar agreed to be interviewed. He still had wistful memories of Ann. McNamar called her a "gentle, amiable maiden, without any of the airs of your city belles, but winsome and comely." He recalled her cherry-red lips and "bonny blue" eyes. From McNamar, Herndon was able to piece together a more complete account of the Lincoln-Rutledge romance.

McNamar was born in Scotland but grew up in New York. Seeking his fortune out West, he drifted into New Salem around the same time Lincoln arrived in the village, in 1831. Ambitious and industrious, within three years McNamar held a half interest in a general store and owned a farm. Ann Rutledge was a seventeen-year-old schoolgirl when McNamar began courting her. They fell deeply in love and were going to be married when McNamar informed Ann that he had to return to New York to check on his elderly father. Ann promised to wait. McNamar mounted a tired old horse—a "veteran" from the Black Hawk War of 1832—and bid his fiancée farewell. His journey home was fraught with drama. In Ohio he came down with a fever, and for an entire month he wavered between delirium and unconsciousness. When he recovered, McNamar resumed his journey east. He finally wrote his first letter to Ann Rutledge when he arrived in New York.

The long delay in communicating with his fiancée had apparently resulted in Ann thinking she had been deserted. McNamar's relationship with this good woman was "all up" due to his bad luck and negligence. McNamar tried to explain his travails. Another letter from McNamar followed, this one "less ardent in tone." Back home, Ann lost faith. In time, the letters from McNamar ceased altogether. Then Ann wrote a letter of her own. She informed McNamar of Abraham Lincoln's interest in her and asked for McNamar's formal release from their engagement. Weeks passed, and when it became obvious that McNamar would not respond, Ann formally accepted Lincoln's marriage proposal. That, at least, is the story Herndon claimed he got from McNamar.

McNamar did not bear Abraham Lincoln any ill will. "I had every reason to believe him my warm, personal friend," he told Herndon. He realized that leaving New Salem and failing to communicate in a timely fashion had left him "far behind in the race" for Ann Rutledge's hand in marriage, giving Abe Lincoln the edge to make "rapid strides" and win Ann's heart. And throughout her struggle over which beau to choose, McNamar believed that Ann behaved honorably.

Herndon's research also led him to Ann's grave. On a gloomy Sunday morning he found the burial site about seven miles outside Petersburg in what is now known as the Oakland Cemetery. On the headstone the date of her death was inscribed as August 25, 1835. Herndon pondered the grave and put his thoughts down on paper. He found himself in the spirit of the "beautiful and tender dead. . . . [A] sad, solemn place." Like a good reporter with an eye for the telling detail, Herndon observed the name on the headstone abutting Ann's. It was her brother David Rutledge. Ann was buried next to David, resting "sweetly on his left arm."

One month after his return from New Salem, Herndon was ready to announce to the world the existence of Ann Rutledge. He would make the revelation in a lecture, which he delivered the night of November 16, 1866, at the Old Courthouse in Springfield.

Lectures were a popular form of mass entertainment in those days. Generally a minister would give the invocation, followed by a performance from a local pianist. Then came the featured speaker. Herndon was a skilled

orator and flamboyant writer. He was also disgusted with the deification of
Lincoln, whom he believed to be a great but not perfect man. Early Lincoln
historians were writing hagiographies, and Herndon took to calling those
first published works "humbug." "I love Lincoln dearly—almost worship
him, but that can't blind me," Herndon wrote a friend. He believed that Lincoln rightfully deserved the moniker Honest Abe, but Lincoln was not at all
times and to all people "absolutely Honest." "He was an exceedingly ambitious man—a man totally swallowed up in his ambitions," Herndon said.

The lecture in Springfield the evening of November 16, 1866, made history and altered forever how Americans would view their greatest president
and his relationship with his wife. Herndon wrote the entire fifteen-
thousand-word address in longhand and had five hundred copies printed
and copyrighted in advance. No admission fee was charged, and when the
seats were all taken and the hall quieted down, Herndon stepped before the
lectern and began his oration. Herndon informed his audience that he was
about to deliver a "long, thrilling, and eloquent story." Foreshadowing the
condemnation he knew would be coming his way, Herndon said it was his
sacred duty to reveal "one of the world's most classic stories."

Herndon launched into the story of New Salem, "the dead village of the
dead," and of Ann Rutledge—"the beautiful, amiable, and lovely girl of
nineteen" and the two men she had been engaged to, Abraham Lincoln and
John McNamar, and the inner turmoil she had suffered in choosing the
man she would marry. In her conflict Ann became sad and restless. "She
suffered, pined, ate not, and slept not." And then the fever struck her down
and she died. Herndon read directly from the notes of his October interview with McNamar. "Abraham Lincoln loved Miss Ann Rutledge with all
his soul, mind, and strength. They seemed made in heaven for each other."
And when Ann died, the future president "slept not, ate not, joyed not." Ann
Rutledge was the true love of his life, Herndon maintained. She was in fact
"the woman he should have married." After her death Lincoln could never
love another and indeed abstained from using the phrase "yours affectionately" in his letters or using the word "love" even in his letters to Mary Todd,
whom he married seven years after Ann's death. Lincoln's marriage to Mary
was nothing but "domestic hell," Herndon asserted. "For the last twenty-
three years of his life, Mr. Lincoln had no joy."

The lecture lasted about ninety minutes. The *Illinois State Journal* in
Springfield found Herndon's revelations so scandalous it refused to write
about the lecture the next day, reporting only that printed copies of

Herndon's speech could be purchased at news depots in the city for anyone interested. It took several days for the news to circulate around the nation. The *Chicago Tribune* denounced Herndon for defaming Lincoln's memory. Letters deploring Herndon poured into the law office that he had once shared with Lincoln. Lincoln's old friend Isaac Arnold wrote Herndon that he had sullied "the greatest & . . . the best man, our country has produced." The prominent Chicago lawyer Grant Goodrich wrote Herndon: "You are the last man who ought to attempt to write a life of Abraham Lincoln." Reports of Herndon's lecture reached Europe. In Dundee, Scotland, the Reverend James Smith, the former minister of the First Presbyterian Church in Springfield who was now the United States consul in Dundee (appointed by Lincoln), sent a scathing letter to the *Dundee Advertiser* calling Herndon's lecture "a most cruel . . . and malignant attack upon his heart stricken widow." The Lincoln children, Smith bitterly wrote, were being cast as "sons of a man who never loved their mother." Smith's blistering letter was reprinted in the *Chicago Tribune* and elsewhere.

Herndon had braced himself for some degree of criticism, but nothing prepared him for the ferocity of the attacks. "If such things must be, so be it," he wrote to a student admirer at the University of Pennsylvania School of Law. "I cannot be a liar—I must be brave, and keep my self respect, or sink. When you hear men scolding me, please say to them—'Do you know what you are talking about?'" As the storm raged, Herndon gained key support from Ann Rutledge's brother, Robert B. Rutledge. Although Rutledge corrected some of the facts, he called the lecture bold and "mainly and substantially true."

In Chicago, Mary Lincoln and her son Robert had been reduced to a state of utter despair. Until this time, the name Ann Rutledge had been unknown to Mary. She claimed Lincoln had never spoken of this Rutledge woman in their entire twenty-three years of married life. To know that every major newspaper in America was now reporting that Ann Rutledge was the true love of Lincoln's life was more than she could bear.

Robert sought advice from Justice David Davis. "Mr. William H. Herndon is making an ass of himself," he wrote Davis. He compared the Herndon lecture as fit for print only in a publication such as the *New York Ledger*, a weekly newspaper popular with women and filled with romantic features of love and marriage. "I am getting seriously annoyed at [Herndon's] way of doing things. If you have seen his lecture on 'Abraham Lincoln & Ann Rutledge,' I have no doubt you will feel the impropriety of such a publication even if it were, which I much doubt, all true." Yet Robert had to admit that Herndon's long association as his father's law partner endowed the revelations with the ring of truth. "He speaks with a certain amount of authority from having known my father so long." Robert appealed to Davis for advice and wondered whether Davis could come up with a plan to keep Herndon at bay. Although the clock could not be turned back regarding the Springfield lecture, what Robert now feared was Herndon embarking on a national lecture tour. That was something he was determined to stop. "Do you think it would be advisable to write to him?" Robert asked Davis. "He is such a singular character that I am afraid of making matters worse, but I think something ought to be done to stop his present course." In the end, Robert decided the best way to bring an end to Herndon's lectures was to make a direct appeal in person.

Robert traveled to Springfield the first week in December and went to Herndon's law offices. The two men eyed each other with reciprocal contempt. Herndon had known Robert since he was a bratty youngster running wild with his brothers Willie and Tad in the Lincoln & Herndon law firm. The office, on the second floor of a brick building facing the state capitol, was reputed to be the "dingiest and most untidy law office in the United States, without exception." Abraham Lincoln was mostly to blame for the chaos and disorganization. He would pile documents on his desk until the pile became a wobbling mountain of paperwork. On top, a handwritten note from Lincoln read: "When you can't find it anywhere else, look in this."

In his sixteen years with the firm, Herndon had always respectfully called his senior partner "Mr. Lincoln." He had held his tongue even on those occasions when the Lincoln boys would wreak havoc in the office, destroying furniture, spilling ink, and tossing pencils into the spittoon. Herndon once even accused the boys of "pissing" on the floor. He wanted to "wring the necks of these brats and pitch them out of the windows" but he knew that Lincoln would not tolerate any abuse or criticism of his children.

Now Robert Lincoln sat before him, a smug young man of twenty-three, a Harvard graduate, here to set Herndon straight on the matter of Ann Rutledge and the public humiliation of his mother. The tension between the two men was evident. It seemed to Herndon that Robert was looking to pick a fight. "I kept my temper and he couldn't fight because he had no one to fight with," Herndon later said. As Robert tried to explain how the Ann Rutledge lecture had injured his mother, Herndon stared disapprovingly at him, thinking the young man as arrogant and cold as ever. Assessing his character, Herndon concluded that Robert was certainly more Todd than Lincoln—"a cold little soul—his mother's child." The meeting ended without any resolution, although Herndon came away convinced that Robert's agenda was to intimidate him into silence. If anything, it made the cranky Herndon more determined than ever to complete his book.

Robert returned to Chicago and pondered his next move. Herndon had always been a puzzle to him. When he was attending Harvard, Robert had received several bizarre, "pseudo philosophical" letters from him that he thought proved Herndon had lost his mind. Certainly, he was unconventional. Herndon experimented with American Transcendentalism, which rejected traditional religion and held that an individual could achieve a heightened spiritual state through the power of intuition. Emerson and Thoreau were prominent transcendentalists, but Herndon took it beyond an interesting new way of thinking; he actually came to believe that he was clairvoyant and could read minds.

Robert decided to pen a follow-up letter to Herndon. Wisely, this time he tempered his arrogance and struck a conciliatory note. "All I ask is that nothing may be published by you, which after careful consideration will seem apt to cause pain to my father's family, which I am sure you do not wish to do. I hope that you will consider this matter carefully, My dear Mr Herndon, for once done there is no undoing." In a second letter, written on Christmas Eve, Robert asked Herndon to return a book his father had left behind in the Lincoln & Herndon law office. Robert explained that he wished to give it to a family friend. Herndon sent an obnoxious reply saying the book had already been disposed of and that, in any event, when he was elected, President Lincoln had informed him that everything in the law office was now Herndon's property, to do with as he pleased. More alarmingly, Herndon said in the letter that he planned to continue researching his Lincoln biography.

It was the final breach. "I infer from your letter," a bitter Robert wrote in response, "but I hope it is not so, that it is your purpose to make some considerable mention of my mother in your work—I say I hope it is not so, because in the first place it would not be pleasant for her or for any woman, to be made public property in that way."

Meanwhile, Mary Lincoln organized her own campaign to attack Herndon's credibility. Like Robert, she tried to enlist the support of David Davis in his role as associate justice on the United States Supreme Court.

The Ann Rutledge story was a myth, Mary claimed. It was a "malignity" concocted by that "drunkard" Herndon—"this miserable man!" Mary said that Abraham Lincoln had made Herndon his law partner "out of pity," and taken him into his office "when he was almost a hopeless inebriate." One can imagine Mary's rage when Davis responded that there was nothing wrong with a man, even someone as great as Abraham Lincoln, having a romantic fling in his youth. To which Mary indignantly responded, "As you justly remark, each & every one has had a little romance in their early days—but as my husband was truth itself . . . I shall assuredly remain firm in my conviction that Ann Rutledge is a myth—for in all his confidential communications, such a name was never breathed. Nor did his life or his joyous laugh lead one to suppose his head was in any unfortunate woman's grave—but in the proper place with his loved wife & children."

Mary Lincoln was much more appreciative of the Rev. James Smith's unconditional support when his letter, published in the *Dundee Advertiser*, was reprinted in the *Chicago Tribune*. She wrote Smith a letter in which she referred to Herndon as a "ruined man."

"If W.H. utters another word and is not silent with his infamous falsehoods in the future his life is not worth living for I have friends, if his low soul thought that my great affliction had left me without them. In the future he may well say his prayers. 'Revenge is sweet,['] especially to womankind, but there are some of mankind left who will wreck it upon him. He is a dirty dog."

If the letter reads like a curse placed upon the head of William Herndon, perhaps in some mysterious way it worked its magic. Following his Ann Rutledge lecture, it almost seemed that "God himself was against Herndon," writes the Lincoln historian David Herbert Donald. "Everything he did turned out wrong." Herndon gave up the practice of law to focus full-time on researching his Lincoln book. He moved his family to a farm six miles north of Springfield that his father Archer deeded to him in 1867. It was six hundred acres of fertile bottomland, ideal for corn, but Herndon had the notion of planting fancy fruits. In his first year managing the farm, which he renamed Fairview, Herndon planted grapevines, apple, peach, plum, and pear trees, and exhausted his savings with the purchase of new livestock—a herd of sixty cattle, twelve horses, and sixty hogs.

Apparently, all of Herndon's knowledge about farming came from books. One old neighbor pitifully said of Herndon: "He could not raise anything but Hell." The plagues that afflicted Herndon became very nearly biblical in breadth: "His fruit trees died, his potatoes were eaten by beetles, his cows were mutilated by a vicious dog, his mule was killed, his hogs had the cholera," wrote Donald. When it seemed that his financial situation could not get any worse, it sank even lower. In 1868, the bank foreclosed on Herndon's Springfield house. At age fifty-three, Abraham Lincoln's former law partner found himself forced to work the fields of his farm as a manual laborer. His drinking was now out of control. A neighbor reported seeing Herndon so intoxicated he was "hauled home from town just like you would a hog on hay in the back end of the wagon. . . . They unloaded him with his jug of whiskey—he would lay up stairs drunk for a week."

FOUR MONTHS AFTER William Herndon delivered his notorious Ann Rutledge lecture, Elizabeth Keckley received an alarming letter from Mary Lincoln. The former First Lady was in grim circumstances. "It will not be startling news to you, my dear Lizzie, to learn that I must sell a portion of my wardrobe. . . . I cannot live on $1,700 a year. . . . Now, Lizzie, I want to ask a favor of you. . . . I want you to meet me in New York, between the 30th of August and the 5th of September next, to assist me in disposing of my wardrobe." Lizzie was not surprised. She understood that Mary's gowns, shawls, furs, and jewelry represented the widow's only true assets. And the timing made sense. Early September signaled the start of the fall season for the fashionable set in New York.

It was a dilemma for Lizzie. Her dressmaking store in Washington was thriving. Even with the change in administrations, she was still the most sought-after seamstress in the nation's capital. Business was so good she could turn away prestigious clients. When President Andrew Johnson's daughter, Martha Johnson Patterson, asked Lizzie to come to the White House to fit her for a new dress, Lizzie politely but firmly declined, saying she never cut or fitted anyone outside her shop. Clients had to come to her. Martha Patterson, aged thirty-nine, was living in the White House and serving as her father's hostess in place of her invalid mother, who would make only two public appearances as First Lady. A modest and tactful woman, Martha once said of her family, "We are plain people, from the mountains of Tennessee, called here for a short time by a national calamity. I trust too much will not be expected of us." Nevertheless, she refused to come to Lizzie's shop for the fitting and found a more accommodating dressmaker.

Leaving for New York at the peak of her busy season would be a burden, but Lizzie knew she could not refuse Mary Lincoln. In Lizzie's words: "She was the wife of Abraham Lincoln, the man who had done so much for my race." Several letters were exchanged as Mary and Lizzie conferred on strategy. Both women were aware that the sale of Mary Lincoln's wardrobe was fraught with risk, and represented a "delicate business." The important thing, they both agreed, was reaching Mary's financial goals without public fanfare.

September came around. Lizzie closed her shop on the tenth and awaited a final set of instructions from Mary. A letter finally arrived five days later from Chicago. Its contents puzzled Lizzie. Mary was apparently already on her way to New York. The letter directed Lizzie to proceed to New York immediately, arrange for lodgings at the St. Denis Hotel, and wait there for Mary's arrival. Mary Lincoln said she would be traveling incognito, under the name Mrs. Clarke. Lizzie pondered this set of instructions. It was perplexing. For one thing, it was surprising that Mary was traveling alone, without a male escort. For another, Lizzie had never heard of the St. Denis Hotel, which she assumed meant it was a second-rate establishment. Lizzie decided to stay put until she heard from Mary again. The next three days filled her with anxiety. When no letter or telegram came, Lizzie at last decided she could not wait any longer; she packed her bags and made haste for New York.

Lizzie arrived in the great metropolis the evening of September 18, 1867. She stood on the street outside the station, having no idea how to get to the St. Denis Hotel. Then she walked up to Broadway and boarded a stage. She asked a gentleman sitting next to her if he could please let her know when they reached the St. Denis Hotel.

"Yes, we ride past it in the stage," he told her. "I will point it out to you when we come to it."

"Thank you, sir."

After a while the man announced, "This is the St. Denis." He pulled the strap, and when Lizzie got off she found herself standing on the pavement in front of a six-story brick building at 799 Broadway, at the corner of E. Eleventh Street.

There was a separate entrance for women, and Lizzie rang the bell. A bellboy appeared, and Lizzie asked whether a Mrs. Clarke was registered at the hotel. The boy said he would check, and Lizzie followed him inside. It was there, at the front desk, that she saw her old friend Mary Lincoln. The two women, who had not seen each other in two years, shook hands.

"My dear Lizzie, I am so glad to see you." Here was Lizzie Keckley at last, and the relief in Mary's voice was understandable. Mary turned to the hotel clerk. "This is the woman I told you about," she said eagerly. "I want a good room for her."

The clerk studied the mixed-race woman. He was a dandy, "highly perfumed," and, according to Lizzie, extremely rude. "We have no room for her, madam," the clerk informed Mary.

"But she must have a room. She is a friend of mine, and I want a room for her adjoining mine."

The clerk said officiously, "We have no room for her on your floor. Friend of yours, or not, I tell you we have no room for her on your floor. I can find a place for her on the fifth floor."

It was humiliating. Here was the former slave whose son had been killed in battle fighting for the Union army, tasting the bitter bile of bigotry in the North. Apparently, the fifth floor held the designated quarters for black people. To her credit, Mary said, "Well, if she goes to the fifth floor, I shall go too, sir. What is good enough for her is good enough for me."

"Very well, madam." The clerk, still oblivious to the fact that he was dealing with the Great Emancipator's widow, agreed to give them adjoining rooms. Channeling her years as the demanding First Lady of the United States, Mary sharply ordered him to send her bags up to her new room— "and have it done in a hurry."

Following the bellboy, Mary and Lizzie took the stairs to the fifth floor. They were both out of breath when they reached their rooms. Lizzie was shocked to see the accommodations. Mary's was a nasty three-cornered room, barely furnished. "I never expected to see the widow of President Lincoln in such dingy, humble quarters," Lizzie said.

"How provoking!" Mrs. Lincoln exclaimed as she sat exhausted in the chair, still panting from the five-story climb. The aging tornado still had some fight in her. She made a vow to speak with the hotel manager in the morning and give him a "regular going over." Now it was time for the two old friends to become reacquainted. "I was almost crazy when I reached here last night and found you [had] not arrived," Mary told her. Mary said she had even sent Lizzie a telegram saying she was "frightened to death" at being alone in New York. (The desperate telegram, which Lizzie finally retrieved when she returned to Washington, read as follows: "Come, I pray you, by next train. Inquire for MRS. CLARKE. Room 94. . . . Come by next train, without fail. Come, come, come. I will pay your expenses when you arrive here. I shall not leave here or change my room until you come.")

It was getting late, and Lizzie was starving. Mary remained in the room while Lizzie went to the dining hall in the lobby. A waiter seated her at a corner table. She was giving him her order when the maitre d' was suddenly hovering over her.

"You are in the wrong room," he told her.

"I was brought here by the waiter," Lizzie said.

"It makes no difference. I will find you another place where you can eat your dinner."

Lizzie wearily rose from the table and followed him out. She understood exactly what was going on. "It is very strange that you should permit me to be seated at the table in the dining room only for the sake of ordering me to leave the next moment."

"Servants are not allowed to eat in the dining room. Here, this way." He led her to the servants' hall but found the room locked, and nobody could find the key. "Very well," Lizzie finally said. "I will tell Mrs. Clarke that I cannot get any dinner."

The man scowled at her. "You need not put on airs!"

When Lizzie returned to the room her eyes were flooded with tears. She told Mary what had happened. "The insolent, overbearing people," Mary remarked. Lizzie went to bed hungry.

The following morning Mary woke up Lizzie at 6:00 A.M. The two women got dressed and, not wishing to provoke another incident, left the St. Denis and walked up Broadway until they found a restaurant serving breakfast. At last the famished Lizzie was able to eat. After the meal, Mary and Lizzie strolled along Broadway and soon found themselves at Union Square Park. Sitting on a bench, they took in the scene. The oval-shaped park, enclosed by an iron picket fence, featured a magnificent fountain as the centerpiece and a huge equestrian statue of George Washington by the American sculptor Henry Kirke Brown. (In three years' time, another Brown work of art—a larger-than-life bronze statue of Abraham Lincoln— would be dedicated in the southwest corner of the square where Mary and Lizzie now sat.) These were the final days of summer, and a flock of children danced and played around the two women sitting on the bench. They made quite a pair; the tall regal mulatto, born of a black woman and her white slave master, and the stout Mrs. Abraham Lincoln, her famous face concealed behind her double black widow's veil.

Mary informed her companion that she had brought several trunkloads of clothes with her from Chicago, and they were now in storage at the St. Denis Hotel. She had deliberately selected the obscure hotel because she did not wish to be recognized at a better-known establishment. Mary said she had already communicated with the diamond brokerage firm of W. H. Brady & Co. seeking an appraisal of her jewelry. Although she was asking "outrageous prices," evidently there was interest there; a representative from the firm had made an appointment to see "Mrs. Clarke" at the St. Denis to inspect her possessions.

At noon, Mary and Lizzie returned to the hotel. A few minutes later, Samuel Keyes, a partner at W. H. Brady—a firm that had apparently been selected at random by Mary Lincoln after she saw its ad in the *New York Herald*—knocked on her door. Keyes was a clever and manipulative fellow. On the previous day when she had stopped by the brokerage company, at 609 Broadway, he had scrutinized Mary's jewelry and noticed her name inscribed in one of the rings she was trying to sell. Now, alone with Mary and Lizzie in the St. Denis Hotel, Keyes asked Mary outright whether she was President Lincoln's widow. Perhaps too eagerly, Mary confided that indeed it was true—she was the Mary Lincoln. Never particularly appreciative of anonymity, Mary evidently determined that it was time to declare her identity. Her masquerade had lasted exactly one day.

Keyes, an earnest Republican, was elated. Mary displayed for Keyes the shawls, dresses, and fine lace garments that she said she was compelled to sell. Keyes agreed that it was a despicable state of affairs. Then Mary complained about the treatment of Lizzie Keckley at the St. Denis, and an outraged Keyes urged her to move to another hotel right away. He recommended the Earle Hotel on Canal Street. Mary, Lizzie, and their new business associate Mr. Keyes took a carriage downtown. Unfortunately, the Earle Hotel was booked. Even after informing hotel management that she was Mary Lincoln (so much for concealing her identity from wide public knowledge), there was still no room available. They next tried the Union Place Hotel, where they secured several rooms under the name Mrs. Clarke.

Samuel Keyes became a regular visitor, but now the senior partner in the firm, William H. Brady himself, came with him. Keyes and Brady familiarized themselves with the goods for sale and assured Mary of their fantastic worth. The smooth-talking Brady in particular made a persuasive case. "Place your affairs in our hands, and we will raise you at least $100,000 in a few weeks," he promised. But that guarantee came with a caveat. Brady informed Mary that to earn full value he would have to let it be known that the merchandise came from Mary Lincoln. The notoriety of her name and the martyrdom of her good husband would ensure their lucrative sale.

While Keyes and Brady took on the jewelry, Mary and Lizzie dealt with the clothes. Several appointments were lined up with secondhand merchants who came to the hotel room to inspect the garments. "They were hard people to drive a bargain with," Lizzie remarked. Disappointed with the offers, Mary and Lizzie tied up a bundle of dresses and shawls and went door-knocking along Seventh Avenue, then as now the fashion district of the city. But the merchants proved to be tough negotiators and bid "little or nothing" for the stock. Mary was disgusted and exhausted.

By now, the Union Place Hotel was buzzing with excitement. Mary's trunks were being stored in the lobby, and though her name had been rubbed down from wear and tear, the faint outlines of the letters remained. The first reports of Mary Lincoln's presence in New York started appearing in the city's newspapers. Keyes and Brady were delighted by the publicity. Drumming up interest in Mary's jewels would surely be good for business. Mary now found herself under the domination of these two hucksters, and also in their debt, as they had loaned her six hundred dollars for hotel and living expenses.

An odd scheme was concocted. From her room at the Union Place Hotel, Mary agreed to write a letter to Brady offering for sale her shawls, a lace dress, a diamond ring, and several furs. The total value exceeded twenty-four thousand dollars. Only her "peculiar and painfully embarrassing" circumstances compelled her to take such humiliating measures, she told Brady in the letter. She urged Brady to conduct the sale in a manner that would stir up "as little comment as possible." Privately, however, Mary gave Brady permission to show the letter to the city's leading Republican politicians. The tactic was pure shakedown. Brady was gambling that the Republican leadership would purchase the items quietly and in confidence rather than let it be said that Abraham Lincoln's widow was "in want."

As Mary wrote the letter, Lizzie stood at her side. It distressed the dressmaker to see such language being committed to paper. Lizzie suggested that the words be softened.

"Never mind, Lizzie," Mary said dismissively. "Anything to raise the wind. One might as well be killed for a sheep as a lamb."

Brady went around the city showing the letter to several influential

Republicans, including the former New York representative Abram Wakeman, who was now serving as surveyor of the Port of New York in charge of the port's entire inspectional force, and Henry Wikoff, a womanizing rogue and former White House confidant of Mary Lincoln. But Wakeman, Wikoff, and the other Republicans who were shown the letter failed to take the bait. Not one item was sold in this ham-fisted manner.

With the New York City press corps hot on her trail, Mary paid her hotel bill and left Manhattan for a brief stay in the country with Lizzie. Three days later they returned and checked into yet another hotel, the Brandreth, on Broadway. This time Mary registered under the name "Mrs. Morris." By now Mary appeared to be completely under the spell of William Brady, and, after relentless goading by the diamond broker, Mary signed off on a new stratagem: Her wardrobe from her White House years would be placed on public exhibition. Trunks filled with Mary's clothes were delivered to the W. H. Brady & Co. offices on Broadway, and Mary authorized Brady to initiate the sale. An official announcement was made in the newspapers, and handbills were circulated around the city.

It was now time to go home. Mary packed her bags and Lizzie accompanied her to the train station for the trip back to Chicago. The dressmaker was to remain behind in New York and keep an eye out for Mary's interests. But in her wake, Mary left a firestorm. Brady, with Mary's permission, had turned over to the *New York World* all the letters she had written him regarding the sale of her clothes and jewelry. The very morning of Mary's departure, the pro-Democratic newspaper published the material but mischievously spun the story into an attack on the Republican Party, contending that the party of Lincoln was rebuffing his widow in her time of financial crisis. One letter quoted Mary as accusing the Republican Party— "for whom my husband did so much"—of "unhesitatingly depriving me of all means of support" and leaving her in a "pitiless condition."

The next day the *World* fueled the scandal by publishing another letter from Mary Lincoln to William Brady. This document concerned Abram Wakeman, the surveyor of the Port of New York.

"Please call and see Hon. Abram Wakeman," Mary's letter stated. "He was largely indebted to me for obtaining the lucrative office which he has held for several years, and from which he has amassed a very large fortune. . . . Therefore he will only be too happy to relieve me by purchasing one or more of the articles you will please place before him." The letter was loaded with innuendo—corruption by Wakeman and a shakedown on the part of Mary Lincoln. Mary's two-week New York excursion was degenerating into a full-scale debacle for the Republican Party.

From William Brady's point of view, the scandal was a blessing. The opening day of the sale, hundreds of fashionable New Yorkers appeared at his store just a few doors south of Houston Street to have a look at Mary Lincoln's clothes. The showroom was jammed with curious shoppers, and Brady himself—the P. T. Barnum of diamond brokers—could be observed managing the chaos and supervising his sales staff. Spread out on a piano were Mary's dresses from her four years in the White House. On a lounge in the showroom her luxurious shawls were also displayed. Every so often a bargain hunter would hold a garment in front of herself and measure it for size. A dress trimmed in gold and worth an estimated four thousand dollars was kept in a box and shown only to women of means who expressed a special interest in it.

Newspaper coverage of the event was almost universally contemptuous. Lizzie Keckley kept a clip of a nasty article from the *New York Evening Express* noting that some of Mrs. Lincoln's dresses were jagged and frayed at the seams, with tattered lining. One dress appeared soiled with a yellow crystalline powder—evidently a camera flash had blasted the dress while Mary was posing for a photograph. Discriminating shoppers holding aloft another dress observed that it was stained under the armpits with Mary's own perspiration. Some of the outfits were deemed out of fashion and it was remarked that most of them were cut low-necked—"a taste which some ladies attribute to Mrs. Lincoln's appreciation of her own bust." One wealthy patron entered the Brady establishment and made a big show of examining all the merchandise. She was looking for a particular shawl made in China—a gift she claimed she had mailed to Mary Lincoln as an inducement to get President Lincoln to sign the Emancipation Proclamation. The dowager desired to acquire the shawl once again, but she did not find it in the pile at Brady's.

The sale was a complete flop. Thousands came to look, but very few to buy. A symbol of the disrespect accorded Mary Lincoln came in the form of a pledge book that customers were asked to sign before they entered Brady's showroom. Although admission was free, people were encouraged to contribute at least one dollar in support of President Lincoln's widow. But the pledge book was a mockery. People signed their names and then filled the pledge line with the mortifying amounts of a penny or a dime. Somebody calling himself the Committee to Save Us from National Disgrace donated seventy-five dollars. Of course it was a joke at Mary Lincoln's expense.

Mary found herself under attack by Democrats for political corruption and by Republicans for desecrating the memory of Abraham Lincoln. All the old scandals from her stormy White House years were dredged up. The newspapers of the defeated South were particularly vicious, with one Georgia publication calling Mary repugnant and a "mercenary prostitute." In her home state, the *Chicago Tribune* published a letter stating that the actions of the former First Lady "make us blush for our country and for our womanhood."

On board the train to Chicago, a prosperous-looking man with a middle-aged paunch sat reading that morning's *New York World*, absorbed in the story of Mary Lincoln and what newspaper headlines were now branding the "Old Clothes Scandal." He started a conversation with another passenger seated next to him.

"Are you aware that Mrs. Lincoln is in indigent circumstances and has to sell her clothing and jewelry . . . to make life more endurable?"

The other fellow replied, "I do not blame her for selling her clothing, if she wishes it." At least, he said with a sneer, it would give her the funds to pay for her funeral.

The passenger gripped the *World* newspaper in his fists and indignantly retorted, "That woman is not dead yet."

Neither man could have imagined that the stout little lady sitting across from them and overhearing the conversation was Mary Lincoln, her face hidden behind her double black mourning veil.

The train pulled into the Chicago depot. Waiting for her at the station was her "darling little Taddie." She had left him almost three weeks earlier, and now he was there to greet his adored mother. Mary and the boy embraced, and "his voice never sounded so sweet."

Then she went home and saw Robert. Nothing was ever the same for her again.

7
Breach and Betrayal

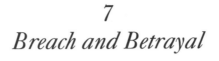

MARY LINCOLN TOOK Tad home to 460 West Washington Street. They were boarding in a good neighborhood with the builder Coles and his wife, and Mary appreciated everything they were doing for her, calling them a "very kind, good, quiet family, and their meals are excellent." Mary had her own parlor and a bedroom that was "sweetly furnished."

It was Saturday night. Tad, affectionate as always, clung to his mother. But the joy of Mary's homecoming ended abruptly when Robert showed up. He was distressed beyond words and almost maniacal in his rage. He had just returned from an enjoyable vacation out West in Cheyenne, Wyoming, with several male friends, and now the Old Clothes Scandal was exploding on the front pages of the *Chicago Tribune*. That morning, the *Tribune* had reprinted the letters, previously published in the *New York World*, that Mary had written to William Brady. Robert was beside himself; his mother had never before heard him use such language. He was threatening to take his own life, and he "looked like death."

As her son went on berating her, Mary could not stop weeping. She retired to her bedroom but could not sleep. On Sunday morning she sat at her writing table and composed a short but poignant "My Dear Lizzie" letter to her companion, who had remained behind in New York. "I am writing this morning with a broken heart after a sleepless night of great mental suffering. I weep whilst I am writing. I pray for death this morning. Only my darling Taddie prevents my taking my life." She said that in the next few days she expected another round of "newspaper abuse" coming her way. Then she ordered Lizzie to get to William Brady and his partner Keyes and immediately inform them "not to have a line of mine once more in print." Even Mary was coming to the realization that it was time to pull back on the attention. She ended the letter with these pathetic words: "I am nearly losing my reason." Her prediction of more abuse being heaped upon her proved accurate. "The Republican papers are tearing me to pieces. . . . If I had committed murder in every city in this blessed Union, I could not be more traduced." Just days later came this pitiable communication to Lizzie: "I am friendless. What a world of anguish this is and how I have been made to suffer. You would not recognize me now. The glass shows me a pale, wretched, haggard face, and my dresses are like bags on me."

To her acquaintance Rhoda White, widow of a New York judge, she put forth a disingenuous defense. "Never was an act committed with a more innocent intention than mine was. Having no further use for the articles proposed to be sold—and really requiring the proceeds—I deposited them with an agent & I presumed no publicity would result from it. I was not more astonished than you would have been to see my letters in print." Of course, Mary made no admission to Mrs. White of her collusion with these men, which had now led to publication of these embarrassing—even incriminating—letters. It was finally dawning on Mary that Brady and Keyes were not true friends to her. As she wrote Lizzie Keckley: "I begin to think they are making a political business of my clothes, and not for my benefit either."

Seeing his mother ridiculed on front pages across America was a nightmare for the guarded and private Robert. He was now a lawyer, licensed to practice in the state of Illinois following a year of studying law at the offices of Scammon, McCagg & Fuller and taking law classes at the Old University of Chicago. Robert had already set up his own law firm, partnering with Charles T. Scammon, the son of Jonathan Young Scammon. The Scammon & Lincoln law offices at 1 Marine Bank Building in downtown Chicago was a venture that could not fail, at least on paper. Robert Lincoln, son of the Great One, opening a law firm with the son of Chicago's most eminent lawyer.

Unfortunately, Charles Scammon was a huge disappointment to the president's eldest son. Just three months into the partnership Scammon simply took off on a "succession of sprees," as Robert described it. Scammon stopped communicating with his partner, and, through word of mouth, Robert heard the young lawyer was somewhere in the East—"under treatment" for alcohol abuse. The relationship became so ruptured and antagonistic that Robert took to calling Scammon "utterly worthless." In

Robert's words: "I cannot tell you to what extent his debauches damage me personally." Even Samuel W. Fuller, a partner in Scammon, McCagg & Fuller, was urging Robert to disassociate himself from the young man. As a courtesy, Robert went to the senior Scammon and informed the distinguished attorney that he intended to dissolve the partnership with Charles Scammon. Apparently, no objection was raised; the father was fully conscious of the issues involving his ne'er-do-well son.

The shame of Mary Lincoln's Old Clothes Scandal, as it had been dubbed by the newspapers, could not have come at a more discomforting time for Robert. There he was, struggling to build a practice, which, with his "utterly worthless" partner, was already on shaky ground, and now he also had to deal with his mother, who was engaged in a war of words with the leadership of the Republican Party. One urgent task for Robert was informing his fiancée of the situation. On October 16 he poured out his troubles in a heartfelt letter to Mary Harlan in Washington. One can imagine her reading the letter, and bracing herself for what lay ahead with Mary Lincoln as her mother-in-law. "I suppose you have seen some of the papers so there is no need of detailing what I was told they were full of," Robert wrote. "I did not read them. The simple truth, which I cannot tell to anyone not personally interested, is that my mother is on one subject not mentally responsible."

It was an extraordinary thing to declare, and it laid the foundation for the drama that would one day lead to the utter sundering of the Lincoln family. Robert said he had consulted with several professionals whom he trusted, and they had advised him that nothing could be done regarding the state of his mother's mental health. It was, he noted, "terribly irksome." He told his fiancée: "The greatest misery of all is the fear of what may happen in the future. . . . I have no doubt that a great many good and amiable people wonder why I do not take charge of her affairs and keep them straight but it is very hard to deal with one who is sane on all subjects but one." That subject, of course, was money. Robert wrote that he had tried to assume more responsibility for his mother's financial affairs, but she found his interference offensive. "You could hardly believe it possible, but my mother protests to me that she is in actual want and nothing I can do or say will convince her to the contrary."

Curiously, around this time, the theme of insanity that was laid out in Robert's private correspondence with his fiancée started to appear in newspaper articles. Four days after Mary Lincoln returned from New York, the

Chicago Journal reported, "The most charitable construction that Mary Lincoln's friends can put on her strange course is that she is insane." The *Chicago Journal* was a newspaper with close connections to Chicago's Republican power brokers, and it had been founded by the lawyer who had taken Robert under his wing, Jonathan Young Scammon.

Another article that reads as if it came directly from Robert, or a close associate, appeared in the *Boston Daily Evening Transcript*, which in its day was the newspaper of record for that city. It described Robert as "intelligent, quiet, industrious, unassuming, courteous." It went on to point out that Robert "resembled his father, not his mother. . . . The conduct of his mother is as deep a mystery to him as to all of her friends, and the only theory he can suggest in her defense is that she is insane." If Robert was indeed the source of these stories, it surely was shameful conduct on his part. For, in distancing himself from Mary, he was attempting to rescue his reputation at his mother's expense. It is also interesting that Robert—or somebody close to him—sought to put it out there that he was more like his mythic father than his notorious mother. It was of course a ludicrous assertion. In every way imaginable—down to his physical frame—Robert surely was more a Todd than a Lincoln.

But nothing came close to the pure libel of a letter to the editor published in the *Chicago Tribune* and signed by the anonymous reader who called himself "B." The commentary compared Mary Lincoln to the Empress Carlotta of Mexico, who went insane following the overthrow and execution of her husband, the Emperor Maximilian.

"Many who have known Mrs. Lincoln for years, have for a long time unhesitatingly affirmed that her mind was wrecked, and that an insane asylum must be eventually her home. The evidences of her insanity, in a thousand ways, are not wanting." The letter then went on to the subject of Robert Lincoln. "There is a son who inherits the virtues of the father and whom we would all shield with parental affection if we could. The comments of the press, which he must silently bear, pierce his heart. . . . We say at the same time to him, we love and respect you, and so long as you walk in your integrity, no act of another can rob you of our warmest affection."

The Old Clothes Scandal persuaded Robert Lincoln and David Davis that it was time to finally settle the Abraham Lincoln estate. Mary had been seeking a distribution of the president's assets since 1865. Now, just one month after the eruption of the scandal, and two and a half years after the assassination, it was a done deal. In November 1867 it was announced that

Abraham Lincoln's estate totaled $110,000 and would be divided between his widow and two surviving sons. Mary only learned about the arrangement when she picked up a copy of the *Illinois State Journal*. She was outraged that neither Justice Davis nor her son had shown her the courtesy of notifying her of this important development. "The papers are abounding with notices of settlement of the estate, and the amount left each of us," she wrote Davis. "As I have not heard a word from Robert on the subject, I consider it necessary that I should be quite as well-informed as the Press—regarding our own business."

From the newspaper reports, Mary also learned for the first time that Robert was receiving about $250 a month from the estate—almost double her allotment. Robert had also received additional dollars to renovate his bachelor apartment at the Opera House. Understandably, Mary, now living with Tad as a boarder, saw this as a betrayal. She could not understand why Robert was given everything he asked for, while her requests for funds to buy and keep up a home of her own were routinely rejected. Mary's share of Abraham Lincoln's estate came to thirty-six thousand dollars, the approximate equivalent of a half million dollars today. Her boys split the rest, with Robert receiving a lesser share because Davis subtracted the extra money he had previously distributed to him.

The timing of the settlement certainly seems suspicious. Mary, who could be so savvy about certain things and oblivious to others, understood it for what it surely was—a deliberate derailment of her effort to sell off her clothes. Her son, Mary confided to Lizzie Keckley, was in collusion with Davis. "R. is very spiteful at present, and I think he hurries up the division to cross my purposes." The reports of Mary's inheritance received national attention, and any sympathy her financial plight may have been generating vanished overnight. Thirty-six thousand dollars was a vast sum of money. Mary Lincoln was no longer the desperate, poverty-stricken widow of the man who had saved the Union. Now she was a wealthy woman.

The strain between Mary and Robert continued to mount. She was looking forward to his departure for an extended Thanksgiving holiday in the Rocky Mountains with several friends including Edgar Welles and Norman Williams, a wealthy young Chicago lawyer who was engaged to the daughter of the chief justice of the Illinois Supreme Court. Robert would be "out of the way" for three weeks, Mary told Lizzie Keckley almost gleefully. She would use the opportunity to push ahead with William Brady's proposal to circulate a hundred and fifty thousand handbills promoting the sale of her wardrobe. It was one last marketing ploy aimed at turning things around and bringing in real revenue. Incredibly, after all the misery they had caused her, Mary was still not ready to abandon her futile commercial enterprises.

In New York, Lizzie Keckley was facing a financial crisis of her own. She was desperately anxious to return to Washington and reestablish her dressmaking business, but Mary insisted she remain in New York, where she could keep an eye on Brady and Keyes. Meanwhile, Lizzie earned a little money here and there sewing. Taking advantage of her connections in the black community, she arranged to live rent-free in various apartments in Manhattan, but by November she was "wretchedly low-spirited." Communicating once again her desire to return to Washington, Lizzie received this frosty reply from Mary Lincoln: "Can you not, dear Lizzie, be employed in sewing for some of your lady friends in New York until December 1?" Mary promised to send money, just not now. After a bleak Christmas in New York, Lizzie implored Mary yet again to be released. Mary answered with a suggestion that Lizzie join her in Chicago. "Had you not better go with me and share my fortunes, for a year or more?"

Lizzie's bond with the former First Lady now became a subject of national speculation. At Mary's request, Lizzie gave an interview to the *New York Herald*, then the largest circulation newspaper in America. In the *Herald* article, Lizzie was described as Mrs. Lincoln's "faithful negro servant" and perhaps the only loyal friend the former First Lady had left in the world. The newspaper revealed that when Mrs. Lincoln came up with the ill-conceived notion of selling her clothes, "she first consulted her former modiste, Mrs. Elizabeth Keckley, upon whose judgment and discretion she had great reliance."

In the elite ranks of America's black leadership, including the great abolitionist Frederick Douglass, the fact that a former slave had become Mary Lincoln's source of strength engendered pride, and high regard for Lizzie. For advice, Lizzie reached out to the pastor of her church in Washington, the distinguished African American orator Henry Highland Garnet. Garnet went up to New York and accompanied Lizzie to a strategy meeting with Horace Greeley, the editor of the *New York Tribune*. Steer clear of Messrs. Brady and Keyes, Greeley counseled. Continuing to allow Mrs. Lincoln to associate with those two characters would be imprudent.

Lizzie also pitched Frederick Douglass the proposal that collections be taken up for Mary Lincoln in black churches across the United States.

Douglass, then forty-nine, was willing to join Garnet on a national lecture tour to raise money for Mary—anything to aid the "widow of the man who broke the fetters of our enslaved people." Douglass sent Mary Lincoln a gracious letter expressing his eagerness to sign up for the tour. But Douglass also appreciated the volatile state of racial relations in America and recommended that he not be given top billing on the lecture circuit—nor should his name be placed at the bottom. Instead, he advised, "sandwich me between."

Initially, Mary Lincoln was enthusiastic about Douglass's participation. "Whatever is raised by the colored people, I solemnly give my word, at my death it shall all, every cent, be returned to them." Mary promised that if fifty thousand dollars were raised, Lizzie would receive five thousand at her death. In a peculiar assurance to Lizzie, Mary wrote, "I cannot live long, suffering as I am now doing." But then something happened that caused Mary to abruptly change her position. She sent Lizzie a letter with this mortifying pronouncement: "I want neither Douglass or Garnet to lecture in my behalf." Sympathetic as she had been to abolishing slavery, Mary Lincoln evidently could not abide asking for handouts from black Americans. It just would not do, although she appreciated the effort. "[Most] of the good feeling regarding my straitened circumstances proceeds from the colored people; in whose cause my noble husband was so largely interested. . . . Mr. F. Douglass and Mr. Garnet will always have my most grateful thanks. They are very noble men." Still, it was terribly humiliating for Lizzie, who now had to notify Douglass and Garnet that Mary would not accept their assistance after all.

While she was struggling to survive hand-to-mouth in a strange city, Mary thought Lizzie had to have read the newspaper accounts about her inheritance. Trying to forestall trouble, Mary wrote Lizzie: "By the time you receive this note, you will doubtless find the papers raving over the large income which we [she, Robert, and Tad] are each said to have." Without getting into the specifics, Mary claimed that the "fabulous" sums quoted in the newspapers were "utterly false." In another letter, Mary erroneously claimed that she was expecting to receive only twenty-five thousand dollars once the estate was settled, not the thirty-six thousand being accurately reported. "I mention about the division of the estate to you, dear Lizzie, because when it is done the papers will harp upon it."

New Year's Day 1868 came and went with no joyful celebration for either woman. In early January came news that sent Mary into a panic. Lizzie notified her that those two New York hucksters, Brady and Keyes, had sent Mary's entire wardrobe off to Providence, Rhode Island, for the first stop in a traveling road show scheduled for North America and Europe. An admission fee was to be charged, with a percentage going to Mary. Lizzie had signed off on the tour without first consulting with Mary. Mary was furious. "Why did you not urge them not to take my goods to Providence? For heaven's sake see K.&B. when you receive this, and have them immediately returned to me, with their bill. I am so miserable I feel like taking my own life. My darling boy, my Taddie alone, I fully believe, prevents the deed." This was it for Mary. Brady and Keyes were officially finished.

Mary vented further, panicked about what her son Robert would say if he heard about it. "This exhibition must not be attempted. R. would blast us all if you were to have this project carried out. . . . I am positively dying with a broken heart, and the probability is that I shall be living but a very short time. . . . Go to B.&K. and have my clothes sent to me without further publicity. . . . I am feeling too weak to write more to-day. Why are you so silent? For the sake of humanity, if not me and my children, do not have those black clothes displayed in Europe. The thought has almost whitened every hair of my head. Write when you receive this."

Yet there was more disturbing news to come. Lizzie informed Mary that she was planning to donate several "sacred relics" of Lincoln memorabilia in her possession to Wilberforce University, the first college in America to be owned and operated by African Americans. Wilberforce was named for the eighteenth-century English abolitionist William Wilberforce. The Ohio institution held a special place in Lizzie's heart because her son George had attended Wilberforce before he was killed in battle during the Civil War. The historical treasures Lizzie intended to donate to the university included the cloak and bonnet worn by Mrs. Lincoln that fateful night at Ford's Theatre, on which could still be seen the "life-blood" of President Lincoln; and a pair of gloves that President Lincoln had worn at his last inaugural reception. The gloves still bore the marks of the thousands of hands Lincoln shook that day.

Lizzie said she had received numerous lucrative offers for the garments and turned them all down because they were too blessed to sell. But she was willing to donate them to Wilberforce University in memory of the president whom she revered. In a strange twist of fate, a building on the Wilberforce University campus had burned to the ground in 1865, on the same day as Lincoln's assassination. The pile of rubble where the building once stood had come to have symbolic importance to the campus and African Americans everywhere. To raise the necessary funds for a new building, Lizzie wrote to Wilberforce's president, Bishop Daniel H. Payne, and suggested putting Mrs. Lincoln's cloak and bonnet on exhibit. An admission fee would be charged with the proceeds going to benefit Wilberforce University. When Mary read Lizzie's letter she was livid, and fired off a response which revealed once again that Robert Lincoln's reaction was at the forefront of her concern.

"R. would go raving distracted if such a thing was done. If you have the least regard for our reason, pray write the bishop that it must not be done. How little did I suppose you would do such a thing. . . . This exhibition must not be attempted. R. would blast us all if you were to have this project carried out." Lizzie backed off and never sent the relics to Wilberforce.

Finally, Mary was ready to sever her relationship with Brady and Keyes. She sent Lizzie a list of clothes she wanted sent back immediately, among them a Russian sable boa and cape, a chinchilla coat, sable cuffs and muff, a camel's hair shawl, and a black llama shawl. Mary fretted that her clothes had been "pulled to pieces" during the weeks that they had been on public display. She sent Brady a sharply worded letter demanding the return of "all goods unsold," which fundamentally meant her entire wardrobe, since, after all this time, only a few items had been bought. In return, Brady wrote out an invoice in the amount of $824 for expenses. After some haggling, Mary paid the bill. She mailed the check to Lizzie and authorized her to deliver it in person to the untrustworthy Brady, with this warning: "[D]o not give him the check until you get the goods—and be sure you get a receipt." So in the end, her attempt to sell off her old clothes and jewels resulted in a net loss for Mary, to say nothing of the damage to her reputation and her broken relationship with Robert.

But it was not over. Another thunderbolt was coming Mary's way, this time from the person she least suspected would ever betray her.

LIZZIE KECKLEY STARTED scaling down her communication with the former First Lady, and Mary Lincoln was becoming frantic with worry. "Write me every day," came one plea. "I am greatly disappointed, having only received one letter from you since we parted." Then: "After your promise of writing to me every other day, I can scarcely understand it. I hope to-morrow will bring me a letter from you. How much I miss you cannot be expressed." Then this: "Write me, dear Lizzie, if only a line. I cannot understand your silence. . . . I am feeling so friendless in the world." Finally, "Your silence pains me."

Lizzie was now living in a boardinghouse on Broome Street in lower Manhattan, then a rundown area relegated to some of the poorest New Yorkers. The owner of the house was a woman named Mrs. Bell—a cousin of William Slade, who had worked as a White House messenger in the Lincoln administration, and become chief steward in charge of all White House servants when Andrew Johnson assumed the presidency. Lizzie had once employed one of Slade's relatives as a seamstress when her Washington dressmaking business was thriving. Now Slade was returning the favor, and had arranged for Lizzie to stay at his cousin's Broome Street house. It was conveniently close to the William H. Brady brokerage firm, and Lizzie spent many daylight hours at the Brady showroom looking out for Mary's interests. In evenings, she sat at a desk in her lonely room on Broome Street and wrote and wrote—not letters to Mary, as she would have wished, but a manuscript.

From Mary Lincoln's viewpoint this would become the most hurtful kind of book. It was a memoir of Lizzie's life as a slave, her journey to freedom, her years as Mary Lincoln's White House confidante, and, most provocatively, her role in the notorious Old Clothes Scandal of 1867. This was why Mary had not heard from Lizzie. Lizzie had evidently started to write the book in October or early November, after Mary's departure for Chicago, when she was left in New York in crushing misery and poverty. She wrote in secret, without informing Mary of what she was working on. The manuscript pages piled up as Lizzie worked tirelessly with a ghostwriter, James Redpath, a well-known journalist and friend of Frederick Douglass. It is likely that Douglass had put Lizzie in contact with Redpath, and possible that he also encouraged Lizzie to write the book.

Redpath was born in England in 1833 and immigrated to America with his family when he was seventeen. He started writing for Greeley's *New York Tribune* when he was just nineteen. In 1855 he was sent to Kansas to cover the war between Free State and proslavery forces. His dispatches were the first to bring the firebrand John Brown to national attention; his biography of Brown, published after the doomed raid on Harper's Ferry, was a bestseller, and Redpath donated most of his royalties to Brown's widow and surviving children.

For weeks now the other boarders at Mrs. Bell's had seen Redpath joining Lizzie in the parlor every night. He reviewed and edited Lizzie's previous night's writing and set the objectives for that evening's work. Lizzie lacked confidence in herself as a writer and wondered whether she could actually write a book, as she had no formal education, but Redpath encouraged her. A trust developed between the journalist and the novice memoirist. Lizzie turned over to him all the letters Mary Lincoln had written to her, although she later insisted that she had made him promise not to include any of them in the final manuscript. She had believed that somehow Redpath would use his writer's skills to weave the letters into the narrative without quoting them verbatim. At least that was the assurance he had given her. Lizzie later claimed she did not know that the twenty-four letters Mary had sent her during the height of the Old Clothes Scandal would be published as an addendum in the book.

It is possible that Lizzie also had assistance from another prominent writer, Jane Grey Cannon Swisshelm. Born in Pittsburgh, Mrs. Swisshelm became a teacher at age fourteen, and moved to Louisville, Kentucky, with her husband when she was twenty-one. Encountering slavery for the first time, she became an outspoken abolitionist, wrote many antislavery articles, and started her own small national publication, the *Saturday Visitor*, advocating women's rights and the abolition of slavery. Vigilantes, in an uproar over her editorials, broke into her newspaper office and tore apart the printing press, but vandalism did not diminish Mrs. Swisshelm's commitment to social reform. During the Civil War she moved to Washington, volunteered as an Army nurse, and got to know Mary Lincoln.

When Lizzie published her memoirs Mrs. Swisshelm was fifty-three years old. Some historians believe that Mrs. Swisshelm, working with Redpath, whipped Lizzie's book into shape in order to advance a political and social agenda. It was important for the nation to know that a mulatto woman had become a trusted confidante of the Lincoln family and could even be literate. (When she was an old woman, in 1901, Lizzie gave an interview to the *Minneapolis Register*, saying that she dictated her memoirs to a stenographer and that two journalists rewrote and polished the book, giving credence to the evidence that Redpath was not the only ghostwriter involved. One additional ghostwriter has been mentioned as a possible co-author: Hamilton Busbey, a journalist who later became the owner and editor of *Turf, Field, and Farm* magazine.)

Sometime in early spring 1868, two weeks after Lizzie had delivered Mary Lincoln's check to William Brady, she turned in her final manuscript to the firm of G. W. Carleton & Company in New York, publishers in

America of Victor Hugo and Charlotte Brontë. The full title of Lizzie's book was *Behind the Scenes, or, Thirty Years a Slave, and Four Years in the White House*. The sole writer's credit was given to Elizabeth Keckley, identified on the book's cover this way: "Formerly a slave, but more recently modiste, and friend to Mrs. Abraham Lincoln." There was no acknowledgement of any coauthors. Curiously, the book was marketed as a novel. But this was a sleight of hand, a calculation by the publishers to discourage litigation by the Lincoln family. Everyone recognized the book for what it was: an exposé.

Then, as now, book publishing was all about marketing. Carleton & Company saw a window of opportunity in the Old Clothes Scandal and put the book on fast turnaround. On April 19, 1868, less than two months after Lizzie had delivered her manuscript, news of Lizzie Keckley's book exploded on the front page of the *Chicago Tribune*. The headline blared, BEHIND THE SCENES, and below that, THE HOME LIFE OF PRESIDENT LINCOLN.

"In a few days, G. W. Carleton & Co. of New York will publish a book called, 'Behind the Scenes,' by Elizabeth Keckley." The article called Lizzie a "colored woman of more than ordinary intelligence, and a decided European cast of countenance."

"I have often been asked to write my life, as those who know me know that it has been an eventful one," the book began. Clearly anticipating hostile reaction, Lizzie explained that she was writing it for the purpose of putting Mrs. Lincoln "in a better light before the world." If the work was breaching Mrs. Lincoln's confidence, Lizzie argued, it was excusable, because Mrs. Lincoln's reputation had been impugned by others.

Behind the Scenes struck a raw nerve in America, still reeling from the Civil War and the emancipation of five million slaves. *Putnam's Magazine* declared it "ought never to have been written or published," and should not be read by "any sensible person." The *New York Times* questioned whether Lizzie Keckley actually wrote *Behind the Scenes* and suggested she should have "stuck to her needle." It judged the book's revelations to be "gross violations of confidence." Members of her own race who feared a backlash among their white employers also denounced Lizzie.

Predictably, the *New York Commercial Advertiser*, controlled by the Republican Party boss Thurlow Weed, who was always ready to pounce on anything that made Mary Lincoln look bad, recommended *Behind the Scenes* as a "literary thunderbolt" filled with "startling" information. Another reviewer praised Lizzie's writing style as straightforward and graceful—"notwithstanding she was born in slavery and passed thirty years of her life in bondage." By far the most unsettling reaction came later that year from an anonymous writer who was obviously threatened by the implications of *Behind the Scenes*—that a black woman could become a successful businesswoman and close confidante of the president's family, and then publish a literate memoir. Under the pen name "A. Lincoln Fann," this author published a crude and racist parody, *Behind the Seams*, by a Nigger Woman Who Took in Work from Mrs. Lincoln and Mrs. (Jefferson) Davis. The word "nigger" appears six times in the first paragraph. The lampoon, priced at ten cents a copy, was "based" on the life of a "Betsey Kickley," who was so illiterate she had to sign her name with the letter X.

The searing criticism shocked Lizzie. She defended herself in a letter sent to her publisher and later printed in the *New York Citizen*. Indignantly, she wondered whether the furor over her book could be attributed to her dark skin—"and that I was once a slave."

"As I was born to servitude, it was not my fault that I was a slave; and, as I honestly purchased my freedom, may I not be permitted to express, now and then, an opinion becoming a free woman?"

Mary Lincoln read the book in early May. The contents of *Behind the Scenes* crushed her spirit. The anecdotes Lizzie told of Abraham Lincoln in the White House were as intimate as any that had ever been written about an American president's family. Mary was mortified to see twenty-four of her letters written to Lizzie during the Old Clothes Scandal published in their entirety as an appendix in the book. They exposed Mary's role as the mastermind in this scandalous affair, not the injured party, as she had sought to portray herself. The book also divulged Mary's enormous level of debt, which up until then had been a private quandary known only to the former First Lady, her creditors, and the Republican national leadership.

Mary sulked in shame in her rented quarters on West Washington Street in Chicago. A quiet fury built within her, and it was aimed at the principal source of her torment: Lizzie Keckley. Once so dearly loved, Lizzie now became that "colored historian." Lizzie also had to face Robert Lincoln's wrath. For a man as sensitive and guarded as Robert was, to a neurotic degree, *Behind the Scenes*, and in particular the publication of his mother's intimate correspondence, was a true blow—not only to his obsessive need for privacy, but also to his ego. When he read his mother's letters to Lizzie, in which words such as "maniac," "raving," "spiteful" were used to describe him, he was devastated. The "colored historian" had made them public, but they had been penned by his own mother. Robert came across, not as the brave and virtuous son of the great Abraham Lincoln, but as his mother's petulant and mean-spirited son. As if that were not enough, the book came out just as he was attempting to build his law firm and prepare for his impending marriage to a senator's daughter.

Horrified by the attention the book was receiving, Robert worked his contacts, and like an invisible hammer he came down hard on Carleton & Company, demanding that the publishers withdraw the book from circulation. Without any public pronouncement, the publishers did quietly make it almost impossible to find a copy in stores, and *Behind the Scenes* swiftly disappeared from the marketplace. Despite a firestorm of publicity and national exposure, it was a failure; only a few hundred copies were sold in the entire United States. If Lizzie had expected a windfall, she must have been deeply disappointed. She made less than five hundred dollars on the book, though she did leave a legacy of extraordinary anecdotes for future Lincoln historians.

It was a great lesson for Robert in how to wield the mighty authority of his name. He was on his way to becoming a power broker. And it would not be his last effort at censoring history.

Lizzie came to regret publishing the book. Few bought it, and she tried to apologize to Robert Lincoln in person but he irritably told her to go away. Lizzie held on to her cherished Lincoln artifacts, including the blood-stained cloak and bonnet Mary Lincoln had worn the night of the assassination, for thirty-five years. Then, desperate for cash, she sold them to a Chicago candy manufacturer and collector for $250. In 1892, at the age of seventy-four, she moved to Ohio and became head of Wilberforce University's department of sewing and domestic science arts. After she suffered a stroke she returned to Washington and ended her days in the most pathetic of circumstances, dying in her sleep, in 1907, at the National Home for Destitute Colored Women and Children. She was eighty-nine. Among her personal effects was a photograph of Mary Lincoln that hung on the wall of her room.

The publication of *Behind the Scenes* was for Mary Lincoln the final degradation. She made a decision. The time had come for her to go into exile and leave this "ungrateful Republic." She would take Tad with her and "flee to a land of strangers." There, she prayed, she would find peace and refuge.

8
Exile

THE GUESTS INVITED to the wedding of Robert Lincoln and Mary Harlan started assembling at 7:30 Thursday evening at the H Street townhouse of the bride's parents. The spacious parlor was fragrant with bouquets of flowers and, as a dramatic flourish, a wall of roses formed the monogram M and R in honor of the bride and groom.

Only thirty-three people had been invited to the wedding, and this was causing a strain between Mary Harlan and her friends. One of them was Minnie Chandler, the Iowa Wesleyan College student who had so assiduously followed every detail of Mary's romantic life from the distant town of Mount Pleasant. Minnie was distressed beyond words to learn that the wedding, which she had thought was taking place in late autumn, had been unexpectedly moved up. Only by happenstance did she discover that she had not been invited. The insult wounded Minnie Chandler's pride, and in the letter she wrote to Mary, her emotions spilled out. "Miss Harlan, Sunday though it be, the peculiar circumstances indeed which I am about to relate ... must excuse me. My instincts seldom mislead me Miss Harlan & it is with deep regret that I this morning heard of your perfidy. There I was, obliged to smile sweetly upon a gentleman while he told me that Miss Harlan was to be married this week.... Words fail to describe my astonishment."

Perhaps Minnie Chandler would have been more understanding had she known why Mary Harlan had felt compelled to push up her wedding date. It was at the insistence of Mary Lincoln, who in the wake of the humiliating Old Clothes Scandal, had declared her intent to start a new life in exile overseas. Mary had booked passage for an Atlantic crossing for herself and Tad, embarking October 1, 1868. Suddenly, everything had to be accommodated to her itinerary.

James Harlan was Senator Harlan again, having resigned his post as interior secretary in disgust over the Reconstruction policies of President Andrew Johnson. In 1867 he was reelected United States senator from Iowa. He greeted every wedding guest as they arrived at his Washington home. Among them were Edgar Welles, Mrs. Edwin Stanton and her son Edwin Jr., and President Lincoln's last treasury secretary, Hugh McCulloch. Mrs. Charles Scammon, the wife of Robert's estranged alcoholic law partner, became sick en route from Chicago and could not make it. She sent two thin gold bracelets as gifts.

The Harlans were a pious family, conservative in both dress and manner. (Senator Harlan's tenure as interior secretary is most notable for the firing of Walt Whitman, then working as a clerk in the Indian Affairs Bureau, for publishing the "dirty book," *Leaves of Grass*.) The mother of the bride, Ann Harlan, wore a simple wine-colored silk dress with long sleeves, point lace collar, and a single string of pearls. But nothing could compare with the morbid attire of Mary Lincoln, who, the *Washington Star* reported, wore black mourning clothes, just as she had every day since her husband's death. She was in "deep mourning," the *Star* said, "without any jewelry or ornaments whatsoever." Not even the marriage of her son could lift her public display of grief. It was the first time she had returned to Washington since the assassination, and being physically present in the city filled her with "natural horror."

"The terror of having to proceed to *Washington* to witness [the wedding] almost overpowers me," Mary confided to her friend Rhoda White. But she was anxious to see her son's marriage to a "young lady who is so charming & whom I love so much."

Robert Lincoln wore a black wool broadcloth suit with a single gemstone in his necktie, and white gloves. He seemed full of happiness. At 8:00 P.M. the bride made her appearance. Mary Harlan's wedding gown was rich white satin, with long sleeves, a long train, and a fan-shaped bow in the back. Her light brown hair was woven into strands, and her veil, fastened with a garland of orange blossoms, was white and very full. "The entire dress, although plain, was exceedingly tasteful and rich, aiding though not adding to the beauty of the bride." She and Robert took their places in the center of the parlor. Officiating was Bishop Matthew Simpson of the

Methodist Episcopal Church. Bishop Simpson was well known to the Lincoln family—he gave the sermon at President Lincoln's funeral in Springfield. The ceremony was solemn and earnest, with Simpson reciting the traditional wedding liturgy of his church: "To have and to hold from this day forward, for better for worse, for richer for poorer, in sickness and in health, to love and to cherish till death do us part." Robert and Mary were pronounced man and wife, and the bishop was the first to congratulate the bride and groom, followed by the Harlans and Mary Lincoln.

The wedding party celebrated with a dinner catered by James Wormley, a freeborn black chef who had learned his cooking skills as a steward at the Metropolitan Club and in the haute cuisine kitchens of Paris. Wormley's catering service was said to be Washington's finest, well regarded for using fresh ingredients that he grew on his farm in northwest Washington and seafood that was caught daily in Chesapeake Bay. People raved about his turtle soup. For this one special evening, an exception was made to the prohibition of music in the Harlan home, and a vocalist was called in to entertain the guests. But as the *Washington Evening Star* reported, "Owing to the sad circumstances connected with the death of President Lincoln in this city, now nearly four years ago, it was determined by the families of both the bride and groom that the ostentatious displays customary on such occasions should be avoided."

The next day, the newlyweds left Washington in high style, on a special private car attached to the 12:30 P.M. train to New York. Accompanying the bridal party were Mary Lincoln, Edgar Welles, and Edwin Stanton Jr. Tad remained behind in Washington with the Harlans for several more days to get reacquainted with the city he remembered from his youth in the White House. The caterer James Wormley was also on the train and kept the party well fed with his wonderful creations. As the train approached Baltimore, a bittersweet parting took place. This was as far as Mrs. Lincoln was going. The Lincolns were splitting up, and Mary did not know when she would see her eldest son and his bride again. It gave her some comfort to know that Robert was married. She adored her new daughter-in-law and considered the marriage to be the only "sunbeam in my sad future." "I have known & loved the young lady since her childhood," Mary Lincoln confided to Mrs. White. "I consider this marriage a great gain—A charming daughter will be my portion & one whom my idolized husband loved & admired since she was very young." Mary's only regret about the wedding was its small scale. Ever focused on money issues, she complained that her son should have invited more guests, for that would have meant "an immense assortment" of gifts.

Mary Lincoln disembarked at Baltimore, and the chartered train continued on to New York, where Robert and his bride spent the first few days of their honeymoon at the Hoffman House, a hotel at Broadway and Twenty-fourth Street. Meanwhile, Mary checked into Barnum's Hotel, considered the most luxurious in Baltimore.

Later that evening came drama. Mary was seated alone in the Barnum's dining room at a table very close to the door when she suddenly felt dizzy— "everything appeared black before me." Her head spinning, she tried to stand but found herself sinking to the floor. A distinguished-looking gentleman came to her assistance and escorted her back to her room. Henceforth, to avoid the embarrassment of another public fainting spell, she took all her meals in her room. She blamed the episode on the "after effects" of the wedding in Washington.

During the five days before she would be leaving for Europe, Mary remained secluded in her room. Now the most important thing to her was organizing a proper farewell. She believed she was being driven from the land of her birth, and she wanted as many people as she could muster to record her departure for history. In the next few days, she reached out to her dwindling band of friends. She wrote letters and sent telegrams imploring them to come to Baltimore to see her off from the pier. She was most determined that a woman named Eliza Slataper be present.

Mary and Mrs. Slataper, the wife of a civil engineer from Pittsburgh, had met only three months earlier in Cresson Springs, a fashionable resort town in western Pennsylvania known for its medicinal spring water, high in mineral content. Like Mary, Mrs. Slataper was interested in spiritualism, and Mary actually considered her new friend to be a gifted clairvoyant. Mrs. Slataper had promised to see Mary off, but now she wrote that she was ill and could not make the journey to Baltimore. Mary was beside herself; she sent Mrs. Slataper four letters over eight days, plus follow-up telegrams, beseeching her to come. The fact that Mary had met the woman just three months earlier can be taken as evidence of the state of her loneliness and despair. "I have just sent you a telegram—praying that you may immediately come down here. . . . I shall be lonely beyond expression without you—*come to me*. . . . Do come if you love me." Then: "Leave P[ittsburgh] Sunday morning at 11 A.M. You will arrive here in 13 hours—If you value my peace—*come*." Evidently, Mrs. Slataper sent Mary a telegram reiterating that she was sick, and not able to make it, to which Mary responded dismissively: "you are quite well enough & I may never see you again." Finally, two days before her departure, Mary resigned herself to the fact that Mrs. Slataper was not coming. "Can I begin to express my disappointment at not seeing your dear face before I leave this blessed land? Instead of yourself, your telegram came this morning. . . . How anxiously I have been expecting you within the last week, *you will never know*. The hours are drawing near for us to leave. . . . No more happy hours with you for a long time, perhaps never again in this world."

Ann Harlan brought Tad up from Washington, and then the senator's wife hastily returned home. Even she was not willing to extend her stay for a day or two to witness Mary's departure. She had been Mary Lincoln's last hope for a friendly face at the pier.

Tad was understandably conflicted about leaving America. He adored his new sister-in-law, and she and Robert had wanted him to live with them. Mary Lincoln grumbled that her youngest son was becoming a "little obstinate" and "argumentative" about the trip. "Poor child, he doubtless feels like a victim." But he was still the dutiful boy with the big heart who would never think of abandoning his widowed and ailing mother. The former White House mischief-maker-in-chief was now a tall and lanky lad of fifteen, still dealing with the issues of his youth and struggling to catch up to the educational level of his peers.

October 1, 1868, the day of departure, was here. Mary and Tad checked out of Barnum's Hotel and took a carriage to the Baltimore docks where they boarded a transatlantic steamer, the *City of Baltimore*, owned by the Inman Line, the smallest of the three great British shipping companies, after Cunard and White Star. *City of Baltimore*, commissioned in 1855, was a fast vessel and for a time held the world record for greatest run in a single day— 390 miles. Tickets cost one hundred dollars in pure gold, but Mary and Tad did not pay a dime. The wealthy German-Jewish banker Joseph Seligman paid their fare in full. Seligman had come to America in 1836. Twenty-five years later, the immigrant peddler of jewelry, knives, and dry goods was advising President Lincoln on financial affairs of state. Seligman and his brothers, like the Rothschilds, were bankers on an international scale. Moved by Mary Lincoln's plight, Seligman had financed the widow's exile.

Forty other passengers who booked passage on *City of Baltimore* stood on the deck cheerfully waving at friends and family. Mary, wearing her black mourning clothes, with loyal Tad at her side, could only watch.

Perhaps she gazed out at the faces on the pier hoping beyond reason to see her friend from Pittsburgh, Eliza Slataper. But there were no familiar faces out there. No one had come to bid her farewell.

A flotilla of tugboats hauled the ship out of the harbor, and *City of Baltimore* steamed into Chesapeake Bay and then into the vast expanse of the Atlantic Ocean. The weather off the coast of Baltimore that day was unseasonably warm, the water tranquil. The passengers had a peaceful night's rest. But at dawn Mary and Tad and the others on board were awakened by monstrous ocean swells. What followed were ten straight days of hideous weather that became a nightmare for everyone.

"I never had an idea before what sea sickness was," passenger Charles Tilghman recounted in a letter written at sea to his mother, Agnes. Tilghman, twenty-two years old, came from an aristocratic family from the eastern shore of Maryland. He had just been graduated from medical school and was on his way to London to continue his studies. Sick to his stomach, Tilghman went three days "without tasting a mouthful" of food. When eight bells tolled for dinner, only four of the forty passengers aboard showed up in the dining room. The worst of the storm came on the third day, when *City of Baltimore* "encountered a fearful gale." It became impossible even to stand. Passengers hid under tables as shattered china rained down on them. Women and children wept with fear and prayed for mercy. The ship's captain said that in forty years of crossing the Atlantic, this was the worst storm he had ever experienced. "There was no sleeping done that night," Tilghman wrote. Sixteen hours later, the storm abated, but for days the ocean remained "tough but bearable." By now, young Tilghman had earned his sea legs, and came to appreciate the adventure. He even stood on the deck and hung on for dear life as huge waves swept over it. *City of Baltimore* was "as much out of the water as in. . . . There is a peculiar attraction about it and I shall be sorry when we see land." They passed just four ships during the entire transatlantic voyage. The captain told Tilghman that the storm had apparently blown all sailing vessels off the established sea-lane.

As everyone on board waited out the storm, they got to know one another. Tilghman was eager to detail to his mother every quirk of his fellow passengers. One couple on honeymoon was bickering relentlessly. "She says she didn't know what she married him for, and he says he wishes she was at home." Then there was Mary Lincoln—"first on the list" of prominent passengers. "First—certainly on vulgarity," Tilghman remarked.

For some reason, Mary also took a dislike to Tilghman, and at one point, before they were even introduced, accused the young physician of ungentlemanly behavior. By the Southern code of conduct in which both Mary and Charles Tilghman had been raised, no remark could be more stinging. It is possible that Mary recognized the Tilghman name and knew that a relative, Lloyd Tilghman, had served as a brigadier general in the Confederate army before his death in battle in 1863. In his letter to his mother, Charles Tilghman spewed forth venom, calling Mary Lincoln vulgar in every way—in "figure, face, cleanliness, and conversation." Declared Tilghman: "She is fit only for a fishmarket." He and Mary avoided each other for the entire trip, a challenging feat considering that the ship, bow to stern, measured only 330 feet. Tilghman's only gracious observation about the Lincolns came when he reported a Tad Lincoln sighting. "She has her son Taddie with her, the one who figures conspicuously in the photographs of his illustrious father in family life."

The food on board *City of Baltimore* did not suit everyone's taste. Turkey with pineapple was one of the signature meals. Tilghman's sophisticated palate managed to tolerate the Dutch-influenced menu with its bland meats topped with thick syrups and sugar. But he warned his family that should Cousin Sam ever contemplate sailing to Europe, he should not sail on the *City of Baltimore*. On the frigid and rain-slicked day of October 15, Land's End, the westernmost tip of the English coast, came into view. A few hours later, *City of Baltimore* docked in Southampton. For Tilghman, the voyage was at an end. He disembarked and posted his letter to his mother, then went on to London to continue his medical education. But for Mary and Tad, the journey continued until the ship arrived in the German port city of Bremen. From Bremen, with all their trunks, they made their way to Frankfurt, on the Main River. This was where Mary had chosen to live in exile, close to the therapeutic sulfurous spas of Baden-Baden.

The next several weeks of hectic activity were focused on organizing life in a foreign land. Mary and Tad shared a single room at the Hotel d'Angleterre for thirty dollars a week. The hotel was close to the Zeil, Frankfurt's premier shopping district—a dangerous setting for a compulsive shopper like Mary Lincoln. The first priority was to find Tad a school. Mary was a great admirer of the strict and exacting discipline of German education. Recommendations at the hotel led her to Dr. D. Hohagen's Institute, a boarding school at No. 17 Kettenhoftstrasse. The student body consisted of several "well-behaved German and English boys." The rector was Dr. Hohagen, who agreed to Mary's stipulation that Tad be instructed in English as well as German. Tad was enrolled on October 26, 1868. Tuition for the first quarter was 150 florins, or about $88. Even this modest amount Mary had trouble paying. She wrote to Robert requesting that he forward the payment directly to the institute, and then followed up with a letter to David Davis, asking him to remind Robert to send the money. Tad settled into living at the school, and Mary could only hope he would, as she put it, "make up for lost time."

Meanwhile, Mary got to know Frankfurt. Here, in this ancient European city, for the first time since her husband's assassination, Mary found a degree of peace and contentment. A thriving community of American expatriates lived at the Hotel d'Angleterre and she found them to be generous and embracing. American consul-general William Walton Murphy and his wife, Ellen, resided on the same floor as Mary, and Murphy took special care of the former First Lady. An appointee of the Lincoln administration, the Michigan-raised Murphy was a "rough diamond . . . one of the most uncouth mortals that ever lived," according to the memoirs of the American diplomat Andrew Dickson White. But Murphy had also been a shrewd and effective promoter of the Union cause during the Civil War and had excellent relationships with Frankfurt's two leading banking families, the Rothschilds and the Seligmans. Murphy was a protégé of William Seward, and in regular dispatches kept the secretary of state informed about the 378 American citizens residing in Frankfurt, including Mary Lincoln and Tad.

In early December, Mary received her first letter from Eliza Slataper. Any ill will Mary may have harbored toward Eliza for failing to give her a bon voyage in Baltimore vanished the moment she opened the letter. "In this distant land, how can I sufficiently express the great pleasure your kind letter has afforded me," Mary wrote back. Characteristically for Mary, she admitted to being lonely and isolated while boasting about the extravagance of her surroundings. "We have quite a little colony at our hotel—which is considered the aristocratic one. . . . All the nobility stop here, counts, dukes & duchesses abound in the house, and on my table their cards are frequently laid. Yet in consideration of poor health & deep mourning I have of course accepted no dinner invitations & have kept very quiet."

Through Mary's correspondence with Eliza, we get a sense of her life in Frankfurt. The shops, Mary said, were very beautiful, but she complained about the German merchants who straight away raised prices when they saw an American approaching. She did rave about one bargain. A well-known Frankfurt seamstress who made dresses for Prussian nobility and Queen Victoria's daughter was charging Mary only one-fifty a yard for rich silk fabric trimmed with crepe. In America, during the Civil War, similar material had cost Mary ten dollars per yard. Predictably, Mary ordered black, for yet another mourning cloak. "I like Frankfurt exceedingly," Mary wrote. She was "enjoying *peace*, which in my deepest, heart rending sorrow, I was not allowed in my native land." She listed her circle of acquaintances at the Angleterre Hotel. In addition to Consul-General Murphy and his wife, there were Mr. and Mrs. Henry Mason. Mason was a descendant of Pilgrims and founder of Mason & Hamlin, one of the earliest American piano and organ manufacturers. As fate would have it, General Robert Allen of the United States Army, and his wife and daughter moved into a suite at the hotel in early December. This was the same military officer who had lived in Springfield in 1837 and held the ball at which Mary had her first memorable encounter with William Herndon—leaving Herndon on the dance floor after he had compared her to a serpent.

Mary expressed a longing for several features of American comfort she found lacking in Frankfurt. She pined for a glass of ice water because the water in Frankfurt was "impossible & really dangerous to drink"—a bold statement considering the appalling state of the water Mary drank when she lived in Washington and Chicago. Wine was universally consumed in Frankfurt, but Mary marveled that she had yet to run into a drunkard. Nobody on the street ever seemed to be intoxicated. Even the notoriously gloomy German winter had been accommodating Mary so far. The weather was mild enough for Mary to let the fire in her room die out. Robert and his wife wrote often. At this point, Mary Lincoln's relationship with her new daughter-in-law was idyllic, and Mary missed her family very much. Tad, however, was still bewildered, perhaps wondering what he was doing in Germany. "He likes his school & is a most affectionate, amiable tempered child—he is *recovering* from his homesickness."

Mary complained that the high cost of living overseas was becoming an unbearable burden. "I am charged the highest prices & I am living in one room, in the most economical manner." Also, the mild winter she had been enjoying took a predictable turn for the worse, and her Frankfurt physician urged her to go to Italy until it improved. Because she could not travel alone, she would have to hire a maid or companion to accompany her. Once again, Mary's obsessive fear of poverty was pushing her into worry and misjudgment. She deluged Washington, D.C., with requests for a three-thousand-dollar annual pension. In an open letter addressed to the United States Senate, she sent this impassioned plea:

I am a widow of a President of the United States whose life was sacrificed to his country's service. . . . By the advice of my physician I have come over to Germany to try the mineral waters and during the winters to go to Italy. But my financial means do not permit me to take advantage of the advice given me, nor can I live in a style becoming to the widow of the Chief Magistrate of a great nation, although I live as economically as I can. In consideration of the great service my deeply lamented husband has rendered to the United States, and of the fearful loss I have sustained by his untimely death—his martyrdom, I may say—I respectfully submit to your honorable body this petition, hoping that a yearly pension may be granted me so that I may have less pecuniary care.

It was a tempered and poignant document. But Mary was not as diplomatic in her private correspondence with David Davis when she asked the Supreme Court justice to use his influence to lobby on behalf of her pension bill. Noting newspaper reports that Congress was considering raising the salary of President-elect Ulysses S. Grant to the sum of one hundred thousand dollars a year, Mary spat out: "My husband was Commander in Chief & directed every move Grant ever made—Surely, surely with ill health upon me & physicians bills that often *appall* me—*I will be remembered*."

As Congress considered Mary's pension bill, a strange scandal flared. Several European newspapers reported the improbable story that a German nobleman with the equally improbable name Count Schneiderbutzen was romancing Mary Lincoln. There were even published accounts that asserted they were engaged. The story was picked up in America, where it became material for satire that, apparently, some people read as legitimate news. Count Schneiderbutzen was the grand chamberlain to the Duke of Baden and managed the duke's household staff. This led the *New York World* to deride the widow of the great Abraham Lincoln for considering marriage to a glorified manservant. The *World* ridiculed Schneiderbutzen as a "short-of-funds count" who was now in "ecstasies at securing an heiress." Schneiderbutzen was even accused of ordering his tailor to cut down Abraham Lincoln's clothes to fit the count's small stature. "Poor little S, we don't begrudge him a stitch of the sacred wardrobe. He will have earned it before he is done with Mary Lincoln," the *World* boorishly reported.

As usual, American newspapers were all too willing to believe the worst of Mary Lincoln. The story was, of course, a fabrication, probably stoked by the penniless Count Schneiderbutzen to get attention. Mary became very upset when Tad came home with a ten-day-old London newspaper that carried a report of her "engagement" to Schneiderbutzen. She was in bed with a migraine and a "burning pain" in her spine when Tad handed her the newspaper. "I am in a most trying and humiliating position," she remarked after reading the *Times*. She called it "vile and wicked trash" and wanted it to be known to everyone that she "knows no such person as *this* Count." Behind her mortification was a very real concern that the bogus account of her engagement might ruin her chances for a congressional pension.

One of Mary's genuine friends in Frankfurt was a pastor and writer from Boston who had served as a chaplain in the army during the Civil War. F. W. Bogen, who was fluent in German, had been a passenger on *City of Baltimore*. He had been kind to Mary and Tad, and used his language skills to assist in expediting the removal of Mary's trunks from the ship. While Mary was getting settled in Frankfurt, Bogen often stopped by the Angleterre to check on her health. He also knew Senator Charles Sumner of Massachusetts—Mary Lincoln's truest friend in the United States Senate—and sent Sumner a letter depicting Mary's life in Frankfurt. "She lives very retiredly in the Hotel d'Angleterre, occupies only one room, sees few friends." Mary ate all her meals in her room—"in order not to be exposed to the gaze of the curious," Bogen reported. Room service, about four dollars a day, added to her expenses. Bogen confirmed Mary's suspicion that her fame as Abraham Lincoln's widow resulted in merchants charging her a premium on the presumption that she must be rich to have been married to the great American hero.

When the German winter returned with a vengeance around the first of the year, 1869, Mary's doctors insisted that she travel south for relief. Italy was her first choice, but it was deemed too expensive, so Mary settled on Nice, in the south of France. Nice had been a destination for British winter tourism since the early 1700s, but when Mary arrived, around the first of February 1869, Nice's transformation into a playground for the rich and famous was still several decades away. The contrast between frigid, bleak, Frankfurt and sunny Nice was almost indescribable for Mary. She marveled that she could keep her hotel window open all day. Her view of the azure Mediterranean filled her with a sense of tranquility. Flowers bloomed in the garden—in February! For the first time in her life, she breathed in the enticing aroma of orange trees. "I live out in the open air & am gradually finding myself grow stronger day by day, for I had been very sick in

Frankfurt," she wrote Eliza Slataper. And it was a relief to be away from the attention of the hostile American press. "Oh if you were only with me here! Was there ever such a climate, such a sunshine, such air? You cannot turn for flowers, beautiful bouquets, thrust into your very face. I never return from my walks without my hands being filled—and yet to me, they bring sad, deeply painful memories."

Mary was in Nice when her open letter pleading for a pension was read before the United States Senate. Charles Sumner generously requested that the pension be fixed at five thousand dollars a year for the duration of Mary Lincoln's life. After a prolonged and contentious debate on the floor of the Senate, on the last day before the Fortieth Congress adjourned, the vote was taken. Twenty-seven senators voted against the resolution that would have made Mary Lincoln the only former First Lady to be granted a government pension. Twenty-three were in favor, and sixteen senators were absent or failed to record a vote. Mary's controversial record as First Lady, the Old Clothes Scandal, and the fact that Abraham Lincoln's estate had left her well-provided-for, all worked against the resolution. Her exile in Europe, and now the salacious claim that she was engaged to a good-for-nothing German count, contributed to the negative vote. Politically, it was difficult to justify spending public dollars on a woman who was so polarizing. F. W. Bogen could only shake his head at what he perceived to be the injustice of it. "Her husband, the Constitutional commander in chief of the army and navy of the U.S., fell by the ball of an assassin, during the war. The widow of a private even . . . who died in the service of the U.S. receives a pension."

It was now March 16. The south of France was still enchanting, though it came as a revelation to encounter so many Americans there, enjoying that faraway jewel. They were everywhere, Mary remarked, and she was pitiless in describing her nouveau riche countrymen—"you can always recognize them, very often, by their loud voices, so *early* as ten or eleven in the morning, VELVET COSTUMES &&—*Full dress.*" But the time was at hand to return to Frankfurt, and Taddie.

It took three full days of tedious and constant travel by rail and coach to reach Frankfurt. She arrived on the morning of March 22, and immediately sent a messenger to the boarding school with instructions to bring Tad home for a few hours for a visit with his mother. Mary had been gone for just six weeks, but in that time Tad had experienced a growth spurt. She could not believe how tall he had become. His face was still full of color, but Mary was upset to see him looking so thin. The heavy German food he was being fed at Dr. D. Hohagen's Institute was not agreeing with him. Thereafter, Mary arranged with the school to allow Tad to return to the Angleterre Hotel each night and join his mother for dinner, then go back to the school before lights out.

Five months after her wedding, Mary Harlan Lincoln became pregnant. The young bride had had a difficult first trimester. She wrote her mother-in-law that she was not feeling well, but had not yet informed her that she was pregnant. In the same letter, the twenty-two-year-old bride wondered whether she was too young to have a child. It seems she had read about a controversial nineteenth-century feminist who called dual housekeeping duties and motherhood "an uncomfortable state of existence for a young married lady." Not picking up the signals, Mary Lincoln advised her daughter-in-law that there was plenty of time for babies. "Have a good rest and enjoy yourself *free* for a year or more to come." But of course it was too late to follow her mother-in-law's advice.

Abraham Lincoln's first grandchild, a girl, was born October 15, 1869, after eight hours of labor. A doctor, a nurse, and Mary Harlan Lincoln's mother, Ann Harlan, were with her during the delivery. Robert stayed up all night awaiting the birth of what he called a baby as "fat and healthy as one could wish." Four hours later he dashed off a letter to his mother in Frankfurt announcing the joyous news. The baby was as yet unnamed, which perhaps indicated some tension within the family over the matter. Mary Lincoln, who could not believe she was a "grandmamma," fully expected the newborn to be named after Mrs. Harlan. As Mary Lincoln herself acknowledged, according to the custom of the day, Ann Harlan was "entitled" to have the baby named after her since she was the grandmother who had been present at her birth. There was the added complication that there were already two Marys in the family—"rather too much." Mary Lincoln was probably being coy when she claimed she could not recall Ann Harlan's first name, was it Angelica or Anastasia? "I abominate ugly names," Mary wrote to Sally Orne. It was certainly indicative of Mary's thorny character that she could make such a fuss over the baby's name. The family crisis was averted when in a subsequent letter from Robert Mary Lincoln received the delightful news that the baby would in fact be christened Mary, though to avoid confusion, the child would forever be called Mamie.

Mamie's birth after so much family heartbreak also, unfortunately, marked the first sign of a rupture in the relationship between Mary Lincoln and her daughter-in-law.

At the beginning, Mary Lincoln's letters were filled with the kind of worldly and sensible advice a young wife who had just given birth to her first child might appreciate.

"You should go out *every day* and enjoy yourself—you are so very young and should be as gay as a lark," Mary counseled her daughter-in-law. "Trouble comes soon enough, my dear child, and you must enjoy life, whenever you can. We all love you so very much—and you are blessed with a devoted husband and darling child—*so do go out* and enjoy the sunshine."

Letter after letter followed. Well-meaning or overbearing? That was open to interpretation. "Do not allow the baby to walk too soon or she will become bowlegged. . . . Don't mope around the house. Attend operas and concerts." When Mrs. Lincoln offered to pay for an extra nurse to free Mary Harlan Lincoln from the burdens of full-time motherhood, Robert was no doubt infuriated. "If I was in Chicago," Mary Lincoln wrote, "I would take young Miss Lincoln out for afternoon carriage rides, so her young mother can be as gay as a lark."

Mary Lincoln went on a buying binge in Europe that mortified her son and daughter-in-law in Chicago, but it delighted her to be spending her money on the baby—"the dainty dresses, little sashes and shawls, not to mention . . . the precious little shoes for the dear little feet.

"That blessed baby, how dearly I would love to look upon her sweet young face. . . . I never see anything particularly pretty—that I do not wish it was yours."

One expensive item in particular incurred Robert's wrath. It was a long embroidered cloak that his mother had purchased in one of her promenades on the Zeil in Frankfurt. To a compulsive shopper such as Mary, the Zeil was a dreamland filled with charming little stores "full of bargains." When Mary had seen the cloak, fit for a princess, she had had it gift-wrapped and sent to Chicago for her first grandchild. It was characteristic of Robert that he did not appreciate it as a generous gift from his mother, and just let it go. From his rigid perspective, it was yet another symptom of her lunacy in matters of money. She could barely pay her hotel bill, yet she showered Robert's little family with extravagant and wasteful presents. He informed his mother in no uncertain terms that the cloak was just too elaborate by Chicago standards, and it had actually "frightened" his wife. He also objected to the length of the cloak. Offended, Mary wrote a stern note back that she addressed directly to her daughter-in-law: "Robert writes that you were quite frightened about the baby clothes. Certainly they were made of the simplest materials & if they were a little trimmed there was certainly nothing out of the way. The *baby* is *not* supposed to be able to walk out in the street this winter & being carried in a nurse's arms, certainly a simple embroidered clothes—is not too much for people in *our station* of life. The very middle classes in Europe dress their children quite as much & as I do not consider ourselves in that category I would not care what the MEAN & ENVIOUS would say. However, I will send no more be assured."

Mary's expenses were out of control. When Tad's boarding school let out for the summer, mother and son embarked on a tour of Paris and London, followed by seven wonderful weeks in Scotland. They returned to Frankfurt in late August via Brussels and an excursion to the site of the Battle of Waterloo before—ten days late—Tad resumed his education at Dr. D. Hohagen's Institute. The semester had already started. Only then did Mary realize that she could no longer afford the comforts of the Angleterre Hotel with its congenial community of American expatriates. She found accommodations at the cheaper Hotel de Holland. Once more, she was following the depressingly familiar pattern of her years in Chicago: Her standard of living had begun to slip downward.

It was there, at the Hotel de Holland, that Mary had a surprise visitor. Her cherished friend from Philadelphia, Sally Orne, was just starting a three-year tour of Europe. She was traveling with her brother, two young daughters, a maid, and a valet. Mrs. Orne had arrived in Frankfurt from Hamburg late one evening and found all the rooms at the Angleterre Hotel booked. She had been redirected to the Hotel de Holland, not the sort of place for someone traveling in the high style befitting the wife of a wealthy Philadelphia carpet manufacturer. Nevertheless, Mrs. Orne checked into the Hotel de Holland at 10:30 P.M. and made the surprising discovery that Mary Lincoln was living in Room 72. When she was taken to her old friend's room, Mrs. Orne was shocked at what she saw.

"I followed the waiter to the *fourth story* and the back part of it too— and there in a small cheerless desolate looking room with but one window—two chairs and a wooden table with a solitary candle—I found *the wife the petted indulged wife of my noble* hearted just good *murdered* President Abraham Lincoln." Mrs. Orne reported her findings in a letter to Senator Charles Sumner, who she knew was leading the congressional crusade to secure a pension for Mary Lincoln. "Can you believe it?" she asked Sumner. "—it would be hard to say which overcame me most—the painful meeting or *the place*—My very blood boiled within my veins and I almost *cried out—shame on my countrymen*—Mrs. Lincoln was completely overwhelmed with grief—her sobs and tears wrung my own heart and I thought at the moment if her *tormentors* and *slanderers* could see her—they surely *might be satisfied.*"

Mrs. Orne sat with Mary in her dim fourth-floor room until three in the morning. Their conversation became so loud that the guest in the room next to Mary's knocked on her door and grumbled, "Ladies, I should like to sleep some." The two women giggled like schoolgirls at a sleep-away party. Another guest actually complained to the front desk, and a waiter was sent upstairs at 2:30 in the morning to ask the two American ladies to quiet down. Here at last was a dear companion from the old days to ease the pain of Mary's isolation and loneliness. "I sat by her side listening to her tales of sorrow until the night was far spent," Mrs. Orne told Charles Sumner. "Through the long night as her tears flowed unceasingly I would ask myself can this be the once so justly proud wife of Abraham Lincoln . . . in a far distant land—*alone, unprotected* and *impoverished by circumstances best known to herself* that she cannot afford to even keep a *maid to be with her*. . . . To say *she lives retired* does not express the manner of her life—she lives *alone*. I never knew what the word *Alone* meant before."

Mrs. Orne informed Sumner of the ugly rumors circulating in Europe that Mary Lincoln had been an accomplice to her husband's assassination. Many ignorant Europeans actually believed that the former First Lady was forced into exile because she had had a role in the assassination. The misinformation had even reached the servants at the Hotel de Holland, who were treating her with scorn. "It seems to me Abraham Lincoln might call for vengeance from the ground—and yet his *loving gentle big* heart—with all his *sensitiveness*—whilst breaking over the cruelties practiced upon his wife of his bosom—would in his agony cry out 'Father forgive them.'" As to claims that Mary Lincoln was insane, Mrs. Orne had this to say to Sumner: "As it has been suggested by some that Mrs. Lincoln is partially deranged, having seen her so recently it may be proper for me to say to you that I have watched her closely by day and night for weeks and fail to discover any evidence of aberration of mind in her, and I believe her mind to be as clear now as it was in the days of her greatest prosperity and I do believe it is unusually prolonged grief that has given rise to such a report."

Sally Orne came from a politically connected family. Her brother Charles O'Neill, who was traveling with her, was a Republican congressman from Philadelphia. Mrs. Orne was also "immensely wealthy"; her husband the carpet merchant was the president of the Union League in Philadelphia and very involved in national Republican Party politics. "She came from Hamburg in search of me," Mary wrote in awe. "We are together all the time. She is a very lovely woman and will remain here some time, she says, to be with me. I feel quite made up." For Mary, Mrs. Orne's visit was also affirmation of supernatural intervention. She revealed this to her friend Eliza Slataper, another true believer in the hereafter and the powers of the paranormal. According to Mary, Mrs. Orne had had an "irresistible impulse" to leave Hamburg for Frankfurt, and by some mystical occurrence, ended up at the Hotel de Holland, where she announced to her daughters, "I have a presentiment that Mrs. Lincoln is in this house." Before Mrs. Orne had removed her bonnet, "she was in my room."

It saddened Mary when Sally Orne had to move on to Paris, but Mrs. Orne promised to do everything in her power to lobby Congress and win the former First Lady her pension. Coincidentally, Mrs. Orne's husband, James, was vacationing with President Grant in Long Branch, New Jersey. In those days Long Branch was the Hamptons of America, renowned for its sand dunes and sun-kissed beaches. It was Grant's favorite seaside resort. Grant and Orne were chatting on the beach when the president turned to the carpet merchant and said, "Mr. Orne, it shall be my first duty, when Congress reassembles, to see that Mrs. Lincoln has her pension." Representative O'Neill made the bold prediction that Congress would authorize the pension that winter. The expectation of victory made Mary ecstatic. Sally Orne seemed to her to be a savior sent from heaven.

And then, almost overnight, Mrs. Orne stopped writing.

Mary continued to reach out to her friend in letters, and no detail of her forlorn existence was too small to be left out. A needle prick on the index finger of her right hand became infected. Mary could not believe such an ordinary mishap from sewing could cause her such agony. Her right hand became grossly inflamed. A doctor bathed the wound in bandages and salve but the pain kept her up at night for the good part of a week.

In November, Tad stayed out of school for three days to nurse his mother at her bedside as she lay stricken with what she called "neuralgic headaches"—probably debilitating migraines. "In his loving & tender treatment of me at all times, & very especially when I am indisposed—he reminds me so strongly of his beloved father." Thanksgiving was approaching, and a dejected Mary beseeched Mrs. Orne to return to Frankfurt with her two daughters to spend the holiday with her and Taddie. There was no response. A week later, Mary bitterly complained about her uncarpeted room at the Hotel de Holland. "*Death* would be far preferable to me than my present life, believe me." Meanwhile, Mary criticized Mrs. Orne for celebrating a "gay & delightful" life in Paris. Such were the burdens of friendship with Mary Lincoln. Thanksgiving week, a letter from Mrs. Orne finally arrived. In it was a special gift for Taddie—a stamp depicting the face of his martyred father. "You are an exceedingly naughty woman to neglect me so long," went Mary's sullen reply. "My bright little comforter Taddie is of course with me to day and we have been *speculating* upon your silence as lonely friends often will & we fear that you are sick—I trust that such may not be the case—and that you may be rather enjoying yourself in the gay world of Paris. . . . The darkness is very great—we can only pray that the dawn is at hand."

Christmas 1869 brought more misery. The Lincolns' second holiday season in exile found Mary prostrate in bed with another incapacitating migraine. Mary sent her son to an English-speaking druggist, and he was given a self-prescribed medication that Mary called the "blue mass." Mary took an "*unconscionable dose*," and it apparently knocked her out of commission for several days. She asked Tad to fetch her Frankfurt doctor, but the best treatment the physician could come up with was mineral water and the peculiar recommendation that Mary wear flannel pajamas. Tad dutifully went out and purchased a pair for his mother. "Taddie is like some old woman with regard to his care of me." Once again Tad's good heart brought back memories of his father: "[His] dark loving eyes—watching over me, reminded me so much of his dearly beloved father's—so filled with *his* deep love."

Four days after Christmas, with Mary still confined to her bed, Tad came home with a week-old copy of the *Times of London*. Edwin Stanton was dead. President Lincoln's secretary of war had passed away just four days after his Senate confirmation to the United States Supreme Court. Stanton had taken the oath of office on his deathbed, thereby setting a record for the shortest tenure in Supreme Court history. "In my present weak state the news almost overwhelms me," Mary wrote. At the same time, Mary could not stop herself from lashing out at President Grant, who was publicly noncommittal on the issue of her pension. "*Where is Grant all this time*—Where is his *memory* of my husband—who made him *just what he is*. . . . Did not my husband elevate him from obscurity . . . & most truly place him on his present pinnacle of greatness?" She accused Grant and his wife, Julia, of being "intensely SMALL selfish people," heartless and utterly indifferent to the suffering of Abraham Lincoln's widow.

New Year's Day 1870 heralded a new decade and offered Mary a slight measure of comfort. As she lay on her sofa, racked with unbearable back pain, ten well-wishers came to pay their respects, including Consul-General Murphy and his son, two Frankfurt physicians, and three lady friends. Tongue firmly planted in cheek, Mary noted that the notorious Count Schneiderbutzen "did not present himself." But her back pain worsened; she described it as a "sharp, burning *agony*" down her spine. Her doctors placed her in a plaster cast that went from her shoulders to her lower back. Not long after Edwin Stanton's death, Mary heard news from home that made her blood boil. Wealthy Republicans had raised the astounding sum of $111,000 in support of the widow Stanton and her family, and in just a few weeks. She considered it an outrage that Stanton's widow was living in the "handsomest residence" in Washington while Abraham Lincoln's widow was lodging on the third floor in an uncarpeted room in a "disconsolate boarding house"—minus a servant.

Tad was now sixteen. The former mischief-maker-in-chief was developing into a fine young man. At Dr. Hohagen's boarding school he studied German, English, and French. He also took dance lessons and drawing. As he was still struggling to keep up with his classmates, Mary hired an English professor to serve as his private tutor. His speech impediment showed marked improvement from rigorously reading aloud under the tutelage of a German elocution teacher. In time, Tad mastered "perfect articulation." These lessons did, however, have one unintended consequence: Due to Tad's mimicry of his German teacher's diction, Abraham Lincoln's son spoke English with a slight Teutonic accent!

An adolescent now, Tad started taking an interest in personal grooming. He used expensive soaps and oils, and tamed his unruly dark hair with mounds of perfumed ointment. His striped brown trousers had to be lengthened to keep up with his growth spurts. In his effort to adapt to life in Germany, he bought a new pair of ice skates and enjoyed skating on Frankfurt's frozen lakes. He also visited the Frankfurt zoo, toured the Black Forest, and accompanied Mary on an excursion to the city of Heidelberg. A new form of entertainment that was sweeping Europe, called the cyclorama, also awed Tad. It was a colossal 360-degree painting that depicted a great moment in history, usually an epic battle. The viewer stood in the center of the panoramic scene, and the effect was to be present at that momentous historical event. Music and a narrator added to the experience.

Cycloramas traveled from city to city, much like movies would decades later. Tad was so enthralled he went twice.

Like his mother, Tad found the German winters disagreeable. The school had inadequate heating, and he often shivered in class. He was susceptible to respiratory infections, and his guardianship records show a troubling number of visits to doctors. He suffered from weak lungs.

In May 1870, Mary was shopping for schoolbooks for Tad in downtown Frankfurt when she stopped by the English Reading Room library to peruse the latest British and American newspapers. She was zealous about keeping up with events at home. But this time, as she skimmed a British newspaper, her heart stopped. Reading the article, Mary learned for the first time that the Senate Committee on Pensions had voted to indefinitely table her pension bill. The full report of the committee was devastating. It put Mrs. Lincoln's net worth at $58,756, including the $22,000 Congress had already authorized as payment of President Lincoln's salary for the year of his assassination. In hurtful language, the committee concluded that Mrs. Lincoln was living "royally" and beyond her means. It even insinuated that there were other alarming facts relevant to the Mary Lincoln issue that were "probably not needful to refer to, but which are generally known." As she was reading the article, Mary collapsed on the spot and had to be assisted into a carriage. Her physician was sent for, and, after examining the patient, he evidently threw up his hands. Thinking this woman was impossibly demanding, and never got better, the physician came up with the only prescription that made sense to him at the time: an immediate change in scenery. He recommended the famous spas at Marienbad. Twelve hours later, she was taken to the Frankfurt railroad depot, traveling light by Mary Lincoln's standards—just two carpet satchels packed with clothes.

When she arrived in Marienbad, Mary felt exhausted. She could barely straighten her back, and there were days when she lay helpless on the bed in her third-floor hotel room. She remained there for six weeks, and slowly regained her strength. The famous salt baths were working their magic on Mary Lincoln's feeble bones.

Meanwhile, high political intrigue was taking place in Washington. The House of Representatives passed a bill along straight party lines authorizing a three-thousand-dollar annual pension for Mary Lincoln. It was now up to the Senate. Once again, Mary's most loyal friend in Washington, Senator Charles Sumner, spoke eloquently in its favor. Senator James Harlan of

Iowa found himself in an awkward position because his daughter was married to Robert Lincoln. Politically, he could not come out publicly and endorse the measure. Privately, however, he worked the floor in support of Mary Lincoln. On the day before the Senate was to adjourn for the summer, the pension issue went before the full body. It was an extraordinary session. Never in history had a First Lady been discussed in such poisonous language. Senator Richard Yates, a Republican from the land of Lincoln, rose and accused Mrs. Lincoln and her family, the Todds, of sympathizing with the rebellion "all through" the Civil War. "There are recollections and memories, sad and silent and deep, that I will not recall publicly, which induce me to vote against this bill. . . . A woman should be true to her husband. . . . Mr. President, the occasion does not require, and I shall not, so far as I am concerned, go into details. Mr. Lincoln's memory is sweet to me. God almighty bless the name and fame of Abraham Lincoln."

The life of exile Mary Lincoln had chosen for herself and Tad did not help her case. "Why should she be an absentee from America?" asked Senator Justin Morrill of Vermont. "Did not Mrs. Madison win fame by staying here at home? In my judgment her brilliant boy had much better be educated here at home under American institutions than to be educated abroad, where he will not grow up in the principles of his father." Pennsylvania's senator Simon Cameron, who had served as Lincoln's first secretary of war, came to Mary's defense. Cameron took the floor and brought the Senate chamber back to the year 1861, when Lincoln and his family arrived in Washington for the inauguration. "The ladies, and even the gentlemen, the gossips of the town, did all they could to make a bad reputation for Mrs. Lincoln, and tried to do so for the president. They could not destroy him, but they did . . . destroy the social position of his wife. I do not want to talk, and I say, let us vote."

The time came to cast their votes. The tally went: twenty-eight in favor, twenty opposed. Nearly a third of the Senate abstained or were not present. President Grant signed the bill that very day. It took two days for the news to reach Mary in Europe. It came via a transatlantic telegram from James Orne. Mary expressed "unbounded gratitude" to the Ornes for their role in securing its passage. The three thousand dollar annual payment ensured her financial future, though she grumbled that she thought she deserved six thousand.

It was typical of Mary's hard luck that, as soon as this crisis was settled, another immediately arose in its place. In her letter thanking James Orne, written July 16, 1870, Mary straightforwardly reported that the "agitation in Europe is very great." That was an understatement.

Three days later, France declared war on Germany. It was the start of the Franco-Prussian War.

The city of Frankfurt was under threat of invasion. A French expeditionary force crossed the Prussian border and advanced on the city of Saarbrücken, just seventy miles from where Mary and Tad lived. In France, there was euphoria. "Our Army has taken the offensive and crossed the frontier and invaded Prussian territory," the French general staff announced. Crowds rejoiced in Paris. Church bells rang. In Frankfurt, there was panic. Mary and Tad watched with alarm as the 400,000-man German army mobilized for war. The streets of Frankfurt became jammed with soldiers moving to the front. Americans were urged to evacuate the city. One month later, the French army was trounced at the Battle of Sedan. France's ruler, Napoleon III, was in tears as he surrendered his sword and 88,000 of his soldiers to William I, King of Prussia. The Franco-Prussian War was brief, but historically momentous. Napoleon III became the last ruling monarch of France. His defeat ushered in the Third Republic. The German states unified under the Prussian king, who proclaimed himself kaiser of the German Empire. And the Germans annexed Alsace-Lorraine, arousing hostility between the two nations that would not be resolved until after World War II.

For Mary Lincoln and Tad Lincoln, the Franco-Prussian War also had profoundly personal consequences. Germany was now in a state of political convulsion. After living in exile for two years, they had to flee Frankfurt.

They arrived in Liverpool in September 1870, and went by rail to the town of Leamington, situated in the geographic center of England, about three hours from London. Once again, Mary was drawn to a resort famous for its salty waters that professed to cure aches, pains, and undefined female maladies. The healing powers of Leamington's waters had been known since Roman times, but it was Queen Victoria's visit, in 1858, that had put Leamington on the map. Mary and Tad intended to make a new life there, and, as in Frankfurt, Mary's first priority was getting Tad established.

She hired a young English tutor who came with excellent references, and Tad worked with him from eight in the morning until one in the afternoon. A long break followed, until 5:00 P.M., when lessons resumed. At seven, they called it a night. Tad's only day off was Sunday. He never deviated from this routine. He seemed to have found a new focus in his studies, and it delighted Mary to see her son so engaged. "Study more than he does now he could not possibly do," Mary wrote her daughter-in-law. It seemed to Mary that Tad was studying for "dear life," as if to make up for lost time.

Mary frequently traveled to London, and became engrossed in a book that had just been published to acclaim in Europe, *The Gates Ajar,* by the American writer Elizabeth Stuart Phelps. *The Gates Ajar* was a spiritual novel of life in the hereafter, where heaven was a place of reunion and rec-onciliation with lost loved ones. The book became a sensation, selling more than one hundred thousand copies, with American sales driven by women who had lost husbands, sons, brothers, and fathers in the Civil War. Its theme of earthly loss and sorrow held obvious appeal for Mary Lincoln.

The damp English climate took its toll on Mary; she suffered from a persistent cough, possibly bronchitis, and she was growing weary of sight-seeing. It tore her apart that she had yet to hold her granddaughter Mamie—"That blessed baby, how dearly I would love to look upon her sweet young face." Tad also worried her. "He has become so heartsick and at the same time his English education has become so neglected." He was "almost wild" to see his brother and baby niece Mamie. Home beckoned.

In November, Mary took Tad to London. They were boarding at a house at No. 9 Woburn Place in Russell Square, near the British Museum. One afternoon, as they were riding in a carriage to a downtown London bank where Mary's letters were being forwarded, their conversation turned to the Christmas holiday. Mary was thinking of traveling to Italy to join her friend Mrs. Mathew Simpson, the wife of the bishop who had married Robert and Mary Harlan. She longed to warm her weary bones in the Italian sun. But she also knew that Tad was at a crossroads. In a trembling voice, she told her son that the Cunard ship *Russia* was sailing the following Saturday for New York, and Tad could spend Christmas with Robert and Mary Harlan Lincoln in Chicago and see his little niece for the first time. As soon as she had made the suggestion, she regretted it. A transatlantic ocean voyage in winter was not something she could sanction. "To trust my beautiful, darling *good* boy to the elements, at this season of the year makes my heart faint within me," she wrote her daughter-in-law. They would wait until spring. Tad's years in exile were coming to an end. He was turning eighteen. He had spent three Christmas holidays abroad. It was time.

Passage was booked on the *Russia* in May. Tad and Mary were going home.

Neither expected the tragedy that would befall them in America.

9
Woman of Sorrow

THE *RUSSIA* WAS a beautiful ship. Nautical experts marveled at the symmetry of her three-mast design, and she was reputed to be one of the fastest vessels in the Cunard fleet. With her steam engine and full spread of its sails, the *Russia* could cross the Atlantic in eight days, depending on wind and weather. Her skipper was Cunard's senior officer, Captain Theodore Cook.

There were 235 first-class passengers who boarded in Liverpool on April 29, 1871. Perhaps the most prominent was that hero of the Civil War, General Philip Sheridan, accompanied by his staff of two generals and three army captains. Britain's Third Earl of Ellesmere, on his way to Canada to hold talks with the governor-general, was also on board with his wife the Countess of Ellesmere. And then there were Mary Todd Lincoln and her son Tad.

The ship crossed the Irish Sea and hugged the southeast coast of Ireland before turning northwest, where it picked up the Great Circle Route to New York. Mary's stateroom was cramped, just nine feet wide, with two bunks. There was a porthole for fresh air and sun, a plush couch, washstand, and mirror. An oil lamp supplied light for reading. The dining room was the ship's main social hub. Mary, Tad, and the other passengers sat on padded seats at a long table bolted to the floor and conversed over the din and the vibration of the ship's single propeller. They enjoyed every imaginable manner of meat—fried, boiled, stewed, and steamed. Roast shoulder of mutton and rump steak were two specialties, and for dessert there was pudding and jam tarts.

Even with these comforts and accommodations, it was another brutal voyage for the Lincolns. The *Russia* encountered a major gale in the mid-Atlantic, and the voyage was set back two full days. "Rough was no name for it," Mary said. "We certainly thought we were doomed to destruction." It surely reminded Mary of the hideous weather during her first crossing of the Atlantic on the *City of Baltimore*. During the worst of the storm the *Russia*'s captain ordered all passengers confined to their berths for three days. "When we did go out on deck we were almost frightened to death, for the waves were actually mountains high and the swell was so tremendous. We were tossed about like a leaf," said Mary.

In Chicago, an anxious Robert Lincoln monitored the ship's progress. He wrote David Davis: "I am expecting Tad to be here any day as the ship on which he left England is now overdue at New York." His little brother's prospects were obviously on Robert's mind. "I have not thought much as to what I shall advise Tad to do. He is now past eighteen & entitled to be consulted. I have no fears about him if he is as good a boy as I am told."

Russia finally pulled into New York Harbor on May 11. For Mary, the voyage had been alternately terrifying and monotonous—"nobody could be more glad than I was when it was over." It was standard federal policy for all passengers to sit in quarantine for three days, but rank had its privileges. The cutter *Bronx* of the United States Revenue Marines sailed out to meet the *Russia* and pick up General Sheridan and his people. Mary was delighted when she and Tad and the British earl and his wife were invited to join Sheridan's party and bypass the quarantine.

Sheridan, known as "Little Phil," stood only five-foot-five. Abraham Lincoln once memorably described him as a "brown, chunky little chap, with a long body, short legs, not enough neck to hang him, and such long arms that if his ankles itch he can scratch them without stooping." When the Civil War had started, Sheridan had been thin, chiseled and just thirty years old. Hard drinking and a gargantuan appetite eventually ballooned his weight to two hundred pounds.

A military band playing "Hail to the Chief" greeted General Sheridan on the dock. Although the ceremony was meant for the Civil War hero, Mary glowed. She had not experienced the soaring pomp and circumstance since her years as the indulged First Lady of the United States. President Grant had sent Sheridan to Europe to observe the Franco-Prussian War, and a reporter for the *New York Times,* who was at the dock to interview him about his impressions of the French and Prussian armies, was quite startled to see Mrs. Lincoln back from Europe and young Tad with her. "Mrs. Lincoln delighted to be home in her native land," the reporter wrote.

"Tad speaks English with a foreign accent and Mrs. Lincoln is looking well, but yet seems oppressed by her husband's death."

Mary and Tad found their way to the Everett House in New York, a fashionable residential hotel on Union Square. One of her first visitors was her old friend Rhoda White. The two widows became reacquainted. Another visitor was John Hay, who had once served as President Lincoln's private secretary. Hay was now living in New York and writing editorials for the *New York Tribune*. He was taken aback at the sight of Tad, whom he had not seen in six years. The Tad Lincoln he knew from the White House was the "absolute tyrant" of the executive mansion—shrewd, lawless, and with a "very bad opinion of books and no opinion of discipline." But here in New York, there stood a fine and gracious young man. Hay realized that the terrible shock of President Lincoln's assassination had sobered and "fixed" Tad Lincoln. He was deeply impressed that Tad had remained at Mary Lincoln's side through three years in exile. It was indicative of a benevolent tenderness beyond the teenager's years, and strangely at variance with the "mischievous thoughtlessness" of his childhood. Hay and Tad chatted. Hay found him a "cordial, frank, warm-hearted boy" and "greatly improved" by his time abroad.

Mary and Tad had one more caller. She was a "lady reporter" from the *New York World* who arrived at the Everett House unannounced and requested an interview with the former First Lady and her son. The reporter found Mrs. Lincoln dressed as usual in deep mourning, "stout as ever," and very pale.

"I have come, Mrs. Lincoln, to welcome you home again, and to see if you will grant me a few moments conversation."

The former First Lady found it impossible to turn down a high-profile platform like the *World*, and she agreed to be interviewed, telling the reporter, "I am willing to spend a few moments with you, although I feel very ill with a sick headache."

"Very much obliged to you, madam. Will you please tell me where you intend to reside?"

Mary said she was on her way to Chicago to live temporarily with her son Robert. "Beyond that I cannot tell you."

"Then you do not intend to return to Europe?"

"I cannot tell. I may, and I may not. I have enjoyed my journey abroad exceedingly and like the European style of living very much, but home seems very pleasant and I was very glad when I landed in America again."

"Did you find that the memory of your husband, our late president, was respected abroad?"

"Everywhere," Mrs. Lincoln responded. "His shocking death seems to have overcome all prejudice the people in Europe may have had against him for political reasons. This was, of course, exceedingly gratifying to us. People spoke of him as if they honored him greatly, and I know that the manner of his death made all persons his friends." With that, Mary pronounced herself too ill to continue and asked Tad to take her place. With all her flair for drama, she exited the room. Tad and the reporter were left alone, and he did not relish the idea of speaking to her, telling her that he "didn't like getting into the newspapers." The reporter thought Tad's name was Thaddeus, which was a common mistake. Like many Americans, she assumed Thaddeus was his given name and did not know that Tad had actually been named after Abraham Lincoln's father, Thomas. She noted Tad's smooth skin and cheeks flushed with good color, and in the article that was published in the *World* the next day, she wrote that he seemed to be in "perfect health."

Tad told the reporter that the Lincolns wished above all to live quietly and in private.

"It has been rumored in the papers that your mother intends marrying again." It was that ridiculous Count Schneiderbutzen story rearing its head once more. She asked straight out: "Is that true?"

"That's all nonsense," Tad said. "I wish folks wouldn't talk so much about my mother. There's no truth whatever to that report. People say pretty near what they like nowadays." Tad went on to call the political war over his mother's pension an "abominable shame." He said, "Such a fuss as she has had is enough to discourage any woman."

"You have been studying in Germany, have you not?"

"Well, yes, I have been at school there and speak German very well."

"Did you like the people as well as your mother did?"

"Yes, we liked them very well. They were very kind to us everywhere."

"Did you find that they spoke well of your father?"

"Yes, they liked him very well."

"Which do you like best—Europe or America?"

"Well, we both like home best, after all. It somehow seems more comfortable here." With that, Tad had had enough, and brought the interview to an end.

Mary and Tad arrived in Chicago on May 15. Robert Lincoln and his family were living in a "charming" three-bedroom house at 653 Wabash Avenue, perfect for a young professional couple starting out. Here, for the first time, Mary Lincoln saw her granddaughter Mamie. She and Tad stared in wonder at the apple-cheeked nineteen-month-old toddler who was Abraham Lincoln's first grandchild. On the surface, in these first hours of joyful reunion, the gathering seemed harmonious. Mary wrote Rhoda White that her eldest son and his wife were "rejoicing over our arrival."

"We are received with so much affection here and notwithstanding the confined limits of this charming little home my son Robert, who is all that is noble and good and his lovely little wife will not hear to our removal." There was not a hint of family acrimony in her letter to Mrs. White. But in truth, relations between Mary Lincoln and her daughter-in-law were already seriously strained. Within days of Mary's arrival, the situation became unbearable; Mary Harlan Lincoln could not stand to be anywhere near the overbearing Mrs. Lincoln. They disagreed about everything—the servants, the home decor, and the proper method of raising Mamie. Young Mary unburdened her heart to her friend Anna Eastman, who wrote back these supportive words: "There could be no sweeter daughter-in-law and true friend to her than you dear, if she would only do half way right."

Mary Lincoln decided it would be best if she and Tad found other accommodations. Around this time, Tad started coughing. The teenager had always been susceptible to bronchial infections, and this one at first seemed like just another bad chest cold, something he may have caught during the voyage on the *Russia*. Mary cared for him while she arranged for new lodgings at Clifton House—that "den of discomfort and dirt"—and her return to the boarding life she loathed. Their move from Robert's house was delayed for a few days so Tad could try to regain his strength, and on Saturday, mother and loyal son checked into Room 21. Mary could not believe she was once again viewing life "from the window" of an apartment at Clifton House. "My husband, so fondly indulgent, would have shrunk back in horror if he could have imagined *his* loved family, *thus* domiciled."

Meanwhile, Mary Harlan Lincoln received a telegram that her mother Ann was gravely ill. Young Mary scooped up the infant Mamie and hastily boarded a train to the nation's capital to help out. Perhaps part of her was relieved at the summons as it gave her a ready excuse to get out of town, and Mary Lincoln's sight.

Two days after Mary Lincoln had written Rhoda White that things in Chicago could not be more blissful, she wrote to tell her friend that Tad was "confined to his bed to day with a severe cold." His condition steadily deteri-orated. Two weeks later, Mary Lincoln's next letter to Mrs. White contained these ominous words: "My dear boy, has been *very very* dangerously ill."

Tad was in physical agony, afflicted with a cough so severe that each deep breath he took was like a knife plunging into his chest. Two of Chicago's leading physicians were called to Clifton House to examine the teenager. Dr. Charles Gilman Smith was a graduate of Harvard University and the University of Pennsylvania School of Medicine. He had moved to Chicago when he was twenty-nine and built a thriving practice catering to the carriage class. He had a fine physique, a good singing voice, and he was a professor of children's diseases at the Chicago Hospital for Women and Children. Assisting him was Dr. Hosmer A. Johnson, a distinguished pro-fessor at the Chicago Eye and Ear Infirmary. Dr. Johnson, like Dr. Smith, had impeccable social credentials.

When they listened to Tad's chest with a stethoscope they could hear the splash of fluid in his body. Tapping the rib cage produced a dull percussive sound. There was an unmistakable lateral bulge on the left side of his body.

The diagnosis was determined to be dropsy. Today we know it as pleurisy.

Pleurisy is a viral infection. It is not a disease in itself, but symptomatic of one. In Tad's case, the underlying cause was probably tuberculosis, which had gone undiagnosed for years. Looking back, it explains much of his medical history: his susceptibility to colds when he was a student at the Brown School in Chicago, and his recurring visits to the doctor in Frank-furt. Months shivering in Dr. Hohagan's unheated classrooms probably aggravated his condition.

Drs. Smith and Johnson did what they could. They also brought in an eminent lung specialist, Dr. Nathan S. Davis, a founder of the American Medical Association and dean of the Chicago Medical College. Dr. Davis was fifty-four years old when he examined Tad. Many of his colleagues con-sidered him the greatest physician and diagnostician they had ever known. But in the nineteenth century, there was no cure for pleurisy or for TB. For pain relief, Mary was probably advised to place hot compresses soaked in homeopathic herbs on Tad's chest. The doctors also prescribed opium-based syrup, sold under the brand name Ayer's Cherry Pectoral, Mrs. Winslow's Soothing Syrup, or McMunn's Elixir of Opium. They may also have told Tad to hold a pillow tightly against his chest when he coughed.

For a while it seemed that the care Tad was receiving was working. Mary was impressed with all the medical personnel—she called them "excellent physicians." Credentials aside, she also would have appreciated their high social standing in Chicago. For ten straight nights Mary sat at Tad's bedside. It was a touching role reversal from their days in Frankfurt when Tad would skip school to nurse his mother through her migraines and crippling back pains. Now it was Mary's time to show the deep bond of love that connected mother to son. On June 8 Dr. Davis returned to Clifton House and examined Tad again. Using all his diagnostic skills and three decades of experience in the science of auscultation, Dr. Davis listened to the pattern of Tad's breathing and determined that his left lung was still partially filled with water, but there was some evidence of improvement since his last checkup. Overall, the prognosis was hopeful. Dr. Davis informed Mary that her son's youth, combined with vigilant care and the "mercy of God," would carry him through this ordeal. Mary and Tad were left alone in Room 21. In a rare moment of peace, Tad closed his eyes and fell into a fitful sleep. Exhausted herself, Mary sat at her desk and unburdened herself to Rhoda White. "May we *ever* be sufficiently grateful should his precious life be spared. Dr. Davis, a very eminent lung physician, says that *thus far* his lungs are *not at all* diseased although water has been formed on part of his left lung, which is gradually decreasing. . . .With the *last* few years *so filled* with sorrow, this fresh anguish bows me to the earth."

Tad's fever subsided, and he was even able to eat a little. But in late June, his condition took a turn for the worse. His lungs were now so filled with mucus and bacterial fluid that he could not lie down and breathe. He was made to sit in a permanent upright position, like a gruesome statue, even at night when he tried to sleep. A chair was brought in with a bar built into its armrests. In this manner, when Tad managed to nod off, at least the bar would keep him from slipping to the floor. The infection was spreading.

In June, yet another eminent physician was called in for consultations. He was Dr. C. G. Smith, considered the city's foremost pediatrician. He saw Tad every day for an entire month. Chicago's medical elite had now come together as a team with the sole objective of saving the life of Abraham Lincoln's youngest son. One procedure that was apparently considered by the physicians was thoracocentesis. It was a standard course of treatment for dropsy that involved opening the chest cavity above the third rib and inserting a trocar, or three-sided needle, into the pleural space. The putrefied fluid would then be drained through a syringe. But there were grave risks associated with all surgery performed in the nineteenth century. In the case of thoracocentesis, the major concern would have been the accidental laceration of the lung. (A Boston patient once said, "I would sooner send a bullet into the chest than plunge in a trocar.") Tad's doctors rejected thoracocentesis as too risky.

As the executor of Abraham Lincoln's estate, David Davis traveled to Chicago to assess the condition of his young charge for himself. He walked into a deathwatch. Tad was soaked in sweat. Seeing his spiked fever, shortness of breath, and stabbing chest cough, it was obvious to Davis that Tad was dying. "Tadd [sic] Lincoln is dangerously ill," the Supreme Court justice wrote that night. "If he recovers, it will be almost a miracle. The disease is dropsy on the chest. He has been compelled to sit upright in a chair for upwards of a month. His mother is in great affliction. I saw him and her on Saturday—it made me feel very sad. He seems a warm hearted youth."

It was the fourth deathbed vigil Mary Lincoln had endured: first her son Eddie, dead in 1850 at age three; then Willie, dead at age eleven from cholera; the martyred Abraham Lincoln in 1865; and now her cherished son Tad, eighteen years of age. "As grievous as other bereavements have been, not one great sorrow ever approached the agony of this," Mary said. One scorching night early in July, Tad, barely clothed, tried to lift his feeble body out of the chair, but collapsed in a heap. On Tuesday, July 11, he surprised everyone when he showed true improvement. Hopes soared, and Robert Lincoln, witnessing this promise of a miracle, wrote to his wife in Washington: "Mr. Thomas Lincoln has been picking up for the last two or three days and is to all appearances improving, his face has lost some of its expression of distress."

But Tad's recuperation was an illusion. Two days after Robert had informed his wife that Tad was on the road to recovery, he had to tell her that his brother had suffered a relapse and was going fast. The great diagnostician Dr. Nathan S. Davis had the sad duty of notifying the Lincolns that at this point, Tad's death was inevitable. Robert tried to do everything to lift Tad's spirits. He showed him a new photograph of baby Mamie, taken in Washington and mailed by Mary Harlan Lincoln. Love of family had been the foundation of Tad's character, and seeing the photo of the niece whose birth had brought him back to America brightened the closing hours of his life. It was, Robert said, "really the last pleasure he had on earth." Robert related the distressing scene in Room 21 to his wife: "I am sorry to tell you that Tad seems to be losing ground. Yesterday was very hot and oppressive and he got in a bad way during the night. . . . I have just now come from him and he is looking and feeling better, but Dr. Davis says he can see nothing to found any hope of his recovery upon and that he can live only a few days. . . . To-day there is a fine breeze and the air is really delightful—all of which makes him feel better but really have little or no effect upon his trouble. He is looking dreadfully."

Eleven o'clock Friday night. Tad was asleep. In the hotel room observing the stricken teen were Mary, Robert, and two private nurses hired to help out. Robert decided to take a break and get a few hours' sleep at home. He left his brother in the care of the three women and returned to his own bed on Wabash Avenue. As he explained to his wife, "Tad appeared a great deal better. He was stronger and looking well and the water was reduced a good deal in his chest. Thursday was very close and oppressive and it pulled him back very much. Friday afternoon he seemed to rally again and at eleven P.M. was sleeping nicely with prospects of having a good night, so I left him with mother and his two nurses and went to the house." But at 4:30 in the morning Robert was awakened by an urgent knock on his front door. A messenger sent by Mary told him that he had to return immediately to the hotel. When Robert arrived at Clifton House he saw at once that his brother was "failing fast."

"He was in great distress and laboring for breath and ease but I do not think he was in acute pain." Tad lingered for another three hours, until 7:30 Saturday morning, July 15, when he "suddenly threw himself forward on his bar and was gone." His heart, compressed by the effusion of bodily fluids, just gave out.

His body was taken to Robert's house, and a service was held the next day. Senator Harlan arrived from Iowa, where he had been campaigning, although, curiously, Mary Harlan Lincoln remained behind in Washington. The young people who attended Bible studies class with Tad when he had been living in Chicago came as a group and, no doubt with a mixture of lurid fascination and horror, stared into the open casket that held the body of their famous classmate. Mary Lincoln sat on a sofa, dazed, looking "truly the woman of sorrow that she was." Next to Mary, Robert sat on one side, and on the other was the Reverend Dr. John Howe Brown, pastor of the Presbyterian Church on Thirty-first Street. The house was filled with mourners standing in the parlor and halls, and even on the staircase and balcony.

Tad's obituary in the *Chicago Tribune* made mention of his physical resemblance to his father. It was also noted that Master Lincoln bore his mortal illness with "great patience and resignation." Overall, the coverage was poignant and appropriate. The *State Journal*, taking note of Tad's well-known and "unfortunate imperfection of speech" pointed out that with scholarship and discipline Tad had "succeeded in entirely overcoming the impediment." The newspaper also praised Tad's moral fitness to carry the name Lincoln. In Germany, where young men his age routinely consumed beer and wine, it was noted with pride that Tad was committed to temperance and "refused to taste or have anything to do with intoxicating beverages of any kind." While Tad was praised for facing death with valor, Mary continued to absorb the potshots of what she called the vampire press. One newspaper actually speculated in print that Tad's demise might finally cause Mary Lincoln to go insane, although her hometown newspaper, the *Illinois State Journal*, sympathetically described the former First Lady's grief as "beyond expression."

In New York, John Hay penned a moving tribute to Tad in the *New York Tribune* that recalled the "tricky little sprite who gave to that sad and solemn White House of the great war the only comic relief it knew." Hay went on: "He was so full of life and vigor—so bubbling over with health and high spirits, that he kept the house alive with his pranks and his fantastic enterprises. . . . Early in the morning you could hear his shrill pipe resounding through the dreary corridors of the Executive residence. The day passed in rapid succession of plots . . . and when the president laid down his weary pen toward midnight, he generally found his infant goblin asleep under his table or roasting his curly head by the open fire-place." Hay recalled his encounter with Tad just eight weeks earlier. "The Tad Lincoln of our history ceased to exist a long time ago. The modest and cordial young fellow who passed through New York a few weeks ago with his mother will never be known outside of the circle of his mourning friends. . . . In his loss the already fearfully bereaved family will suffer a new and deep affliction, and the world, which never did and never will know him, will not withhold a tribute of regret for the child whose gayety and affection cheered more than anything else the worn and weary heart of the great president through the toilsome years of the war."

Tad's body was taken to the St. Louis & Alton Railroad depot, where it was placed on a chartered train to Springfield. A distinguished group of mourners boarded the private car: Robert Lincoln, his father-in-law Senator Harlan, Senator Lyman Trumbull of Illinois, Supreme Court Justice David Davis, former Illinois congressman Isaac Arnold, Rev. Brown and his wife, and the Chicago lawyer Jonathan Young Scammon. Following the pattern she had set years before with the funerals of her children and President Lincoln, Mary Todd Lincoln remained behind, too shattered by grief to witness the internment of yet another loved one. Reverend Brown's wife stayed with Mary to offer what comfort she could. The train pulled into the Springfield railroad station at 3:50 A.M., and Tad's coffin was transported to the home of Mary Lincoln's sister Elizabeth Edwards and her husband Ninian. There, it was placed in the same parlor in which Abraham Lincoln and Mary Todd had been married in 1842.

Illinois was experiencing one of the hottest summers on record. The day before Tad's funeral, the thermometer in Springfield reached 114 degrees. At nine in the morning, the coffin was carried out of the Edwards' parlor and transported to the First Presbyterian Church. Fittingly, the pallbearers were six young people who had known Tad when he was a frisky terror living in Springfield before his father became president. The pallbearers carried the beautiful rosewood casket, decorated with wreaths of immortelles, into the church and placed it in front of the pulpit. The church was packed, with space in the front row reserved for Robert and the immediate relatives, including three of Mary Lincoln's sisters. A dirge played on the organ opened the services, after which Rev. Brown invoked the divine blessings. The text was from Isaiah: "But they that wait upon the Lord shall renew their strength; they shall mount up with wings as eagles; they shall run and not be weary; they shall walk and not faint." A prayer was offered for Mary Lincoln. Then the casket was placed on a hearse and, with a solemn line of mourners following, driven to Oak Ridge Cemetery on the outskirts of the city. Much had changed since Abraham Lincoln had been buried there in 1865. The property, once a pristine forest, was now the site of construction and activity. Roads had been laid out and an iron gate installed around the cemetery—all to accommodate the enormous crowds who made the pilgrimage to the tomb of Abraham Lincoln.

The vault was opened and Tad's coffin was taken inside. There, his mortal remains were laid to rest in the same tomb that held his beloved brother Willie, and Eddie, the brother he had never known. Most of all, he was with his father again.

Now Tad was gone, and Robert Lincoln became the sole surviving son of Abraham and Mary Todd Lincoln.

10

The Wanderer

ROBERT LINCOLN INSISTED that his mother stay with him at his home on Wabash Avenue, but ten days later, he just walked out the door and left her there. His strength was all "used up," he told a friend, and, under doctor's orders, he went west, to the Rocky Mountains. The slow and agonizing death of his brother had left him in a state of paralyzing despair; he may have even been close to a nervous breakdown. His need to leave was so urgent that he could not even tell his mother about it in person. Robert notified Mary by letter that he had had to go "by order of his physician, being so ill and worn out."

Robert was supposed to remain in the Rockies for two weeks; he stayed an entire month.

Mary could not believe that she had been left by herself in this state of deep anguish—"entirely alone, in my fearful sorrow." Her only companion at this time was a boarder who lived in the spare bedroom. Mary reached out to her friend Eliza Slataper in Pittsburgh. "From the depths of an agonized bereaved heart" she begged Mrs. Slataper to come to Chicago and keep her company—even if for a day or two. "I have been prostrated by illness—& by *a grief*—that the grave alone can soften." Tad had been dead nearly a month, and Mary told Mrs. Slataper that she was desperate to see a kindly face. "I am entirely alone, in my *fearful sorrow. Come, come, come to me.*"

Robert returned in late summer, but, as he admitted to his "second father," David Davis, "There is no use trying to disguise the fact that things are very gloomy here." Mary Lincoln was still living with him, and her inconsolable grief did not improve with the passage of time. She described herself as "utterly prostrated." Her heart fluttered with "violent palpitations." The best recommendation her doctors could come up with was "perfect quiet." She even canceled the visit Mrs. Slataper had planned, writing, "As anxious as I am to see you I feel that it is best that we do not meet." She further unburdened herself to David Davis, writing him: "Dear Judge, I well know how deeply you sympathize with us, in our great sorrow. My beloved boy was the idol of my heart and had become my inseparable companion. My heart is entirely broken, for without his presence the world is complete darkness."

In 1871 Chicago's population was 330,000, surpassing St. Louis and making it the fourth-largest city in the United States. With the explosive growth came an unparalleled business boom. Great fortunes were being amassed, and the law offices of Robert T. Lincoln, at No. 1 Marine Bank Building, were thriving.

In October, John Hay went to Chicago to visit Robert. Hay had written that beautiful tribute to Tad Lincoln, and now President Lincoln's former private secretary was able to extend his condolences to the Lincoln family in person. Mary Lincoln was still living at Robert's while her daughter-in-law remained in Washington with baby Mamie. Mary Harlan Lincoln had now been gone for three straight months. Whether this state of affairs was a consequence of her mother's grave illness or her mother-in-law's continued presence on Wabash Avenue remains a matter of conjecture.

It was Sunday, October 8, 1871, Hay's thirty-third birthday, and although it was fall, Chicago was experiencing one of the hottest and driest years on record. Between July, when Tad Lincoln died, and October, less than three inches of rain had fallen on the city. It was a parched matchbox.

There was a quirky story in the Chicago newspapers that day. On Saturday night, the adventurer George Francis Train gave a lecture at Chicago's Farwell Hall. Train was internationally famous for his 1870 breakneck journey around the world. He had left New York City for San Francisco, then continued west on to Japan, Hong Kong, Egypt, Marseilles, and Liverpool before returning to New York exactly sixty-seven days later. The adventure is credited with inspiring Jules Verne's *Around the World in Eighty Days*, and it was widely assumed that the book's protagonist, Phileas Fogg, was based on Train. But that Saturday evening at Farwell Hall in Chicago, George Francis Train became an object of ridicule when he suddenly announced, "This is the last public address that will be delivered within these walls! A terrible calamity is impending over the city of Chicago! More I cannot say, more I dare not utter." The next day, Train's premonition was reported in the Sunday *Chicago Times*, which dubbed him the Prince of Blatherskites.

At about 9:00 P.M., with Train's dire prediction just twenty-four hours old, flames were seen shooting out of a barn owned by Patrick and Catherine O'Leary, of 136 De Koven Street. Mrs. O'Leary kept five milking cows inside the barn. Though there is no evidence to support the myth that the fire started when Mrs. O'Leary's cow kicked over a kerosene lantern, it is an indisputable matter of record that the first flames of the Great Chicago Fire came from the O'Leary barn. In an instant the structure was engulfed; the flames spread north and east, whipped up by gale-force winds that sometimes approached 60 miles per hour. In less than ten minutes, two entire city blocks had been consumed by fire. The flames were unstoppable; they raced up Canal Street and turned west at Mather. A shower of "red snow" rained down on the city, burning embers that floated into open windows, igniting mattresses and curtains as people slept in their homes. Flaming shingles were blown off roofs and hoisted across the Chicago River by the high winds. Now the North Side was hit by this missile attack. Twenty city blocks were ablaze.

At 653 Wabash Avenue, Robert Lincoln, his mother Mary, and their houseguest John Hay watched with mounting panic as the city around them became a raging inferno. The Lincoln house was soon in real danger of going up in flames. They all fled for their lives into the streets of Chicago. What they encountered was sheer terror, and the end of law and order. Refugees escaping with their valuables bundled in blankets were being robbed by bands of intoxicated thugs. On the North Side, the foreman of a firefighting unit trying to save the city ordered his men to turn the water hoses on a rowdy mob of three hundred drunks.

No great building or personage was immune. The Dearborn Street headquarters of the *Chicago Times*, which just that morning had mocked George Francis Train for his premonition of disaster, went up in flames as its editorial staff struggled to put out a special edition. The last-minute bulletin on the front page read: "The entire business portion of the city is burning up, and the TIMES building is doomed." The roof at the Western Union offices caught fire, and, as the flames consumed the building, an Associated Press reporter transmitted the first news reports of the disaster to the world. The historic five-story Tremont House, the hotel Mary Lincoln and her two sons had lived in when they moved to Chicago after President Lincoln's assassination, went down in flames at 3:00 A.M. Former Illinois congressman Isaac Arnold, who three months earlier had accompanied Tad Lincoln's casket on the funeral train to Springfield, was now in the fight of his life, as roaring flames surrounded his residence at Erie and Pine.

On Terrace Row, Chicago's most exclusive address, Robert's mentor, the lawyer Jonathan Young Scammon, lived in a magnificent mansion facing Lake Michigan. Scammon was out of town on business, and his wife, Maria, was on her own. Concerned about her safety, Robert and Hay crossed the Chicago River on one of the bridges that remained open and made their way to the North Side. They found bedlam outside the Scammon residence. Workmen were carrying the precious contents of Scammon's immense library out of the mansion and loading it on wagons to be carted off for safekeeping. Mrs. Scammon was personally directing the enterprise. Many of the books reflected Scammon's personal interest in the philosophy of Emanuel Swedenborg, the Swedish Christian mystic who lived in the eighteenth century and claimed to have visited heaven and hell and spoken with angels and demons. Some say Swedenborg was a visionary; others called him a charlatan. The relevant fact is that Jonathan Young Scammon was a practicing Swedenborgian and owned one of the world's foremost collections of works by the mystic. These literary treasures, along with a giant globe of the earth, were being carried out of the mansion.

Robert immediately advised Mrs. Scammon to put a stop to the evacuation of the mansion. He informed her that it could complicate potential insurance claims should any property be damaged. Remain calm and stay put, Robert advised her, adding that Terrace Row, at least for the time being, did not appear to be in any imminent danger. Maria Scammon considered what Robert said. Then she went to the fourth floor of her mansion and peered out at the city landscape that lay before her in flames.

Maria Scammon was very fond of Robert, but his advice that she should remain where she was sounded officious and even ridiculous. No doubt she appreciated Robert's concern; it was an act of physical daring for him and John Hay to cut a swath across the city in these perilous hours. But she chose to ignore what Robert had advised, and ordered the teamsters to continue with the evacuation. It was a good thing she did. At noon, the fire came roaring down Terrace Row. Not one mansion on the row was left standing.

It is believed that Mary Lincoln spent the first night of the Great Chicago Fire along the shores of Lake Michigan. Thousands of terrified citizens, rich and poor, converged on the lake, thinking that the water afforded them natural protection against the encroaching flames. Flying sparks cascaded down from the skies and fell on the panicked multitude. Smoke from belching flames blinded their eyes. Young girls covered their heads with shawls to stop the embers from torching their hair. Holes were dug in the sand, and women and children climbed into them for shelter, leaving just an air hole through which they could breathe. Others, who could feel the scorching heat from burning buildings along the shore, jumped into Lake Michigan and stood in water up to their neck so their clothes would not catch fire.

The Crosby Opera House, where Robert Lincoln had lived as a young bachelor, was lost at 5:00 A.M. *Chicago Tribune* publisher Joseph Medill ordered his stone building at Dearborn and Madison abandoned after the presses in the basement started to melt. Medill asked each of his employees to take home a bound volume of the *Tribune* dating back to 1860. It meant the world to a newspaperman like Medill to rescue those archived editions and preserve his legacy.

On Monday night at eleven o'clock, rain started to fall. The wind died down. As dawn broke on Tuesday, it was time to survey the damage. The fire had killed between 200 and 300 people. Another 100,000 had been left homeless—nearly a third of the city's populace. More than 17,000 buildings had been destroyed. Downtown Chicago no longer existed. The *Chicago Tribune* suspended publication for two days until it found a small printing press on the West Side. Its first story on the fire appeared on Wednesday, October 11: "During Sunday night, Monday and Tuesday, this city has been swept up by a conflagration which has no parallel in the annals of history. . . . A fire in a barn on the West Side was the significant cause of a conflagration which has swept out of existence hundreds of millions of property, has reduced to poverty thousands who, the day before, were in a state of opulence." A letter written to his brother by William H. Carter, president of the city's board of public works, vividly portrays Chicago in the immediate aftermath of the Great Fire. "Our beautiful city is in ruins," Carter said. "The greatest calamity that ever befell a city is upon us. . . . The Homestead, built by my own hands out of my own hard earnings, is gone—a total wreck. It was the first home I could call my own, where my children were born. . . . Good Bye to 46 Van Buren St. It went up in a cloud of fire and desolation is all around it."

The renowned landscape architect Frederick Law Olmsted was sent to Chicago by the *Nation* magazine to report firsthand on the destruction. He found a field of ruins a mile wide and four miles in length—approximately comparable to the area of Manhattan between the Battery and Central Park. "The distinguishing smell of the ruins is that of charred earth," Olmsted reported. "Besides the extent of the ruins what is most remarkable is the completeness with which the fire did its work." But the spirit of the city impressed Olmsted. The cleanup was proceeding in a driving, steady, and organized manner. Legend has it that one enterprising citizen was seen "poking about" in the still-smoldering ruins near the *Tribune* building, picking out bricks that had cooled off enough to be used again. The very morning that the flames died out, the first building to rise from the ashes was erected. It was a tiny shed constructed with wood planks at 59 Union Park Place by a Ukrainian contractor, William Kerfoot. Announcing to the world that he was open for business, Kerfoot put up this crude, handwritten sign: ALL GONE BUT WIFE CHILDREN AND ENERGY.

While the city was still a smoldering ruin, Chicagoans were already thinking about tomorrow.

For Mary Lincoln, still shaken by Tad's death, Chicago after the Great Fire must have seemed like hell on earth. Wabash Avenue lay in ruins. Every house was down, Robert's included. The only structure on Wabash that was spared total destruction was the Methodist church. Certain letters and documents written by Abraham Lincoln that Robert kept stored in his home were lost forever in the conflagration. Fortunately, the preponderance of Abraham Lincoln's presidential papers was safely locked away in Bloomington, Illinois, 130 miles away, under the care and custody of David Davis. But Robert's entire law library was destroyed, and his downtown law office also was a total loss.

Finding Chicago uninhabitable, Mary once again packed her bags. Just a few days after her city became a wasteland, she found refuge forty miles west in the small town of St. Charles, Illinois. There, her face covered by a heavy black veil, she appeared at the front desk of the Howard House Hotel and registered as a guest under the name Mrs. May.

To certain people in the United States, the Howard House Hotel, at the corner of Third and Illinois Streets, was a magical place that tugged at them with an irresistible force, for this was the residence of Caroline Howard, the most famous spiritualist in the West.

Caroline Howard was sixty years old when Mary Lincoln checked into her hotel. During her long marriage to Leonard Howard she had given birth to fourteen children, five of whom died in infancy. The Howards were among the earliest settlers of St. Charles, arriving from New York State in

1837. Leonard Howard built a large Greek revival house for his family on the east side of the Fox River. They lived a simple life and earned extra money taking in boarders; five boarders were residing with the Howards during the 1850 census, all from Ireland. At some point, the Howards bought the hotel in St. Charles and renamed it Howard House. Among spiritualists, Mrs. Howard was considered the real deal, blessed with the power of conjuring the spirits of the dead and serving as a medium between those grieving on mortal earth and their loved ones in the hereafter. Just as grieving Civil War widows had made the spiritual novel *The Gates Ajar* a best seller, so they now flocked to St. Charles to participate in the regular séances held in the Howard House Hotel lobby.

It was shrewd of Mary Lincoln to use a false name when she registered as a guest. In that era, a woman put her liberty at risk if she publicly declared herself to be a spiritualist. Mary was surely aware of the case of Elizabeth Packard, the wife of an Illinois minister who was institutionalized in 1860 for three years because of her declaration of faith in the spiritualist movement. But Mary Lincoln fooled no one when she registered as Mrs. May; Caroline Howard very quickly determined that the refugee from the Great Chicago Fire was Abraham Lincoln's widow.

Special arrangements were made, and Caroline Howard invited the former First Lady to her home at 516 S. Sixth Avenue, where her privacy could be guaranteed. Every day Mary would leave her room at the Howard House and climb into a boat to be rowed across the Fox River. After she had disembarked on the east side of town, she would be taken to Mrs. Howard's home, where the psychic put on quite a show. First the parlor was darkened. Then Mrs. Howard entered a self-induced trance. Out of the stillness Mary suddenly heard the sound of tapping—presumably spectral beings trying to communicate from the "other side." There was no doubt in Mary's mind that Mrs. Howard was a medium, putting her in direct communication with the spirits of her martyred husband and her beloved sons. Mary was so appreciative that she gave Mrs. Howard's daughter a gift of a shawl, which was treasured in the Howard family for more than 120 years before it was sold at auction in the 1990s.

Mary's journey into the supernatural took her next to the bleak village of Moravia, in upstate New York, about thirty miles from Syracuse, the heart of what Mary's biographer, Jean H. Baker, called "dark parlor country." Twenty-three years earlier, on the night of March 31, 1848—curiously, the eve of April Fools Day—two sisters, Magaretta Fox, fourteen, and the eleven-year-old Catherine Fox—claimed to be awakened by a strange and relentless knocking or rapping on their bedroom door in the farmhouse where they lived in the village of Hydseville, not far from Moravia. They said that a spirit they called Mr. Splitfoot was communicating with them from beyond. The story of the Fox sisters reached the townspeople, and very soon dozens of people went to the house and swore they could hear the inexplicable tapping. Over the ensuing weeks, hundreds more followed. A local lawyer took affidavits from the Fox family, published the documents in book form, and the fame of the Fox sisters and the mysterious manifestations at the farmhouse spread around the world. The girls held exhibitions, charged admission, and sure enough, even skeptics came away baffled after hearing the bizarre rapping of Mr. Splitfoot. The likes of Horace Greeley, James Fennimore Cooper, Harriet Beecher Stowe, and William Cullen Bryant all attended their séances. In 1871, after a private session in Moravia, Mary Lincoln believed that the gifted Fox sisters had put her in communication with the spirit of Abraham Lincoln.

The story of the Fox sisters threatened to come undone when a dubious doctor in Buffalo concluded that the tapping sound was a result of sleight of hand—or in this case sleight of knees. The girls appeared to be blessed with the singular skill of adjusting their kneecaps with a loud clack. To prove his point, the Buffalo physician stretched their legs out on cushions; while they were in this position, there was no hocus-pocus racket from the spirit world—just dead silence. Of course, to true believers such as Mary Lincoln, the experiment was immaterial. (It was not until 1888, during a lecture at the Academy of Music on Fourteenth Street in New York City, that Margaretta Fox made a full confession, announcing to the world that she had the unique talent of snapping the joint of her big toe. She then proceeded to demonstrate in the splendid acoustical surroundings of the Academy of Music, and the great hall resounded with the echo of her toe crackling. "I began the deception when I was too young to know right from wrong," she admitted. "It is the greatest sorrow of my life.")

After her experience with the Fox sisters, Mary went to New York City, and there she encountered the most barefaced charlatan of them all.

His name was William Mumler.

Mumler had been an engraver for the high-end Boston jewelers Bigelow Bros. & Kennard. In his spare time he dabbled in photography. One day, so the story goes, as he sat for a self-portrait, he experienced a strange tingling sensation on his right arm. When he developed the plate he was startled to see the ghostly image of a young woman standing next to him. Mumler realized with a shock that it was his cousin, now dead twelve years. On that day, the business of spirit photography was born. Mumler circulated his photograph just as the spiritualism movement in America was proliferating. He quit his day job at Bigelow Bros. and set up a studio on Washington Street in Boston. Controversy over his work drove him out of the city, and in 1869 Mumler moved to Manhattan, where he charged up to ten dollars a photograph.

Today, photographic special effects are routine. Any image can be manipulated or created through Photoshop with the click of a computer mouse. But in the 1860s and 1870s, photography was a new art form. Just how Mumler managed his feat of ghostly invention was a mystery. We know that as an engraver he was artistic, and it has been suggested that he painted the image of the spirits using quinine bisulfate paint, which, when developed in a photographer's darkroom, comes out white. Or Mumler may have double-exposed the metallic photographic plate. Whatever his technique, his photographs dazzled the world.

Mumler's career took a detour after the mayor of New York ordered his arrest for criminal fraud. The showman P. T. Barnum was so offended by Mumler's deceit that he agreed to testify as a prosecution witness during Mumler's seven-day trial. He presented the judge with a photograph of himself with Abraham Lincoln floating over his shoulder. Barnum, who is sometimes credited with the adage "there's a sucker born every minute," said his Lincoln photo came from a photographer he hired to prove that Mumler's photographs were "humbug." Although the case was dismissed by the trial judge for lack of evidence, Mumler's credibility suffered a blow when it was shown that the same "spirit" appeared in several of his photographs, and was very much a living breathing man.

Nevertheless, Mumler's business remained in operation, and in 1872, a heavily veiled woman went to his studio and said she would like to sit for one of his spirit photographs. She called herself Mrs. Tydall. Mumler picks up the story:

> "I requested her to be seated, went into my darkroom and coated a plate. When I came out I found her seated with a veil all over her face. The crepe veil was so thick that it was impossible to distinguish a single feature of her face. I asked if she intended to have her picture taken with her veil. She replied, 'When you are

ready, I will remove it.' I said I was ready, upon which she removed the veil and the picture was taken."

According to Mumler's account, he retreated to his darkroom where he dipped the tintype into a chemical soup and developed the photograph. Only then, as the picture materialized, did he recognize the woman with the heavy jowls as Mary Todd Lincoln, for behind the stout lady stood an ethereal image of Abraham Lincoln, tall, saintly, his hands gently positioned on his widow's shoulders. It was a shocking, brilliantly realized picture. For Mary, it was photographic proof of the supernatural presence of her husband, hovering over her life not as a ghost haunting her days, but protective and wondrous.

With growing appreciation of the trickery that could be achieved in the darkroom, over time the novelty of spirit photography died out. What had once cost ten dollars a photograph could soon be had for the bargain-basement price of thirty cents at one of the numerous spirit studios that had sprung up around the nation. Mumler died in poverty in 1884, and the Mary Todd Lincoln portrait—the last she ever posed for—was his most enduring work.

Mary spent the summer of 1873 taking in the spa at the elegant Stephenson House in St. Catharines, Ontario. The waters at St. Catharines were drawn from an artesian spring so rich in salt and mineral content it had to be diluted before it could be consumed. As a bottled elixir, St. Catharines water was in huge demand in the United States. Before slavery was outlawed in America, St. Catharines, situated twelve miles across the border from Niagara Falls, was a terminus of the Underground Railroad. Mary encountered many of the escaped slaves who had remained there after the Civil War to work at Stephenson House. Invalids, arthritic patients, and women with undiagnosed nervous disorders flocked there for the purported healing powers of the mineral baths. Curiously, Stephenson House also became a favorite of several leaders of the old Confederacy, including Robert E. Lee and Jefferson Davis.

Mary returned to Chicago for a rare joyous event in the Lincoln family—the birth, on August 14, 1873, of her second grandchild, a boy who was blessed with perhaps the most illustrious name in American history: Abraham Lincoln II. Robert and his wife sensibly decided early on to call their son Jack. To bequeath a name such as Abraham Lincoln II was too much of a burden for anyone to bear, particularly one so tiny. It was said that the boy would be permitted to use his given name once he had proven himself worthy.

Mary Lincoln stayed for a time at Robert's rebuilt home on fashionable Wabash Avenue, playing with her granddaughter Mamie, now a winsome little girl of four, and getting to know baby Jack. But for Mary Lincoln and Mary Harlan Lincoln, living under the same roof had never been a good fit, and Mary Lincoln soon switched to hotel lodgings. By now, the relationship between the two Marys had completely ruptured. For some reason lost to history, Mary Lincoln had become "violently angry" with her daughter-in-law. Robert later maintained the conflict started over some minor affair—a "trifle," in his words—but whatever the origin of her anger, it was something his tempestuous mother had found unforgivable.

Mary Harlan Lincoln could be just as hardheaded; she had refused to greet or speak to her mother-in-law when she came to Wabash Avenue to visit the children. Now the young mother would not allow Mary Lincoln to set foot in her home. She was still permitted to see her granddaughter Mamie, but their visits were usually restricted to Mary's hotel room. On at least one occasion the Lincoln family nanny took little Mamie to the hotel where Mary Lincoln, in conversation with the nanny, proceeded to give her daughter-in-law quite the "tongue-lashing—in absentia." The nanny became so upset at hearing the "insulting remarks" she walked out of the room and loyally reported the incident to the Lincolns. Robert was infuriated that his mother would assail his wife "in the presence of my little girl."

Mary Harlan Lincoln had had enough, and warned her husband that if her mother-in-law ever lived with the family again, she would leave with the children and never come back. Robert had already suffered almost a full year of separation from his wife when she had gone to Washington to care for her mother and taken her time getting back. He was not about to lose his family again. It may also have been around this time that Mary Lincoln discovered something about her daughter-in-law that she found exceedingly troubling: The young mother of two was a closet drinker—it was her "dark secret," according to the historian Jean H. Baker, and quite astonishing for a woman who was raised in a strict Methodist household by teetotaler parents. The evidence concerning Mary Harlan Lincoln's drinking is sketchy. Her mother-in-law made one cryptic allusion to it in a letter in which she wrote about praying daily for her son Robert's continued temperance—presumably a real challenge in a household where alcohol was being abused. How Mrs. Lincoln found out about Mary Harlan's drinking, if the allegations were indeed true, is unknown; what is clear is that she no longer considered the Lincoln-Harlan marriage to be the only "sunbeam in my sad future," as she had called it when her son married Mary Harlan in 1868.

Dr. Willis Danforth, forty-seven years old, was Mary Todd Lincoln's gynecologist, with offices at 1224 Wabash Avenue. Danforth knew that she suffered from chronic urinary tract infections—she referred to it as "my running waters"—the result of a damaged urethra following the birth of Tad in 1853. In November 1873, Danforth paid a house call on Mrs. Lincoln, expecting to conduct a routine physical examination of the patient, followed by a straightforward conversation about her gynecological issues. He was truly shocked at what followed. According to Dr. Danforth, Mary Lincoln entered a self-induced trance to conjure up the dead. She then told Dr. Danforth that she was "possessed" by the spirit of a dead Indian who was inside her head pulling bones out of her cheek and wires out her eyes— "particularly the left one." Every so often, the Indian spirit would lift her scalp and then lower it back in place. After the perplexed Danforth had listened to his patient, his official diagnosis was "nervous derangement and fever in her head." He prescribed chloral hydrate.

Chloral hydrate is the oldest sedative in medicine. A German scientist first synthesized it in 1832, and by the time Mary Lincoln started taking choral hydrate it had become one of the most widely prescribed sleep-inducing depressants in the United States. Chloral hydrate is prescribed to this day, for stress or as a sedative before surgery, but its use is strictly limited to two weeks or less because of the risks of dependency.

During one of his house calls, Dr. Danforth left Mary Lincoln five packets of chloral hydrate in powdered form. That same night, in a state of extreme distress, Mary swallowed the entire supply. The next day she wrote Danforth a note asking for more.

"Please oblige me by sending about 4 powders. I had a miserable night last night & took the 5 you left. What is to become of this excessive wakefulness, it is impossible for me to divine."

Danforth's treatment continued on and off until March 1874, when he started to see Mary almost daily, right through September. It seems likely that by this time Mary had become addicted to chloral hydrate. During one of her last physical checkups, she blurted out a premonition: The spirit of her late husband had come to her, and by numerical tapping on the table, like some Morse code from the spirit world, conveyed the exact date of her own death to her. She was going to die in days, on September 6, 1874. And her son Robert Lincoln was to meet his doom the following year, in 1875, around the tenth anniversary of the assassination of Abraham Lincoln. Mary became so convinced of her impending death that she wrote Robert a letter detailing instructions for her funeral. The letter was placed in a sealed envelope addressed: "*For Robert T. Lincoln, Esq. To be opened by him, immediately after my death.*" Dated August 1874, the letter in its entirety read as follows:

August 1874
Being fully impressed with the idea, that my stay on Earth, is growing very short, I think it is best, to commit my last wishes to writing, knowing full well that my dear son will carry them out.

I wish my remains to be clothed in the white silk dress, which will be found in the lower drawer of the bureau in my room. I desire that my body, shall remain for two days (48) hours, without the lid of the coffin being screwed down. On the 3d day, after my death, Professor Swing [Reverend David Swing, minister at the Fourth Presbyterian Church], acceding, I wish the coffin taken to the latter's church, he preaching the funeral sermon from the 23d Psalm.

Yea, though I walk through the valley of the shadow of death, I will fear no evil; for thou art with me; thy rod & they staff they comfort me. My coffin I wish to be of solid rosewood, but massive silver plate with this inscription.

Mary Lincoln
Died_____

He, giveth his beloved sheep.
On the fourth, 4th day of my decease, I wish my remains placed beside my dear husband & Taddies' on one side of me.

Of course September 6 passed without incident. Danforth diagnosed Mary Lincoln with "debility of the nervous system." It was his medical opinion that Mary's disorder was symptomatic of mental illness, because he could find nothing "arising from physical disease." He ordered her confined to the calm of her hotel room, where she remained for twelve weeks, until November.

After all these dispiriting months of solitary existence in her Chicago hotel room, wanderlust struck Mary Lincoln once more, and she informed Robert that she was heading south, to Florida, for the winter. Robert must have absorbed the news with a mixture of anxiety and relief. The journey to Florida would physically separate his disapproving mother from his unhappy wife, and he could use the peace. But Robert was also profoundly concerned about his mother's state of mind. It gave him some measure of composure to know that she would be traveling with a trustworthy companion, her maid Mrs. Richard Fitzgerald, the mother of the future vaudeville star Eddie Foy. Mrs. Fitzgerald had been hired by Robert to serve as his mother's companion, security guard, maid, and nurse. She was there to look out for Mary and keep her out of trouble.

Eddie Foy was sixteen years old when his mother started working for Mary Lincoln in 1872, years before young Eddie made his mark as a comedian and dancer and patriarch of the celebrated vaudevillian family act The Seven Little Foys. In the meantime, Foy's mother served as Robert Lincoln's eyes and ears. Eddie Foy had clear recollections of his mother's employment in the House of Lincoln. "Mrs. Lincoln had always been a woman of rather unusual disposition," he wrote. "After her husband's assassination she fell into a deep melancholy and after her son Tad died, she suffered from periods of mild insanity. She had many strange delusions. At these times she thought gas was an invention of the devil and would have nothing but candles in her room. At other times, she insisted on the shades being drawn and the room kept perfectly dark. . . . The position was a trying one and Mother gave it up twice, but each time the kinsmen induced her to come back after she had had a short rest."

Accompanied by the game Mrs. Fitzgerald, Mary Lincoln boarded a train for her first excursion into the Deep South since the end of the Civil War and the emancipation of the slaves. She stopped first in Chattanooga, Tennessee, and then went on to Savannah, Georgia, where the arrival of the Great Emancipator's widow was big news. She changed hotels when her visit was revealed in the local newspaper, which described her as looking in "feeble health." It was not until the end of November that she finally reached Jacksonville, Florida. The rest of the journey was an exotic excursion via steamship down the Saint Johns River, inhabited by alligators, manatees, bald eagles, and dolphins, until she arrived at her final destination, the resort city of Green Cove, Florida. Just as the explorer Ponce de Leon had once searched for immortality in the Florida swamplands, invalids now flocked to the natural sulfur springs of Green Cove for their curative properties. The treatment was known as taking the "boil"—a gush of crystal blue water, always at a temperature of seventy-eight degrees, that boiled out of a fissure twenty feet below the surface of the spring at a rate of three thousand gallons a minute.

Mary avoided the resort hotels, and, for privacy reasons, stayed at Mrs. J. T. Stockton's out-of-the-way boardinghouse, where she drew the shades and kept to herself day and night. For more than three months she remained there with her nurse Mrs. Fitzgerald. Then came the night of March 12, 1875, when a dark premonition took hold of her. Mary became utterly obsessed with the idea that her son Robert was dying. She demanded to be taken to the Western Union telegraph office in Jacksonville, about twenty miles away. Mary was so certain of her forewarning that she sent the telegram to Robert's new law partner, Edward Isham, rather than directly to Robert. After all, how could Robert respond to her urgent message when he was at death's door?

"My Belief is my son is ill[.] Telegraph me at once without a moments delay—on Receipt of this I start for Chicago when your message is received[.]" Mary ordered the telegraph operator to dispatch her message right away—"without fail."

In Chicago, Edward Isham received what must have been the most perplexing telegram of his life and showed it to Robert. He and Robert pondered the bizarre message, and Robert decided that the best course of action would be to send his mother a telegram reassuring her that he was in fine health and there was nothing to worry about. But ninety minutes later, another desperate message arrived from Mary in Jacksonville. This time the telegram was addressed directly to Robert.

"My dearly beloved Son Robert T. Lincoln rouse yourself—and live for my sake[.] All I have is yours from this hour. I am praying every moment for your life to be spared to your mother."

The next morning, as Robert fretted in Chicago, Mary Lincoln, accompanied by Mrs. Fitzgerald, returned to the Western Union office in Jacksonville, where the manager, John Coyne, showed Mary the reassuring telegram Robert had sent her. He tried to put the former First Lady's mind at rest, saying everyone back home was fine. But Mary refused to hear any of it and wrote out another muddled communiqué that she telegraphed to Robert: "Start for Chicago this evening[.] hope you are better today[.] you will have money on my arrival."

Nothing could dissuade her. Coyne watched as Mrs. Lincoln, with Mrs. Fitzgerald at her side, strode out of the Western Union office, presumably to arrange transportation for Chicago.

Three days later Mary Lincoln's train pulled into the station in Indianapolis. The information about her precise location was sent to Robert from a telegraph operator who had been asked to be on the lookout for the widow Mrs. Lincoln. Robert was informed that his mother was connecting to the noon train to Chicago, via the Kankakee, Illinois, line. That gave him Mother's exact time of arrival.

Robert would be waiting for her at the railroad depot in Chicago.

II

The Trial

MARY LINCOLN WAS startled to see Robert waiting for her when the train pulled into the railroad depot in Chicago. She stepped onto the platform and saw for herself that her premonition, this sense of dread, and her certainty that Robert was dying, had been a delusion after all. Mother and son greeted each other warmly, and Robert insisted that Mary come over to the house and stay with his family. She declined, preferring to stay at the Grand Pacific Hotel because she and Mary Harlan Lincoln were not on speaking terms.

The city that Mary returned to was in the throes of a remarkable rebirth, having taken heed of Joseph Medill's famous editorial, published in the *Tribune* three days after the Great Chicago Fire: "All is not lost. . . . Chicago still exists. . . . We have lost money, but we have saved life, health, vigor and industry. Let the Watchword henceforth be: *Chicago Shall Rise Again.*"

The Grand Pacific, rubble following the Great Chicago Fire, was now grander and bolder than the original edifice. Its second incarnation was designed in the palazzo style, giving it a cosmopolitan European facade. Seven million bricks had gone into the construction of the six-story exterior. The lobby, known as the Grand Exchange, was overflowing with entrepreneurs and businessmen from the East Coast and Europe, smoking cigars and reading the world's major broadsheet newspapers. Lunch was served between one and three in the afternoon, dinner from four-thirty to six, followed by tea between six and nine, then supper from nine till midnight. European guests were astonished at the quantity of milk that Americans could consume at meals. Wine was rarely served. The activities at the Grand

Pacific were reported daily in the Chicago newspapers. It was a beat, like the police department, covered by a reporter; four inches of space were devoted daily to the hotel's menu for that day, and a list of its prominent guests.

Mary moved into a third-floor room costing forty-five dollars per week. That night she and Robert had supper in the hotel dining hall and talked things over. The decor took one's breath away. The dining hall had an immense frescoed ceiling, seven gas-lit chandeliers, and a red and black marble floor. Robert was awed that after her long journey from Florida, his mother did not seem at all fatigued. He assured her of his good health, but during their conversation she blurted out something that Robert found very unsettling. Mary said that on the morning she had boarded the train at Jacksonville to return to Chicago, an attempt had been made on her life—somebody had given her coffee to drink that was laced with poison. Robert's heart sank when he heard her tale. It reaffirmed his conviction that his mother was mentally unbalanced. He decided that he had to stay at her side, and checked into a third-floor room adjoining hers.

Mary slept well that first night back, but the next evening, with Robert again occupying the room next to hers, there were problems. As Robert lay in bed, he heard a knock. He opened the door and saw Mary standing there in her nightgown and robe. She said she was afraid to spend another night alone. He sent his mother back to her own room, but a few minutes later he heard yet another knock. It was Mary again, pleading with him to allow her to sleep in his room. Robert relented and gave her the bed while he slept on the lounge. This arrangement was repeated for several nights: Mary and Robert would bid each other good night, a short time would pass, and then that knock on the door would come. Robert found it impossible to get any sleep. Finally, he had had enough; he told his mother that if she did not stop interrupting his sleep, he would leave the hotel and she would be on her own.

It was now April 1. In just thirteen days the United States would mark the tenth anniversary of the assassination of Abraham Lincoln. Robert went to look in on his mother and found her in her room half-clothed and in an agitated state. She told him there was a "wandering Jew" in the lobby waiting for her. This man was returning a purse he had stolen from her in Florida. It sounded like another crazy, implausible story. Before Robert knew what was happening, his mother was heading down the hallway to the "vertical railway"—the Grand Pacific Hotel had one of the nation's first elevator systems powered by steam. Robert caught up with her, and as they stepped into the elevator, he decided that he must bring this madness to a halt. He ordered the elevator operator to come to a stop, and told the half-dressed Mary to return to her room at once. She refused. Then Robert placed his arms around Mary and gently prodded her out the elevator. Mary turned on him. "You are going to murder me!" she screamed. She found a chair to sit on in the hallway, and then said that the wandering Jew was communicating with her from behind the wall. Robert was horror-stricken. All of Chicago was going to go up in flames again, the voice was warning her, she told Robert. She looked at him as the voice behind the wall said that Robert's house on Wabash Avenue would be the only one left standing after the fire. She could leave her trunks there, where they would be safe.

Robert put Mary back in her room, and when he left the hotel, there was no doubt in his mind that something had to be done about Mother on two fronts, medical and legal. First, he consulted with his personal physician, Dr. Ralph N. Isham, who was his law partner Edward Isham's nephew. Dr. Isham was forty-four years old in 1875. Born in upstate New York, he had earned his medical degree from Bellevue Hospital Medical College in Manhattan, and in 1855, moved to Chicago and married Katherine Snow, daughter of one of Chicago's earliest settlers, George Washington Snow. The marriage elevated Isham to the ranks of the city's elite. He and his wife had four children and a full domestic staff consisting of a cook, three servants, and a coachman. A surgeon, Isham believed himself to be unqualified to make a judgment about Mary Lincoln's mental health, and put Robert in contact with one of the nation's foremost specialists in diseases of the mind. He was Dr. Richard J. Patterson, owner of Bellevue Place, a private asylum for women, in Batavia, Illinois, about forty miles outside Chicago. Robert met with Dr. Patterson on April 10 and described his mother's symptoms. Patterson charged ten dollars for the consultation.

On the legal front, Robert, perhaps recalling the adage attributed to Abraham Lincoln that the lawyer who represented himself had a fool for a client, hired the distinguished Chicago law firm of Ayer & Kales, which then engaged as cocounsel the state's leading expert on insanity law, Leonard Swett, who had an office in the same building as Ayer & Kales. There was the added bonus that Swett had been a cherished friend of Abraham Lincoln and knew Mary Lincoln. With Swett organizing everything, a topflight team of the city's leading physicians was assembled to provide the most expert medical advice for this delicate situation, with all its historical and political implications. It was no coincidence that three of the six doctors who were hired had also been involved in the desperate race to save the life of Tad Lincoln four years earlier. Now they came on board to establish whether Tad's mother was to be declared insane. Drs. Charles Gilman Smith, Hosmer Allen Johnson, and Nathan S. Davis were working together once more, this time on behalf of Robert Lincoln. Three new members of the Mary Lincoln insanity committee joined them: her gynecologist, Dr. Willis Danforth; Dr. James Stewart Jewell, an expert on mental disorders and the founder of a medical publication that exists to this day, *The Journal of Nervous and Mental Diseases*; and Dr. Patterson, the owner and superintendent of Bellevue Place.

On May 8, Danforth made a house call at the Grand Pacific Hotel to examine Mary Lincoln. It seems likely that he did this at the behest of the committee—certainly a contravention of ethics if one judges Danforth's professional conduct by modern standards. He had not seen Mary since he had treated her the previous fall, when she had told him her premonition that she would die on September 6, 1874, a date that had come and gone without incident eight months earlier. Now Mary sat down with Danforth for an agreeable conversation in her room. She seemed in good spirits, further evidence that Mary, when she wanted to, could still turn on the charm. Florida had been "pleasant," he recalled her saying, and she had marveled at the semitropical Florida scenery. It had been a joy, she said, to be back in the Deep South where she had been raised, as she took such took pride in the customs and manners of the Southern people. Danforth was impressed with her clear mindedness. Mary seemed rational and at ease. Then, out of nowhere, she repeated the disturbing accusation she had made to her son that someone had tried to poison her on her journey to Chicago.

Mary's account went like this: At a wayside station stop just outside the main Jacksonville train terminal, she ordered a cup of coffee, and, as she drank it, she realized it had been laced with poison. Then, in the oddest feature of the story, Mary recounted that she proceeded to order a second cup of coffee, also laced with poison, which she drank in the expectation of inducing an overdose that might cause her to vomit. It was a peculiar and mystifying yarn. What made it so strange, Danforth thought, was that it was obviously a hallucination, and yet the rest of her conversation seemed perfectly rational.

Eight days later, the six consulting doctors gathered for a Saturday meeting at 2:00 P.M. at the Ayer & Kales law firm. Leonard Swett was there, and so was Benjamin Ayer, senior partner at Ayer & Kales. They listened as Danforth filled the group in on the details of his conversation and examination of Mary Lincoln. Next, it was Robert Lincoln's turn. Ever the cautious lawyer, Robert chose each word with deliberation, not wishing to exaggerate or minimize his mother's troubles. But whatever he said, it was enough for the doctors to unanimously conclude that Mary Lincoln was insane and should be institutionalized. They made this assessment even though Danforth was the only physician in the group to have personally treated Mary.

Swett got to work. He asked Robert to request from the six physicians formal letters for the record stating their diagnosis. It was absolutely critical that every doctor commit "in writing to pronounce her insane," Swett said. Then a team of Pinkerton detectives was hired to keep tabs on Mary Lincoln. The detectives put the former First Lady under round-the-clock surveillance, positioning themselves in the Grand Pacific Hotel lobby or outside the elevator on the third floor where they could observe Mary's activities and keep an eye out for any visitors entering her room. A list of potential witnesses was drawn up. Based on what they were hearing from the maids and waiters about Mary's out-of-control behavior at the Grand Pacific, there would be plenty of ammunition for the trial. Nothing, however, could move forward without an endorsement from United States Supreme Court Justice David Davis, executor of Abraham Lincoln's estate.

Analyzing the situation, Davis urged everyone to proceed. "I believe her to be a fit subject for personal restraint," Davis said, using the mildest phrase he could muster for court-ordered institutionalization. He said he feared the consequences "unless action is taken soon." He added that if Swett, in assessing the evidence, thought he could obtain a verdict of insanity, "then proceedings should be commenced at once." But Davis expressed worry over what would happen if Mary were brought to trial and acquitted. Such a verdict, the Supreme Court justice said, "would be disastrous in the extreme, but this must be risked." Davis made clear that the principal goal in this sorry business was getting Mary help, but also protecting the good name and political future of his protégé Robert Lincoln. Mary Lincoln must be dealt with before she committed an act that would lead to another scandal. The opportunity to remove her from the public arena and put her in a place where she could be watched and controlled, he said, "should not be lost."

Very quietly, Robert solicited the support of Mary's family—the Todds, through her influential first cousin, John Todd Stuart, the former mayor of Springfield who had once been Abraham Lincoln's law partner. Robert sent Stuart two urgent letters, and when he had not received an answer, he sent a telegram. Finally, Stuart responded, but noncommittally. A Democrat who had once run for Congress in 1862 as the candidate of the party opposed to Lincoln's policies, Stuart agreed in principle that a conservator should be appointed to assume control of Mary's property and assets, but he was "not so sure about the necessity of *personal restraint*," meaning incarceration in a mental asylum. The concept of putting Mary Lincoln away against her will was troubling Stuart; it seemed heartless and left a bad taste in his mouth, though he added, "I have no doubt but that she is insane."

Two days after meeting with the doctors at Ayer & Kales, the Pinkerton detectives assigned to tail Mary Lincoln reported seeing several people "regarded by us as suspicious" entering her room. The identity of these men was never established. Robert also learned from the Pinkerton team that his mother was carrying one thousand dollars cash that she must have received through the sale of a government bond. To Robert, this accelerated the need for action—she had to be stopped before she depleted her assets. But the most shocking development was the news that Mary was carrying fifty-six thousand dollars worth of government securities on her person. Apparently distrusting banks, and paranoid about another Chicago fire breaking out, she had sewn her fortune into pockets hidden in her petticoat.

Time was running out. Swett prodded Robert to act now—before "the loss of her bonds through sharpers," a nineteenth-century term for con men. Robert gave his final authorization to proceed, at which point Swett hopped into a cab and went around the city reinterviewing key witnesses to be called at trial. He came away convinced that the case against Mary was even "very much stronger" than he, Swett, had anticipated. Now Robert, as the petitioning party, had to take one more step to institute official court proceedings. Illinois state law required that he fill out a form known as the "Application to Try the Question of Insanity." Robert's petition stated that "*his mother, Mary Lincoln, widow of Abraham Lincoln, deceased*, a resident of Cook county, is insane, and that it would be for *her* benefit and for the safety of the community that *she* should be confined in the Cook County Hospital or the Illinois State Hospital for the insane." The petition listed all the witnesses to be subpoenaed who were prepared to testify that his mother, "the said Mary Lincoln is absolutely *non compos mentis*." It ended with these words: "your petitioner prays that a Warrant be issued for a jury of *twelve* good and lawful men, to determine the truth of the allegations in the foregoing petition contained . . . and that said *Mary Lincoln* be declared an insane person after due hearing and proof, and that a Conservator be appointed to manage and control her estate."

Robert filled out the application the morning of May 19 at the Cook County Courthouse. Judge Marion R. M. Wallace signed a warrant for Mary Lincoln to appear before his court at 2:00 P.M. the same day. The trial would take place in just a few hours.

Now there was no turning back.

That same morning, May 19, Mary Lincoln went on a shopping excursion to State Street and stopped by one of the city's finest department stores, Gossage's. She made a rash and inexplicable purchase—eight pair of lace curtains costing six hundred dollars—even though she had no home of her own to hang them in, and ordered them to be delivered to her at the Grand Pacific Hotel. By early afternoon, she had returned to her room. She heard a knock, and, expecting the curtains, opened the door. It was the bundle boy from Gossage's with a package tucked under his arm. But to her surprise there also were two other gentlemen standing there. The first was Samuel Turner, manager of the Grand Pacific, and the other was that distinguished Chicago lawyer Leonard Swett. Mary accepted the delivery and then invited the two men inside. She was a little embarrassed because her hair was unkempt and she was not dressed for visitors. When Mary apologized for her appearance, Swett told her, "Never mind your hair, Mrs. Lincoln, sit down here."

She knew Turner from her two-month-long stay at the hotel, and she had the highest regard for Swett. He was fifty years old with a long face trimmed with chin whiskers. Like Abraham Lincoln, he had a keen legal mind and interesting features. People often remarked that Swett resembled President Lincoln, though Swett carried more bulk and was not as tall. He had known her beloved husband since 1849, when the two lawyers rode the Illinois court circuit on horseback and buggy, serving at various times as opponents and cocounsels. Once they were defending a man on trial for murder and Lincoln was stricken with doubt. "The man is guilty," Lincoln told Swett. "You defend him. I can't." Swett won the case.

Swett got right to it. The dialogue that follows was recorded in a letter by Swett so vivid in its detail that thirteen decades later it still has the power to transport the reader back into that room with Mary Lincoln. He told Mary, "I have got some bad news for you."

At this announcement, Mary blinked, and Turner, the hotel manager, left the room. Evidently, his assignment was to escort Swett to the room and then beat a hasty retreat. Mary and Swett were now alone.

"Mrs. Lincoln," Swett began, "your friends have with great unanimity come to the conclusion that the troubles you have been called to pass through have been too much and have produced mental disease."

Mary absorbed the words and wondered out loud whether Swett was insinuating that she was crazy.

"Yes," Swett answered. "I regret to say that is what your friends all think."

She responded formally, "I am much obliged to you, but I am abundantly able to take care of myself and I don't need any aid from any such friends." But it was dawning on her that something serious was stirring. "Where is my son Robert?" she demanded. "I want him to come here."

Swett answered portentously that she would soon see Robert in the courtroom.

"What court do you mean? Who says I am insane?"

"Judge Davis said so, and your cousin John T. Stuart. Robert says so. And as I do not want to throw the responsibility of this upon others, I say so." Then Swett pulled from his pocket the letters written by four physicians who all believed Mary Lincoln was insane. Mary looked over the names and, with the exception of Willis Danforth, quite reasonably pointed out, "I haven't seen these physicians. They do not come to see me, they know nothing about me. What does this mean?"

Swett kept his voice low and steady. He informed Mary that he had with him a warrant for her arrest. Two policemen were waiting outside, and if she did not accompany him voluntarily, he would turn her over to them. There was no option, Swett informed her—she had to come, and unless she went with him right now, he would be forced to "seize" her. The lawmen were authorized to handcuff her and haul her into court, where the judge was waiting. It was about 2:30 P.M. Swett implored Mary to put on her bonnet and go with dignity, but Mary refused, and she used the only weapon at her disposal—her fierce tongue. With bitter sarcasm she pointed out that as long as Swett was attending to the business of insane people, "allow me to suggest that you go home and take care of your wife. I have heard some stories on that subject about her." This must have cut to the bone, for Swett's wife, Laura, was an invalid, and it was said that she never left the house. Swett later said that when Mary spoke to him that way, she "wounded me . . . worse than bullets would."

Tears were now streaming down Mary's face. "And you my husband's friend, you would take me and lock me up in an asylum, would you!" Mary called out the name of Abraham Lincoln and begged him to "drive" Swett away. But she was now coming to the realization that she had no choice, and she asked Swett to give her a moment of privacy while she found something more suitable to wear to court because her dress was muddy from her morning shopping excursion. Swett shook his head and suggested that she use the closet if she really wanted to change clothes. Mary could not believe it. "Why won't you leave me alone for a moment?"

"Because, if I do, Mrs. Lincoln, I am afraid you will jump out of the window."

Mary indignantly stepped into the closet, and when she emerged she was wearing a simple black widow's dress and a black crepe veil over her face. Swett addressed her. "Will you take my arm, Mrs. Lincoln?"

"No, I thank you," Mary answered bitterly. "I can walk yet."

They took the elevator to the lobby. Outside the hotel two carriages were waiting, with police at the ready. Inside one of the carriages sat the lawyer Benjamin Ayer. Again Swett offered Mrs. Lincoln his arm to climb into the carriage. "No, Mr. Swett. I ride with you from compulsion, but I beg you not to touch me." It was just a short distance to the Cook County Courthouse at Hubbard and Dearborn, and when they arrived there, Swett opened the huge mahogany door for her. When Mary peered inside the courtroom she froze. She was about to face one of the most remarkable proceedings in American trial history. County Court Judge Marion R. M. Wallace was waiting for her, and a twelve-man jury had already been impaneled. The witnesses were all assembled. The insanity trial of Mary Todd Lincoln was ready to begin.

Swett coaxed her in. "Come right along, Mrs. Lincoln. Robert is in here and I will sit by the side of you." She hesitated a moment before stepping inside. A reporter for the *Chicago Tribune* was present, and in his article he recounted the first moment he had seen Mrs. Lincoln enter the courtroom. "The lady was pallid, her eye was watery and excited, and her general appearance that of one suffering from nervous excitement. She was attired in a plain black suit, and was neat and comely of appearance." As she walked inside, Mary saw her son Robert sitting in the well of the courtroom. Every feature of his face seemed to be marked with sadness, and his eyes were suffused with tears. Swett led Mary to the defendant's chair and sat her down. Then he went over to Robert and informed him sotto voce that his mother was already bitterly denouncing him. Swett, a master of courtroom tactics, told Robert, "We must act as though we were her friends. Come sit beside her."

Robert stiffly positioned himself next to his mother, but no words passed between them. Mary listened as Swett informed her, "You are entitled to counsel. Your old friend, Mr. Arnold, is here. He was your husband's friend and maybe you would rather have him and Robert sit by you than have any stranger brought in here." Swett was being clever and manipulative. Counsel had been arranged for Mrs. Lincoln and it would be Isaac Arnold. Swett waved, and in an instant, the sixty-year-old Arnold had replaced him at the defense table. Mary considered Arnold. The two shared a special bond—Arnold, a former Republican member of the House of Representatives, had been the last person at the White House to bid Abraham Lincoln farewell the night of the assassination.

It was at about eight o'clock on April 14, 1865. Mary Lincoln, dressed for the theater and looking fetching in a pink bonnet and a scooped white dress and gloves, sat in the coach as Isaac Arnold came running up the White House driveway waving his arms to get the president's attention. President Lincoln, wearing a high silk hat, backed out of the carriage and asked his old friend if this matter, whatever it was, could wait. He was already late for the performance of *Our American Cousin*. "I am going to the theater," he told Arnold. "Come and see me in the morning." Arnold stepped away and Lincoln rejoined the First Lady in the coach. The presidential valet placed a heavy shawl over Lincoln and the horses trotted off to Ford's Theatre. Arnold stood there and watched as Lincoln looked back at the White House one last time. Mary Lincoln had every reason to have faith in Isaac Arnold. They had remained in contact in the years since the assassination, and not long ago Mary had sent Arnold a gift—a set of Shakespeare's works.

The jurors were seated on the west side of the courtroom, and perhaps never before had such a distinguished panel been assembled. These were not twelve men randomly selected out of a common jury pool and named to the panel after *voir dire*. Judge Wallace had handpicked the jurors, and they included some of the leading citizens of the city. Sitting in the foreman's chair was Lyman Judson Gage, a senior executive at the Merchants Loan & Trust Company. Gage would one day serve as secretary of the treasury under William McKinley and Theodore Roosevelt. Seated next to Gage was United States Representative Charles Benjamin Farwell, who would one day be elected to the United States Senate from Illinois. And

Mary Lincoln must have been astonished to see in the jury box Dr. Samuel Blake, who in 1871 was one of the physicians consulted during her son Tad's fatal illness. Under Illinois statute, insanity trials required the presence of at least one physician on the jury, and Judge Wallace had selected Dr. Blake. The remaining jurors had equally impressive backgrounds. There was Thomas Cogswell, co-owner of the downtown jewelry firm Cogswell-Weber that catered to the carriage trade; J. McGregor Adams, partner in Crerar & Adams, the largest railway supply firm in the Midwest; the wealthy factory owner and foundryman James A. Mason; William Stewart of Stewart & Aldrich; the real estate developer Silas Moore; the wholesale grocery magnate Henry Durand (for which the Durand Art Institute at Lake Forest College is named); and Charles M. Henderson, whose shoe and boot factory C. N. Henderson & Co., was one of the largest shoe manufacturers in the Midwest. The only man who could be categorized as an archetypal American citizen was D. R. Cameron, an out-of-work bookkeeper. Perhaps Judge Wallace selected him as the token representative of the people. With the exception of the bookkeeper, these were all gentlemen of the city's elite, businessmen or political figures whom Robert Lincoln probably socialized with, or knew by sight or reputation. It has been speculated that Judge Wallace wanted the jurors to be so notable that no one could challenge the verdict in this sensitive case. Perhaps an equally sound interpretation was that the judge also wanted no surprises.

The shocking news that former First Lady Mary Lincoln was on trial for insanity flashed through the court building. In quick order every seat was taken, and extra chairs had to be brought in to accommodate the rush of spectators and newspaper reporters. Every now and then when Mary Lincoln turned her head, revealing her profile, they caught a glimpse of her ghostlypale skin.

It was an extraordinary situation. There Mrs. Lincoln sat, having been brought to court under threat of arrest as a defendant in a trial for which she had received no prior notification. She was given no opportunity to organize a defense or question the jurors who had been impaneled without her knowledge or presence. And her counsel was not a lawyer of her own choosing, but a lawyer handpicked by opposing counsel Leonard Swett. It was hard to believe that the target of this farce was the widow of the martyred American president, although it should be noted that the Illinois statute governing the guardianship of the insane was considered progressive when compared to statutes of other jurisdictions, because it required a trial by jury. Only three states—Illinois, Kentucky, and Indiana—mandated jury trials for the involuntary commitment of an "idiot" or lunatic.

The proceedings at the Cook County Courthouse may have followed the strict letter of the law, but even Isaac Arnold seemed to have doubts about its fundamental fairness. Just as testimony was about to begin, he rose from the defendant's table, went up to Swett, and told him that he had concerns about the "propriety" of defending Mrs. Lincoln, but he phrased it in a way that suggested he believed Mary to be insane, and so—in all honesty—he could not defend her. Swett was shocked. In his carefully constructed choreography, this last-minute affliction of cold feet was an unwelcome and disturbing snag. Speaking bluntly, Swett spat out, "That means that you will put into her head that she can get some mischievous lawyer to make us trouble." Swett would have none of it. "Go and defend her, and do your duty."

At this sharp rebuke, the rebellion was over. Arnold beat a hasty retreat back to the defense table. Perhaps he had concluded that he was ethically bound by his prior commitment to those two power brokers, Leonard Swett and Robert Lincoln. There was, possibly, another important consideration—his relationship with David Davis. As Mary Lincoln's biographer, Jean H. Baker, has pointed out, Arnold had ambitions to write the definitive biography of President Lincoln. To produce such a work, however, required access to the Lincoln Papers, which were under the control Justice Davis, the executor of the Lincoln estate. Davis had not only legal authority over the documents, but physical as well. They were stored in his vault in Bloomington, Illinois, and for Arnold to access the material for his Lincoln biography, Davis would have to sign off, and so would Robert Lincoln.

Whatever the reason, Arnold returned to his assigned role. All was now ready. Testimony was about to commence.

The courtroom became very still as the first witness was called to the stand. He was Dr. Willis Danforth, Mary's gynecologist and the doctor who had prescribed chloral hydrate for her. Danforth made an imposing witness. He was one of the city's leading physicians and a member of the faculty at Hahnemann Medical College and the Chicago Homeopathic Medical College. He was also a war hero. Although he had been thirty-five and married when the Civil War broke out and thus ineligible for the draft, he talked his way into the army because of his belief that "my country was bigger than my family." He served, not as a surgeon as one would expect with his education, but as a captain in the cavalry.

As Danforth took the stand, Leonard Swett remained seated at the prosecution table, looking spent and exhausted. He later told David Davis that he was so "used up" by the ordeal of coaxing Mary Lincoln to court that he had to ask his cocounsel, Benjamin Ayer, to take over direct examination. The able Ayer guided Danforth through his testimony, and the jurors listened as he related how he had examined Mary Lincoln for the first time in 1872, and then again in November 1873, with treatment continuing for several weeks for "nervous derangement" of the head. The *Chicago Tribune* carried an account of Danforth's testimony: "She had strange imaginings; thought that some one was at work at her head, and that an Indian was removing the bones from her face and pulling the wires out of her eyes. . . . She complained that some one was taking steel springs from her head and would not let her rest; that she was going to die within a few days, and that she had been admonished to that effect by her husband. She imagined that she heard raps on a table conveying the time of her death, and would sit and ask questions and repeat the supposed answer the table would give." (As it turns out, Mary Lincoln's description of wires being pulled out of her head may have been her way of describing the agonizing experience of migraine headaches. There is evidence to suggest that she struggled with debilitating migraines for many years.)

Just a week ago, Danforth testified, he had called on Mary Lincoln in her room at the Grand Pacific Hotel, and they had had an agreeable conversation about her recent stay in Jacksonville. The account of Danforth's testimony continued: "She appeared at the time to be in excellent health, and her former hallucinations appeared to have passed away. She said her reason for returning from Florida was that she was not well. She startled him somewhat by saying that an attempt had been made to poison her on her journey back. She had been very thirsty, and at a wayside station not far from Jacksonville, she took a cup of coffee in which she discovered poison. She said she drank it, and took a second cup, that the overdose of poison might cause her to vomit." Danforth said it was his opinion that Mary Lincoln was insane.

Dr. Danforth was excused, and the name of the next witness was called. He was Samuel Turner, manager of the Grand Pacific Hotel. Turner recounted that Mary checked into the hotel on March 10. She was a pleasant and undemanding guest until a strange incident that took place on April 1. Turner said that on that day, Mary had come to his office with a shawl wrapped over her head. She wanted to speak with him at once about some "strange sounds" she was hearing on the third floor. He agreed to go with her and investigate. In the room, Turner said, he looked around and everything seemed fine—he heard nothing abnormal. He left Mary Lincoln and returned to his office. In short order Mary was back in the lobby, this time asserting that a man intent on molesting her was lurking in the hallway outside her room. A skeptical Turner accompanied her back to the third floor, looked around one more time, and saw no suspicious characters. All at once, Mary claimed that she needed to see a gentleman by the name of Shoemaker in Room 137. Turner tried to tell Mary that Room 137 did not exist. When she insisted, Turner accompanied her to the first floor, and they looked into every conceivable variable—Rooms 27, 107, 127, and so on. They found no one named Shoemaker. Turner said Mary became "greatly excited," even inconsolable, and could not be quieted down. She was afraid to be left alone and insisted that Turner find another female boarder for her to share a room with that night. The hotel manager showed her to a room where she spent the night with a hotel servant, assigned to be her companion. Prodded under direct examination, Turner said he absolutely believed Mary that was deranged and should not be left alone. Turner testified to one more subject of interest. When asked if Mary had ever had any visitors during the ten weeks since she had checked into the hotel, he responded that he was aware of just one—her son Robert Lincoln.

Isaac Arnold rose to cross-examine the witness, but it was a lame effort at putting up a defense.

"Did Mrs. Lincoln look as if she had fever?" Arnold asked. Apparently, he was attempting to lay a foundation for arguing that Mary's hallucinations might have been the result of a temporary disorder due to physical, not mental, disease. But Turner did not bite. "Her face was as white as it is today," he answered.

A parade of hotel employees followed Turner to the stand. The housekeeper, Mrs. Allen, testified that Mary suffered from "nervous excitement" and would continuously pace back and forth across her small room and stay awake at night. Twice Mary asked that Mrs. Allen sleep in her room to keep her company. Mary's closet was packed with deliveries from downtown stores that she never opened. Just last Wednesday, Mrs. Allen said, she saw Mrs. Lincoln in a "very much excited" condition, mixing several different powdered medications together into one glass and swallowing the mixture. (Could the drug cocktail explain Mary's hallucinations and peculiar behavior at the hotel?)

Another housekeeper, Maggie Gavin, was responsible for cleaning Mrs. Lincoln's room and changing the linen. Her testimony was gripping and disturbing. She said she had heard Mrs. Lincoln "complain frequently that people were speaking to her through the wall." Sometimes Mrs. Lincoln heard voices coming to her out of the floor. She claimed that her pocketbook had been stolen, but Maggie Gavin said the pocketbook was in the bureau drawer the whole time. On one recent occasion, the housekeeper said, Mrs. Lincoln had called her over to the window and pointed to a plume of smoke billowing from a chimney down the street. Chicago is burning down, Mary cried out. Fear of another conflagration was a recurring nightmare for many Chicago citizens—the Great Chicago Fire had occurred less than four years before and was still a terrifying memory. But this was simply smoke from a chimney. Maggie Gavin said Mrs. Lincoln was a pack rat—her closet was filled with packages from State Street department stores that she had never opened, and she went "out shopping at least once a day and sometimes twice."

A waiter who worked in the hotel dining room was the next witness. John Fitzhenry said he had been summoned to Mary Lincoln's room and found the former First Lady "casually dressed," in a state of wild agitation and shrieking, "I am afraid! I am afraid!" Then she made the strangest demand: she ordered Fitzhenry to find the tallest man in the Grand Pacific dining room and bring him to her room.

Dr. Ralph Islam, Robert Lincoln's personal physician, was called to offer his expert analysis of Mary's state of mind. Isham read for the jury the urgent telegrams ("My belief is my son is sick . . .") that Mrs. Lincoln had sent from Jacksonville.

Three other doctors who had met the previous week to consider the evidence against Mary Lincoln followed Isham as a witness. Drs. Davis, Smith, and Johnson were unanimous in their conclusion that Mrs. Lincoln should be institutionalized. Johnson said that, based on the evidence he was hearing in court, Mary Lincoln was "deranged" and should be sent to a private asylum. Smith said it was his opinion that Mrs. Lincoln was of unsound mind.

Isaac Arnold put up a perfunctory cross-examination of the doctors. With Dr. Smith, he established under cross that Mrs. Lincoln's insanity was due to "events in her recent history" and was not hereditary in nature. This was most likely a maneuver; to state for the record that insanity did not run in the Todd family (Robert, after all, was half Todd) was designed to appease Robert Lincoln. But Arnold never raised an objection about the fundamental issue: admitting into evidence expert medical testimony by physicians who had never personally examined Mary Lincoln, with the exception of Dr. Danforth. It must have been a demoralizing blow to Mary to see these esteemed physicians who had labored so long to save the life of her son Tad, and understood how grieved she was by his death, now testify that she was insane.

With Isaac Arnold barely presenting a defense, the case against Mary was a lock. The testimony of so many witnesses, from the immigrant house-keeping staff of the Grand Pacific Hotel to the city's most distinguished doctors, seemed irrefutable. The stage was now set for the star witness, and late in the afternoon Benjamin Ayer called out the name Robert Lincoln. Mary looked on with glacial composure as her son rose from his seat to take the stand. The handsome young man's face grimaced with the "unpleasant-ness of the duty he was about to perform, and his eyes were expressive of the grief he felt," according to one reporter in the courtroom. Robert began with a recitation of his family's tragic history and the assassination of his father, on Good Friday, April 14, 1865, followed by the long and excruciating death of his brother Tad. All at once, Mary's severe expression gave way to tears, and she buried her face in her hands. Robert said his determination to go to court and have his mother declared insane was upsetting but neces-sary, and in her best interests. "She has been of unsound mind since the death of Father; has been irresponsible for the past ten years," he told the court.

Ayer steered Robert to events of three weeks before, when Mary, in a state of hysteria, abruptly ended her stay in Florida and hurried to Chicago to determine for herself if Robert was at death's door. Robert said he had found her frenzy about his health bewildering, since he had "not been sick in ten years."

He said that he had gone to the Chicago railroad station to greet his mother when her train pulled into the station, and after she had declined to stay at his house on Wabash Avenue, accompanied her to the Grand Pacific Hotel. Robert testified that he arranged for a room next to Mary's so he could be close by during this crisis, but his mother kept waking him up at night to stay in his room because she was terrified of being alone. After sev-eral nights of this bizarre behavior, Robert said he had had enough.

"I told her that if she did not stop such proceedings I would leave the hotel."

Then Robert's testimony turned to his mother's finances. Just three weeks before he had found her carrying in her petticoat all the money she had in the world—$57,000 in bonds and securities, an extraordinary sum in those days. What if somebody robbed her? She'd be penniless. Then there was Mary's recent buying binge. In the past few weeks, she had spent $450 on three watches for Robert (he returned all three to the jewelers) and $200 on soaps and perfume. He expressed concern that she was on a path to financial ruin, frittering away her savings on frivolous purchases. How could any balanced woman spend $600 on lace curtains, as she had that very morning at Gossage's, when she had no home to hang them in? Still in a state of deep widow's mourning, his mother never wore jewelry, yet she continued to purchase expensive bracelets and rings.

Robert was asked whether he genuinely believed his mother to be insane.

"I do not regard it safe to allow her to remain longer unrestrained. . . . She has no home, and does not visit my house because of a misunderstanding with my wife. She has always been kind to me. She has been of unsound mind since the death of her husband, and has been irresponsible for the last ten years. I have no doubt my mother is insane." It was the first public exposure of the clash between Mary Lincoln and Mary Harlan Lincoln, and for Robert, making the revelation in open court with newspaper reporters present must have been an insufferable experience.

He testified that he had consulted with Mary's cousin, John Todd Stuart, and with Justice David Davis of the U.S. Supreme Court, and both of these venerated men of honor had advised him to take this difficult course of action. Robert said they had agreed that his mother could no longer remain "unrestrained." She was, he told the jurors, "eccentric and unmanageable."

Robert was excused, but he was quickly recalled to clarify what to him must have been an imperative issue. He was asked by Ayer whether insanity was hereditary in the Todd family, and he answered that it was not. Again, Robert seemed fixated on establishing that there was no genetic predisposition toward madness that ran in his blood.

Robert was the last of the seventeen witnesses called by the plaintiff, and now Judge Wallace turned to Mary's attorney and asked him to begin his case. Incredibly, Isaac Arnold stood before the judge and announced that he would not call a single witness on behalf of Mary Lincoln. He would not even call Mary to the stand to give her an opportunity to establish before the world that she was sane, as in her heart she believed she was. The only thing the jurors ever heard from Mary were her audible gasps of refutation during her son's testimony. Mary Lincoln was very capable of speaking for herself in public. Isaac Arnold's failure to call her as a witness in her own defense left her with no defense at all.

Now the wily Leonard Swett, who had taken a back seat during the afternoon of testimony, rose to deliver his closing summation to the jury. He kept it succinct. Presumably, he believed the testimony presented in court was so compelling that there was not much left to say, except how sad but necessary it was to bring Mary Lincoln to trial. The jurors had heard from seventeen witnesses in a remarkably short time—just three hours. Perhaps the speed of the trial was indicative of how smoothly turn the wheels of justice when the fix is in. The evidence, he told the jurors, was overwhelming. "The weight of her woes was too great for her," and he asked them to return with a verdict "without delay." No official court transcript of the trial survives. Surely Isaac Arnold must have made some form of closing argument but, evidently, his remarks were so unremarkable that none of the Chicago newspapers thought them newsworthy enough to report in their lengthy accounts of the trial.

The jurors rose and left the courtroom to begin deliberations. A court recess was declared, but very few of the reporters or spectators went anywhere. Perhaps they sensed that more high drama was about to follow. Robert approached his mother and offered his hand. Mary grasped it, and for the first time that day, the voice of Mary Lincoln was heard in court. Some reports quoted her as saying, "Oh, Robert, to think that my son would do this to me." Another reporter heard it a slightly different way: "Robert, I did not think you would do this." Whatever the precise quote, Robert's "response was stifled by the spring of tears" that flowed down his face. He could not speak. Observing this heartbreaking picture, Swett tried to persuade Mary that this was being done for her own good, but Mary shook her head. One reporter overheard her use the word "persecution."

Inside the jury room, deliberations were proceeding at an accelerated pace. For jury foreman Lyman Judson Gage of the First National Bank of Chicago, they came to be layered with matchless hypocrisy. In 1875, the year of the trial, Gage was thirty-nine, a respected banker and financier. But many decades later, following his retirement as U.S. treasury secretary, Gage revealed himself to be a follower of Madame Blavatsky, a Russian-born psychic whose claims of psychic powers included feats of levitation, telepathy, and out-of-body projection. She was also said to be skilled at materialization—the power to produce physical objects out of nothing. Madame Blavatsky founded the Theosophical Society in New York City, in 1875, so it is unlikely that Gage was a follower of the charismatic spiritualist at the time of the trial; he may well have been disposed to believe in spiritualism. It is a supreme irony that the jury foreman in the Mary Lincoln trial—laced as it was with testimony about spirits, voices in the walls, and premonitions of death—spent the last days of his life at an ashram in Point Loma, California.

All this, however, was in Gage's future. Now, on May 19, 1875, the issue for Gage and the other jurors in the deliberation room was the fate of Mary Lincoln. The physician, Dr. Samuel Blake, who had been appointed to the panel as required under Illinois law, commanded everyone's attention. As previously noted, Dr. Blake had at one time been Tad Lincoln's physician. In treating Tad, Dr. Blake told his fellow jurors, he had observed Mary Lincoln firsthand, and could speak with authority about her mental condition. Mary Lincoln, he said, suffered from "dementia or degeneration of the brain tissue." There was no hope for her, Dr. Blake assured the jurors, and the disease would become "progressively worse."

With this assurance, the jurors had heard enough. They deliberated for about ten minutes before filing back into the courtroom.

As jury foreman, it was Gage who was responsible for announcing the verdict, the language of which was dictated by statute:

> We, the undersigned, jurors in the case of Mary Lincoln alleged to be insane, having heard the evidence in the case, are satisfied that the said Mary Lincoln is insane, and is a fit person to be sent to a State Hospital for the Insane; that she is a resident of the State of Illinois, and the County of Cook; that her age is fifty-six years; that the disease is of unknown duration; that the cause is unknown; that the disease is not with her hereditary; that she is not subject to epilepsy; that she does not manifest homicidal or suicidal tendencies, and that she is not a pauper.

Many years later, in 1921—six years before his death at age 91—Gage wrote a letter to a collector of Lincoln memorabilia in which he explained his role in the trial. (Gage's memory of certain details of the trial was sometimes incorrect.)

I remember the fact of that trial or examination quite distinctly, although I could not possibly name any one of the other eleven men who constituted the trial jury, nor could I name the judge who presided.

Little or no effort was made to defend the accused. . . . There seemed to be no other course than for the jury to find the lady guilty as charged. . . . The trial was privately conducted, and I doubt if there was any press publicity given to the case. It did not appear the accused was violently insane, but suffered from phobias or occasional insane delusions. She imagined at times that the city was afire and became greatly excited. She also had a kind of phobia for purchasing on credit goods for which she had no use. The evidence went to show that she bought large quantities of things, had them sent to her rooms, where they were thrown into her closet and the wrappers containing them never taken off.

I knew the lady before the circumstance above named occurred, but not very intimately. She seemed to be a woman of rather superior mind, and of high nervous temperament, and susceptible of intense feeling.

It is rather a startling fact that the leading physician who testified against her [Gage is probably referring to Dr. Willis Danforth] afterwards told me privately that there was no doubt whatever of the fact of her mental abberation [sic]. He told me in substance that it was a case of dementia, or degeneration of brain tissue, that she would steadily degenerate and that within a year or a year and a half, or two years, she would die. . . . That is about all I can say in this connection.

As the verdict came down, Mary listened with a vacant stare. Then she asked her lawyer what it had all meant. Isaac Arnold had to tell her that she would be institutionalized immediately. Judge Wallace declared that the most suitable facility was Bellevue Place, in Batavia, Illinois, about forty miles outside Chicago. There she would be placed under the care of Bellevue's superintendent, Dr. Richard J. Patterson, who was present in court.

There was one more humiliation for her to bear. Robert urgently whispered something to Swett. The lawyer rose and directly addressed Mary Lincoln.

"Mrs. Lincoln, you have $56,000 of money and bonds on your person, and one of the unpleasant necessities of this case is that you must surrender these." He reminded Mary that he could obtain a court order and have the sheriff forcibly take the money if she did not give it up voluntarily. "I hope you will not impose that necessity on me," he said. Swett suggested that she turn the money over to her son. But Mary shook her head and said Robert could never have anything that belonged to her again. Swett tried another approach.

"Here is Mr. Arnold," he said, noting the presence of Mary's lawyer who had put up such a tepid defense. "Would you surrender them to him?"

Mary considered this and consented to the arrangement. But there was a problem—the bonds were hidden in her undergarments. "Certainly, you would not be indelicate to me in the presence of these people. Please take me to my room. It is so hot here."

"Yes, Mrs. Lincoln, I would be glad to take you to your room. Nothing remains but these bonds. Now if you will promise me after you get there that you will give them to Mr. Arnold, we will go there."

Mary nodded. "I am very much fatigued and need rest," she said.

Mary, Swett, and Arnold left the courthouse through an underground tunnel. It was a short ride back to the Grand Pacific, and when they entered the third-floor hotel room, Swett immediately closed the door, found some paper, and wrote the following: "Received of Mary Lincoln $50,000." He handed the receipt to her.

"Fifty-six thousand dollars," she said without hesitation.

Swett stood corrected. "I beg your pardon," he said, and wrote out a new receipt with the accurate amount. "Now, Mrs. Lincoln, the receipt is all right, but we haven't got any bonds."

Mary burst into tears. "And you are not satisfied with locking me up in an insane asylum, but now you are going to rob me of all I have on earth. My husband is dead and my children are dead and these bonds I have saved for my necessities in my old age. Now you are going to rob me of them." With that final outburst she stepped into a corner of the room and pulled up her skirt. She tried, but did not have the physical strength to tear open the secret pockets she had sewn into her petticoat. She called Arnold over. Together, they ripped the pockets apart, and out spilled fifty-six thousand dollars in government bonds and securities.

Dusk had fallen. Arrangements were made for Mary to be kept under observation for the rest of the night. A housemaid was hired to stay with her in her room, and two Pinkerton detectives were positioned right outside her door. Under no circumstances, they were instructed, was Mary Lincoln to be permitted to leave the premises. Swett went home, exhausted from what must have been one of the most profoundly draining days of his life. He told David Davis: "To have advanced on a battery instead would, it seems to me, have been a real relief."

But the drama was not over yet.

The next day, as Robert Lincoln sat in his law office making final arrangements for the private night train that would take his mother to Bellevue Place in Batavia, a messenger from the Grand Pacific Hotel arrived. Mary had escaped! Robert found Swett and they hurried over to the hotel. When they got to Mary's room they saw to their enormous relief that she had returned, but the story that unfolded was truly alarming.

Mrs. Lincoln had made some excuse to the housemaid and talked her way out of the room. She then strode right past the Pinkerton guards, who were too awed by the intimidating widow of Abraham Lincoln to try to stop her. All they could do was tail her to the lobby. Mary made her way to the hotel pharmacy, Squair & Co., and ordered a two-ounce bottle of laudanum and two ounces of camphor, a thick ointment with an intense aroma used in the nineteenth century as a local anesthetic. Laudanum was an opium-based medication popular in Mary Lincoln's time for treating colds, menstrual cramps, headaches, and even tuberculosis. It was all the rage as a painkiller and sleeping aid, with doctors prescribing it without fully understanding its addictive properties. Among the upper class of the Victorian era laudanum was considered a wonder drug. Its use was so widespread that sometimes it was even sweetened with sugar and spoon-fed to cranky and teething infants.

Mr. Squair dealt with Mary's order. She explained that she needed the laudanum and camphor for a bath she was preparing for her arthritic shoulder. Finding the story hard to believe, Squair, who was fully aware of that day's court verdict declaring Mary Lincoln insane, bought some time by telling her to return in ten minutes. Then he watched as Mary walked out of the hotel and climbed aboard a carriage. The cab took her down the block to Rogers & Smith, a pharmacy at the corner of Clark and Adams. The clerk there, after getting some hand signal from the Pinkerton detective and the frantic Mr. Squair, who had followed her into the store, also refused to fill the order. Mary tried a third drugstore, William Dole's, but there too the pharmacist refused to hand over the drug. Now Mary hopped back into the cab and returned to the Grand Pacific, the conscientious Mr. Squair in hot pursuit. Squair found Mary Lincoln inside his store waiting for her order to be filled. He went behind the counter and prepared a harmless concoction of burned sugar and water, and handed Mary a four-ounce bottle. Then she stepped out, and somewhere between the lobby and the third floor hallway, gulped down the entire contents in a bid to end her life. Mary returned to her room and waited for the end, but nothing happened, not even an upset stomach. After twenty minutes or so, she once again boldly strode past the hapless Pinkerton guards and returned to Squair & Co. There she demanded another ounce of laudanum—the first order was too weak, she complained. This time, the suspicious Mary went behind the counter to watch Squair prepare the order. It was a battle of wits between two clever people. Squair told Mary that he kept laudanum in the storage room in the basement. Alone now in the cellar, Squair once again prepared a harmless brew of burned sugar and water. To add a measure of authenticity, he pasted on a label: "Laudanum—poison." Mary Lincoln took the bottle and swallowed the liquid in the hotel lobby.

Robert Lincoln and Leonard Swett were outraged when they put the pieces of the story together. They turned on the servant who had been left in charge, and the woman confessed that she had been been "outwitted, although she had tried to do her duty."

"It is perfectly frightful to think how near she came to poisoning herself," Swett wrote to David Davis. They were furious with the Pinkerton detectives, and resolved to stay in the hotel room until Mary's departure time to ensure there were no further embarrassments. The Chicago police were also called for assistance, and a police officer from the armory was assigned to stand guard over Mrs. Lincoln's room.

In these last hours of freedom, Mary settled down, as her son and Swett hovered over her. She became a surprisingly thoughtful and gracious hostess. She continued to insist that she was sane, and her institutionalization was a conspiracy by Robert and David Davis to steal her money. But she apologized to Swett for some of the cruel things she had said to him about his invalid wife. When evening came, it was time to go. They all left for the train depot in time to catch the 5:15 Northwestern express to Batavia.

This time Mary Lincoln accepted Swett's helping hand and climbed on board the private car that had been arranged for the journey. It was the most deluxe accommodation Robert could arrange, reserved for the director of the railroad and available only to well-heeled passengers willing to pay a premium for travel "in all its appointments," including cooking and sleeping accommodations. Five of Mary's trunks were already on board. Mary turned to Swett and asked him to visit her at the asylum. When Swett assured her he would be there in ten days' time with his wife, Mary responded, "Don't wait ten days; come next week." Boarding the train with Mary were Robert Lincoln, Isaac Arnold, and Dr. Patterson, owner and superintendent of Bellevue Place.

Seeing Mary depart on the train, Swett said, was "painful beyond parallel." But in these last few moments, he was struck by her quiet grace. She was a true lady, thought Swett.

The train pulled out of the depot. The mental asylum was forty miles away.

12

Insane Asylum

IT TOOK JUST ninety minutes for the train from Chicago to pull into the depot at Batavia, Illinois. From there it was a short carriage ride to the mental asylum, where Mary Todd Lincoln's admission was recorded in a bound volume titled "Patient Progress Reports for Bellevue Place."

"Mrs. Mary Lincoln admitted today. Age 56—Widow of Ex-President Lincoln—declared insane by the Cook County Court May 19—1875. Case is one of mental impairment which probably dates to the murder of President Lincoln—More pronounced since the death of her son, but especially aggravated during the last 2 months."

Bellevue Place, situated in the breathtaking Fox River Valley, had once been a private school academy known as Batavia Institute, but it was renamed Bellevue Place when Dr. Richard J. Patterson purchased the building and turned it into an exclusive sanitarium for the "insane of the private class." Only women of wealth and "quiet, unexceptional habits" were accepted as patients, but Bellevue could still be a harrowing place to experience. On the day Mary Lincoln entered the institution there were twenty other patients. Most suffered from depression and debilitating melancholia; all were "ladies of position and culture." Pins, needles, scissors, and pens were kept away from those who were suicidal, though a Mrs. Munger managed to steal a knife from the kitchen and plunge it into her stomach. One elderly patient heard "whispers in the air," and voices in her head. A troubled young woman from Chicago passed her days at Bellevue Place doing "dainty" needlepoint, but Dr. Patterson was concerned about her because she was refusing to eat; she had dropped forty-seven pounds in just three months. Several patients were epileptic. In those days, a social stigma was attached to epilepsy, and epileptics were treated as outcasts to be sent off to mental institutions. The haunting music of Beethoven and Chopin filled the asylum hallways. It was played by an accomplished pianist who was incarcerated there. The top floor housed the most serious cases. There, one patient was a catatonic; another used the floor of her room as her toilet. One woman's head was shaved because she could not stop pulling her hair out. Screams from these tortured souls resounded throughout the building.

Dr. Patterson's core conviction was that mental illness could be cured through peace, quiet, and a bucolic setting. Consequently, he turned the sixteen-acre grounds into a landscape adorned with soothing flower beds, hammocks, lawn chairs, and a greenhouse where one thousand roses bloomed. Everything was designed for rest. Fresh air, a healthy diet, and above all peaceful relaxation were the fundamental ingredients of his treatment. Physical exertion was severely restricted, limited to piano playing, the occasional croquet game on the lawn, and as a special treat, a carriage ride into town. A regimented life with simple and undemanding activities such as sewing and arts and crafts was what Dr. Patterson thought was best for his patients.

Robert Lincoln considered it a "blessing" that Patterson was able to take on his mother as a patient. Patients at Bellevue were treated firmly but humanely and with courtesy. Patterson was a reformist who professed that the mentally ill should be contained with the least physical restraint possible. There were no shackles or straitjackets at Bellevue. He prescribed medicine only when "absolutely necessary," although this policy did not stop him from distributing chloral hydrate at bedtime. To steady his patients' nerves he sometimes even prescribed marijuana, or served beer, or eggnog laced with two teaspoons of whiskey.

Bellevue Place was a family business. Patterson's redoubtable wife was the sanitarium's matron, and a son, John, the in-house gynecologist and his father's chief medical assistant. The ratio of staff to patients was impressive: twenty patients cared for by a dozen nurses and assistants.

Mary Lincoln was shown up the spiral staircase to her room on the second floor. It was simply furnished but clean, with just a single bed, a bureau, rocking chair, lounge, and a clock on the wall. She slept well that first night, but the morning of her first full day there she was understandably nervous—her pulse was one hundred, but according to the daily patient progress report, Mary seemed content, talkative, and even "cheerful." She took a long walk on her third day of incarceration and familiarized herself with the lovely grounds, and the next day she went out for her first carriage ride into town.

Robert Lincoln came to see her on May 26, and came away impressed with the facility and his mother's acceptance of her situation. The typical fee for a Bellevue patient ranged from fifteen to twenty-five dollars a week, but Mary's rate was the highest, forty-five dollars, because she had one of the better rooms, with a private bath; unlimited access to a carriage for rides into Geneva or Batavia; and a private attendant to bring meals to her room and do her laundry and other menial chores. This attendant was also a paid informant who spied on Mary through the wooden slats in her adjoining room. She was told to report any suspicious or strange behavior to Dr. Patterson, who would then presumably pass the information on to Robert. Because Mary was finicky about beds, Robert also arranged for his mother to have a clean new mattress.

In preparation for Mary's incarceration, the bars on her windows had been replaced by a decorative screen, but upon consideration of her suicide attempts on the night of May 19, Patterson decided to enhance the level of security, and installed strong wire mesh in the windows. The object, he declared, was to keep Mary safe in her room while making security "as unobjectionable as it is possible." Mary had more freedom than most of the other patients to roam the grounds and head into town whenever she wanted, as long as asylum personnel accompanied her. Sometimes she had the privilege of eating dinner with the Pattersons, who lived on the first floor. Every now and then she went downstairs to chat with Mrs. Patterson, and she showed her good heart when she befriended the Pattersons' retarded daughter, Blanche. But at night, like everyone else, Mary was locked in her room, with the key kept in the possession of her personal attendant.

The second week of her incarceration, something happened to Mary. Bellevue's patient records indicate that she became "very melancholy," and "quite restless and uneasy." She spent entire days in her room. Robert came to see her on June 2 and then again on June 17, and he also noticed a change in her behavior—"he thought her not quite so cordial in her manner toward him as at previous visits." Apparently, they had had a disagreement about a trunk that Mary was supposed to send back to Chicago, and Robert had become very cross with her. By early July, Mary had sunk into a depression and was refusing to get out of bed. On July 5, she just burst into tears. The staff sometimes found her prickly and fickle; she would make an appointment for a carriage ride in the morning and, when the time came, put off the ride until the evening, and later cancel it altogether. Some of the staff complaints against Mary seem picayune. They accused the former First Lady of being "capricious" about her food. For breakfast she would order corn bread, but when it was placed before her, ask for rolls instead. This pattern repeated itself at supper when she would ask for griddlecakes and then refuse to touch them.

So passed six excruciating weeks. Mary was in a low-key state of rebellion that she was clever enough to keep in check. But within her a rage was boiling. She had probably come to the realization that the court proceedings that had resulted in the declaration of her insanity had been a true circus. And she also came to realize the full scope of her son's treachery. The old adage that even paranoids have enemies proved true for Mary Lincoln. Those sketchy characters lurking in the hallway at the Grand Pacific Hotel that she had thought were intent on molesting her were, it turned out, real. They were Pinkerton detectives who had been hired by Robert to keep her under surveillance. The feeble defense put up by her old friend Isaac Arnold galled her. There was a whiff of malfeasance about the trial; it now must have become obvious to her that had Arnold acted as a true advocate, he could have demolished the case against her.

As she thought these issues through in those terrible days of loneliness, Mary Lincoln had an unexpected visitor. Martha Rayne was a reporter with the *Chicago Post & Mail*. In a city with a tradition of sharp journalists, Martha Rayne was considered one of the best. Born in Nova Scotia, Rayne began her newspaper career in Boston and then headed to Chicago, where she was hired by the *Tribune* to write women's features under the pen name Vic. Now she was working for the *Post & Mail*. Just five days before she arrived at Bellevue to see Mary Lincoln, she had scooped her male competitors by obtaining the first interview with General Philip Sheridan and his bride Irene Rucker. The Sheridan marriage was stirring national interest because he was forty-four and his bride was only twenty-two. Combative and resourceful—two essential qualities in any great street reporter—Rayne showed up at Bellevue Place on July 8 without an appointment. The first thing that struck her was the physical beauty of the place. She could not imagine a more enthralling setting, with its undulating hills and the Fox River threading its way through the quaint town of Batavia. Bellevue Place was situated on a natural elevation and reminded her of a gentleman's mansion rather than an institution for the insane. Rayne may have been an intrepid reporter, but she had to admit that as she stood at the front door and rang the bell, her first instinct was to flee.

"Cold chills assailed me, and I anticipated blood curdling cries and heart-rendering appeals as soon as I entered the unhappy domain."

Dr. Patterson himself opened the door, and Rayne presented her business card to the handsome physician. She was surprised when he invited her inside and showed her to his office. After some pleasantries, Rayne got to the point. How was Mrs. Lincoln, she inquired. Patterson guardedly informed her that Mrs. Lincoln was resting and giving him "little trouble" and was quite content at Bellevue. Now Rayne came to the true purpose of her visit. She would like to pay her respects to Mrs. Lincoln in person. Patterson informed her that Mrs. Lincoln "positively refused" to see any visitors, but he was willing to send up the reporter's calling card. Rayne waited. Later she recalled, "I anticipated nothing less than a refusal." But to Rayne's astonishment—and the doctor's—Mrs. Lincoln sent word down that she would be happy to see this lady from the *Post & Mail*. Rayne followed the doctor up the stairs, her heart racing at what was surely to be the greatest scoop of her career.

When the door opened she found herself in a plainly furnished room with a brightly colored three-ply carpet. There sat Mrs. Abraham Lincoln. The martyr's widow rose at once and cordially shook hands with the thirty-nine-year-old reporter, and invited her in. Mrs. Lincoln was dressed in black, with white lace ruffles at the neck and cuffs. Her hair, graying fast, was carelessly coiffed in a knot with a coronet braid. She looked worn and ill, Rayne thought, and her eyes seemed "lusterless." The reporter was startled at the condition of Mrs. Lincoln's fingers, which were "uncared for" and never at rest. Mary wore no ring. The former First Lady was perfectly ladylike and rational, and when she spoke of her late husband her words were tender and evocative. The two women shared several mutual friends, including the writer Noah Brooks, and Mary asked after them. Cut off as she was from the outside world, Mrs. Lincoln asked whether there had been any arrests in the murder of Sharon Tyndale, the former Illinois secretary of state who was shot to death during a robbery outside his house in Springfield. Mary wanted all her Chicago friends to know how much she missed them, and she made a point of bringing up the names James and Myra Bradwell. James Bradwell was a retired Cook County judge and former state legislator, and his wife was the prominent publisher of the *Chicago Legal News*.

When the interview was over, Rayne rose to leave. Mary handed her a handsome bouquet of flowers from a crystal vase on the table and insisted that she accept it. They shook hands and Mary bowed graciously. In that gesture the reporter was reminded of Mary Lincoln's glorious past, when she had entertained ambassadors and senators in the White House. She left Mrs. Lincoln to her memories, and her solitary existence, in her dismal little room.

The article that was published five days later in the *Post & Mail* was vivid, sympathetic and, from Dr. Patterson's point of view, utterly affirmative. Rayne's portrayal of life at Bellevue, with its "pleasant lawn seats, rustic chairs and croquet games," made the place seem more like a first-class resort than an insane asylum. The ambiance at Bellevue was rosy even for Patterson's retarded daughter. In this portrayal, Blanche was fair and delicate, "a girl of much culture," and Patterson was depicted as a serene genius and Mary Lincoln's savior. Mary Lincoln "could not be in a better place for her complete restoration," Rayne concluded. "Here she has no responsibility of thought or action. The noise and panorama of the streets cannot bewilder her. . . . She is unaware of the slightest restraint; and can read, write, ride, or walk at her pleasure. She orders her meals as she would at home, and is served in her room, or at the family table as she prefers."

No doubt Martha Rayne accepted the congratulations of her editors at the *Post & Mail* for another great exclusive. Robert Lincoln was probably not thrilled that the story had been published at all, but on the whole he could not have taken issue with anything Rayne had written. One woman who read the article that day had an entirely different reaction. Mary Lincoln's friend, the so-called lady lawyer of Chicago, Myra Bradwell, read it not as an intriguing feature story on life at Bellevue Place, but as a desperate cry for help. The critical passage for Mrs. Bradwell came at the end of the interview, when Martha Rayne was getting ready to leave. According to the *Post & Mail* report, Mrs. Lincoln "alluded very feelingly to her attachment to Judge Bradwell's family." It struck Myra Bradwell as a curious thing for Mary to say. Of all the people she could have reached out to, why did Mary mention the Bradwells by name? Not long ago, James Bradwell had drawn up Mary's will. Myra wondered whether there was a hidden message here. Could Mary Lincoln be using the pages of the *Post & Mail* to let the Bradwells know that she needed them to come to her assistance?

Right then, Myra decided to take the train to Batavia and visit with her friend. She said she had to "satisfy myself in regard to Mrs. Lincoln's insanity."

Today, in the twenty-first century, Myra Bradwell is a forgotten woman. Jane M. Friedman, a law professor at Wayne State University in Detroit tells the story of calling the librarian at the Myra Bradwell Elementary School in Chicago's South Shore neighborhood in the early 1990s, seeking material for a biography she was researching about the woman for whom the school was named. The school had nothing on Myra Bradwell. "In fact," the librarian stated, "I don't even know who Myra Bradwell was." In 1875, she was one of the most famous women in America.

Myra Colby Bradwell came from a family with a long and distinguished history of political dissent. Two descendants on her mother's side fought at Bunker Hill, and her parents were prominent in the antislavery movement in Illinois. Intellectually gifted, Myra started reading the law in the days following her marriage to the young attorney James Bradwell, with the goal, she would explain later, of working and thinking "side by side" with her husband. She was thirty-eight when she took the Illinois bar examination, passing with highest honors. Myra's formal application for a law license was denied twice by the Illinois Supreme Court—first "by reason of the disability imposed by your married condition"—and then, when that logic was questioned on appeal, simply because she was a woman. When Myra Bradwell appealed to the United States Supreme Court, the country treated her lawsuit as a comedy, with the *New York World* calling Myra that "she-attorney." The only way Myra could win, according to the *Nation*, was if the nine justices of the Supreme Court had "all gone crazy." The state of Illinois considered the case such a foregone conclusion that when oral arguments in *Bradwell v. Illinois* were heard before the Supreme Court in 1873, it did not even send a lawyer to make a presentation. The vote was eight to one against Myra Bradwell, with the majority of justices declaring in derisory language that the idea of a married woman taking on a career independent of her marital duties was "repugnant" and must be resisted.

"The paramount destiny and mission of woman are to fulfill the noble and benign offices of wife and mother. This is the Law of the Creator," read one justice's concurring opinion. Justice David Davis voted with the majority. Chief Justice Salmon P. Chase, the father of that formidable Washington hostess Kate Chase—once Mary Lincoln's nemesis—was the lone dissenter.

The state's refusal to license Myra to practice law in some ways proved to be a blessing, as it allowed her to focus her energies on running the *Chicago Legal News*. Myra was the publication's founder, publisher, business manager, and editor-in-chief. Under the motto *Lex Vincit* (Law Conquers) it became the most widely circulated legal newspaper in America, reporting on the most important cases of the day. Though Myra had no license, through its pages and her editorial positions on equal rights for women and the treatment of the insane, she became an influential policy maker. In effect, if not in actuality, she was America's first woman lawyer.

The Bradwells and the Lincolns had known each other for years. Following President Lincoln's assassination, Myra had helped ease Mary's transition into private life, advising her on where to live in Chicago. One reason Mary purchased her house on West Washington Street was that the Bradwells owned a house down the block. James Bradwell served as Mary's personal attorney when she had need of one, and had drafted her will. In Mary's opinion, Bradwell was a true gentleman—"a just, good man & a lover of *truth*."

Myra Bradwell took the train from Chicago and, following a good dinner, spent the night at a hotel in Batavia. The following morning she arrived at Bellevue Place. Her first impression was one of awe. The grounds were lovely and artistically landscaped, but then she saw the bars on the windows. "I looked anxiously around, hoping I might possibly see my friend. . . . I knew well how fond she was of such strolls. But not a person did I see anywhere around. I ascended the steps of the house and rang the bell. Almost immediately the door was opened by a portly, fine-looking gentleman." (The dialogue that follows is taken directly from Myra Bradwell's account.)

"Is this Dr. Patterson?"

"It is."

Myra introduced herself, and the courteous Patterson invited her into his office.

"Doctor, I have called to see Mrs. Lincoln. She is a dear friend of mine and I thought I would like to see her a few moments, with your permission."

As Myra recalled it, a "cloud" passed over the doctor's face as soon as she spoke the name Mrs. Lincoln. It was an expression, she said, "which I can best describe as flinty, took the place of what before was agreeable."

Patterson told her, "Madam, have you a line from her son, Mr. Robert Lincoln?"

"No, sir, I didn't suppose that was necessary."

"Where are you from, madam?"

"From Chicago."

"Well, madam, you cannot see her unless you have such a paper."

Myra was not going away so fast. She asked the doctor about Mary's medical condition and then wondered why Abraham Lincoln's widow was not allowed to have visitors.

"Well, madam, she is no better—for meddlesome people come here to see her, calling themselves her friends, when in reality they come out of self-interest only."

Myra's back stiffened. "Doctor, please, don't attribute such a motive to me. I assure you my visit is only out of pure kindness to Mrs. Lincoln."

"I did not refer to you, madam."

"Well, doctor, as you are not willing for me to see her, will you allow me to leave a note for her?"

"No, madam, there is no necessity for that. It would only disturb her mind and while she is under my care I shall not permit her to be disturbed either by visitors or letters."

"If she is permitted to see such persons as you choose, and is not permitted to receive letters except from such, *she is virtually a prisoner, is she not?*"

"Madam, she is no more a prisoner than other patients I have under my care."

Patterson kept looking at his watch—"a gentle hint, probably, that I was trespassing on his time." Myra knew that her welcome was at an end and asked to be allowed to remain at Bellevue Place until it was time for her train to leave. Patterson hesitated a moment, then said, "You can sit in here," ushering Myra into the parlor. She sat there and waited for a time, and an odd thing dawned on her: not one person, staff or patient, had passed by. "It struck me as being rather strange, inasmuch as I had heard his patients had the freedom of the house, but this, clearly, must be an erroneous impression of a good-natured public." Myra pondered the moment and made an interesting and bristling observation. If in the future she were to find herself in an asylum such as Bellevue Place, and could see no way out, "it would take but a few days to make a raving maniac of me." She tried to put herself in Mary Lincoln's shoes: "Surrounded by those whose reason is dethroned, kept a prisoner to all intents and purposes, having no voice as to who shall see me or call on me . . . knowing that I was constantly watched and every move known; soon, very soon, would all interest in life cease, and if death did not end the darkness that moved over me, the seal of insanity would surely be written upon my brain, and all that remained of life would go out in that hour."

Patterson was not the first man to underestimate Myra Bradwell. The next day, Myra's article was published in the *Bloomington Courier* newspaper, under the headline: IS THE WIDOW OF PRESIDENT LINCOLN A PRISONER? Patterson must have been apoplectic when he saw it. The subhead was: NO ONE ALLOWED TO SEE HER EXCEPT BY ORDER OF HER SON.

Myra said in her report that she had made the visit to satisfy herself about Mary Lincoln's insanity—"of which so many have of late expressed doubt." The article was more than a journalistic exposé. Myra was what Leonard Swett had feared would happen if he didn't tell Isaac Arnold to do his duty and "defend" Mary Lincoln at her insanity trial, otherwise, "you will put into her head that she can get some mischievous lawyer to make us trouble." Mary Lincoln had finally found herself a mischievous lawyer.

On Robert's next bimonthly visit to Bellevue, he brought his daughter Mamie along to lessen the inevitable tension of an encounter with his mother. Mary Lincoln was delighted, and it took her mind off the mournful memories of the day, the fourth anniversary of Tad's death. It filled her with joy to see her namesake granddaughter. That evening, after Robert and Mamie had left, Mary went downstairs and had a long chat with "Dr. P.," and for the first time asked him about an early release from Bellevue. What if she were to move to Springfield and live with her sister, Elizabeth Edwards? she speculated aloud. Patterson's response was predictably negative. As he understood the family dynamics, he said, Mary and her sister were not even on speaking terms. Mary pooh-poohed such a notion. "It is the most natural thing in the world to wish to live with my sister," she told Patterson. "She raised me and I regard her as a sort of mother."

The conversation was very troubling to Patterson, whose treatment mandated a steady drone of mind-numbing serenity. At Bellevue, even spicy food was banned on the theory that it overstimulated the central nervous system. In Patterson's experience, it could take years of therapy before Mary Lincoln could even think about winning her freedom. By law, Mary's stay at Bellevue was indeterminate and she could be released only after it was established by the court that her reason had been "restored."

Mary's friends around the nation were beginning to make inquiries about the wisdom of keeping her locked up. Robert tried to deflect the issue by spreading the word that the Fox River Valley was "the most beautiful country west of New York." His mother did not have to mingle with the other patients, she had the key to her own room and she dined at her "own private table." Bellevue Place was more like a hotel than an insane asylum,

Robert maintained. But questions lingered. While Mary's dearest companions acknowledged her occasional mania, lapses in good judgment, and compulsive shopping, did it really have to come to this—an insane asylum? Sally Orne, Mary Lincoln's kindhearted comrade from Philadelphia who was so ready to lend a hand in the battle for Mary's government pension, wrote Robert a letter demanding an explanation. Robert responded with a "My dear madam" letter to Mrs. Orne in which he acknowledged "some of my Eastern friends have criticized the public proceedings in court, which seemed to them unnecessary." He went on:

"Six physicians in council informed me that by longer delay I was making myself morally responsible for some very probable tragedy, which might occur at any moment," he explained to Mrs. Orne. Painting a rosy picture of Bellevue Place, he assured Mrs. Orne that his mother was not being held against her will in a snakepit state institution. "My Mother is, I think, under as good care and as happily situated as is possible under the circumstances. She is in the private part of the house of Dr. Patterson and her associates are the members of his family only. With them she walks and drives whenever she likes and takes her meals with them or in her own room as she chooses, and she tells me she likes them all very much." Robert conceded that the damage had been done to his reputation by his mother's stinging courtroom comment. ("Oh, Robert, to think that my son would do this to me.") "The expression of surprise at my action which was telegraphed East, and which you doubtless saw, was the first and last expression of the kind she has uttered and we are on the best of terms," Robert claimed. "Indeed my consolation in this sad affair is in thinking that she herself is happier in every way, in her freedom from care and excitement, than she has been in ten years. So far as I can see she does not realize her situation at all." Here Robert was stretching the truth. One could even argue that suggesting his mother was *non compos mentis* and oblivious to her situation was an outrageous deceit. Robert told Sally Orne that his mother faced a bleak future. "I can tell you nothing as to the probability of her restoration. It must be the work of some time if it occurs. Her physician who is of high repute is not yet able to give an opinion. . . . I can only do my duty as it is given me to see it. Trusting that I am guided for the best."

The insidious letter worked its charm. It was Robert, the noble son doing his duty, who was to be pitied. Mrs. Orne, who was spending the summer in Saratoga, New York, sent him a warm and respectful response, indicating that she had totally bought his propaganda.

"It is a great comfort to hear from your own self, of the loving care and wise guidance which your dear Mother is under," she told Robert. "Not that I ever had one doubt of that, for I know too much of your goodness as a son from her own lips. . . . I can readily see how comfortable your dear Mother is made by your thoughtful care, and can with you believe her happier than she has been for years. Dear precious one! How my heart goes out towards her in love and affection! . . . God give you strength to bear up under this chastening, and crown your days with happiness that such a son of such a father most justly deserves."

It was time for Robert's next bimonthly trip to Batavia, and once again he brought his delightful little treasure Mamie along. This time Mary had two expensive dolls for her granddaughter to play with. During the visit, Mary asked Robert's permission to communicate with her sister in Springfield. It was a deft manipulation by Mary, and when the visit was over, Robert informed Dr. Patterson that he would have no objection to his mother sending a letter to Mrs. Edwards. The medical logs recorded that the correspondence with Mary's elder sister was "at Mr. Lincoln's suggestion." Robert and Mamie headed back to Chicago, and as soon as they left, Mrs. Lincoln called for a carriage to take her into town so that she could mail her letter to her sister. Accompanied by a driver and her personal attendant, Mary went to the post office, posted the letter, and then immediately returned to Bellevue. When she got back, she told the medical staff that the ride into town had been "very pleasant."

But Mary was up to something. The letter to Mrs. Edwards was not the only correspondence she mailed out that day. There was a second letter. Somehow Mary had slipped it past Dr. Patterson and his vigilant wife and the snooping attendant. It was a desperate appeal for help.

The letter was addressed to Myra Bradwell's husband, James. Apparently, Mary, in a black hole of information, was unaware of Myra's first effort to see her, and of her extraordinary exposé published in the *Bloomington Courier*. Lost to history for more than 130 years, Mary's letter to James Bradwell was recently discovered by the historian Jason Emerson. It stated:

> May I request you to come out here just so soon as you receive this note. Please bring out your dear wife, Mr. Wm Sturgess and any other friend. Also bring Mr. W. F. Storey with you. I am sure you will not disappoint me. Drive up to the house. Also telegraph to Genl. Farnsworth to meet you here.

The letter set in motion an unexpected chain of events. Evidently, the Bradwells had followed through on Mary's request and sent a telegram to Farnsworth asking him to see the former First Lady. The very next day, July 29, General John Farnsworth, a flamboyant former Illinois congressman, appeared at Bellevue Place. He was able to get there so quickly because he lived in a limestone mansion in St. Charles, about five miles north of Bellevue Place. Physically imposing, bald, with a long narrow beard, Farnsworth had organized the Eighth Illinois Cavalry during the Civil War and seen action against J. E. B. Stuart, rising to the rank of brigadier general of volunteers. Farnsworth had stood at Lincoln's deathbed—a fact that surely attached him sentimentally to Mary—and he allied himself with the Radical Republicans and voted to impeach Andrew Johnson, which also endeared him to Mary. In 1872, as the political winds shifted to voices of moderation and national conciliation, Farnsworth had been voted out of office.

Dr. Patterson was shocked to see Farnsworth, who candidly informed the doctor that Mary Lincoln "wrote him a note yesterday asking him to come." At that moment, Patterson realized that he had been hoodwinked by Mary Lincoln. As he wryly noted in the medical log, "This note [to Farnsworth] she must have put in the office yesterday when she claimed to have written only to her sister." The good doctor was shrewd enough to realize he could not deny somebody of Farnsworth's stature access to the martyred president's widow. Farnsworth was shown to Mary's room and sat with her for several hours. When he came downstairs he found Patterson waiting for him, and directly informed the doctor that Mary Lincoln was demanding her liberty.

"She wanted him to help her," Patterson wrote in the medical log entry that day. "She makes no complaints—Says she feels under some restraint— Looks better than when he saw her last." Spinning Farnsworth's words, Patterson wrote that Farnsworth "thinks *she does not talk like a sane woman* but still she would hardly be called insane by those who used to know her—he thinks she has been on the border of insanity for many years." Farnsworth put forth a compromise proposal to Patterson: What if Robert Lincoln were to remain conservator of Mary's property while his mother went free? Under this arrangement, Farnsworth suggested, Mary "would not do much harm."

Farnsworth left Bellevue but told Patterson he would be back—next time with his wife.

Heartened by the visit from Farnsworth, Mary Lincoln came down the spiral staircase and handed the Pattersons a letter, requesting that it be mailed out that day. When she left, Patterson examined the envelope. It was addressed to Mary's old washerwoman in Chicago. His antenna was now on full alert; Patterson opened the envelope. It probably did not surprise him to see that he was being duped again, for inside it was another letter that Mary was smuggling out, addressed to one of her cronies who she was attempting to enlist in her struggle for freedom. Patterson confiscated the letter and sent it on to Chicago—"in care of Mr. Robt Lincoln."

The day of high drama was not over yet. In late afternoon, the train from Chicago pulled into the Batavia station, and out stepped the prominent Chicago couple James and Myra Bradwell. They hired a carriage to take them to Bellevue Place, and when they got there they demanded to see Mrs. Lincoln.

Patterson's mouth must have dropped when he saw the Bradwells at the front door of Bellevue Place. That beastly woman was back. Having just contended with the unexpected visit of General Farnsworth, he now had the formidable Bradwells to deal with. He had to wonder just how far Mary's duplicity had reached.

Patterson had been able to swat away Myra Bradwell's first visit as a passing annoyance, one he did not even bother to record in his daily medical log. But this second call was something else, and very worrisome. She had her husband with her, and he was an influential former judge and state legislator. Patterson plainly understood that he had no choice but to show the Bradwells to Mary Lincoln's room. The three old friends had an emotional reunion. Mary would later write, "When all others, among them my husband's supposed friends failed me in the most bitter hours of my life, these loyal hearts, Myra and James Bradwell, came to my assistance . . ." The visit lasted until 7:30 P.M. It was, said Patterson, "a long call," and when it was over, the Bradwells came down the spiral staircase and informed the asylum owner that Mrs. Lincoln should be set free and allowed to live in Springfield in the "tender loving care" of her sister Elizabeth Edwards.

The next day, Mary Lincoln made a point of reaching out to "Dr. P." With the exposure of her smuggling operation, it was time to make peace with the medical staff. It was a stressful meeting. She expressed concern that Patterson would not "trust her again." Patterson was prickly about her "deceit," and said Mary was at liberty to write to whomever she pleased— "but that she ought to be open about it." In the future, he told her, she should send all her correspondence directly to Robert Lincoln and let him judge what should be forwarded. As Robert was her court-appointed conservator, Patterson said, it was the only "fair and right" thing to do.

Events elsewhere were moving at a quickening pace. James Bradwell wrote Mary's cousin, John Todd Stuart, in Springfield that Mary "feels lonesome" and she was finding Bellevue Place to be "unendurable." Myra Bradwell was given the task of communicating directly with Elizabeth Edwards, woman to woman. "I cannot feel that it is necessary to keep her thus restrained," she wrote Mrs. Edwards. "I love her most tenderly and feel sorry to see one heart ache added to her already overburdened soul." Myra told Mrs. Edwards that Mary "feels her incarceration most terribly and desires to get out from behind the gates and bars" and to live with her in Springfield.

Next, Myra paid a visit to Robert Lincoln's law office. On the surface, Robert was calm and deliberate, but he surely was seething inside, and about to make the critical mistake of underestimating Myra Bradwell's lawyerly skills. Myra presented Robert with an interesting proposition: Would he, as Mary's conservator, permit his mother to live with Lizzie Edwards in Springfield? Robert thought about it and said he would raise no objection, assuming that his Aunt Lizzie was agreeable, which he quickly maintained he was certain she would not be. In fact, he said, with a trace of condescension in his voice, he would personally go to Batavia and escort his mother to Springfield if Aunt Lizzie ever agreed to allow his mother to live with her. Then he laid out a condition that he probably assumed could never be met. He said that Dr. Richard Patterson would have to sign a "certificate of recovery" before Mary Lincoln could be released. Both parties sitting in Robert's law office knew this was unlikely to happen. Myra left the meeting dispirited, but still plotting. The next week she returned to Bellevue Place and was greeted by a more conciliatory Dr. Patterson, who permitted her to spend the night in Mary's room. The two women shared the same single bed, a common bonding experience in nineteenth-century America.

The next morning, August 7, was a quiet summer Saturday at Bellevue. As was his custom, Patterson left for Chicago, where he kept office hours one day a week. Myra Bradwell went downstairs at around ten o'clock in the morning and announced that she was going into the town of Batavia, but would return in the afternoon. Three hours later she was back, but she had a gentleman with her. He identified himself as "Mr. Wilkie of Chicago." Mrs. Lincoln was called downstairs and introduced to Wilkie. Then the accommodating Bellevue staff allowed everyone—Mary, Myra, and this man Wilkie—to go to Mary's room, where they talked for two hours. Myra and Wilkie caught a late-afternoon train to Chicago, with Myra promising to see Mary again very soon.

When Patterson returned to Bellevue and heard about Wilkie, he was beside himself. Once again Myra Bradwell had outfoxed him. He felt certain it was no coincidence that the Bradwell woman had picked a Saturday— Patterson's only day off—to pull another fast one. He wrote an angry letter to Myra in which he protested the practice of inviting strangers to see Mary Lincoln without his knowledge.

"In making future visits, if any should be made . . . I will thank you to select some other day than Saturday, the day when it is well known I am absent from the home." Meanwhile, Patterson wondered about this man Wilkie and who he could be. He would find out soon enough.

At this point Patterson had just about had it. He found Myra Bradwell to be so insulting. She had even had the temerity to call him "Mr. Patterson," ignoring his medical degree. Patterson was also under severe financial pressure. Even with everything going right, Bellevue Place was never going to be a great business. It was becoming apparent to him that the continuing presence of Mary Lincoln was a distraction, and posed a threat to his reputation. Abraham Lincoln's widow was just too high profile a patient to suit Patterson's sensibilities. He took pen in hand and wrote to Robert Lincoln announcing a stunning medical miracle. After less than three months at Bellevue Place, it seemed that Mary Lincoln was no longer insane. "I am happy to say that both mentally and physically, Mrs. Lincoln is greatly improved, and as she has expressed a desire to live with her sister, Mrs. Edwards, I see no reason medically why she may not do so unless her condition should change for the worse." How Patterson had achieved this wondrous cure he did not say. But the good doctor who said madness took years to cure, if ever, was now saying that Mary Lincoln should be released after just eleven weeks. Obviously, he just wanted her out of there.

In Chicago, Robert read the letter from Patterson and realized he was facing a public relations nightmare. He could not believe this betrayal. Just forty-eight hours before he had sent his Aunt Lizzie a cunning but dishonest letter in which he declared his utter opposition to his mother's release. Myra Bradwell, Robert warned his aunt, was the "high priestess in a gang of Spiritualists and from what I have heard it is to their interest that my mother should be at liberty to control herself and her property." Now he had to back off, and it was humiliating. The day after he received the declaration from Dr. Patterson that his mother was "greatly improved," Robert wrote a new letter to Aunt Lizzie in which he said that Myra Bradwell had called on him at his law office, and "we had a long talk." Robert now said he had "no objection" to his mother's release, though he continued to believe she was "not entirely 'right.'" Then he added an embarrassing correction: "I said in my [last] letter to you that I understood that Mrs. Bradwell is a spiritualist. . . . I was misinformed."

Robert went down to Bellevue Place on August 13 to visit with Mary, but he spent a large part of his time there strategizing with the flustered Patterson, as they tried to figure out how things had gotten so out of control. It was that Bradford woman who they blamed most—she was a "pest and a nuisance," Robert told Patterson. By now, Robert had also figured out the identity of this mysterious Mr. Wilkie from Chicago. He gave Patterson the troublesome news that Franc Wilkie was a top writer at the *Chicago Times*. It was an "outrage," Robert declared, and now both men braced themselves for another newspaper exposé orchestrated by Myra Bradford.

The more Robert thought about it, the more he realized what a mortifying disaster this was turning into. He had arranged for the institutionalization of his own mother in the most public manner imaginable. He had testified at her trial, and newspapers across the world had quoted him as saying he had "no doubt that she was insane." And now she was going to be set free. Robert stalled for time. He sent Aunt Lizzie another letter in which he said that he wondered whether she was aware of what she was getting into. Then he dropped a bombshell: His mother, Robert claimed, had nearly destroyed his marriage with her craziness, and had once tried to kidnap his daughter Mamie. She had "suggested to a lady (who told me of it with some alarm) the idea of running away with the child," Robert wrote. The insanity trial, Robert informed his aunt, divulged "only a part of the facts, which forced me to act. I would be ashamed to put on paper an account of many of her insane acts—and I allowed to be introduced in evidence only so much as was necessary to establish the case." Plus, Mary was doing so well at Bellevue, he assured his aunt. Those reports of "bolted doors and barred windows" were melodramatic drivel put forth by Myra Bradwell. In fact, Robert added, the only restraint at Bellevue was a "white wire netting such as you may see often to keep children from falling out of the window." He also candidly admitted to Mrs. Edwards his concern that, if Mary were to be released, she could cause another scandal like the notorious Old Clothes Scandal of 1867.

"If you have in your mind any plan by which my mother can be placed under care and under some control which will prevent her from making herself talked of by everybody, I hope you will tell it to me—I do not know who is willing to assume such an undertaking, nor do I believe any one could succeed in it unless backed by the authority of the law, as is Dr. Patterson—He is a most excellent and kindhearted man & as she knows his authority, he has absolutely no trouble with her."

The letter worked its magic, because Lizzie Edwards started to ask everyone involved in releasing Mary Lincoln to her custody to slow down. First, she made it clear that she had always intended Mary Lincoln's stay in Springfield to be a "visit" only—more like an extended holiday than a permanent dwelling arrangement. She now said that she was unwilling to "assume any responsibilities" in caring for her sister. Moreover, she added, her own health was too questionable to take on such a challenge. She was feeling "feeble," and dealing with her own issues of "nervous prostration." She regrettably informed Robert that due to her medical condition she was now "a most unfit person to control an unsound mind." And she apologized to Robert. "After hearing all the facts from you—her position, and difficulties in your family—I do not see, that you could have pursued, any other course." Now Robert had the duty of letting his mother know that she would not be released from Bellevue anytime soon.

"I am dreadfully disappointed that Aunt Lizzie writes me that she is not well enough to have you visit now, but I am going to try to arrange it with her very soon. . . . You must trust me that I can and will do everything that is for your good, and you must not allow yourself to think otherwise."

It was a crushing disappointment for Mary Lincoln. "It does not appear that God is good, to have placed me here," she wrote the Bradwells. "I have worshipped my son and no unpleasant word ever passed between us, yet I cannot understand why I should have been brought out here."

Robert was not finished with his campaign to sabotage her release. His next objective was to muzzle that pest and nuisance of a lady lawyer, Myra Bradwell. On August 14 he wrote a letter to Myra:

"I visited my mother yesterday and I could not help observing . . . a renewal in degree of same appearances which marred her in May and which I had not noticed in my last four visits. I do not know of any outside causes for this unless it is the constant excitement she has been in since your first visit. . . . In view of what I have seen and which I regard as a distraction of the good accomplished by two months and a half of quiet and freedom from all chances of excitement, I am compelled to request that you visit her less often and not at all with persons with whom I am not acquainted."

The next day, in coordination with Robert, Dr. Patterson notified James and Myra Bradwell that he was forbidding any future communication or visitation with Mrs. Lincoln.

"So much discussion with the patient about going away tends to unsettle her mind and make her more discontented and should be stopped," he told the Bradwells. "She should be let alone. She should never have been subjected to this unnecessary excitement."

No doubt pleased with his plotting, and secure in his belief that he had outmaneuvered the Bradwells, Robert took his family on a two-week summer vacation to the resort town of Rye Beach, in Westchester County, New York.

Meanwhile, the Bradwells made their next move. First Myra Bradwell took the train to the state capital and called on Elizabeth Edwards. After speaking with Myra and hearing the full story from her point of view, Aunt Lizzie now came to the realization that her nephew Robert had been manipulating her with stories of kidnapping plots and gangs of spiritualists. She now understood that all Mary Lincoln wanted to do was get out of Bellevue and live in peace with her sister. Lizzie Edwards wrote an irate letter to her nephew.

"I have just had a call from Mrs. Bradford, on an errand from your mother," Aunt Lizzie informed Robert. She told Robert that she had been more than willing to permit Mary to live with her but "shrank from the responsibility after your statement of her condition." But she now had come to the conclusion that Robert had "misapprehended my intention."

"I now say that if *you will bring* her down, *feeling perfectly willing*, to make the experiment."

Aunt Lizzie made just one stipulation, that Robert hire a "competent" white woman to help care for Mary.

With this pledge of commitment from Mrs. Edwards, the Bradwells had achieved a fundamental component of the next phase of their campaign to liberate Mary Lincoln. Now it was time to pour the public pressure on Robert Lincoln and Dr. Richard Patterson.

James Bradwell sent Patterson a strongly worded letter that was promptly leaked to the Chicago newspapers in which he demanded that Mary Lincoln be released into the custody of her sister.

"No, Doctor, if you have the good of Mrs. Lincoln at heart, I am sure that you will see that she is taken to her sister. . . . She pines for liberty. Some of the best medical men in America say that it is a shameful to lock Mrs. Lincoln up behind grates as she has been, and I concur with them. I believe that such confinement is injurious to her in the extreme, and calculated to drive her insane. . . . Will you take the responsibility and run the risk of the American people saying hereafter that it was the restraint of your institution that injured Mrs. Lincoln and proved her ruin?" Bradwell finished off his letter by threatening that unless Patterson complied, he would seek a writ of habeas corpus to "open the door of Mrs. Lincoln's prison house."

Then Myra Bradwell invited a reporter from the *Chicago Times* to her home on Michigan Avenue. The powerful interview was published the next day.

"I have always had the tenderest regard and love for Mrs. Lincoln," Mrs. Bradwell told the reporter, "and during her stay in Florida received many long and beautifully written letters from her. I was inexpressibly shocked when I learned of her alleged insanity, and of her confinement in an asylum at Batavia. I wondered what could have occurred to unbalance her mind so suddenly. It was a matter of the greatest surprise and astonishment to me."

The reporter asked, "Do you think Mrs. Lincoln is insane?"

"I will be frank with you in answering that question. I think Mrs. Lincoln has no more cause for being continued behind bolts and bars than any other person whose sanity is not questioned. She is no more insane than I am."

Myra claimed that Robert Lincoln had agreed to release his mother to the custody of his aunt Lizzie Edwards on the condition that Dr. Patterson issue a certificate of recovery.

"Has Dr. Patterson signed such a certificate?" the reporter asked.

"He has, but it has not yet been delivered to Mrs. Lincoln." In actuality, Patterson had signed no such document.

"Did you learn whether Mrs. Edwards would receive her sister?"

Myra said, "I did. I made a visit to Springfield. I had a long conversation with her. She promised to receive her sister and take care of her. Mrs. Edwards is a lady of fine feelings and cultivation. She has a beautiful home, surrounded by lawns and flowers. It is just the place for a sorrow-burdened heart like Mrs. Lincoln to find repose and peace." Myra revealed that upon her return to Chicago from Springfield, she went to see Robert Lincoln at his law office, but he had "gone East"—vacationing with his family in New York. "Nothing can be done until his return," Myra told the newspaper.

The Bradwells' boldest stroke came next. Myra finally gave the *Chicago Times* the go-ahead to publish Franc Wilkie's account of his exclusive visit with Mary Lincoln seventeen days before. The timing of its publication proved profound and strategic.

The *Chicago Times* was an odd champion to take up Mary's crusade. The irascible Wilbur F. Storey, a Democrat and a Copperhead who opposed Abraham Lincoln's war policies and the abolition of slavery, ran the newspaper. Mary Lincoln may have loathed Storey's politics, but she knew the publisher to be an iconoclast who refused to deal with Chicago's political and business establishment on bended knee. "It is a newspaper's duty to print the news and raise hell," went Storey's journalistic creed. Analyzing the landscape of Chicago newspapers, with the *Tribune* on one end of the political spectrum and the *Times* on the other, Mary had counterintuitively picked Storey's plucky *Times* to campaign for her release. It turned into a masterstroke. Storey had assigned his top writer to interview the former First Lady, Franc Wilkie, a veteran war correspondent who had known Mrs. Lincoln in Washington.

Wilkie wrote an extraordinary article, filled with passion. REASON RESTORED, the headline proclaimed, FOR HER PHYSICIANS PRONOUNCE HER AS SANE AS THOSE WHO SENT HER THERE.

Recently a representative of the *Times*, in quest of scientific facts by means of personal observation, visited the institution of Dr. Patterson at Batavia, and while there was introduced to Mrs. Lincoln by a mutual friend who happened to be there at the same time. . . . The lady appeared in very good spirits, and her mind was clear and sprightly. After some preliminary conversation she invited the gentlemen to her room to obtain a view of the pastoral landscape from that source, and to pursue the interesting conversation already begun. . . . This opportunity . . . to discover the exact condition of her mind, so far as he was able to do so, by drawing her into conversation on all possible topics in which he deemed her to have been interested, either pleasantly or painfully during her life. If there were any weak points in her mind, he was determined to find out what they were. If she were brooding over any circumstances of her sad life, he was bent on finding out what it was. Her visit to London was alluded to, and thoroughly discussed. Little Tad was with her there, and she alluded to the child, now dead, but whose memory is very dear to her, with all the warmth and affection a fond mother might be expected to exhibit. There was, however, NOT A SIGN OF WEAKNESS or any abnormal manifestations of mind visible. She conversed fluently and rationally about her wanderings in England. She narrated her experiences in Germany. . . . During all this time she not only exhibited a sound and rational judgment, but gave evidences of the possession of uncommon powers of observation and memory.

Concerning Mr. Lincoln she related anecdotes illustrating his extreme good nature. She conversed about the assassination. No mental weakness, under any possible test, could be discovered. . . . She very keenly described the characters she had met abroad, showing that she possesses great powers of analysis. She gave her view of foreigners, and foreign matters, concerning which she exhibited great apprehension and acuteness of mind. She also spoke of the books she was engaged in reading and the life she led. Her health at present, she observed, was superb. She had never been better.

Wilkie asked Mrs. Lincoln about her state of mind in Florida, when she had sent those disturbing telegrams to her son, and her subsequent bizarre behavior at the Grand Pacific Hotel. According to the explanation Mary gave Wilke, "She had been suffering somewhat from fever, and her nervous system was somewhat shattered. She was prostrated, and any eccentricities she might have manifested then, if any, she attributed to this fact."

Mary told Wilkie that the iron bars that bolted the door to her room made her feel like a prisoner, but the worse part about being at Bellevue Place was "the presence of insane people in the house, whose wild and piercing screams she sometimes heard." She worried that remaining at Bellevue would in time "unseat her reason."

Wilkie's article ended with these words set in upper case type: "The representative of the *Times* became convinced that her mind was in A PERFECTLY SOUND AND HEALTHY CONDITION. . . . The gentleman departed thoroughly convinced that whatever condition of mind Mrs. Lincoln may have been in previously, she is unquestionably *compos mentis* now, and ought not to be deprived of her liberty."

Robert returned from his Rye Beach vacation incensed at the Bradwells and distressed that the tide of public opinion was turning so fervidly against him. The son of the Great Emancipator found himself cast as the villain, denounced in Sunday church sermons across the land for institutionalizing his widowed mother. Even admirers of Robert Lincoln acknowledged that this "was not Robert's finest hour," and pointed to his "perversely legalistic" way of thinking, which had boxed him into a corner with no face-saving way out.

At the eleventh hour, Robert initiated one more desperate maneuver. On September 4 he hired Dr. Andrew McFarland, former president of the Association of Medical Superintendents of American Institutions for the Insane, to consult on his mother's case. McFarland was a specialist in the treatment of spiritual mania. Any woman who claimed to speak to the spirit world was, by definition, a lunatic, according to Dr. McFarland.

McFarland arrived in Chicago in the "strictest secrecy" and registered at a hotel for the night under an alias. The next morning, September 8, he proceeded on to Batavia, arriving at Bellevue Place and conducting a "protracted, confidential" interview with the former First Lady. In McFarland's opinion, Mary Lincoln needed to remain institutionalized. To release her now could result in tragedy, McFarland told Robert. He pointed to "features of her case that give me grave apprehensions as to the result unless the utmost quietude is observed for the few ensuing months, beyond which all reasonable hope for restoration must be abandoned." For his professional services and expenses, McFarland charged $341.

The McFarland report gave Robert the expert medical opinion he needed to keep his mother incarcerated at Bellevue. But then a strange thing happened. Robert never used McFarland's analysis. The fight just went out of him. Demoralized and defeated, Robert gave up. At last he seemed to recognize that he had been outwitted by his "insane" mother and the "lady lawyer" Myra Bradwell.

On September 11, 1875, Mary Lincoln was permitted to leave Bellevue Place. She had been institutionalized for three months and three weeks, and her release made the medical record books—it was the shortest incarceration in Bellevue Place history. Not long before her release, Mary was taken to Bellevue's office, where the beleaguered Dr. Patterson and his wife told her they wanted her to state for the record whether she had been "unkindly or improperly treated" during her stay at Bellevue—"whether the least impropriety had been shown her."

"No—not at all," Mary assured them.

Mary was driven to the railroad depot in Batavia to catch the nine o'clock train to Chicago, in the company of a nurse recommended by Dr. McFarland named Anna Kyle—the "suitable white person" Lizzie Edwards had insisted Robert hire to help care for Mary. Miss Kyle's salary was sixteen dollars a month. McFarland warned Robert that the nurse lacked refinement and culture, though she made up for it with her "good disposition, sagacity and presence of mind," qualities he predicted she would need with Mary Lincoln.

It took them ninety minutes to reach Chicago. A dour Robert Lincoln met them at the station. Then everyone waited for the 3:40 P.M. train to Springfield. Once again, Robert had arranged first-class accommodations for his mother—and why not, as the trip was paid for by funds from Mary's estate, still under Robert's control as court-appointed conservator. It was the railroad president's private car, and even with the presence of the son who had betrayed her, Mary must have been delighted to be traveling in such high style. She was on her way to her new home, and the loving embrace of her sister.

13
"Monster of Mankind"

WHEN MARK TWAIN wrote *The Gilded Age: A Tale of Today* he was satirizing greed and corruption in post–Civil War America:

> What is the chief end of man?—to get rich. In what way?—dishonestly if we can; honestly if we must. Who is God, the one only and true? Money is God. God and Greenbacks and Stock.

Indeed, the book's title has ever since branded an era.

Robert Lincoln also became an icon of the Gilded Age, but not for inventing a remarkable new machine or creating a bold business that redefined American commerce. Robert's path to riches and power came through the magic of his name.

It was said that had Abraham Lincoln lived, he would have retired to Springfield, or perhaps Chicago, which his wife would have preferred, and opened a law practice with his son. Now Robert Lincoln's law partner was Edward Swift Isham, seven years his senior. They made a good team. Robert was the perfectionist, the tenacious researcher who prepared for trial, while Isham focused on courtroom presentation. It was a reversal of his father's relationship with William Herndon, in which Abraham Lincoln was the public face of the partnership and Herndon performed the drudgery. On those occasions when he appeared in court Robert proved himself an able and quick-thinking litigator. Once he was representing the plaintiffs in a civil case filed against a bankrupt and "hopelessly insolvent" businessman named Windet. Robert rose to his feet to examine the defendant and pronounced Windet's name with the accent on the first syllable.

"Mr. Win-*det*," the witness corrected Mr. Lincoln, accenting the last syllable.

"I beg your pardon, sir," Robert answered, "but I think that I am to be excused for not knowing whether to associate more of wind or debt with you."

For Robert it was a flicker of his father's famous droll humor, and the courtroom roared with laughter.

As Chicago rose from the rubble of the Great Fire of 1871 Isham & Lincoln prospered. Fevered land speculation propelled the local economy, and Isham & Lincoln did its fair share of real estate and insurance law. The bulk of its practice was corporate, and it allowed Robert to associate himself with the leading businessmen of the Gilded Age. The firm represented the Pullman Palace Car Company, Commonwealth Edison, Chicago Elevated Railways, and Marshall Field & Company. Robert personally drew up wills for three of the city's leading citizens: Marshall Field, the *Chicago Tribune's* Joseph Medill, and William L. Newberry, who had made a fortune in railroads, real estate, and banking. Robert enjoyed socializing with men of high rank. He was a charter member of the Chicago Club and took an active role in forming the Chicago Bar Association. He also served as a vice president of the Chicago Historical Society. Through these gatherings Robert networked and socialized and made the connections that elevated his law firm into prominence.

Two months after Mary Lincoln was released from Bellevue Place, Robert's wife Mary Harlan Lincoln gave birth to their third child, a daughter who they named Jessie, after Mary Harlan's sister who died at the age of six. Baby Jessie joined a lively brood. Mamie was now an enchanting child of six, and brother Abraham Lincoln II (Jack) was two.

Just eight weeks after Jessie's birth, Mary Harlan Lincoln received word that her brother William was gravely ill. Will, as he was called, was a lawyer who had gone West seeking a cure for tuberculosis. For a time he had lived in Colorado, but he was in San Francisco when the Harlan family learned that the young man, who was just twenty-four, was hemorrhaging in the lungs. In Iowa, James Harlan was fighting for his political comeback, once again seeking the Republican nomination to the United States Senate, when a telegram arrived saying that Will was on his deathbed. The thought of his son "dying among strangers, thousands of miles from home" anguished the senior statesman. Joined by his wife, Ann, James Harlan boarded a fast train to the West Coast. The race to get to the dying Will in time was closely followed by the *Iowa State Register* newspaper, which reported that in his "lonely trip to meet his son, the hearts of . . . all true Iowans will follow him." Mary Harlan Lincoln, still recovering from a difficult pregnancy, also went to San Francisco, and Will Harlan was surrounded by his loved ones when he died, on January 20, 1876. Mary Harlan Lincoln returned with her bereaved parents to Mount Pleasant and stayed with them a full month before going home to Robert.

Everyone expected great things from Robert Lincoln, and speculation about a life in public service had followed him from the start of his legal career. He had the name, and in politics that meant the world. There was even talk of Robert as a future candidate for president of the United States, although, temperamentally, he was ill suited to a calling in the public arena. No episode had better demonstrated his tin ear for politics than his destructive management of his mother's insanity proceedings.

Even though he had once admitted to having an "almost morbid" fear of such a life, Robert's wife was eager for him to enter politics. Mary Harlan Lincoln had grown up in Washington a senator's daughter, and the happiest years of her life were spent in the dynamic social swirl of the capital that could seem so enthralling to a young woman in times of national upheaval. Against his better judgment, in April 1876, Robert threw his hat into the ring and ran for his first public office, as a member of the Board of Supervisors in the village of South Chicago, about ten miles south of downtown Chicago. South Chicago was populated by Irish Catholic immigrants, Swedes, Scots, and Germans who provided skilled labor for the city's steel and grain industries. Robert ran as a Republican on a clean government platform, denouncing local government as a "gang of robbers" who voted themselves "enormous salaries for doing nothing." He won the election but remained in office just a single year. Politics made him uncomfortable. Plus, he hated publicity, did not like having his photograph taken, and would have preferred never to see his name in a newspaper—qualities that certainly did not suit him for political life. When he learned that the wife of John Nicolay, his father's former private secretary, was abandoning Washington because she could not tolerate the heat and humidity, Robert could not wait to inform his wife that not everyone loved Washington as much as she did. "I shall tell my wife about Mrs. Nicolay leaving Washington on account of the climate." Robert was content to remain in Chicago.

During the historic presidential election of 1876, Robert Lincoln, in spite of his aversion to public speaking, which he once morosely described as looking upon a "vast sea of human faces," campaigned in support of Governor Rutherford B. Hayes of Ohio. Hayes had earned a glorious record in battle during the Civil War. Wounded three times, he had had four horses shot out from under him, and rose to the rank of major general. While fighting during the Shenandoah Campaign in 1864, Hayes was nominated for congressman from Cincinnati but refused to campaign for office, saying, "I have other business just now. Any man who would leave the army at this time to electioneer for Congress ought to be scalped." When he ran for president in 1876, the country was exhausted from eight years of scandal under President Grant. Hayes lost the popular vote by 250,000 to Governor Samuel J. Tilden of New York, but it was the Republican Hayes who ended up in the White House after some backdoor dealing with the electoral college in one of the most disputed elections in American history. For the next four years, Hayes, once so highly regarded for his personal integrity, found himself ridiculed as *Rutherfraud* B. Hayes.

Hayes was grateful for Robert Lincoln's support, and when Robert sent him a congratulatory note, an appreciative Hayes wrote across the letter: "From a son worthy of his illustrious father, Abraham Lincoln." Hayes even offered young Mr. Lincoln the post of assistant secretary of state, even though Robert had had no experience in foreign affairs and no government background except for the year he had served as a supervisor in the village of South Chicago. Privately, Robert was tempted, and also deeply touched, but after consulting with his wife, his law partner Edward Isham, and a few other associates, he turned the offer down.

"He is building up a lucrative practice, and to go away now for any considerable length of time would be to sacrifice it," Hayes was privately told. Robert sent President Hayes a letter saying he had given "grave consideration" to the offer but felt compelled to focus on his law practice "for at least some years yet to come." Interestingly, the assistant secretary of state job ultimately went to Robert's friend John Hay, launching that talented young man on a brilliant diplomatic career that would one day make him secretary of state under William McKinley and Theodore Roosevelt.

Robert now had a friend in the White House, and he used his influence to obtain patronage appointments for a tight little circle of friends, including a Chicago businessman, as minister to Switzerland, and another crony as a collector of Internal Revenue for the Chicago district. In one gesture of goodwill on behalf of the Todd branch of his family, Robert asked President Hayes to name a cousin whom he had never even met, Miss

Mattie Dee Todd, postmistress of Cynthiana, Kentucky. Although she was a Democrat and her father had served in the Confederate army, Mattie Todd received the appointment and remained postmistress for sixteen years.

The Gilded Age was serving Robert Lincoln well. But in the background was the nagging problem of his mother that would not go away. Robert was thirty-two years old when he received a most alarming letter from Springfield, where his mother Mary was living. It was from his Aunt Lizzie's husband, Ninian Edwards.

"I am sorry to say that your mother has for the last month been very much embittered against you and has on several occasions said that she had hired two men to take your life. On this morning we learned that she carries a pistol in her pocket."

ELIZABETH EDWARDS'S HOUSE on Second Avenue in Springfield held profound memories for Mary Lincoln. Mary first went to live with her sister in 1839, at age twenty-one, and it was in this house that she had married Abraham Lincoln. Now, thirty-five years later, she was back, a convicted lunatic estranged from her only surviving son.

Elizabeth Edwards was five years older than Mary. She was a stern-looking woman with a pinched face, and hair parted in the middle and pulled back into a severe bun. Her husband, Ninian Edwards, was a lawyer and former state legislator. His father had been the territorial governor of Illinois and later, when Illinois was admitted into the Union, the state's first governor. Elizabeth and Ninian went down in history as the disapproving in-laws who opposed Mary Todd's marriage to the gangly young Kentuckian Abe Lincoln. They considered him unschooled and uncouth, a backwoodsman not up to their social level. William Herndon quoted Mrs. Edwards as calling Lincoln a "cold man . . . not social . . . abstracted." And Ninian had a troubled and envious relationship with his brother-in-law. He mortified Lincoln when he switched parties to become a Democrat and actually supported Stephen Douglas for president in 1860.

Now, in Mary's bleakest hours, Elizabeth was offering her home as sanctuary. For those first weeks following her release from Bellevue Place in September 1875, Mary Lincoln's transition was trouble-free. She was given her own private room with curtains. The only glitch came when, just a week after her arrival, Anna Kyle, the nurse hired by Robert to serve as his mother's full-time companion, had had enough, and quit. A nurse named Amanda, whom Mary knew from Bellevue Place, was hired to replace her.

But other than these grating personnel issues, the "experiment," as Elizabeth Edwards called it, was going well. Mary ended her estrangement with her sister Frances Todd Wallace, who was married to a Springfield doctor, and also mended her relationship with her sister Ann Todd Smith. The two had severed connections when Mary was First Lady and heard that Ann was ridiculing her behind her back as an "overdressed queen." In this time of need, Mary and her sisters were willing to forget the past and dine and take tea together.

Elizabeth was delighted and rather astonished to witness these heartfelt scenes of reconnection. Mary was behaving in the most "affectionate manner," although not affectionate enough for her nurse Amanda. She evidently preferred working at a mental asylum to caring for Mary full-time, and returned to Bellevue Place after a month in Springfield. She was replaced by a woman who was hired to do Mary's wash and attend to her in every way.

The experiment seemed to be a resounding success, and Aunt Lizzie was able to enthusiastically report to Robert that his mother was taking daily carriage rides and greeting old friends who came to the Edwards's house to pay their respects to her "with a manifestation of cheerfulness and pleasure." Even Elizabeth admitted this was something she had never expected. On November 5, after two full months of steady observation, Aunt Lizzie felt comfortable in telling Robert, "I have no hesitation in pronouncing her sane, and far more reasonable, and gentle, than in former years." Aunt Lizzie explained that Mary's bizarre conduct in Florida and Chicago that triggered her sister's insanity trial had been due to a combination of fever and general ill health, and the side effects of prolonged use of chloral hydrate, which contributed to Mary's hallucinations. "Surely the evidence of derangement exhibited last Spring, must have arisen from physical disorder—she informs me that her health was poor before going to Florida, and during her stay there, and on her return, was often conscious of the presence of fever—moreover, had used Chloral very freely, for the purpose of inducing sleep—Those causes, had doubtless much to do, with producing the sad result. As far as I can judge, she is capable of taking care of her interests. . . . The reunion with her family, receiving the calls of former acquaintances, and returning visits, has already had a very beneficial [effect] upon her spirits."

Instead of taking pleasure in the glowing account, Robert was dismayed. Everything he had predicted would happen upon his mother's release from Bellevue Place ("See if I am not correct, when the time comes," he had written) was proving dead wrong. Robert picked and chose his way through Aunt Lizzie's letters, looking for symptoms of his mother's mental illness that could reaffirm his conviction that she needed to be reinstitutionalized. For example, he learned that Mary wanted to purchase a new veil, bonnet, and shawl. To Robert this was proof that she had yet to conquer her uncontrollable mania for shopping. Robert also wanted Aunt Lizzie to know that his informants had let him know that Mary had turned over silverware inscribed with the name "Lincoln" to a Chicago spiritualist named Mrs. Farwell.

Elizabeth Edwards sighed in worldly resignation at Robert's accusations. In her own sensible way, she tried to set her nephew straight. She wrote back clarifying several points. First, the silverware allegation was a complete falsehood. It was true that Mary had donated her silverware, but it was to a charitable home, and Mrs. Farwell had no connection with spiritualism. She was just a nice lady. And Aunt Lizzie said that Mary deserved a new bonnet. "I quite agree with her that her dust-soiled veil bonnet and shawl were too shabby for her to wear in visiting or churchgoing," she wrote Robert. If shopping gave his mother pleasure, so be it, accept it. "It has always been a prominent trait in her character to accumulate a large amount of clothing, and now that she has the means, it seems to be, the only available pleasure," Aunt Lizzie said. "Is it not best, that she should be indulged in it, as a matter of expediency? I hesitate to presume to oppose what I really think she is entitled to enjoy." Aunt Lizzie had a fundamental appreciation for the fact that it was Mary's money anyway.

Robert tried to strike fear in his aunt's heart by reminding her that the Democrats now controlled Congress and they could vote to revoke his mother's pension, but Elizabeth probably rolled her eyes at this manufactured crisis, because the furor over his mother's pension was yesterday's news. No politician was making an issue of it now. Aunt Lizzie advised Robert to back off. "If you determine to become indifferent to what you cannot prevent—you will insure yourself a greater degree of repose of mind than you have known for years. Excuse me for making such suggestions, as the experience of long years has taught me the most availing remedy in life's trials. . . . Let them alone when you have done what you could."

Mary was making it known to everyone that she could never be completely free until she had full custody of her money. Elizabeth took up the fight in a November 12, 1875, letter in which she told Robert there was "no evidence of derangement" and appealed to him, "for the sake of peace and quietness . . . yield your Mother the right to control her possessions." To assure everyone that she had no intention of squandering her assets, Mary pledged to make a local Springfield banker, Jacob Bunn, trustee of her government bonds. These bonds would remain with the banker, "undisturbed during her life," as she lived off the interest and her three thousand dollar annual government pension. In this same letter Aunt Lizzie assured Robert that in his mother's current will, drawn up by James Bradwell, Robert was the sole beneficiary with the exception of twenty thousand dollars that Mary was bequeathing to her granddaughter Mamie.

The mention of the will may have unintentionally backfired, as Robert was sensitive to whispers that his true purpose in institutionalizing his mother was to obtain possession of her fortune and protect his inheritance. Robert sought out the advice of Justice David Davis, who was in Washington for the fall 1875 session of the United States Supreme Court, and enclosed in the envelope his Aunt Lizzie's letters so that Davis could see what he was up against. Once again Robert was fixated on that new bonnet his mother wanted to buy.

"I merely mention it to you to say that one of the last deliveries [before] she went to Batavia was four new bonnets all of which are in her trunks at Mrs. Edwards & none of which she has ever worn—It is an indication to my mind that no radical change has taken place since last spring," he informed Davis. Robert went on to accuse his mother of donating the silverware to a "Clairoyant woman" who lived just a few blocks from his house in Chicago. "This I have been told by three different persons."

"How gravely [Mrs. Edwards] misjudges on the general subject of my mother's devotion to spiritualism," Robert maintained. "She hardly thinks of anything else and almost her only companions were spiritualists." Clearly frustrated with his Aunt Lizzie, he told Davis, "I cannot help feeling that she is taking a pretty short turn on me."

Like Robert, David Davis refused to rejoice at the news that the widow of the man who appointed him to the Supreme Court seemed to be thriving in Springfield. After reading Elizabeth Edwards's letters and reflecting all day on the problem, Davis concluded that the present state of affairs regarding Mrs. Lincoln was "not encouraging." As Robert had once blamed that "pest" and "nuisance" of a woman Myra Bradwell, Davis now set his ire on Elizabeth Edwards. She was "officious" and "intermeddling" and in ignorance of the "real situation."

"She has no conception of your mother's real condition & evidently does not believe that Spiritualism has anything to do with it while you & I know differently. . . . Your mother has evidently convinced Mrs. Edwards & her other relatives that she is unjustly restrained of her liberty." But Davis also recognized the political reality. "You cannot now send her back to Batavia," he told Robert. "There is no other way left since the Springfield visit—you could not get her back to Batavia."

Robert was biding his time. Under Illinois statute, his mother had to wait a full year from the date of her insanity conviction before seeking the restoration of all rights and property and the discharge of Robert as her conservator. Meanwhile, Leonard Swett, under Robert Lincoln's directive, was already meeting in private chambers with Judge Wallace, who had presided over the insanity trial. Swett and Wallace, in consultation with Robert, were trying to work things out. Robert was certain that Judge Wallace would "order whatever Mr. Swett and I think best," but only when his year as court-appointed conservator was up, in June 1876.

Sensing that Robert was being obstructionist, Mary hired a former Illinois Republican governor, John M. Palmer, who was in private practice in Springfield, to represent her interests. Palmer argued that there was no legal reason to wait until June 1876 as long as all the parties signed off on an agreement to discharge Robert as conservator right away. For Palmer, stepping into the Lincoln family feud was rife with sensitivity. Abraham Lincoln was a god to him and he wanted Robert and also his client Mary Lincoln to know that he saw himself as a peacemaker, not a litigator. "I write under the influence of motives of a different character," he informed President Lincoln's son.

As Christmas 1875 came around, Ninian Edwards was warning Robert that his mother was "very much embittered" and impossible to reason with on the subject of her bonds, which she wanted immediately restored to her control. The holiday season brought more distress to Mary Lincoln—she was "impatient and unhappy" and completely fixated on securing her money. Part of her discontent was the ordeal of facing winter in Springfield. As a woman suffering from arthritis and the aches of old age, Mary would have preferred to spend the cold weather months in Florida, or perhaps California, but Robert refused to allocate funds for a trip. As she shivered in Springfield, she blamed her son.

On January 14, 1876, Ninian Edwards wrote his nephew a remarkable letter. Once again he reminded Robert that for the last month Mary had been "very much embittered." And then he made the disturbing revelation that "on several occasions [Mary] said that she had hired two men to take your life."

"On this morning we learned that she carries a pistol in her pocket. . . . She says she will never again allow you to come into her presence—We do not know what is best to be done—Your aunt says nothing will satisfy her until she has possession of her bonds, and her advice is that all her rights should be restored to her as soon as possible. . . . Nothing else will satisfy her—Gov Palmer advises me to inform you of her threats and to her carrying the pistol—He is of opinion that by consent her bonds may be restored to her. If you think it best to come down you had better not come direct to our house but advise me where to meet you—Except on the subject of the restoration of her bonds and her purchases she is as rational as I ever knew her—Please do not let her know that I have written to you on the subject—The information in regard to the pistol you can learn from others."

Ninian was panic-stricken. His big fear was scandal and the shame it could bring on his household. The next day he sent his nephew another letter. "Elizabeth thinks she could get [the pistol] from her. . . . We do not think she would use it for the injury of anyone." Aunt Lizzie tried to calm everyone down. She wrote Robert a letter of her own. "Your Uncle is perhaps unnecessarily excited upon the subject of the pistol," she said. While acknowledging, "there may be a danger to herself and others," Aunt Lizzie sought to downplay the existence of a plot to assassinate Robert Lincoln and suggested that he write to Ninian asking him to investigate. In this crafty way Ninian would be authorized to make inquiries, interrogate Mary, and confiscate the weapon "without exciting her suspicions of our being the informant." Elizabeth Edwards searched for the revolver and on one occasion looked through her sister's handbag when Mary was not around but could not find it. Where Mary was keeping the weapon at the ready, no one knew.

In Chicago, it was finally time for Robert to say I told you so. This "pistol business" demonstrated what he had been saying all along—his mother was indeed insane. He told his aunt and uncle that his mother's possession of the weapon was a "great concern," but he was fatalistic about his own physical safety. He expressed more worry that "something unforeseen may happen," meaning that Mary might injure herself or someone in the Edwards household. Robert tried to explain that the doctors who had advised him the year before to keep Mary institutionalized "were very urgent in expressing their opinion that no one could foretell the possible freaks which might take possession of my mother." This was precisely why she should be returned to Bellevue Place, he said, "where no catastrophe could happen." While he was not directly threatening to send his mother back to Bellevue, the implication was there, and Robert wanted his aunt and uncle to realize that, other than the "idea" that it was an insane asylum, there was actually "nothing unpleasant" about Bellevue Place. Before actually mailing the letter, Robert showed it to his law partner Edward Isham, who advised against sending it, probably because he thought it would cause an uproar from Mary Lincoln and her new lawyer, John Palmer. The letter was never mailed.

Robert was certain that his mother was slipping into one of her manic manifestations. The "freaks," as he called them, were taking over. Mary was spending half the day with dressmakers, and shopping in Springfield's finest stores, ordering dresses to be sent directly to her room, bypassing her vigilant and wary sister. Robert also received a letter from Mary asking that he send her a clock, candelabra, whip, seashells, engravings, several books, and six paintings she had stored in Chicago. Mary the pack rat wanted to redecorate her room in the Edwards house. Then she sent Robert another letter—"more than a dozen pages long"—demanding "my this and my that." Robert showed his mother's letters to his wife, and together the couple could only conclude that the request was "plainly irrational and the emanation of an insane mind." They were "worn out & forgotten" items, worthless junk, and Robert refused to "go near them." He was getting fed up with the endless Sturm und Drang, and bitterly suggested that his three Springfield aunts "who now have charge" of Mary Lincoln handle the next scandal that he was certain was inevitable. Leonard Swett was also urging Robert to do everything he could to return Mary Lincoln to Bellevue Place. The allegation that she was plotting to kill her son incensed Swett, though Ninian Edwards now regretted ever having made the accusation. He had come to the belief that Mary was the victim of gossip and her own rhetorical excess. Elizabeth Edwards agreed that the account of Mary and the pistol was probably a hoax, but the damage was already done.

Things were threatening to spin out of control. Ninian Edwards understood that only one man could get through to Robert. In May 1876 Ninian journeyed to Bloomington in central Illinois. There on a flat stretch of prairie land stood an elegant three-story yellow brick Victorian mansion. It was the magnificent 36-room home of Justice David Davis. With the United States Supreme Court now in summer recess, the 300-pound power broker was home, enjoying the fruits of his labor. Ninian stood in awe at the sumptuous English carpeting, the rare Italian marble, and the features that made the Davis mansion a model of modern-day comforts, with indoor plumbing, hot and cold running water, a central furnace, and gas lighting. Ninian went to see Davis to set the record straight on Mary Lincoln. He also informed Davis that Mary had hired a New York lawyer to assist Governor Palmer in her fight to restore her bonds and revoke the jury's finding of insanity. When the meeting between the two old friends was over, Davis wrote Robert Lincoln a letter in which he told his protégé flat out that it was time to stop this destructive war with his mother.

"By appointment Mr. Edwards came to see me today," Davis reported, "and I am satisfied that you had better consent to the discharge of your mother.... Mr. Edwards & his wife both believe her to be sane.... They will testify to her sanity—Can we oppose it? Ought we to oppose it?—Can we afford to have a [trial] which is sure to come?"

Davis concluded, "I have after mature reflection, come to the conclusion that it is better for your happiness to give free consent to the removal of all restraint on person or property—and trust to the chances of time."

It must have been a kick in the teeth for Robert to read this letter from the man he considered to be his second father. He wrote Davis back, wondering whether his mother intended to launch a personal attack on him in court. Davis responded: "I do not believe that any raid on you is contemplated." So it was over. David Davis was advising Robert that it was time to just let it go.

On June 15, 1876 at 2:00 P.M. Cook County judge Marion R. M. Wallace beckoned two gentlemen in his courtroom to approach the bench. They were Leonard Swett and Robert Lincoln.

"If it pleases the court," Swett began, whereupon the distinguished lawyer said Mr. Ninian Edwards of Springfield wished to present a petition from Mary Lincoln.

Ninian came forward, adjusted his eyeglasses, and said, on behalf of Mary Lincoln, that he was asking the court to discharge her son Robert as conservator and permit her to resume the full management of her affairs. Ninian Edwards requested that Judge Wallace issue a court order restoring "all the rights and privileges" enjoyed by Mary before the insanity verdict a year before.

When Edwards was finished, Swett informed the judge that Robert Lincoln supported the petition. Now Swett asked for a jury to be sworn in. Twelve men, including one physician as required by law, were brought into the jury box and seated. Unlike the prominent jurors selected for the insanity trial in 1875, these were ordinary citizens. With the panel seated, Ninian Edwards was called as the first witness and sworn in. It is said that lawyers make the worst witnesses, and this was certainly true of Ninian Edwards. Tense and uneasy on the witness stand, he stumbled through his testimony, the gist of which was that Mary Lincoln "has been with me for nine or ten months, and her friends all think she is a proper person to take charge of her affairs."

Judge Wallace looked at Robert Lincoln, who rose and, speaking for the first tine in court that day, and said he desired "immediate action" on the petition. He presented to the court his final report as conservator of his mother's estate, showing that Mary Lincoln had assets worth $81,390, including $58,000 in stocks and bonds, $1,029 in cash, and the rest in personal jewelry and of course those famous lace curtains from Gossage's department store, now valued at $549.83. Robert then asked the court to relieve him from further responsibility in the management of his mother's affairs.

That was all. Testimony was concluded. Ninian was the only witness called. The jury retired, and in just as short a time as it had taken the other jury a year before to declare Mary Lincoln insane, these Chicago citizens returned, and the verdict was read into the record. It was said that deliberations lasted the length of time it took for all twelve men to affix their signatures to the verdict sheet.

"We the undersigned jurors in the case wherein Mary Lincoln, who was heretofore found to be insane, and who is now alleged to be restored to reason, having heard the evidence in said cause, find that the said Mary Lincoln is restored to reason and is capable to manage and control her estate." And with that, Mary Lincoln was no longer a convicted lunatic.

The jurors were dismissed and Leonard Swett, Ninian Edwards, and Robert Lincoln left the courtroom. Ninian arranged for a telegram to be sent to Mrs. Lincoln in Springfield: "All right," it stated. "We will send them," meaning her bonds—indicating a full vindication.

Outside the court, however, Robert was up in arms. He had thought the arrangement was that his mother would be determined to be a fit person to run her financial affairs—which did not necessarily mean that she was sane.

The Lincolns in the White House:
A mezzotint adaptation of a
painting by the artist Francis B.
Carpenter, showing Mary, Willie,
Robert, Tad, and President
Lincoln. *Courtesy, The Lincoln
Museum, Fort Wayne, Indiana.*

The last photograph taken of
President Abraham Lincoln before
his assassination in April 1865.
*Courtesy, Abraham Lincoln Presidential
Library & Museum (ALPLM).*

Mary Todd Lincoln, First Lady. *Courtesy, Abraham Lincoln Presidential Library & Museum (ALPLM).*

Mary Todd Lincoln, in 1863 when she was forty-five, dressed in deep mourning over the death of Willie Lincoln. *Courtesy, The Lincoln Museum, Fort Wayne, Indiana.*

Robert Todd Lincoln, taken in 1863, in his senior year at Harvard. The handsome Robert would not enter the army until January, 1865. *Courtesy, The Lincoln Museum, Fort Wayne, Indiana.*

Thomas "Tad" Lincoln, probably taken in 1858, three years before he became the "tricky little sprite" in the White House. *Courtesy, The Lincoln Museum, Fort Wayne, Indiana.*

"Tad" Lincoln, prankster-in-chief, is standing sentinel over the White House in July 1861 in his Zouave uniform. Tad inked in the mustache and beard. *Courtesy, The Lincoln Museum, Fort Wayne, Indiana.*

Willie Lincoln, the brightest and most promising of Lincoln's sons. President Lincoln said of Willie, "My poor boy, he was too good for this earth." *Courtesy, The Lincoln Museum, Fort Wayne, Indiana.*

Mary Harlan, a senator's daughter, and the future Mrs. Robert Todd Lincoln. *Courtesy, Abraham Lincoln Presidential Library & Museum (ALPLM).*

Mary Harlan Lincoln on her wedding day. "Like the Harlan she was and the Lincoln she had become." *Courtesy, Hildene, the Lincoln Family Home, Manchester, Vermont.*

Robert T. Lincoln at age twenty-five, in 1868, the year he married Mary Harlan. *Courtesy, The Lincoln Museum, Fort Wayne, Indiana.*

Mary Todd Lincoln, depicted in William Mumler's notorious spirit photograph, with the "ghost" of Abraham Lincoln hovering over her. The 1872 photo was believed to be the last ever taken of Mrs. Lincoln. *Courtesy, College of Psychic Studies, London.*

Tad Lincoln. A rare photo of the former White House mischief-maker, taken not long before his death. His mother said of him, "In his loving & tender treatment of me . . . he reminds me so strongly of his beloved father." *Courtesy, The Lincoln Museum, Fort Wayne, Indiana.*

Mamie Lincoln, 1874, at age four. Abraham Lincoln's first grandchild, whom he never knew. *Courtesy, The Lincoln Museum, Fort Wayne, Indiana.*

Abraham Lincoln II, born with the most illustrious name in American history. The family called him Jack. This photo was taken in either 1880 or 1881 in Chicago. *Courtesy, The Lincoln Museum, Fort Wayne, Indiana.*

Robert Todd Lincoln, father of three, in the Gilded Age. *Courtesy, Hildene, the Lincoln Family Home, Manchester, Vermont.*

The three Lincoln grandchildren, taken in 1883 in Washington, when their father was serving as secretary of war. Mamie (left) was fourteen, Jack was ten, and Jessie eight. *Courtesy, The Lincoln Museum, Fort Wayne, Indiana.*

Abraham Lincoln II, posing in a photographer's studio with a large-wheeled bike. Asked about his resemblance to the Great Emancipator, Jack said, "I would like to be as good, as kind and as wise as he was, but not so tall; he must have bumped his head many times." *Courtesy, The Lincoln Museum, Fort Wayne, Indiana.*

Abraham Lincoln II in Versailles, on his deathbed. "We are desperate here," his father said. *Courtesy, The Lincoln Museum, Fort Wayne, Indiana.*

The two surviving Lincoln granddaughters, Mamie and Jessie. *Courtesy, Hildene, the Lincoln Family Home, Manchester, Vermont.*

Mamie Lincoln's wedding portrait. She married the historian Charles Isham on September 2, 1891. The photograph was taken by Queen Victoria's official photographer. *Courtesy, The Lincoln Museum, Fort Wayne, Indiana.*

Jessie Lincoln, the beautiful family "wild-child," dressed in the fashion of the day, with a feathered hat. She would marry three times. *Courtesy, The Lincoln Museum, Fort Wayne, Indiana.*

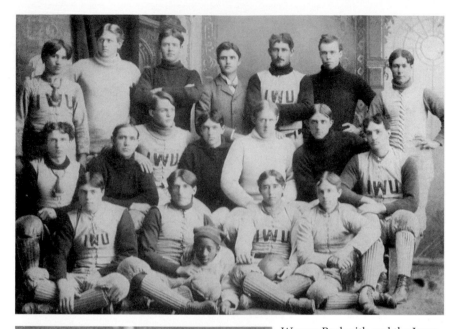

Warren Beckwith and the Iowa Wesleyan College football team. Beckwith is standing, on the far right, with hand on his hip. *Courtesy, Iowa Wesleyan College archives.*

Mamie Lincoln and her son, Lincoln, who was born severely cross-eyed. His eyes were later corrected by surgery. *Courtesy, The Lincoln Museum, Fort Wayne, Indiana.*

Lincoln Isham and his father, Charles Isham, lawyer and historian. *Courtesy, The Lincoln Museum, Fort Wayne, Indiana.*

Warren Beckwith, in World War I. On his way to the front lines in France, he looked up his ex-wife, Jessie, but she refused to let him see their two children. "She said there was no point to it, to let the past be, and that was the end of that." *Courtesy, The Lincoln Museum, Fort Wayne, Indiana.*

Jessie Lincoln Beckwith, single mother, around the year 1912, with her children, Peggy Beckwith, fourteen, and Robert Todd Lincoln Beckwith, eight, in a sailor suit. *Courtesy, The Lincoln Museum, Fort Wayne, Indiana.*

Jessie Lincoln in middle age. She would be disinherited by her parents, but still supported by the family trust fund. *Courtesy, Hildene, the Lincoln Family Home, Manchester, Vermont.*

Robert Todd Lincoln, tycoon and elder statesman. The photograph, a gift to his granddaughter, Peggy Lincoln Beckwith, was signed, "from her affectionate grandfather." Though dated April 30, 1913, the photo was taken years earlier. *Courtesy, The Lincoln Museum, Fort Wayne, Indiana.*

Robert Todd Lincoln Beckwith. Asked what he did for a living, Abraham Lincoln's great-grandson said, "I'm a spoiled brat." *Courtesy, Hildene, the Lincoln Family Home, Manchester, Vermont.*

Peggy Beckwith, future mistress of Hildene. She rarely wore a dress, preferring a flannel shirt and knickers. *Courtesy, Hildene, the Lincoln Family Home, Manchester, Vermont.*

Abraham Lincoln's great-grandchildren, Bob and Peggy Beckwith. *Courtesy, Hildene, the Lincoln Family Home, Manchester, Vermont.*

Lincoln Isham, the eldest great-grandson. Content to strum a guitar, compose little ditties, and spend winter evenings at the Stork Club. *Courtesy, Hildene, the Lincoln Family Home, Manchester, Vermont.*

Bob Beckwith and his sister, Peggy. Bob had three wives. Peggy never married. She once said, "It always provokes me when people stare and say, 'There's Lincoln's great-granddaughter.' It's just my luck he was related to me." *Courtesy, Hildene, the Lincoln Family Home, Manchester, Vermont.*

Jack Coffelt, the last Lincoln's chauffeur, in a studio portrait. "A very good con man, and a very violent guy." Could he be D. B. Cooper? *Courtesy, Coffelt family.*

D. B. Cooper: FBI artist's rendering. The Cooper case from 1971 remains the only unsolved skyjacking in U.S. history. *Courtesy, FBI.*

The Last Lincoln. Robert Todd Lincoln Beckwith in old age, around the time of his scandalous second marriage. "A sad end to the last descendant of one of America's greatest heroes." *Courtesy, Hildene, the Lincoln Family Home, Manchester, Vermont.*

To him, this was an important distinction. Had the court not deemed his mother "restored to reason," Robert's enduring certainty that his mother was mentally ill could have been stated for the record. Robert and Swett turned on Ninian. They blamed him for the court's declaration; as far as Robert was concerned, Ninian had gone too far. Ninian said he was "mortified." He explained that he had a distracting eye infection that made it uncomfortable for him to be on the witness stand. And he was thrown off when Judge Wallace kept asking him to speak up. Ninian felt ashamed. He had thought that the only issue before the jury was "the question whether she was a fit person to have the care, custody and control of her property. They were not called upon to try the question of her sanity, and I regret very much that the verdict stated she was 'restored to her reason.'"

In Springfield, Mary Lincoln was overjoyed. She sent Ninian's seventeen-year-old grandson, Edward Lewis Baker Jr., running off to the offices of the *Illinois State Journal*—the newspaper edited and owned by his father—to get the word out. She wanted every important newspaper in the country to report her victory, and some did, including the *Chicago Times*, which had led the crusade to have her released from Bellevue Place. A HAPPY DENOUEMENT, the *Times* headline read. But Mary discovered to her dismay that in news, timing is everything. Rutherford B. Hayes had on that day received the Republican Party nomination for president. It was a busy news day, and Mary's court victory was relegated to a single sentence in the *New York Tribune*: "A jury has decided that Mrs. Abraham Lincoln is restored to reason."

Four days after the verdict, Mary unleashed her fury. She had been waiting an entire year for this moment. Now she was free to say what she really thought of her son. Mary wrote to Robert on June 19, 1876. Now, with the bonds in her possession and her sanity legally restored, she let loose.

It began without salutation, and it went as follows:

Robert T. Lincoln:
Do not fail to send me without *the least* delay all my paintings . . . my silver set . . . my silver tete-a-tete set also other articles your wife appropriated & which are *well known* to you, must be sent, without a day's delay. Two lawyers and myself have just been together and their list coincides with my own & will be published in a few days. Trust not to the belief that Mrs. Edwards's tongue has not been *rancorous* against you all winter & she has maintained to the very last

that you dared not venture into her house & our presence. Send me my laces, my diamonds, my jewelry—My unmade silks, white lace dress. . . . I am now in constant receipt of letters, from my friends denouncing you in the bitterest terms, six letters from prominent, *respectable* Chicago people such as you do not associate with. As to Mr Harlan [Robert's father-in-law]—you are not worthy to wipe the dust from his feet. Two prominent clergy men have written me since I saw you—and mention in their letters that they think it advisable to offer up prayers for you in Church on account of your wickedness against me and High Heaven. . . . Send me all that I have written for, you have tried your game of robbery long enough. . . . You have injured yourself, not me, by your wicked conduct."

She signed the letter, "Mrs. A. Lincoln."

A shaken Robert read the letter in Chicago, and a follow-up letter that arrived several days later in which Mary called him a "monster of mankind." Robert brought both documents to Leonard Swett. He let Swett write the response, which was addressed to Ninian Edwards. It was a lion's roar:

> Now with such a son bearing patiently for ten years, after all his past sad family history the terrible burden of his mother's approaching insanity putting off any steps restraining her until seven of the most prominent physicians say to him professionally there is danger of her jumping out of her window every week at Batavia, permitting her to be restored the first day the statute permits it, mainly at your request, and when you yourself say that she is not in her right mind, giving her also, mainly at your request, every dollar of her principal [sic] and all the interest accrued, when it was his judgment that it would be better to pay it in monthly installments—I say with such a son and such a mother, shall we, friends of the family, permit her to go about with a pistol, avowing her purpose to shoot him, or shall we permit her to break him down and ruin him by harassing and annoying him.

Swett was not finished. He said that Robert would return nothing to Mary unless Mary acknowledged that the items she was demanding had once been gifts to Robert Lincoln and his wife. To return them without such an acknowledgment, Swett said, would be to suggest that they had been "improperly procured," when in fact they were presents from his formerly loving and generous mother. Next, he uttered a menacing warning of his own. If Mary Lincoln tried to slander or pursue Robert in any way, "I shall, as a citizen, irrespective of Robert, or any one . . . have her confined as an insane person, whatever may be the clamor or consequences." Before sending the extraordinary letter to Ninian, he showed it to that behind-the-scenes manipulator, David Davis, who approved its strong language.

The letter was delivered to Ninian Edwards, and Mary read it. Under Ninian's guidance, Mary retreated. She was now promising, in the presence of Ninian and her sister Elizabeth, that she would "neither bring any suits against Robert nor make any attacks on him."

As it had done to her son, the fight had exhausted Mary. She was determined to leave Springfield. Even with the public restoration of her good name, she understood that people still looked on her as mentally unbalanced.

"I cannot endure to meet my former friends, Lizzie," she told her sister. "They will never cease to regard me as a lunatic, I feel it in their soothing manner. If I should say the moon is made of green cheese they would heartily and smilingly agree with me. I love you, but I cannot stay. I would be much less unhappy in the midst of strangers."

It was time for Mary Lincoln to go into exile one final time.

14

Secretary of War

OVER THE NEXT four years, the law firm of Isham & Lincoln prospered, and for Robert it meant the steady accumulation of wealth. In time, a forgiving nation seemed to have pigeonholed Mary Lincoln as a hysterical eccentric, and collectively chosen to overlook Robert's conduct in the matter of his mother's institutionalization. By 1880 the new president-elect, James A. Garfield, was seriously considering naming Robert Lincoln his secretary of war.

Garfield, a former Union general, won the general election with a plurality of just 9,464 votes out of more than nine million cast. As with any dark-horse victor, Garfield now had the task of accommodating the various factions of his divided party as he pondered the makeup of his cabinet. Joseph Medill, the influential owner and editor of the *Chicago Tribune*, and a client of Robert Lincoln's, met with Garfield about a week after the election and pushed for young Lincoln's appointment. Robert Lincoln would be popular with the electorate, Medill argued, and there was the added bonus that Robert was identified with the pro-Grant wing of the Republican Party, known as the Stalwarts, which had supported Grant's running for a third term. The Republican senator from Illinois, John A. Logan, was also backing Robert for a cabinet post. Logan was a fiery political partisan known as "Black Jack" for his jet-black hair and eyes, and swarthy complexion. He had been an able army general during the war, a winner of the Congressional Medal of Honor for valor, and he was now a leader of the Illinois branch of the Republican Party that had backed Grant's nomination and that Garfield was anxious to mollify with a cabinet appointment. Logan and Medill, working together, pushed for Robert's nomination. There was one other factor working in Robert's favor: Garfield was looking for geographic balance in his cabinet, and naming Robert Lincoln would satisfy the president-elect's requirement for a cabinet officer from Illinois.

"I quite agree with you that the selection of Robert Lincoln would please the people of Illinois and the whole nation," Medill wrote Logan.

At some point it became public knowledge that Robert Lincoln was under serious consideration for secretary of war, and for some battle-scarred veterans of the Civil War, the revelation provoked a storm of outrage. One political friend of Garfield called Robert "a boy" and wondered how the president-elect could justify appointing someone with Lincoln's limited military background to the role of secretary of war. Former president Ulysses S. Grant did little to squelch the rumor that he also was opposed to Lincoln's selection. Why Grant would find the nomination so objectionable was understandable. Robert's service in the army had consisted of two months in the closing days of the Civil War as a captain on Grant's personal staff. He had received his commission following his graduation from Harvard after President Lincoln had written Grant that his son, then twenty-two, "wishes to see something of the war before it ends." Grant assigned Captain Lincoln to public relations duty, escorting Washington officials who were touring the front lines in Virginia. Now Robert Lincoln was under real consideration as secretary of war. Privately, Grant, then fifty-eight years old, expressed grave misgivings. In a letter to Senator Logan, he spoke of his "profound respect and esteem" for the memory of President Lincoln, but reading between the lines, it was clear that Grant was skeptical about Robert Lincoln's qualifications.

"I write to you on the subject of a cabinet position for Illinois," Grant told Logan. "I do not desire to give any recommendation. You mentioned in a letter to me the name of Robert Lincoln. . . . It would, in my estimation, be an injury to him to give him an office that would take him from his profession. To give him a position in which he could not sustain himself well in might be still more injurious. Has he had the sort of practice that would enable him to prove acceptable as Attorney General? If so, it would help him in his practice when he retired. If otherwise it would hurt him. You can judge better his fitness than I can." The message was clear: If Garfield wanted Robert Lincoln in his cabinet, he should offer the young lawyer the attorney general post, not the War Department.

Watching from the sidelines as Garfield weighed his options, Robert neither lobbied for the post nor placed himself out of the running. In January

1881, two months before Garfield's inauguration, Robert gave Senator Logan an illuminating summation of his life.

> I am somewhat in doubt. I would certainly be glad to be associated with the administration. My own conviction however, is that situated as I am, I could not in justice to my family take any office which interfered with my present means of livelihood. This is perhaps not a patriotic way of looking at things. . . . Mr. Isham and I have been together for eight years and our professional business is I think probably the largest in Chicago. I am 37 years old, in good health and am in receipt of a professional income which not only enables me to live in comfort but added to my other small resources encourages me to think that by handling my affairs properly I may be able to make a reasonable provision for my children. I like my present way of life and think I would not like a political career.

Peering into the future, Robert said he could perhaps see himself entering public service in ten years' time, once he had accumulated the "fortune" he was determined to make. But, as to Garfield, he left some wiggle room, inviting Logan to "argue me out of my present notions" and extending his appreciation for everything the senator was doing on his behalf.

Finally, in late February, Garfield formally offered Robert the post of secretary of war. Robert accepted on March 2, just six days before Garfield and his vice president, Chester A. Arthur, were to take the oath of office. The Senate confirmed Robert's nomination on March 5, along with those of the entire Garfield cabinet, which included Secretary of State James G. Blaine from the state of Maine.

Mary Harlan Lincoln and the three children waited until May to join Robert in Washington. Mamie, Jack, and Jessie became fixtures at the White House, where they were invited to play with Garfield's youngest children. Although Jack Lincoln was only eight years old, he was already showing a fine regard for history, so perhaps he appreciated the symbolism of Abraham Lincoln's grandson roving about the White House family quarters. The Garfields had five children who had survived infancy, and the second youngest, Irwin, aged ten when his father became president, developed a reputation as quite the White House terror. Not since Tad Lincoln had a presidential son caused as much havoc as Master Irwin Garfield.

Sometimes he would tear down the marble staircase on a high-wheeled bicycle and steer straight into the East Room. Even Taddie would have been impressed!

Mary was delighted to be back in Washington, where her parents still lived in their townhouse on H Street, but she made an interesting comment to a writer that suggested a struggle with personal demons. Mary Abigail Dodge was a former governess and essayist who lived in the household of her cousin, Secretary of State James G. Blaine. Miss Dodge disliked attention and wrote under the pen name Gail Hamilton (for the place of her birth, Hamilton, Massachusetts). She often accompanied Blaine and his wife to parties and events in Washington, and her diaries from that era illuminate Washington society circa 1881. One entry, in March, was about her invitation to a White House dinner where she met the president and First Lady, Lucretia Garfield.

"Mrs. Garfield thanked me ever so much for coming and the President nearly squeezed my hand off," she wrote. Then President Garfield made a haunting remark to the writer. At the time, he was engaged in a difficult battle with the Senate over the confirmation of one of his nominees, and Miss Dodge paraphrased what he told her: "The Senate may take him out in front of the Capitol and shoot him, but they will never make him withdraw [the] nomination."

Another diary entry described a dinner party for a British diplomat at which Miss Dodge was introduced to the new secretary of war and his wife, Mary.

"Robert Lincoln looks like his mother rather than his father," Miss Dodge, who was then forty-eight, wrote in her diary. She and Mary got along well, and Mary invited the writer to call on her the next morning. Miss Dodge thought Mary eye-catching and interesting.

"She says she knows that I shall like [Robert], that he is thoroughly good, and honest, and noble. She has almost everything to make her handsome but health, and I told her so and that she ought to move Heaven and earth to get that, and she said it did her good to hear me talk—it encouraged her so, and she meant to devote herself this summer to getting well, so as to come out strong next winter. She seems very sweet, and simple, and attractive."

The undefined reference to poor health seemed to suggest that Mary suffered from neurasthenia, a disorder afflicting many upper-class women of her time, including her mother-in-law. Virginia Woolf was another famous sufferer. The symptoms include general lassitude, irritability, anxiety, and depression. In extreme cases, a woman could sometimes declare herself an invalid and remain confined to her bed for years. Today, the illness might be diagnosed as chronic fatigue syndrome, but in the 1880s, doctors had no clear understanding of the syndrome and usually prescribed bed rest and a change in scenery as a cure.

ACROSS THE OCEAN, in the French village of Pau, in the foothills of the Pyrenees Mountains, a stout little lady with white hair and a bent back was following the career of Robert Lincoln with a strange mixture of veneration and contempt.

Mary Lincoln, former First Lady of the United States, living in European exile for the second time in her life, was indulging herself in a whimsical fantasy. It started after she had read an article in the *American Register*, a weekly English-language newspaper published in Paris but available in Pau for the thriving expatriate community. The *Register* ran an article about her son Robert Lincoln and his illustrious legal career, and how he would surely one day—and not a distant day at that—become a contender for president on the Republican ticket.

"You can imagine how elated I felt, in my quiet way, over such a prospect," Mary Lincoln wrote. "I began to study over in my mind, with such a *certainty* in view, what never once occurred to me to do in my good husband's time notwithstanding articles that often appeared in the papers, that 'Mrs Lincoln was the power behind the throne.'"

Mary found herself daydreaming of the return of the Lincolns to the White House. Imagine, "Little Mamie with her charming manners & presence, in the event of success, will grace the place." Interestingly, Mary's fantasies of her granddaughter running about the White House where her Tad and Willie had once played never extended to her other two grandchildren, Jack and Jessie, who, as far as she was concerned, remained nonentities. Mary even allowed herself the pleasure of pondering the names of the future President Robert Lincoln's cabinet. She wrote how she would recommend at least one "superior" man to the cabinet, and, remarkably, it was Leonard Swett, the lawyer who had persuaded a jury to have her declared insane in 1875. But even in this whimsy, Mary still found the bile within her to denounce her son—"*The* young man who makes *no* concessions to the *Mother*, whom he has so cruelly & unmercifully wronged."

Mary Lincoln never congratulated her son on his triumphant appointment as secretary of war. Neither, for that matter, was Robert willing to reach out to his mother to bury the hatchet. Mother and son had not exchanged a single word since 1876. Very few people had the nerve to ask Robert about his mother. One who did was Henry Darling, an essayist, clergyman, and future president of Hamilton College in New York. Where was Mary Lincoln? Darling ventured. "Somewhere in Europe," came Robert's dour reply, adding that he did not "know her present address." But more than just an ocean divided mother and son.

Just as the shame of the Old Clothes Scandal had sent Mary into foreign exile in 1868, now the indignity of having been branded a lunatic had driven her to France. The idea started to take shape in the days after the Cook County court ruled her restored to reason. This time, she had justification for her paranoia, because Robert—that "monster of mankind" son of hers—was threatening to have her reinstitutionalized if she caused any trouble. So, Europe beckoned. In Europe she could live in anonymity, without the stigma of being a lunatic, somewhere where Robert could not have her arrested again. Only Mary's sister Elizabeth and brother-in-law Ninian, and very few others in Springfield, knew that she was leaving the United States. Mary had sworn them all to secrecy. One other relative was let in on the furtive travel arrangements, Mary's seventeen-year-old grand-nephew, Edward Lewis Baker Jr. Bright, dark-haired, and even-tempered, Lewis, as he was called, was the son of Edward Baker Sr. and Elizabeth Edwards's daughter Julia. Baker Sr. was the coproprietor of the *Springfield State Journal*, that reliable mouthpiece for the Lincoln administration. (Lincoln was sitting in Baker's newspaper office waiting for word from the Chicago convention in 1860 when he received the news of his Republican Party nomination.) In 1876, Baker and his wife were living in Argentina following his appointment as U.S. consul in Buenos Aires. His son, young Lewis, was staying with his grandmother Elizabeth Edwards when Mary Todd Lincoln moved in, following her release from Bellevue Place, and he was a witness to all the turmoil that played out in the Edwards's household in the ensuing year.

Great-Aunt Mary Todd Lincoln fascinated Lewis, who was pondering a career in journalism at his father's newspaper. Where others found Mary grating and impossible, Lewis was enthralled by her stories of the Civil War and her gossipy recollections about the famous statesmen of the Lincoln era. For her part, Mary appreciated the flattering attention of this charming young man, who was about the age Tad was when he died. Even if Mary loathed Lewis's parents, the pair had a special connection. "Love crowned you at your birth," she once told Lewis, as she recalled how at his christening in 1861 she had sent his mother a bottle of water from the river Jordan in Palestine. Mary regaled Lewis with her usual overbearing adoration. "I believe that face of yours, loved by so many persons, *so* abounding in intelligence, good looks, & sweet sympathy, was watered by this same Jordan water." Then, recalling her own dear sons Willie and Tad, she told Lewis, "I have been called upon to surrender two of the loveliest sons that God ever gave to a Mother, possessing exactly your attributes."

As Mary packed to leave the United States, she asked Lewis to at least accompany her to New York, where she was booked for passage to France on October 1. They left Springfield in early September. Elizabeth Edwards went with them to the depot, and there, as Mary and Lewis prepared to board the train to Chicago, the two sisters who, over the years, by turns, had experienced so much affection and conflict, flew into each other's arms, and Mary burst into tears: "I go into exile and alone," she said.

Elizabeth watched the train leave the platform. Some time later, when she was authorized to apprise Robert Lincoln of his mother's whereabouts, she wrote him a letter. Elizabeth was ruefully apologetic about having kept Mary's travel plans so hush-hush until now, but she was blunt in her explanation: His mother, she informed Robert, had found it necessary to "place an ocean between you and herself."

"I often wonder Dear Robert if the course I have been constrained to pursue has at all dissatisfied you. The truth is I only, from the beginning of this unpleasant matter, wished to do my duty." Perhaps playing to Robert's receptivity to anything incriminating about his mother's actions, Elizabeth let him know that, shortly before her departure, Mary had gone on a buying binge.

"It may yet turn out that all parties have been too indulgent," Elizabeth admitted. "If so, the consolation will be in having erred in the side of humanity." Elizabeth told Robert not to worry—"a sense of loneliness will cause her return sooner than she contemplated—the improvement in her social feeling was quite manifest during the stay here—and among strangers she will yearn for home times."

Mary Lincoln first went south, to Kentucky, and the city of her birth, Lexington. Just as Tad had once served as his mother's steadfast protector, now Lewis Baker sat at his great-aunt's side as the train from Chicago rumbled past Indiana and through Ohio before reaching the bluegrass region of

Kentucky and, the "Athens of the South," Lexington. Mary showed her young companion the graves of her parents and the site of her childhood home on Short Street, where a fire had long ago razed the house. Mindful that Lewis was still an easily bored teenager, Mary took him on an excursion to the longest cave in the world, Mammoth Cave, which even in 1876 was a popular tourist attraction. The plucky old lady must have made quite the picture as she and Lewis explored that eerie world of absolute blackness. It was a labyrinth that extended 367 miles, a "grand, gloomy and peculiar" world of wonder.

From Lexington, the intrepid Mrs. Lincoln and her young charge went to Philadelphia for the Centennial Exposition, a celebration of the nation's one-hundredth birthday, and the first major world's fair to be held in the United States. Before it closed on December 31, 1876, the exhibition would draw almost ten million visitors (including repeat guests)—about 20 percent of the population of the United States. As Mary and Lewis walked the fair grounds overlooking the Schuylkill River, they marveled at the new inventions that heralded American genius in the Gilded Age. Alexander Graham Bell was demonstrating the telephone, and when Emperor Dom Pedro of Brazil put the device up to his ear, he quickly dropped it in shock, shouting, "My God, it talks!" The Centennial Exposition also saw the first wide-scale appearance of a practical typographic machine, later to be known as the typewriter; the introduction of Heinz tomato ketchup; and the nation's first soft drink, Hires Root Beer ("Greatest Health-Giving Beverage in the World"). Perhaps Mary and Lewis sampled that long yellow fruit with the funny name, "banana," that was causing a sensation at the fair. It was considered such an exotic treat that it was served on a plate with a knife and fork, and at an exorbitant price—ten cents.

Mary and Lewis arrived in New York the last week in September, and Lewis was left to explore the city on his own while Mary went shopping. When Mary was done, she had added six trunks of clothes to her hoard. In what was believed to be her first excursion to the theater since *Our American Cousin,* in 1865, she saw the Howard family production of *Uncle Tom's Cabin,* with Gertrude Howard playing Topsy. It was still relatively early in the run of the play, which would go on to be performed continuously in the United States for a remarkable eighty years.

On October 1, Mary and Lewis took a carriage to the Barrow Street pier in lower Manhattan, and it was there, after four weeks of travel and steady companionship, that Lewis bid his great-aunt bon voyage. Lewis had just twenty-seven dollars in pocket money to make his way back to Springfield.

Mary boarded the *Labrador*, a 394-foot steamship with two funnels and three masts rigged for sail. *Labrador* sailed under a French flag and was owned by Compagnie Générale Transatlantique. Under ideal conditions, the ship could cross the Atlantic in eight days. Of course, Mary had her usual luck with transatlantic voyages—it took twelve stormy days to make the passage. On board she made the acquaintance of a distinguished Frenchman, Louis de Berbieu, a widower who was traveling with his young daughter. This man Berbieu, who was understood to be of "royal descent," charmed the former First Lady with his Continental elegance and good heart. His presence made the stormy passage tolerable. When Mary arrived in the city of Le Havre, the port of call for French ocean liners, at the mouth of the Seine in Normandy, she found to her delight that M. de Berbieu had notified the port agents that the widow of the great Abraham Lincoln was traveling alone and required assistance. Mary's trunks were collected and sent through customs "without opening an article of baggage," she gloated. "Such kindness, deference & attention it is impossible for me to describe."

As she recuperated from her ocean voyage in her hotel room, Mary wrote "dear Lewis" how thankful she was for his companionship in America. "*Words* are impossible to express *how* near you are to my heart. Such attention, such kindness as you have shown me in the past year I can say no more." Her son Robert was dead to her, but now she had Lewis.

Mary loved France. Every morning at eleven a carriage carrying a coachman and a footman called on her at her hotel for a drive around the city of Le Havre. Mary appreciated the courtesy, particularly as the owner of the carriage accompanied her on these excursions. "It is pleasant to be thus received," she admitted. The famous bookstore Galignani's in Paris sent her Francois Guizot's handsomely bound five-volume *History of France*, and Mary, who read and spoke fluent French, started to read the story of "this beautiful land."

It was now time for her to proceed on to her final destination. She boarded the steamer *Columbia* and went 357 miles down the Garonne River to Bordeaux, in southwest France. At Bordeaux she boarded a train, and five hours later she arrived at the Grand Hotel, in Pau, in the foothills of the Pyrenees Mountains.

Among Americans of the privileged class, Pau was a treasure. Mary had known about it since her time in Frankfurt with Taddie, when she had recommended the village to Sally Orne after hearing that Mrs. Orne's daughter

Susie had been stricken ill in Paris. Napoleon had vacationed in Pau, and Marie Antoinette tended to a small garden when she had summered there. Pau was famous for its perfect climate, clean air, and curative mineral springs. In the center of the village from which the Pyrenees mountain range could be seen stood a magnificent castle, the Château de Pau. Mary was surprised to see so many English people, which did not please her. The English fascination with Pau had begun in the time of Wellington, who had left a garrison of troops behind in the village. During the nineteenth century the English flocked to Pau, and everywhere Mary could see that country's cultural influences—tearooms, fox hunting, polo, croquet, cricket, and the first eighteen-hole golf course in continental Europe.

The village of Pau welcomed the famous American widow, and the mayor, accompanied by two adjutants, paid her a courtesy call. But as with most seasonal resort towns, Mary soon found Pau to be "a very expensive place," and it was not long before she became suspicious of the villagers. She held particular distrust for the civil servants who worked in the post office, whom she blamed for causing delays in the delivery of the checks mailed to her by her Springfield banker, Jacob Bunn. "There is a carelessness, I fear, at the P.O. here," she complained to her sister Elizabeth. Now she was calling the French "superficial," "covetous," and "peculiar." Mary even asked Bunn to enclose her checks in an envelope without a return address, because she suspected the post office employees of identifying the package as coming from an American bank. In not too long a time she was attacking the French as "the *most unprincipled, heartless, avaricious people* on the face of the earth."

"With the exception of a *very few*, I detest them all."

She kept up with the political news from home by regularly reading the *American Register* and the *Illinois State Journal*, to which she subscribed. She followed the 1876 election impasse between Rutherford B. Hayes and Samuel J. Tilden with concern, as she worried that it could provoke another civil war. When she read that Hayes, the ultimate victor in the election crisis, had appointed a former Confederate army lieutenant colonel to be his postmaster general, she was outraged.

For family news, Elizabeth Edwards was her main source. In March 1877 came word of the sudden death of Elizabeth's granddaughter Florence, at age four. Mary's brother-in-law Ninian suffered a stroke and lost the use of his right arm. Mary also maintained a regular correspondence with dear Lewis, expressing deep "regret" about his decision to skip college and head straight into journalism, which Mary warned would lead to a love of politics that was "anything but desirable in a young man."

Mary felt isolated in Pau and told her sister that she had only a few friends and lived "very much alone." Thoughts of her son Robert haunted her. "'My Gethsemane' is ever with me," she said, referring to the biblical garden where it was said that Judas Iscariot betrayed Christ. It had been two years now since her release from Bellevue Place, but Mary said Robert's responsibility for her institutionalization still rankled "deeply in my heart." He was a "bad son" who had "cruelly persecuted" his own mother. "That wretched young man, but *old* in sin, has a fearful account yet to render to his Maker! And God does not allow sin to go unpunished," she wrote Lewis.

Growing up, Mary confided to Lewis, Robert had always been a cold character. "In our household he was always trying to obtain the mastery on all occasions," although he never dared show any insolence to his brothers or his mother when Abraham Lincoln was present. "It was a great relief to us all when he was sent East to school," Mary said, "*then* we had a most loving peace.—So different from our other sons—he was always persecuting them and my husband so tender & loving—always said he never knew from whence such a mean nature came." It was a shocking thing for any mother to put on paper, even with the bad blood that now existed between Robert and Mary, and it certainly contradicted Mary's letters in years past in which she heaped praise on her son's superior qualities. There were shades of truth in both depictions.

In Springfield, Elizabeth Edwards took on the role of mediator and tried to make peace between the Lincolns. Mary had been sending little French trinkets for her granddaughter Mamie, that Elizabeth would then forward to Robert. Perhaps in this fragile line of communication there was the foundation for a reconciliation. Of course, it must have rankled Robert Lincoln and his wife that only Mamie—and not all three of their children—was the object of their grandmother's generosity.

In spring 1879, Elizabeth boldly asked Robert to write to his mother in France and initiate a dialogue. Robert refused. Rather sheepishly, he said that he was "afraid a letter from me would not be well received." If communicating with his mother would do any good, Robert said, "I would write to her at once & not think I was making any concession, for I have not allowed her anger at me to have any other effect upon me than regret that she should so feel and express herself toward me. As to interfering to control her in any way, I assure you and I hope you will so write to her, that under no possible circumstances would I do so." For the first time, Robert let slip his regret in instigating court proceedings against his mother. "If I could have foreseen my own experience in the matter, no consideration would have induced me to go through it."

And so the years passed. By 1879, after three years in Pau, Mary was desperate to experience the bonds of family again. She took delight in a new photograph of Lewis that he had sent her, but it made her miss home more. One day in late June, as a grand procession celebrating the summer solstice marched beneath her hotel window, Mary sat at her little desk and wrote Lewis, acknowledging how "*far* removed" she felt from family and how she longed to be in the midst of the "tight little circle" in Springfield. World-renowned French cuisine could not compare to the southern-comfort cooking she had known at home, and she proceeded to list the dishes she longed for with mouthwatering delight—the "*waffles, batter cakes*, egg corn bread—are all unknown here—as to biscuits, light rolls && they have never been dreamed of—not to speak of *buckwheat cakes*."

Once again she blamed Robert for her banishment.

"*Very* reluctantly I left you all and it was only for *self protection* that I did so. Of this, dear Lewis, you are *fully* aware."

Mary's wanderlust took her to Paris, Vichy, Avignon, Marseilles, and the seaside resorts of Biarritz and Saint Jean-de-Luz, near the Spanish border. She even made brief excursions to Rome and Naples. Now in her sixties, she was in delicate heath, suffering from diabetes, cataracts, rheumatism, probably high blood pressure, a bad back, and "great bloat"—an undiagnosed disorder that for a time caused her body to balloon. For one horrible week, wrapped in flannel pajamas, with her throat swollen and her chest congested, Mary wondered about the effects on her health of living in a high-altitude climate such as Pau's.

Yet she never stopped traveling. One must admire the endless curiosity of the little old lady who, even when afflicted with so many physical discomforts, was still cutting a swath through southern Europe.

She was back in Pau in time to experience a disgraceful episode involving former president Grant and his wife Julia Dent Grant.

Following his eight years in office as president, Ulysses S. Grant and Julia Grant embarked on a world tour that took them to the Far East and Europe, and kept them abroad for more than two years. In December 1879 their travels took them to Alhambra, Spain, and the crypts of Ferdinand and Isabella. Julia Grant was a homely woman with crossed eyes, but she loved being the center of attention. It has been said that no woman enjoyed being First Lady more than Julia Grant, and no one left the White House more grudgingly. On the last day of her husband's term of office, after preparing a luncheon for Rutherford and Lucy Hayes, Julia let loose a "floodgate" of tears as she sat in her carriage at the Washington railroad depot.

In Alhambra, the crown of Queen Isabella was placed upon the former First Lady's head. "It is too heavy for my American head," Julia protested, and the crown was removed. The Grants were greeted with cheers in Valencia and Barcelona. And then, as Christmas neared, they arrived in Pau. The former president and his wife were honored with a parade, a reception, and a six-course dinner at the Hôtel de France. Dessert was a special treat concocted for the Grants by the hotel chef—bombe à la Vicksburg. But in all this celebration, where was Mary Lincoln? It was almost inconceivable that the Grants were not made aware of her presence in the tiny village, as she was certainly the most famous American to be living in permanent residence there. Yet Mary had not been invited to any of the festivities honoring the Grants.

Julia Grant tried to explain this unforgivable breach of etiquette in her memoirs. "I learned the night before we left that Mrs. Abraham Lincoln was there and I was very, very sorry that we had not learned this sooner, as it was now too late to make her a visit. We had our tickets and our train, a party was going with us and we could not at this late hour change out plans." Julia Grant's excuse stretched credibility, and it is probable that she was snubbing Mary Lincoln for humiliations she had caused the Grants when she had been First Lady. No doubt they were aware that Mary often called the general a "butcher" during the Civil War and claimed he had "no regard for life. . . . He loses two men to the enemy's one." When she had been First Lady, Mary, who had suspected Julia of harboring First Lady ambitions, once lashed out at her for seating herself in the First Lady's presence. "How dare you be seated until I invite you!"

"I suppose you think you'll get to the White House yourself, don't you?"

Julia answered that she was perfectly content with her present situation as the wife of General Grant and that she was in a far more exalted position than she had ever expected to attain.

"Oh, you had better take it if you can get it," Mary retorted. "'Tis very nice."

An aide to General Grant described the 1865 incident as "altogether a hateful experience."

That same month of December 1879, personal catastrophe came to Mary Lincoln when she suffered a stupid little accident that in a split second made her a near-cripple. Mary was standing on a stepladder, hanging a painting over the mantle, when she fell, hitting her back on the corner of a table. Three weeks later she was still in her hotel room recuperating from her "poor broken back." Doctors set her body in plaster. Her left side was in unremitting pain; she was, she wrote Lewis, a "broken hearted sorrowing woman" shriveled down to one hundred pounds. But even in this bedridden and wretched condition Mary still found the strength to lay waste to her enemies. Although she suffered from cataracts she possessed an eagle eye for envy, and had spotted one short article—"a little paragraph," she called it—noting that President John Tyler's widow Julia was applying for a congressional pension. Even though it was Mary's long battle for a three-thousand-dollar annual pension that had opened the door to all former First Ladies seeking relief from the government, she was furious, yet saw no hypocrisy in her position. Mary Lincoln had more in common with Julia Tyler than either woman would have cared to admit. Julia Tyler was flirtatious and daringly feminine for her time. She was also reckless about money. As First Lady, she was attacked for her regal and "queen-like" behavior (Julia instituted the practice of playing "Hail to the Chief " when the president entered the room on a state occasion). Although born in New York, Julia was a proud Southerner by marriage. She praised slavery as a civilizing influence and argued that slaves lived better than the poor of London. But after the Civil War, she found herself on the wrong side of history. Mary Lincoln considered her a "*fearful* Secessionist," and called her demand for a pension "impudent." (Congress authorized a twelve-hundred-dollar pension in 1881.)

By March 5, 1880, a full two months after her fall, Mary was still in physical agony, requiring "*absolute* rest," and under doctor's orders to stay in bed. But after four years abroad, she was finally determined to return to Springfield. At age sixty-two, her days of wanderlust were coming to an end.

Mary made arrangements for her homecoming with her usual efficiency, and the attention to detail of an experienced world traveler. First class passage was booked on the steamship *Amérique*, departing Le Havre on October 15, 1880. Mary sent her trunks ahead and notified her Springfield banker, the reliable Jacob Bunn, to hand over $125 to her grandnephew Lewis Baker. With these funds Lewis would make his way east in time for Mary Lincoln's arrival in New York, sometime around October 25. Mary expressed two wishes for her journey. The first was that "by all that was merciful" Lewis would make all his connections and be there to greet *Amérique* in New York Harbor; the second was that on both sides of the Atlantic she be exempt from paying any duty on her "immense array" of trunks.

Mary Lincoln was not the only famous woman on the ship; the other was the great French actress Sarah Bernhardt.

Sarah Bernhardt was thirty-six when she sailed for the United States for the start of her first American tour, and she was already the most celebrated actress in the world. Mark Twain said of her: "There are five kinds of actresses: bad actresses, fair actresses, good actresses, great actresses—and then there is Sarah Bernhardt." She had bedded most of her leading men and led one of the most public lives of the nineteenth century. Every detail of her existence seemed to be known, even her sexual peccadilloes. Apparently, she never experienced an orgasm; as her biographer put it, she was an "untuned piano" and vulnerable everywhere "except in the right place."

The Divine Sarah entered her cabin at six in the morning, October 15, 1880. As a celebrity, she was accorded special attention. Flowers were everywhere, and her initials, embroidered in red, hung from a banner wall to wall. "What a profusion of the letters S. B.!" she exclaimed. Her maid Félice moved into the adjacent cabin while the rest of Miss Bernhardt's entourage was assigned to cabins on the other side of the ship. It was a misty day with a gray sea and no visible horizon. For three days Sarah remained in her cabin in a state of "utter despair," weeping hysterically, missing France, and dreading her American tour. On the fourth day, she got out of bed. It was seven at night and she went on deck for fresh air. As she strode up a flight of stairs, she passed an elderly woman dressed in black. The woman's face, she recalled, was sad and "resigned." Suddenly, a violent wave slammed against the ship and the two women were thrown headlong down the steps.

"I immediately clutched hold of the leg of one of the benches, but the unfortunate lady was flung forward. Springing to my feet with a bound I was just in time to seize hold of the skirt of her dress, and with the help of my maid and a sailor, we managed to prevent the poor woman from falling head first down the staircase. Very much hurt, though, she was, and a trifle confused; she thanked me in such a gentle, dreamy voice that my heart began to beat with emotion."

What followed next was a most extraordinary encounter.

"You might have been killed, madame, down that horrible staircase,"

Sarah Bernhardt said, in the golden voice that was renowned for its clarity and perfect diction.

With a sigh of regret the woman replied, "Yes, but it was not God's will." She looked intently at one of the most famous faces in the world. "Are you not Madame Hessler?"

"No, madame, my name is Sarah Bernhardt."

The woman knitted her brow and said in a mournful, scarcely audible voice, "I am the widow of President Lincoln."

Sarah reeled in shock. She wrote in her memoirs, "I had just done this unhappy woman the only service that I ought not to have done her—I had saved her from death. Her husband had been assassinated by an actor, Booth, and it was an actress who had now prevented her from joining her beloved husband. I went back to my cabin and stayed there two days, for I had not the courage to meet that woman for whom I felt such sympathy, and to whom I should never dare to speak again."

The *Amérique* was notorious in France for being a hard-luck ship. On its first voyage under the name *Amérique*, in 1874, it encountered a violent gale and was abandoned by its 235 passengers and crew one hundred miles off Brest, France. The ship, one of the largest in the world, with a passenger capacity of nine hundred, was assumed to be lost at sea until British sailors found it drifting in the English Channel. Three years later, on its way to New York, *Amérique* found itself stranded off the coast of Seabright, New Jersey. On another voyage, it collided with an Icelandic vessel and foundered on the shoals off Newfoundland. Such was its reputation that the ship's owners, Compagnie Générale Transatlantique, had difficulty convincing the French public that the *Amérique* was seaworthy. Sarah Bernhardt was aboard the vessel at all only because the shipping line had offered her impresario "excellent terms." (*Amérique* was finally put out of its misery in 1895 when it was wrecked off the coast of Colombia and sold for scrap.)

At 6:30 A.M., October 27, after twelve terrifying days at sea, including an "abominable snowstorm," the *Amérique* pulled into New York Harbor. With its arrival, Mary Lincoln had to face one more indignity. A flotilla of steamships flying the French flag came out to welcome Sarah Bernhardt. More than twenty newspaper reporters were on hand to interview the famous actress who was the subject of so much interest in America for her talent and scandalous love life. On the dock, a great throng of fans waited to cheer her appearance. Then a reporter for the *New York Sun* observed an old woman watching the spectacle from the deck of *Amérique*, "almost unnoticed."

"She was dressed plainly; her face was furrowed and her hair was streaking with white." The reporter then realized—"this was the widow of Abraham Lincoln."

"When the gangplank was swung aboard, Madame Bernhardt and her companions ... were the first to descend. ... The gates were besieged." Mary Lincoln, with the other passengers, followed the Bernhardt entourage down the gangplank. It was a struggle for Mary to walk, and she had to lean on the arm of Edward Lewis Baker Jr. Her grandnephew had done well—he had fulfilled his promise to be there when the *Amérique* reached port. As Mary and Lewis tried to make their way through the surging crowd, the *Sun* reporter saw a police officer, who evidently did not recognize Mrs. Lincoln, place his hand on her shoulder and order the former First Lady to "stand back."

"She retreated with her nephew into the line of spectators," the reporter wrote.

Sarah Bernhardt's carriage made its way through the crowd. The actress climbed on board, and with her manager was driven off to the Albemarle Hotel. The gates were swung open and now Mary Lincoln and the other passengers who had been told to wait were permitted to leave. Mary told Lewis that she was not upset to be so jostled. She had long ago made peace with her life of shadows in her native land.

15
Deathwatch

AFTER FOUR MONTHS in office, President James A. Garfield was going on vacation. He woke up Saturday morning, July 2, 1881, and went to check on his two youngest children, Abram and his little White House terror, Irwin. The boys would be leaving today for a month-long stay at the family farm in Ohio, while Garfield and his two oldest sons, Harry and James, would be taking the train to Garfield's alma mater, Williams College in Massachusetts, where the president would deliver the commencement address and attend his twenty-fifth class reunion.

Shortly after 9:00 A.M. Secretary of State James G. Blaine arrived at the White House. Garfield's train was leaving in a half hour and Blaine had arranged to drive the president to the depot. Garfield bid farewell to the White House servants and climbed into the State Department carriage. With Blaine at the reins, the president was taken to the Baltimore and Potomac Depot, at B Street off Sixth.

"How much time have we, Officer?" Garfield asked a policeman on duty as he stepped out of Blaine's carriage.

"About ten minutes, sir."

Harry and James Garfield were waiting on the train platform for their father. Four members of Garfield's cabinet were also at the railroad station: the secretary of the treasury, the postmaster general, the secretary of the navy, which was then a cabinet-level post, and Secretary of War Robert Lincoln. All these men and their wives had been invited by Garfield to accompany him on the special presidential train to Williams College.

In the carpeted waiting room, a short, rumpled man of forty with intense eyes and a black beard watched as President Garfield and Secretary of State Blaine entered the railroad station. His name was Charles Guiteau. A self-aggrandizing sociopath, Guiteau claimed to be a lawyer, but in truth he worked as a bill collector. He had volunteered for the Garfield-Arthur campaign of 1880, and, after incessantly pestering campaign officials to give him a platform for a public speech, he was invited by vice presidential candidate Chester A. Arthur to speak at a rally of black voters, on Twenty-fifth Street in New York City. Although Guiteau spoke for just a few moments before he got stage fright and scurried from the platform, in his delusional mind his oration was the turning point in the election. On the day after Garfield and Arthur took the oath of office, Guiteau showed up in Washington, expecting to be rewarded with a prestigious diplomatic post in the new administration. First, he asked to be named minister to Austria; then he demanded the post of American consul in Paris. Garfield's people dismissed him as a crackpot.

Now, as Garfield and Blaine strode into the train station side by side and walked right past him, the disgruntled office-seeker stood at the ready. From his pocket, Guiteau pulled out a snub-nosed handgun with an ivory handle that he had purchased at a gun shop on F Street for ten dollars. Six feet from the president, Guiteau opened fire. The first shot grazed Garfield in the right arm.

"My God! What is this?" Garfield called out.

A second later another shot rang out. It hit the president in the back, just above the waist. It took Garfield's legs out from under him. Blaine turned and took a step toward the shooter; his first instinct was to give chase, but he stopped when he saw the president lying in a pool of blood. Passengers at the depot were now screaming, "There he goes!" as Guiteau, still gripping the pistol, ran for the exit. He got a step or two from the station before his path was blocked by a police officer. "Stop him!" came the cries. "He shot the president!" Guiteau's pistol was confiscated and he was hauled back into the station.

Fifteen seconds after the first shot had rung out, Robert Lincoln was at the president's side. He found Garfield on his back, his eyes closed, his face as pale as death. Robert ran out of the station, found his driver, and ordered him to get a doctor. Then Robert rushed back to his fallen president. Inside the station it was bedlam. An angry mob surrounded Guiteau shouting, "Lynch! Lynch!" One spectator knocked the assassin's hat off. Now, in the custody of two cops, Guiteau was escorted away. But he wanted the world to know who had been responsible for shooting the president. "I did it. I will go to jail for it. I am a Stalwart, and Arthur will be president."

As Blaine kept the crowd back, Robert Lincoln stood over the president. Garfield's distraught sons Harry and James knelt at his side, their faces streaked with tears. Garfield whispered something in James's ear, and then a remarkable thing happened—the president reached his hand out to Robert Lincoln, the son of the first United States president to be assassinated. Robert grasped it and held it tight. Perhaps in some instinctive way Garfield sought to comfort Robert.

"I don't think this is serious," Garfield said. "I will live."

By now, Garfield was surrounded by doctors. One medical man who worked for the city health department gave the president brandy and waved ammonia smelling salts under his nose. Then a mattress from a Pullman Palace Car was retrieved. Garfield was hoisted onto it and carried into a private chamber on the second floor of the depot. They turned Garfield on his side and the doctor slipped his finger into the hole in his back to probe for the bullet. Garfield was informed that the wound did not appear to be mortal.

"I thank you, Doctor," he said, "but I am a dead man." The president insisted on being transported back to the White House.

He was taken to a bedroom in the southeast corner of the presidential mansion. Eleven doctors crammed into the room, but the physician who took charge was Dr. Willard Bliss, whom Robert Lincoln, in his capacity as secretary of war, had selected to lead the medical team. Bliss and the others took turns probing the wound in Garfield's back; some poked with a finger or a metal rod, trying to determine the path the bullet had taken into the president's body. No surgical gloves were used, for in the United States, the sterilization of hands and medical instruments was not yet standard procedure. Blood poured from the wound and stained the bed, and the president could not stop vomiting. The consensus of the medical people was that any attempt to operate and dig out the ball would almost certainly prove fatal to the president.

Garfield was worried about his wife, Lucretia, who was vacationing in the oceanside resort of Long Branch, New Jersey, with their little girl Mollie. He dictated a telegram to her through an aide, Colonel A. F. Rockwell: "The President wishes me to say to you that he has been seriously hurt, how seriously he cannot yet say. He is himself, and hopes you will come to him soon. He sends his love to you."

Now Garfield turned to Dr. Bliss. The two men had grown up together in Ohio, and he asked his old friend what his chances were, man to man. Bliss told him, ". . . you cannot live long."

James Blaine entered the bedroom. Garfield told his secretary of state how much he loved him, then asked him what he knew about the assassin. Blaine told him it was Charles Guiteau. Garfield recognized the name. "Why did that man shoot me? I have done him no wrong."

Briefing reporters on the president's medical condition, Robert Lincoln said, "When I first entered the room he was seized with an attack of vomiting and I was alarmed, but the president, turning to the physician in attendance, said, 'That is the result of the hypodermic injection you gave me a while ago, wasn't it, Doctor?'" Garfield was the one who was trying to cheer everyone up. Robert was so moved by the president's valor he could not speak any further without breaking into sobs, and the press briefing came to an end. A reporter later wrote, "The scene undoubtedly called to his [Robert's] mind a similar tragic event in his own family history." Secretary Lincoln became the first man to bear witness to two presidential death-watches. It was a bleak and dispiriting entry in the history books.

Secretary of State Blaine's wife, Harriet, organized the wives of the Garfield cabinet, and for those first twenty-four hours everyone took turns nursing the stricken leader. Only Mary Harlan Lincoln failed to participate, for reasons unknown.

Robert Lincoln met with the other cabinet members in emergency session, with James Blaine running things as the highest-ranking cabinet secretary in the line of presidential succession. A telegram, under Blaine's name, was sent to Vice President Chester A. Arthur in New York. "It is the judgment of the Cabinet that you should come to Washington to-night by the midnight train." The telegram was loaded with political intrigue. Arthur's only government experience before becoming vice president was as collector of the Port of New York in the Grant administration. Like Robert Lincoln, he was a Stalwart, steadfast in his support of the spoils system of government in which civil servants were appointed for their party loyalty rather than their competence. Now, should Garfield die in office, Arthur was poised to take over, but he was in a quandary. As soon as Guiteau's utterance, "I am a Stalwart and Arthur will be President," became public knowledge, he knew that the country would be thinking: Was Charles Guiteau a patsy of the Stalwarts and even of Arthur himself? He foresaw a replay of the distrust that had afflicted the unfortunate Andrew Johnson after Abraham Lincoln's assassination.

At the White House, Bliss gathered his team of doctors and announced that he would, from that moment, become the sole physician in charge. He said he was acting at the directive of president and Mrs. Garfield and would require only a few consulting physicians—the others could go home. An uproar ensued. Some of the doctors questioned Bliss's surgical skills. Bliss responded, "If I can't save him, no one can." He overestimated his gifts as a healer, for President Garfield was already doomed—not by Guiteau's bullet, but by the medical treatment he was receiving. When Bliss probed the wound with his bare finger he inadvertently created a path that led everyone to assume, erroneously, that it was the path the bullet had taken. After the other members of the medical team each took his turn probing the path Bliss had made, what had been a three-inch entry wound had become a twenty-inch gouge. One doctor had actually reached into the wound up to his wrist trying to reach the bullet.

In those bleak and desperate hours, Robert Lincoln was heard to mutter, "How many hours of sorrow I have passed in this town."

On Sunday afternoon Robert Lincoln and the other members of Garfield's cabinet climbed into two carriages waiting outside the White House and rode to Independence Avenue, to a townhouse across from the Capitol where Arthur was staying. Arthur bounded down the steps and shook hands with the gentlemen, first with his rival Blaine, then with Lincoln and the others. Arthur invited the seven cabinet officers inside and served tea and lunch. Later that evening, the vice president went to the White House and tried to see Garfield, to no avail, though he was permitted to sit briefly with Lucretia Garfield and pay his respects. Then he was escorted into the cabinet room where Lincoln, Blaine, and the others were waiting. "I pray to God that the president will recover," he said. Indirectly addressing the whispers of his possible role in the assassination, he told the men, "God knows I do not want the place I was never elected to."

For weeks, Garfield lingered between life and death. Daily, and sometimes hourly, medical bulletins were issued from the White House to keep the nation updated on the president's condition. Robert Lincoln, in his public statements, reiterated the official line that the government was functioning normally. Privately, he was deeply concerned. As he wired his political patron, Senator Logan of Illinois, "The President's condition is very alarming." Three days later, Robert informed Logan, "The President had a natural movement with which surgeons are much pleased." But to his friend John Hay he wrote, "I wish I felt better about the President. He is an awfully wounded man."

On July 23 Garfield's temperature spiked, and he came down with chills, indicating an infection. On August 14 he suffered an unrelenting attack of projectile vomiting, followed four days later by a swelling of the neck and a ghastly flow of pus that discharged through his mouth, nose, and ears. The infection was spreading. The cabinet was informed that the president's death appeared imminent. Vice President Arthur was told to stand by. THE END EXPECTED, read one newspaper headline. Then, remarkably, President Garfield rallied.

In the first week of September, he was moved out of Washington to the resort town of Elberon, New Jersey, near Long Branch. The risk of transporting him, his doctors concluded, outweighed the peril of keeping him in Washington, with its fetid air and malaria and the stinking Potomac River. Garfield was taken to a cottage near the Elberon Hotel. Positioned in a bedroom with a breathtaking view of the ocean, the president, breathing in the salt air, exclaimed, "This is delightful." When Robert Lincoln was shown into Garfield's sickroom, a big show was made of it, meant only to reassure the people that the wheels of government continued to turn. Not wishing to burden the president, Lincoln advised Garfield that the war department was running smoothly, and there was nothing urgent that required his immediate attention. When a reporter for the *New York Tribune* interviewed Robert after his meeting with the president, he maintained the deception.

"There is really nothing for me to tell you about the war department. It goes on in a routine way."

The reporter probed. "Do you expect any Indian troubles?" (Chief Sitting Bull, whose forces had wiped out Lieutenant Colonel George Armstrong Custer and the Seventh Calvary at the Battle of the Little Bighorn, had surrendered three weeks earlier, ending a five-year manhunt.)

Secretary Lincoln replied that there might be a "little trouble" with the Indians but he doubted there would be "any serious disturbances." He also indicated that he was confident that Garfield would recover.

But Robert was aware that the end was near. Death finally came on September 19, seventy-nine days after Garfield had been gunned down. "How it hurts here!" Garfield cried out, his hand positioned over his heart. An aide,

David Swain, came forward with a glass of water that Garfield gulped down. "Swain, can't you stop this. O, Swain!" Lucretia Garfield rushed in and held her husband's hand. Dr. Bliss leaned over his body and listened with his ear for the president's heartbeat. He detected a slight fluttering, but twenty minutes later, the heart of the forty-nine-year-old president gave out.

"It is over," Bliss said.

Lincoln and the other members of Garfield's cabinet submitted their resignations. In so doing they were following political protocol. Arthur sensibly refused to accept the resignations and asked every holdover from the Garfield administration to remain in office. But this was a political calculation designed to gain the confidence of a grieving nation. Arthur soon began to pick off the old cabinet members one at a time. The first to go was the treasury secretary, William Windom. Not surprisingly, next was Secretary of State James G. Blaine, Arthur's old political enemy and leader of the Half-Breeds faction of the Republican Party that supported civil service reform. The others followed, and before the end of the calendar year, every cabinet officer had been replaced, with one exception—Robert Lincoln.

In fall 1880, after four years of exile in France, Mary Todd Lincoln returned to Springfield a stooped, gray-haired old lady, "prostrated by illness, the light of life and joy blotted out for her." Mary once again moved into the home of her sister Elizabeth Edwards. Almost immediately, there was tension between the two sisters. Mary had brought with her a mind-boggling sixty-five trunks and crates that Elizabeth was gracious enough to store in two rooms at the back of the house, but it was hard for a woman of Elizabeth's small-town frugality to fathom how anyone would need all these things. The trunks weighed an estimated four tons and actually caused the floor to buckle in the center.

During Mary's earlier stay with her sister, following her release from Bellevue Place, she had socialized with family and old friends. This time, she lived like a hermit, "shrinking and sensitive," according to her niece Katharine Helm. Even when she was persuaded to go for a carriage drive, she demanded that the curtains be drawn. In her bedroom, Mary insisted on living in near total darkness. With the cataracts she suffered from, the darkness soothed her ailing eyes, but it also matched her desolate spirit. To this eye malady, Mary added a melodramatic dimension: She claimed she had been rendered nearly blind by incessant weeping. Springfield treated her as a curiosity, strange and a little crazy. Children found it hard to believe that she could be the widow of the great Abraham Lincoln.

Mary and Elizabeth bickered without end. After about six months, the burden of caring for Mary was crushing the mettle of the saintly Elizabeth Edwards, who poured out her resentment in a letter to her half-sister Emilie Helm. Elizabeth complained that Mary was so demanding she was requiring "every moment" of her time. She was also a hypochondriac: "Her enjoyment of a darkened room does not accord with my ideas of enjoying life," Elizabeth said. The newspapers, ever eager to pursue a degrading Mary Lincoln story, claimed she was exaggerating her illness. The *Chicago Tribune*, time and again favoring Robert Lincoln's point of view in its coverage of the Lincoln family, claimed that Mary's "immediate friends here consider her ailments to some extent imaginary." Mrs. Lincoln, the newspaper told its readers, was being "well cared for" by members of her sister's family. It also said that a physician who was often called to examine Mary found it so "unnecessary" that he sometimes refused to send her a bill. Grudgingly, the newspaper acknowledged that while Mrs. Lincoln was "not in good health," the American public could "rest assured" that she was well provided for financially and medically. Adopting this theme, the *New York Times* reported, "Mrs. Lincoln is not really sick." According to the *Times*' mean-spirited account, Mrs. Lincoln suffered from a "hysterical condition."

"Her sufferings are wholly imaginary. She could live for many years."

One of those who helped care for Mary was her great-niece, Mary Edwards, the sixteen-year-old granddaughter of Elizabeth Edwards. Mary Edwards became Mary Brown, and she would live well into the twentieth century. In 1956, when she was ninety years old, she vividly recalled Mary Lincoln's eccentricities in an interview published in *Life* magazine. To put it bluntly, Mrs. Brown said, Mary Lincoln was "a lot of trouble."

"It was very hard on Cousin Robert. He suffered a lot and his mother wouldn't speak to him and said he was a robber, that he had stolen her silver and her jewelry."

The great-niece could still recollect the screaming matches that erupted between Mary Lincoln and Elizabeth Edwards.

"Aunt Mary had a lot of money that she kept in a money belt, even under her nightdress, but sometimes she hid it in other places. One day she said Grandmother had stolen her money. Mother was there—she always got along with Aunt Mary because she never argued with her like Grandmother did. Well, Aunt Mary had a commode with a piece of Oriental carpet on top—she kept it beside her bed. Mother and Grandmother got her up on that, and Grandmother dived her hand in under the mattress and there was a big roll of bills."

The floor of the house creaked under the weight of Mary's trunks, Mrs. Brown recalled in the 1959 *Life* interview, under the headline, AN OLD LADY'S LINCOLN MEMORIES.

"In the room next to her Aunt Mary had 65 trunks. Grandmother's maid left because she was afraid to sleep under that room, with all that weight. The trunks were filled with bolts of curtain materials and dress goods. Aunt Mary had a lot of clothes in her trunk made out of elegant foreign material she brought abroad, and she had basted it together to look like dresses—to escape customs duty. She wouldn't stop buying. . . . She had about a hundred shawls. Every day she got up and went through these trunks for hours. Grandmother said it was funny, if Aunt Mary was so sick, that she was able to be up all day bending over her trunks."

The *Life* magazine writer asked Mrs. Brown, "Was Mrs. Lincoln really as ill as she imagined those days when you were sitting with her?"

"She had terrible headaches," Mrs. Brown answered. "And she was puffed up. . . . Her fingers swelled up and she had to take off her wedding ring. . . . She took a lot of bottles of 'restorative,' it was recalled, and it had a paregoric in it, same as opium, but you could get those things without prescriptions then."

In May 1881, Robert Lincoln traveled west to inspect Fort Leavenworth, in Kansas. At the time it was the main U.S. Army base in the military campaign to drive out the Native Americans. On his way back he took time off from War Department duties to stop in Chicago to help his wife prepare for the family's permanent move to Washington, where Robert had been living alone since his confirmation as secretary of war. Robert was pleased to be back on Wabash Avenue in a spirited household filled with three loving youngsters; very soon they would all be under the same roof in Washington. But he was facing a difficult undertaking: the time had come to settle things with his mother.

Robert took the train to Springfield, taking with him his daughter Mamie, the special little treasure, now a little lady of twelve, who could always touch Mary Lincoln's heart. They stayed at the Leland Hotel, and the next morning, a Sunday, he took Mamie by the hand and they went to the home of Elizabeth and Ninian Edwards.

Mary Lincoln and her son had not spoken a word to each other in five years, and their hostility toward each other must have been apparent. Nevertheless, Mary took great pride in Robert's rise to the position of secretary of war, and she was at a point in her life where she could be forgiving. This reconciliation was the result of five years of arduous mediation by Elizabeth Edwards, and the presence of that cherished little girl helped heal the hurt. Robert told his mother he was sorry for the way he had treated her, and begged her to accept his apology. He said he had come to forget the past, and asked her to love him again. In that moment all of Mary's fury seemed to dissolve.

Pointedly, the encounter did not last long; later that evening, Robert dined with the governor of Illinois and two military aides from the war department who were traveling with him, Adjutant General Richard Drum and Judge Advocate Thomas Barr. Then, he and Mamie left for Chicago on the midnight train, and when he returned to Washington, it was with his family in tow. Robert was content to have made peace with his mother, but probably couldn't help but wonder what mischief the old lady might be up to next. Meanwhile, the Robert Lincolns settled into a handsome rented white-brick house on Massachusetts Avenue, just east of Thomas Circle.

It wasn't long before Mary stirred things up again. Though her eyesight was murky with cataracts and she could barely walk, just a few weeks after President Garfield's assassination, the indomitable Mrs. Lincoln took to the road once more. Mary headed east, first to the spa at St. Catharines on the Canadian side of Niagara Falls, and then on to New York City, where she arrived at the train depot so "thoroughly exhausted" the hackman, as drivers were called in those days, had to lift her into his carriage. Mrs. Lincoln told the driver to take her to West Twenty-sixth Street, off Broadway. This was the location of Dr. E. P. Miller's Home of Health, and Mary checked into a grimy room that she facetiously called "choice." Part hotel, part Turkish and Roman bathhouse, the Home of Health occupied three buildings at Nos. 37, 39, and 41 on West Twenty-sixth Street and offered the latest remedy for pain, hydroelectric therapy. Every day Mary would position herself in the sitz bath (a name taken from the German word *sitzen*, meaning to sit), a special bath of saltwater that covered only the hips and buttocks, while the upper body, arms, legs, and feet remained dry. She also tried out the hydroelectric bath treatment, which entailed fully immersing herself in a tub of water through which an electric current was passed, to stimulate her muscles and improve her blood circulation. The tub had special safety features, including legs set on rubber pads to prevent fatal electric shocks.

In New York, Mary's personal physician was Dr. Lewis Sayre, a *Mayflower* descendant and old childhood acquaintance from Lexington. Sayre was one of America's best-known doctors and the father of orthopedic surgery. His textbooks were the standard reference for a generation of medical professionals. One of his great innovations was the Sayre jacket to treat curvature of the spine; it encased the patient's entire trunk in plaster of Paris. When Mary Lincoln arrived in New York, Sayre had just been elected president of the American Medical Association.

As stories about Mary's hypochondria continued to circulate, at Mary's urging, Sayre became Mary Lincoln's public advocate. He called a newspaper reporter to say how appalling it was that anyone would accuse Mrs. Lincoln of hypochondria or question the seriousness of her medical condition. Sayre said he could confirm that Mrs. Lincoln was physically "incapacitated" and required constant care, including a full-time nurse. Further, he said, something had to be done to help Abraham Lincoln's widow financially.

The Sayre interview set in motion a flurry of articles in which Mary Lincoln once again returned to the front pages of America's leading newspapers. One reporter who went to Dr. Miller's hotel found Mary Lincoln in her "plainly furnished" room on the second floor and spent two hours with the former First Lady.

"Mrs. Lincoln sat propped up with pillows on a sofa," he wrote. "She cannot move without assistance. Her chief physical ailment is a spinal disease, caused by a severe fall received while she was in Europe. She is, in fact, deserted and next to friendless."

It was also becoming evident that, despite their Springfield reconciliation, Mary had not forgiven her son. A prominent New Yorker who had recently spoken with Mrs. Lincoln, and was interviewed on condition of anonymity, said he had asked Mary Lincoln why Robert was not more helpful.

"Her son Robert was now Secretary of War, and I could see no reason why he should not be requested to give her some aid," he said. "I was sure he could do so, and would if he knew she was in need. Mrs. Lincoln begged me not to do so, saying her son had a large family and needed all he had. But I told her I would do it, and if he refused I would write to President Arthur. I know Mr. Arthur very well, and I proposed to lay the matter before him and to insist that if Lincoln didn't assist his mother he should be turned out of the Cabinet."

There was very little doubt, this source said, that Mrs. Lincoln and her son were not on the best of terms. He then went on to relate the story of Tad Lincoln's death. Tad had been Mrs. Lincoln's "favorite son." When the teenager realized he was dying, he threw his arms around his mother's neck and cried out, "O mother, to think I must be taken away, and you left to live with Robert!" That, at least, is the story Mary Lincoln wanted out there.

To Robert's chagrin, the renewed attention his mother was receiving came as President Arthur, in office just twenty-nine days, was leading a procession of dignitaries to Yorktown to celebrate the centennial of the British surrender. The entire Washington diplomatic corps had been invited to accompany the president on a steamer down Chesapeake Bay for a grand naval review, fireworks, and patriotic speeches. Arthur's cabinet was on board, along with the cabinet wives, including Mary Harlan Lincoln. Much to her discomfort, Mary found herself engaged in a discussion about her mother-in-law with President Arthur and the American businessman Cyrus W. Field. Interestingly, after the festivities, Mary Harlan Lincoln went directly to New York, and for the first time in years, visited with her mother-in-law. It must have been a remarkable encounter. Now Mary Todd Lincoln could say in interviews that she found herself alone in the world but for two exceptions—"her son Robert and his wife, Mary, who visit her at intervals of two or three weeks."

Around this time, the financial trouble of another presidential widow was also receiving attention. The frail and stoic Lucretia Garfield was only forty-nine when her husband was assassinated. Now she was a grieving widow with five children to support, having returned to Ohio to live on the family farm. Congress was considering authorizing a five-thousand-dollar annual pension for the woman. When Mary Lincoln heard this, she girded herself for one final pitched political battle. If Lucretia Garfield deserved five thousand dollars, why not Mary Lincoln? Mary sought out an old ally from Springfield, Reverend Noyes W. Miner, who was now pastor at a Baptist church in New Jersey. She invited Miner and his wife to visit her at Dr. Miller's Home of Health. They were appalled at what they saw. Mary sat in the room unable to walk, "almost blind," and without a nurse or a companion to assist her. A few days later, an indignant Miner stirred the pot by recounting his encounter with President Lincoln's widow before his audience of Baptist ministers who were in New York for their national convention.

Prodded by Mary, when the Forty-seventh Congress returned following Christmas break in 1882, Miner took her case to Washington. He had with him a set of instructions from one of the country's great political strategists—Mary Lincoln. The most important thing, Mary advised the Baptist minister, was the "absolute necessity" to be there when Congress convened on January 5. "Leave no one *untalked to*," she advised him. "Overpower them all by your good words." The near-blind invalid who could not walk down a flight of stairs without assistance seemed to be completely clued in to the Washington power elite. She gave Miner the names of eight important congressmen he absolutely had to collar—Logan, Springer, Hewitt, Cox, Anthony, Singleton, Ingalls, and Cameron. She fretted about her old foe David Davis, who had resigned his seat on the Supreme Court; he was now the United States senator from Illinois and the newly elected president *pro tempore* of the Senate, second in line to the presidency should Chester A. Arthur die in office. "He will prove himself an ungrateful villain in the matter," Mary predicted. And one more thing, Mary told Miner—"be kind enough NOT to say a word about bonds." Shrewd counsel, as Mary thought it prudent not to remind Congress that although she was pleading poverty, she still had considerable assets that at the time totaled eighty-four thousand dollars.

Mary wrote her advice to Miner on the morning of January 3, 1882, from her miserable room at Dr. Miller's Home of Health. She must have been in one of her manic states, because at 5:00 P.M. that same day she sent Miner a follow-up letter with one additional instruction. She had thought of something important that she had to tell him.

"*Do not* approach Robert T. Lincoln," she warned.

Victory came with surprising ease. With the country still recovering from the trauma of the Garfield assassination, national pride mandated that Lucretia Garfield and the other living presidential widows be accommodated. Without much debate, Congress voted to authorize Mrs. Garfield a five-thousand-dollar pension, and raise Mary Lincoln's pension from three thousand to five thousand, plus fifteen thousand in back payments. The other two surviving presidential widows—Julia Tyler and Sarah Polk—also received five-thousand-dollar pensions.

But the vote failed to bring much joy to Mary. In her paranoia, she suspected that that old villain David Davis was working behind the scenes to derail the bill with a presidential veto. And even after Arthur signed the measure into law, a new worry plagued Mary. Where was the check? "Until I see the $15,000—I will not believe it," Mary said. When February came and still no check had arrived, Mary was frantic.

On February 14, 1882, after complaining about the "miserable" food, Mary left Dr. Miller's Home of Health, declaring the place to be "very false" and a "swindle." She checked into the Grand Central Hotel to recuperate from the hydroelectric treatment that had left her in a state of exhaustion. It also galled her to read that a public subscription had raised the astonishing sum of $360,000 for the beloved Lucretia Garfield. Why, Mary wondered, had she become such a polarizing figure in America? Why had her country turned against her?

"Mr. Miner," she said, "what have I done that I am so persecuted by the press. I am a poor, lonely woman; my husband is dead, and two of my sons are dead; my health is shattered and I am almost blind from constant weeping. I try to keep myself secluded from the world but I cannot escape them; they will follow me and say hard and cruel things about me. I long to leave the world and be at rest."

The time had come for her to return to Springfield. Mary arranged to have her invalid's chair sent on ahead, and asked her grandnephew Lewis to meet her at the Springfield depot when her train pulled in at seven in the morning on Friday, March 24. She went to her sister Elizabeth's house and sequestered herself in her little room, with curtains drawn, for the next three months.

Mary Lincoln had one more tribulation to face before death came to her. In the last weeks of her life, she was stricken with an outbreak of boils. The pus-filled abscesses erupted all over her body; the misery it brought her was biblical, like Job's. It was July 15, 1882. Did anyone in Mary's family realize the magnitude of the day? It was the eleventh anniversary of the death of Tad Lincoln.

The end was near. Dr. T. W. Dresser, Mary's physician, was summoned, and Robert Lincoln was notified by telegram in Washington. Mary told her loved ones that she knew she was dying. Those were her last words. At one o'clock the following morning, she slipped into a coma and never awakened. Like Job's, her life had come to represent the epitome of suffering. But her last hours were peaceful and serene. She had not appeared to be in any pain. Her physician was holding her hand to check her pulse with his timepiece when her heart just stopped. The precise time was noted as 8:15 in the evening. She was sixty-four years old.

Robert immediately left Washington for Chicago to gather his wife and children so they could travel together as a family to Springfield for the funeral. Mary Harlan Lincoln had been vacationing in Colorado Springs with Mamie, Jack, and Jessie when she received Robert's telegram informing her of his mother's death. They all boarded the next train to Chicago, but when Robert arrived to pick them up, something happened: Mary refused to attend the funeral. Even now that her mother-in-law was in her casket, Mary Harlan Lincoln could not bear to be in the same room with her. Officially, it was announced that Mrs. Robert Lincoln was confined to her house due to "ill-health," and unable to make the journey.

When the secretary of war reached Springfield, he went directly to his aunt Elizabeth's house on Second Street. Elizabeth had ordered an open casket, which met with Robert's approval. Robert went to the parlor and looked at his mother, at her hands folded across her chest, and her mouth shaped into a slender smile. She wore her wedding ring—the ring Abraham Lincoln had placed on her finger when they were married in the very house where Mary Lincoln now lay in repose. She had not been able to wear it for the last year or so of her life because her fingers had been swollen by diabetes. But on the day of her funeral, the ring, worn thin with age, was where Abraham Lincoln had put it on her wedding day. It was of Etruscan gold, inscribed, "A.L., to Mary, Nov. 4, 1842. Love is Eternal."

At ten o'clock the casket was removed from the Edwards home and taken directly to the First Presbyterian Church. To the mournful and steady meter of Beethoven's funeral march, it was borne inside by an honor guard of pallbearers that included Governor Shelby Cullom, Judge Samuel H. Treat, and Mary Lincoln's Springfield banker, Jacob Bunn. It was positioned on a bier draped in white velvet. Robert Lincoln and his three aunts—Mary Lincoln's sisters—took their seats in the front pew reserved for the family and honored dignitaries. Everyone agreed that the Reverend James Reed's sermon was touching, yet glossed over nothing. When Abraham Lincoln was killed in 1865, Reed said, Mary had died with him.

"The lightning that struck down the strong man unnerved the woman. The sharp iron of this pungent grief went to her soul," Reed said. The marriage of Mary and Abraham Lincoln brought to the minister's mind two tall and stately pine trees he had observed the previous summer in the Allegheny Mountains. The trees stood on a rocky ledge and had grown so close to each other that they were united at the base, with interlocking roots penetrating the soil. But the taller of the trees had been struck by lightning years ago, leaving it scarred and dead, while the small tree lingered in fellowship until it too died in solidarity. "Both trees had suffered from the same calamity. They had virtually been killed at the same time," Reed said. And so it was with Mary Lincoln.

As the choir sang "Rest, Spirit, Rest," the casket was borne out of the church. The funeral procession, with Robert at its head, proceeded in carriages to Oak Ridge Cemetery on the outskirts of the city. A huge crowd lined the streets of Springfield. By order of the governor and mayor, all government offices were closed for the funeral. Every business and every store in the city was shut down. It was the largest gathering of mourners in Springfield since the funeral of President Lincoln in 1865. Ahead rose the magnificent obelisk that marked the Lincoln tomb where the remains rested of Abraham Lincoln, and the sons—Eddie, Willie, and Tad—Mary Todd Lincoln had borne him. Mary's casket was carried into the catacomb. A final prayer was spoken. At last, Mary would be with her beloved husband and sons.

16

The Man Who Could Be President

THE BURDEN OF collecting Mary Todd Lincoln's lifetime of possessions fell to the woman who refused to attend her funeral—her daughter-in-law Mary Harlan Lincoln.

Mary Todd Lincoln's things were transported by rail to the town of Mount Pleasant, Iowa, where a large room on the third floor of the Harlan family home was cleared out to make space for sixty-five trunks. The Harlan house was set on a broad tree-lined street on the campus of Iowa Wesleyan College. It had wide porches on three sides, a long galley inside, and parlors in the front and the rear. The most magnificent room in the house was the library, where an entire tier of books was a sad reminder of Will Harlan, Mary's brother who died of tuberculosis at age twenty-four. They were his law books.

Mary spent months organizing her late mother-in-law's goods. One summer day she invited her cousin Florence Snow to see what she had accomplished. Florence followed Mary up the stairs, and when she entered the storage room she could not believe that Mrs. Abraham Lincoln could have amassed so much property in one lifetime. Mary made a remark about her mother-in-law's "mania" for shopping and showed Florence around. Piles of clothes had been set up on long trestle tables with index cards indicating where they were going to be shipped. Some items were destined for Lincoln relatives; others, of historical value, were to be sent to institutions such as the Smithsonian Institution and the Chicago Historical Society. Mary Lincoln had been dead two years, but the task was so time-consuming there were still several trunks her daughter-in-law had yet to open. They were lined up against the wall awaiting her inspection. But the most demanding part of the work was over.

Mary sighed. "And here am I," she told her cousin, "decided [sic] what to do with this unconscionable accumulation." In all these months of sorting and organizing the collection, Mary still could not summon a kind word about her late mother-in-law.

Florence looked around in wonder. Many of the woolen garments were sprinkled with red pepper. Mary explained that this was to keep the moths out.

"It's mighty lucky I could have this room with so many windows," Mary remarked. She showed Florence the hundreds of children's outfits and trinkets her mother-in-law had purchased for the three Lincoln grandchildren. Mary said she intended to give them to Mamie, Jack, and Jessie, and to the children of friends and servants employed by the Lincoln family. Then Mary showed Florence the gowns that the former First Lady had worn on state occasions in the White House during the Civil War. Holding the garments aloft, Mary said they would one day make splendid gifts for her two daughters. Florence could tell that Mary was "heavily burdened" by the immensity of the task, and told her how much she admired her for taking it on. Mary responded that this was her chore and she would see it to its completion—"like the Harlan she was and the Lincoln she had become."

It seemed that the Lincolns were doing everything they could to eradicate Mary Todd Lincoln from the annals of family history, or at least diminish her role in it. Little Mamie, who had been named after the former First Lady, was now informed that she had actually been named after her mother. Mamie was a charming girl of fifteen with a shapely chin, delicate neck, and pretty mouth. She wore her thick brunette hair in two braids around her head—an appealing young lady on the brink of womanhood, as Florence Snow described her. One day Florence asked Mamie what it meant to be the progeny of the Lincoln bloodline. It was an honor, Mamie replied, but then, she said, she considered herself just as much Harlan as Lincoln.

"She did not speak of her Grandmother Lincoln," Florence recounted.

Robert Lincoln also made a peculiar effort at shaping and manipulating history's depiction of his mother. He reached out to acquaintances and members of his family and asked them to send him all of his mother's correspondence related to her "distressing mental disorder." He made no secret of what he planned to do with the letters. He intended to burn them. He wanted nothing less than the systematic destruction of any records pertaining to his mother's mental crisis—and with them, his own distressing role in her institutionalization. But there came a point when even Robert realized it was an exercise in futility. Letters written by Abraham and Mary Lincoln were already collector's items; there was such an explosion of interest in America for anything related to the life of the sixteenth president that a name had been coined for it—Lincolniana. It would be impossible for Robert to gather everything, as he later acknowledged, telling a friend, "I long ago came to the conclusion that one could not imagine a more hopeless work than an effort to collect [the letters] or even a large fraction of them." But he still managed to retrieve "hundreds" of his mother's letters and earmark them "for destruction."

As his wife sorted and catalogued Mary Todd Lincoln's things and raised the children, Robert Lincoln carried on as secretary of war. He was the last man standing from the Garfield cabinet, and insiders were predicting that he was on the way out, to be replaced by someone whose thinking was more in line with the current administration's. But other "considerations" stopped President Chester A. Arthur from firing his war secretary—undoubtedly, the political impracticality of dumping the son of the Great Emancipator. Privately, Robert may have welcomed the boot from President Arthur. He was having a miserable time at the war department. His heart just did not seem to be in it. He expressed a longing for the "independence" of Chicago, and complained to his friend John Hay that Washington's climate was making his children sick.

At age forty, Robert started to develop a middle-age paunch. He weighed 190 pounds and his face was broad and square, so unlike his gaunt and haunted-looking father's. He wore a chimney-pot hat and grew a sweeping mustache and a short-cropped but thick brown beard. His full head of hair was not yet showing any flecks of gray. He almost always wore black.

For most of the day he sat behind his mahogany desk at the War Department. His top aide, Thomas Barr, was positioned in a corner of the office, while two male clerks who could take dictation waited outside. Cabinet meetings were held twice a week, at noon, at the White House. Robert usually wrapped up his workday at four in the afternoon. A late night at the office was 6:00 P.M., though he would often go home with a briefcase full of paperwork and newspapers and continue working into the evening—a box of Henry Clay cigars at the ready—in a small bedroom on the second floor that he had converted into an office.

There were 25,000 troops in the army—a number fixed by statute—with most of them stationed out West to deal with Indian uprisings in Arizona and New Mexico. The Apache warrior Geronimo was the only remaining Indian chieftain who refused to recognize the authority of the United States in the West; at one point more than one-fourth of the U.S. Army and five hundred scouts were assigned to his capture. The commanding general of the United States Army was Lieutenant General Philip Sheridan, and there was "considerable friction" between him and Robert Lincoln, resulting in an exchange of several "very pointed" letters which indicate that the secretary of war considered Sheridan insubordinate, and threatened to go to President Arthur if he refused to bow to civilian authority.

Sheridan and Lincoln were different kinds of men, and their clashes had more to do with personality than government policy. "Little Phil" Sheridan came from a hardscrabble background. He had a "bad attitude" at West Point and was suspended for a year after he had threatened to run a classmate through with his bayonet. He graduated thirty-fourth in a class of fifty-two. After his valiant record in the Civil War, Sheridan led U.S. forces in the military operation against the Indian nations in the West. He lived with a Native American mistress during this tour of duty—the daughter of a chief—and was condemned for a wisecrack he made to the Comanche chief Tosawi, known as "Silver Knife," in 1869. During peace talks, the Indian leader told Sheridan, "Me, Tosawi; me good Injun." Sheridan is said to have answered, "The only good Indians I ever saw were dead." Along the way, the quote surfaced as the notorious, "The only good Indian is a dead Indian." It rankled Sheridan to be reporting to Robert Lincoln, whom he considered to be unqualified to lead the United States Army.

Temperamentally, Robert may have been ill suited to run a department in which a certain esprit de corps was essential to great leadership. Nothing proved this more than his disastrous handling of the Greely expedition to the Arctic.

Adolphus Greely was an ambitious army second lieutenant serving in the signal corps. In the late 1870s he was named commander of an Arctic expeditionary force that was to establish meteorological and magnetic observation posts in the northern reaches of Greenland. Greely thought his expedition would rank in importance with Lewis and Clark's. But Robert Lincoln was indifferent to the polar initiative; he considered it to be a "pseudoscientific wild goose chase into nowhere," and a diversion from the

War Department's primary mission—opening the West and defending settlers from Indian attack. Although Congress had appropriated twenty-five thousand dollars for the expedition, Lincoln put off signing the necessary paperwork that would have authorized Greely to purchase supplies such as arctic footwear, windproof lanterns, chronometers, and other scientific equipment. Frustrated with the delay, Greely called on Lincoln and demanded to know why he was defying the will of Congress. Lincoln could not believe the impertinence of a *lieutenant* making demands on the secretary of war. He signed the paperwork but he could never forgive Greely.

In 1881, Greely and twenty-five soldiers left for Grinnell Land, 600 miles from the North Pole. Their major food supply was an excellent source of energy and protein called pemmican—dried buffalo meat mixed with fat, cranberries, and cherries. Greely and his men set up a chain of stations for scientific observations; collected specimens, weather and tidal data; and explored the northern reaches of the Earth. He came within 450 miles of the North Pole, a record.

Disaster struck in summer 1882 when a relief ship loaded with supplies and reinforcements found its way blocked by ice and failed to reach Greely. The following summer, another relief vessel split apart in the Arctic ice and sank. In Washington, Robert Lincoln reacted with all the insouciance of a merciless industrialist of the Gilded Age; he declared that, for the time being, nothing could be done because of the impracticality of sending out another rescue ship. He informed Congress that it was "only a matter of conjecture" that Greely and his men were in any real danger. Privately, however, he let it be known that he had to assume Greely and the twenty-five soldiers had perished. Lincoln, it was said, "did not see any use throwing away more money for dead men."

There was a groundswell of protest, led by Greely's devoted wife Henrietta Greely, and her public campaign shamed Lincoln and the Arthur administration. Congress authorized unlimited funds to launch a rescue operation, but even though Greely was army, the mission was pointedly assigned to the navy. On May 1, 1884, the USS *Thetis* and two other navy ships under the command of Captain Winfield Scott Schley left New York Harbor and sailed north. Six weeks later they found the Greely expedition encamped at Pim Island in the northernmost region of Canada. There were only seven survivors out of the original force of twenty-six men. Eighteen men had starved to death; Greely executed another solider for stealing rations. Only one of Greely's soldiers had the strength to wave a feeble greeting to the *Thetis,* then fell flat on his face on the ice. Greely was so weak he had to be carried aboard on a stretcher. Captain Schley reported that had he been delayed just two days he would have found the entire Greely expedition dead of starvation.

The survivors returned to the United States on August 1, 1884, landing at Portsmouth, New Hampshire, and came ashore on their own feet to a hero's welcome. Secretary of the Navy William Chandler was present to offer his congratulations, but Robert Lincoln was conspicuously absent. Chandler read a message from Lincoln in which the war secretary praised Captain Schley for his "inestimable services," but mentioned not one word of the three years of suffering Greely and the other surviving members had endured. Nor was Lincoln present a week later when Greely and his men landed in New York City. Greely also learned to his dismay that he had been passed over for promotion to captain, and he always assumed that Robert Lincoln had been behind the rebuff.

Greely would not be officially recognized for heroism until 1935, when, at the age of ninety-five, living in Washington, and expressing concern about the rise of Adolph Hitler, he was awarded the Congressional Medal of Honor—only the fourth man in U.S. history to be so honored for peacetime heroism (Charles Lindbergh, Richard Byrd, and Byrd's pilot Floyd Bennett were the others). Until his final days, Greely considered Robert Lincoln responsible for the needless deaths of his men.

Within the army, Robert's actions were deemed a betrayal of the military code of honor. Could this truly be the son of the Great Emancipator, whose anguish over the loss of his soldiers during the Civil War was so evidently etched on his forlorn face? General William Hazen, the chief of the signal corps, held true scorn for the secretary of war and took the extraordinary step of openly demanding a congressional investigation. In private correspondence sent to Lincoln, he blamed him for the loss of life suffered by the Greely expedition.

Robert Lincoln warned the general to keep the issues between them confidential. But Hazen arranged to meet with a reporter from the *Washington Evening Star* in a quiet corner at the Ebbitt Hotel, and during the on-the-record interview he told the reporter what he really thought of Robert Lincoln. It was a bold, but unforgivable, breach of the military rules of conduct. The next day, President Arthur informed the general that he should consider himself under arrest. The *Chicago Tribune,* in keeping with its long history of support for Robert Lincoln, even in the most challenging of circumstances, wrote of General Hazen: "If ever an officer deserved to be court-martialed for infraction of army discipline and for disrespect to his superiors it is Gen. Hazen." Hazen was found guilty, but his sentence was simply a public rebuke, which he deemed a vindication, and he was permitted to continue to run the signal corps.

In fairness to Robert, he was a solid administrator. Previous war secretaries openly let the department run itself. For years, the most powerful civilian in the department was not the secretary of war, but the chief clerk, who was given carte blanche to run the day-to-day operation while the secretaries focused on politics and big-picture policy. But under the assertive—some would say arrogant—Robert Lincoln, there was no question who was in charge. "He is absolutely at the head of the department . . . and he yields none of his power or authority." Robert brought a good-government sensibility to the running of a department that was notorious for its casual corruption. He streamlined the army budget and found one million dollars in efficiencies, and took steps such as refusing to look the other way when army officers put in for all-expenses-paid vacations to New York City under the pretext of visiting West Point.

Revenge was a powerful stimulus for Robert. He demonstrated his capacity to hold a grudge when he learned that Ward Hill Lamon, the author of *The Life of Abraham Lincoln*, a book he despised, was seeking the position of postmaster for the city of Denver. Robert used his influence in the Arthur administration to scuttle the appointment. Later, when he was questioned about it by an incensed Lamon, Robert took pleasure in letting his father's devoted companion and bodyguard know that he took personal responsibility for sabotaging the appointment. He admitted that he had told the postmaster general of the United States that naming Lamon postmaster of Denver would be "personally offensive to me." And he went on to explain why. He referred to the first paragraph on page 10 of Lamon's book, in which, citing the research of William Herndon, Lamon claimed it was possible that Abraham Lincoln's parents had never married. It was an "insinuation which was especially offensive," Robert wrote Lamon, and "an astonishing exhibition of malicious ingratitude on your part towards your dead benefactor."

Lamon was furious. He had fallen on hard times and had been counting on a dependable government payroll. He had also been around long enough to remember Robert Lincoln as the irresponsible Harvard snob who had misplaced the briefcase containing his father's inaugural address.

Lamon wrote Lincoln back and revealed that he was at work on a new book—an investigative biography of the secretary of war. The threat touched a chord in Robert—his pathological aversion to media attention and the glare of the spotlight. He sought the counsel of David Davis, who knew Lamon from the old days when Davis, Lamon, and Abraham Lincoln all rode the Illinois court circuit.

"I appeal to you in the name of the great dead, and in the name of your living friends, not to publish anything concerning Robert T. Lincoln," Davis wrote Lamon. "It would grieve me beyond measure, and many besides, who have loved you and Mr. Lincoln." Lamon never published the book. Most likely, he never even seriously worked on it—he just knew that even his threat to publish it would be enough to give Robert many sleepless nights.

In the closing days of 1883, Robert and Mary Lincoln were shocked to hear that Henry Rathbone had murdered his wife, Clara Harris.

Rathbone was a young army major engaged to marry Clara Harris when they unexpectedly received an invitation to accompany President and Mrs. Lincoln to the theater, on Good Friday, April 14, 1865—this, after Robert Lincoln and General Ulysses S. Grant and Mrs. Grant had turned the First Lady down. Rathbone, the son of the former mayor of Albany, and Clara Harris, the daughter of Senator Ira Harris of New York, were sitting in the presidential box at Ford's Theatre when John Wilkes Booth shot the president in the back of the head. When Rathbone stepped forward to apprehend the assassin, Booth slashed him with a dagger and cut a deep wound in his arm, from elbow to shoulder. Clara Harris's white satin dress was saturated in blood that everyone assumed was Abraham Lincoln's. Actually it was Rathbone's. Clara could not bring herself to wash the dress, and later that summer when she returned to her family's cottage in Loudonville, New York, outside Albany, she took the bloodstained dress with her and left it hanging in her bedroom closet. The months passed.

On the first anniversary of Lincoln's assassination, Clara said she was awakened in the night by the sound of laughter. She told her family it was the ghost of Abraham Lincoln, chortling as he had on the night of his assassination, when he was enjoying the comedy *Our American Cousin* moments before Booth fired the fatal shot.

Rathbone had married Clara Harris in 1867, and they had had three children. Like Mary Todd Lincoln, the haunted Rathbone had spent the next decade of his life seeking treatment at spas and searching for a cure for his delusions, unbearable headaches, and undefined physical maladies. All the while, the bloodstained white dress hung in the closet, because Clara could not bring herself either to wash it or destroy it. With the dress still hanging—some would say entombed—in the closet, she had the closet bricked off. The years passed. In 1883, the Rathbones were living in Hanover, Germany, where Henry was serving as U.S. consul. On Christmas Eve, shortly before dawn, Rathbone entered his wife's bedroom, pulled out a revolver, shot his wife, and then stabbed himself six times. In some ways it was a replay of that night in the presidential box at Ford's Theatre, but this time Rathbone pulled the trigger and wielded the dagger. Rathbone survived, and spent the rest of his life in an asylum for the criminally insane in Hildesheim, Germany. (Rathbone died of natural causes in 1911.)

What happened next to Clara's white satin dress is quite a story. Rathbone's son, Henry, who had been thirteen when his mother was murdered, grew up to become a United States representative from upstate New York. In 1910, he tore down the brick wall in his mother's closet in Albany. The bloodstained dress was still there, and he set it on fire. He said it had been the source of the curse that had haunted his family.

Some say Ford's Theatre itself was cursed. Following Lincoln's assassination, the federal government seized the building and ordered that it never again be used as a place of entertainment or public amusement. The Ford family was paid a hundred thousand dollars in compensation, and the building was turned into a records facility for the War Department. On June 9, 1893, Ford's Theatre collapsed, killing twenty-two federal clerks.

The 1884 Republican nomination for president was shaping up to be a slugfest between Chester A. Arthur and James G. Blaine, and there was serious talk of Robert Lincoln entering the field as a dark-horse candidate. No matter his personal shortcomings, nothing seemed to stain Robert Lincoln; such was the residue of his father's legacy. The *New York Times* pushed for Lincoln's nomination, saying in an editorial, "What stronger name could be presented to the convention, what name more certain to secure a hearty endorsement than that of Robert T. Lincoln." The secretary of war was "entirely acceptable to every group and faction of the party and has the confidence of all Republicans," the *Times* noted.

The *Chicago Tribune* also advocated Robert Lincoln for president, although the newspaper had to concede that Robert was not a born politician. "I do not think he is overfond of public life," said the *Tribune's* man in Washington, T. C. Crawford. "If he is he has a most skillful way of concealing it. He dreads an interview for newspaper publication as any small boy would a visit from the dentist." As a loyal member of Arthur's cabinet, Lincoln was irritated by talk of a presidential bid, and let it be known that he was "heartily" for the incumbent president's nomination. The truth was that Robert wanted nothing more to do with Washington. "I know that he has become tired of his position in the Cabinet," said the *Tribune*'s Crawford. Robert even considered resigning as war secretary, but, under the circumstances, he had to stay on; he knew that his resignation would be misinterpreted as a sign of disloyalty to President Arthur.

The Republican convention was held at the Crystal Palace in Chicago in June 1884. Blaine led on the first ballot, with Arthur in second place. Robert Lincoln sent word to his old ally Leonard Swett that under no circumstances should his name be placed in nomination for president or vice president. All the same, he received four votes. With the convention deadlocked, Lincoln's count rose to eight votes by the third ballot. Two young Republican rabble-rousers—Theodore Roosevelt and Henry Cabot Lodge—tried to rally the convention under Lincoln's banner. Another dark horse was former General William Tecumseh Sherman, but the Civil War hero ruled himself out with the statement that, to this day, remains the clearest, most definitive assurance that a person has no interest whatsoever in running for office: "If drafted, I will not run; if nominated, I will not accept; if elected, I will not serve." Blaine finally won on the fourth ballot. His opponent in the general election was the Democratic governor of New York State, Grover Cleveland.

The campaign of 1884 became infamous for unrelenting mudslinging. Cleveland, a foe of Tammany Hall, was deemed to be the candidate of good government, later known as "Grover the Good." So it came as a shock when the *Buffalo Evening Telegraph* revealed that Cleveland was paying child support for an orphan he had fathered out of wedlock. "Ma, Ma, where's my Pa?" became the taunting phrase chanted at Cleveland campaign events. It looked as if Blaine was headed to victory. Then came one of the great blunders in American political history. Blaine was giving a speech in New York when, in his presence, a Protestant clergyman launched into a denunciation of the Mugwumps—Republican defectors who were supporting Cleveland—saying, "We are Republicans, and don't propose to leave our party and identify ourselves with the party whose antecedents have been rum, Romanism and rebellion." The slur galvanized Catholic voters in New York. Even though Blaine's mother was a Roman Catholic of Irish descent and his sister was a nun, the former secretary of state was attacked as being anti-

Catholic. Blaine lost New York by just over one thousand votes, and it cost him the election in the Electoral College. Grover Cleveland became the first Democrat to be elected president since Abraham Lincoln's predecessor, James Buchanan, in 1856.

On February 25, 1885, a farewell dinner was held for the outgoing Arthur administration. It was an important social event, and all of the wives of the cabinet officers were expected to attend. Once again, Mary Harlan Lincoln failed to appear.

The Lincolns returned to Chicago in June, and Robert resumed the practice of law. The firm, having added a third partner, the well-connected William Gerrish Beale, was now called Isham, Lincoln & Beale. Beale was the first president of the prestigious Mid-Day Club, a private club that served sumptuous lunches to Chicago's leading professionals and businessmen. Edna Ferber fictionalized the Mid-Day Club as the Noon Club in her novel *So Big*, and her description of its exclusive membership certainly matched the three named partners in Isham, Lincoln & Beale: "Successful young Chicago business and professional men whose clothes were made at Peel's, who kept their collars miraculously clean in the soot-laden atmosphere of the Loop; whose shoes were bench made; who lunched at the Noon Club on the roof of the First National Bank where Chicago's millionaires ate corned beef hash whenever that plebeian dish appeared on the bill of fare."

The Lincolns became the pioneers of Chicago's Gold Coast. They found a handsome piece of corner property at 60 Lake Shore Drive, not far from Lincoln Park, and hired the architect Solon S. Beman to design a beauty of a house. It made an impressive statement with its brown brick and red sandstone facade topped by a high-pitched roof covered with dark slate. Inside there were twenty rooms, enormous tubs in the bathrooms, a carved staircase, ornate fireplaces and oak walls in the reception hall, and mahogany in the drawing room.

Robert was involved in all phases of the design and construction process, and his extraordinary—some would say obsessive—attention to detail could be seen in a letter to Beman in which he reminded the architect that there must not be any "white flaws" in the stone ordered for the front stairs. One wonders what Mary Todd Lincoln would have thought had she lived long enough to see her son residing in such splendor. Robert's neighbors included the banker and future treasury secretary Franklin MacVeagh and the dry goods merchant Potter Palmer, who had made a fortune with his "no questions asked" returns policy. The city even permitted Robert to string wires across Lincoln Park to power his house with electricity. What else could the Chicago Park Board do when the request came from the son of the national hero for whom the park was named? In return, Robert and his neighbors agreed to pay the costs of lighting the borders of Lincoln Park.

Robert and Mary watched the mansion go up with pride, though they lamented the slow pace of construction. "I am camping in my new home and can't get the painters off the first floor though they promised to be done a month ago," he complained to his friend John Nicolay. But his gratification was evident just two months later. "We are now getting really settled after six years of vagabonding—nothing but the sheriff or undertaker shall ever move us."

The race for the 1888 Republican nomination was coming down to perennial candidate James G. Blaine and two former treasury secretaries, Walter Gresham and John Sherman, the future author of the Sherman Anti-Trust Act and younger brother of General William Tecumseh Sherman. And once again there was Robert Lincoln hovering as a dark horse. Sizing up Lincoln's chances, the influential magazine *Harper's Weekly* noted that "sentimental considerations . . . are of great weight in practical politics." The *Republican* newspaper in Springfield, Massachusetts, called Lincoln the best secretary of war in recent times and just the man who could unite the divided party. Other publications were openly antagonistic. One newspaper in Omaha remarked, "It is curious how some papers hang on to the name of young Lincoln in discussing Presidential possibilities. . . . There are a hundred men in Omaha his superior."

The distress that two presidential assassinations had caused Robert left him deeply skeptical about public service. "I have seen too much of the wear and tear of official life to ever have a desire to reenter it," Robert candidly remarked. "Though I was but a boy when my father became President, I can well remember the tremendous burden he was called upon to bear. . . . I have seen enough of Washington official life to have lost all desire for it. The Presidential office is but a gilded prison. The care and worry outweigh, to my mind, the honor which surrounds the position." Contemplating his future at age forty-four, Robert said he anticipated living another twenty-five years. Even in this moment of reflection, he was viewing life through the calculus of an actuarial table. "I wish nothing better than to spend those years in my professional work," he said. "I am not willing, either, to have them embittered by an unsuccessful candidacy."

The Republican Party's national convention was held at the Crystal Palace in Lincoln's hometown of Chicago, giving him a strategic edge over his rivals. But Robert was nowhere to be found. Such was his disdain for the process that he actually fled the country. Reporters found him in England, in a hotel at Grosvenor Square in London, in the company of his favorite traveling companion—his daughter Mamie.

Republican party leaders who opened the *Tribune* on the morning of June 22, 1888, read Robert declare, "I am here to avoid the bother of politics and business and to get a rest." He then indicated his public support for Walter Gresham of Indiana. The convention went with a dark horse from Indiana, but it was not Gresham. When the votes were counted, the victor was Benjamin Harrison, grandson of the first president to die in office of natural causes, William Henry Harrison, who had served just thirty days and eleven hours.

Robert Lincoln and little Mamie stayed in London for ten weeks. When their ship docked in New York Harbor, Robert led Mamie down the gang-plank. He was wearing those quintessential trappings of the English gen-tleman—a bowler hat and a Scotch tweed suit from Poole's.

The election of 1888 was one of the most fraudulent in Americacan his-tory. Grover Cleveland won the popular vote but lost in the Electoral Col-lege. When a thankful Benjamin Harrison told the Republican Party boss Matthew Quay, "Providence has given us the victory," Quay responded, "Providence hadn't a damn thing to do with it." Quay said that Harrison, whom he found to be cold and unappreciative, would "never know how many Republicans were compelled to approach the gates of the peniten-tiary to make him President."

One week after Harrison was inaugurated president, a messenger appeared at the Washington homes of the two United States senators from Illinois, Shelby Cullom and Charles Farwell. They were informed that Pres-ident Harrison wished to see them at ten o'clock the following morning at the White House. Harrison cordially greeted the two Republicans. After some chitchat, the new president came to the purpose of the meeting. He said he wished to appoint an "Illinois man" to the post of minister to Great Britain.

"I am thinking of sending Robert T. Lincoln over there," President Har-rison said. The senators were delighted. This was the first they had heard that Lincoln was even under consideration.

President Harrison continued. "He has the experience in public life, he is well known and well thought of in all parts of the country. I believe his selection would give satisfaction not only in your state but everywhere else."

Cullom and Farwell heartily endorsed the nomination. Minister to Great Britain was the single most important foreign mission in the diplomatic service. It was a wonderful tribute to the state of Illinois, and they urged Harrison to send the nomination to the Foreign Relations Committee at once. The senators assured Harrison that Lincoln would be confirmed within a week. Harrison smiled, "He doesn't know anything about it yet."

The next day a reporter for the *Tribune* came to the offices of Isham, Lincoln & Beale. He was shown into Robert's office and found the lawyer behind his desk, grinning.

"You have heard of your appointment as Minister of Plenipotentiary and Envoy Extraordinary to the Court of St. James?"

Robert's smile broadened. "That's a high-sounding title for a plain man."

"Will you accept it?"

"I have not had time to give the matter a thought," Lincoln said. He had been officially informed of his nomination just a half hour before, in a telegram. "I did not know that my name had even been contemplated for the place. It is a total surprise."

The reporter asked, "You have been to England?"

"Yes, several times. I was abroad for six months in 1872, and also last summer."

"How do you like London?"

"A pleasant city."

"Have you many friends there?"

"A few." With that, Lincoln dismissed the reporter. Although he had sworn never to serve in government again, Lincoln accepted the president's nomination for one very self-serving reason—the "social benefits" that his family would be accorded as the American minister in England. His father may have been born in a log cabin, but Robert Todd Lincoln considered himself a full-blown member of the American aristocracy.

Lincoln went to Washington in early May and paid a courtesy call on President Harrison, then had private talks with Harrison's new secretary of state—none other than the "Plumed Knight" himself, James G. Blaine, his old colleague from the Garfield administration. Then Robert returned to

Chicago for a farewell dinner in his honor at the Union League Club. The next night, five hundred friends paid him tribute at the Chicago Club.

Lincoln gathered his family; everyone would be going to London. They went by rail, first to Washington and then on to New York. Mamie Lincoln was now nineteen years old, her brother Jack was sixteen, and Jessie thirteen.

In New York City, the Lincolns boarded the steamship *City of Paris* on May 15, 1889, and set sail for London—and personal catastrophe—on the other side of the Atlantic.

II.

Second Generation

17
Abraham Lincoln II

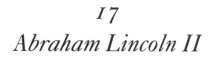

ABRAHAM LINCOLN II loved the sea. When he was a boy, and his father was secretary of war, the sturdy little fellow known as Jack was a regular passenger on the presidential yacht USS *Dispatch,* and became the sailors' pet. A navy tailor even fashioned a man-of-war uniform for the youngster. So Jack was in his element on the *City of Paris.* Traveling with the Lincoln family was Robert Lincoln's newly appointed personal secretary, Charles Isham, a distant cousin of his law partner.

The voyage lasted seven days. When the ship docked in Liverpool on March 22, 1889, the new American minister to the Court of St. James, along with his family, boarded a train to London. The entire American legation greeted the Lincolns on their arrival in the English capital, including the distinguished career diplomat Henry White, who was first legation secretary.

Robert presented his credentials to Queen Victoria at Windsor Castle. A few days later, all eyes in Victoria's court were fixed on Mary Harlan Lincoln and Mamie as they were shown into the drawing room at Buckingham Palace and introduced to the monarch, who was then in the fifty-second year of her reign. Although her husband, Prince Albert, had died twenty-eight years earlier, Victoria was still in a state of mourning, and wore black, as she would every day for the remainder of her life. How very like the widow of Abraham Lincoln! Queen Victoria had been an admirer of President Lincoln, and she was curious to meet the Great Emancipator's granddaughter. The wife of the new American minister to England wore a black silk dress and diamond earrings, and carried a bouquet of purple flowers. After shaking hands with the queen, Mary Lincoln introduced her daughter

Mamie to Victoria. Mamie looked "fresh and pretty" in a lovely debutante's gown of white peau de soie and simple pearl ornaments; she carried a corsage of pure white exotics and maidenhair fern.

Jessie Lincoln was just fourteen years old, and deemed too young to attend an occasion of such magnitude as meeting Queen Victoria. Undoubtedly, she was upset at being excluded, but when she was later allowed to attend a party at the Foreign Office, she had her own brush with British royalty. The Prince of Wales—the future King Edward VII—was there, and Jessie was dying to meet him. She approached Mary King Waddington, the American-born wife of the French ambassador, to arrange an introduction. It was not such a simple request. The Prince had recently injured his knee and walked with a cane, but Mrs. Waddington was willing to try. She approached the heir to the British throne and informed him that Abraham Lincoln's granddaughter would very much like to be presented to him. The Prince of Wales rose and hobbled over to Jessie, and they shook hands. They chatted for a few minutes, and Jessie was quite taken with him. The prince, at age fifty-one, still seemed to be able to make the hearts of American girls flutter. He told her how much he had esteemed President Lincoln, and then suggested that she tour the Foreign Ministry and meet the other distinguished guests.

"Thank you very much," Jessie said, "but I don't want to see anything else. I only wanted to see the Prince of Wales, and now that I have seen you and talked to you, I don't want to do anything more."

Mary Lincoln set up house at 2 Cromwell House, South Kensington, London, and the three Lincoln children began their exploration of the city. Everyone who came in contact with Abraham Lincoln II remarked how much in looks and intellect he resembled his martyred namesake. Jack himself was fascinated by his connection to the Great Emancipator. Robert Lincoln's junior partner, William Beale, had once found him on the floor of his father's law library with a map of Civil War battles spread out before him. Jack kept referencing an open book beside him. He was re-creating the key battles of the war, hour by hour. "He was fond of the history of the late war," Beale said. "He was ready to discuss this situation or that in which General Grant and others had found themselves."

Jack rarely used his given name, and when he did it was to considerable effect, as in this story that circulated at the time. Jack was at bat playing baseball in a vacant lot in Washington when he connected hard with the ball and it went crashing into a kitchen window. The irate homeowner came charging out, and all the boys scattered. Only Jack Lincoln refused to flee. He stood there white-faced and trembling with fear, still clutching the bat, and prepared to take his punishment like a little man.

"Is this your ball, and did you break my window?" the irate homeowner screamed into the boy's ear, giving Jack a "good shaking."

"Yes, sir," Jack replied.

"What is your name?" "Abraham Lincoln, sir."

According to the story the man walked away as if he had seen a ghost, and left young Jack standing in the field. Later that day, Jack told his father what had happened. Robert, who was then serving as secretary of war, chastised the boy for breaking the window but also praised him for taking responsibility in the face of the homeowner's wrath.

A family friend from Mount Pleasant, Iowa, where Jack had spent many happy summers, commented on how much he had grown and wondered whether he would be as tall as his grandfather, to which Jack cleverly replied, "I would like to be as good, as kind and as wise as he was, but not so tall; he must have bumped his head many times."

Jack attended University School on Dearborn Avenue in Chicago, a college prep school for boys on the North Side. He was a gifted student, and studied Latin, Greek, math, and English literature. "Study came easy to him," said the principal, Professor C. N. Fessenden. "He was the first boy in the school to get through his lessons. Then he was ready to help the others. The result was that he was popular. His schoolmates looked up to him, besides liking him. Jack was a grave boy, deliberate in his speech and actions. He had much of the Lincoln blood in his veins." Lest he be accused of embellishing Jack Lincoln's intellect, Fessenden could only say, "Don't imagine that I speak flatteringly. He was the best student in my school."

When Jack was fifteen, he was called on in class for a singular assignment. He rose, assumed the position behind his desk, and started to recite the Gettysburg Address. Imagine his pride as he delivered the lines purposefully and with a straightforward dignity. An exceptional honor was accorded Jack that same year when a statue of Abraham Lincoln, designed by the American sculptor Augustus Saint-Gaudens, was unveiled in Lincoln Park in Chicago. It was the masterpiece *Standing Lincoln*, a life-size bronze of a humble Lincoln rising from a chair, preparing to address the American people. Thousands of citizens turned out for the dedication ceremony and watched in awe as Abraham Lincoln II pulled aside the American flag to reveal the statue. People stood silently, riveted by the inspiring moment, until cheers broke the deep hush. Many who had known President Lincoln personally wept.

Robert Lincoln had Jack's future all planned out. The boy would follow in his father's footsteps. First, he would spend a year at Phillips Exeter Academy, then he would go on to Harvard and become a lawyer. And who could tell what would happen after that, blessed as he was with the most illustrious name in American history?

In the summer of 1889, while his sisters Mamie and Jessie remained in London, Jack Lincoln was sent to France to absorb the language in preparation for his entrance exams to Harvard. Arrangements were made for him to attend school in Versailles. He was sixteen.

Playing tennis in Versailles one afternoon, Jack felt something strange under his arm. It was an accumulation of boils that had formed into a nasty cluster—a carbuncle. It was a staph infection, sometimes a sign of poor hygiene that perhaps originated with just a minor cut on the surface of the skin. At first it was a mild irritant, of "little consequence." It should have cleared up in a week or two. But the carbuncle kept growing, and Jack's French doctors determined that surgery was necessary. Robert Lincoln and his wife Mary were notified, and the alarmed parents arrived in France in early November. Just as the finest doctors in Chicago had been called upon to treat Tad Lincoln for pleurisy in 1871, now Robert and Mary Lincoln assembled France's most esteemed healers. Docteur Jules-Émile Péan, perhaps the best-known surgeon in Paris, was called on to perform the operation. Docteur Péan had been one of the first French doctors to use aseptic surgical instruments, and was credited with inventing the arterial clamp and the haemostatic forceps used to control bleeding during surgery. Such was his fame that in 1891 the artist Toulouse-Lautrec made Docteur Péan the subject of perhaps his most celebrated work, *Docteur Péan en train d'operer*.

Jack's surgery took place on November 6. Mamie Lincoln, just having turned twenty, and Jessie, fourteen, went to Paris, escorted by their father's private secretary, Charles Isham, to be with their ailing brother.

Docteur Péan cut away at the mass of dead tissue. The surgical incision was long, running almost the entire length of Jack's arm, from underarm to elbow. It was hoped that the sloughing process would allow the infection to drain. While Jack recuperated, Robert Lincoln updated his London legation secretary, Robert S. McCormick, the son-in-law of *Chicago Tribune* owner Joseph Medill, on Jack's condition.

"Jack's carbuncle is running its course and has now begun the healing process, which is expected to take a full week. He is easy and comfortable and we are all settled down in fair comfort to await the time when we can return."

Eleven days later, Lincoln remained optimistic. "Jack continues to improve slowly and we see no reason to doubt his recovery." Jack was suffering a slight fever, which at its worst reached 102 degrees Fahrenheit. "He is weak and emaciated but cheerful and his appetite continually increases," Robert Lincoln reported. That afternoon, Jack was fed beef juice. He pleased his apprehensive parents when he joked that he would have preferred beefsteak. They promised him that by the next day he could eat something more bountiful. The Lincolns were still in Paris on Thanksgiving. On November 28, Robert Lincoln, in a letter to McCormick on diplomatic business, wrote as an aside at the bottom of the page, "Everything seems to go on well with Jack, and the Dr. thinks he will be able to begin 'sitting up' out of bed in 4 or 5 days."

Christmas was just ten days away, and Robert and Mary Lincoln were now filled with anxiety. Although their son's fever was almost down to normal, the teenager seemed to be deteriorating, and showing no desire to get out of bed. He could not even sit up. "On the whole he is not booming," Robert noted. Christmas Day found the Lincolns gathered around Jack's bed. The ugly wound running under his arm refused to heal, and Robert was forced to admit that his son was "getting weaker instead of stronger, and we are not happy about him."

Word got out that the grandson of Abraham Lincoln was in a medical crisis. John Hay, occupied with writing his monumental ten-volume history of Lincoln with John Nicolay, was frantic. "We were very anxious all day yesterday—the morning papers having announced the dangerous illness of your boy in Versailles—yet we hoped for better news today; and this morning he still lives and there is further hope," he wrote Robert. "We trust and pray the improvement may continue and that his youth and strength may soon restore him to perfect health again. Any other result would be too dreadful to contemplate."

Robert took a brief break from his vigil to write Hay back. "You can imagine it has been a very anxious time here," he told his old friend. He expressed awe that the French surgeon dared to perform the operation on the son of so famous a personage. "Another man would not have had the nerve to cut as he did for the danger. . . . The shock of the operation is very great."

Jack kept his mind alert, reading newspapers and "light" books. He was eating well and digesting his food (he could not abide French food, and refused to eat anything that had not been cooked by his mother), and to look at him, one would think he was on the road to a slow but steady recovery. His mother was a pillar of strength. Mary refused to leave his bedside, and not once was she out of range of his voice.

Robert and Mary, now starting to lose confidence in the team of French physicians, were thinking about transporting Jack back to London. "I am very sorry to say that we are able to get little encouragement, tho the doctors say the case is not desperate. Mrs. Lincoln and I have had talks which result in our feeling that there is little help for Jack here." Weighing the risks of transporting his son to London, a frustrated Robert concluded, "The possible dangers are no greater than his present situation—while good may come. Of course we shrink, with him so ill, from leaving the reasonably comfortable quarters we are in . . . and from undertaking the hardships of a journey on French railways—but, as I said, we are desperate here and we must try some change."

With McCormick and his wife acting as facilitators, a Chicago doctor who was living in London agreed to leave at once for Paris to examine Jack Lincoln. Dr. H. Webster Jones was a graduate of Yale and a former director of the Chicago Relief and Aid Society. He arrived in Paris on January 13 and Robert met him at the train station. Jack was slipping, the disheartened Robert Lincoln informed the doctor. Overnight, young Lincoln had been feverish and was coughing. Another ganglion had materialized on Jack's arm. Robert took Jones to Versailles and they arrived just as the French physicians were performing a new surgical procedure. Without administering anesthesia, they were tearing away at the diseased tissue. Jones was impressed by Jack Lincoln's pluck. "He won all my sympathy and admiration," he said. "The boy deserves to get well! His courage and hope are boundless." He said Jack had behaved "heroically" during the operation on his open wound. But Jones was also critical of the French, warning Robert that they were taxing the boy's endurance and "capable of doing him great harm."

Jones advised the Lincolns that it was "imperative" they take their son out of France and home to London without delay. But Jones said he could offer little expectation of success; the boy was just too far gone.

"Jack's disease is not simply carbuncular, tho that title covered all its earlier phenomena," Jones wrote McCormick. "At any rate, as now appears it so affected the springs of life as to have undermined his recuperative powers, till there is little left to build upon."

Jack left Versailles on January 17. Accompanying the teenager to Calais were his parents, Dr. Jones, and Charles Isham. The Lincoln party crossed the English Channel on a steamship, with Jack enduring the difficult passage reclining on a swinging bed, which may have exacerbated the seasickness he experienced as the vessel approached Dover. A special hospital railroad car was provided for Jack on the final leg of the journey to London. Jones could not believe Jack Lincoln's fortitude. The boy, he said, was "never braver." All told the trip took thirty-six hours—the route eased by Robert's wealth and diplomatic status.

Jack was taken to the Lincolns' home at 2 Cromwell House, where two of London's leading physicians were waiting to see him. They examined him, and assured his anxious parents that there was reason for optimism. There was no evidence of septicemia or pneumonia. Jones and his British colleagues determined that if the boy was to be saved, they would have to attack the underlying reason why the wound would not heal. A fourth physician was brought into the case. Sir James Paget, First Baronet, was *surgeon extraordinary* to Queen Victoria. When Sir James examined Jack Lincoln he was seventy-six years old, too old to perform surgeries, but he was still England's most esteemed medical consultant. Cases were sent to him for "final judgment." Slightly built, with a long face and bright eyes, he and Robert Lincoln probably got along because Sir James appreciated brevity and disliked clever people. "To be brief is to be wise," he liked to say.

Sir James seemed to agree with Dr. Jones's private assessment of the French physicians. They were butchers. "Two of the most distinguished English surgeons say they never saw or heard of an operation performed in a manner of this and that they're without any experience to guide them in trying to make it heal," Robert wrote John Hay.

One week later, Jack was teetering on the edge of death from blood poisoning. The "great cut" under his arm was now a foot long. The carbuncle had burrowed a channel into Jack's blood system, spiking his fever. His pulse grew weaker, and his breathing became labored. It was as if a great weight had been placed on his chest. Robert Lincoln had seen this before, and he must have thought himself cursed, for his son was suffering the agonizing death throes of pleurisy, as his brother Tad had nineteen years before. Dr. Jones said the "pleuritic effusion" was evident on the left lung, and causing life-threatening distress to the heart. The open wound was "obstinate," and would not heal.

Prayers were offered from church pulpits on both sides of the Atlantic.

The popular London preacher Joseph Parker, speaking from City Temple, the largest nondenominational church in England, asked his parishioners to pray for the Lincoln family.

"We now commend unto Thee the son of the American minister," Parker said. "He is sick, we trust not nigh unto death; but Thou knowest the pain of his father's heart and the trouble of the whole household." In the United States the gloom was acute. A country that was set to embrace the young man blessed with the exalted name Abraham Lincoln II now stood ready for a national deathwatch.

Robert was almost apologetic when he wrote John Hay. "I am sorry to write you again about our boy. . . . [H]is wound does not heal. He's very weak. In short, it is hard to see that he is recovering."

On February 27, 1890, a final, desperate operation to remove the infected tissue was performed at 2 Cromwell House. Three days later, "Jack passed a very restless night." Hope mixed with despair. After four months of setbacks and remissions, the end came, on March 5 at 11:00 A.M. Robert was in his drawing room talking with his first secretary, Henry White. Suddenly, Mamie Lincoln came rushing in.

"Go upstairs quickly!" she screamed.

Ten minutes later, a forlorn Robert Lincoln came down the staircase and found White anxiously awaiting him. The only thing Robert could say was that "all was over."

"The end came rather suddenly at last," White told his wife, Margaret.

A telegram was sent to Mary Lincoln's father, James Harlan, which he received at 8:00 A.M. Iowa time. Senator Harlan took the news hard. The official cause of death was listed this way: "Carbuncle under arm 4 months[,] pleurisy 4 weeks." Privately, Dr. Jones was blaming the French doctors for bungling the case. "Whether Jack gets well or not I shall always be of the opinion that French surgery was his greatest foe."

Americans mourned not just the boy's death, but also the end of the male line of Lincolns. "The boy had the characteristics of his grandfather and was visualized by many as the reincarnation of the martyred President," wrote the *Illinois State Journal*. The death was a blow, not just to the Lincoln family, but also to the "people of the United States."

The body of Abraham Lincoln II was temporarily interred at Kensal Green Cemetery in London; a small private service was held at 3:00 P.M. on April 7. Robert Lincoln asked Henry White to accompany him in the carriage with a clergyman who was to say a few words. After services were over,

Lincoln and White headed back to London alone in the carriage. In a curious way the friendship between the two diplomats represented the reconciliation that was taking place in post–Civil War America. White came from a socially prominent Maryland family that had sympathized with the South. When the war ended with the defeat of the Confederacy, the Whites moved to France, where Henry White completed his education. Now forty, he was offering himself as a source of comfort to Robert Lincoln in this time of grief.

"When we got to Kensington Gardens I persuaded him to send away the carriage and walk there, which he did for an hour and enjoyed it," White told his wife. Lincoln confided something to White: He was not really interested in returning to the practice of law. He had maintained his association with the firm of Isham, Lincoln & Beale only because he dreamed of the day when Jack would take over the practice. It was all "for Jack's sake, to keep the place open for him." White was stunned when, for the first time, Robert spoke about his mother. "He also told me a lot about his trouble with his mother, and seemed generally most confidential," White said. But White kept the conversation private for the rest of his life and never divulged what Robert had said about Mary Todd Lincoln.

White was invited to have dinner with the Lincolns that night. He was a little apprehensive, not wishing to intrude on their privacy, but Robert's wife insisted. White spent the evening with Robert and Mary, and reported to his wife that he had "cheered them all a good deal." But the anguish of Jack's death was never far from the surface. "It certainly is a most horrible break in their lives."

Robert's heartbreak was evident in the letter he wrote to John Hay, one month after Jack had died.

"Jack was to us all that any father and mother could wish and beyond that, he seemed to realize that he had special duties before him as a man, and the thoroughness with which he was getting ready was a source of the greatest pride to me. I did not realize until he was gone how deeply my thoughts of the future were in here." His wife, as always in delicate health, "surprised us all in not breaking down," Robert confided to Hay. "I would not have believed that any human could have stood the strain of the months as she did." Robert said, of all the misfortunes he had faced in life, this was "the hardest."

Mary Lincoln, accompanied by her two daughters Mamie and Jessie, went home to America in August, expecting to remain there for at least six months. Left to his grief, Robert occupied himself with diplomacy. In September, he accepted an invitation to vacation at Andrew Carnegie's estate in Scotland.

The following month, the time came for the duty Robert had been dreading: the exhumation of Jack's body from its burial site at Kensal Green Cemetery. He returned to the United States with the coffin on the steamship *City of New York*. From New York, the coffin was transferred to a private car on the Pennsylvania Railroad; it arrived in Springfield at six A.M., November 8, 1890. He had just one companion with him during this miserable journey—his old friend Edgar Welles, the son of Abraham Lincoln's secretary of the navy, Gideon Welles. Edgar was now a vice president of the Wabash Railway Corporation. At Springfield, Robert and Edgar, along with the coffin, remained in the car, sidetracked at the depot, for three hours. Then, at 9:00 A.M., a delegation that included Senator Cullom, Governor Joseph Fifer, former governor Richard Oglesby, and representatives from the Abraham Lincoln Monument Association arrived in four carriages, accompanied by a hearse. Jack's coffin, made of antique English oak with silver trimmings, was adorned with a silver plate bearing the name Abraham Lincoln II and the date of his birth and death. It was lined with lead and hermetically sealed. The coffin was placed on the hearse and the cortege proceeded at once to Oak Ridge Cemetery, where it was carried into the monument and positioned inside the family crypt to the right of Tad Lincoln. Then a marble slab was placed over it. Robert turned to the distinguished delegation present.

"Gentlemen, I thank you for this kindness."

That was all. No prayers were given. There was no other ceremony. Jack's mother was not present. It was said that Mary Lincoln's "delicate health" prevented her from attending the final internment of her son.

The remains of six Lincolns now reposed in the Lincoln Monument: Abraham Lincoln, Mary Todd Lincoln, their sons Eddie, Willie, and Tad, and now their grandson, Abraham Lincoln II.

Two crypts were yet to be occupied. They were reserved for Robert and his wife.

18

Tycoon

THE DEATH OF Abraham Lincoln II was a shattering blow to a family engulfed in misfortune. But it had one positive consequence: a romance developed between Mamie Lincoln and her father's private secretary, Charles Isham.

Charles had first gotten to know Mamie aboard the ship *City of Paris* when the Lincolns sailed to London. There could not have been a dreamier setting than crossing the Atlantic Ocean that spring of 1889, with Robert on his way to assume the post of minister to the Court of St. James. Whatever flirtations may have taken place on the vessel, six months later they blossomed into full affection when Charles was given the task of escorting Mamie and her sister Jessie to Versailles to be with the ailing Jack Lincoln. In those terrible days, when Mamie Lincoln's sole occupation was watching her adored brother suffer, Charles was a comforting and soulful presence. The role of protector suited Charles, and something in his stiff and formal manner clicked with Mamie. Perhaps he reminded her of her father.

Because of their age difference, Charles was a surprising choice for a beau; he was born in 1853, making him sixteen years older than Mamie. Intellectually, however, he had it all: degrees from Harvard University and Harvard Law School, and another law degree from the University of Berlin. Slightly built and a dapper dresser, Charles was a noted scholar and historian who had once served as head librarian at the New York Historical Society. When he met Mamie, he had just completed editing the most important work of his career, the five-volume letters and papers of Silas Deane, America's first foreign diplomat. Socially, he was also of the correct class. Charles Isham came from a distinguished New York family; his father

William Isham was president of the Metropolitan Bank of New York. Charles approached his romance with Abraham Lincoln's first grandchild with all the deliberation and consideration of a diplomat on a sensitive foreign assignment. There were multiple issues to think through: Mamie was not just the boss's daughter; Robert Lincoln was also his distant cousin Edward Isham's law partner. All this meant that Charles had to conform to the strictest conventions of courtship.

In the Victorian era, the ultimate goal of girls in England and the United States was marriage. By the time they had turned eighteen, finding the right man was the priority, and if they had not married by age twenty-three it could be seen as a mark of failure. Mamie Lincoln and Charles Isham were both introspective, and their age difference did not seem to trouble either of them. As the oldest of three siblings, Mamie possessed poise and maturity beyond her years. It was said that she seemed ten years older than her age. And their personalities blended well; in short, they were a good match.

After Jack's death, his heartbroken sisters returned to America with their mother to live in Mount Pleasant and recuperate from the nightmare. Charles Isham also went home, and settled in New York. He attended church every Sunday, went to the theater and the opera, and continued his research work with the New York Historical Society. He also corresponded with Mamie, and, with Robert Lincoln's blessing, Mamie and Charles became engaged. Mamie was introduced to her future in-laws, the Ishams, at a dinner in New York, on February 25, 1891. The following day, Mamie, Jessie, and Mary Lincoln boarded the steamship *Saale* and returned to England. Charles remained in the United States but was back in London by July.

The time had come to let the world know that Abraham Lincoln's first grandchild was to be married. The formal announcement of the engagement was made during a gala ball thrown by Henry White and his wife, the socially connected Margaret Stuyvesant Rutherfurd, at the Whites' country estate near Bracknell, about an hour outside London. Back in Iowa, the news was reported in the Mount Pleasant newspaper with the gusto generally reserved for a royal wedding. Charles Isham, it was said, "must be pure and brave as Sir Galahad himself to be worthy of such a maiden's heart and hand."

As the wedding date approached, Robert Lincoln found a young man who could in some measure fill the void left in his life by Jack's death. The dashing Larz Anderson III was appointed the American legation's second secretary. Young Anderson's pedigree was impeccable, as one would expect from a Robert Lincoln appointment: Phillips Exeter and Harvard University, the Hasty Pudding Club, and a year at Harvard Law before Robert Lincoln persuaded him to enter diplomacy. And Lincoln knew Larz's father, the retired Civil War general Nicholas Longworth Anderson of Ohio.

When Larz arrived in England, in August 1891, to assume his diplomatic post, he checked into the Burlington Hotel on Cork Street. He was flabbergasted by the capacity of British servants to cater to the upper class. His first night, he encountered the "quietest and most respectful of valets," who folded his clothes and polished his boots. In the morning, a tempting tray of toast with little pats of unsalted butter and a delicious pot of tea with thick cream were set before the young American envoy. Larz took a hansom cab to the legation and found that Minister Lincoln was already gone for the day, but he ran into the able Henry White, who took the young man by the arm and walked him straight out of the building and on to his London house for a tour. That evening, Larz was invited to the Lincolns for dinner. He became a bemused observer of the frenzy preceding the Lincoln-Isham wedding, which had London abuzz. He recounted how he was besieged by newspaper reporters seeking any morsel of information he could share with them. No detail was too insignificant.

"One gave me a printed list of questions to fill out and return," he wrote his parents. "They even wished to know who would make the bride's bouquet and provide the refreshments. Reportorial cheek is as great here as in America."

The Lincolns, each in their own way, found the excessive attention distasteful. Confidentiality and an absolute insistence on privacy were powerful ingredients in Robert Lincoln's makeup. His wife's reclusive nature and her hazy "delicate health" reinforced this sense of family mystery. Mamie Lincoln was very much the product of her parents' sensibilities. Her wedding could have been the society event of the season, but she wanted something understated and quiet. As for the intrusive press, the Lincolns would just have to put up with them as graciously as they could.

The wedding took place Wednesday, September 2, 1891. The day started out bleak and wet, but the sunshine broke through in the early afternoon as the guests arrived at the Holy Trinity Church in the leafy London suburb of Brompton. There were only sixty guests. No written invitations were sent; instead, everyone was notified by word of mouth as to the date and time. Mary Lincoln sat in the front row with Jessie. Charles Isham's parents and his sisters from New York were there. From Chicago came the department store tycoon Marshall ("the customer is always right") Field and his wife Nannie, and Robert's law partner Edward Isham and his wife Frances. The Henry Whites; Larz Anderson III, who served as an usher; and several foreign ambassadors were also present. It seemed strange to have a wedding for only sixty guests in a church that could seat 1,505; the place must have felt depressingly empty. There were no bridesmaids.

As a boys' choir sang the hymn "Oh God! Our Help in Ages Past," Mamie Lincoln made her grand entrance with her father at her side. The bride wore a white satin dress trimmed with orange blossoms, and a lace veil. She held a prayer book. Robert escorted Mamie down the grand aisle to the altar, where she and Charles knelt before the Anglican clergyman, Frederic William Farrar, chaplain to the speaker of the House of Commons, who pronounced them man and wife.

The wedding, coming so soon after his son's death, failed to lift Robert out of his melancholia. According to Larz, Robert was drained, and desperate for rest, just before he departed for the Isle of Jersey off the coast of Normandy. When he returned, he found in Larz a young man he could mentor like the son he had lost, with the kind of hopeful enthusiasm he had once reserved for Jack. "I am prepared to say that he is one of the finest types of the American gentleman I have ever seen. He is a man to be proud of," Lincoln wrote Larz's father.

When Mamie and Charles returned from their honeymoon they decided to make New York City their home, and in fall 1891 they left for the United States. Now Jessie Lincoln, sixteen years old, wrote to her grandfather, James Harlan, "Wouldn't it be lovely if I could go home to you? I could plant seeds and flowers and make everything lovely." The following spring, Mary Lincoln decided that she too had had enough of life in London, and moved back to Chicago with Jessie. Robert found himself on his own, miserable, and with a job that failed to offer much stimulation.

The work of legation minister could be excruciatingly dull. Although there were interesting struggles in the years Lincoln served in London, including free trade issues and a dispute with Canada over the slaughter of seals, he found himself spending much of his day dealing with the boorish behavior of American citizens who came to the legation with letters of introduction from politicians back home and demanded theater tickets and other special considerations. Thank goodness Robert had two capable aides in Henry White and Larz Anderson III to keep the legation running efficiently.

In diplomacy, a legation was not up to the status of an embassy. It was a ceremonial distinction, but it also raised practical issues that were infuriating for someone with Robert's thin skin. Although he represented a great foreign power, technically, Lincoln ranked lower than the ambassador of a small nation. It was galling that the conventions of diplomacy required him to wait at the end of the line at social functions while the ambassadors of far lesser powers were received. In diplomacy, little errors in judgment also had a way of blowing up into awkward scandals. When Queen Victoria's grandson, the Duke of Clarence, second in line to the British throne after his father the Prince of Wales died of influenza at age twenty-eight, the queen demanded to know why the president of the United States, alone, among all heads of state, had not sent condolences to her. In fact, President Harrison had written her a warm message of commiseration, but the correspondence was forwarded to the British Foreign Office for processing, where it was delayed by a bureaucratic snag. All the other heads of state had sent their sympathies directly to Queen Victoria.

Lincoln spent Christmas 1891 with the Henry Whites at their country estate outside London. Christmas morning, Master Jack White and his kid sister Muriel serenaded their parents' guests with holiday carols. An elaborate breakfast buffet was laid out, and then came the exchange of gifts. In the afternoon everyone went to the pond to skate and take a brisk hike around the property. Lincoln seemed to be coming out of his shell. "The Minister was regaining his spirits," Larz wrote his parents, "and his sunny disposition began to show itself again. It was very enjoyable to see him happy and talking at a tremendous rate. He insisted on sitting up till all hours."

Robert Lincoln became a grandfather on June 8, 1892, when Mamie gave birth to a son, Lincoln Isham, the third-generation Lincoln in the direct line since the Great One. Robert received the news in a telegram from his son-in-law Charles, and wrote back, "I was very glad to know that the most anxious part of [Mamie's] ordeal had been safely passed. In the absence of any later news I am trusting that she is still going on well. Give her my best love and congratulations on this achievement which puts us all in another category." Then Robert wondered whether his wife Mary had been present during Mamie's labor to hear her grandson's "first exclamation of disgust at this beastly world." It was a peculiar and discouraging thing for Robert to say. Even in this moment of exultation—the birth of a grandson—he was tortured by his family's miserable run of misfortune.

The next presidential race was coming around, and Robert found himself yet again the subject of speculation in the United States and Europe that he might run for president. He was attending a dinner party in London, in February 1892, when Mary King Waddington, the French ambassador's wife, teased him about occupying the White House one day. "The papers say he is to be the next President," Mrs. Waddington wrote in her diary. But Robert was dismissive of such chatter. "He assured us there was no possible chance of it," Mrs. Waddington said, "and no one would be as sorry as he himself if ever the thing came to pass." Mrs. Waddington had to agree. "It certainly would be difficult to be a second President Lincoln."

Robert made plans to cross the Atlantic in early October, in time to thrust himself into the closing days of the presidential election, which was pitting the incumbent Benjamin Harrison against former president Grover Cleveland. As he was about to leave London by train for Liverpool, a messenger from the legation arrived to inform him that he had been chosen as a pallbearer at Alfred Lord Tennyson's funeral. The much-loved poet laureate of the United Kingdom had passed away at age eighty-three on October 6. Robert had to make an immediate judgment call—and he chose to continue his voyage. It turned into a rough passage. The steamship *Etruria* was rolled by wind and rain, but on his arrival in New York, Robert was caught in a tempest of a different nature. He had miscalculated the impact of Lord Tennyson's death on the British people. The funeral at Westminster Abbey for the author of *The Charge of the Light Brigade* had been, it turned out, a ceremony of national mourning; that Robert had been chosen to be a pallbearer, and did not cancel his trip, was seen as a rude and ill-mannered snub to a British icon.

Robert went on to Chicago, and, in the Land of Lincoln, he plunged into a vigorous round of campaign speeches in which he attacked the Democrats and urged voters to support President Harrison. Today, an American diplomat taking leave of his foreign post to campaign for a presidential candidate would be denounced for misuse of office, but in the late nineteenth century, no one noticed. Regrettably for Lincoln, President Harrison was resoundingly defeated. Even Illinois, where Lincoln's speechmaking was expected to carry the day for the Republicans, Grover Cleveland won by a margin of twenty-six thousand votes. Robert knew his days as minister to England were numbered.

Robert spent Christmas in New York at the Murray Hill Hotel, and signed off on an amazing gift for Mamie and Charles—a Georgian townhouse on East Thirty-eighth Street. Construction commenced in early 1893 on the fourteen-foot-wide brick mansion; it had seven fireplaces, a three-hundred-bottle wine cellar, and its own elevator. Robert also commissioned a twin townhouse next door that he intended to someday give to Jessie. On December 28, Robert, accompanied by Mary and Jessie, sailed for England out of New York Harbor on the White Star Line's SS *Teutonic*. The Lincolns were treated to a special send-off—a thirteen-gun salute, fired from the military battery stationed on Governor's Island. They arrived in London on January 4, 1893, and Lincoln, in preparation for his inevitable departure, wrote a pro forma letter of resignation, something that was expected of every foreign emissary upon the election of a new president.

Grover Cleveland took the oath of office on March 4 (this was prior to the ratification of the Twentieth Amendment to the United States Constitution that moved up the inauguration date to January 20). It took less than a month for the Cleveland administration to exact its revenge. The new secretary of state, Walter Q. Gresham, notified Robert that President Cleveland had accepted his letter of resignation. Son of the Great Emancipator or not, Robert Lincoln was out of there. It was a double blow, coming from Gresham, because Robert Lincoln had endorsed him for president in 1888.

All that was left to do in London was say good-bye. Robert and Mary dined with Queen Victoria at Windsor Castle, the queen pronouncing him "pleasant and sensible" company in her diary. Robert returned to Windsor with his official letter of recall, and, on May 16, he left London. The entire American legation accompanied Robert on the Eagle train to Southampton to give their boss a fitting bon voyage. As the Lincoln luck would have it, Robert was the last American minister to England. By Act of Congress the position was elevated to ambassador, and Robert's replacement, former senator Thomas F. Bayard, became the first U.S. representative to Great Britain with the official rank of ambassador. No longer would the United States have to take a back seat at the Court of St. James.

Robert returned to Chicago disenchanted, and disengaged. Wallowing in self-pity, he wrote a friend, "I feel about 900 years old." To John Nicolay he said, "I wonder if you are getting to feel so miserably old as I do. My daughter and her baby live a thousand miles away and the whole future seems, miserably, so many days to be passed." With the death of Jack Lincoln, the shop, as he referred to his law office, "ceased to interest me," and Robert extricated himself from Isham, Lincoln & Beale.

There was another important factor that made Robert abandon the law.

The world of business was where true wealth could be attained, and it was in this arena that Robert was determined to make a name for himself as an entrepreneur and titan of industry. He quickly found himself on the ground floor of the founding of two great public utilities, the Chicago Telephone Company and the Chicago Edison Company, which elected him to the board of directors. But most of his focus was on the entrepreneur George Pullman, who named Lincoln special counsel for the Pullman Palace Car Company.

As any great fortune, George Pullman's began with an inspired idea.

George Mortimer Pullman was a country-store clerk and carpenter from New York State when he took a night train out of Buffalo and was appalled at the primitive conditions inside the car. The typical train meal consisted of hard tack beef, a recipe from the Civil War which baked all the moisture out of the beef to give it a long shelf life, and doughnuts so stale they were called "sinkers" because you had to dip them into coffee to make them fit for human consumption. It was during this serendipitous journey that Pullman came up with the concept that would make him one of the wealthiest men in American history: leasing and servicing luxury train cars to the railroads for first-class passengers. Pullman stayed up all night drawing designs for sumptuous railroad accommodations. He named his business the Pullman Palace Car Company. The deluxe accommodations in his luxury train car—chandeliers, leather seats, and plush upholstery—made it seem like a hotel on wheels. Freshly prepared gourmet meals were served in the dining car, and on long-distance routes passengers could spend the evening sprawled out in the comfort of a sleeping car.

The passenger service was presided over by a class of people experienced in catering to the whims of the white upper class—former slaves of the plantation South. George Pullman made a point of hiring "the blackest man with the whitest teeth." Travelers called the porters "boy" or "George," after the practice of naming them after their slave master, or in this case, after the company president. The work was endless: carrying luggage, dusting, cleaning the washrooms, polishing spittoons, stoking the fires, lighting gaslights, shining shoes, pressing pants, replacing towels, keeping the guests happy, and remaining on call day and night. Not for nothing were they called the World's Most Perfect Servant. The harsh reality for black people was that becoming a Pullman porter was probably the best job they could obtain in post–Civil War America.

In 1880 George Pullman purchased four thousand acres ten miles south of Chicago and renamed it—what else—the town of Pullman. Then he commenced construction on America's first planned community. As his architect he hired Solon Beman, who had designed Robert Lincoln's mansion on Lake Shore Drive. To an outsider, the town of Pullman was a dynamic and progressive creation. The humble brick houses were clean, and designed to look like English row houses. Every house had running water, indoor plumbing, gas, a cellar, and a pantry. There was regular municipal garbage removal, and, by town regulation, all the lawns had to be watered and maintained. The sewage system was state-of-the-art for the late nineteenth century and comparable in efficiency to that of the city that was reputed to have the best sewage system in the world, Berlin. The finest building in Pullman was the Arcade—America's first indoor shopping mall. It had a spectacular glass roof and a wide central passageway with shops on each side, a bank, post office, restaurant, and an elegantly furnished community theater that seated eight hundred people. The library, on the top floor of the Arcade, contained six thousand books, all donated by George Pullman from his personal collection. Cosmetically, the town of Pullman was a huge improvement over the fetid working-class neighborhoods of Chicago where the working poor lived in squalor. But Pullman was no worker's paradise either.

In 1885, Richard Ely, a professor at Johns Hopkins University, was sent by *Harper's Magazine* to investigate life in Pullman. Ely held a doctorate in economics, but he had a novelist's flair for capturing little episodes that revealed some essential meaning. When Ely visited the Pullman town library, he was awed by the expensive Wilton carpeting, plush-covered chairs, and artwork on the walls. This ostentatious display of wealth was pure George Pullman; he surrounded his Pullman workers with the trappings of prosperity because he thought it would improve their character. Some called Pullman's library a gracious act of charity; others could argue that the library was breathtaking in its condescension.

Pullman, one of the richest men in America, charged a three-dollar annual fee for the use of his library. The public library in Chicago was, of course, free. But Ely found that in Pullman, "nothing is free." There were no homeowners in Pullman; everyone was a tenant, and everything was the property of the Pullman Palace Car Corporation. Independent newspapers, public speeches, and town hall meetings were prohibited. The one church that had been built in Pullman was not in use because no denomination could afford the annual rent; a Presbyterian diocese offered two thousand dollars, but George Pullman rejected it as insufficient. The town clerk and treasurer were not elected; they were officers of the company. A tenant who was found to be in violation of Pullman regulations could be evicted on ten days' notice. "Spotters" roamed the town, informing on violators or those who spoke out against the company or talked about joining a labor union. Ely concluded that the residents of Pullman were a "servile people," afflicted with a pervasive sense of insecurity.

"The power of Bismarck in Germany is utterly insignificant when compared with the power of the ruling authority of the Pullman Palace Car Company in Pullman," Ely reported. "Here is a population of eight thousand souls where not a single resident dare speak out openly his opinion about the town in which he lives.... Pullman is un-American."

Then came the Panic of 1893—the most serious collapse of the economy in United States history up to that time. Precipitated by a run on the gold supply and a tightening credit squeeze, it resulted in a stock market crash and the bankruptcy of more than fifteen thousand businesses. Unemployment soared to 20 percent. The railroad industry was hit hard; the Philadelphia & Reading Railroad ceased operations. When orders for sleeping cars plummeted, George Pullman cut production at his factories, laid off two thousand workers, and reduced wages by an average of 25 percent. But Pullman refused to scale back the rates he charged his tenants for rent and utilities; on average, they totaled fourteen dollars a month, as much as 40 percent more than the rates in surrounding communities. Nor would he lower prices for food at the company stores; despite the economic crisis, he still insisted on squeezing out a 6 percent annual profit from the town of Pullman's operation. Because the rents were automatically deducted from their paychecks, workers found themselves trapped in a form of debt slavery. One Pullman employee worked 120 hours with overtime and was issued a take-home paycheck for a grand total of seven cents.

On May 7, 1894, and then again on May 9, a delegation of forty-six leaders from the American Railway Union, Local 269, met with Pullman and other company officials and demanded the restoration of full wages. Pullman addressed the men and flat out refused to buckle. The next day, three committee leaders were fired without explanation. The workers saw it as an obvious act of retaliation and breach of good faith. At a mass meeting held on May 11, a vote was taken to strike, and the men walked off the job, shutting down all of Pullman's operations. The union sought arbitration. Pullman responded: "We have nothing to arbitrate." Eugene V. Debs, the founder of the American Railway Union, launched a boycott of all Pullman cars, ordering his union members to refuse to attach them to other trains. Railroad management reacted by firing the switchmen. By late June, the walkouts and reprisals had spread to twenty-seven states and involved more than 150,000 workers. It was the first national strike in U.S. history. The nation's transportation system was paralyzed. The mail could not be delivered. Somehow, a simple local issue involving the town of Pullman had escalated into an epic battle between labor and business.

And where was George Pullman during this chaos? He was on vacation with his family, in the village of Elberon, New Jersey, where he owned a seaside mansion. Pullman's indifference to the national crisis infuriated even the pro-business *Chicago Tribune*, which attacked his "absurd stubbornness." Secretary of State Gresham called on Pullman to resign as company president. The mayor of Chicago begged Pullman to negotiate. Pullman's imperious policy even cost him the support of natural allies such as the Republican power broker Mark Hanna, who called him a "damned idiot."

"Arbitrate, arbitrate, arbitrate!" Hanna said. "A man who won't meet his men half-way is a God-damn fool!"

The stage was set for violence. When a brick-throwing mob of two thousand strikers at the Rock Island Railroad Yard refused to obey an order to disperse, the U.S. marshal asked President Cleveland to send in federal troops. Cleveland called out six thousand infantry and cavalry. The soldiers confronted throngs of striking workers who were rioting in the streets. Trains were flipped over, boxcars were torched, and arsonists set fire to seven buildings at the Chicago world's fair. The worst day of violence was July 7, when soldiers fired into a crowd of ten thousand unionists and mowed down twelve civilians.

Even George Pullman came to the realization that something had to be done. He cut short his vacation and took the train to New York to meet with senior Pullman Company executives. Standing at his side was former secretary of war and minister to Great Britain, Robert Lincoln. It came as a shock for Americans to learn that the son of the Great Emancipator was now the right-hand man of the tyrant of Pullman Township whose intractability was throwing the United States into a vortex of violence and anarchy. When Pullman and Lincoln stepped off the train from New Jersey, a crowd of reporters swarmed all over them. Lincoln quickly asked Pullman, "Shall we take a cab to the Brevort House?" ending the barrage of questions. But first, they had breakfast at the Murray Hill Hotel. It was not Lincoln's finest moment; the memorable "let-them-eat-cake" line was picked up in newspapers everywhere.

By late July the strike had been broken. George Pullman conceded nothing on wages or his management of Pullman Township, and agreed to rehire his workers only if they renounced the union. The trains started to run again, and on August 2, the Pullman factories reopened. But Pullman's national reputation as a visionary businessman was in ruins, and he was reviled in Chicago. The social reformer and future Nobel Peace Prize laureate Jane Addams, the founder of Chicago's Hull House, compared Pullman to Shakespeare's King Lear, the tragic ruler whose misjudgments brought about his downfall. The Democratic governor of Illinois, John Altgeld, a progressive who loathed Pullman and Robert Lincoln, toured the town of Pullman a month after the strike had ended and found families facing starvation. He appealed to George Pullman. "The men are hungry and the women and children are actually suffering. . . . Something must be done at once." When Pullman informed the governor that there was nothing he could do, Altgeld wrote another personal appeal, telling the mogul, "Some of these people have worked for you for more than twelve years. I assumed that even if they were wrong and had been foolish, you would not be willing to see them perish."

Three years after the strike, Pullman was at his desk at the Pullman Building in Chicago when he complained of "hot spells." He left work at 5:00 P.M. and went home to his three-story gray stone mansion at Prairie and Eighteenth. Pullman's wife, Hattie, was away, shopping in New York. At 4:30 the following morning Pullman called his body servant to his bedside and said he was not feeling well. His personal physician was summoned, but it was too late. The tycoon died of a heart attack at 5:00 A.M. at age sixty-six. It was said that the lingering stress of the strike had killed him.

Pullman, who had been fully aware that his workers held him in contempt, had left instructions with his wife to take steps to prevent the theft or desecration of his body. His remains were first wrapped in tarpaper. Then asphalt was poured into the coffin. Pullman's burial took place in the strictest secrecy, at the stroke of midnight, at Graceland Cemetery. The coffin was lowered into a hole eight feet deep and thirteen feet wide. It was more like a pit than a grave. Then concrete was poured over the coffin, and eight railroad T-rails, bolted together by two long rods, were placed on top of the concrete. More concrete was poured in. Pullman's grave became a tomb of stone and steel, leading the sardonic journalist Ambrose Bierce to remark, "It is clear the family in their bereavement was making sure the sonofabitch wasn't going to get up and come back." The burial process took two full days, and it made an indelible impression on Robert Lincoln.

Speculation mounted over who would be named Pullman's successor. The most logical choice was company vice president Thomas Wickes, or a former general, Horace Porter, who had been a Pullman vice president based in New York before his appointment as ambassador to France. The board of directors met in November and surprised everyone by appointing a three-man executive committee consisting of Robert Lincoln, Marshall Field, and the retired dry goods merchant Henry Hulbert to run the company. Field had his own business empire to worry about and Hulbert was sixty-six years old and lived in Brooklyn. By default, Lincoln was put in charge—named president pro tempore, and issued the full powers of the presidency. He was fifty-four years old.

President Cleveland had appointed a federal Pullman Strike Commission, and the Pullman Company was under siege. Lincoln faced colossal challenges. In testifying about the company's hiring policies, he told the commission members that "the old southern colored man makes the best porter on the car. He is more adapted to waiting on passengers and gives them better attention and better manner." Lincoln revealed himself to be a creature of his times.

When the commission report was issued, the Pullman Palace Car Company was condemned for charging excessive rent to the residents of Pullman Township.

In 1898 the Illinois Supreme Court ruled that the company could continue manufacturing sleeping cars and trains but could not govern an entire ward of Chicago, inhabited now by more than twelve thousand citizens. Preparations were made for the city of Chicago to annex the township. All two thousand brick houses were sold to the highest bidder.

Robert Lincoln was no longer under serious consideration as a candidate for the U.S. presidency. It was hard for folks to believe that the son of the Great Emancipator had become the president of a company that was notorious for union-busting and corporate greed. His countrymen were now all too willing to accept as truth even the most preposterous rumors about his activities. One strange tale was that Robert Lincoln was the "ringmaster" of an elite corps of businessmen who met regularly for lunch at the Chicago Club to determine who would receive invitations to the city's exclusive balls and society events. Only families at the "apex of the social scale" were eligible—Chicago's so-called Gilded Three Hundred. "It is a long way from Abraham Lincoln, the nation's savior, to Robert Todd Lincoln, the patron of the Gilded Three Hundred," sputtered the *Fresno Weekly* newspaper. "The lamp of genius burns it out right quickly. It is apt to leave no glimmer to the next generation."

Robert Lincoln was now a corporate tycoon. He and Mary, even though they were still subjected to the glare of the public arena, were delighted to be out of government service. Robert's mother, Mary Todd Lincoln—that lightning rod for notoriety—had now been dead for more than a full decade. But another Lincoln woman was about to take center stage. And a new scandal was just around the corner.

19
The Newlyweds

JESSIE LINCOLN WAS the prettier of the two Lincoln girls, with delicate features, a narrow waist, and hair piled high on her head in a waterfall of curls. Jessie was enrolled as a student of voice and music at the Iowa Wesleyan Conservatory of Music, but her mind was not on her studies. She was a young woman in love.

His name was Warren Wallace Beckwith, and he was the star quarterback on the Iowa Wesleyan College football squad. A gifted athlete, he played professional baseball for one season in 1896 with the Texas League, where he became a fan favorite and developed quite the roguish reputation. His teammates called him "the dude." Another of his monikers was "the lady-killer." It was said that he would never leave the clubhouse without first combing his thick brown hair, and he always carried a mirror in his pocket so he could check himself out just before he headed to the diamond. In 1897 Beckwith tried out for the Chicago Cubs. That was the same season the Chicago team beat Louisville 36-7, a club record for runs scored that stands to this day. But Beckwith's father ordered his son to return to Iowa Wesleyan, where he was now—at age twenty-two, a big man on campus, a sinewy athlete with a cocky confidence that women found irresistible. College did not hold much curiosity for young Beckwith, who had a "decided aversion to educational matters." Nor was he interested in a career. One report called him reckless and irresponsible, a "harum-scarum young fellow."

Beckwith came from a prominent family. His father, Warren Beckwith, had been a cavalry captain during the Civil War and settled in Mount Pleasant, where he became road master of the Chicago, Burlington and

Quincy Railroad. A great uncle, Lewis Wallace, had served as the youngest general in the Union army, and later as governor of the New Mexico Territory. General Wallace was best known as the author of *Ben-Hur: A Tale of the Christ*, a top-selling novel of the nineteenth century. The book, still in print, has been filmed three times, most famously in 1959. Lewis Wallace was seventy years old when his rascally nephew started courting Abraham Lincoln's granddaughter.

Robert Lincoln made it known to Jessie that under no circumstances would he accept Beckwith as a son-in-law; he ordered her to stop seeing the young man. But the rebellious Jessie continued her furtive romance with Warren, and in early November 1897, just a few days after Jessie turned twenty-two, the young couple applied for a marriage license at the Mount Pleasant town clerk's office. They swore the clerk to secrecy, but blurted out enough details for him to realize that Jessie's parents were in the dark about their plans. The marriage was to be performed at a friend's house later in the week. Jessie and Warren said they planned to keep their marriage a secret for a full year to give the Lincolns a chance to get to know Warren better and accept him into the family.

The young lovers left the town offices confident that their scheme would work—and ran straight into a buzz saw. The clerk had telephoned Robert and Mary Lincoln and informed them that Jessie had just this day applied for a marriage license. Mr. and Mrs. Lincoln raced into town, panic-stricken that their daughter was about to throw away her future. Though Jessie was in the middle of a semester, they hauled her back to Chicago with them, assuring her that in time she would forget all about Warren Beckwith. A full week passed.

On the morning of November 10, Jessie told her mother she was going shopping and would be spending the day with friends on the South Side. Jessie stepped out into a perfect, unusually mild fall day and made her way to the Northwestern Train Depot, where she rendezvoused with the man she loved. The lovers boarded the next train to Milwaukee—a city with laws that accommodated quick marriages—and arrived there at 1:45 P.M. They got into a carriage and asked the driver to recommend a justice of the peace. He knew just where to take them, to 581 Twelfth Street, the home of the appropriately named Orlando P. Christian, pastor of the Methodist Episcopal Church on Sherman Street. It was 2:30 P.M. when they knocked on his door. Reverend Christian invited Jessie and Warren into his parlor, and, after a few routine questions, agreed to perform the marriage ceremony. He

went to his desk, found the necessary paperwork, placed Jessie and Warren
under oath, and asked them to swear to their names and ages. He was
shocked to hear Jessie Lincoln identify herself, and asked whether she was
Robert Lincoln's daughter. Jessie told him the truth.

Two witnesses were required, and the pastor called for Mrs. Christian,
and a neighbor who sometimes filled in as a witness, Mrs. Henry J. Baum-
gaertner, the wife of the president of the Milwaukee Common Council.
Everyone gathered in the parlor. Once more, Christian placed Jessie and
Warren under oath, and then, in the presence of the two witnesses, he performed the ceremony. As the Reverend Christian pronounced them man
and wife, it occurred to Christian that he had never married a couple that
seemed as somber and responsible. After the little group offered their congratulations to the couple, Jessie and Warren informed them that they had
eloped. This was the first time in his career as a clergyman that Christian
had married a runaway couple. It came as a blow to him, but there was
nothing he could do. They were of legal age, and by law, the Beckwiths were
married.

Jessie and Warren took their leave. Outside, the cab was still waiting for
them, and off they trotted to the Plankinton House Hotel in downtown Milwaukee. With 450 rooms and a massive dining hall, it was one of the premier
hotels in the city. Warren Beckwith registered as "Mr. and Mrs. Warren Wallace" and paid the bill in advance. The newlyweds went to their room, and at
some point ordered room service and ate a late lunch. There was not much
time; Jessie was in a big hurry to get back to Chicago before her parents suspected anything. In the early evening, a waiter passing the Beckwiths' room
found the door wide open. The newlyweds were already gone.

Jessie and Warren caught the 4:00 P.M. train to Chicago, and on the trip
back they decided that Jessie would inform her parents that evening that
she had eloped. Meanwhile, Warren would check into a hotel in Chicago
while she worked things out at home, and await word from Jessie. Two
hours later, they parted company at the Northwestern station. Warren made
his way to Clifton House while Jessie took the first hansom cab she could
find and hurried home. When she entered the Lincoln mansion at 60 Lake
Shore Drive, it was just in time for dinner. Everyone sat down in the dining
room. The conversation was casual. Robert and Mary asked about Jessie's
day, still under the illusion that she had gone shopping with friends on the
South Side. Jessie froze, and said nothing to dissuade them of that notion. It
was the moment she should have seized to let her parents know that she was

now a married woman. After dinner, she went up to her room and closed the door behind her.

A half hour later, the deception was over.

Robert and Mary were about to go to bed when the telephone rang. It was eleven o'clock at night and a reporter from the *Chicago Tribune* was checking out a tip that Jessie Lincoln had eloped. Apparently, Robert had a good laugh over that one. He put the phone down and, with Mary, went up to Jessie's room on the second floor and told his daughter that a reporter was on the line claiming she and Warren Beckwith had gotten married. A moment later the Lincolns staggered out of the room. It had really happened. Their daughter Jessie was now Mrs. Warren Beckwith.

Mary Lincoln went for the phone and the *Tribune* reporter was still holding. "The message is more than true," Mary said. "My daughter was married at Milwaukee this afternoon, and the elopement, if you wish to call it that, has already occurred. She was married without my knowledge and against my advice."

Mrs. Lincoln was asked why she was so opposed to the marriage.

"I simply objected to Mr. Beckwith," she said. But she knew there was nothing she could do when faced with a headstrong daughter who was in love with a bad boy. "My daughter is of age, and there is where the matter stands. She is in her room now and Mr. Beckwith is somewhere in the city, I understand."

Robert Lincoln took the phone from Mary. He wanted to hang up, but the reporter managed to get in one final question: Was reconciliation with the newlyweds at all possible?

"You can understand that I don't want to talk about that," Robert responded.

Robert Lincoln wanted to ring Warren Beckwith's neck—if he could find the lad. And the more he learned of the illicit romance between Jessie and this ne'er-do-well Beckwith, the more irritated Lincoln became. It must have been the worst kept secret in Mount Pleasant, because when Beckwith had left to meet up with Jessie in Chicago, several players from the football team had gone to the depot to offer him their congratulations and give him a big sendoff.

A newsman was sent to the Lincoln mansion later that night, and when he got there the house was pitch black except for one light emanating from the latticed window of Jessie's room. It seemed that the Lincolns' youngest daughter was still awake.

The story broke in the Chicago newspapers the following morning. Readers could not get enough of this delicious little scandal. To make matters worse for Robert Lincoln, on the very day that news of the elopement hit the front pages, his appointment as temporary president of the Pullman Palace Car Company was officially announced. For the Chicago newspapers, it was just too good to be true. Every detail of Warren Beckwith's life was investigated, and lurid pleasure was taken in pointing out the young man's lack of prospects. "It is said of him that he has never been thrown upon his own resources and has devoted himself to such athletics as boxing, ball playing, and bicycle riding," ran one account. The *Chicago Chronicle* called Warren an "unpleasant youth" but at least gave him credit for having outfoxed Jessie's exceptionally "watchful" parents. It was said that Jessie and Warren had been secretly engaged for at least two years.

The press besieged the Lincoln mansion. Robert cringed, then stepped outside to face the horde of reporters. He distributed a written statement that could only be interpreted as deeply derogatory in its references to his new son-in-law.

"About a year ago my daughter and young Beckwith became sweethearts while she was visiting her mother's old home at Mount Pleasant, Iowa," said Robert, who was described by one reporter as "exceedingly angry."

"Both Mrs. Lincoln and I objected to the young man. We broke off the attachment, separated the young people, and thought that settled it. While Miss Jessie was in Mt. Pleasant, on a recent visit, it seems the attachment was renewed, unknown to us. We still disapprove of the young man as much as we did at the outset. He is not satisfactory to us to be the husband of our daughter. He is the son of Capt. Beckwith, a good friend of Mrs. Lincoln's family at Mt. Pleasant—and the father is altogether an estimable old man. It is the son, not the father, we are opposed to."

The statement went on, "I do not know anything about the details of the ceremony. I do not know what business the young man engages in, but he was in some business or other in Mt. Pleasant. Jessie is now here at home with us. I do not know anything about the whereabouts of Mr. Beckwith nor of his plans. We did not know of the secret wedding until Mrs. Lincoln questioned our daughter in her room after dinner, when she admitted having gone to Milwaukee and being married secretly in the afternoon. That's all there is to it."

The next morning reporters were still camped in front of the Lincoln mansion. Everyone wanted to talk to Warren Beckwith, but no one knew where to find him. As the *Chicago Tribune* pointedly noted, "His whereabouts appeared to be a secret to every one but his bride." It was rumored that he was somewhere in Chicago waiting for a summons from Robert Lincoln. When Robert emerged, it was obvious that the Lincolns had gone through another rough night, and that nothing had been settled.

"Have I seen Mr. Beckwith?" he snapped in response to a reporter's query. "Have I seen him? Well, I think not! And, furthermore, I have no desire to see that young gentleman. I shall not extend my pardon to him according to my present ideas. I refuse to talk further about the matter. The facts of the trip to Milwaukee are quite correct and I shall only devote my time to disposing of Mr. Beckwith."

"Is Mrs. Beckwith at home?" another reporter asked.

It took a moment for Robert to realize that the reporter was referring to his daughter Jessie. "Who? Mrs. Beckwith? Yes, I suppose she is. At least she should be here."

"Will the couple reside at home?"

"Well, my daughter will remain, I think, but as to that gentleman, I have nothing at all to say."

Lincoln was asked to spell out his objections to Warren Beckwith as a son-in-law. Lincoln was measured in his response. "Mr. Beckwith belongs to an excellent and reputable family, I believe. What I hold to be grounds for our objection to the match I would rather not say."

For the next few days, the Lincolns were adamant that Jessie stay at home. One melodramatic columnist even suggested that Jessie was being kept a prisoner. "It is a pity when Abraham Lincoln freed the colored women of the south that he did not at the same time liberate the white ones of the north. The people of the elegant set of Chicago are showing that they are a bit independent in their ideas for they are asking each other, 'Who is Robert T. Lincoln that he should say he is so much better than anyone else?'"

A blast of cold weather descended on Chicago, and the gloomy sky matched the miserable mood inside 60 Lake Shore Drive. Only a handful of the Lincolns' most intimate advisers and friends—"none but the most near and dear"—were allowed in to visit with Mary and Jessie, and when they arrived it was to commiserate, not celebrate, the marriage. One of those who came to consult with Robert Lincoln was John Runnells, general counsel of the Pullman Company. Runnells met with the new Pullman president at 9:00 A.M. and remained several hours. It was frustrating for Robert to be dealing with this family uproar while the Pullman board of directors was gathering in urgent session at corporate headquarters. Pullman stock was a blue chip favorite of widows and charitable trusts, and the stock price was being carefully monitored around the nation in these turbulent weeks following the death of George Pullman. When Robert managed to sneak out of the house Saturday morning, he headed straight to the Pullman office building downtown to catch up on work. Even there a newspaper reporter from the *Chicago Journal* who was staking out the building waylaid him.

"I do not care to discuss my affairs in public anymore," Robert told him. "I have nothing to add to what I have already said."

For Jessie, one bright note was a kind letter from her cousin, Mary M. Kelly, who was about her age. "Congratulations and best wishes for a long and happy married life," Mary Kelly wrote. "We all wish you were with us tonight as we are having a little party. Having had a honeymoon myself, however, I correctly understand that you prefer being where you are." Apparently, Mary Kelly was not fully up to speed about the wretched state of Jessie the newlywed.

In Milwaukee, Christian was shocked to read that the simple little marriage ceremony he had performed had been blown into the society scandal of the year. The clergyman felt compelled to let Robert Lincoln know what had happened in his parlor that day.

"I understand that you do not particularly blame me for my part in the transaction as I was totally ignorant of who they were until they came to answer the question that I am required to put to them before performing the ceremony," he wrote Lincoln. He pointed out that Jessie and Warren were of legal age, and, besides, he did not feel it was his position to probe into their personal lives. Then he took the liberty of ministering to Robert Lincoln. "I believe that you have it in your power to lift her up in this sphere in which you have so carefully trained her to occupy. The eyes of the world are upon you and all are anxiously awaiting your decision. Let me entreat you to rise in the spirit of your noble and dearly beloved father and in one master stroke strike the shackles from the hands and lives from those who do dearly love each other. I'm thoroughly convinced that your daughter can never truly love another and what is home without true love abiding? I pray you give the young man a fair trial and if he then proves unworthy you shall have washed your hands of all responsibility."

Holed up at Clifton House awaiting word from Jessie, the beleaguered bridegroom was overwhelmed by the maelstrom of all those hurtful and humiliating articles exposing him as a loafer, and decided that he had better do something to restore his good name. On November 11, he got word to Jessie that he would find a job working for his father in Aurora, Illinois, headquarters of the company he co-owned, Western Wheel Scraper Company, which manufactured a horse-drawn carriage that graded dirt and gravel roadways. Warren wanted to make himself worthy of Jessie Lincoln. He told his bride that "for the life of me" he could not understand why her parents were so opposed to the marriage.

"Keep up the good heart," he advised Jessie. "Father will help me I know for a good start and there I will make it a success. I care nothing of what your father may personally think of me. His impressions are wrong as anyone who really knows me will confirm. I really am truly going to make a life-long effort and attain success for you."

But before Warren could launch his career at the Western Wheel Scraper Company, there was one more football game to play. He checked out of Clifton House and returned to Mount Pleasant, intending to rejoin his teammates at practice for Monday's big game against the Fighting Scots of Monmouth College. His arrival at the train depot was covered by the press with the hoopla afforded the homecoming of a local war hero, and though his bride was not with him, he was "not disconsolate," the *Mount Pleasant Daily News* reported.

"Warren Wallace Beckwith, who eloped with Miss Jessie Lincoln, returned to the city last night apparently not more concerned by the hubbub he has raised than if he had just scored a touchdown or made a 45-yard dash. . . . That he had returned home was no indication that he had given up his bride or bowed in submission to his imperious father-in-law. He is a true athlete and when he gave his word to the captain . . . that he would be here Friday to practice for Monday's hard game with Monmouth his captain knew that nothing would detain him."

Warren told reporters that he intended to remain in Mount Pleasant and get in one full day of practice before returning to Chicago to bring back his bride—"in spite of paternal objections." Mount Pleasant applauded the local boy who had made good by marrying into the Lincoln family. "Everybody he met on the streets wanted to shake hands with him . . . on account of his nerve as well as his good fortune in securing such a lovely bride." That afternoon Warren showed up for football practice at the campus of Iowa

Wesleyan and was surrounded by teammates who showered him with goodwill. He wore a bright new jersey that he said he had bought on his wedding trip.

In Chicago, even in the face of the relentless pressure from her parents, Jessie was determined to stick with Warren. She let them know that she intended to move out of the mansion and live with Warren at her grandfather's house in Mount Pleasant. The Lincolns came to a decision. It was time to get together with the Beckwith clan and work this out.

At ten-thirty Saturday morning, Jessie and her mother descended the stone steps of the Lincoln mansion, climbed into a waiting carriage, and drove to the Union Railroad Station, where they boarded a train to Aurora. True to form, they did everything they could to ensure privacy. Jessie, wearing a wide-brimmed hat with a plume, covered her face with a veil. Although she carried a pass permitting her to ride free on the Pullman sleeper car, Jessie sought more deluxe accommodations and paid the full seven-dollar fare for a private stateroom. Mother and daughter hurried through the train station hoping they would not be recognized, and the moment they stepped into the car they closed the curtains. From Mount Pleasant, Warren Beckwith also boarded a train to Aurora, and on Sunday afternoon, November 14, at the home of his parents, the newlyweds saw each other for the first time since they had eloped.

It vexed Captain Beckwith to see his son made the figure of national mockery, when in truth the Beckwiths came from a distinguished family that traced its roots back to Robert the Bruce, the warrior king of Scotland. Captain Beckwith was a substantial personage who owned a 1,600-acre Iowa farm where he raised trotting horses and a herd of 150 purebred Hereford cattle. He had five children; Warren was the youngest. Luzenia Porter, his first wife, had died in 1880, and Captain Beckwith was now married to Luzenia's sister Sarah.

An uneasy truce was declared between the Lincolns and the Beckwiths. Mary tried to talk Jessie into accompanying her to New York to buy a wedding gown, and the blankets, linens, and sheets that all brides required for a proper trousseau. But Jessie may have perceived this to be a ruse to separate her from Warren, and she refused to go along. Instead, she accompanied Warren on the last train out to Mount Pleasant. Mary Lincoln must have been apoplectic.

The newlyweds arrived in Mount Pleasant just before midnight. Word of their homecoming was telegraphed ahead, because half the town, including the Iowa Wesleyan football team and Warren's numerous cousins, had gathered at the depot to cheer this triumph of young people in love. Everyone roared when the train pulled into the station and the newlyweds stepped onto the platform. A "great throng" surrounded Jessie and Warren and let out three hearty hip-hip-hurrahs. The next day, Warren played opposite Monmouth, and two days later he took the field against the Keokuk College of Physicians and Surgeons, defeating them by the lopsided score of 48-0. Evidently, even then, medical school students were not known for their skill on the gridiron.

The game also marked the first time that the *New York Times* covered the Iowa Wesleyan Tigers versus the Keokuk Medics. But with Jessie Lincoln Beckwith sitting in the stadium, this game was an important social event. Warren's brothers and sisters sat with Jessie, and she applauded with gusto when her husband took to the field. It was pointedly observed that Jessie's parents were not at her side. Warren was complimented for playing "as good a foot ball game as he ever did in his days of single blessedness." In a post-game interview following the victory against Keokuk, Warren was asked about his relationship with his in-laws. He answered that he did not expect any reconciliation but would like it to happen for the sake of his bride. He also shot down a rumor that Mr. Lincoln had offered him a position with the Pullman Palace Car Company. No, Warren said, he would not be going to Chicago to work for Mr. Lincoln. Instead, he planned to finish out the semester at Iowa Wesleyan and then work for his father, Captain Beckwith, although in what capacity he could not say. Warren said he just wanted to settle down in Mount Pleasant with Jessie.

The realities of married life very quickly struck the newlyweds. Jessie was pregnant. She sought the comforts of home in Chicago, where she was now an intriguing figure to her society friends; they could not believe she had had the nerve to run away and elope, and now, in such quick order, become pregnant. "I have not written you before because I have not had sufficient control of language to express myself suitably," wrote one mesmerized socialite cousin of Jessie's. "Now that the 'deed is done' . . . I am anxious to see the bride and groom of such celebrity." The underlying message was that Jessie had married laughably beneath her.

Warren followed her to Chicago and found work at the Chicago Gas Light & Coke Company. The job with his father did not pan out, which was a shame because the Western Wheel Scraper Company turned out to be a terrific business. Captain Beckwith and his two partners found themselves at the cusp of modern road building in America. The days of smoothing out roadways with a pick, shovel, and wheelbarrow had given way to employing the scraper, a strange-looking machine resembling a mechanical spider, that, when dragged by a team of horses, could grade and level rough roads. Western Wheel Scraper manufactured the world's first road grader, and it was the beginning of a huge industrial concern that would in the next century merge with Austin-Western, makers of giant earthmoving equipment. In a curious way, Robert Lincoln's Pullman Palace Car Company represented a dying industry, while Captain Beckwith's Western Wheel Scraper anticipated the historic national shift from rails to roads. Unfortunately, in the year 1898, Warren did not have the wisdom to imagine America in the twentieth century. He just wanted to play some ball.

With his wife entering her fourth month of pregnancy, to the utter shame of his family, Warren tried out for the pro baseball team in Ottumwa, Iowa. He signed with the club in early March 1898, but his playing days lasted a mere two weeks. He was booted off the team after his stepmother, Sarah, approached the manager and implored him to release Warren from his contract. Warren was given a good talking-to and Sarah reminded him that he had to start making a living and get serious about his life. Robert Lincoln also made it known that he would provide "suitable employment" for Warren, but only if he quit baseball.

Before Warren could settle on his next move, the battleship *Maine* was blown up in Havana harbor. Whipped into hysteria by the jingoistic press, Congress declared a state of war between the United States and Spain on April 25, 1898. President William McKinley issued a nationwide call for 125,000 volunteers, and Warren Beckwith signed up with 5,000 other men from Iowa. Patriotism aside, one wonders whether Warren saw the war as a way out of a miserable situation at home. His unit, Company F of the Fifteenth Iowa infantry volunteers, mustered at Camp McKinley in Des Moines, and then shipped off to Jacksonville, Florida, for training. Warren never saw action in Cuba; after one hundred days, with the capitulation of Spain, the war came to a sudden end. Cuba was granted independence, and the United States acquired Guam, Puerto Rico, and the Philippine Islands, and became a true world power. Not for nothing did Robert Lincoln's friend John Hay, now serving as McKinley's secretary of state, call the conflict that "splendid little war."

Warren was still in uniform when he received word of the birth of his first daughter. Mary Lincoln Beckwith was born August 22, 1898, just nine months plus twelve days from the day Jessie and Warren had eloped. In keeping with Lincoln family tradition, and to avoid an impossibly confusing effusion of Marys in the family, the baby was given a nickname at birth by which she would be known for the rest of her life: Peggy.

Warren was granted a military furlough, and made his way to Chicago. When he strode into the Lincoln mansion at 60 Lake Shore Drive, he was presented with a stout little tot with puffy cheeks, an alert face, and exquisite baby skin. Warren was delirious with pride over the baby's lineage. By one account, the impulsive young father was sent on an errand to fetch a bottle of milk. He galloped through the streets calling for other riders to stand aside—he had the right of way because he was bringing milk for Abraham Lincoln's great-granddaughter.

The birth of baby Peggy changed the family dynamics. Warren found his father-in-law Robert Lincoln to be more accommodating, even embracing. Perhaps the former secretary of war appreciated that his son-in-law wore the uniform of the army he had once reigned over. It was his "interfering" mother-in-law, Mary Harlan Lincoln, who was now the problem. Warren found her bossy and overbearing. It seemed to him that Mrs. Lincoln regarded baby Peggy as a surrogate for the son she had lost when Abraham Lincoln II died. It upset him to have Mary usurp his role as Peggy's father, and she also appeared to be poisoning his relationship with Jessie. Many years later, Beckwith would remark, "There has been talk that I didn't get along with Robert Lincoln but that's not true. I was a frequent visitor at his home and he was always very nice to me. Mrs. Lincoln was always interfering in our marriage. . . . Mrs. Lincoln said she was lonely since the death of her son." In so many ways, it was a peculiar replay of the troubled relationship between Mary Harlan Lincoln and her late mother-in-law, Mary Todd Lincoln.

With the war over, Warren was discharged from the army, but he would still be gone for months at a time, working railroad jobs or cattle ranching in Oklahoma, or at his father's property in Iowa, drifting, trying to find his way.

Mary Harlan Lincoln's father did not live to see the new century dawn. On Sunday, September 30, 1899, former senator James Harlan contracted a severe cold. Somehow he managed to preside over the induction ceremonies of the new university president at Iowa Wesleyan. Two days later, with his death imminent, Robert and Mary Lincoln were summoned, and arrived in time to comfort the old man in his final hours. He "bade his daughter an affectionate 'good night.'" Those were his last words. Harlan lost the power of speech and died the following day at age seventy-nine. His funeral was the largest gathering that had ever been held in Mount Pleasant. The public schools and government offices closed, and Main Street shops and businesses were draped in mourning. Students from Iowa Wesleyan College served as guards as his body lay in state, and it was said that every man, woman, and child in Mount Pleasant passed the coffin.

As New Year's Eve 1899 came around, Americans were buoyant. Snow was falling on New York City that Sunday evening when the eighteen hundreds passed into history and a new century was born. The hub of national celebration was not Times Square but lower Manhattan. A mass of humanity had gathered around Trinity Church, and when the clock struck midnight everyone erupted into the "Star Spangled Banner," followed by "Auld Lang Syne" and "Yankee Doodle Dandy." Steamboats and ferries in the Hudson River blasted their horns, and factories set off steam whistles.

It was a different country then. The population was seventy-six million, and more than sixty percent of the people lived on farms. Automobiles were a rare sight on the roads, and at a price tag of fifteen hundred dollars, available only for the very wealthy. Horses and buggies remained the dominant mode of transportation. Only a few homes of the rich were powered by electricity. Most streets and homes were still lighted by gas. The tallest skyscraper in the nation was at 15 Park Row in Manhattan, near City Hall; it stood twenty-nine stories high. Eggs cost twelve cents a dozen, sirloin steak twenty-four cents a pound. The average worker made twenty-two cents an hour.

In Chicago, at age fifty-six, Robert Lincoln was ten years older than the life expectancy of the average American male. Mary Lincoln was fifty-three. As president of the Pullman Palace Car Company, soon to be renamed the Pullman Company, Robert was now an eminent businessman. As the Gilded Age faded into memory, professionally, he had every reason to be content. It was now the Age of Optimism, or as some called it, the Age of Confidence. In Buffalo, New York, then the eighth-largest city in America, preparations were under way for a new world's fair. It was to be known as the Pan-American Exposition. President McKinley would attend. And as fate would have it, so would Robert Lincoln.

20

Presidential Curse

PRESIDENT MCKINLEY'S CHARTERED train left Canton, Ohio, bound for Buffalo on September 4, 1901. The train had every luxury available in early twentieth century travel, including two Pullman sleeper cars, a day coach, and a separate car for baggage. On board were the twenty-fifth president and his wife, Ida Saxton McKinley, their two nieces, and Mrs. McKinley's personal physician, maid, and nurse. Mrs. McKinley suffered from epilepsy, and there were more people associated with her care and comfort than with the president's, who had with him two White House stenographers, a Secret Service detail, and his secretary, George Cortelyou.

The train proceeded at a leisurely pace so as not to upset the fragile First Lady, and detoured to Cleveland, where it picked up a third McKinley niece. Finally, at 5:30 that evening, the train pulled into the station at Dunkirk, outside Buffalo. A welcoming committee of local dignitaries, including the mayor of Buffalo and John Milburn, the president of the world's fair, greeted the presidential party. The McKinleys spent the night as guests at Milburn's house on Delaware Avenue.

September 5 was a perfect golden day in Buffalo. A horse-drawn carriage carrying the McKinleys like two crowned heads of Europe pranced down Lincoln Parkway and stopped at the entrance gate to the world's fair, where a boy reached out and said, "Here's a program for you, Mr. President." McKinley grinned, dug into his pocket, and handed the boy a dollar coin, but the lad took a step back and refused to accept the money. "No, sir," he said, "that's a present." Before fifty thousand spectators, McKinley spoke about America's limitless potential, and when he was finished, the enormous crowd erupted in cheers. Some called it the greatest speech of McKinley's life.

The next day McKinley visited Niagara Falls with one hundred invited guests, and then returned to the exposition, once again entering via the Lincoln Parkway gate. A vast throng had already assembled outside the Temple of Music, where the president was to hold a reception to which the general public had been invited. At 4:00 P.M., as an organist played a Bach sonata, the temple doors were flung open, and the public streamed in. McKinley called out, "Let them come!" and the crowd applauded and lined up where the president stood, in the middle of the great hall, to shake his hand. He was protected by a detachment of soldiers, local police, and Secret Service, but the crowd was swelling by the second. A twelve-year-old girl went up to the president, and he shook her hand and fixed a gentle smile on her. McKinley, whose two daughters had died in infancy, had a special way with children.

In line behind the girl was a twenty-three-year-old man dressed in black. His name was Leon Czolgosz. McKinley's security detail took note of the man's right hand, wrapped in a handkerchief, presumably from some injury. McKinley bowed and extended his hand in greeting. Less than a foot of space separated the president from Czolgosz. It was 4:07 P.M. Suddenly, Czolgosz pushed the president's outstretched hand aside and opened fire. Two pistol shots rang out. The handkerchief had been concealing a .32 Iver-Johnson six-shooter. The first bullet grazed the president's chest. Before anyone could react, Czolgosz, an anarchist, pulled the trigger a second time. It blasted McKinley in the stomach. The president stared at the assassin in amazement and then fell back into the arms of a Secret Service agent.

"Am I shot?" the president asked.

The agent tore open McKinley's vest and saw the gaping hole in his stomach. "I'm afraid you are, Mr. President."

A six-foot-six black waiter, James "Big Jim" Parker, grabbed Czolgosz from behind in a chokehold and yanked him down. "You son of a bitch!" Parker shouted. "You've shot the president!" Police wielding billy clubs pummeled Czolgosz, and the crowd tore at his clothes and screamed, "Lynch him!" and "Hang the bastard!" The president, clutching his stomach, was assisted to a chair. McKinley motioned for his private secretary, George Cortelyou.

"Cortelyou, my wife, be careful about her; don't let her know."

McKinley's gaze drifted to his assassin. The man's face was a bloody pulp after cops and soldiers had delivered blow after blow. "Let no one hurt him," McKinley gasped.

At that moment, a train was approaching the Buffalo station carrying a most distinguished passenger, Robert Lincoln. President McKinley had extended an invitation to Lincoln to meet with him at the Pan-American Exposition. Lincoln wielded great influence in the McKinley administration. The secretary of state was his friend John Hay, and the secretary of the treasury was Lyman Gage, the prominent banker from Chicago who had served as foreman of the jury that had declared Mary Todd Lincoln insane in 1875.

The train pulled into the Buffalo station, and Lincoln was about to disembark when a great commotion broke out. Word of the national tragedy had traveled like lightning. It was almost impossible to believe that another American president had been shot, the third in thirty-six years.

Lincoln insisted on proceeding to the exhibition grounds, where he encountered twenty-five thousand citizens assembled outside the hospital where McKinley had been taken. In this chaos Lincoln was somehow able to weave his way to the hospital entrance. The *New York Times* account of September 6, 1901, reported that Lincoln had visited with the president in his grievously wounded state. McKinley died six days later.

Lincoln was now the only man in history to be associated with three presidential assassinations—his father's, Garfield's, and now McKinley's. This bizarre, almost mystical correlation is a historical oddity that remains relatively obscure except among researchers of presidential assassinations. The sobriquet, the Presidential Angel of Death, that has been attached to Robert Lincoln's name over the years, has most recently been joined by Jinxy McDeath, a creation of the writer and social commentator Sarah Vowell.

Watching McKinley die was another wrenching experience, even for a man who expected the worst in all circumstances. Lincoln thought he was cursed, and let it be known that from then on he would no longer appear at any presidential function. His despair was evident in a letter he wrote to Vice President Theodore Roosevelt, on September 18, after he had succeeded McKinley as president.

"I do not congratulate you for I have seen too much of the seamy side of the Presidential Robe to think of it as a desirable garment."

Several years later, Lincoln was invited to have lunch at the White

House. He respectfully declined. In private correspondence he acknowledged his belief that his presence had spelled doom for three presidents: "If only they knew, they wouldn't want me there," he said of the White House invitation. Still later, Lincoln, as a gray eminence of the Republican Party, was asked whether he would attend an event at which the president would be present. "No, I am not going and they'd better not invite me," he said, "because there is a certain fatality about presidential functions when I am present." Robert vowed never to set foot in the White House again.

The same month of McKinley's assassination, Robert Lincoln decided that something must finally be done about his father's remains. He went to Springfield in his private rail car and took a carriage to the site of the Lincoln Monument in Oak Ridge Cemetery, where his parents and three brothers lay buried. What he saw displeased him. The Lincoln Monument had been officially dedicated in 1874, but it was already in a state of disrepair. As part of the renovation work under way, Abraham Lincoln's coffin had been removed from its sarcophagus and placed in a temporary shallow grave, which must have upset Robert beyond words. Before the coffin was returned to the tomb, Robert was insisting that his father be reburied in an impenetrable block of rock, just as George Pullman had been. He had legitimate reasons for his concern. In 1876 a gang of thieves had broken into the Lincoln tomb at night, intending to steal the corpse and hold it hostage for two hundred thousand dollars ransom. Abraham Lincoln's coffin was actually halfway out of the sarcophagus when Secret Service agents, who had been tipped off to the plot, burst in and arrested the grave robbers.

In accordance with Robert Lincoln's instructions, heavy construction equipment was hauled in to dig a huge ten-foot-deep gravesite. On September 26, 1901, twenty-three people gathered in the utmost secrecy to bear witness to an historic event: the reburial of Abraham Lincoln. An extraordinary thing happened next. A debate arose among the official observers: Considering all the rumors that the body was not that of President Lincoln, and the impenetrable design of his permanent resting place, should not the coffin be opened to positively identify the remains, and put the rumors to rest once and for all? Some argued that opening the coffin would be a gross desecration. In the end, they decided it had to be done.

Two plumbers went to work. With hammer and chisel they cracked the lead-lined casket just over the body's head and shoulders. As they lifted a piece of the lead, a rancid odor, "harsh and choking," wafted out. All those present removed their hats as a sign of respect, and leaned in for a look. It was Abraham Lincoln, beyond any doubt. The most famous face in American history was remarkably unchanged, though it now had a chalky, unearthly texture, like that of a bronze statue. But the coarse black whiskers, the wart on his cheek, all his features, were still there—even his melancholy expression. It had been thirty-six years since Lincoln's death, and the embalming process had preserved everything, including his facial hair, except for the eyebrows, which were strangely gone.

"I saw that top-knot of Mr. Lincoln's hair—his hair was course and thick, 'like a horse's,' he used to say—and it stood high in front," said one of the witnesses, J. C. Thompson. "When I saw that, I knew that it was Mr. Lincoln."

Some items in the coffin were not holding up as well. The president had been buried in the suit he wore at his second inaugural. Now it was stained with yellow mildew. And there were bits of red, white, and blue fabric, specks from the now-disintegrated American flag he had been buried with.

After having absorbed the image that would haunt many of those present for the rest of their lives, everyone agreed that the remains in the coffin were those of Abraham Lincoln. There was not one dissenting voice. It was time to put President Lincoln to rest. The plumbers soldered the piece of lead back into place and sealed the coffin. One of the witnesses was a thirteen-year-old boy, Fleetwood Lindley, whose father had kept him out of school for the day to observe the historic event. Young Fleetwood held on to one of the leather straps as the coffin was lowered ten feet to the bottom of the grave. Then two tons of cement was poured inside. When the cement hardened, it became an impregnable mountain, as Robert Lincoln, who was not present, had demanded. Fleetwood Lindley said he was not frightened when he stared into the face of Abraham Lincoln. It was only later that night that the full impact hit him. "I slept with Lincoln for the next six months," Lindley would tell *Life* magazine. When he died in 1963 at the age of seventy-five, Lindley became the last living person on earth to have seen Abraham Lincoln's face.

Jesse Lincoln Beckwith gave birth to a stillborn child, in 1901. Three years later, on July 19, 1904, she had a son, who was given the grand name Robert Todd Lincoln Beckwith. Like his sister Peggy, Robert was immediately issued a moniker. Everyone in his family would call him Bob, or Bud, and sometimes Buddy. Jessie had had a difficult pregnancy; Robert Lincoln worried that his daughter was not faring well, and further, that his namesake was a "dreadfully fat baby." Even with the birth of a son, Warren

Beckwith's marriage to Jessie was irretrievably broken. Warren was having trouble holding a job; for a time he worked as a railroad brakeman, then went to Oklahoma to try cattle ranching. One day he came home to find that Jessie had moved out. He tracked her down at her mother's house in Mount Pleasant and called her on the telephone to find out when she would be coming back.

"When I get ready," Jessie snapped. Warren was offended by her flippant answer. He informed her that he had a job lined up in Springfield, to which she replied, "If you get some work to do you wouldn't be so lonesome."

Two years later, in 1906, Mary Lincoln invited Jessie and the grandchildren to accompany her to London. Warren, of course, had not been invited, and he did not want his family to go. If they did, he threatened Jessie, he would divorce her. Time had healed nothing; if the Lincolns had thoroughly disdained Warren in 1897 when he had married Jessie, now they loathed him. Privately, Mary and Robert even explored the possibility of legally adopting Peggy and the infant Bud. It was Jessie's innocent question—"in case I should die could [Warren] take the children?"—that had started the Lincolns thinking about it.

"I think [Jessie] would be willing for us to adopt the children if that would help out any," Mary wrote her husband.

Beckwith hired a lawyer to discuss terms of a divorce. The lawyer went to the Harlan house in Mount Pleasant to talk things over with Jessie, but only Mary Lincoln was home. Most mothers would probably have told the lawyer to return another day; Mary Lincoln, however, had no problem with sitting down with him and negotiating terms. When the lawyer informed Mary that Warren Beckwith would be filing for divorce on grounds of desertion, she replied that there would be no resistance to it from the Lincolns.

"I agree with you that this Jessie affair had better be settled now without too much delay," Mary wrote Robert. On Abraham Lincoln's birthday, February 12, 1907, certainly a curious date for the case to appear on the court docket, Jessie and Warren Beckwith presented themselves in district court in Henry County, Iowa. Warren was granted his application for a decree of divorce, while Jessie was awarded full custody of the children. Neither party sought alimony or child support from the other. That was the last time they saw each other. Warren Beckwith also disappeared from the lives of his children. He would never see Peggy or Bud again.

Robert Lincoln's best friend was the Chicago department store merchant

Marshall Field. They were as close as brothers and went everywhere together. But the ill wind that had often come up in Robert's life had a strange way of blowing in whenever Marshall Field was present. Field had become a business icon for his "give-the-lady-what-she-wants" store policy. He followed two basic personal rules of finance—never borrow and always pay cash—and, like Robert Lincoln, he despised unions.

In March 1905, Lincoln and Field were on a golfing vacation in Augusta, Georgia, when Field slipped on ice and broke a bone in his right ankle. He had to use crutches for the rest of the trip. On New Year's Day 1906, somebody had the bright idea of playing winter golf in the freezing cold at a country club in Wheaton, Illinois. The foursome consisted of Robert Lincoln, Marshall Field, Field's personal assistant, and his nephew. Using red golf balls, they played eighteen holes in knee-deep snow. The game wore Marshall Field down. A few days later he developed a sore throat, but did not change his plans for a business trip to New York. There, he was stricken with pneumonia. Doctors treated the tycoon in his suite at the Holland House, and Robert Lincoln rushed to New York from Chicago and visited with his ailing friend. Robert's former law partner, William Beale, who now represented Field, came in on the Twentieth Century Limited and spent the whole day at Field's bedside. The speculation was that Field was dictating a change in his will. He died the next day at age seventy-two, devastating Robert, and sending him into a deep depression.

"Mr. Field's death is a great affliction to me for he had been my intimate friend and companion and we depended greatly upon each other for our recreation," Robert wrote his aunt, Emilie Todd Helm. While Robert had the reputation of being an imperious tycoon, he was emotionally fragile and had a high-strung temperament that, in times of crisis, left him on the edge. After Field's death he suffered a nervous breakdown. His doctors sent him to Augusta to recuperate. "I am still fit for nothing whatever," he admitted to Aunt Emilie a month into his stay. "It is no worse but it is most discouraging to see one day come after another without any visible improvement." In his quest for what he called "perfect rest," Robert decided to leave Augusta and head north to Hildene, the magnificent twenty-four-room mansion he had built in Manchester, Vermont, in 1904.

Lincoln had named it Hildene because the house was built on a gentle slope, and "dene" was the old English word for valley. It was, Lincoln maintained, his "ancestral home," but as Abraham Lincoln had been born in a log cabin in the backwoods of Kentucky, people were forced to wonder what ancestry Robert Lincoln was referring to. The Lincolns lived in high style at Hildene, with a permanent domestic staff of three maids, a butler, valet, chef, chauffeur, groomsman, coachman, and private secretary. He also retained a local doctor, C. M. Campbell, who was on call twenty-four hours a day when Robert was at Hildene. Robert's letters portray a sickly worry-wart, now aging and preoccupied with his health. "I hope you are very well," went one memorable letter to John Nicolay. "I am sorry to say that I am not." He called his condition "nervous dyspepsia" or "nervous prostration." In the winter of 1905, he was laid up for three months, during which time he said he "did absolutely nothing whatever." Even after all that bed rest, he said he still required at least several more months before he could think of getting back to work.

Golf gave Robert his greatest pleasure. Hildene was still in the design phase when he had purchased ten shares of stock in the Ekwanok Country Club in Manchester. In 1904, he was elected its president. Golf at Ekwanok was intense, and taken seriously. The strictest rules of the game were enforced, and there was never such a thing as "winter play," in which a golfer, under certain conditions, could improve his lie on the fairway. When he was residing at Hildene, Robert played eighteen holes most afternoons, sometimes, when he was tired, stopping at the sixteenth hole because it was closer to the clubhouse. His regular foursome consisted of local business leaders, including the president of the Albany Trust Bank and the owner of the Albany Car Wheel Company. Caddies at Ekwanok made fifteen cents a game. Hard liquor was prohibited. The most popular drink served at the Ekwanok clubhouse was ginger champagne and lemonade.

Robert could wax poetic about the game of golf. "I have just come in from eighteen holes of golf in which I think I played the best game I have ever done," he wrote his private secretary at the Pullman Company in Chicago, in 1906. The social scene at Ekwanok was formal and hierarchal, with the Lincolns at the summit. When Robert entered the clubhouse, he was greeted with awestruck silence. Having the son of the Great Emancipator as a founding member was considered a great honor. Abraham Lincoln had ended slavery, saved the Union, and debated grand principles of nationhood. Now, the most contentious issue his son Robert faced was whether golf should be played on Sundays. He was in favor of it, but most of the country club membership was opposed. Robert became so identified with the game of golf that he was offered the presidency of the United States Golf Association, but, just as he had done when he was told the presidency of the United States could be his for the asking, he turned the position down.

Even on warm summer days in Vermont, Robert maintained his stiff formality. When he went into town, he always wore a dark suit and hat. On the rare occasion when his reclusive wife accompanied him, she also dressed in black and wore a large-brimmed black hat. It was an event when Robert's handsome open coach pulled up to the National Bank in downtown Manchester, drawn by two, sometimes four horses. His coachman would help him out of the carriage, and children would crowd around him and ask for his autograph. Robert, now in his early sixties, would oblige, and hand the youngsters ten cents for good measure, which may explain why they sought his autograph.

Chicago remained their legal residence, but Hildene became the Lincolns' true home. Mary was usually the first of the high-society summer residents to appear in Manchester for the start of the season, on April 15, arriving on the train from New York City. Robert would show up two weeks later. The Lincolns were also always the last to leave in the fall, before the first snow. Although Robert stayed on as president of the Pullman Company, it proved impractical to run the day-to-day operations of such a huge company from Vermont; his real value to Pullman was as a figurehead and ambassador of goodwill. One duty he did spend a great deal of his time on was deciding who would be issued annual passes to ride on Pullman sleeper cars free of charge.

ROBERT LINCOLN ADMITTED that he was "rather dreading" the coming centennial celebration of Abraham Lincoln's birth. President Taft had invited the Lincolns to accompany him to Springfield in the presidential car, but Robert declined, citing ill health and the advice of his doctor. Perhaps the real reason was the assassination curse he thought was hanging over his head, but Robert did end up attending the centennial ceremonies, though he traveled to Springfield in his own private Pullman car.

On February 12, 1909, speeches paying homage to the memory of the great American, Abraham Lincoln, were delivered in every large city in the nation. Chicago—with more than fifty commemorations, including a speech at Lincoln Park given by a then-little-known academic, Dr. Woodrow Wilson, the president of Princeton University—basically shut down. Robert Lincoln pulled into Springfield on Friday morning, February 12. With him was his wife, a contingent of executives from the Pullman

Company, Ambassador James Bryce of Great Britain, and Mary Bryan, the wife of the orator William Jennings Bryan.

At 10:00 A.M., Robert and Mary and the other distinguished guests arrived in a caravan of eighteen carriages at the Lincoln Monument for a solemn remembrance. As he stood in silent meditation, in a bitter wind and freezing drizzle, Robert's eyes sparkled with tears, and he choked back sobs as a sixteen-piece band played a funeral dirge. In one of her rare public appearances, Mary Lincoln stood next to her husband. In a howling wind, an honor guard of old veterans from the Civil War who had heeded President Lincoln's call to arms, stood at attention with fixed bayonets. These were the men who loved Lincoln best, and even in this miserable weather they refused to relinquish their posts until dusk fell. There was one sour note to the day for the Lincolns. A feature article on the front page of the *Illinois State Register* headlined LINCOLN AND HIS WOOING told the story of Abraham Lincoln's love affair with Ann Rutledge, and concluded, "Had she and Lincoln married, there is reason to believe the future president's home life might have been happier." It was the story that would not die. Even in this glorious moment, the Lincolns found themselves still beleaguered by William Herndon's discovery.

A poignant moment came when Robert made an unannounced visit to Abraham Lincoln's home, at Eighth and Jackson. The house, now a state museum, was packed with tourists who were there for the centennial celebration. On display in the dining room were a sugar bowl and creamer, and a large silver bowl from which ice cream had been served at the wedding of Abraham and Mary Lincoln in 1842. The room was sweet with the aroma of old-fashioned jelly and pound cake laid out on serving trays. Robert asked to see the bedroom he had slept in when he was a boy, and requested a moment of privacy. He stayed in the room for some time, alone with his thoughts.

At 5:00 P.M. the Springfield chapter of the Daughters of the American Revolution held a reception at the Lincoln house for invited guests. Robert's wife was asked to attend but sent her regrets. Once again, the newspapers reported her absence in the most generous terms, writing simply that she was "unable to be present."

At a mass gathering at the Springfield Tabernacle, at First and Adams, ten thousand people heard the three-time Democratic nominee for president William Jennings Bryan deliver a rousing address in honor of the sixteenth president. When the band played that haunting southern melody

"Dixie," a gesture of reconciliation that Abraham Lincoln would surely have appreciated, there was a ripple of applause. And at a male-only banquet at the State Arsenal building, that went well past midnight, old soldiers in Union blue filled the grandstands in what was called a "beautiful, brilliant, iridescent" evening of tribute and speeches. Robert Lincoln, as the guest of honor, sat on the dais. He had issued the strictest instructions that he was not to be introduced or made to give a speech. No black Americans had been invited to the banquet. Their only presence was a letter from the educator and author Booker T. Washington that was read to the guests. There was a hue and cry over the ban, and the black populace of Springfield ended up holding a separate celebration at the city's St. Paul's A.M.E. Church that same night. There, they heard the Reverend L. H. Magee declare, "I would rather be one of that great number of black devotees than toastmaster at a so-called 'Lincoln banquet' at twenty-five dollars per."

Robert Lincoln and his party left Springfield for Chicago the following morning in his private car.

There was one other commemoration of Abraham Lincoln's centennial that was of perhaps even greater magnitude than the one held in Springfield. It took place at a dirt-poor farm three miles outside Hodgenville, Kentucky. President Theodore Roosevelt had only twenty days left to his term in office, but he chose to celebrate February 12, 1909, at the site of the lob cabin that had been the birthplace of Abraham Lincoln. Shamefully, none of Lincoln's blood descendants attended the ceremony designating his birthplace as a national historic site. Roosevelt and his advisers were not surprised by this affront; as his top military aide, Major Archibald Butt, confided in a letter to his sister-in-law, "I hear that Bob Lincoln . . . does not relish the perpetuation of this cabin." Butt went on to say that he did not necessarily fault Robert Lincoln for distancing himself from his family's log-cabin origins. "I cannot blame him. The very thought of it, having seen it once, would make any member of his family shudder with horror. It does not bear the stamp of poverty alone, but degradation and uncleanliness."

Most of the people who cheered President Roosevelt that day in Hodgenville were poor Kentucky country folk—not the sort of crowd Robert Lincoln usually found himself with. To get to the site of the Lincoln farm meant traversing some of the worst back roads in Kentucky. Though the state had made a valiant effort to smooth out the roadbed for President Roosevelt's visit, it was still a rough three-mile carriage ride from the train depot in Hodgenville for the president and his wife.

At the dedication ceremony, eight thousand spectators watched as Roosevelt mounted a chair to give them a better view of him. A fine specimen of gray granite hung suspended in the air by a giant derrick as Roosevelt gave his inspiring Lincoln speech, and, at his signal, the granite cornerstone was lowered into place. The president, just fifty-one years old, grabbed a shovel and applied the first trowel of mortar to mark the start of construction of a memorial to Abraham Lincoln on these sacred grounds. A special honor was given to Isaac T. Montgomery, an elderly African American who had once been a slave of Jefferson Davis. It seemed fitting that it was he who placed a copy of the Emancipation Proclamation inside the cornerstone. Montgomery then made a brief and moving speech in which he called himself "one of the former millions of slaves to whom Lincoln gave freedom."

Three months later, Robert Lincoln did appear in the town of Hodgenville, on Memorial Day, for another dedication—this one of a bronze statue of his father that had been created by the American sculptor Adolph Weinman. Robert had contributed one thousand dollars to the statue's erection, and agreed to participate in its unveiling and dedication. As usual, Robert arrived in his private Pullman car. City fathers picked him up at the train depot, and he was taken by carriage to the center of the little county seat, where he must have been mortified to suddenly find himself at the head of a parade, right behind the marching band. He was driven to the statue, which was draped in flags, but the honor of pulling the cord was accorded to his elderly aunt, Emilie Todd Helm, his mother's half-sister, whom Robert had picked up in Louisville. The statue was unveiled, revealing a magnificent work of art: a seated and contemplative Abraham Lincoln, six feet in height. Robert Lincoln was on the speaker's platform listening to the orations extolling his father, when it became obvious that he was in distress. His shoulders were shaking with emotion, and he seemed to be on the verge of tears. After the ceremony, he had to be helped from the platform. The left side of his body felt numb; he was in a state of "almost complete collapse."

Robert insisted on being taken back to the railroad station where his private car was at the ready. He ordered the train to leave Hodgenville immediately, his sudden illness having forced him to cancel plans to visit his father's birthplace, just three miles away. (Robert Lincoln said it "grieved" him that he was unable to visit the site of the Lincoln log cabin and indicated that he wanted to return in the fall. He said that he desired to "walk over the farm and drink from the spring." He never did make the trip.) Some might contend that this was a blessing for Robert. While most Americans regarded Abe Lincoln's humble beginnings as the embodiment of the American experience, for Robert, his family's destitute origins were a source of embarrassment and shame. He had always maintained that the storybook history of his father's lowly birth had been grossly exaggerated. He was also ambivalent about the memorial now under construction at the site; on at least one occasion he had actually suggested that the log cabin be torn down to end the perpetuation of the "myth" of Abraham Lincoln's childhood poverty. There was also an ongoing dispute about the authenticity of the log cabin that had become a national shrine.

Robert returned to Vermont, where his daughter Mamie and her husband Charles had purchased a summerhouse not far from Hildene. Mamie was devoted to her father. She had bought a Kodak, the first camera manufactured for amateur use, and photographed Robert on the Ekwanok golf course. The Ishams also maintained a residence in New York City, at 15 E. Sixty-sixth Street, and they had one of the first telephones to be issued in the city, with the number PLAZA 1146. In New York and in Manchester, Mamie led a life of rectitude and correctness. In this regard, she was the spitting image of her parents and the very model of Victorian womanhood. Robert's only issue with Mamie was that her marriage had failed to produce more heirs. Lincoln Isham was the Ishams' only child.

Jessie Beckwith was a single woman now, and Robert and Mary Lincoln became proxy parents to Jessie's children, Peggy and Bud. Peggy loved Hildene, where there were buttons to summon the butler in all twenty-four rooms. Her childhood summers there were magical times. Robert Lincoln was a doting granddad, and bought her a pony for her ninth birthday, a sensitive age for Peggy because her parents had divorced that year. Jessie did not take kindly to the pony's coloring; she thought it just did not suit her little girl, and wanted the animal sent back, but Peggy threw a fit, and the pony stayed on at Hildene. Keeping up with his grandchildren was physically exhausting for someone of Robert's age and infirmities, but evidently he enjoyed them, particularly Peggy. He found her more interesting than Bud, probably for the simple reason that she was older, and at least he could communicate with her. He also introduced Peggy to golf (when she became an adult she could shoot a respectable one hundred on the men's course), and advised her to carry a little notepad around at all times to jot down her thoughts and ideas. The Lincolns loved the youngsters very much, and appreciated having them around, but sometimes it became a burden.

Robert once remarked, "things are getting where very little bother unduly troubles us both." One can sympathize with the Lincolns, who had to have wondered: Where are the parents? Who is supposed to be raising these kids?

With Jessie's painful marriage to Warren Beckwith finally at an end, Robert and Mary Lincoln were praying that her impetuous days were behind her. How wrong they were.

21
Family Secrets

IDA TARBELL COULD not believe she was having tea with Robert Lincoln. To be in this magnificent parlor drinking tea with the son of her idol Abraham Lincoln was so unimaginable to her that she could scarcely concentrate on what he was saying. She scrutinized Lincoln's face searching for something that bore a resemblance to the visage of the Great Emancipator, but Tarbell said, "There was nothing. He was all Todd," plump and perfectly groomed, with "the freshness which makes men of his type look as if they were just out of the barber's chair."

Tarbell was forty years old when Robert Lincoln agreed to see her. She was writing for *McClure's Magazine* and was several years away from publishing the book that would make her famous, *The History of the Standard Oil Company*, an exposé on the business practices of John D. Rockefeller. Had Lincoln known that the middle-aged woman sitting across from him pleasantly sipping tea would go down in history as one of the founders of muckraking journalism, he surely would have made some excuse and left the premises. But Tarbell's work on Rockefeller was in the future. At the time of her meeting with Lincoln, her project was a biography of Abraham Lincoln, to be published in monthly installments by *McClure's*, then a popular illustrated competitor to the *Atlantic Monthly*.

Lincoln routinely rejected all inquiries from authors seeking interviews about his father, but the call from Tarbell was different because she had shrewdly gone through an intermediary, Emily Lyons, a well-liked society figure in Chicago whom Tarbell knew from Washington. "Come to Chicago," Emily Lyons had told Tarbell. "I'll see that you meet Robert Lincoln."

Tarbell arrived in Chicago and found herself in Mrs. Lyons's house having tea with Robert Lincoln. As the hostess, she said, "Now, Robert, I want you to give her something worthwhile." Lincoln chortled. No one but the droll Emily Lyons would dare to speak so frankly to him. "Of course, if you say so, Emily," he answered, feeling more amused than put-upon. But then he looked at Tarbell and told the writer that he could offer her very little assistance. He had no new revelations to give her. But as a favor to Emily Lyons, there was one thing he would be willing to do. Robert promised to release to her a photograph of Abraham Lincoln that had never been published before.

Ida Tarbell was delighted. An exclusive photograph of President Lincoln would be a coup for her magazine. Arrangements were made, and, true to his word, Robert Lincoln saw that Tarbell received the photograph. It was a wonderful image, filmed in the daguerreotype process. According to Robert, it was the earliest photo portrait of his father in existence. It had been shot, he believed, in 1846 or 1847, during his father's first term in Congress. It took Tarbell's breath away. "This was a Lincoln which shattered the widely accepted tradition of his early shabbiness, rudeness, ungainliness," Tarbell wrote. "It was another Lincoln, and one that took me by storm." Tarbell was truly appreciative when Robert Lincoln granted her the rights to publish the picture, but that was all she would ever receive from the Prince of Rails.

Several years later, after the publication of Tarbell's *The Life of Abraham Lincoln*, Robert agreed to see her again in his office at the Pullman Company. Away from the social setting of Mrs. Lyon's parlor, he was all business. Although he was perfectly pleasant, his eyes seemed "harder to me in his office than over Mrs. Lyon's tea table." Tarbell's *The Life of Abraham Lincoln* was credited with doubling the circulation of *McClure's Magazine*, and Robert Lincoln had found himself unexpectedly pleased with the book's publication. He thought Ida Tarbell had done a masterful job of assembling his father's story.

Sitting in Robert Lincoln's office, Tarbell, thinking that she had earned the family's trust, decided it was time to ask Robert Lincoln for the mother lode—full access to Abraham Lincoln's presidential papers, the near-mythic collection of correspondence, memoranda, letters, and private records amassed during President Lincoln's political career, including his turbulent White House years. For Lincoln historians and journalists, it was the holy grail. To Tarbell's formal request, Robert's response was immediate and decisive. "Impossible," he said. "They are in the safety vault of my bank. I won't allow anybody to see them." He said he feared that publication of the documents could prove embarrassing to many prominent people who were still alive. "I fear misuse of those papers so much that I am thinking about destroying them." Ida Tarbell could not believe what she had heard. The idea of Robert destroying the historical documentation of the greatest crisis in American history sent her into the "greatest panic." She wondered if he could be serious. His next remark was: "I think I will burn them."

Robert had granted access to the Lincoln Papers only once, to John Nicolay and John Hay, who had written the authorized Lincoln biography. Nicolay and Hay had worked on their ten-volume book, totaling 4,700 pages, for sixteen years—after they had reached a private understanding with Robert: In return for exclusive rights to the Lincoln Papers, Robert could censor any document or language he deemed inappropriate for publication. Fulfilling their commitment, in 1884, the authors sent Robert a draft of their multi-volume epic, in which Hay acknowledged, "Every line has been written in a spirit of reverence and regard. Still, you may find here and there words or sentences which do not suit you. I write now to request that you will read with a pencil in your hand and strike out everything to which you object. I will adopt your view in all cases whether I agree with it or not." When Robert sent back the manuscript, Hay and Nicolay saw that it had been heavily edited. Hay assured Robert that he would abide by all the fixes. "I don't think there is a word left in it that would displease you. But of course before final publication I shall give you another hack at it, with plenary blue-pencil powers."

In the first four volumes, which related to Abraham Lincoln's early years, Robert had deleted several anecdotes regarding his backwoods grandfather, Thomas Lincoln, and, in effect, sanitized his father's life in Kentucky and Indiana. (The pompous Robert even considered his father's much-loved nickname, "Honest Abe," to be an "epithet," spoken in the wilderness by a "civilization which did not know how to express itself with propriety.") How beholden were Nicolay and Hay to Robert for access to the Lincoln Papers? The dedication page is worth noting: "To the Honorable Robert Todd Lincoln . . . in token of a lifelong friendship and esteem."

Robert tried to dissuade historians of the notion that the Lincoln Papers contained anything of importance. He told Ida Tarbell, "There is nothing of my father's there that is of value—Nicolay and Hay have published everything." But everyone suspected that this was a feint. For Tarbell and other historians, the issue was not what Nicolay and Hay had published, but what they had not. What secrets would the Lincoln Papers reveal about the president and his administration and the prosecution of the war? Would Robert ever allow access to the papers, or would he follow through on his threat to burn them? Robert wrapped up the meeting with Tarbell with words that echoed in her mind: "I won't allow anybody to see them."

In 1911, after ten years of service as corporate president, Robert Lincoln announced that he was resigning from the Pullman Company for reasons of ill health but would stay on as chairman of the board. Although he had enjoyed the privileges associated with the title, Robert had grumbled about the heavy demands that went with running a huge company like Pullman, which, he had said "gives me great anxiety and leaves me no leisure." Had he stayed on, he told a friend, he would have died from the stress.

The presidential election of 1912 was the last election cycle in which Robert Lincoln was seriously considered as a potential Republican nominee. The party was split between the progressive wing, led by former president Theodore Roosevelt, and the conservative, probusiness faction headed by the incumbent president, William Howard Taft. Fearing a split in the popular vote, Republican power brokers put out a feeler to Lincoln in the form of a letter from his golfing chum, George H. Thacher, president of the City Savings Bank of Albany. Would Lincoln, Thacher inquired, consider entering the race as a compromise candidate, someone acceptable to both party blocs? Lincoln sent his response back five weeks before the start of the Republican convention.

"I am nearly sixty-nine years old and a year ago was forced to give up the conduct of a business, the Pullman Company . . . If I had tried to keep on, I should now, I am sure, be dead." Lincoln said he was also "sure" that if he accepted Thacher's proposition, he would be dead within thirty days. "So barring accidents the foursome will go on." This reference to golf gave rise to the myth that Robert Lincoln was more interested in playing golf than becoming president. When Lincoln's letter to Thacher was made public, in 1957, it was reported under the grossly misleading headline: LETTER REVEALS LINCOLN'S SON DECLINED PRESIDENTIAL BID TO KEEP UP HIS GOLF GAME.

After 1912, the Republican leadership finally got the message that Lincoln was just not interested in holding electoral office, leading a sassy *Washington Post* reporter to declare Lincoln to be the only man in history "who has declined the Republican nomination."

Around this time, the Lincolns made it known that they were leaving Chicago. The mansion at 60 Lake Shore Drive was sold for sixty thousand dollars to Charles Monroe, an executive with the Chicago public utility. All their goods, including the invaluable Lincoln Papers, were shipped to Washington, where the Lincolns had purchased a magnificent three-story brick showplace at 3014 N Street in Georgetown. Here the Lincolns would spend their winters. The rest of the year was reserved for Hildene. Everywhere Robert went, the Lincoln Papers accompanied him. It seemed that he could not bear to have them out of his sight. Or perhaps he wanted to ensure they would not fall into unauthorized hands. Every April the servants would cart eight trunks of the precious documents and deposit them on board Robert's private railroad car for the journey to Manchester. Every fall the papers would make the same trip in reverse, back to Washington.

That national treasures were handled in so careless a manner kept Herbert Putnam up at night. Putnam, a Harvard graduate who had studied law at Columbia, was the first professional librarian to hold the post of Librarian of Congress. He tried to convince Robert Lincoln that the Lincoln Papers should be deposited with the Library of Congress for safekeeping. It was a delicate dance. Putnam knew he had to handle Lincoln with all the sensitivity he could muster. He informed him that the papers of nine presidents, including all the greats and near-greats—Washington, Jefferson, Madison, Monroe, Jackson, Polk, and others—were in the custody of the Library of Congress. Should not the most esteemed president of all join these illustrious leaders? "Is there any chance that it may be placed in the National Library?" Putnam wrote Lincoln, pointing out the library's "commodious" safe. Lincoln replied that the subject of his father's papers was "often on my mind."

"If my son was still alive, I should probably leave the papers in his hands, but as it is, I think it my duty to select some depository for them, just what it will be I am not yet prepared to say." The correspondence continued for years, with Putnam working Lincoln the way a good journalist works a skittish source. He deftly reminded Lincoln of the dangers of "fire and accident" that could result in the total loss of the Lincoln Papers, and suggested that Robert at least consider leaving the collection in the secure confines of the Library of Congress until the issue of accessibility to the public was worked out. Putnam was deferential, but relentless. He enlisted the support of Charles Moore, chairman of the Fine Arts Commission and a dinner companion of Lincoln's. "We have known so many collections to be lost by fire, and so many papers destroyed . . . that we are always apprehensive," Moore wrote Lincoln. Even Ida Tarbell, in a revised and updated edition of her *Life of Abraham Lincoln,* made a public appeal urging Robert to bend, writing in the preface:

"The collection of original Lincoln letters and documents owned by Mr. Robert Lincoln . . . is of supreme importance. It is to be hoped that Mr. Lincoln will one day place his collection in the Congressional Library."

Jessie Lincoln Beckwith was living with her two children, Peggy and Bud, in a mansion her father had bought for her in Georgetown, down the block from the Lincolns' townhouse on N Street. The move to Washington had reinvigorated her; she had joined the capital's smart set, mixing with socialites and diplomats, and it was in this milieu that she had started to date Ned Johnson.

Frank Edward "Ned" Johnson, scion of a prominent banking family from Norwich, Connecticut, had first made a name for himself as an artist, studying for five years at the prestigious Academy of Fine Arts in Munich. The earliest public showing of his watercolors took place when he was twenty-two. At his great-grandfather's Norwich mansion, the library and reception room were turned into a gallery, and all of Norwich society was invited for the viewing. Two years later, Johnson was displaying his work at Thurber's, an art gallery in Chicago, to fine reviews. The *Chicago Post* praised his "native talent" and the *Times-Herald* his "brilliant coloring" and technical skills.

The great adventure of Johnson's life took place in 1911, when he was commissioned by the Smithsonian Institution to study the cave dwellers of the Sahara desert. He set sail for Europe and was gone for two years. When he returned to the United States, he wrote three articles for the *National Geographic* magazine, reporting on his encounters with a tribe of six hundred Arabs who lived in caves hewn into the Tunisian mountainside. The natives could run up to fifty miles a day without taking a drink of water. The people there had never set eyes on a fruit or a vegetable. It was dangerous business. The paths up the mountains were like polished marble from centuries of hard use. "A stumble meant sudden death," Johnson wrote. "It is difficult even for the mountain goats born and bred there." His lectures at the Cosmos Club were popular and well attended by Washington society figures. One columnist called him the "Adonis-like archeologist." Johnson was now not just a watercolor painter but a nationally recognized archeologist, explorer, and lecturer.

At the height of his celebrity, Johnson asked Jessie Lincoln Beckwith to marry him. He was forty-two, she forty.

"Mrs. Beckwith has been so conservative, so wary of the masculine sex, owing to her disastrous venture with young Beckwith, that it seems absurd to link her with a matrimonial rumor," reported one society columnist. The article said that Robert and Mary Lincoln were at first "strongly opposed" to her marriage to Ned Johnson, but they were now "reconciled to the match." Perhaps Jessie's parents did not want her to make the same mistake twice. But they surely must have appreciated the lovely little note Johnson sent to Mary Lincoln, saying, "I thank you and Mr. Lincoln with more than words can express for giving me permission to marry Mrs. Beckwith."

"The man is Frank E. Johnson," Robert Lincoln wrote his cousin. He said Johnson came from a "good family."

"Mary and I think well of him and are glad there will be somebody of good sense to look out for her and her children when we are out of the ring."

Word of the wedding got out, and some clever reporter from Iowa had the bright idea of tracking down Warren Beckwith for a reaction. He found Beckwith living in Cedar Rapids. Nothing had been heard from the former husband of Jessie Lincoln in more than a decade, and, judging by the reporter's account, he seemed to be as lost as ever. He had remarried in 1907, to a woman named Blanche Cutter, whom he had met in Aurora, Illinois, and they had a son, Philip. When the reporter with the *Cedar Rapids Republican* had found Beckwith on the golf course and informed him that his ex-wife was getting married, Beckwith was apathetic. "He seems inclined to shun the limelight and concerns himself more with the fact that he finished the afternoon six up over his opponent than he does over his former wife's remarriage," said the newspaper account. Yet after all these years Warren still resented the way the press had depicted him when he had eloped with Jessie in 1897. He said he was "tired of the rot that the newspapers have been printing about my escapades as a ballplayer and a break man."

The specter of Warren Beckwith reared up again just a month before Jessie's marriage to Ned Johnson. Anne Dodge, a friend of Jessie's from Iowa, sent her a letter in which she told her of a strange encounter with Beckwith. He was a changed man, Anne claimed, and was going through hard times. No longer was he the lithe young athlete who had captivated Jessie at Iowa Wesleyan College. Now he seemed forlorn and depressed. And he missed Peggy and Bud, his children with Jessie. He wondered whether he could at least have a photograph of them. In her letter, Anne Dodge expressed how Beckwith felt about Jessie.

Jessie, he said it was all every bit of it your mother's fault, that if it hadn't been for her you and he would be living happily together with your children now but that your mother was determined to separate you from him from the start and that she succeeded. And Jessie, now comes the part I think you should know. He said he had always loved you and you alone and always should love you the best in all the world! That there was only one woman in the world that he had ever really loved and that was Jessie Lincoln.

Warren's new wife had been a good friend to him when he needed one, but even she understood that Jessie would always be his "sweetheart."

Anne Dodge was quite stinging in her assessment of who was to blame for the collapse of the Lincoln-Beckwith marriage.

I think it terrible for a mother-in-law to interfere between a man and his wife and wreck the happiness of a man and the woman and their offspring! If there are differences let the man and woman settle them between them but let no one else come in and separate them and cause a tragedy that has been brought about in your life and Mr. Beckwith's. It is a crime and comes from interference!

It was quite a lot for Jessie to digest, coming just four weeks before her wedding to Ned Johnson.

The Lincoln clan gathered at Hildene, and, on June 22, 1915, in a ceremony performed by the Reverend Sidney Kingman Perkins of First Congregational Church in Manchester, Jessie Lincoln Beckwith was married for a second time. Only immediate family was present, including Peggy Beckwith, now seventeen, and Bud, a chubby-cheeked eleven-year-old. The *Washington Post* called it a "wedding of wide interest" but noted inaccurately that Jessie was the "only surviving granddaughter of President Abraham Lincoln." Jessie's sister, Mamie Lincoln Isham, had been keeping such a low profile in New York City that, evidently, people had forgotten she was alive.

These were the twilight years for Robert Lincoln. He had the strength to play just eight holes of golf, with the habit of twisting his face into a silly grimace when he putted. Robert and Mary celebrated their golden anniversary at Hildene in 1918. Medically, something always seemed to be troubling Robert. He suffered severe headaches and double vision and was diagnosed with a painful foot disorder. He had chronic conjunctivitis. But he could still appreciate the occasional fine cigar. His favorite brand was the Bismarck Invincible, ordered by the box from the Virginia Club in New York, sometimes as many as five hundred at a time. He also developed a fondness for, of all things, Budweiser beer. One of his favorite pastimes was observing the planets and stars in a small observatory he had built on Hildene, about eighty yards from the "Big House." The domed structure contained a six-inch refracting telescope, which was mounted on a secure pedestal with all the necessary controls to track and rotate with the celestial bodies. It was a painstaking, deliberate hobby that perfectly suited his exacting personality. As a self-taught amateur astronomer, he relied on *Elements of Practical Astronomy* and *Whittaker's Almanac* as guides.

Robert was very close to his daughter Mamie and her husband Charles, who had only one child, Lincoln Isham. The boy had suffered a wretched childhood, burdened, as he was, with a crippling inferiority complex. Very few photographs of him exist, but those that survive show a child born with severely crossed eyes. Sometime in his teenage years or early twenties he must have had an operation, because the next set of photos show a handsome young man with a normal line of sight. Linc was born with his grandfather's incapacity to tolerate slights, and was deeply hurt by them. Though he had been smart enough to be accepted at Harvard, he did not see it through. His "frail body was unequal to the strain," and he suffered what may have been a nervous breakdown. He tried to do his part in World War I by driving an ambulance for the American Red Cross, and, in 1919, his father, in an apparent reference to Linc's mental breakdown, was able to report that the "disturbing state of mind he labored" was showing signs of improvement.

Regrettably, Charles would not live to see his son's wedding. He died at age sixty-six, on June 9, 1919, just three months before Linc was married.

The bride was Leahalma Carrea (sometimes spelled Leaholma Correa). A children's book author, she was said to be the same age as Linc, twenty-seven, though there were some reports that she was actually much older. Leahalma was born in Spain of aristocratic heritage and lived on Lexington Avenue in Manhattan with her daughter Frances from her first marriage. The wedding took place on Saturday, August 30, 1919, at the Church of the Transfiguration in New York, better known as the Little Church Around the Corner. In keeping with Lincoln family tradition, or perhaps because Leahalma was a divorcée with a child, the wedding took place in complete secrecy. None of Linc's relatives were informed of it. His mother Mamie was summering at her country home near Hildene in Vermont when she heard the news, and after a four-day honeymoon, Linc and his bride drove up to Manchester to visit with her.

In 1917, Warren Beckwith surfaced yet again. He had been serving in World War I as a captain of field artillery, and found himself passing through Washington on his way to the front lines in France. He decided to look up his former wife and called her on the telephone to say he wondered whether he could see Peggy and Bud.

"She said there was no point to it, to let the past be, and that was the end of that," Warren said. It was the last time he ever tried to communicate with his and Jessie's two children.

Meanwhile, Jessie could not stay out of trouble. Robert Lincoln received a bizarre letter from his son-in-law Ned, in which the explorer accused Jessie of adultery. Another Lincoln scandal was brewing, and Robert must have read the letter with a cold fury. Johnson wrote that he had arrived home unexpectedly in Washington to find that his wife had fallen in love with another man. The gentleman had not only assumed Johnson's place in Jessie's heart but also in his bed, for he was now living with Jessie. His name was Robert Randolph, and he came from a distinguished Virginia family that traced its origins back to colonial times. Jessie casually notified Johnson that she was going off on a cruise on board Randolph's yacht— "without a chaperone."

The marriage was finished. Johnson found work as a diplomat and moved to Cuba. Writing from the American mission in Havana, he informed Robert Lincoln that he wished to divorce Jessie on grounds of "desertion from bed and board," but he would be willing to consider less scandalous grounds such as "incompatibility of temperament." He suggested that Robert Lincoln, who after all was a lawyer, prepare the legal documents.

"If you have the papers prepared and forwarded to me to be acknowledged and sworn to before the proper officials in Havana, it will keep things quiet . . . as I know that you and Mrs. Lincoln do not want any publicity, neither do I."

The letter cost Johnson a lot of respect in the eyes of his father-in-law. "What a damned fool that man is, to expect me to do this business for him!" Robert Lincoln declared.

The divorce was an embarrassment for two prominent families, the

Lincolns and the Johnsons of Norwich. Ned Johnson's mother, Alice Johnson, wrote a letter to Mary Lincoln, one heartbroken mother to another, Mrs. Johnson wondering whether she was "half the cause" of the breakup, because her son had been spending "far too much" time in Norwich caring for his ailing grandmother. During the time that Ned was away dealing with this family medical emergency, Jessie's eyes had evidently started to wander, and Robert Randolph had made his move.

"I shall always love Jessie and her children, even if my son failed to make them happy, as I hoped he could and would. . . . Ned only said how can a man love a woman who is on a small yacht for two months with another man. . . . Give her my love and tell her that I only wish for her happiness wherever she passes her life. No one daughter could have been nearer or sweeter to me." Jessie had appeared to be hard up for money, and had sold the diamond ring Johnson had given her when they were married. And she had the nerve to ask her estranged husband for a thousand-dollar loan— "ASAP." The Johnsons were outraged. "It seems like a bad dream," Alice Johnson told Mary Lincoln. "One can only hope she will pass out of this bad dreamy state and be her own dear loving self once more."

The divorce was handled with a minimum of fuss and publicity, but the exasperating Jessie was making her father's blood boil. In 1920 she was determined to buy Woodstock Farms, a historic Federal-style plantation built in 1840 on the banks of the Piankatank River in Middlesex County, Virginia. She had fallen in love with the property at first sight. But there was one problem. The bank refused to approve a mortgage unless her father co-signed. Jessie was in a panic. "The thought of forgoing this and spending the rest of my life in second-rate apartment houses is hard to face," she wrote her parents. "It makes me very blue. Momma would probably say that this feeling on my part is one more proof of insanity but I think you can appreciate my point of view." Robert Lincoln wrote Jessie a tough-love letter in which he wondered how "a married daughter of your age having two children long past the age of infancy" could find herself in such a financial mess. He accused her of being a victim of her own "caprice." Having said all this, Robert informed Jessie that he was raising her trust fund allowance by ten thousand dollars, to the sum of twenty-five thousand dollars a year. Jessie breathed a sigh of relief.

"I did not expect you to increase my income nor dreamed of asking it. . . . It is needless to tell you *how deeply grateful I am.*" Jessie was able to proceed with the purchase of Woodstock and the surrounding 150 acres.

For Robert Lincoln, the time had come at last to turn over the Lincoln Papers to the Library of Congress. The transfer was conducted with all the secrecy and planning of a military operation. On May 10, 1919, at 9:00 A.M., a wagon pulled up to the Lincoln mansion in Georgetown. Eight trunks of documents dating from 1834 to 1865 were carried out of Lincoln's house, placed in the back of a wagon, and transported to the Library of Congress.

Lincoln had his Washington lawyers from the firm McKenney & Flannery draw up the necessary formalities. It was a deed of gift, with the critical stipulation that the Lincoln Papers remain sealed in a vault and barred from public scrutiny or private review for twenty-one years from the date of Robert Lincoln's death. Lincoln signed the deed, had it witnessed by a notary, and then personally delivered it to Herbert Putnam at the Library of Congress. Later that day, Putnam wrote Lincoln a letter of acknowledgement in which he expressed "profound satisfaction" on behalf of the United States government. Privately, however, Putnam must have been disappointed. He was sixty-two years old in 1923. If Robert Lincoln should die this year, which seemed unlikely, it would be 1944 before the Lincoln Papers could be opened. Putnam had to wonder whether he would ever live to see the day.

The Lincoln Papers were locked in compartment 19, on the third floor of the Manuscript Division. Putnam personally wrote the labels that were affixed to the cases:

> PAPERS OF ABRAHAM LINCOLN
> Given by Hon. Robert T. Lincoln
> With proviso that they are
> *not to be opened*
> until twenty-one years after his death.

Not everything of historical value was turned over to the Library of Congress. Four years after the documents were carried out of Lincoln's Georgtown townhouse, Robert's close friend Horace G. Young saw something at Hildene that truly disturbed him. Young was the retired general manager of the Delaware & Hudson railroad corporation. He lived in Greenwich, Connecticut, but summered in Manchester, and was a member of the Ekwanok Country Club. He was one of the so-called "Lincoln Foursome" who played golf daily with Robert.

One day in August 1923, Young said he walked in on Lincoln at Hildene and found his friend "surrounded by a number of large boxes and with many papers scattered about the floor, and with the ashes of many burned papers visible in the fireplace." Young asked Lincoln what he was doing and Lincoln replied that he was "destroying the private papers of his father, Abraham Lincoln." Young was shocked. "No one had any right to destroy such papers—least of all" Abraham Lincoln's son. Robert told Young that he "did not care and intended to continue his destruction." That night, an agitated Young went to see his friend, Nicholas Murray Butler, the president of Columbia University, who had just arrived in Manchester for a summer holiday. Butler was staying at the Equinox Hotel.

"You are the only person who has any influence with him," Young told Butler. "He is going to burn a lot of his father's papers. For God's sake, see him at once!" The following morning an alarmed Butler went to Hildene to look into it himself. He said he had found Lincoln sitting in front of a fireplace, reading a newspaper, the wood logs aflame. The two men caught up on the day's events. Butler was a renowned diplomat and scholar whom Theodore Roosevelt had found so impressive he called him Nicholas Miraculous. (Butler would go on to serve as Columbia University's president for forty-three years. In 1931 he would win the Nobel Peace Prize for work promoting the Kellogg-Briand Pact, which renounced war as an instrument of foreign policy.) As Lincoln and Butler chatted, Butler noticed a large "old-fashioned" trunk sitting next to the bookshelf. He asked Lincoln whether he was going somewhere. When Lincoln said no, Butler asked about the trunk.

"Well," said Lincoln quietly, "it contains only some family papers which I am going to burn."

Butler could not believe what he was hearing. So Horace Young's account was true. "What are you going to do?" he asked Lincoln. "Burn your family papers!" Not many men would challenge Robert Lincoln in his own home, but Butler lost his patience. "Why, Robert Lincoln, those papers do not belong to you. Your father has been the property of the nation for fifty years, and those papers belong to the nation. That you should destroy them would be incredible. For heaven's sake do not do anything like that!"

Lincoln listened to Butler's arguments. For one full hour the debate went back and forth until, finally, Lincoln agreed to preserve the material.

"All right," he said, "but no one must see them while I live."

"Very well," Butler said, "then deposit them in the Library of Congress and fix a date before which they shall not be opened."

Some historians have questioned Butler's account because the presidential papers had already been turned over to the Library of Congress. But Butler was certain of the facts, and he related the story twice, first in an article in the *Saturday Evening Post* and again in his autobiography, *Across the Busy Years*, published in 1939. Perhaps the documents in question were not part of the official presidential papers. Perhaps they related to Mary Todd Lincoln's life. Regardless of what they were, *something* historically noteworthy was set on fire at Hildene that summer, according to two men of "inviolable integrity"—Robert's own golfing chum Horace Young, and the future Nobel laureate Nicholas Murray Butler.

On Memorial Day, May 30, 1922, fifty-seven years after Lincoln's assassination, the Lincoln Memorial was dedicated. Robert arrived in formal attire, white-bearded and requiring a cane, with his wife Mary, now an old lady of seventy-six. The photograph of Mary Lincoln, fleshy with a double chin, was the last known picture ever taken of her. It was in profile, furtive and glancing, shot almost as an afterthought, symbolic of her shadowy life. As fifty thousand Americans watched, Robert Lincoln was helped up the marble steps by a military honor guard.

Before him rose the most beloved monument to a political leader ever to be built in America. It was a sitting Abraham Lincoln, nineteen feet tall, made of Georgia white marble. Carved into the wall behind the statue were these words, written by the art critic Royal Cortissoz: "In this temple as in the hearts of the people for whom he saved the union the memory of Abraham Lincoln is enshrined forever." On the southern wall of the monument was an inscription of the Gettysburg Address, and on the northern wall, Lincoln's second inaugural address. A mural depicted the Angel of Truth freeing a slave. The statue's hands and face were a marvel, modeled from plaster casts of Lincoln made during his lifetime. And the location was perfect. The monument faced east, toward a long reflecting pool. Behind, to the west, across the Potomac, rose Arlington National Cemetery and the stately mansion of General Robert E. Lee. To the east loomed the Washington Monument and Capitol Hill. Before his death, Secretary of State John Hay had promoted this location as the ideal site for the Lincoln Memorial. He argued that, like the man, the Lincoln Memorial should stand alone, distinguished and serene. Looking upon the completed memorial, Hay's good taste was evident for the nation to see. It was a magnificent structure, pure of line and flawless.

The principal speakers were President Warren Harding and former president William Howard Taft, now the Chief Justice of the United States. Obviously no one in this distinguished group was superstitious about sharing the stage with Robert Lincoln, the man with the "presidential curse" hanging over his head. Amplifying devices carried the speakers' voices into the distant reaches of the mall, and the event was broadcast on radio. Congress came as a body. The full foreign diplomatic corps was also present, including the ambassador from Germany, marking the first American ceremony at which Germany had been officially represented since the declaration of war in 1917. One would think Ambassador Otto Wiedefelt would have been on his best behavior, but he arrived late and kept leaving his seat like a restless child, leaning against one of the Doric columns for a better view. One other strange occurrence detracted from the ceremonies. As President Harding spoke, an airplane appeared out of the sky and circled the mall at a low altitude. Embarrassed that it might be an army plane, Secretary of War John Weeks stood between two columns and frantically waved his arms to signal the pilot to fly away.

Robert Lincoln refused to speak at the ceremony. He had made it clear to the event organizers that "no notice whatever" should be taken of him. For eight long years he had seen the Lincoln Memorial slowly rise from a swampy marshland on the banks of the Potomac, and now that it was completed he was filled with pleasure. It was not in his nature to succumb to sentiment, but this gift to his father's memory was a national treasure. Robert would often have his chauffeur detour to the mall. As they approached the Lincoln Memorial, Robert would call out, "Stop the carriage, stop the carriage!" He would look up at the great white temple and fix his eyes on the incandescent statue of his noble father.

"Isn't it beautiful?" he would say.

As for the Great Emancipator's wife, somebody at the White House had noticed an embarrassing oversight. There was no portrait of Mary Todd Lincoln on display. It was an American tradition that every First Lady was honored with an official White House portrait. The portraits of seven first ladies hung in the Vermeil Room, sometimes known as the Gold Room, on the first floor. Other portraits were scattered about, but nowhere was a portrait of Mary Todd Lincoln to be found. She had been overlooked.

Lieutenant Colonel Clarence Sherrill, director of public buildings and grounds for the District of Columbia, contacted the Lincolns and diplomatically broached the question of what should be done about this odd state of affairs. Sherrill had a reputation as one of the brightest military officers in Washington, having graduated second in his class from West Point in 1901. It took a while for the Lincolns to get back to him.

In 1924, Mary Lincoln informed Sherrill that "having given considerable thought to the matter," the Lincoln family had reached a decision. It would be honored to have a portrait of Mary Todd Lincoln hanging in the White House with those of the other first ladies. Mary Lincoln said the responsibility for commissioning a portrait artist would be hers, and that she expected the final product to be an "appropriate" painting of her mother-in-law, suitable for display in the White House. In August 1925 the portrait of Mary Todd Lincoln was completed, but as anything associated with Mary Todd Lincoln and the Lincoln family, it was handled like a state secret.

The artist hired by the Lincolns turned out to be Katherine Helm, the daughter of Mary Todd Lincoln's half-sister, Emilie Todd Helm, who famously had been invited to live in the White House by Abraham Lincoln after her husband, a Confederate general, had died in the Civil War. Though Miss Helm was a competent artist, it was hard to see any resemblance to Mary Todd Lincoln in the portrait she delivered. But the Lincolns were satisfied with the work, and had the Lincoln family lawyer, Frederic Towers, arrange the details. He requested that the traditional installation ceremony be handled in a low-key manner, without public fanfare. First Lady Grace Coolidge was consulted, and it was determined that the most fitting place for the portrait would be on the second floor, near Mrs. Coolidge's own portrait on the same wall. It was a magnanimous gesture by the incumbent First Lady. (The portrait of Mary Todd Lincoln now hangs, appropriately, in the Lincoln Bedroom.)

On July 26, 1926, two masons from the town of Manchester went to Hildene to repair the plastering outside Robert Lincoln's bedroom. It was 8:00 A.M., and the workmen were making quite a racket. Lincoln's manservant entered the bedroom to see if the noise was disturbing Mr. Lincoln. He found the master of the house dead in his bed. Had Robert Todd Lincoln lived six more days, he would have turned eighty-three.

Lincoln passed away from a cerebral hemorrhage brought on by arteriosclerosis. He had been in failing health for two years. His chronic conjunctivitis had to be treated each morning with eye drops by a family physician making a daily house call. The day before his death he had eaten breakfast in bed and ventured out for a customary twenty-mile motor cruise around Manchester in his chauffeured automobile. He retired that evening at his usual hour in good spirits and probably read in bed, as was his habit, before turning out the lights. "His passing was quiet," said his lawyer Frederic Towers. "He simply went to sleep to wake up, to wake up no more."

The news was flashed across America. Robert's obituaries poignantly noted that he was the last of the Great Emancipator's immediate family to bear the Lincoln name.

The funeral two days later was marked with utmost simplicity and privacy; only the immediate family and just a few friends were invited to attend. The six-hundred-dollar coffin was placed in the reception room at Hildene, and when the bell tolled 4:00 P.M., the Reverend D. Cunningham Graham of Congregational Church in Manchester read the Twenty-third Psalm. At the family's request, Tennyson's "Crossing the Bar" ("And may there be no moaning of the bar, When I put out to sea") was read. The coffin was borne from the house by Lincoln's two grandsons, Lincoln Isham and Bud Beckwith. Joining the young pallbearers were Lincoln's lawyers from Washington, Norman Frost and Frederic Towers. The last two surviving golfers from the "Lincoln Foursome," Horace Young and George Thacher, were also present, as was Robert's long-ago neighbor from Chicago, Prentice Porter. The coffin was placed inside a hearse and driven down a mile of private road to Dellwood Cemetery, which adjoined the Lincoln property. The entire funeral party gathered inside the vault where a final prayer was offered. It was over.

There were no words of committal. Here the body would rest until the family could arrange transportation to Springfield, where Robert Lincoln would be buried in the Lincoln tomb with his parents, his three brothers, and his cherished son, Abraham Lincoln II. Just four years earlier Robert Lincoln had reaffirmed his wish to be buried in the family vault in Springfield. "Within it are entombed the bodies of my father and my mother and my only son, and it is arranged that my wife and myself shall be entombed there," he said.

Robert Lincoln's long life was over. The time had come for the third generation of Lincolns to assume their place in American life. And in twenty-one years from the date of Robert's death, the mythic Lincoln Papers would finally be opened. The clock was ticking.

III.

Third Generation

22

The Lincoln Isham Waltz

THE LINCOLNS WERE in a state of profound grief. Sunday evening, after the funeral, Mary Lincoln suffered an uncontrollable fit of weeping, the first real tears she had shed "since Papa left us." When she regained her composure, Mary went to check on her granddaughter, who was spending the summer at Hildene. She found Peggy in her room, sprawled out in bed with her head buried in the pillow. Much overcome—as we all are, Mary thought. Mary and Peggy had a quiet dinner together, with Mary putting on a brave face. "She does not know that I weep," Mary told her daughter Jessie.

Sixteen days after Robert's death, "a thought came to me," Mary wrote. "And it was this: that the beloved one should be interred in the Arlington Cemetery at Washington instead of within the crypt at Springfield." Mary said after "prayerful" consideration, her mind was made up: "I knew I was right." She proceeded to set the wheels in motion. One could sympathize with her reasoning. For his entire life Robert had lived in the shadow of Abraham Lincoln. "You know our darling was a personage who made history independently of his great father and should have his own 'place in the sun,'" Mary told Katherine Helm. Left unsaid was perhaps another consideration—that Mary, who would one day be buried next to Robert, could not abide the thought of spending eternity in the same tomb with her mother-in-law.

With the onset of cold weather in the fall, Mary Lincoln and Peggy Beckwith left Hildene for Washington, taking the body of Robert Todd Lincoln with them. The commission to design and build a suitable tomb for her husband was awarded to James Earle Fraser, who had apprenticed under Augustus Saint-Gaudens, sculptor of the colossal *Standing Lincoln* in

Chicago. Working out of his Manhattan studios, Fraser carved a six-foot-high, ten-foot-long clay model, and then, once Mary had signed off on the design, he sculpted Robert's sarcophagus out of pink granite from the Stony Creek Quarry in Connecticut. The army selected a splendid burial site for the former secretary of war—on the eastern slope of Arlington, in a direct line to the Lincoln Memorial. On March 14, 1927, Robert Lincoln was laid to rest. Three years later, Mary Lincoln arranged for the body of her son Abraham Lincoln II to be exhumed from the Lincoln tomb in Springfield and transported to Arlington, where it was buried next to his father's. Army regulations at the time prohibited the inscription of minors' names, so Jack's grave was unmarked. But at last father and son were together again.

Five months after her father's death, Jessie married her lover, Robert John Randolph, in Washington, on the day after Christmas, 1926.

Robert Randolph was a descendant of William Randolph, who had emmigrated from England in 1674. In Virginia, there were few names more esteemed than Randolph. Robert Randolph tried his hand at engineering, then went into banking, working out of the Baltimore branch of the Equitable Trust Company of New York—but what he was best at was marrying well. His first wife had been the New York heiress Vera Schuyler Schermerhorn. The couple had had one son, Robert Jr., who, when his father married into the Lincoln family, was sixteen years old and attended boarding school at the Berkshire School in Sheffield, Massachusetts. It was an embarrassment to Robert Randolph that he refused to, or could not afford to pay the $7,500 in arrears for child support and tuition that his ex-wife claimed he owed.

Randolph and Jessie lived off the largess of the Robert Todd Lincoln estate, now in the control of Mary Lincoln and valued at $2.4 million, the rough equivalent of $30 million in today's dollars. Most of the assets were held in two blue-chip stocks, Con Edison of Chicago, and Nabisco, then called the National Biscuit Company, which dominated the American market for mass-produced cookies and crackers.

In the spring, Mary Lincoln returned to her beloved Hildene and spent a quiet summer there—her first since the death of her husband. Peggy Beckwith kept her company. October came. Soon it would be time to leave for Washington, before the weather turned.

That month, an unexpected visitor drove up the long private dirt road that led to Hildene and asked to see Mrs. Lincoln. She said her name was Myra Pritchard. She introduced herself as the granddaughter of Myra

Bradwell, the "lady lawyer" who had outfoxed Robert Lincoln and fought so relentlessly to free Mary Todd Lincoln from her incarceration at Bellevue Place, in 1875. Mary Lincoln must have been shocked. Mrs. Pritchard, a former championship golfer from Battle Creek, Michigan, related a remarkable story.

When Myra Bradwell had died thirty-four years before of cancer, she had bequeathed her personal papers to her daughter Bessie. When Bessie died, the papers passed on to her daughter, Myra Pritchard. Mrs. Pritchard told Mary Lincoln that she had come to Hildene as a courtesy. She wanted to let the Lincoln family know that she had written a book, *The Dark Days of Abraham Lincoln's Widow, as Revealed by Her Own Letters*. The contents of the book were groundbreaking: Mrs. Pritchard had in her possession thirty-seven "lost" letters written by Mary Todd Lincoln to Myra Bradwell at the height of the insanity scandal and in its aftermath. The letters had been passed down through two generations of Bradwell women with the understanding that they would be published upon the death of Robert Lincoln.

That time had now arrived.

Mrs. Pritchard told Mary Lincoln that she had a signed contract with the publishing firm of J. H. Sears & Company, and first serial rights to the book had been purchased for the sum of five thousand dollars by *Liberty Weekly* magazine, a popular general interest magazine, second in circulation only to the *Saturday Evening Post*. The magazine intended to publish excerpts from the book over nine issues.

Mary Lincoln stayed calm. The most important thing, she realized, was to avoid immediately making an enemy of this woman. She needed time to think things through, consider all the issues, and consult with her advisers. She got Mrs. Pritchard to agree to come to Washington and meet with her again in a few weeks.

As soon as Myra Pritchard had gone, Mary set about notifying those two able Lincoln family lawyers, Towers and Frost. Towers expressed admiration for Mary's tactics. As he put it, "It is better to have Mrs. Pritchard as a friend than to offend her."

Mrs. Pritchard met with Towers and Frost the following month at their law offices, at which point she handed over her 111-page manuscript. The two lawyers read the text, and the lost Mary Todd Lincoln letters that formed the foundation of the book, and immediately recognized its potential to bring a heap of embarrassment to the Lincoln family. The letters, written between 1872 and 1878, threatened to resurrect the whole disgraceful business involving Mrs. Lincoln's insanity trial. The lawyers knew that Robert Lincoln, who had struggled so mightily to erase his mother from the annals of history, would never have sanctioned publication of the material. The time had come to bring down the Lincoln hammer. They began with the debatable premise that Mrs. Pritchard did not own the copyright to the letters, thus she did not have the legal authority to have them published. The estate of Robert Lincoln held the copyright, meaning Mary Lincoln. But things could be worked out, they told Mrs. Pritchard. Mary Lincoln would be willing to buy her out.

Myra Pritchard went home to consult with her lawyer. One week later, she folded. The Lincolns were just too powerful. Further, she had no desire to offend Mrs. Lincoln, or to engage in costly copyright litigation. And there was an added incentive to seal the deal—twenty-two thousand dollars that Mary Lincoln agreed to pay for the rights to Mrs. Pritchard's book and all of the original Mary Todd Lincoln letters. At the end of January, Mrs. Pritchard canceled her publishing contract with J. H. Sears. An executive at the publishing company was ordered to return all of Mrs. Pritchard's materials and manuscript posthaste. The outcome bemused him, and he marveled at the clout of the Lincolns.

"All I can say is that it sews her up as tight as a drum," he said, referring to Mrs. Pritchard's settlement with the Lincolns. "In point of fact, I think if she is apprehended reading a book about Lincoln, or mentioning his name or the name of his lady, she is likely to subject herself thereby to imprisonment for life, if indeed not summary execution."

Mrs. Pritchard was frustrated beyond words, and not just because of the hours she had put into writing her first book: She fully anticipated that the Lincoln family would set fire to the Mary Todd Lincoln letters that her grandmother, Myra Bradwell, had left her descendants. Myra had been paid a handsome sum, but she also understood that this was not what the crusading Myra Bradwell had had in mind when she bequeathed the Mary Todd Lincoln correspondence to her heirs. Mrs. Bradwell had wanted these letters to establish the fact that Mary Todd Lincoln had been maligned by history, and that she was not the insane shrew depicted in folklore, but a misunderstood and sympathetic victim who had been deplorably treated by her son.

For Robert Lincoln's widow, in her Georgetown mansion when she signed off on the negotiations with Mrs. Pritchard, the crisis was over. The

Lincolns' history had once again been successfully censored—or so she thought.

In just a three-year period following her wedding to Randolph, Jessie Lincoln borrowed close to a hundred thousand dollars. She continually wrote checks, earmarked "allowances" to support her husband, one for $151, another for $650, and so on. Randolph was on a spending spree, "and it was the Lincoln money he was spending," said Gerald Ballentyne Jr., a Virginia auctioneer who knew the family. Randolph bought a Franklin sports coupe with a rumble seat, a Rolls-Royce, a Willis-Knight sedan, and several vintage Model Ts. The stables at Woodstock Farms, Virginia, where they lived, were converted into a garage, and now the finest cars in America were parked in stalls where thoroughbred horses had once been raised.

Mary Lincoln was inclined to indulge her daughter, and cosigned a seventy-thousand-dollar loan Jessie had obtained from the Liberty National Bank in Washington. At the same time, for basic living expenses, Jessie was dipping into her mother's interest income. This became a source of friction between Jessie and family lawyer Frederic Towers, who considered her seriously reckless in money matters. He undoubtedly viewed her as a spoiled brat whose parents had coddled her through three problematic marriages. Now she and her third husband were threatening to bleed the Lincoln family assets dry. Jessie seemed to forget that the nation was in the grip of the Great Depression, and Towers had to remind her that her mother's inheritance, while comfortable, had been "considerably reduced" by the impact of the economic crisis.

"It is not fair for her, not fair to her, and not fair to the rest of the family that one member of it should absorb almost a staggering portion of Mrs. Lincoln's income," the straight-shooting lawyer wrote Jessie. "Do you not see that this cannot go on? Do you not agree with me that it is my duty under the circumstances to advise Mrs. Lincoln that no matter how much she may want to go on with the loans . . . the time has come to stop." Otherwise, Towers warned her, the Lincoln trust, no matter the size of its fortune, could not "survive."

Jessie read the letter, and then let Towers have it. First, she found it necessary to remind the lawyer that she did not take for granted the "comforts and luxuries of life" that she enjoyed. She knew it was a blessing. "Since your advent you can see me only as occupying a superficial place in the family. . . . This is not a true state of the case!" Jessie wanted the lawyer to know that "underneath the froth" of her relationship with her mother, the two Lincoln women shared a "deep and abiding love . . . I have fought her fights and shared her joys and sorrows."

Towers responded, "You know I have no axe to grind and that my motives in this matter are unselfish . . . but when I see that to continue to lend you money at the rate of $30,000 to $40,000 a year is bringing your mother's margins of safety close to the vanishing point it is time to tell her so. If I cannot do this for her I might as well quit and engage myself in some useful pursuit." Ending on a note of conciliation, Towers said, "I think I appreciate your love for her. I know I appreciate her love for you. There is no greater or more unselfish love than that of a mother for her child."

Mary Lincoln found comfort in the Christian Science Church—just as her late mother-in-law Mary Todd Lincoln had sought reassurance in spiritualism.

Mary Baker Eddy, who was born in 1821 in Bow, New Hampshire, had had a spiritual awakening when she was forty-four. She was walking on an icy sidewalk in Lynn, Massachusetts, when she slipped and landed on her spine. "The physician attending me said I had taken the last step I ever should," Mrs. Eddy wrote. As she lay on her bed she asked for her Bible, and by "divine guidance," she recounted, she came upon a passage in Matthew: "And lo, they brought to him a paralytic, lying on a bed . . . and Jesus said to the paralytic, Be of good cheer, child, thy sins are forgiven. . . . Arise, and take up thy bed, and go unto thy house. And he arose, and went away to his house." It was, she said, her "Great Discovery." It taught her "how to be well." According to Mrs. Eddy's account, her reading of the passage produced a surge of strength within her, and she "got out of bed and walked." Thus was born the First Church of Christ, Scientist. Illnesses could be cured not by doctors, but by prayer. Healing came not from surgery or medicine, but from a higher sense of God. For a family that had lost Tad Lincoln and then Abraham Lincoln II despite the finest medical care available, the Christian Science faith proved to be seductive.

It was Mamie Isham who had introduced her mother to the church's controversial teachings. Mamie had joined in 1897, and Mary Lincoln became a member the following year. Jessie was also intrigued. Once, she requested a personal audience with Mary Baker Eddy, but Mrs. Eddy declined to see Abraham Lincoln's youngest granddaughter, telling an aide, "No, not today."

Abraham Lincoln's three great-grandchildren were now adults, all of whom were living the existence of the idle rich.

Linc Isham and his wife, Leahalma, had an apartment in the swanky Carlyle Hotel in Manhattan. Linc dabbled in investments, but retired at an early age to take up the guitar and the mandolin. He wrote several songs, which were never published, with the amusing titles "Baghdad Billy," "Baby I Love You," "Madam Bombay," "Congo Las Vegas," and "The Lincoln Isham Waltz." Linc purchased a historic tavern in Manchester, Vermont, in 1927, and spent summers there, close to Hildene. He had true affection for "good old Vermont." As Linc put it, he liked to "get a good whack at golf," and, as his grandfather had before him, he served as president of the Ekwanok Country Club, but for one term only, from 1936 to 1937.

He was also a fixture of New York café society in the Roaring Twenties, when New York City had as many as one hundred thousand speakeasies during the Prohibition era. Fifty-second Street between Fifth and Sixth Avenues was said to be the "wettest" block in the United States. Linc's hangout was the Stork Club, then on Fifty-first Street, run by the flamboyant saloonkeeper Sherman Billingsley. Linc Isham could be assured of a good table there, where he mingled with movie stars, blue bloods, showgirls, prizefighters, and politicians. Ernest Hemingway, J. Edgar Hoover, Al Jolson, and Ethel Merman were all regulars, and the gossip columnist Walter Winchell proclaimed it "New York's New Yorkiest place." Linc's other speakeasy haunts were Club Napoleon on West Fifty-sixth Street, where the membership card featured a likeness of the little emperor; the Showplace, on Broadway; the Silouette Club, on West Fifty-second Street; and a joint at 72 East Fifty-sixth Street that was so in-crowd it did not have a name. Many of these places were equipped with a secret back door for a quick getaway in the event of a police raid.

Linc's marriage to Leahalma Carrea was childless, and Linc never made a big thing of his family legacy. He was in Dorset, Vermont, during the second week of February one year when he called the municipal office and spoke to a probate judge, Margaret Doherty, about an estate issue that was coming up.

"Hello, Margaret, this is Lincoln. I plan to come down Wednesday or Thursday to see about some letters."

"Well, better come Wednesday. Thursday we are closed for the holiday."

"Closed for the holiday? What holiday?" Lincoln Isham asked.

Judge Doherty could hardly believe it. "Lincoln's birthday, of course. You should know."

Isham responded, "Oh, I forgot. I'm as bad as grandpa."

Robert Todd Lincoln Beckwith, known as Bud in his youth, now called himself by its more adult variation, Bob. He had had a complicated childhood. He had been through three fathers—his biological father Warren Beckwith, then Ned Johnson, and now Robert Randolph. He developed a terrible stutter, which he blamed on insecurities resulting from his thorny family life, and this severe speech defect would torment him for the rest of his days. Education was never a priority for Bob Beckwith. He attended Sidwell Friends, a private Quaker school in Washington, founded in 1883. "Without going into details I will say that he did not distinguish himself as a student," the school archivist said of him.

Jessie determined that a little military discipline might be just the thing for her son. In 1919, she sent Bob off for six months to the New York Military Academy at Cornwall-on-Hudson, but it was not a happy experience. He had a mediocre academic record in his single semester there, earning a 74 average grade and flunking French with a 61. He got a 78 in math and a 72 in the course that one would have expected the great-grandson of Abraham Lincoln to excel in—American history. Conduct earned him his best grade, an 84. Jessie transferred Bob out of military school in winter 1920, and enrolled him in the first migratory boarding school in America, the Adirondack-Florida School. In the fall, students attended classes in Onchiota, New York, twenty miles from Lake Placid in the Adirondacks, and after Christmas break, classes would resume in Coconut Grove, Florida. In this regard the school echoed the seasonal travel pattern of the student body's aristocratic parents. How much education was accomplished as the students followed the sun was open to debate. Conditions were ritzy, with a heavy emphasis on outdoor activities, like canoeing in the Adirondacks, and sailing a thirty-five-foot sloop in Florida. The male heirs to the Firestone and Vanderbilt fortunes, and J. P. Morgan's grandson, all attended Adirondack-Florida.

The Lincoln legacy must have gone a long way, because Bob, despite his mediocre academic record, was accepted into his grandfather's prestigious alma matter, Phillips Exeter. He lasted only two years, and opted not to go to college. Preparing for years of toil and achievement through years of education was not in Bob's character. He quoted his mother as forever telling him, "You'll never work, so don't try." Jessie justified this dubious philosophy in the context of charity, saying to her son, "You'll just be taking a job away from someone who needs it."

In the Roaring Twenties, Bob Beckwith was living with his mother and her third husband at the Georgetown townhouse on N Street, down the block from his grandmother's mansion. He was short and round, more Todd than Lincoln, with a bad-boy charm and an alarming lack of ambition. When the subject of what he did for a living came up in conversation, he liked to respond, "I'm a spoiled brat." He said it for the shock value. Unfortunately, the wisecrack appeared in several newspaper interviews over the years, and helped shape the negative perception of the Lincoln heir. Bob did endeavor to emulate Abraham Lincoln in one area—he took to imitating his great ancestor's signature.

Bob was fixated on fast cars, and into often got into a jam behind the wheel. In 1925, at a time when travel by road could be very dangerous, during one of the first cross-country excursions across America by automobile he was pulled over for speeding in Omaha. He confounded his family by posing for a news photographer, grinning from ear to ear, proudly showing off his traffic ticket. One Sunday in the 1920s, he and a friend, Paul Rawling, started out for Woodstock, the family farm in Virginia. It was 8:30 at night. Between the two of them they only had two dollars. "After we had gone maybe 70 miles I began to feel a bit sleepy so I let Paul take over the wheel," Bob wrote his grandmother Mary Lincoln. "Paul is not a very good driver but as I had taken the car past the most dangerous places I thought this was safe, especially as I warned him. . . . That is where I missed my guess. While I was taking a little nap Paul misses a corner." Bob's friend drove the car straight into a ditch, demolishing the front end. According to Bob's account, he "bummed" a ride to Fredericksburg and used his last two dollars to buy a train ticket back to Washington. He was still trying to figure out how to raise the cash to pay for towing and repairs when he arrived home and saw a letter from Mary Lincoln waiting for him. He tore it open and, as luck would have it, there was a handsome check inside. After he breathed a sigh of relief, Bob sat down and wrote her a "Dearest Granny" thank-you note. "Thanks, Granny, for your wonderful present. As usual I was broke and this time it was more than welcome."

Peggy Beckwith, six years older than her brother Bob, was twenty-eight when her mother married Robert Randolph. Peggy had grown up in Washington and attended the Madeira School, a finishing school for girls, founded in 1906 by a Vassar graduate, Miss Lucy Madeira. In those days, before its move to a lush two-hundred-acre campus in Virginia, the Madeira School was located on Nineteenth Street near Dupont Circle in downtown Washington. Graduates of the school went on to attend the finest colleges for young women in America—Madeira was a direct feeder into Vassar, Smith, Wellesley, and Bryn Mawr. But Peggy Beckwith cut her own path, and it did not include debutante balls or higher education. As someone said of Peggy, "She should've been a man."

Rather than hunt for an eligible husband, Peggy preferred to hunt deer in Vermont. She grew into an expert outdoorswoman. She hiked the woods around Hildene and went canoeing, fishing, and hunting, feeling more comfortable in a man's flannel shirt and knickers than a dress. She cut her flaxen hair short, above the ears, like a boy. As to the inevitable questions about her sexuality, Peggy was never known to have had a relationship with a man. Neither did she ever have a woman as a lover, or at least none that has been revealed. But when she sought company at all, she clearly preferred women. Mostly, she just wanted to be left alone.

In late 1929, when the aviatrix Amelia Earhart was at the peak of her fame, Peggy Beckwith appeared at the Washington Airport and enrolled in flying classes under the name M. L. Beckwith. She became proficient in takeoffs, spiral climbs, and three-point landings. At some point she confided to her flight instructor, Lieutenant Howard French, that she was Abraham Lincoln's great-granddaughter. They both got a kick out of soaring in the sky above Washington and circling the majestic Lincoln Memorial. Word leaked out that Lincoln's great-granddaughter was taking flying lessons, and reporters descended on Washington Airport and filed cheery stories about the Lincoln heiress who had abandoned "tea frills for flying togs." One magazine article noted that when Peggy flew, she would wear knickers, boots, heavy woolen socks, a man's shirt, sweater, and an old hat. Stating the obvious, the article pointed out that Peggy "doesn't give a rap about clothes or how she looks." Nor did she care that she was overweight. Abraham Lincoln, the article jovially speculated, "would have liked this great-granddaughter of his immensely just because of her courage and her indifference to public opinion."

Flying was no passing fancy for Peggy. She was dead earnest about it and spent four thousand dollars on a De Havilland Gypsy Moth biplane. She had a reputation as a cautious pilot who avoided reckless stunts, but Mary Lincoln found her granddaughter's passion worrisome. Vermont flying, because of the sudden downdrafts and the mountainous topography, could be a challenging exercise for any pilot, especially one with limited solo experience like Peggy. Sometimes she would come home from an afternoon of soaring in the air over Manchester to find her grandmother in tears, having persuaded herself that Peggy would get killed in a plane crash. Her mother Jessie also poured on the guilt.

But there were others at Hildene who were thrilled when Peggy went up in her plane because it meant a fleeting break from the demands of an imperious and demanding boss. Peggy was now overseeing Hildene, which was one of Manchester's largest employers. In the summer, fifteen men were hired to keep the lawns and gardens in first-class condition. The grounds were so extensive that the sound of lawnmowers could be heard cutting grass all day, and then resume the following morning. In the summer, mowing the lawns of Hildene was truly a never-ending task. The Lincolns also employed a butler, a workforce of maids, a chauffeur, and a cook. Running Hildene was like managing a factory, and Peggy was doing it.

One of Abraham Lincoln's supreme gifts was his empathy for people. He genuinely loved common folks, and it helped make him a great man. But his flair for leadership eluded his great-granddaughter. Peggy would look out on the magnificent grounds of Hildene from her perch at the second-floor window and survey the acreage that surrounded her. It was Lincoln land, and all the working stiffs she saw below, toiling on the property, had better know they worked for her. Sometimes when she saw something displeasing, she would grab a megaphone and bark orders. When she thought she was being ignored, she would put a bugle to her lips and blow. It was a clarion call that got everyone's attention, and it did not endear Peggy to the Hildene staff. For the workers, it was a relief—truly liberating—when Peggy took off in her plane. She would fly every other day, weather conditions permitting. "That's the only time we knew she wasn't around to be watching us," said a gardener who was fired by Peggy when she found him sleeping on the job.

Mary Lincoln was eighty-eight years old when she made a decision about what would happen to Hildene after she had passed on. Jessie was shocked when she was officially notified that, under the terms of a new will drawn up by Mary Lincoln, all of Hildene would be bequeathed to her sister Mamie.

"It was a stunning blow," Jessie wrote her mother. She had been under the impression that Hildene would go to her daughter Peggy. Although she had "absolute confidence in Mamie's abiding love," Jessie felt betrayed. "You told us that you were leaving Hildene to Peggy, (and told me not to tell . . .)" Jessie had to wonder what was going on, and asked her mother whether "your feeling for me has decidedly changed."

"Sometimes (<u>only</u> sometimes) I grit my teeth when I think of all the fruit of my toil at Hildene being turned over in your will to [Mamie] instead of to Peg. I wonder if some awful thing that I have done that caused you to change your mind. It is unthinkable to face seeing poor Peg turned out of the only place she loves on earth—and what is worse—it would be right on top of losing you! Can't you change it?"

On September 29, 1934, Mary Lincoln responded. It had been raining all day in Vermont, and Peggy, now thirty-six years old, was somewhere poking around. Ten days earlier, Bruno Richard Hauptmann had been arrested for the kidnapping and murder of the Lindbergh baby. The following day, Adolph Hitler would announce his expansion of the German army and navy and the creation of a German air force, in violation of the Treaty of Versailles. The planet was set on the path toward the second World War. But Mary Lincoln had to put aside the great events taking place in the world because something profoundly personal was on her mind that day. She struggled to find the words to explain to her youngest daughter why Hildene was going to Mamie, and only Mamie. She began the letter with a term of endearment that she used when writing to Jessie—"My Dearest Petticoat."

I do not feel like writing a long letter today but I do want you to know how I feel about Peg, and Hildene—I talked with Papa about my Will many years ago, and when I suggested that perhaps Peg should have it he replied, 'Do you think she is <u>steady</u> enough?' He no doubt had in mind her age and did not refer to any personality traits of character—<u>he loved her</u>. When I made my last Will (the sixth) four years ago this month I gave the Hildene question much serious thought. I decided our eldest child should properly inherit the place, certainly for her lifetime, and I gave instructions that this should be done, but that the property on Mamie's death should go to Peg, <u>for good and all</u>. . . . It will be Peggy's, <u>absolutely</u>. . . . <u>Nothing</u> you have done, <u>ever</u>, has had any influence with me in the making of my Will, and I think Hildene is dealt with, as Papa could have liked—I have simply tried to be as fair as I could be to all of my family, without fear, or favor, as my present will is now four years old I think it is evident that nothing you have said, or done, has had anything to do with the manner in which I dealt with Hildene, at that time. With a heart full of love, as ever, Mama.

There was nothing to be gained by reciting the long list of grievances in Jessie's melodramatic life, starting with her elopement with Warren Beckwith, cheating on her second husband, and now her marriage to the aristocratic wastrel Robert Randolph. At least Jessie now knew that Hildene would be passed on to her daughter Peggy upon Mamie's death.

Three years later, Mary Harlan Lincoln was dead. It was a slow decline due to old age. The family knew the end was coming, and in the final week of her life her two daughters and her granddaughter were in constant attendance at her bedside. Death came on March 31, 1937, at her mansion in Washington. Peggy went to check up on her grandmother at ten at night. "She was sleeping like a baby," Peggy said. A nurse stayed with her grandmother through the evening. "She said gran slept quietly all night but that she noticed the pulse getting weaker. Then the breathing stopped and that was all." Her passing at age ninety was "a most peaceful one," Peggy said.

The obituaries described Mary as the "popular and gracious" cabinet wife and the most "charming diplomatic hostess" in London when her husband served as minister to the Court of St. James. They pointed out how generous she had been to the people of the United States, donating to the nation the Lincoln family Bible, the Bible on which President Lincoln took his oath of office, and the letter Queen Victoria wrote to Mary Todd Lincoln after the assassination. These treasured Lincoln relics were now on display in a glass case at the Library of Congress. Nothing was said of her poisonous relationship with her mother-in-law, though the *Chicago Tribune* did take notice of Mrs. Lincoln's reclusive personality and how she and the entire Lincoln family "shunned publicity on all occasions."

She was buried in Arlington National Cemetery, next to her husband's "place in the sun" and the grave of their son Abraham Lincoln II. One week later, two Lincoln family lawyers, the steady team of Norman Frost and Frederic Towers, opened Mary Lincoln's last will and testament. It revealed that up until 1935, Mrs. Lincoln had intended to bequeath all of Hildene to her granddaughter Peggy. But in June 1936, she amended her will with a codicil that left Hildene to her daughter Mamie Lincoln Isham, now a widow of twenty years. Mamie was also left the N Street mansion in Washington, and all her mother's jewelry and clothing.

Jessie had every right to feel disinherited and affronted. There was no house for her. Jessie did inherit the cars—a 1928 Chrysler Sedan valued at $50, a 1927 Lincoln Sedan valued at $150, and the Ford station wagon worth $250. However, both Jessie and Mamie were well provided for. The Lincoln women were to live off the income from the three-million-dollar Mary Harlan Lincoln trust fund. Mary Lincoln also directed that, following the death of her daughters Mamie and Jessie, the trust fund would go to her three grandchildren, Lincoln Isham, Peggy Beckwith, and Bob Beckwith. There was one other interesting clause worth noting, and it was something that would have profound consequences for the Lincolns in the decades to come. If none of the three grandchildren had blood heirs of their own, it was Mary Lincoln's wish that upon the death of her last direct blood descendant, the trust fund be divided among three institutions close to her heart: the American Red Cross, Iowa Wesleyan College, and the First Church of Christ, Scientist.

As the new mistress of Hildene, Mamie Lincoln Isham spent the next year redecorating the estate while she continued to live in her townhouse at 19 E. Seventy-second Street in Manhattan, and her summer place in Dorset, Vermont. Mamie was a true Lincoln, distrustful of the public spotlight, wary of being perceived as trading on her great name. Although she was a Christian Scientist, she was choir mother of Grace Church in Manhattan.

Mamie finally moved into Hildene in June 1938, a frail, sickly woman of sixty-nine. Of all the Lincolns of the second generation, she was the one who most looked like Abraham, tall and stooped with deep-set gray eyes, and very shy. Sadly, Mamie would never live to enjoy Hildene. Six months after she moved in, on November 21, 1938, she died following surgery at a New York City hospital.

Hildene now belonged to Peggy Beckwith.

23
"I, Robert Todd Lincoln . . ."

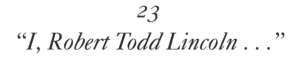

PEGGY BECKWITH WAS forty in 1938 when she became mistress of Hildene, and it was increasingly improbable that she would one day bear any children.

Linc Isham was forty-six, content to strum a guitar, compose little ditties, and spend winter evenings at the Stork Club in New York City.

Robert Todd Lincoln Beckwith's choice for a life partner was Hazel Holland Wilson, who was twenty years older than Beckwith when they married. Hazel lived in Chevy Chase, Maryland, and worked as a secretary at the General Electric Co. when she met Beckwith. Hazel's brother, Jim Holland, introduced them at a party with the words, "I'd like you to meet my sister." She was a statuesque woman with a theatrical widow's peak and down-to-earth style. She was also a widow with two children, Doris and Raymond, who was just ten years younger than his stepfather.

There was friction when Bob Beckwith brought Hazel home to meet the Lincolns. The age difference was bothersome, and even though Jessie appreciated Hazel's charm, she saw the handwriting on the wall and its implications for the Lincoln bloodline. It exasperated Jessie that her son—the last hope for the continuation of the family dynasty—had picked for a wife a woman who was already beyond childbearing age.

Into Bob Beckwith's life came Hazel's daughter Doris. Beckwith welcomed her as family, and though he never formally adopted her, Doris Wilson came to be known as Doris Beckwith, socialite and debutante. Beckwith arranged for her transfer to Holten-Arms, a prestigious all-girl prep school that Jacqueline Kennedy would one day attend. She was introduced into society at a supper dance before a full orchestra at the Columbia

Country Club in Chevy Chase, Maryland, in January 1940. Twenty-seven other debutantes were presented that night, but all the attention in the *Washington Post* coverage was focused on the exquisite blonde Doris, who was identified as Robert Todd Lincoln's great-granddaughter. She wore a white gown with a fitted beaded bodice and short puffed sleeves, full skirt, and gold slippers. Dinner was seafood á la Newburg, and among the handsome young bachelors forming the stag line was an American University student from Chevy Chase, Robert Crans, whose father worked in the engraving division at the U.S. Treasury Department. Young Crans definitely had his eyes fixed on Doris. The Lincoln family took a keen interest in making this a special night for the debutante. From Vermont, Peggy Beckwith generously paid for her corsage and boutonnières.

"My goodness," an appreciative Doris wrote Peggy. "I didn't even think I would ever have one orchid let alone all these beauties." To her step-grandmother Jessie, whom she affectionately called Muzzie, Doris wrote, "The party was so wonderful that I didn't even need a glass of the perfect champagne to make me feel elated."

When the United States entered World War II, Bob Beckwith was too old to serve, though the Coast Guard did commandeer his yacht. Robert Crans signed up in September 1942.

Crans was six-foot-two and so thin that he had to go on an eating binge to meet the Navy's minimum weight requirement, 165 pounds. He received his commission in the U.S. Navy Air Corps, and on September 18, 1943, one week after he had earned his wings at the Navy Training School in Pensacola, the handsome young ensign married Doris Beckwith at the Sulgrave Club in Washington. Bob Beckwith gave his stepdaughter away. For her wedding veil, she wore a Brussels lace veil that had once belonged to Mary Todd Lincoln—a gift from Peggy. Immediately after the reception, Doris changed into a beige suit and mink fur, and the newlyweds were off to Pensacola.

Crans spent the war years hunting German submarines in the Atlantic, test-flying seaplanes, and training navy pilots. By the end of World War II, the skinny kid from Chevy Chase who had married into the Lincoln family had filled out considerably; he weighed 220 pounds.

Up in Vermont, Peggy Beckwith did what she could for the war against fascism. She planted a victory garden, canned vegetables, conserved gas, and sent care packages to soldiers stationed overseas. She also taught first aid at the local school and won a merit badge from the U.S. military for her work as a plane spotter. Her mother did not care much for Franklin D. Roosevelt, so in 1940, when he broke political tradition and ran for an unprecedented third term, Jessie joined a Wendell Willkie club to support the Republican Party nominee. But when war was declared, Jessie pitched in. She sponsored a number of British youngsters through the Save the Children Fund, and contributed to the Red Cross.

During World War II, the nation's capital was deemed vulnerable to aerial attack, and a number of precious historical documents were transported out of Washington for safekeeping. The original Gettysburg Address and Lincoln's second inaugural address were evacuated to the Bullion Depository at Fort Knox, Kentucky. In a top-secret operation conducted three weeks after Pearl Harbor, the Lincoln Papers were removed from the Library of Congress and shipped to the campus of the University of Virginia in Charlottesville, where they were placed in a vault at the Alderman Library. They would not be returned until August 1944.

On July 27, 1949, the clock that had started ticking the day Robert Lincoln had died, in 1926, finally ran out. Twenty-one years had passed since Robert Lincoln's death. The time had come to make the Lincoln Papers available to the American people.

Two dozen of the greatest Lincoln scholars of the age met for a celebratory dinner in a large banquet room at the Library of Congress and awaited the stroke of midnight. The poet and Lincoln biographer Carl Sandburg was there, passing the hours strumming his guitar and singing songs from the Civil War era. So was General Ulysses S. Grant III, President Grant's grandson. One noted Lincoln researcher held his cane aloft and declared, "Not since that morning in the Petersen House [where Abraham Lincoln died] have so many men who love Lincoln been gathered together in one room." Moments before midnight, everyone was escorted across the street to the library annex and taken to the manuscripts division on the third floor, where they gathered in front of a huge safe. Eric Sevareid of CBS and ABC's John Daly (the future host of *What's My Line*) were there to cover the historic event. Ruth Painter Randall, the future biographer of Mary Todd Lincoln, and wife of the great Lincoln scholar Professor John G. Randall of the University of Illinois, described it as the most exciting night of her life. "There was a hush and then dead silence," Mrs. Randall said. "Midnight struck." Then, Luther Evans, the Librarian of Congress, stepped in front of the safe and solemnly read from Robert Todd Lincoln's deed of gift. "It sounded," said Mrs. Painter, "like what it really was, a voice from the tomb."

"I, Robert Todd Lincoln . . . sole surviving child of Abraham Lincoln and the absolute owner of all of the letters, manuscripts [and] documents . . . left by my father . . . do hereby give the same in perpetuity to the United States of America." At that, a librarian worked the combination and unlocked the safe. The door swung open as flashbulbs exploded and newsreel cameras whirred. For those present, said Mrs. Painter, the suspense was unbearable as the mythic Lincoln Papers were unveiled—eighteen thousand individual documents from the life of Abraham Lincoln. Lincoln's great-grandson, Bob Beckwith, showed up only for the formal ceremony, which took place later that day at the more reasonable hour of four in the afternoon. Beckwith had been assuring everyone that nothing of historical importance would be found in the Lincoln Papers, just as his grandfather had predicted. But the Lincoln descendants, who could be so dense on matters related to their illustrious forebear, were once again mistaken. The Lincoln Papers, said David Mearns, director of the library's reference department, "had been well worth waiting for."

"Here, for the first time, was Abraham Lincoln three-dimensional, whole, intelligible."

In the closing years of her life, Jessie Lincoln moved to Hildene, where Peggy could take care of her. A kitchen was installed on the second floor because Jessie had trouble climbing stairs. There were some suggestions that Jessie's weight ballooned to four hundred pounds in these final years, a disturbing state of affairs for a woman who had once been the loveliest of all the Lincoln grandchildren.

In case there was any doubt, Peggy wanted everyone at Hildene to know who was running the place. "I am the boss," she would tell the staff. If anyone had an issue, she would say, "You ask me."

The Hildene workers remembered Jessie as a painfully shy woman who rarely engaged any of them in conversation. The one-time Lincoln wild child died at Rutland City Hospital in Vermont on January 4, 1948, at age seventy-two. Services were held three days later at Hildene and she was buried at Dellwood Cemetery in Manchester.

All three of Jessie's husbands survived her. The explorer and artist Frank Edward Johnson would live until 1955. Her last husband, Robert Randolph, had a rough time of it after Jessie's death. All through the 1930s he had been receiving $416 a month from a $425,000 trust fund Jessie had set up for him when they were married. At the time of Jessie's death, he was living at the mansion Robert Lincoln had built for Jessie at 2908 N Street in Washington, but after Jessie's death, the house was sold, and Randolph, that descendant of noble Virginian blood, had nowhere to go. He moved into a hotel in Burlington but could not afford the rates. To their credit, Peggy and Bob established a trust fund for their stepfather that assured him of a reliable source of income in his old age. Randolph died in April 1952 in Washington, and was buried in Arlington National Cemetery.

And what of Jessie's first husband, the disreputable Warren Beckwith? His last communication with Jessie had come during World War I, when he tried to talk to his ex-wife on the telephone as he passed through Washington on his way to France. In 1952, an enterprising reporter for the *Chicago Tribune*, seeking an "epilog to the Abraham Lincoln story," found Warren living in a splendid house overlooking the Pacific Ocean in La Jolla, California. He was seventy-eight years old and had snow-white hair, but he was still trim, and in good spirits. Typical of Beckwith, sports was still on his mind. He complained that he could not golf or go hunting as much as he would like to because of a recent heart attack. But he was happy to talk.

"I guess the Lincolns were surprised when Jessie and I eloped. They hadn't wanted us to get married, but why shouldn't we? We were sweethearts at college." He was still blaming Mary Harlan Lincoln for the dissolution of his marriage with Jessie. "She kept taking Jessie and our children away from me. Mrs. Lincoln said she was lonely since the death of her son, Abraham Lincoln II. When Mrs. Lincoln took Jessie and our children to London in 1906, I said I was going to get a divorce. Mrs. Lincoln said I couldn't get one, but I showed her. I charged Jessie with desertion and got the uncontested divorce in 1907 in Mount Pleasant. I didn't ask for custody of the children because they were with Jessie, and she and her family were much better able to support them than I was. I never saw Jessie or the children, but friends sent me pictures of them. I only learned about Jessie's death in 1948 from the newspapers. I hadn't seen her since 1906."

Like Jessie, Warren Beckwith went through three marriages. Following his divorce from his second wife, Blanche Cutter, Warren married a silent movie actress, Vera Ward of Asheville, North Carolina, in 1924. They had a son, Warren Wallace Beckwith Jr., who became an oceanographer with the Scripps Institute in La Jolla.

It was a shock for Peggy and Bob to read that their biological father was not only alive but that they had two half-brothers. However, they made no effort to reach out to their father or to Philip and Warren Jr. Three years later, in 1955, Warren Beckwith died, at age seventy-five.

There was another surprise awaiting Peggy and Bob when their father's will was filed for probate. Warren Beckwith had left a "large fortune," and two-thirds of the estate was to be divided among Warren's four children, Peggy, Bob, Philip, and Warren Jr. (Most of the assets were from the estate of his father, Captain Beckwith, the cofounder of the Western Wheel and Scraper Company, who died in 1905.) It was not until around 1980 that Bob Beckwith saw an image of his father for the first time, when he was shown a photograph by a Lincoln historian. Now he knew how much he resembled his dad. Peggy seemed more curious about the man. She kept a history and genealogy of the Beckwith clan in her library at Hildene.

There is an unsettling footnote to the Warren Beckwith story. His family suffered many unexpected and violent tragedies over the years, comparable even to the Lincolns'. Warren's oldest brother died in the Far East during a trip around the world. Another brother committed suicide. His sister Florence died of diphtheria, and another sister, Emily, shot herself in 1935 while living with Warren in Albuquerque.

Peggy Beckwith considered herself a real farmer. There was an old saying in Vermont that Peggy espoused: "As the fellow says, 'Here it is Monday, tomorrow is Tuesday, the next day Wednesday, half the week gone and not a lick of work done.' Time goes fast on a farm." The gene of eccentricity ran deep in Peggy Beckwith. One of her peculiarities was a devotion to wild creatures that was so extreme, some would say it bordered on lunacy. She had a pet Angora rabbit she let roam Hildene to its heart's content. She found two baby raccoons on the road one night, brought them home, and gave them full use of a bedroom on the second floor. Then she had a carpenter saw the bedroom door in half to create a Dutch door so she could look in on them. The stench of urine and feces coming from the room was overpowering, even for Peggy, and she installed a dozen deodorizer lights to deal with it. At some point the rambunctious raccoons figured out how to climb their way out of the bedroom, but Peggy did not seem to mind, and permitted them the run of the mansion. The raccoons went after everything, pulling electrical switches out of the walls and turning on the faucet in the bathtub. One day the water overflowed and leaked through the ceiling below, but Peggy refused to lock the creatures in a cage. Instead, she ordered her staff to disconnect the bathroom faucets. The raccoons came first.

When Peggy's friend Bernice Graham was invited to tea at Hildene, she could not believe the deterioration that had befallen Robert Lincoln's mansion. Raccoon claw marks had scratched the beautiful wood paneling, and the carpeting was a soiled and revolting mess. The raccoons were everywhere; Bernice saw one critter climbing the mantel. "I will admit I was taken aback, to say the least." A magnificent Aeolian pipe organ, one of the largest privately owned such insruments in the world, with 1,000 individual pipes and 242 rolls of music, stood in the entrance hallway of Hildene. In the old days, before radio, the Aeolian organ—a gift from Robert Lincoln to his wife—would send orchestral music resounding through Hildene, like a built-in stereo sound system. Maintenance was a chore, and the organ needed to be played every day to keep it in running order. But Peggy was indifferent to this gem, and now the network of pipes hidden within the walls of Hildene had become a nesting place for a horde of mice.

Peggy's devotion to her three dogs, particularly her beagle, Bugie, reached the level of absurdity. She cut a hole in the top of her new convertible Corvair so her dogs could poke their heads out and enjoy the breeze. (Her cars were modified in other ways. To accommodate her short stature, a block was built on top of the pedal so she could reach the gas.) All of her animals were overindulged. Bugie was so overweight she could not climb the stairs, so Peggy had an electrician power up Hildene's obsolete elevator for the dog.

Never concerned about her looks or health, Peggy let herself go. For breakfast she usually ate a doughnut. Dinner was a veal cutlet or roast lamb. There was always dessert, lemon pie pudding or Jell-O. As she was a chain smoker, her breathing became heavy and labored. Peggy was also a pack rat. She could not throw anything away—shades here of her great-grandmother Mary Todd Lincoln. Piles of newspapers and magazines cluttered Hildene. The observatory where Robert Lincoln would stargaze and survey the surface of the moon also fell into disuse; Peggy turned it into a boiling factory to make maple syrup.

To cut costs, Peggy scaled back the staff. One by one the live-in servants left by attrition or retirement. Peggy was left with a household staff of just a cook and two chambermaids, though she had help running the farm. During her reign over Hildene, the great estate built by Robert Lincoln fell into a state of dilapidation equal to the notorious Grey Gardens of East Hampton, New York, the squalid twenty-eight-room mansion occupied by Jacqueline Kennedy's unconventional aunt and first cousin.

Like her great-grandmother, Mary Todd Lincoln, Peggy could sometimes display the temperament of a volcano. The slightest infraction could send her into a paroxysm of rage. Due to a misunderstanding, Iowa Wesleyan College sent Peggy a fundraising letter that noted her involvement in the Mary Harlan Lincoln Club. The college's use of the Lincoln name was always a sensitive issue for Peggy because she did not want to be accused of ignoring her Harlan roots for the more glamorous Lincoln lineage. Peggy read the letter and was angered.

> To be addressed as a member of an organization I have never heard of . . . is indeed amazing. I shall be very interested to find out just who did organize this "CLUB" and presumably made me a member. . . . Since they dreamed up this "splendid idea" of tying Robert Lincoln around James Harlan's neck, any letters I receive from "Iowa Wesleyan" go straight into the wastebasket unopened. . . . Let us set the record straight: I'm not a member of the "Mary Harlan Lincoln Club" and, thank you, I shall not join it.

Peggy never appreciated being associated with Abraham Lincoln. "It always provokes me when people stare and say, 'There's Lincoln's great-granddaughter.' It's just my luck he was related to me." Comments like that did not endear Peggy to the tight-knit community of Lincoln scholars. Nor did they appreciate her fundamental ignorance of Civil War history when she was quoted as saying that Abraham Lincoln and Robert E. Lee were "good friends." She seemed to have inherited her grandfather Robert Lincoln's lack of tact in comments meant for public consumption. Every now and then, usually around the time of President Lincoln's birthday, a reporter would track her down, seeking some meaningful comment about the great man's life. In 1954 she was quoted as saying that if Abraham Lincoln "were alive today he would be an Eisenhower Republican."

At some point Peggy started to make herself scarce whenever February 12 came around. She once found a reporter staking out Hildene, waiting for Lincoln's great-granddaughter to emerge. When the reporter saw the obese lady in jeans and workman's boots heading up the driveway, he couldn't have imagined she was a Lincoln. When he asked how long he would have to wait before Peggy Beckwith would appear, she snapped, "Forever! Now, get out of here." Peggy usually took the phone off the hook on Lincoln's birthday, but in 1963 she was caught off guard when a reporter for UPI managed to get her on the phone, and questioned her about the civil rights movement. Peggy let loose with comments that bewildered the nation.

"We're Southerners," she said, "but I don't think of the South as a separate culture. It's part of the Union. The aggression of the federal government in forcing integration concerns me, and I disagree with the stand taken by Attorney General Robert Kennedy on this matter. People and animals just don't like strangers. . . . When strangers are suddenly thrown together, people and animals alike bristle." In another interview on race relations, Peggy said, "It's not the color of the skin that causes all the trouble. It's whether you like the individual. And you can't be forced to like an individual." Peggy was asked whether Abraham Lincoln would have taken a similar laidback approach to civil rights. "I can't say," came her answer. "I'm as far away from him as anybody else." Lincoln scholars would probably have agreed.

DOWN IN VIRGINIA, another Lincoln was living off the land, but he never let his hands get dirty. Peggy's brother Bob Beckwith liked to call himself a "gentleman farmer of independent means," a quaint phrase that suited Beckwith entirely, denoting as it did the landed gentry from another century. Woodstock, the plantation Beckwith inherited from his mother Jessie, was a working farm with pecan trees, corn, hay, and sweet beans. There was a small herd of forty Black Angus cattle and a single bull. Mostly, Beckwith drank and entertained while Woodstock's overseer, Allie Shackleford, ran things. Bob Beckwith had three great passions in life: fast cars, boats, and beautiful women, and living off the Mary Harlan Lincoln trust fund facilitated his relentless pursuit of all three.

On the country roads and in the town of Saluda, Virginia, Beckwith was a reckless speed demon. Once, he was stopped by a Middlesex County deputy sheriff and issued a speeding ticket. "You might as well write me another, because I'm driving back the same way," he informed the officer. On another occasion, he drove his Cadillac through a stop sign at fifty-five miles per hour. "Whoops!" he said. "Get that one on the way back." His wife Hazel, sitting in the passenger seat, gave him hell. George Shackleford, the overseer's son who helped out at Woodstock, said he had pulled Beckwith out of two wrecks and had once found him hanging upside down in a pickup truck that had flipped over.

Beckwith had an edgy wit and, sometimes, a tense relationship with his wife, who wore heavy makeup and styled her hair in a high bouffant with a bold streak of gray. Her nails were always done. Everyone at Woodstock was pitching in one year to harvest the bean crop, even Hazel. Not Beckwith, though. Hazel muttered something about her husband "being of no use." Everyone stopped, then watched as Beckwith, at an exaggerated snail's pace, bent and picked a single bean. "Here, I picked one," he said, and then strode off.

Weekends at Woodstock, the Beckwiths entertained. Among Bob's closest friends were Dr. Thomas Grove and his wife, Emily. Grove was a country doctor with offices in Saluda who appreciated the fine Chivas scotch whiskey on hand at Woodstock. He found it a kick to be socializing with Abraham Lincoln's great-grandson. But Emily Grove was troubled by the arbitrary way Beckwith stored historically important Lincoln relics. Beckwith had taken Emily to the shed near the main farmhouse so she could see the exquisite antiques from the time of Lincoln, including a liquor cabinet with a retractable rolltop cover and brass feet, which she could not stop raving about.

"Why in the world are you letting it stay out here in ruins?" she asked Beckwith.

"Would you like to have it?"

Emily took about a second to respond. "Indeed I would and I'll keep it in better condition than you've been doing here."

Beckwith shrugged. "Just take anything you want. We're not going to use it."

Emily pondered the possibilities. Inside was a treasure trove of Lincoln memorabilia. But being a gracious southern lady she politely declined, though she did take the cabinet—"and enjoyed it ever after." The cabinet remains with the Grove family to this day.

Bob Beckwith first met Dr. Grove when Bob's stepdaughter Doris suffered a medical emergency at Woodstock and required a doctor. Grove rushed over to the plantation. Beckwith was impressed that the physician would make a "country call." They really hit it off when they discovered that they were both high-level Freemasons. After Grove finished treating Doris, he noticed that Beckwith's hands were shaking from Parkinson's disease. Beckwith explained that he had tried everything to control the tremors but nothing had worked. The shaking had become so bad that when he tried to drink coffee it would spill over the cup and scorch his hands, so he had to switch to a tall glass and add ice. Dr. Grove prescribed a new medication that had just come on the market, and a few days later a grateful Beckwith called Grove and said that for the first time in years he had been able to enjoy a hot cup of coffee, "and my hand didn't shake."

Because of Beckwith's severe stutter, dinner-table conversation with him could turn painfully uncomfortable. "Come on, Bob, spit it out," Doris teased him one evening. Everyone at the table laughed nervously, but the wisecrack did not seem to upset him. He had a certain technique for dealing with his speech impediment—tapping his knuckles as a reminder to slow down, or putting his words into lyrics and singing his part of the conversation. Sometimes, though, he got so fed up with his own helplessness that he would spew out a curse. But at the table, his stutter could also imprison him in glum silence.

Dinner at Woodstock was formal, and served promptly at six. In the summer, Bob wore a white starched dinner jacket. During the rest of the year his dinner attire was a blue blazer and tie. The butler was a black man named McKinley whose wife, Esther, worked as the cook. Elsewhere in the Western world the finger bowl stood on the edge of extinction, but not at Woodstock. McKinley made certain one was placed before each guest at the end of every meal.

Beckwith kept two cocker spaniels, Bing and Bang. "Don't get too close to Bang," he liked to chuckle. On warm days he would dive into the Piankatank River that ran along the property, with Bing and Bang swimming loyally alongside their master. George Shackleford pitched in during the summer months, when Beckwith needed an extra hand.

Shackleford can still recall the day back in the late 1950s when Beckwith asked him to haul boxes down from the attic. Shackleford loaded everything onto the back of the pickup truck, and then he and Beckwith drove to the banks of the Piankatank, and dumped the boxes in the river to construct a barrier reef to halt beach erosion. At some point, curiosity got the better of young Shackleford and he reached into a box and pulled out a handful of documents. He was astonished to see that they were from the Lincoln family archives. Some of the material displayed the Pullman Company letterhead. "All that stuff should have been saved," Shackleford said.

Beckwith may have been incredibly irresponsible when it came to preserving history, but he could be generous with his money. When Allie Shackleford died after nearly fifty years as overseer at Woodstock, Beckwith set up a trust fund and paid Allie's widow her late husband's full salary. The payments continued for fifteen years, until the day she died.

Beckwith's marriage to Hazel had its ups and down, with indiscretions on both sides; Hazel's was set in motion when the Beckwiths built a swimming pool at Woodstock. The pool was a fiberglass design, with water pumped directly from the Piankatank River. George Shackleford remembers the day the pumps were turned on and the pool filled with water that was brown from river silt. Then the chlorine and filters kicked in and the water turned crystalline blue. One day, because of bad weather, the contractor who built the pool was invited to spend the night at Woodstock. Two years later he was still there. Hazel's affair with the man became the worst-kept secret in Saluda. "Oh my God, it was wide open," said Dr. Grove's son, Tom. "Bob didn't talk about it. He was too much of a gentleman to talk about it. I can only imagine it was a slap in the face."

The affair ended badly. George Shackleford and his mother were home when Hazel telephoned and "she was in a state of hysterics," Shackleford said. Hazel and her lover were engaged in a ferocious fight. George and his mother rushed over to the main house and came upon a disturbing scene. There were broken dishes everywhere. The kitchen walls were splattered with eggs. Hazel was standing there looking disoriented, and she was holding a .22-caliber target pistol in her hand, aiming it at the contractor, who was on his way out the door.

"Better stop," Hazel told him. He never turned around, and Hazel dropped the weapon. Shackleford picked it up and recognized it from the gunroom on the second floor, part of the collection of weaponry left by Jessie Lincoln's third husband, Robert Randolph. Shackleford was relieved to see that the pistol did not have any rounds in it.

Treasured Lincoln relics at Woodstock had a way of disappearing. Thomas Grove was shopping at an antiques shop on Main Street in Fairfax, Virginia, in 1964 when he saw an interesting sideboard, a piece of furniture popular in the nineteenth century for displaying china and serving meals. Grove studied the veneer closely.

"I think I've seen this before," he told the antiques dealer.

"I don't think so."

Grove looked at the dealer. "It's the old Lincoln sideboard."

"How did you know that?"

"I used to eat on it," Grove said. He just walked out of the store in disgust and wondered what other treasures from Woodstock were being lost, either through Beckwith's neglect or his misguided generosity. It seemed that everything at the farm was starting to fall apart, and Woodstock was going downhill just like Hildene. The yacht which had been commandeered by the Coast Guard during World War II fell into such a state of disrepair it had to be scuttled. The compass was saved, and every layer of brass and copper was stripped until the vessel was down to its wood hulk; then it was torched. People in Saluda saw the smoke rising on the horizon and for a while feared that Woodstock was on fire.

Hazel Beckwith died of congestive heart failure on April 27, 1964, at Sibley Memorial Hospital in Washington. She was eighty years old. Her husband was sixty. Three days later, services were held at Gawler's Chapel on Wisconsin Avenue. Peggy Beckwith was supposed to fly down for the funeral of her sister-in-law, but by two in the afternoon, she was a no-show. Had she missed her flight? Her brother insisted on delaying the start of services. Finally, two hours late, an out-of-breath Peggy showed up. The story that quickly got around the chapel was that on the Eastern Airlines flight coming down, Peggy became ensnared in her seat. She was so overweight she could not lift herself out, and airline personnel actually had to take the seat apart to free her.

For comfort, Bob Beckwith had Margaret Fristoe to turn to. Maggie was a petite, outgoing, and stylish woman in her mid-thirties. She worked as a manicurist at the Statler Hotel in downtown Washington, at a time when it was not unusual for men of leisure to engage in a little pleasant luxury and have their nails cut and buffed. As a young United States senator from Massachusetts, John F. Kennedy was a regular Statler client. Bob Beckwith started going there, too.

"He would come in and of course he just fell in love with her," Maggie's daughter, Lenora Hoverson, said.

Maggie's husband, James Fristoe, was a lieutenant colonel in the United States Air Force, assigned to the intelligence division. A steady and disciplined career officer, Fristoe said he had met Bob Beckwith on several social occasions and found him to be pleasant enough. "I didn't hold any animosity. Frankly, the marriage was not all that solid." Fristoe said he had been stationed at military bases around the country during the time when his wife was seeing Beckwith, and he became aware of the relationship. He decided to remain married to Maggie, he said, for a very practical reason—he did not want to jeopardize his daughter's eligibility for medical benefits from the military. When he was finally inclined to dissolve the marriage, "I called Maggie and I asked her to divorce me after I met my present wife. I didn't want anything. I just wanted my name. I told her, 'You've been more than fair.'"

When Bob and Maggie traveled together to attend Lincoln-related events and social functions, Maggie was represented as Bob's personal secretary. Four months after Hazel's death, Beckwith and Maggie flew to New York to see the world's fair at Flushing Meadows Park. It was Illinois Day, and a number of distinguished sons and daughters of Illinois had been invited to the gala, including U.S. ambassador to the United Nations Adlai Stevenson, Benny Goodman, Cab Calloway, Steve Allen, Oscar-winning actress Mercedes McCambridge, and Illinois Governor Otto Kerner. Ralph Newman, a Lincoln historian and chairman of the World's Fair Illinois Commission, also invited the three living Lincoln descendants: Lincoln Isham, Peggy Beckwith, and Bob Beckwith. He never expected them to attend.

"For many years all of the leading scholars assumed that the Lincoln descendants were anti-social, unapproachable, and reclusive," Newman said. Lincoln Isham and Peggy Beckwith wrote back, thanking Newman but declining the invitation because of ill health. Newman was not surprised, particularly at Peggy Beckwith's turndown. "She's an odd one," he said of Peggy. "I would call her an eccentric recluse. She's a big, fat gal who doesn't give a damn about Abraham Lincoln, and she's rebuffed any attempts by historians to interview her or look for family papers on the farm." But Newman was thrilled when Bob Beckwith telephoned and accepted the world's fair invitation.

Like his sister, Beckwith had in the past exhibited an unsettling lack of curiosity about Abraham Lincoln and basic civic responsibility. "I was not especially interested," he said in 1962. He let his voter registration lapse and later admitted he had not voted in at least a decade. "I never take part in politics. None of the family does."

Illinois Day, August 26, 1964, was a huge success. The Illinois Pavilion featured a life-size animatronic of Abraham Lincoln created by Disney engineers under the supervision of Walt Disney. The show was called *Great Moments with Mr. Lincoln*. Audiences in the five-hundred-seat theater were dazzled by the mechanical Lincoln arising from its chair. It had forty-eight body movements and fifteen facial expressions controlled from a computer off stage. There was Lincoln frowning, smiling, gesturing with his hands, and reciting the president's speeches through the voice of the actor Royal Dano, who had been chosen by Walt Disney because his voice approximated the historical descriptions of President Lincoln's. (Dano, who is best known for his memorable role as the preacher in the 1983 movie *The Right*

Stuff, also bore a striking resemblance to Lincoln.) It was said that Disney would well up with tears every time he saw the *Great Moments with Mr. Lincoln* presentation. Bob Beckwith, who was usually offended by any Abraham Lincoln–related memorabilia or merchandise that smacked of kitsch, was thrilled to see his illustrious forbearer come to life this way, and declared the talking Lincoln a "wonderful" creation. Perhaps, had he been truly attentive, he might have taken to heart a line from one of the Lincoln speeches uttered by the animatronic Lincoln: "If destruction be our lot, we ourselves might be the authors and finishers."

The next year, Maggie Fristoe accompanied Beckwith to Chicago for the closing ceremonies marking the Civil War Centennial observance. Following a luncheon presided over by Chicago Mayor Richard Daley, Ralph Newman drove Beckwith and Maggie out to Riverside, a village nine miles from downtown Chicago, where they visited the house where Beckwith's parents, Jessie and Warren Beckwith, had lived before their divorce, and where Bob had been born, in 1904. Then Newman drove them to Springfield. Surprisingly, this was Beckwith's first excursion to the city where Abraham Lincoln was launched on his path to greatness. Beckwith was also taken to the Lincoln tomb and to the house at Eighth and Jackson where his great-grandparents, Abraham and Mary Todd Lincoln, had raised their four boys. During the tour in Springfield, Beckwith was introduced to James Hickey, the curator of the Lincoln Collection for the Illinois State Historical Library, and a man who would soon loom large in Beckwith's life story. Beckwith's stutter, said Hickey, made him aloof at times. "In large crowds of people he found it difficult to communicate; however, in small groups he could be the most charming participant. He inherited from his great-grandfather that famous wit and humor. He also inherited the spells of melancholy."

Those who knew Beckwith were certain that if he married again, it would be to Maggie Fristoe. So it came as a shock when, in 1967, he announced that there was a new Mrs. Robert Todd Lincoln Beckwith. It was not Maggie Fristoe.

24
Father Unknown

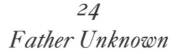

ANNEMARIE HOFFMAN BECAME the second wife of Robert Todd Lincoln Beckwith on November 6, 1967. She was twenty-seven years old. Beckwith was sixty-three. Annemarie was born in Hanover, Germany, in 1940, to Friedrich Hoffman and Elizabeth Schlegel. Those are Annemarie's basic biographical facts. But the complete chronicle of how a beautiful exchange student from postwar Germany came to marry Abraham Lincoln's great-grandson must begin with Bob Beckwith's chauffeur, Bryant "Jack" Coffelt.

Jack Coffelt was born in Joplin, Missouri, on February 20, 1916, at a time when the city was the zinc mining capital of the world. He spent most of his youth in the lawless mining town of Picher, Oklahoma, just across the state border. Picher back then had a population of about thirty thousand. Today it has just eight hundred citizens. It was once a wide-open town with a red light district on Fourth Street and twenty-two bars on Main Street. From downtown Picher to the state line a mile-and-a-half away stood a solid line of "shotgun houses," where a shot of whiskey went for twenty-five cents. "Bar hopping in Picher was an all-day experience," said Picher's local historian, Orville "Hoppie" Ray, who can recall a shooting or knifing at least once a week in Picher's heyday.

Jack Coffelt grew up destitute in this outlaw town, the son of Ottie Coffelt and her husband, Walter, an alcoholic ex-miner who died when Jack was eight. Coffelt's first scrap with the law occurred at age fifteen, when he broke into his grandfather's grocery store in Baxter Springs, Kansas, and stole an assortment of candy bars, gum, and ten dollars in silver coins. His grandfather pressed charges, and young Jack was sentenced to five years in the Kansas State Industrial Reformatory. He was paroled after two years, but at age eighteen Coffelt was back in prison following another burglary conviction. This time, Coffelt was sentenced to a three-year stretch in maximum security at the Oklahoma State Prison in McAlester. He later claimed he had been worked over pretty good in McAlester by the prison guards. He told a parole board he was a professional gambler; elsewhere, he admitted that he had never made an honest dollar in his life.

In 1949, at age thirty-three, he was sentenced to ten years for interstate auto theft and attempted escape. He spent about three years at the federal penitentiary in Atlanta, and, in 1952, was transferred to the federal facility in Leavenworth, Kansas, where he finished out his sentence.

Paroled in July 1955 at age thirty-nine after spending nearly two decades of his life behind bars, Coffelt bounced around the country. He lived in Memphis, where he was said to have pulled off a heist and slipped out of town with a pile of cash, maybe fifty thousand dollars. He lived in Phoenix and in Las Vegas, where he registered as an ex-felon. Then Coffelt settled in a most unusual place—the college town of Lawrence, Kansas, home of the University of Kansas.

Coffelt moved into a two-bedroom apartment at the Meadowbrook Apartments, and it was in these surroundings, for the first time in his life, that he encountered a class of citizens different from the thugs and lowlifes he had known in the penal system. His neighbors were college professors and professionals, the kind of cosmopolitan crowd drawn to the cultural assets of a vital college town. It was here, at the Meadowbrook swimming pool, that Coffelt got to know his neighbor, Barbara McClean, a published poet with a master's degree in English who taught a writer's workshop affiliated with the University of Kansas. Barbara introduced Coffelt into her circle of intellectuals. The ex-con never hid his past. On the contrary, in his gravelly and measured drawl, he relished telling stories of his criminal history. He found a receptive audience in the group of academics who thought it cool and very sixties to be socializing with a bandit.

"He was a hard case, which is understandable because of the way he had lived," said Robert Hoyt, a writer who, with his wife, Jean, socialized with Coffelt. "I remember Jack as a tall, dark-haired man, almost gaunt and with a hang-dog expression. He did enjoy a laugh. His favorite expression, after finishing one of his stories, was, 'And if that ain't true, God's a possum!' Jack implied many times that he went armed, but I never saw signs of a concealed weapon." Hoyt recalled that Coffelt "liked his Jack Daniels," and although he was only in forties, he was already "physically beat up" from the

hard time he'd done in prison. Coffelt exuded a world-weary and sometimes menacing charm that certain women found tempting, even hypnotic.

One wild evening, Coffelt took his friends out to dinner at a fancy steak-
house in Lawrence. He was the center of attention as he spun fantastic—
some would say preposterous—yarns of life in prison. When Jack Coffelt
held forth at the dinner table, it was sometimes hard to distinguish truth
from fiction. When the check came, he whipped out a wad of hundred-
dollar bills and paid the whole thing. He always seemed to have plenty of
cash, which he said he kept tucked in the roof of his late-model Cadillac.

How Jack Coffelt first met Annemarie Hoffman remains murky.
Annemarie spoke with this author only once and very briefly, when I telephoned her on what happened to be her birthday—a birthday she said was
"ruined" by my call. For about a year she had been aware of the book I had
been writing about the descendants of Abraham Lincoln.

"I don't like to talk about that part of my life," she said in softly accented
English. "That part of my life is gone. It happened forty years ago. I put that
story away long ago, as far as I'm concerned." Annemarie made it plain she
wanted the conversation to end, and for me to leave her alone. But I asked
her one more question: How should I deal with the matter of Jack Coffelt in
relation to her life story?

"That's up to you—you're the author."

Robert Hoyt vaguely recalled meeting Annemarie Hoffman in Kansas at
a Jack Coffelt gathering—"a tall blonde in a stunning blue dress." Records at
the University of Kansas show that Annemarie was enrolled as a freshman
in 1964 at the College of Liberal Arts and Sciences and lived in a dorm on
Engel Road in Lawrence, just around the corner from Coffelt's place at the
Meadowbrook Apartments. It seems likely that she and Coffelt would have
known each other in Kansas. Robert Hoyt and other Coffelt acquaintances
recall the ex-con speaking of Annemarie on several occasions. How close
were Annemarie Hoffman and Jack Coffelt? Annemarie may have dropped
a clue in an article that was first published in 1983 in an obscure, now
defunct publication, *Las Vegan Magazine*. The author of the article was
Byron H. Brown, son of James Brown, an ex-con who had been Coffelt's
best friend at the federal penitentiary in Atlanta.

"I do everything Jack orders," Byron Brown quoted Annemarie as
saying. "Whatever he tells me to do I do." (Although Annemarie's name was
not used in the article, Brown's references clearly identify her to insiders as
Annemarie Hoffman.) Jack Coffelt also told Byron Brown, "I never loved

anyone like I loved her." Tough-guy Coffelt said this, according to Brown, "as tears welled up in his eyes."

Following the 1964 academic year at the University of Kansas, Annemarie Hoffman moved to Washington, D.C., where Jack Coffelt had already shifted his base of operations.

Just as Coffelt had proven himself adroit at socializing with Lawrence's in-crowd, he now found himself moving in the "highest circles" of Washington's political and government elite. According to Byron Brown, Coffelt even attended President Lyndon Johnson's inaugural ball in 1965.

Brown also said that he spoke with witnesses who saw FBI director J. Edgar Hoover "throw a warm and friendly bear hug" around Coffelt at a party; he believed that Coffelt was working "both sides of the fence, shrewdly and with finesse," pulling off scams and cons while serving as a police informant. Coffelt himself claimed to be a Mafia bagman, but the story could be another of his tales meant to pump up his reputation.

As Jack Coffelt solidified his connections in the Washington cocktail party circuit, he was introduced to Robert Todd Lincoln Beckwith. The scam artist in Coffelt must have instantly recognized Bob Beckwith as the perfect mark: rich widower, childless, infirm with Parkinson's disease, and none too swift. They became drinking buddies, and Coffelt set about making himself indispensable to the Lincoln heir. He had learned physical therapy in prison, and he applied his skills to Beckwith's aching body. An entranced Beckwith hired him as his chauffeur, handyman, and general factotum. Coffelt drove Beckwith's souped-up Mustang, and in December 1965, Beckwith opened a joint checking account with Coffelt at the Bank of Middlesex in Urbanna, Virginia. Beckwith opened a second joint checking account with Coffelt just after New Year's Day 1967, at the First National Bank of Washington on G Street, where Beckwith had been banking since 1931.

Beckwith was more than three decades older than Annemarie Hoffman when they met. They married on November 6, 1967, in Hartfield, Virginia, the county seat of Middlesex County. That same month, Beckwith added Annemarie's name to the joint checking account he shared with Jack Coffelt at the Bank of Middlesex in Urbana. Nobody was more shocked than Beckwith's long-time companion, Maggie Fristoe. Maggie was out, and the "German girl" was the new Mrs. Robert Todd Lincoln Beckwith.

"I'm telling you, it was like a soap opera," said Maggie Fristoe's daughter, Lenora Hoverson. "Dysfunctional stuff. Crazy stuff."

Annemarie Hoffman, now Annemarie Beckwith, became a United States citizen in January 1968 and enrolled at the College of William and Mary in Williamsburg, from which three United States presidents— Thomas Jefferson, James Monroe, and John Tyler—had received degrees. Now the highly regarded institution was educating the bride of Abraham Lincoln's great-grandson. Beckwith paid for an off-campus room for Annemarie at the Heritage Inn hotel; she went to classes during the week and returned to Woodstock on weekends. Winter passed and then came spring. Annemarie was wrapping up her first semester when, in May 1968, Bob Beckwith saw an envelope addressed to his wife. He opened it and found a medical report inside.

Annemarie was pregnant.

In the past, Beckwith had never expressed much enthusiasm for having children, which may explain why he chose as his first wife Hazel Wilson, who was twenty years his senior. Over time he had come to accept the fact that the Lincoln bloodline would die out upon his death and the death of his sister, Peggy Beckwith, and cousin, Lincoln Isham. Just seven months before he married Annemarie, he told a reporter for the *Chicago Tribune* that it was not an eventuality that particularly irked him. He explained that he was not a man preoccupied with "looking back." In fact, he could not really recall ever asking his grandfather, Robert Lincoln, about Abraham Lincoln. But now the Lincoln heir was holding in his hands a medical report indicating that his bride of seven months was pregnant. Her due date was October, which meant conception had taken place in February, four months into the marriage.

As Beckwith pondered this unexpected state of affairs, he realized that he had better inform his lawyers of the strange and perplexing fact that at age sixty-seven he was to be a father for the first time. He went to Washington, and his first stop was the office of Frost & Towers, the law firm that had represented the interests of the Lincoln family since 1923. Robert Lincoln had first met Norman Frost and Frederic Towers when they were young law students clerking at the white-shoe firm of McKenney & Flannery. When they started their own firm, he had signed on as their first important client. He had the utmost respect for the men, and appreciated their social company as well. All three were avid golfers. Lincoln even built a cottage for Frost and Towers on the grounds of Hildene so they would have a place to stay in Vermont. Towers died in 1959. Frost was still senior partner at the firm, frail at age seventy, but still sharp and ably assisted by his colleague John A. Beck, who specialized in estate issues and corporate litigation.

It was not unusual to see Bob Beckwith at the firm. "He was always coming into the office," John Beck said. The year before Beckwith had notified the lawyers that he was "getting married to this young girl." Now, he was back with an update—his young bride was pregnant.

"That kind of got our attention," Beck recalled. His male vanity in full bloom, Bob Beckwith had made the announcement with a smug self-righteousness that those present found rather sad. Norman Frost was aghast. Frost, whose daughter happened to be married to the great-grandson of President Rutherford B. Hayes, knew the dysfunction of the Lincoln descendants better than anyone. He was genuinely troubled by Beckwith's revelation. Frost was the executor of the Mary Harlan Lincoln Testamentary Trust, which had been set up at her death in 1937, and he was aware of what was at stake. The trust, which had grown to almost six million dollars, was to provide for Mary Harlan Lincoln's daughters, Mamie and Jessie, and their children, Lincoln, Peggy, and Bob. If the three Lincoln grandchildren died without blood heirs, the trust would terminate with the death of the last Lincoln, and the principal would be distributed to three institutions: Iowa Wesleyan College, the Red Cross, and the Christian Science Church.

Frost, in his role as executor of the trust, now raised a delicate matter with Beckwith. Frost was aware that in 1962 Beckwith had been hospitalized for an enlargement of his prostate gland and had had a prostatectomy, resulting in the removal of his prostate. Part of the procedure had involved undergoing a vasectomy, standard practice to reduce the risk of infection. The operation had rendered Beckwith sterile. Had Beckwith deluded himself into believing that he could be the father of the child Annemarie was carrying? Although he had publicly expressed indifference to the fact that he was childless, one lawyer close to Annemarie Hoffman said, "I think Beckwith wanted an heir." But another source close to Bob Beckwith said the Lincoln heir had never for a moment thought he was the father. In any event, Frost and his colleague John Beck were there to set Beckwith straight. Beckwith agreed to make an appointment with his urologist, Dr. Hamilton Dorman. X-rays and a physical specimen were taken, and indeed, Beckwith was found to be "completely sterile." In his doctor's opinion, he could not be the father of the child.

Back at Woodstock Farms, Beckwith confronted his wife. According to his account, Annemarie admitted that he was not the father, but she "refused" to say who was. Revenge was swift. Jack Coffelt was fired as Beckwith's chauffeur, and on May 24, 1968, the joint account Coffelt shared with Annemarie and Beckwith at the bank in Urbana was closed. Coffelt was evicted from the property. Annemarie was next to go. Beckwith's lawyer drew up a document, entitled "Agreement," requiring that Annemarie list the baby's father as "John Doe" or "Father Unknown" on the birth certificate. In return, Beckwith agreed to pay the costs of Annemarie's hospitalization, plus $7,500 to make her go away. Annemarie also agreed to make no claim against the Lincoln/Beckwith estate.

Annemarie was at a crossroads. She was pregnant, and, she said, destitute. She signed the document in September, but would later maintain that she was a victim of "fraud and duress." She accused Beckwith of "taking advantage" of her pregnant condition because he knew that she needed the money to pay her medical expenses. She later denied making any admission to Beckwith that he was not the father.

The next thing she knew, Annemarie was evicted from the farm—"locked out," she said. She moved back to the Heritage Inn in Williamsburg. Her mother, Elizabeth Hoffman, flew in from Germany to help out. Annemarie tried to return to Woodstock on several occasions, but she said Beckwith refused to let her past the front door. She lived in room 3B at the Heritage Inn until she went into labor, on October 13, 1968. Fourteen hours later, at Williamsburg Community Hospital, the baby was born. It was a healthy boy, weighing seven pounds, ten-and-a-half ounces. Despite her signature on the agreement, Annemarie gave him the noble name of Timothy Lincoln Beckwith, and listed the baby's father as Robert Todd Lincoln Beckwith.

Even before Annemarie's release from Williamsburg Community Hospital, Beck and the other lawyers were taking steps to protect the interests of the Mary Harlan Lincoln Testamentary Trust.

"I was practically on the doorsteps of the hospital when the child was born," John Beck said. Beck filed a lawsuit in Williamsburg seeking a declaratory judgment establishing that Timothy Lincoln Beckwith was not the son of Bob Beckwith and demanding that a blood test be conducted on the infant. The lawsuit was filed on behalf of the trust. Beckwith was not a named plaintiff.

"He had no control over the trust," Beck said of Bob Beckwith. "The trustees had the responsibility."

Beck went before Judge Robert Armistead of the Ninth Judicial Circuit of Virginia. At the time, Armistead was presiding over a high-profile murder trial, but he took the time to read the legal papers John Beck had filed, and quickly appreciated the historical importance of the case. "He sniffed this out the minute it came in," said one lawyer involved in the litigation. Beck walked into Armistead's private chambers and took a seat as the judge looked over the court filings. On the wall behind the judge's desk hung a painting of General Robert E. Lee astride Traveller, the Confederate commander's celebrated horse. Beck was taken aback by it. Armistead, having observed Beck's reaction, told him that he was the grandson of a Confederate war hero, General Lewis Armistead, who was killed at Gettysburg. Judge Armistead added that, long after the war, when the Lincoln penny was introduced into circulation, in 1909, General Armistead's widow—Judge Armistead's grandmother—would sit in her rocking chair, lay all the coins in her possession on her apron, and irritably toss away the Lincoln pennies as if they were moldy peanuts. As the judge related this family history, John Beck could only wonder at the strange twist of fate that had dropped the Lincoln trust-fund lawsuit into Armistead's lap. Here was a chance to bastardize the possibly sole living descendant of Abraham Lincoln, Beck thought. But he found Armistead to be a wise and sincere judge.

The lawsuit, under the title, *Norman B. Frost v. Timothy Lincoln Beckwith, Annemarie Hoffman Beckwith, et al.*, was put on the court docket, and sworn depositions were taken from the involved parties.

What happened next brought shame to the House of Lincoln.

It started with rumors of questionable activities at Woodstock Farms.

"There were wild events taking place at Woodstock," said a source who has requested anonymity. "This was not a tranquil place. There was a lot of stuff going on." When I asked for details, my source tactfully responded, "Let's put it this way. The folks there weren't sitting around having tea."

Judge Armistead found the testimony so salacious that he ordered all depositions sealed because he did not want Beckwith or the Lincoln family to face the ordeal of public humiliation. Portions of that testimony can now be revealed for the first time.

The sexual revolution was then in full swing, and Bob Beckwith seemed to be enjoying a hedonistic lifestyle in that era of free love and counterculture. One source described his tight little social circle as participating in what can only be described as "modern-day Roman orgies."

"He was a dirty old man," the source said of Beckwith. "He was so perverted. He'd get his jollies off watching other people have sex." Beckwith was cagey in his testimony when he was deposed, according to sources who have read the sealed transcripts. "Beckwith didn't give up much," said a source, "but what he said was titillating." Neither was Jack Coffelt very forthcoming in his testimony, though the wily ex-convict was described as a "fully engaged participant" in the debauchery at Woodstock Farms. A woman who was deposed was also said to be coy when she was asked to detail the goings-on at Woodstock.

"Did you ever engage in abnormal sexual activities?" she was asked.

"Define abnormal for me," was her answer.

Most of the revelry took place in Beckwith's master bedroom, which was dominated by a portrait of Abraham Lincoln. The sexually charged frolics also went on in Beckwith's apartment at the swank Broadmoor on Connecticut Avenue NW in Washington (where he had moved after he had sold his house in Silver Spring, Maryland, following the death of his first wife, Hazel). Apartment 108 was filled with historical relics from Beckwith's illustrious family, including photographs of his grandfather Robert Lincoln and his mother Jessie. There was also the bust of Abraham Lincoln—a gift from the people of Illinois given to Beckwith when the Illinois Pavilion at the New York world's fair closed in 1965. Surrounded by all of this family legacy, Beckwith committed acts that one source with access to the depositions said were unsettling to say the least.

Was Beckwith the perverted ringmaster, or a pawn, under the sway of Jack Coffelt? The issue became important in the looming court battle over the future disbursement of the Mary Harlan Lincoln trust. "Annemarie's side wanted to establish a record to bolster the idea that Bob Beckwith could have been Timothy's father," said one lawyer involved in the litigation. "They wanted to get to the bottom of the facts behind the birth of the baby and cloak the baby with a presumption of legitimacy." To that end, testimony was obtained establishing that even given Beckwith's age and infirmities, he still had the physical stamina to take part in sexual activities. One major legal hurdle that had to be dealt with was the question of Beckwith's vasectomy. Was it possible that Beckwith had experienced a spontaneous regeneration of the vasa deferentia tubes in the years following his vasectomy? Highly improbable, came the answer from the medical experts, but it was known to happen, although the odds were described as infinitesimal.

Everyone wanted to speak to Annemarie Beckwith and obtain her sworn testimony on the record, but she was not talking. Annemarie was discharged from the hospital October 19, five days after giving birth to Timothy. Six weeks later, she bolted. She and the baby left the United States, reportedly by ocean liner, heading for West Germany. She later claimed that she went into exile because Beckwith had "destroyed her happiness" and rendered her life "so miserable and unendurable" that she was compelled to return to her family in Germany.

Students of history may catch the irony. Annemarie was living in exile with her child, in Germany of all places, just as Mary Todd Lincoln had gone into exile in Germany with her son Tad, in 1868. Annemarie's departure, it should be pointed out, came on the eve of her deposition, and a blood test for Timothy. In the years before the availability of DNA testing, the blood of the child and the two parents had to be obtained to establish paternity. "I never got either," Beck said, referring to Annemarie's deposition and the blood test.

Jack Coffelt was also besieged, and his entire criminal background exposed. John Beck found Coffelt to be an interesting rogue—"a shrewd guy and a real con man. A very good con man, and a very violent guy."

Meanwhile, in a separate action, Bob Beckwith filed for divorce from Annemarie, on grounds of adultery. He asked the court to rule that he could not be Timothy's father. From West Germany, Annemarie countersued, saying it was Beckwith who was the adulterer. She was keeping a low profile in West Berlin, raising Timothy, and moving around, living at various times in Switzerland, Austria, and Italy. Jack Coffelt told the writer Byron Brown that he was "constantly" sending money to Annemarie, and in the process, "draining" his own bank account. Coffelt hired the Memphis lawyer Robert Dobbs to represent him. Dobbs was a well-regarded criminal defense attorney and a trusted Coffelt confidant of twenty years. Dobbs had pulled Coffelt out of several scrapes with the law in the past, and the two men shared lawyer-client privilege, giving Coffelt the confidence that he could tell Dobbs everything.

Coffelt went to Memphis and handed Dobbs what was surely the most attention-grabbing retainer of the lawyer's career—a carved ivory riding crop that had been a gift from the emperor of Japan to President Lincoln, and a gold pocket watch and fob once owned by President Lincoln. The relics had been passed down through the generations of Lincoln descendants until they had fallen into Coffelt's hands. "Jack gave me these as payment for my legal services," Dobbs said; he kept the treasured antiques in the safe in his Memphis office.

One day, when Dobbs learned that his grandson, Brian, then in the second grade, was studying Abraham Lincoln in school, he took the day off from work to take the Lincoln riding crop and watch and fob to show-and-tell for Brian's class. "Dad was old school, American pie," said Dobbs's daughter Debbie. It meant something to have these artifacts in his possession, she said. Surely, the students in young Brian's second-grade class would have been astonished to learn the curious route whereby these historical Abraham Lincoln treasures had come into the possession of a Tennessee criminal defense attorney.

Coffelt, in his ever-present paranoia, was at the end of his rope. Even Dobbs felt uneasy about the case. He told Coffelt in a letter, "I think it would be ill-advised to meet with you at this time unless we could be absolutely certain that you were not being followed." Dobbs closed with a chilling demand: *"Burn this letter."* Instead, Coffelt tucked the letter away in a cookbook. Later, apparently having forgotten the letter was still in the book, he gave it away as a gift. Byron Brown came upon it in 1983, and when he showed it to Dobbs, the wily lawyer had a good laugh, but never disputed its authenticity. "We never put much in writing to each other," he said.

As the Beckwith divorce wound its way through the courts, Annemarie Hoffman Beckwith hired a fine lawyer to defend her. Thomas Penfield Jackson, a graduate of Dartmouth College and Harvard Law School, found Annemarie to be an attractive and sympathetic client. "She was a stranger in a foreign land, and she needed help," Jackson said of Annemarie. From Jackson's standpoint, Annemarie had been thrown into the vortex of the American court system by the strong-arm tactics of the Lincoln family's legal machine. It triggered his sense of ire. As he got to know the facts of the case, he formed the opinion that it was really Annemarie, and not Bob Beckwith, who was the victim. Jackson assigned Patricia Gurne, one of his young associates, as cocounsel. Like Jackson, Gurne came to pity Annemarie. "I felt really sorry for her. She had really been taken advantage of. This was not a matter of a gold digger at work." One of Gurne's assignments was to study up on the science of vasectomy, as Bob Beckwith's capacity to sire a child was certain to be a critical issue.

On July 12, 1976, in Washington, D.C., Superior Court, *Beckwith v. Beckwith* finally came to trial, a full seven years after the couple had split up. The presiding judge in the divorce case was Joseph Ryan. From day one Jackson and Gurne, Annemarie's lawyers, found themselves the underdogs. For one thing, Annemarie was a no-show. She refused to come to court, which incensed Judge Ryan. "He was just irascible," Patricia Gurne said of the judge. Ryan, a devout Catholic, evidently was deeply offended by the prurient evidence in the case, and took out most of his irritation on Jackson. He delayed the trial a week and gave Jackson until July 19 to produce his client, who was still believed to be living in Europe with her son Timothy, now seven years old. Ryan threatened to hold Annemarie in contempt if she and Timothy failed to take the blood test he had previously ordered.

"A trial is a search for truth," Judge Ryan said. "The basic truth to be proved or disproved here involves the parentage of the child. For what appears to be spurious reasons," he said, Annemarie Beckwith was avoiding a blood test for herself and Timothy, "which would aid the court in arriving at the truth."

Elizabeth R. Young represented Bob Beckwith. She was gray-haired and intense, "a bit of an oddball," in the opinion of one of her former adversaries, with a rigid personality and zero sense of humor. Young had known Beckwith for more than forty years. As a young lawyer fresh out of George Washington University's School of Law, she had even witnessed Mary Harlan Lincoln sign her last will and testament, in 1936. But she said that she had never once discussed his Lincoln forbears with Bob Beckwith. "Socially, it's not done," she said, "and in business I talked about what I was paid to talk about." Young came to trial with a solid case. Plus she had one advantage over the other side—a client who was physically present in court. She urged Judge Ryan to sanction Annemarie for refusing to comply with the court-ordered blood tests. "That's what I'm working on right now," she told reporters covering the trial, "to try to find out what we can do."

When the case resumed on July 19, once again Annemarie Beckwith failed to appear. An exasperated Judge Ryan accused the woman of "trifling with this court's jurisdiction." Annemarie's lawyers submitted an affidavit from her in which she claimed that her absence was due to her fear for Timothy's safety. She also said she had been living in Italy in April 1976 when the news broke that Judge Ryan had ordered her and Timothy to take blood tests.

"An acquaintance in Berlin telephoned me to tell me that newspaper articles said Timothy would be a millionaire. . . . Shortly thereafter my residence and place of employment were besieged by representatives of the press wanting interviews with and photographs of me and my son. Anonymous threats to kidnap my son for ransom were telephoned to my apartment. To avoid the publicity and constant harassment, I was forced to leave my employment and place of residence and because of fears for my son's safety I left Europe."

Annemarie and Timothy had flown to the United States and were now living somewhere in Florida, but she was still defying the court and refusing to submit her son to a blood test. She argued that the identity of Timothy's father should not be linked to the divorce proceedings. "I still believe my son should not be involved in any way in this suit between me and my husband. I am concerned for his safety and wish to protect him from publicity," she said in an affidavit. Alluding to the status of the Mary Harlan Lincoln trust fund, Annemarie said she had every right to "protect my son's interests . . . and to protect my own similar interests." Jackson sought to frame Annemarie's disobedience in the context of Timothy's right to privacy, but Judge Ryan was not buying it: he found Annemarie in contempt, in abstentia.

Meanwhile, testimony began in the divorce proceedings. Bob Beckwith was seventy-two years old and in an advanced stage of Parkinson's disease when he was called to the stand. A century before, Mary Todd Lincoln had faced the public ignominy of a trial that ensured history would forever brand her insane. Now her great-grandson was compelled to testify in open court about marital infidelity and his own sexual impotence. Spectators in the courtroom watched uncomfortably as Beckwith physically struggled to take the stand. "He could barely speak—he was sort of pathetic," recalled Gurne. "I remember thinking it was a sad end to the last descendant of one of America's greatest heroes." Beckwith spoke in his halting stutter that could barely be understood, and Gurne had to ask him twice to repeat his name. His testimony was strictly limited. He said he and Annemarie had been married in 1967. He said Annemarie was a native of West Germany. Beckwith acknowledged that it had not been much of a marriage.

"Subsequent to your marriage to the defendant, did you and she live at Woodstock Farms, in Middlesex County, Virginia?"

"No," Beckwith responded. "She lived in Williamsburg, Virginia. I lived in Washington, D.C. We spent brief periods together at Woodstock."

Beckwith was asked to identify a separation agreement that he and Annemarie had signed in 1968, in which his wife acknowledged that, "without the knowledge or consent [of Beckwith] she became pregnant by [another] man."

Beckwith was followed to the stand by his urologist, Dr. Parker Sturgis

Dorman, who testified that his brother, Dr. Hamilton Dorman, had performed a vasectomy on Beckwith in 1962, when he underwent the prostate operation. He said X-rays taken in 1968, the year Annemarie became pregnant, showed that the vasectomy was still effective. In other words, said Dorman, Beckwith was "sterilized in 1962 and has been sterile since that time." Beckwith's internist, Dr. Richard Sullivan, was the next witness. He had been treating Beckwith since 1957. He said in open court that samples taken from Beckwith established beyond doubt that Beckwith was sterile. Both Dorman and Sullivan agreed that Bob Beckwith could not have fathered Timothy Beckwith.

Judge Ryan adjourned the trial for two weeks. On August 4, testimony resumed with the appearance of Dr. Hamilton Dorman, who told how Beckwith had come to him when Annemarie was six months pregnant and asked whether he was capable of siring a child. Dorman said he had conducted tests that determined Beckwith was sterile. "Mr. Beckwith was completely sterile from the time of his operation in '62 to '68, when he came back to me."

One month after testimony concluded, Judge Ryan issued his decision. Bob Beckwith was granted a divorce on grounds of adultery. Judge Ryan said "clear and convincing" evidence established that Beckwith could not be Timothy's father. The boy, Ryan said, was the product of an "adulterous relationship."

Thomas Penfield Jackson filed an appeal, arguing before the District of Columbia Court of Appeals that even if Bob Beckwith was not Timothy's biological father, it did not necessarily mean that Annemarie had committed adultery. What if Annemarie had been "forced" to have relations with another man? What if she had been artificially inseminated? One theory the defense team put out was that "Beckwith arranged and insisted Annemarie go to bed with a surrogate. He wanted a son." But the appeals court upheld Judge Ryan's decision, ruling, "circumstantial evidence can be used to prove adultery." Moreover, the court said no evidence was presented at the trial proving that Annemarie had signed her separation agreement with Beckwith under duress, as she claimed she had.

"In this case, the evidence that Mr. Beckwith was incapable of procreation in 1968, and Mrs. Beckwith's admission that her son had been fathered by someone other than her husband are more than sufficient to support the trial court's finding of adultery."

Although Jackson lost the case, he emerged victorious on one critical point. The appeals court ruled that the issue of Timothy's legitimacy applied to the divorce only and should have no bearing on the ultimate question of whether the boy could one day stake claim to the Mary Harlan Lincoln Testamentary Trust. That matter, the court determined, would have to be decided in a separate action. For Jackson, who would go on to be appointed to the federal bench by President Ronald Reagan in 1982, it was an important concession, ensuring that the "interests of the child" were protected in future litigation involving the disbursement of the Lincoln trust fund.

Now all John Beck could do was wait. The lawyer who represented the Mary Harlan Lincoln trust knew that at some point he would be hearing from all the interested parties.

"We had the money, and they had to come to us to get it," he said.

One day Beck was in his office when his secretary said that Jack Coffelt was there to see him. Beck could not believe it. He instructed the secretary to inform Coffelt that it would be inappropriate for them to have any contact. But through the secretary, Coffelt assured Beck that he was there on another matter having nothing to do with the Lincolns. Beck reluctantly agreed to let the ex-con into his office. Coffelt poured on the charm. He had an amusing story to relate. He said he had just returned from visiting his sister Alvaretta, and it turned out that Alvaretta and John Beck had attended grade school together back in Oklahoma. Beck had a good laugh over that one. He found Coffelt to be a "shrewd guy," and pleasant company, but he was under no illusions about the man's capacity for violence or his role in what Beck believed to be an "attempt to defraud the trust." Beck showed Coffelt the door.

Several years later, Beck received an unexpected call from the FBI. A federal agent was inquiring about D. B. Cooper, the notorious skyjacker who, in 1971, had jumped out of a plane with two hundred thousand dollars in extorted cash, never to be seen again. D. B. Cooper was part of American folklore, the lone wolf who had stuck it to the government. Could it be at all possible, the agent speculated, that Jack Coffelt and D. B. Cooper were the same man?

25

The Cooper Connection

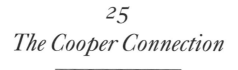

THE LAST OF the Lincolns were dying off. Lincoln Isham passed away on September 1, 1971, in a Bennington, Vermont, hospital at age seventy-nine. He left an estate of $1.5 million, about one-third of which went to his stepdaughter, Frances Mantley. An additional $635,000 went to four longtime employees, and the rest to various charities, including the Red Cross and the Salvation Army. A good neighbor to the end, Isham requested that, to preserve the character of the town, his neighbors in Dorset be offered first crack at purchasing his twenty-two acres of property.

Peggy Beckwith outlived her cousin Linc by four years. She died of colon cancer on July 10, 1975, at the age seventy-six. Obstinate to the end, she had been feeling ill for several years but kept putting off seeing a doctor. She was cremated, and her ashes spread over the promontory near the formal gardens that overlooked her cherished Hildene.

Her will is an interesting document, pure Peggy Beckwith—her dying wishes expressed in exacting detail. She left her brother Bob Beckwith her personal papers and property and all her Lincoln relics, which she never had any use for anyway, once saying, "Why should anybody be interested in all this old stuff we've got around the house?" To Bob's stepdaughter, Doris Crans, whose debutante ball in 1940 Peggy had followed so assiduously, she left the Mary Todd Lincoln bridal lace that Doris had worn at her wedding. The Christian Science Church got the biggest prize of all—Hildene, all four hundred acres of it, including the twenty-four room Georgian revival mansion known as the "Big House," on the condition that the estate be preserved forever "as now laid out." Peggy wanted Hildene to stand for all time as a memorial to her grandparents and her mother, who had designed the breathtaking English gardens. The grounds were extraordinary, but the house was another matter. A private appraisal was conducted and the "Big House" was valued at just one hundred thousand dollars, shockingly low even by 1975 standards. Decades of neglect had finally caught up with Hildene. The appraiser was appalled at what he saw—"seriously damaged," went one comment in his report.

Bob Beckwith came up from Virginia to settle Peggy's estate and inspect and inventory the relics and personal items that had been left to him in her will. There were thirty-five trunks to go through, filled with Peggy's childhood toys, old cameras and photographic equipment, fishing gear, firearms, surveying equipment, and many other interesting artifacts. Beckwith made it known that, in keeping with Lincoln family tradition, Peggy had expressed a desire to have her personal papers burned, and this was carried out.

Peggy's death did have one surprising outcome: For the first time, a Lincoln historian was granted permission to go through all of Hildene's twenty-four rooms in search of historically significant documents. James Hickey, curator of the Lincoln collection at the Illinois State Historical Library in Springfield, was a farm boy from central Illinois who had gotten to know Bob Beckwith during the 1965 centennial observance of the Civil War. "Their personalities meshed," said Hickey's wife, Betty. "They took to each other." Heaven for Hickey was digging through attics, hunting for historical records.

The Hickeys flew to Washington to pick up Beckwith, and there they met Maggie Fristoe, again Beckwith's companion, following his ruinous marriage to Annemarie Hoffman. Maggie stayed behind while Beckwith and the Hickeys flew on to Albany and then drove the two hours to Hildene in Vermont. The date was April 19, 1977. As Hildene came into view, Betty Hickey was awestruck. "But it was like a beautiful woman you saw from a distance. The closer you got the more flaws you saw." She found Beckwith to be a handful. His crankiness, along with his serious medical issues, made dealing with him a challenge. He was also an incurable flirt, even at his advanced age, and held Betty's hand whenever he got the chance.

Beckwith refused to stay overnight at Hildene. He checked into his favorite place in nearby Manchester, the Colburn House, a charming bed-and-breakfast. The Hickeys found a room at a cheaper motel down the road. Mornings, they would pick up Beckwith and head off to Hildene to explore the Big House room by room. Betty Hickey lent a hand keeping Beckwith fed, but he was finding the experience draining, and would only stay a few hours in the morning before he insisted on being driven back to the Colburn House.

"He was diabetic," Betty said. "He needed pick-me-ups. He'd have to have a cookie or crackers or cheese or he'd go to sleep." At Hildene, she kept a kettle on the stove for tea and made sure the water was always hot.

The discovery came on the third day.

Betty was in the attic going through trunks, sorting out Mary Harlan Lincoln's clothes and taking photographs so that everything could be itemized for the lawyers and the archives. There was a vast amount of material to examine, some sixty-nine trunks in the attic alone, plus several thousand books from Robert Lincoln's personal collection. She was in the midst of this daunting task when she heard her husband come up the stairs.

"I found them," a breathless Hickey told his wife. He seemed genuinely thrilled. Betty followed him down to the second floor, to the study where Robert Lincoln had once worked. Outside the room was a staircase, and angled under the staircase was a door that opened "like a cupboard." It was, Betty realized, "a secret door" with a double lock. She looked inside and saw what her husband had just discovered—a bundle of documents, paperwork and twenty-five letters written by Mary Todd Lincoln to her daughter-in-law, Mary Harlan Lincoln, neatly tied with a ribbon and labeled "MTL Insanity File." It was evidence of his problems with his mother that Robert Lincoln had accumulated over the years.

"It was an amazing moment," Betty said. The historical importance of the find was obvious. James Hickey telephoned Peggy Beckwith's estate attorney in Manchester and asked him to come right over and verify the discovery. Meanwhile, Hickey had to convince Beckwith and the Lincoln family lawyer, Elizabeth Young, that the Insanity File should be released to the public. Elizabeth Young was concerned. She had once warned Hickey, "You know, the Lincolns are very private people, and you're getting a little too much into their privacy."

Bob Beckwith weighed his options. One way to go, he acknowledged, was to "destroy the file." But he finally rejected this course of action. There had to be a reason why his grandfather had taken such extraordinary steps to preserve the Insanity File, and Beckwith understood that he had to respect that memory. "I believe he did so knowing that in the future its contents should be made known," Beckwith said of Robert Lincoln.

Under Hickey's guidance, Beckwith turned over the Insanity File to two highly regarded Lincoln scholars, Mark E. Neely Jr. and R. Gerald

McMurtry. Imagine their shock when Neely and McMurtry were invited to James and Betty Hickey's farmhouse in central Illinois, and over scotch, before dinner, Hickey showed them the MTL Insanity File. Between them, the two scholars had worked in the Lincoln field for sixty years, and they had never seen anything like this extraordinary cache. Their book, *The Insanity File: The Case of Mary Todd Lincoln*, was published in 1986, and Beckwith even contributed a short foreword in which he explained his motivation for allowing the material to be published. He tried to strike a diplomatic balance between his two warring ancestors. "I believe that because of this file history will treat my great-grandmother Mary Todd Lincoln more kindly in regard to this very disturbing period of her life and most of all recognize that my grandfather acted in the best possible way towards his mother."

IN 1983, A TWO-PART article appeared in *Las Vegan Magazine*, under the headline, THE DISCOVERY OF D. B. COOPER. It was written by Byron Brown, a young journalist who had been a high school student when he encountered Jack Coffelt for the first time. The article generated very little attention when it was published, and its connection to the Lincoln trust fund scandal is made for the first time in this book.

Byron's account began in June of 1974. He was living in Georgia and thinking about college when his father, James Brown, told him that he was taking a camping trip to the Cascade Mountains of Oregon with an old buddy of his. Would Byron like to join them? Byron said sure. Father and son loaded up the family camper with outdoor gear and took off for the West Coast. But first, they had a stop to make, a thousand miles along their route, in Missouri, where they were to pick up a man named Jack Coffelt. They arrived in Joplin, Missouri, just as night was falling, and checked into a seedy motel on the outskirts of town where the Browns took a room for the night. Coffelt met them there. The room was dimly lit. Coffelt sat on a chair looking straight at Byron. He seemed like a hard case, a dangerous gangster type seemingly from another era.

Byron was aware that his father knew some tough customers. James Brown had been a second lieutenant in the Army Air Force during World War II when he got into the worst jam of his life and was court-martialed for rape. Byron never really knew the details of what had happened. Though James always maintained his innocence, he was convicted, given a life sentence and sent to the federal penitentiary in Atlanta.

Brown had been a newspaper reporter before the war, and was assigned to work on the prison newspaper. That is how he met Jack Coffelt, who was operating the printing press. The two convicts became good friends. Coffelt admired Brown's mind, and together they worked on an autobiographical novel Coffelt was writing, *Cleave the Liquid Sky*. Certain chapters of the original draft of *Cleave the Liquid Sky* had to be written on toilet paper because writing paper was so scarce in the prison. It was a raw and compelling coming-of-age story, but it never found a publisher. There are one or two copies of the manuscript that remain in private hands.

Brown was paroled in 1952 after serving eight years, and proceeded to get his life together. He became a safety engineer for the aerospace industry, married a woman he met in church, and had three children. Meanwhile, Coffelt finished out his federal term at Leavenworth, and after his release, managed to get himself hired by the Lincoln heir, Bob Beckwith, for what Coffelt must have hoped would be the sting of a lifetime. Then everything went bust, and he was fending off a lot of questions about his role in the Lincoln family trust fund scandal.

Coffelt was now sitting in this squalid motel room, forlorn and full of rage. To Byron Brown, there was not much charm about this guy; he was just a mean, dispirited ex-con. What happened next shocked the high school student: Coffelt dropped his pants and hoisted his boxer shorts all the way up his thighs. His legs were "horribly discolored," Byron said, "purple and yellowish bruises blending with the pale skin." Coffelt's face hardened. "Byron, you remember that fella that skyjacked that airplane out in Oregon a few years back? Cooper. D. B. Cooper. You remember him?"

THREE YEARS EARLIER, on Thanksgiving Eve, November 24, 1971, a passenger named Dan Cooper walked up to the Northwest Airlines counter at Portland International Airport and asked about the next plane to Seattle. He paid for a one-way ticket with a twenty-dollar bill. Carrying an attaché case and wearing wraparound dark glasses, Cooper boarded Flight 305, took his seat in the last row, in seat 18-C, and started chain-smoking from a pack of Raleigh filter tips.

As the Boeing 727 taxied from the terminal, Cooper leaned forward and handed stewardess Florence Schaffner a note. Florence, twenty-three, was seated across the aisle from him, preparing for takeoff. Businessmen frequently hit on her, and Florence assumed the passenger in 18-C was another jerk passing her a note to tell her how pretty she looked and ask her out. She stuffed the note in her purse without looking at it. The plane was accelerating down the runway when Cooper leaned across the aisle, and, in a low and raspy voice said, in Florence's ear, "Miss, you'd better look at that note. I have a bomb." She pulled out the note. Written with a felt pen, in capital letters, it read: I HAVE A BOMB IN MY BRIEFCASE. I WANT YOU TO SIT BESIDE ME. Florence took the empty seat next to Cooper. He told her that when the plane landed in Seattle, he wanted two hundred thousand dollars cash and four parachutes, all by 5:00 P.M. "Tell your captain I am taking charge of this plane. These are my demands. Let him read them, and then bring this note back to me. Understand? I want it back."

Florence went into the cockpit and showed the captain and copilot the note. Captain William Scott radioed Northwest Flight Operations that his plane had been hijacked, and relayed Cooper's demands. The pilot was instructed to tell Florence Schaffner to return to her seat and engage Cooper in conversation. Florence sat down next to Cooper and asked to see the bomb. Cooper opened his attaché case and showed her a bundle of red sticks that looked like dynamite, tied together with a tangle of wires and a single battery. As the Boeing 727 circled over Seattle, Cooper ordered a bourbon and water. He paid for the two-dollar drink with a twenty-dollar bill, and, with an air of bravado, told the stewardess to keep the change. This guy had panache, thought Florence, and refused the tip.

On the ground, airline executives and the FBI analyzed the crisis and tried to figure out a course of action. They ordered the crew to cooperate with Cooper in every way. The first description of the hijacker was radioed from Flight 305: "Around 6 feet 1 inch, black hair, age about 50, weight 170 pounds." The news of the skyjacking was flashed across America. A UPI report, relying on a police source, erroneously identified the hijacker as D. B. Cooper. The name, with what one FBI agent would call its "magical combination" of initials, stuck. Dan Cooper was now and forevermore D. B. Cooper.

When the Boeing aircraft landed in Seattle, the plane was refueled. Four parachutes, and a knapsack containing two hundred thousand dollars—ten thousand twenty-dollar bills—were brought aboard. At that point, Cooper allowed the thirty-six passengers to disembark from the plane. As the last passenger filed out, one of the stewardesses called out, "Have a nice Thanksgiving." Cooper released Florence Schaffner and one other stewardess. A third stewardess, Tina Mucklow, stayed aboard with the hijacker, the pilot, and the copilot.

At 7:30 P.M. the airplane took off, with instructions from Cooper to fly at ten thousand feet or under, with flaps and gear down. That would slow the speed to no more than two hundred knots. Five minutes later, Cooper sent Tina Mucklow to the cockpit. "Go in there and stay there. And on your way, pull that curtain between the first-class and economy section. And don't look back." Inside the cockpit, a warning light came on indicating that the hijacker had lowered the aft stairway but it had not locked in place. The Boeing 727 was the only passenger plane equipped with a stairway that, when lowered from the rear section of the fuselage, could allow passengers to exit the aircraft. The copilot got on the craft's PA system.

"Is everything OK back there? Anything we can do for you?"

From the interphone at the flight attendant's station in the rear of the plane, Cooper shouted: "No!" The warning light in the control panel was now indicating that the stairway was fully extended. With one parachute strapped to his chest and the other to his back, the hijacker, his face lashed by sleet and hail, stood on the stairway, and hesitated for a full two minutes. Ten thousand feet below was some of the most rugged terrain in America, a forest of Ponderosa pines just north of the Oregon border and the southern slope of Mount St. Helens. Then he jumped.

D. B. Cooper has never been found, dead or alive. Massive air and ground searches were conducted over the next few weeks. They turned up neither a body nor the two hundred thousand dollars. It remains the only unsolved skyjacking in American history, and one of the great unsolved crimes of the twentieth century.

"A legend was born," said FBI agent Ralph Himmelsbach, the agent in charge of the investigation. Until September 11, 2001, no single event had done more to toughen airplane security in the United States.

Approximately two and a half years later, in the motel room in Joplin, Missouri, Jack Coffelt finished telling young Byron Brown a story that was almost too incredible to believe. "I'm D. B. Cooper. I need your help, Byron. I lost my goddamn money! I dropped it when the parachute opened. Your father has promised to help, but we need your help too. You're young. We're just two old men. You can climb the mountains out there. I'm going to give your daddy half and we're going to buy you a brand new car." He showed Byron his disfigured legs again. He claimed they had been mangled when he crashed into a giant pine tree on the way down. "I've never recovered. It ruined me. I wouldn't do it again for a million dollars." Byron did not know what to believe.

The next morning the three of them climbed into the family camper, and as they drove west toward Oregon, Coffelt elaborated on the D. B. Cooper story. He was standing on the aft stairway aboard the Boeing 727, bracing himself for the right moment to jump, when he lost his grip on the handrail and was sucked out "like a cork out of the bottle," he told Byron Brown. He pulled the ripcord of the parachute strapped to his chest but, to his shock, it failed to open. The reserve pack on his back deployed, but he had not expected its sudden jolt. The bag of cash, weighing twenty-one pounds, which he had bound to his body with a patchwork of parachute cord he had hurriedly tied together, flew off into thin air. He hit the ground, Coffelt said, alive but without the money. That night was the longest, most grueling of his life. Coughing up blood and gasping for air, it took him fifteen hours to claw his way out of the canyon he had landed in. He was gravely injured, but, miraculously, alive.

Since the hijacking he had returned to the Oregon forests twice, in the spring and fall of 1972, in a fruitless search for the missing cash. He had even moved to a suburb outside Seattle, Lynnwood, to be closer to the search area. Calling on the Browns was his last hope.

"That job was my last chance. It meant everything to me. I had nothing to lose." Coffelt told Byron all about his love for Annemarie Hoffman and how he "never loved anyone like I loved her." Coffelt's story was that he had come up with the scheme to skyjack a plane and extort two hundred thousand dollars from the airline after the Lincoln trust fund scandal had blown up in his face. Annemarie was living in exile in Europe, with her son Timothy. Now Coffelt was broke and his health was shot to pieces. He was taking nitroglycerin tablets for heart disease. He was embittered and desperate. He kept saying he had nothing left to lose and he wanted to screw the government. Byron Brown thought that either Coffelt was a total fantasist or he was D. B. Cooper. He could not tell which just yet.

As the trio reached Oregon and set up camp, James Brown pulled his son aside and said, "What are we getting ourselves into?" He was concerned that he had foolishly involved Byron in the commission of a serious federal offense, accessory after the fact. Coffelt also worked on Byron. "You've got to keep your father with me. This is my last chance." After several frustrating days of searching, when a fed-up James Brown threatened to go home, Coffelt's voice was sinister, "You know too much already, James." It terrified young Byron, who sensed that Coffelt was as menacing as he sounded.

James Brown wanted to focus the search at the location where Coffelt had landed and "backtrack from there." But Coffelt was afraid they would be spotted by forest rangers. He thought his knapsack full of cash was farther west, closer to the base of Mount Hood. "I know my money's there," he said. They spent a full week camping out and making their way through the thick underbrush, bickering the entire time. Finally, Coffelt was physically spent, and said he needed to take a break. He was going to go back to his apartment outside Seattle to recuperate for a few days. He told the Browns he would link up with them later.

The next night, July 13, 1974, Byron said he and his father were preparing a meal at the campsite when they saw a car with Kansas license plates creeping toward them. Kansas was "Coffelt country." Then another vehicle, a pickup truck, materialized out of nowhere, and two armed men climbed out. The Browns jumped in their camper and sped off. They never looked back. They felt certain that Coffelt had hired some cronies to eliminate them. Four days of hard driving later, they were back in Georgia.

How believable is Byron Brown's account? His sister, Beth Brown, said that when her father and brother returned from the camping trip, they told her all about Jack Coffelt. She was attending Georgia Tech at the time and can still remember Byron describing Coffelt's nasty leg injuries in vivid detail.

Barbara McClean, the poet who got to know Coffelt when they lived at the Meadowbrook Apartments in Lawrence, Kansas, in the mid-1960s, said that when Coffelt returned to Lawrence in the early 1970s, it was a shock to see him. "He was a walking cripple," she said. He had a "noticeable limp" that he had not had before.

Byron Brown graduated from the University of Las Vegas and became a writer. He knew he had a great story and he was intent on finding out everything he could about Coffelt and D. B. Cooper. "It really took over his life," his mother, Louise, said. Three years later, in 1977, Byron and his father returned to the remote canyon to retrace Coffelt's steps and resume their hunt for the missing money. They never found any cash but they claimed to have uncovered forensic evidence that supported Coffelt's story, including the charred remnants of two parachutes Coffelt said he had set on fire when he landed. Byron set up shop in Las Vegas as a freelance writer and got a Hollywood producer interested in financing his research into D. B. Cooper. The producer's lawyer contacted the FBI to check out Coffelt's criminal history, and that is how the federal agency first linked Coffelt's name to the skyjacking.

To the FBI, the Coffelt tip sounded promising. They compared Coffelt's mug shot with the composite drawing of D. B. Cooper. It looked like a match. The physical description of Coffelt fit. Coffelt was six-foot-one—the approximate height of the hijacker. Also, the age was close. Coffelt would have been fifty-four when the hijacking took place. D. B. Cooper was said to be around fifty. Like Cooper, he was a chain smoker and a big drinker. Then there was Coffelt's past, his many years in prison. D. B. Cooper's jailhouse lingo ("no funny stuff") as he took control of the plane sounded like Jack Coffelt's patter. And why would Coffelt suddenly move to Lynnwood, in Washington State, when he had no previous connection to the Pacific Northwest?

Something the FBI did not immediately know was that Coffelt's lawyer, Robert Dobbs of Memphis, Tennessee, had received a call from Coffelt, from Portland, just before the skyjacking—placing Coffelt in the city where D. B. Cooper boarded the plane. Most significant were the mysterious leg injuries, and Coffelt's claim, through the Browns, that he was D. B. Cooper.

Could this actually be the guy? A full-scale probe was launched under the direction of Ralph Himmelsbach, out of the FBI's field office in Portland. John Beck, the lawyer representing the Mary Harlan Lincoln trust fund, said the FBI reached out to him and asked whether he thought Coffelt could be D. B. Cooper. Beck said, "It sounded pretty far-fetched to me." In any event, the FBI was taking it seriously. Agents looked into Coffelt's prison record under his given name, Bryant, and confirmed that he and Brown had been incarcerated together at the federal penitentiary in Atlanta in the 1950s. At least that part of the story checked out. But Himmelsbach came to eliminate Coffelt as a suspect. He said the FBI concluded that at the time of the hijacking, Coffelt had been a patient at a mental hospital in Illinois. A staff psychiatrist at the hospital told the FBI that due to Coffelt's physical and mental state, there was "no way" he could be D. B. Cooper. But Coffelt's medical records from the facility were subpoenaed just in case.

"We gave Coffelt a pretty good shake," Himmelsbach told me. But he said he ultimately reached the conclusion that "Coffelt did not do it."

By now, the FBI was starting to get fed up with James and Byron Brown's obsession with D. B. Cooper. The Brown family had moved to Ogden, Utah, where James Brown was employed as a safety engineer for Thoikol, the aerospace giant. One day, Louise Brown said, three FBI agents came to her house. She invited them in, and everyone took a seat at the dining-room table. Basically, they wanted to know why the Browns were persisting with this D. B. Cooper business. "They weren't too receptive to what we had to say," Louise Brown said. "One of them said, 'That's a lot of garbage.' I really didn't think they wanted to know the truth. When they left, I thought, Oh my God, what in the world have we gotten ourselves into?"

Byron Brown died suddenly in his sleep in 1998 at the age of forty-one. A rare form of tuberculosis he had picked up in Saudi Arabia, where he had worked as a technical writer, weakened his immune system, and he was felled by an everyday sinus infection. His father, James Brown, died the following year. The Brown family still wonders why the FBI dismissed Coffelt as a suspect so hurriedly.

Ralph Himmelsbach spent eight years of his career at the FBI working the D. B. Cooper investigation. Now retired and living on a farm in the Pacific Northwest, Himmelsbach is bemused by the continued fascination with D. B. Cooper in popular folklore. There are T-shirts, songs, and bumper stickers. Journalists manage to keep the tale alive with fresh theories popping up periodically. The day I spoke with him, somebody from *New York* magazine was driving to his farm for an interview about a possible D. B. Cooper suspect from Minnesota that the writer was checking out. ("Not a chance he's the guy," Himmelsbach told me.) Himmelsbach has been through this many times before: checking out a tip, analyzing the evidence, and, finally, dismissing the suspect and moving on to the next potential "perp."

The D. B. Cooper case was the most important of his career. In 1986 he wrote his own insider's account of the crime, *NORJAK*, the bureau's code name for the investigation. I sent Byron Brown's *Las Vegan* article to Himmelsbach, which he did not recall ever having read. He agreed to review the story and let me know what he thought of it. Two weeks later we spoke again.

"It's a bunch of hokum. It's just a lot of garbage." Himmelsbach was dismissive of everything about Brown's work, including Coffelt's purported admission that he was D. B. Cooper. "Con talk," Himmelsbach called it. "A bunch of old cons telling stories." I asked Himmelsbach if he might modify his estimation of Coffelt as a suspect if it were proved that Coffelt smoked Raleigh filter tips. Eight discarded butts of the brand were found in the ashtray of seat 18-C in the hijacked aircraft. Himmelsbach said that would not mean much because just about every ex-con he had ever encountered smoked Raleigh cigarettes. He said D. B. Cooper wore slip-on loafers when he parachuted out of the airplane at 160 miles per hour and "it's hard to conceive of the possibility that he landed, dusted himself off and walked away." Most likely the hijacker was killed on impact and the body washed away. Or coyotes took care of the carcass. In Himmelsbach's opinion, D. B. Cooper didn't survive the jump.

With all due respect to Himmelsbach, I'm not so sure. Could Jack Coffelt be D. B. Cooper? Did desperation over his failure to assume control of the Lincoln trust fund drive him to hijack a plane and jump out with two hundred thousand dollars in ransom money only to see the moneybag fly off into the wind? The truth may lie buried in a grave in Hawaii. Jack Coffelt moved to Honolulu with his companion, Lorraine "Tave" Gulas, a former airline stewardess who had once been married to the captain of detectives in the Las Vegas police department. Their time in paradise was short-lived. On June 19, 1975, Jack Coffelt collapsed of a heart attack and died at age fifty-nine.

Epilogue
The Last Lincoln

BOB BECKWITH MARRIED one final time. In 1981, Maggie Fristoe became the third Mrs. Robert Todd Lincoln Beckwith.

It was an awkward situation, both for Beckwith and for his stepdaughter Doris Crans. Sometimes, Doris and her husband would run into the Beckwiths at an event at the Columbia Country Club in Chevy Chase. There would be an exchange of social pleasantries and a promise to get together soon, but it never happened. In the old days, Beckwith would come around every Christmas, and Doris would make sure the bar was fully stocked with Dewars and Chivas. Then the Christmas visits had tailed off and now they were just a memory. "It was painful for Mom," said Doris's son, Robert Crans Jr. "She felt estranged from the man she considered her dad."

Doris Crans's husband, Robert, was concerned about the issue of Beckwith's will. He urged Doris to communicate with her stepfather and take a stand about her inheritance before it was too late.

"Come on, honey," he told Doris, "what's yours is yours."

But she refused to discuss the matter. "I don't want to have anything to do with it," she said. Doris was content to have what her mother Hazel had bequeathed her at her death in 1964: two watches, a ring, a necklace, and a set of pearls. "That was all she got and all she wanted," Robert Jr. said.

All around Washington there were the remembrances of Abraham Lincoln's greatness. Bob Beckwith could hear it even in the wind when bells tolled from the tower of the Presbyterian Church on New York Avenue. In 1929, the Lincoln family had donated the brass bells that rang out every quarter hour just four blocks from the White House, with this inscription on the largest bell:

To the Glory of God
And in Memory of Abraham Lincoln
Who Worshipped in This Church
When President of the United States

The other Lincolns were all gone. Beckwith was the last Lincoln—the final blood link to the great Civil War leader who came out of the frontier wilderness and ended slavery in the United States.

In 1983, Beckwith returned to Woodstock Farms in Virginia to live out his final days. Maggie never really took to life on the plantation, and stayed behind in Chevy Chase. Beckwith was in frail health and required constant attention, and Maggie's daughter, Lenora Hoverson, took care of the ailing last Lincoln.

When Lenora's family moved in to Woodstock she was shocked at the condition she found the home in. The core splendor of the two-hundred-acre estate was still evident, with its charming parlor, French lace curtains, and Lincoln family silver. But basic maintenance had been ignored for more than two decades. "The house was going to fall down," she said. After extensive renovations—a new roof with copper gutters, a modernized heating and air-conditioning system—Woodstock recovered its old grandeur. "It was a pricey endeavor, but it had to be done," Lenora said.

Beckwith remained with Lenora and her family at Woodstock for about a year, and then, she said, "we had to put him in a home."

"He had Parkinson's and it caused a lot of depression. It took him down real slowly, and we just couldn't handle him anymore. He became combative."

The last Lincoln spent the last year of his life in a nursing home in Saluda, Virginia. One of his dearest friends, Emily Grove, the widow of Dr. Thomas Grove, tried to visit him. There had been a time after Hazel Beckwith's death when Bob Beckwith had romanced Emily Grove, whose husband had died from a heart attack in 1958 at age forty-four. He had even asked Emily to marry him. "They were good friends, and they were both without spouses," said Emily's son, Tom Grove Jr. "She refused. I told her, 'Mother, why the hell did you say no? It's not like you're a teenager.' My mother was a very Victorian woman. I doubt they ever exchanged a kiss." But in the closing days of Bob Beckwith's life, Emily Grove insisted on seeing her old friend in the nursing home. "She was told no one could visit

Bob," said a Grove family member. "She saw him anyway and she was glad she did."

Bob Beckwith went into convulsions on Christmas Eve, 1985, and died at 6:05 P.M. The Associated Press ran a short obituary, quoting Charles Bristow, proprietor of the Bristow-Faulkner Funeral Home in Saluda, as saying he did not know much about the deceased except that he was President Lincoln's great-grandson. Beckwith's ever-cautious lawyer, Elizabeth Young, was quoted as saying she did not believe Beckwith left any descendants. Private services were held in Chevy Chase, Maryland, and in Virginia. Like his sister Peggy, Bob Beckwith had left instructions to be cremated. His ashes were poured into the Piakatank River that ran alongside Woodstock Farms.

One year later, on December 1, 1986, a teenager appeared in circuit court in the historic city of Williamsburg, Virginia, for a closed-door hearing. For eighteen years the Mary Harlan Lincoln Testamentary Trust had been in a state of legal limbo because of this young man's birth, in 1968. Now Timothy Lincoln Beckwith was making his first appearance in a court of law. He was smart, good-looking, and personable—"and he looked nothing like Bob Beckwith," someone who was present pointedly observed. In the courtroom were lawyers for Iowa Wesleyan College, the American Red Cross, and the Church of Christ, Scientist—the three beneficiaries of Mary Harlan Lincoln's will, provided there was no surviving Lincoln blood heir. Robert Patterson, a lawyer from Richmond, represented young Timothy. After Bob Beckwith had died, they were all there to put their signatures on the dotted line of a settlement agreement that had taken months of negotiations to work out.

Everyone had had to give up something to reach this moment. For Timothy, it meant acknowledging that he was not a blood Lincoln. He agreed to renounce all claims to the trust, which totaled about six million dollars, but in return he was to receive a structured settlement payment of about one million dollars, to be paid out in regular installments followed by a final lump-sum payment.

Iowa Wesleyan College, the Red Cross, and the Christian Science Church were now free to claim their share of what remained of Mary Harlan Lincoln's estate.

For John Beck, the lawyer who represented the trust, that day they had wrapped up a case that had been a source of nearly two decades of frustration and fascination. I asked Beck why he went along with the settlement, given that the divorce court in Washington had determined in 1976 that someone other than Annemarie's husband had fathered her son. "A thousand things can happen in a lawsuit, and it usually does," Beck said. "I have yet to have the perfect lawsuit." Even with the court's finding of adultery, Beck still did not have Timothy or Annemarie's blood test. There was also the strong presumption under common law that a child born while two people are married was the biological offspring of the marriage. Beck realized that it was in everyone's interest to negotiate a deal. No one wanted this case to go to trial. "I thought the interests of the Mary Harlan Lincoln trust had been substantially carried out in the settlement."

At the end of the hearing, everyone shook hands. Timothy was impressively mature and seemed to be a fine young man. Perhaps his mother's legal struggle had made an indelible impression, because after being graduated from prestigious Emory University in Atlanta, Timothy became a lawyer, receiving his law degree from the University of Florida College of Law. At this writing, he is a prosecutor with the Florida state attorney's office, and has a promising future.

Timothy's mother Annemarie is happily remarried and living in the United States. She had this to say about her doomed marriage to the last Lincoln: "It was very unfortunate that I ever met Bob Beckwith."

Woodstock Farms is now a bed-and-breakfast, owned by Bob Beckwith's widow, Maggie Fristoe, and managed by her daughter, Lenora Hoverson, and her husband, John Hoverson. "I don't really push the Lincoln connection," Lenora said. "It's on the Web site, but I don't go whole hog with it. They weren't really my people. It's not my bloodline."

Upon her death in 1975, Peggy Beckwith willed the Lincoln "ancestral home," Hildene, to the Christian Science Church. In 1978 the Church sold it to the Friends of Hildene, who now run it, offering guided tours to visitors.

No name has held more resonance for Americans than Abraham Lincoln. Born in a log cabin in the backwoods of Kentucky, the sixteenth president has come to personify the notion that even the humblest born may become president. But scandal and a sense of entitlement marked the last generation of Lincolns. In place of public service, ambition, and education—the foundations of Abraham Lincoln's genius— his descendants became a symbol for dishonor and decadence in the upper class, to the utter destruction of the House of Lincoln.

Acknowledgments

THIS BOOK COULD not have been written without the books that came before it. Two wonderful biographies of Mary Todd Lincoln were essential research tools: Jean H. Baker's brilliant *Mary Todd Lincoln: A Biography*, published in 1986, and Ruth Painter Randall's groundbreaking *Mary Lincoln: Biography of a Marriage*, published in 1953. *The Last Lincolns* picks up the Mary Lincoln story following the assassination of President Lincoln, but for anyone interested in reading more about the early years and the full-bodied life of Mrs. Abraham Lincoln, the works of Baker and Randall are highly recommended. I am also indebted to that indomitable team of Justin G. Turner and Linda Levitt Turner for their work in collecting and analyzing the letters of Mrs. Lincoln in *Mary Todd Lincoln, Her Life and Letters*. I hope traditionalists will understand my decision to modernize the punctuation of Mary Lincoln's letters because of her excessive use of commas. My goal was to ease the comfort of the reader, without altering in any way the meaning of these invaluable historical documents.

A number of archivists were extraordinarily generous with their time and counsel in guiding me through their libraries and depositories of information about the Lincoln family. A special thanks to Brian Knight, curator of Hildene, the Lincoln Family Home in Manchester, Vermont; Cindy VanHorn, registrar of the Lincoln Museum in Fort Wayne, Indiana; Lynn Ellsworth, archivist at Iowa Wesleyan College in Mount Pleasant, Iowa; Jennifer Ericson of the Abraham Lincoln Presidential Library & Museum in Springfield; and David Pavelich of the University of Chicago's Special Collections Research Center, Joseph Regenstein Library. I also want to express appreciation to the Chicago Historical Society; Jim Tschen Emmons of the

Special Collections Library at the Maryland Historical Society; The Huntington Library, San Marino, California; the Houghton Library at Harvard University; the Milwaukee County Historical Society; the Iowa Historical Society; Julie Bunke at the St. Charles (Illinois) Heritage Center; Faith Damon Davison, archivist at the Mohegan Tribe in Uncasville, Connecticut; and, of course, the Library of Congress. The Friends of Hildene were gracious enough to make me feel welcome during my time there. Lysia A. Bliss, deputy clerk, Williamsburg/James City County Circuit Court, was patient and helpful, as was Willy Conyers, chief clerk of the Washington D.C. Court of Appeals.

Any errors of fact or omission in the writing of *The Last Lincolns* are mine alone.

A first-rate team of research associates helped me gather the information, primary source material, and other historical and legal documentation. I want to particularly thank the indefatigable Molly Kennedy for her great work in Springfield, as well as Jim Nolan and Kiran Krishnamurthy of the Richmond, Virginia, *Times Dispatch*; Mary Seem and Sarah McKeever in Manchester; Liza Horowitz in New York; Lisa Carl in Chicago; Erin Connolly in Minnesota; David Hodes in Kansas, and Jeff Krulik and Karen Needles in Washington, D.C. Daniela Hoffmann of the RTL television network and Filippo Piscopo steered me through archives in Germany and Italy. I am also grateful to Eric Fettmann of the *New York Post*, and to my brother, David Lachman, and my brother, Dr. H. M. Lachman, MD, for allowing me to exploit his excellent book, *Battle of the Gnomes: The Struggle for Survival in a Microbial World*.

Thanks to the many people who agreed to be interviewed during the researching of *The Last Lincolns*. Their names are included throughout the book. A few requested that they not be identified. Beth Brown and Louise Brown were especially generous. Retired FBI agent Ralph Himmelsbach may disagree with the conclusions drawn in this book, but I valued the effort he took to advise me on the issues raised in the chapters of *The Last Lincolns* relevant to the life of Jack Coffelt. Robert Hoyt's recollections were invaluable and he was terrific about putting me in contact with his former acquaintances at the University of Kansas in Lawrence. Robert Crans Jr. and Warren W. Beckwith Jr. were good enough to speak with me about their respective family histories. I hope I was even-handed and accurate in depicting Timothy Lincoln Beckwith and his mother, Annemarie Hoffman. I know I tried my best.

My colleague, the television producer Cindy Galli, was indispensable. I also want to thank Esther Pessin for her hard work and my associates at CBS Television Distribution, and the memory of the late Roger King. Thanks to my friend, Charles Carillo, for his encouragement, and Deirdre Smerillo for her legal work.

Doris Cross made first-rate contributions editing *The Last Lincolns* and very much improved the final product. I also want to thank Rebecca Springer, Iris Blasi, and Michael Goodman for their assistance on the manuscript. Paul B. Brown read an early draft of the proposal and offered me important suggestions. I owe a debt of gratitude to Lisa Sharkey. Two great men, my literary agent Larry Kirshbaum, and my editor, Philip Turner, vice president and editorial director of Union Square Press at Sterling Publishing, were unwavering in their support and enthusiasm for *The Last Lincolns*. Larry and Philip will forever have my appreciation.

That is quite a list of people to thank, but I saved the most important acknowledgment for the end—my wife, the beautiful and talented Nancy Glass, to whom this book is dedicated, along with our children and my parents. Her loving support through these many months of researching and writing were crucial in seeing the book to the end. She was a great champion and also read every word of the manuscript. I thank her, and our children Max, Pamela, and Sloane, for everything.

Notes

PROLOGUE

ix Samuel Turner was in his office when Mrs. Lincoln came in: Testimony of
    Samuel Turner at Mary Todd Lincoln insanity trial, *Chicago Tribune*, 20 May
    1875.

x   She told a housekeeper, Maggie Gavin: Testimony of Maggie Gavin, Ibid.

x   Mrs. Lincoln summoned a waiter, John Fitzhenry: Testimony of John Fitzhenry,
    Ibid.

x   "How I am, to pass through life": Mary Todd Lincoln (MTL) to Mary Jane
    Welles, 11 July 1865, Justin G. Turner and Linda Levitt Turner, eds., *Mary Todd
    Lincoln, Her Life and Letters* (New York: Knopf, 1972), 257. Hereafter, Turner, *Let-
    ters*. Note: I have modernized the punctuation of Mrs. Lincoln's letters without
    altering her meaning, to ease the comfort of the reader. Mrs. Lincoln was a won-
    derful writer but her excessive use of commas can make reading her letters a
    chore.

x   "I have got some bad news for you": Leonard Swett to David Davis, 24 May 1875,
    David Davis Papers, Abraham Lincoln Presidential Library (ALPL), Springfield,
    Illinois. All dialogue cited in prologue between Swett and MTL is drawn from
    this letter.

1. THE PRINCE OF RAILS

3   "For the president, it was probably a single egg": Jim Bishop, *The Day Lincoln
    Was Shot* (New York: Random House, 1955), 21.

4   "It is a good face," the president said. "It is the face of a noble, noble, brave man":
    Ibid.

4   "Well, my son," the president said to Robert, "you have returned safely from the
    front": Ruth Painter Randall, *Lincoln's Sons* (Boston: Little, Brown and Co.,
    1955), 210.

4   The Red Room was the Lincolns' favorite in the White House: Bishop, 28.

5 "He is quite smart enough. I sometimes fear he is one of the little rare-ripe": Abraham Lincoln to Joshua Speed, undated, cited by Randall, *Lincoln's Sons*, 15.

5 living as boarders at the cut-rate price of eight dollars a week: Jean H. Baker, *Mary Todd Lincoln: A Biography* (New York: W. W. Norton & Company, 1987), 99. Baker's book is regarded as the definitive biography of Mrs. Lincoln.

5 "Bobbie will die!": Randall, *Lincoln's Sons*, 16.

5 75 in chemistry, 60 in composition and declamation: John S. Goff, *Robert Todd Lincoln: A Man in His Own Right* (Norman, Oklahoma: University of Oklahoma Press, 1969), 23.

5 In his coat pocket he carried a letter of introduction from Stephen A. Douglas: Ibid., 24.

6 "For what do you remember the year 218 B.C.?": Ibid., 25.

6 Tuition was twenty-four dollars a year: Ibid.,28.

7 "Isn't it too bad Bob's father is so homely?": Ibid., 32. (Lincoln's law partner, William Herndon, wrote: "On his return home Lincoln told me that for once in his life he was greatly abashed over his personal appearance.")

7 "Good," Robert said. "I will have to write home for a check": Ibid., 33, citing *Abraham Lincoln in New Hampshire* by Elwin L. Page.

7 christened the Prince of Rails: Ruth Painter Randall, *Mary Lincoln: Biography of a Marriage* (Boston: Little, Brown and Company, 1953), 185.

8 "Ain't you beginning to get a little tired of his constant uproar?": Robert Todd Lincoln (RTL) to MTL, 2 December 1860, cited by Randall, *Lincoln's Sons*, 81.

8 "'Bob,' the heir apparent to the President elect": *New York Herald*, 16 January 1861.

8 "A. Lincoln, White House, Washington, D.C.": Doris Kearns Goodwin, *Team of Rivals: The Political Genius of Abraham Lincoln* (New York: Simon & Schuster, 2005), 306.

9 "My friends—no one, not in my situation, can appreciate my feeling of sadness at this parting": Ibid., 307.

9 circuitous twelve-day route to Washington: Ibid., 306.

9 Lincoln exploded in anger: Goff, 36.

9 "I have no purpose, directly or indirectly": Goodwin, 328.

9 editorial contributions of [Secretary of State-designate] William H. Seward: Ibid., 324.

10 "so much annoyed, so much perplexed, and for a time so angry": Randall, *Lincoln's Sons*, 88.

10 presence of Mary Lincoln and the children might actually deter an assassination: Ibid., 87.

10 His roommate from Exeter, George Latham: Ibid., 89.

10 [Ellsworth] was like another son to the Lincolns: Ibid., 97.

11 "Do you want to see Old Abe?": *New York Herald*, 13 February 1861.

11 Robert declined with a dismissive wave of his hand: Goff, 37.

11 replace it with a soft felt cap: Goodwin, 311.

12 Lincoln regretted his decision: Ibid., 312.

12 Robert led a chorus of "The Star-Spangled Banner": Goff, 38.

12 in front of his family read out loud the memorable address: Goodwin, 326.

12 At noon, President Buchanan arrived at the Willard: Ibid., 327.

12 Mary and the children were advised to stay away: Baker, 178.

13 "He is sick of Washington": *New York Herald*, 5 March 1861.

13 unwavering in her determination to keep Robert out of harm's way: Katherine Helm, *Mary, Wife of Lincoln* (New York: Harper & Brothers, 1928), 227. Helm was Mary Todd Lincoln's niece.

13 "I know that Robert's plea to go into the Army is manly": Ibid., 227.

14 "Send her to me": Ibid., 221.

14 "Well, we have whipped the rebels at Chattanooga": Ibid., 229.

14 "if I had twenty sons they should all be fighting the rebels": Ibid., 230.

15 "Well, I have just had a great row with the President of the United States": Randall, *Lincoln's Sons*, 150.

15 "Instead of punishing Tad, as I think he ought": Ibid.

15 "If you do not attend to your studies": Ibid., 149.

15 "The president will not be at Commencement": Goff, 57.

15–16 "I returned from college in 1864": Ibid., 60.

16 "My son," the letter began, "now in his twenty-second year, having graduated at Harvard": Abraham Lincoln to Ulysses S. Grant, 19 January 1865, Ibid., 64.

16 "I will be most happy to have him in my Military family": Ulysses S. Grant to Abraham Lincoln, 21 January 1865, Ibid., 64.

17 His escort for the great event was Mary Harlan: Randall, *Lincoln's Sons*, 201.

17 "Robert just now tells me there was a little rumpus up the line": Ibid., 204.

18 "very much as people enter a sick-chamber": General Horace Porter, *The Surrender at Appomattox Court House*. Porter's article on the surrender was reprinted in *Battles and Leaders of the Civil War, Vol. 4*, Robert Underwood Johnson and Clarence Clough Buel, eds. (The Century Co., 1884), 737.

19 At 2:20 P.M. Lincoln ate a simple lunch: Bishop, 21. Jim Bishop's book provides an excellent account of the day President Lincoln was assassinated.

19 Johnson took the oath of office: Goodwin, 698.

19 "I kiss this book in the face of my nation of the United States": Hans L. Trefousse, *Andrew Johnson: A Biography* (New York: W. W. Norton, 1989), 190.

20 Lincoln greeted Johnson with a hearty handshake: Bishop, 152.

20 "Dear husband," Mary said, "you almost startle me": Ibid., 164.

20 "Would you have us be late?": Ibid., 190.

20 "Come see me in the morning": Ibid., 191.

21 "backwards Jupiter": William Hanchett, *Out of the Wilderness: The Life of Abraham Lincoln* (Champaign, Illinois: University of Illinois Press, 1994), 132.

21 They may have studied Spanish together: Goff, 69.

22 "They have shot the President": Wayne Whipple, *The Story-Life of Lincoln: A Biography Composed of Five Hundred True Stories* (Philadelphia: The John C. Winston Company, 1908), 653.

22 "Captain, something happened to the President": Goff, 655.

22 "Captain Lincoln wants to see you at once": Ibid.

22 "It's my father! My father! I'm Robert Lincoln": Bishop, 225.

23 "Take me inside to my husband": Ibid., 236.

23 "Bring Tad. He will speak to Tad.": Ibid., 237.

23 he let forth an "explosive breath.": Ibid., 267.

24 "Take that woman out, and do not let her in again": Ibid., 268.

24 "All at once somebody seized him by the coat collar": RTL to Richard Watson Gilder, 6 February 1909, Illinois State Historical Library.

24 "Now, he belongs to the ages": Some historians contend that Stanton's actual words were, "Now, he belongs to the angels." For an excellent account of the historical dispute over what Stanton said, see Adam Gopnik's article in the *New Yorker*, 28 May 2007.

25 "Oh, Mr. Welles," young Taddie asked, "who killed my father?": Gideon Welles, *The Diary of Gideon Welles: Secretary of the Navy under Lincoln and Johnson, Vol. II* (Boston and New York: Houghton Mifflin Co., 1911), 290.

2. THEM LITTLE DEVILS

26 "They have killed Papa dead": Whipple, 655.

26 They talked into the night, Pendel's voice soothing: Thomas F. Pendel, *Thirty-Six Years in the White House* (Washington, D.C.: Neale Publishing Co., 1901), 42.

26–27 Tad's unusually large head: Helm, 115.

27 next-door neighbor Mrs. Sprigg became "Mith Spwigg": Randall, *Mary Lincoln*, 147.

27 "parental tyranny": Ibid., 101.

28 "wanted to wring the necks of these brats": Ibid, citing William Herndon to Jesse Weik, 8 January 1886.

28 "worshipped his children and what they worshipped": Ibid., 102, citing William Herndon to Jesse Weik, 18 February 1887.

28 "Well, Judge, I reckon we'll have to finish this game some other time": Carl Sandburg, *Abraham Lincoln: The Prairie Years, Vol. II* (New York: Harcourt, Brace & Co., 1926), 280–281.

29 "There goes that Illinois ape": Julia Taft Bayne, *Tad Lincoln's Father* (Lincoln, Nebraska: University of Nebraska Press, 2001), 8. The book was originally published in 1931.

29 Willie was the "most lovable boy I ever knew": Ibid., 3.

30 Many of the worshipers supported the South: Ibid., 12.

31 "It is the order of the Provost Marshal that": Ibid.

31 "If I was a Secesh," Tad boasted: Ibid.

32 When the 230-pound general, who was too fat: Ibid., 15.

32 "Let 'em come," Tad said: Ibid., 28.

32 "Boys, does the president know about this?": Ibid., 44.

33 "Don't you dare bother the president": Ibid., 57.

34 "It's not Pa's looking glass": Ibid., 49.

34 The tutor with the longest tenure was Alexander Williamson: Randall, *Mary Lincoln*, 279.

34 "Julie was reading nobbel books in our house": Bayne, 68.

35 "He had a very bad opinion of books": John Hay, *New York Tribune*, as published in *Chicago Tribune*, 19 July 1871.

35   Tad had a way of taking stock of a new tutor: Randall, *Lincoln's Sons*, 122.

35   "Let him run," Lincoln would say: Ibid., 123.

35   "My whole soul is in it": Francis B. Carpenter, *The Inner Life of Abraham Lincoln: Six Months at the White House* (Lincoln, Nebraska: University of Nebraska Press, 1995), 269.

36   he be given the inkwell as a gift: Gerald J. Prokopowicz, *Lincoln Lore: The Emancipation Inkwell* (Fort Wayne, Indiana: The Lincoln Museum).

36   "Are the president and Mrs. Lincoln aware that there is a Civil War?": Baker, 206.

36   Mary hired Maillard & Company, New York's most expensive caterer: Ibid.

36   "Whew! Our cat has a long tail tonight,": Elizabeth Keckley, *Behind the Scenes, or Thirty Years a Slave, and Four Years in the White House* (New York: G. W. Carleton & Co., 1868), 101.

36   "The Mary Lincoln Polka": Baker, 207.

37   sugar model of Fort Sumter: Randall, *Lincoln's Sons*, 129.

37   "this little fellow": Nathaniel P. Willis, cited by Keckley, 106.

38   "Dear Sir, I enclose you my first attempt at poetry": letter from Willie Lincoln to *Washington National Republican*, cited by Keckley, 99.

39   one of history's three "burning fevers," the other two being malaria and yellow fever: Dr. H. M. Lachman, *Battle of the Gnomes: The Struggle for Survival in a Microbial World* (Enfield, New Hampshire: Science Publishers, 2006), 151.

40   "soldier's disease": Ibid.

40   beef tea, blackberry cordial, and bland pudding: Baker, 209.

40   "I am heartily glad to see you": Randall, *Mary Lincoln*, 285.

41   "You ought to go to bed, Bud," the president said: Bayne, 82.

41   "hopelessly ill": Randall, *Mary Lincoln*, 283.

41   "My poor boy," Lincoln said, "he was too good for this earth": Keckley, 103.

42   "Well, Nicolay, my boy is gone, he is actually gone": Charles M. Segal, ed., *Conversations with Lincoln* (New York: G. P. Putnam's Sons, 1961), 159.

42   The president sent word to the Taft household: Bayne, 82.

43   Mary Lincoln wanted the bouquet preserved: Randall, *Lincoln's Sons*, 131.

43   But on this day his eyes glistened with tears: Ibid., 110.

43   a violent storm had wreaked havoc on the city: Randall, *Lincoln's Sons*, 132.

43   Lincoln's friend William Thomas Carroll, the clerk of the Supreme Court: Ibid.

43   under the sod of his own land: or as Keckley writes: "to sleep under the sod of his own valley," 108.

44   "Please keep the boys home the day of the funeral": Bayne, 82.

44   "Mother, do you see that large white building on the hill yonder?": Keckley, 104.

44   "Who would ever speak to me any more?": Anna L. Boyden, *War Reminiscences: A Record of Mrs. Rebecca R. Pomroy's Experience in War-times* (Boston: D. Lothrop & Co., 1884), 54–55.

44   "This is the hardest trial of my life": Ibid.

44–45   "I was surprised about the announcement of the death of your son Willie": William Florville to Abraham Lincoln, 27 December 1863, Lincoln Papers, Library of Congress (LOC). Florville was known as Billy the Barber in Springfield.

45 "Very imploringly" he begged her to come: Randall, *Lincoln's Sons*, 133.

45 "You have such a power and control, such an influence over Mary": *Mr. Lincoln's White House* (The Lincoln Institute). A similar quote ("You have such control and such an influence over Mary") is attributed to President Lincoln in William H. Herndon and Jesse W. Weik, *Herndon's Life of Lincoln* (Cleveland: World Publishing Co., 1888), 412.

45 "one could scarcely tell she was there": Harry E. Pratt, ed., *Concerning Mr. Lincoln* (Springfield: The Abraham Lincoln Association, 1944), 94.

45 "He begged me with tears in his eyes to remain longer": Herndon, 412.

46 he gave a dozen of them to a lame boy named Tommy: Randall, *Lincoln's Sons*, 139.

46 "Isn't it our kitchen?": Ibid., 141.

47 "You tell my father about him": Ibid., 140.

48 He even mailed Willie's two favorite toy railroad cars: Ibid., 135.

48 He threw himself on the floor and started kicking and screaming: Bayne, 83.

48 a little gun for Tad "that he could not hurt himself with": Randall, *Lincoln's Sons*, 179.

49 "I want to give him all the toys I did not have": Ibid., 181.

49 President of the Confederacy Jefferson Davis was sitting with his wife in the front-row pew: Dallas Tucker, "The Fall of Richmond," *Richmond Dispatch*, 3 February 1902.

50 "From that moment law and order ceased to exist": *Richmond Whig* newspaper, 4 April 1865.

52 The torpedoes were so close to the presidential vessel: William H. Crook (edited by Margarita Spalding Gerry), *Through Five Administrations: Reminiscences of Colonel William H. Crook, Bodyguard to President Lincoln* (New York: Harper & Brothers, 1907), 52.

52 "You are free," Lincoln said. "Free as air": Jay Winik, *April 1865* (New York: HarperPerennial, 2006), 118.

52 "ready for whatever may come": Crook, 54.

53 "I was sure he meant to shoot": Ibid.

53 "If I were in your place, I'd let 'em up easy, let 'em up easy": Winik, 208.

3. LADY IN BLACK

54 "Oh, no, not there": Baker, 247.

54 "I come from Mrs. Lincoln": Keckley, 187.

55 "Why did you not come to me last night, Elizabeth?": Ibid., 188.

55 "There lurked the sweetness and gentleness": Ibid., 191.

55 "a world of agony on his young face": Ibid.

56 "Don't, Mama! Don't cry, or you will make me cry, too": Ibid., 192.

56 "Please come at once to Washington & take charge": Willard L. King, *Lincoln's Manager: David Davis* (Cambridge, Massachusetts: Harvard University Press, 1960), 226.

56 Robert telegraphed a single word: "Come": Randall, *Lincoln's Sons*, 215.

56 "Mrs. Lincoln is very much disturbed by noise": Baker, 248.

57 Later he would say that it was the saddest day of his life: Winik, 356. A compelling account of Lincoln's funeral can be found in Winik's *April 1865*.

59 Perhaps he could have stopped Booth: Nicholas Murray Butler, "Lincoln and Son," *Saturday Evening Post*, 11 February 1939. Butler was the long-time president of Columbia University and a friend of Robert Lincoln.

59 "Our loss is indeed terrible": Randall, *Lincoln's Sons*, 219. RTL wrote the letter to Harvard University professor Francis J. Child twelve days after his father's death.

59 "Don't cry, Mamma; I cannot sleep if you cry!": Keckley, 196.

59 "Pa is dead. I can hardly believe that I shall never see him again": Ibid., 197.

60 Ramsey reported back to Robert on Easter Sunday: Goff, 72.

60 But privately he was informed that his presence was disturbing the First Lady: Baker, 250.

60 "behaved in the most brutal way.": MTL to Sally Orne, 15 March 1866, Turner, *Letters*, 345.

60 "Would you, if convenient, be kind enough to": Randall, *Lincoln's Sons*, 219.

61 His inquiries were so over the top the bartender: Bishop, 137.

61 "Don't wish to disturb you. Are you at home? J. Wilkes Booth": Ibid., 155.

61 "Why was that card of Booth's found in his box—some acquaintance certainly existed": Baker, 250. MTL amplified on her suspicions of Andrew Johnson in a letter to Sally Orne dated 5 March 1866: "*that* miserable, inebriate Johnson, had cognizance of my husband's death. . . . As sure, as you & I live, Johnson, had some hand, in all this."

62 Parker joined the metro police force in 1861: Bishop, 182.

63 "How would you like a little ale?": Ibid., 197.

63 he had in his custody a prostitute he was acquaintaned with: Ibid., 291.

63 "Who is on watch tonight?": Keckley, 193.

64 "Parker knew he had failed in duty": Crook, 74.

64 One of the mourners was the fifteenth president, James Buchanan: Winik, 357.

64 a dangerous crush of mourners who had gathered en masse: account of President Lincoln's funeral from 4 May and 5 May, 1865. *Illinois State Journal* and *Illinois State Register*.

66 "with the written promise that no other bodies, save the president": MTL to Richard J. Oglesby, 10 June 1865, Turner, *Letters*, 244.

68 "Elizabeth, I can never go back to Springfield": Keckley, 200.

68 "I cannot go west with you, Mrs. Lincoln": Ibid., 209.

68 "What are you going to do with that old dress, Mother?": Ibid., 207.

69 The trial lasted a total of fifty days: Edward Steers Jr., *Blood on the Moon* (Lexington, Kentucky: University Press of Kentucky, 2001), 227.

70 Somehow, a superb Japanese punch bowl: Baker, 249.

70 "more precious than gold to my darling husband.": MTL to Sally Orne, 13 January 1866, Turner, *Letters*, 326.

70 "I go hence, broken hearted": MTL to Charles Sumner, 9 May 1865, Turner, *Letters*, 228.

71 In a second-floor bedroom they found something: Randall, *Lincoln's Sons*, 225.

4. CHICAGO

72 she was "in a daze": Crook, 70.

72 "one of the most miserable"cities: Fredrika Bremer, *The Homes of the New World: Impressions of America* (New York: Harper & Brothers, 1853), 605.

74 "a pale, sad little woman in a widow's deep mourning.": Randall, *Lincoln's Sons*, 225.

74 "I am alone.... [My] Husband gone from me": MTL to Oliver S. Halsted Jr., 29 May 1865, Turner, *Letters*, 236.

74 "He was a sad little fellow," Crook said: Crook, 71.

75 "beautiful new hotel" with exquisitely clean: MTL to Oliver S. Halsted Jr., 29 May 1865, Turner, *Letters*, 236.

75 "Mrs. Keckley, how do you like our new quarters?": Keckley, 212.

75 "Ask Mother," Robert said. "I think she will say no.": Ibid., 215.

76 Mary said, "What does A-P-E spell?": Ibid., 217.

76 Tad was "seized with the desire to be able to read & write." MTL to Alexander Williamson, 15 June 1865, Turner, *Letters*, 250.

77 Jonathan Young Scammon, one of the richest men in America: John McAuley Palmer, *The Bench and Bar of Illinois: Historical and Reminiscent* (Chicago: The Lewis Publishing Co., 1899), 73.

78 "contemplating the waves": Baker, 254.

78 "She lived in her letters ... pouring her grief": Turner, *Letters*, 239.

78 "If I have erred, it has been, in being too indulgent": MTL to Alexander Williamson, 15 June 1865, Ibid., 252.

78 "We occupy three very pleasant rooms": MTL to Harriet Howe Wilson, 8 June 1865, Ibid., 242.

79 "which with his natural brightness will be half the battle with him": MTL to Alexander Williamson, 15 June 1865, Ibid., 250.

79 "clerk's salary": MTL to David Davis, 24 February 1867, Ibid., 410.

79 "It is very unbecoming ... when it is remembered": MTL to David Davis, 27 June 1865, Ibid., 255.

79 "intensely selfish": MTL to Anson G. Henry, 17 July 1865, Ibid., 261. Dr. Henry was lost at sea two weeks after the letter was sent to him, when his ship sank en route to Olympia, Washington.

79 "I am glad you are so well situated out here": MTL quoting David Davis in a letter to Anson Henry, 17 July 1865, Ibid., 260.

79–80 "Roving Generals have elegant mansions showered upon them": MTL to Alexander Williamson, 17 August 1865, Ibid., 265.

80 "I board no longer than next spring": MTL to Anson Henry, 17 July 1865, Ibid., 260.

80 "bowed down and heart broken": MTL to Sally Orne, 31 August 1865, Ibid., 269.

82 "Surely there are persons of means": MTL to Alexander Williamson, 9 September 1865, Ibid., 273.

82 "all never worn, scarcely looked at and never shown to anyone": Baker, 259.

82 eighty-four pairs of gloves: Ibid.

82 "It will be a great disappointment if you do not soon forward it to me": MTL to James Kerr, 26 July 1865, Turner, *Letters*, 262.

82 "I propose on the first of next month to rent a room": Randall, *Lincoln's Sons*, 231.

5. THE SENATOR'S DAUGHTER

84 It was a strict rule that only French was spoken in Madame Smith's school: Bayne, 21.

85 "repeated over and over under the critical eye of Madame": Ibid., 22.

85 Prince of Wales's visit to Madame Smith's: Ibid.

86 "puzzle to the faculty": Ibid., 27.

86 Tragedy struck the Harlan family: C. J. King, *Four Marys and a Jessie: The Story of the Lincoln Women* (Manchester, Vermont: Friends of Hildene, Inc., 2005), 49.

87 "Mrs. A. E. Harlan of Iowa": Ibid., 50.

89 "I am so glad you are coming back": King, 74.

89 "wholesome good cheer": Brigham, 204.

89 "There was a constant ebb and flow": Ibid., 204–205.

89 "Mr. New Orleans" and "Daddy Henderson": letters from Minnie Chandler to Mary Harlan, cited by King, 72.

90 "How many are you engaged to now?": Ibid.

90 "How is Bob Lincoln": Ibid., 73.

90 "Taddie is learning to be as diligent in his studies": MTL to Francis B. Carpenter, 15 November 1865, Turner, *Letters*, 284.

91 "a marked character": MTL to Francis Bicknell Carpenter, 15 November 1865, Ibid., 284.

91 "much beloved" in his class: MTL to Alexander Williamson, 26 January 1866, Ibid., 331.

91 "It was the most correct history of his father that had been written": MTL to Francis Bicknell Carpenter, 15 November 1865, Ibid., 284.

92 "exceedingly cold, clear and unpleasant": Ibid., 233.

93 "He could hardly speak so as to be understood": RTL to David Davis, 17 January 1868, David Davis Family Papers, Illinois State Historical Library (ISHL).

93 "I hope you come out of this better than I think you will": Baker, 267.

94 "Be sharp & find out names": MTL to Alexander Williamson, 27 February 1866, Turner, *Letters*, 341.

94 "Be sure of this—a rich reward will be yours": MTL to Alexander Williamson, 6 May 1866, Ibid., 362.

94 "a little relic of my Beloved Husband": Baker, 260.

94 "a warm friend of the Lincolns": Ibid., 261.

94 "Mother's begging letters": Ibid., 260.

94 "I replied to her that there must be some mistake": MTL to David Davis, 12 September 1865, Turner, *Letters*, 274.

95 "that den of discomfort and dirt": MTL to Elizabeth Keckley, 13 October 1867, Turner, *Letters*, 443.

95 Testimony of Tad Lincoln at trial of John H. Surratt: Randall, *Lincoln's Sons*, 235–236.

97 "I told the man that the President was not to be seen": Crook, 45. Crook's account of the visit by "Smith" is based on his published memoirs, not his courtroom testimony.

98 "I think 'Smith' and Surratt were the same man": Ibid., 47.

6. SCANDAL

99 "Robt—I want to give a sketch": William Herndon to RTL, undated, David Herbert Donald, *Lincoln's Herndon* (New York: Knopf, 1948; Da Capo Press edition, 1989), 189.

100 "seemed to glide through the waltz with the ease of a serpent": Ibid., 188.

100 Herndon was not invited to the wedding: Ibid., 189.

100 "My sons and myself fail to understand your meaning": MTL to William Herndon, 28 August 1866, Turner, *Letters*, 384.

101 She could smell liquor on his breath: MTL to her cousin John Todd Stuart, 20 January 1874, Turner, *Letters*, 605. MTL describes Herndon's condition as follows: "When Herndon, presented his disagreeable self to me . . . his appearance & the *air* he brought with him, were so revolting, that I could scarcely ask him to be seated—"

101 "I was born on the 13th day of December, 1823": Article by Herndon, recounting his interview with MTL in 1866, published in *Illinois State Register*, 14 January 1874.

101 "the substance of what she said": Ibid.

101 "kindest man and most loving husband and father": Ibid.

102 "the wonder of the day": Herndon, 106. Originally published in 1888. In 1938, *Time* magazine called *Herndon's Life of Lincoln* "one of the great neglected books of U.S. literature."

103 "She was a woman worthy of Lincoln's love": Ibid., 107.

103 "My heart lies buried there": Ibid.

103 "Disease came upon this lovely beauty" (quotation from *Menard Axis* newspaper): John Y. Simon, "Abraham Lincoln and Ann Rutledge," *Journal of the Abraham Lincoln Association* (1990), 13–33.

104 The "Lincoln Record": Donald, 192.

104 "Did you know Miss Rutledge?": Ibid., 218.

105 McNamar's relationship with this good woman was "all up": Herndon, 109.

105 "I had every reason to believe him my warm": Ibid., 111.

105 "beautiful and tender dead . . . sweetly on his left arm": Herndon's 1866 lecture, "Abraham Lincoln, Miss Ann Rutledge, New Salem, Pioneering, and THE Poem," cited by Donald, 219.

105 "I love Lincoln dearly": Ibid., 206.

106 "the dead village of the dead": Herndon's lecture, "Abraham Lincoln, Miss Ann Rutledge," Ibid., 225.

106 The *Illinois State Journal* in Springfield found Herndon's revelations: Ibid., 229.

107 "the greatest & . . . the best man": Ibid., 230.

107 "sons of a man who never loved their mother": Ibid., 237.

107 "If such things must be, so be it" and "mainly and substantially true": Ibid., 231.

107 "Mr. William H. Herndon is making an ass of himself": Robert Todd Lincoln (RTL) to David Davis, 19 November 1866, David Davis Family Papers, ISHL.

108 "He is such a singular character": Ibid.

108 "I kept my temper and he couldn't fight": Donald, 230.

109 "pseudo philosophical" letters: Ibid., 230.

109 clairvoyant and could read minds: Randall, *Lincoln's Sons*, 242.

109 "All I ask is that nothing may be published by you": Donald, 231.

109 "I infer from your letter": Randall, *Lincoln's Sons*, 245.

109 It was a "malignity" concocted by that "drunkard" Herndon: MTL to David Davis, 4 March 1867, Turner, *Letters*, 414.

110 "As you justly remark": Ibid.

110 "If W.H. utters another word . . . He is a dirty dog": MTL to David Davis, 6 March 1867, Ibid., 416.

110 "God himself was against Herndon": Donald, 238.

110 "he could not raise anything but Hell": Ibid., 248.

111 "hauled home from town just like you would a hog": Ibid., 258.

111 "It will not be startling news to you": Keckley, 268.

111 Early September signaled the start of the fall season: Baker, 272.

111 "She was the wife of Abraham Lincoln": Keckley, 269.

111–117 Elizabeth Keckley's depiction of her journey to New York, her experiences with Mary Lincoln, and the Old Clothes Scandal are detailed in Chapter Fifteen ("The Secret History of Mrs. Lincoln's Wardrobe in New York") of her memoirs.

117 "for whom my husband did so much": Randall, *Mary Lincoln*, 410.

117 "Please call and see Hon. Abram Wakeman": Ibid., 411.

118 "a taste which some ladies attribute to Mrs. Lincoln's appreciation": Keckley, 305.

118 Committee to Save Us from National Disgrace: Baker, 275.

118 "mercenary prostitute": Ibid., 277–278.

119 "make us blush for our country and for our womanhood": *Chicago Tribune*, 7 October 1867.

119 "Are you aware that Mrs. Lincoln is in indigent circumstances": MTL to Elizabeth Keckley, 6 October 1867, published in Keckley, 298.

119 "darling little Taddie": MTL to Elizabeth Keckley, 6 October 1867, published in Keckley, 333.

7. BREACH AND BETRAYAL

120 "very kind, good, quiet, family": MTL to Elizabeth Keckley, 13 October 1867, Turner, *Letters*, 443.

120 "I am writing this morning with a broken heart": MTL to Elizabeth Keckley, 6 October 1867, published in Keckley, 332, and Turner, *Letters*, 440.

121 "Never was an act committed with a more innocent": MTL to Rhonda White, 18 October 1867, Turner, *Letters*, 444.

121 "they are making a political business of my clothes": MTL to Elizabeth Keckley, 2 November 1867, Ibid., 448.

121 Scammon simply took off on a "succession of sprees": RTL to David Davis, 29 July 1867, David Davis Family Papers, ISHL.

122 "I suppose you have seen some of the papers": RTL to Mary Harlan, 16 October 1867, cited in Randall, *Lincoln's Sons*, 250.

123 "The most charitable construction . . . is that she is insane": *Chicago Journal*, cited in Baker, 277.

123 "The conduct of his mother is as deep a mystery": *Boston Daily Evening Transcript*, cited in Baker, 278.

124 "The papers are abounding with notices": MTL to David Davis, 17 November 1867, Turner, *Letters*, 457.

124 Robert was receiving about $250 a month from the estate: Baker, 279.

124 "R. is very spiteful at present": MTL to Elizabeth Keckley, 9 November 1867, Turner, *Letters*, 449.

124 Robert would be "out of the way": MTL to Elizabeth Keckley, 21 November 1867, Ibid., 459.

125 "Can you not, dear Lizzie, be employed": MTL to Elizabeth Keckley, undated, Keckley, 312.

125 Lizzie gave an interview to the *New York Herald*: Keckley, 311.

126 "Whatever is raised by the colored people": MTL to Elizabeth Keckley, 17 November 1867, Turner, *Letters*, 456.

126 "I want neither Douglass or Garnet": MTL to Elizabeth Keckley, undated, Keckley, 312.

126 "They are very noble men": MTL to Elizabeth Keckley, 15 November 1867, Turner, *Letters*, 454.

126 "By the time you receive this note": MTK to Elizabeth Keckley, 17 November 1867, Ibid., 456.

127 "Why did you not urge them not to take my goods": MTL to Elizabeth Keckley, 12 January 1868, Ibid., 468.

127 The historical treasures Lizzie intended to donate: Keckley, 367. Apparently Lizzie Keckley reconsidered her decision to donate the items after MTL raised objections. The items were probably never sent to Wilberforce University.

128 "R. would go raving distracted": MTL to Elizabeth Keckley, 12 January 1868, Turner, *Letters*, 468.

128 "do not give him the check": MTL to Elizabeth Keckley, 29 February 1868, Ibid., 470.

129 Lizzie was now living in a boardinghouse on Broome Street: Keckley, 208.

129 Lizzie worked with a ghostwriter, James Redpath: Jennifer Fleischner, *Mrs. Lincoln and Mrs. Keckly* (New York: Broadway Books, 2003), 316. The book is an excellent account of the friendship between the former slave and First Lady. The author spells the name *Keckly*, which is historically accurate. However, for consistency, I have chosen to stick with the traditional spelling, *Keckley*.

130 It is also possible that Lizzie had assistance from another prominent writer: Randall, *Mary Lincoln*, 414.

131 "In a few days, G. W. Carlton & Co. of New York will publish": *Chicago Tribune*, 19 April 1868.

131 The book struck a raw nerve in America: *African American Review*, 22 March 2000, based on the research of Frances Smith Foster of Emory University.

132 "As I was born to servitude": *New York Citizen*, 25 April 1868, cited in Fleischner, 317.

132 "colored historian": MTL to Rhoda White, 2 May 1868, Turner, *Letters*, 476.

133 she tried to apologize to Robert Lincoln in person: Fleischner, *Mrs. Lincoln and Mrs. Keckly,* 321.

8. EXILE

134 "Miss Harlan, Sunday though it be": Minnie Chandler to Mary Harlan, cited in C. J. King, 74–75.

135 Among the guests for the wedding: *Washington Evening Star*, 26 September 1868.

135 Mrs. Charles Scammon's gift to the newlyweds: MTL to Eliza Slataper, 25 September 1868, Turner, *Letters*, 484.

135 The morbid attire of Mary Lincoln: *Washington Evening Star*, 26 September 1868.

135 "The terror of having to proceed to *Washington*": MTL to Rhoda White, 19 August, 1868, Turner, *Letters*, 481.

135 "The entire dress, although plain, was exceedingly tasteful": *Washington Evening Star*, 26 September 1868.

136 "Owing to the sad circumstances connected with the death": Ibid.

136 "I have known & loved the young lady since her childhood": MTL to Rhoda White, 27 August 1868, Turner, *Letters*, 482.

137 "everything appeared black before me": MTL to Eliza Slataper, 27 September 1868, Ibid., 485.

137 Mary actually considered her new friend to be a gifted clairvoyant: Baker, 283.

137 "I have just send you a telegram": MTL to Eliza Slataper, 25 September 1868, Turner, *Letters*, 484–486.

138 "Poor child, he doubtless feels like a victim": MTL to Eliza Slataper, 21 September 1868, Ibid., 483.

138 The wealthy German-Jewish banker Joseph Seligman paid their fare: Stephen Birmingham, *Our Crowd: The Great Jewish Families of New York* (New York: Harper & Row, 1967), 122 (Syracuse University Press edition).

139 "I never had an idea before what sea sickness was": Charles Tilghman to Agnes Tilghman, 12 October 1868, Tilghman Papers, Maryland State Historical Society.

140 The hotel was close to the Zeil: Baker, 294.

140 The rector was Dr. Hohagen: Randall, *Mary Lincoln*, 417.

141 "make up for lost time": MTL to David Davis, 15 December 1868, Turner, *Letters*, 496.

141 kept the secretary of state informed about the 378 American citizens: Baker, 285.

141 "In this distant land, how can I sufficiently express": MTL to Eliza Slataper, 13 December 1868, Turner, *Letters*, 493.

142 "I am charged the highest prices": MTL to David Davis, 15 December 1868, Turner, *Letters*, 497.

143 "My husband was Commander in Chief directed & every move Grant ever made": MTL to David Davis, Ibid., 498.

143 "short-of-funds count": *New York World*, cited in Baker, 286.

144 "I am in a most trying and humiliating position": MTL to Sally Orne, 16 December 1969, Turner, *Letters*, 535, 537.

144 "She lives very retiredly in the Hotel d'Angleterre": F. W. Bogen to Charles Sumner, 23 November 1868, cited in Randall, *Mary Lincoln*, 417.

144 "I live out in the open air": MTL to Eliza Slataper, 17 February 1869, Turner, *Letters*, 500–502.

145 "Her husband, the Constitutional commander-in-chief": F. W. Bogen, cited in Randall, *Mary Lincoln*, 418.

145 "you can always recognize them, very often, by their loud voices": MTL to Rhoda White, 16 March 1869, Turner, *Letters*, 503.

146 "I abominate ugly names": MTL to Sally Orne, 17 November 1869, Ibid., 522.

147 "You should go out *every day* and enjoy yourself": MTL to Mary Harlan Lincoln (MHL), 16 September 1870, cited by Mark E. Neely Jr. and R. Gerald McMurtry, *The Insanity File: The Case of Mary Todd Lincoln* (Carbondale, Illinois: Southern Illinois University Press, 1986), 172. Courtesy, The Insanity File Collection, The Lincoln Museum, Fort Wayne, Indiana.

147 "That blessed baby, how dearly I would love to look upon": MTL to MHL, November 1870, cited by Helm, 277.

147 "Robert writes that you were quite frightened": MTL to MHL, 22 November 1870, Neely and McMurtry, 174.

148 "I followed the waiter to the *fourth story*": Sally Orne to Senator Charles Sumner, 12 September 1869, courtesy, Houghton Library, Harvard University. The letter details Mrs. Orne's visit with MTL.

149 "Ladies, I should like to sleep some": MTL to Eliza Slataper, 21 August 1869, Turner, *Letters*, 513.

149 "I never knew what the word *Alone* meant before": Sally Orne to Charles Sumner, 12 September 1869, courtesy Houghton Library, Harvard University.

150 "She came from Hamburg in search of me": MTL to MHL, 20 August 1869, Turner, *Letters*, 511.

150 "Mr. Orne, it shall be my first duty": MTL to James Smith, 26 August 1869, Ibid., 514. Smith was the pastor of the First Presbyterian Church in Springfield.

150 "In his loving & tender treatment of me at all times": MTL to Sally Orne, 23 October 1869, Ibid., 520–522.

151 "*Death* would be far preferable to me than my present life": Ibid.

151 "My bright little comforter Taddie is of course with me": MTL to Sally Orne, 28 November 1869, Ibid., 527.

151 Mary took an "*unconscionable* dose": MTL to Sally Orne, 29 December 1869, Ibid., 537–538.

152 "sharp, burning *agony*" down her spine: MTL to Sally Orne, 11 February 1870, Ibid., 546.

152 living in the "handsomest residence" in Washington: MTL to Sally Orne, 11 Feb. 1870, Ibid., 547.

152 Tad mastered "perfect articulation": Randall, *Lincoln's Sons*, 260.

152 It would take a few more years for the cyclorama craze to reach America. The

Battle of Atlanta cyclorama exists to this day, as does the Battle of Gettysburg cyclorama in Gettysburg, Pennsylvania.

153 "probably not needful to refer to, but which are generally known": Quoted from *Congressional Globe*, proceedings of Fortieth and Forty-first Congress, cited in Turner, *Letters*, 556.

153 Mary collapsed on the spot: MTL to Sally Orne, 22 May 1870, Ibid., 560.

154 Congressional debate over MTL's pension: *Congressional Globe*, cited in Baker, 301.

156 "Study more than he does now he could not possibly do": MTL to MHL, 10 September 1870, Turner, *Letters*, 577–578.

156 "To trust my beautiful, darling *good* boy to the elements": MTL to MHL, November 1870, Ibid., 580.

9. WOMAN OF SORROW

157 General Philip Sheridan, accompanied by his staff: *New York World*, 12 May 1871, as reprinted in *Chicago Tribune*, 16 May 1871.

157 There was a porthole for fresh air and sun: Stephen Fox, *Transatlantic: Samuel Cunard, Isambard Brunel, and the Great Atlantic Steamships* (New York: Harper-Collins, 2004), 197.

157 Roast shoulder of mutton and rump steak: Charles Santley, *Reminiscences of My Life* (London: Isaac Pitman, 1909), 147. Santley's description of the food served on board the *Russia* was typical of the ship's menu. He did not travel on the same voyage as Mary Lincoln.

158 "Rough was no name for it": MTL quoted in *New York World*, reprinted in *Chicago Tribune*, 16 May 1871.

158 "I am expecting Tad to be here any day": RTL to David Davis, undated, cited in Randall, *Lincoln's Sons*, 269.

158 "nobody could be more glad than I was": MTL quoted in *New York World*, reprinted in *Chicago Tribune*, 16 May 1871.

158 A military band playing "Hail to the Chief": *New York Times*, 11&12 May 1871.

159 He was taken aback at the sight of Tad: *New York Tribune* article by John Hay, reprinted in *Chicago Tribune*, 19 July 1871.

159 "I have come, Mrs. Lincoln, to welcome you home": *New York World*, reprinted *Chicago Tribune*, 16 May 1871. The reporter interviewed MTL and Tad Lincoln.

161 "rejoicing over our arrival": MTL to Rhoda White, 21 May 1871, Turner, *Letters*, 587.

161 "There could be no sweeter daughter-in-law": Anna Eastman to MHL, quoted in Baker, 307.

161 "My husband . . . would have shrunk back in horror": MTL to Rhoda White, 23 May 1871, Turner, *Letters*, 589.

162 "My dear boy, has been *very very* dangerously ill": MTL to Rhoda White, 8 June 1871, Ibid., 590.

162 Dr. Charles Gilman Smith . . . Dr. Hosmer A. Johnson: F. M. Sperry, *A Group of Distinguished Physicians and Surgeons of Chicago* (Chicago: J. H. Beers & Co., 1904), 141.

162 Many of his colleagues considered him the greatest physician: Isaac Newton Danforth, *The Life of Nathan Smith Davis, A.M., M.D., LL.D.* (Chicago: Cleveland Press, 1907), 173.

163 "excellent physicians": MTL to Rhoda White, 8 June 1871, Turner, *Letters,* 590.

163 "May we *ever* be sufficiently grateful": Ibid.

164 "Tadd [sic] Lincoln is dangerously ill": David Davis to "my dear friend," 12 July 1871, Ward Hill Lamon Papers (LN 132), The Huntington Library, San Marino, CA.

164 "not one great sorrow ever approached the agony of this": MTL to Eliza Slataper, 14 October 1871, Turner, *Letters,* 596.

164 "Mr. Thomas Lincoln has been picking up": RTL to MHL, 11 July 1871, cited by Helm, 293.

164 "I am so sorry to tell you that Tad seems to be losing ground": RTL to MHL, 11 July 1871, Ibid., 293.

165 "He was in great distress and laboring for breath and ease": RTL to MHL, undated but written shortly after Tad's funeral, Ibid., 294.

165 "looking truly the woman of sorrow that she was": quote from unidentified mourner, cited by Randall, *Lincoln's Sons,* 271.

166 "unfortunate imperfection of speech": *Illinois State Journal,* 17 July 1871.

166 "tricky little sprite who gave to that sad and solemn White House": John Hay, *New York Tribune,* 17 July 1871.

167 Illinois was experiencing one of the hottest summers on record: *Chicago Tribune,* 17 July 1871.

10. THE WANDERER

168 His strength was all "used up": Randall, *Lincoln's Sons,* 275.

168 "by order of his physician, being so ill": MTL to Eliza Slataper, 27 July 1871, Turner, *Letters,* 591.

168 "I have been prostrated by illness—& by *a grief*—": MTL to Eliza Slataper, 13 July or 13 August 1871, Ibid., 592.

169 "As anxious as I am to see you I feel that it is best": MTL to Eliza Slataper, 4 October 1871, Ibid., 596.

169 "Dear Judge, I well know how deeply you sympathize": MTL to David Davis, 9 November 1871, Turner, *Letters,* 597.

169 "This is the last public address that will be delivered within these walls!": Robert Cromie, *The Great Chicago Fire* (Nashville: Rutledge Hill Press, 1958), 17. Cromie's book is an excellent account of the fire.

170 But it is an indisputable matter of record: Ibid., 32.

170 "The entire business portion of the city is burning up": Ibid., 86.

171 Scammon was out of town: Ibid., 164.

171 He told her that Terrace Row, at least for the time being: Goff, 96.

171 But she chose to ignore Robert: Cromie, 165.

172 *Chicago Tribune* publisher Joseph Medill ordered: Ibid., 141.

172 "During Sunday night, Monday and Tuesday": *Chicago Tribune,* 11 October 1871.

172 "The greatest calamity that ever befell a city is upon us": letter by William H.

Carter, courtesy, Chicago Historical Society and the Trustees of Northwestern University.

173 "The distinguishing smell of the ruins": *The Nation* magazine, November 1871.

173 "poking about" in the still-smoldering ruins: Cromie, 187.

173 The only structure on Wabash that was spared total destruction was the Methodist church: Ibid.

173 The Howards were among the earliest settlers of St. Charles: *St. Charles Chronicle*, 1 April 1988.

174 they now flocked to St. Charles to participate in the regular séances held in the Howard House: Jeanne Schultz-Angel, *History of St. Charles: The First 100 Years* (St. Charles, Illinois: St. Charles Heritage Center, 2006).

174 she gave Mrs. Howard's daughter a gift of a shawl: *St. Charles Chronicle*, 1 April 1988.

174 "dark parlor country": Baker, 311.

175 The story of the Fox sisters: Ishbel Ross, *Charmers and Cranks* (New York: Harper & Row, 1965); Ashley Fields, Georgetown College; Bob Hoeltzel, historian, Town of Arcadia (New York).

175 Mumler had been an engraver for the high-end Boston jewelers: Troy Taylor, *The Haunted Museum*; Walter E. Woodbury, *Photographic Amusements* (New York: The Scovill & Adams Company, 1896), 22–28.

176 "I requested her to be seated, went into my darkroom": William H. Mumler, *Personal Experiences of William H. Mumler in Spirit Photography* (New York: Colby & Rich, 1875), cited by *The Haunted Museum*.

177 The waters at St. Catharines were dawn from: Alexander Campbell, *The Millennial Harbinger*, Vol. 5, No. 9, 1855, Notes of a Tour to Canada West, No. 1.

178 "violently angry" & "tongue-lashing—in absentia": Betty L. Mitchell, *Timeline* magazine, undated. The author is an historian at the University of Massachusetts.

178 it was her "dark secret": Baker, 310.

179 "my running waters": Baker, 270.

179 "possessed" by the spirit of a dead Indian: Danforth's testimony as reported by the *Chicago Tribune*, 20 October 1875.

179 Chloral hydrate is the oldest sedative in medicine: Palo Alto Medical Foundation (*PAMF Online*); U.S. Drug Enforcement Agency.

179 Chloral hydrate was the ingredient in the original Mickey Finn, named after a Chicago bartender who, in 1903, was accused of slipping it into the drinks of his patrons in order to incapacitate or rob them. Hence the phrase, "slipping a mickey."

179 "Please oblige me by sending about 4 powders": *New York Times*, 9 September 1999, reporting on newly discovered MTL letters.

179 Danforth's treatment continued off and on until March 1874, when he started seeing Mary almost daily: Neely and McMurtry, 11.

179 She was going to die . . . on September 6, 1874: court testimony, reported in *Chicago Tribune*, 20 October 1875.

180 "Being fully impressed with the idea, that my stay on Earth": MTL to RTL, August 1874, Illinois State Historical Library.

180 "debility of the nervous system": *Chicago Tribune*, 20 May 1875; Neely and McMurtry, 6.

181 "Mrs. Lincoln had always been a woman of rather unusual disposition": Eddie Joy and Alvin E. Harlow, "Clowning Through Life," *Collier's* Magazine, 25 December 1926.

181 "feeble health": Neely and McMurtry, 6.

182 "My Belief is my son is ill[.] Telegraph me": Ibid.

182 "My dearly beloved Son Robert T. Lincoln rouse yourself": Ibid.

11. THE TRIAL

184 "All is not lost. . . . Chicago still exists": Cromie, 218.

184 European guests were astonished at the amount of milk: W. G. Marshall, *Through America, Or: Nine Months in the United States* (New York: Arno Press, 1881), 96–97.

185 Mary said that on the morning she had boarded the train: Testimony of RTL, *Chicago Tribune*, 20 October 1875.

185 If she did not stop . . . he would check out of the hotel: Ibid.

186 "You are going to murder me!": Ibid.

186 He and his wife had four children: *Transactions of the Illinois State Historical Society*, 24–25 January 1907.

187 Florida had been "pleasant": Testimony of Dr. Willis Danforth, *Chicago Tribune*, 20 May 1875.

188 commit "in writing to pronounce her insane,": Leonard Swett to David Davis, 24 May 1874, David Davis Papers, ALPL.

188 "I believe her to be a fit subject for personal restraint": Neely and McMurtry, 13.

189 "not so sure about the necessity of *personal restraint*": Ibid.

189 the case against Mary was "very much stronger": Ibid., 15.

189 "Application to Try the Question of Insanity": Ibid., 23.

190 "Never mind your hair, Mrs. Lincoln, sit down here": Leonard Swett to David Davis, 24 May 1874. Davis Papers, ALPL. All the dialogue between Swett and MTL from pgs. 272–274 is drawn from the letter.

193 "We must act as though we were her friends": Ibid.

193 "I am going to the theater": Bishop, 191.

193 Mary had sent Arnold a gift—a set of Shakespeare: Baker, 319.

193 Judge Wallace had handpicked the jurors: names of jurors published in Samuel A. Schreiner Jr., *The Trials of Mrs. Lincoln* (Lincoln, Nebraska: University of Nebraska Press, 1987); Background on Dr. Samuel Blake, Baker, 328; Background on Charles Henderson, *Encyclopedia of Chicago* (Chicago: The Newberry Library, 2004).

195 Only three states—Illinois, Kentucky, and Indiana: Neely and McMurtry, 22.

195 "That means that you will put into her head": Leonard Swett to David Davis, 24 May 1874. Davis Papers, ALPL.

195 Arnold had ambitions to write the definitive biography: Baker, 319.

195 "my country was bigger than my family": Thomas Schwartz, *Journal of Illinois History*, Vol. 6, Summer 2003, 126.

196 "She had strange imaginings; thought that some one was at work at her head": *Chicago Tribune*, 20 May 1875.

197 a gentleman by the name of Shoemaker in Room 137: Neely and McMurtry, 27.

197–198 Testimony from witnesses based on reports from *Chicago Tribune, Chicago Inter Ocean, Chicago Times*, 20–21 May, 1874, and Insanity File Collection, Lincoln Museum. No trial transcript of the proceedings is known to exist.

201 Gage revealed himself to be a follower of Madame Blavatsky: *Time* magazine, 31 March 1930.

202 the disease would become "progressively worse": Baker, 325.

203 "I remember the fact of that trial or examination quite distinctly": Lyman J. Gage to William E. Barton, 20 January 1921, *Barton Collection*, courtesy Regenstein Library, University of Chicago.

203 "Mrs. Lincoln, you have $56,000 of money and bonds": Leonard Swett to David Davis, 24 May 1874. Davis Papers, ALPL.

205 "To have advanced on a battery instead would": Ibid.

206 Mary Lincoln took the bottle and swallowed: account of MTL's suicide attempts from Neely and McMurtry, 34–35; Insanity File Collection, Lincoln Museum; Leonard Swett to David Davis, Davis Papers, ALPL.

207 "painful beyond parallel": Leonard Swett to David Davis, Davis Papers, ALPL.

12. INSANE ASYLUM

208 "Patient Progress Reports for Bellevue Place": Rodney A. Ross, "Mary Todd Lincoln, Patient at Bellevue Place," *Journal of the Illinois State Historical Society*, Spring 1970. The author is an historian whose father ran Bellevue Place from 1946 to 1964.

208 "insane of the private class": Life at Bellevue Place from Ross, Ibid; Baker, 333; Neely and McMurtry, 39–40.

209 even prescribed marijuana, or served beer, or eggnog: Ross, 10; Neely and McMurtry, 39.

209 The ratio of staff to patients: Ross, 10.

209 her pulse was one hundred: Ross, 26.

210 This attendant was also a paid informant: Baker, 332.

210 "as unobjectionable as it is possible": *Chicago Tribune*, 29 August 1875.

212 "Cold chills assailed me": Martha Rayne, *Chicago Post & Mail*, 13 July 1875.

213 Patterson's retarded daughter, Blanche: Baker, 337.

214 "I don't even know who Myra Bradwell was": Jane M. Friedman, *America's First Woman Lawyer: The Biography of Myra Bradwell* (Amherst, New York: Prometheus Books, 1993), 13.

214 "side by side" with her husband: Ibid., 41.

214 "all gone crazy": Ibid., 27.

214 "The paramount destiny and mission": Ibid., 12, 24, 25.

214 "a just, good man & a lover of *truth*": MTL to Jacob Bunn, 31 January 1877, Turner, *Letters*, 324.

215 "I looked anxiously around, hoping I might possibly see my friend": Myra Brad-

well's account of her attempt to see MTL ran in the *Bloomington Courier*, as cited by Friedman, 52–54.

217 "It is the most natural thing in the world": Bellevue Place medical logs.

217 At Bellevue, even spicy food was banned: Baker, 333.

218 "Six physicians in council informed me": RTL to Sally Orne, 1 June 1875, cited by Helm, 295.

219 "It is a great comfort to hear from your own self": Sally Orne to RTL, 8 August 1875, cited by Helm, 297.

219 "May I request you to come out here just so soon": MTL to James Bradwell, undated, cited by Jason Emerson, "The Madness of Mary Lincoln," *American Heritage* magazine, June/July 2006.

220 "This note [to Farnsworth] she must have put in the office": Bellevue Place Medical Logs, Ross, 30.

221 "When all others, among them my husband's": MTL quote from "Presentation of Bronze Bust of Mrs. Myra Bradwell, First Woman Lawyer in Illinois," *Transactions of the Illinois State Historical Society 38*, 1931, cited by Friedman, 51. The quote is attributed to Mrs. Bradwell's friend, Eleanor Gridley.

221 She expressed concern that Patterson would not "trust her again": Bellevue Medical Logs; Ross, 31.

222 "I cannot feel that it is necessary to keep": Myra Bradwell to Elizabeth Edwards, undated, cited by Emerson, *American Heritage* magazine, June/July 2006.

222 Next, Myra Bradwell paid a visit to Robert Lincoln's law office: *Chicago Times*, 24 August 1875; Bellevue Medical Logs.

222 He identified himself as "Mr. Wilkie of Chicago": Bellevue Place Medical Logs; Ross, 32.

223 "In making future visits, if any should be made": Dr. James Patterson to Myra Bradwell, 9 August 1875, cited by Friedman, 55.

223 to call him "Mr. Patterson": Ibid., 57; Insanity File Collection, The Lincoln Museum, Fort Wayne, Indiana.

224 "I said in my [last] letter to you that I understood that Mrs. Bradwell is a spiritualist": RTL to Elizabeth Edwards, 10 August 1875, cited by Friedman, 56; Insanity File Collection, Lincoln Museum.

224 "pest and a nuisance": Bellevue Medical Logs; Ross, 33.

224 his mother "suggested to a lady (who told me of it with some alarm)": RTL to Elizabeth Edwards, 7 August 1875, cited by Neely and McMurtry, 36; Insanity File Collection, Lincoln Museum.

225 "After hearing all the facts from you": Elizabeth Edwards to RTL, 12 August 1875, Neely and McMurtry, 62; Insanity File Collection.

225 "I am dreadfully disappointed that Aunt Lizzie": RTL to MTL, 15 August 1875, cited by Friedman, 58.

225 "It does not appear that God is good, to have placed me here": MTL to James and Myra Bradwell, undated, cited by Emerson, *American Heritage* magazine, June/July 2006.

225 "I visited my mother yesterday": RTL to Myra Bradwell, 14 August 1875, cited by Friedman, 59; Insanity File Collection, Lincoln Museum.

226 "So much discussion with the patient about going away": Richard Patterson to the Bradwells, 15 August 1875, cited by Friedman, 59; Insanity File Collection.

226 "I have just had a call from Mrs. Bradford": Elizabeth Edwards to RTL, 17 August 1875, Neely and McMurtry, 67.

226 "No, Doctor, if you have the good of Mrs. Lincoln at heart": *Chicago Tribune*, 31 August 1875.

227 "I have always had the tenderest regard and love for Mrs. Lincoln": *Chicago Times*, undated.

230 this "was not Robert's finest hour": Neely and McMurtry, 63, 75.

230 "protracted, confidential" interview: Ibid., 72.

230 "features of her case that give me grave apprehensions": Ibid.

230 the shortest incarceration in Bellevue Place history: Baker, 336.

230 "unkindly or improperly treated" during her stay: Bellevue Medical Logs; Ross, 34.

231 "good disposition, sagacity and presence of mind": Neely and McMurtry, 73.

13. "MONSTER OF MANKIND"

232 "Mr. Win-*det*," the witness corrected Mr. Lincoln: Goff, 99. Brigham, 337.

233 Robert personally drew up the wills for three of the city's: Ibid., 98.

233 dying among strangers, thousands of miles from home": Ibid., 287.

234 "almost morbid" fear of such a life: Neely and McMurtry, 78; Goff, 108.

234 "gang of robbers": *Chicago Tribune*, 11 January 1887.

234 "I shall tell my wife about Mrs. Nicolay": Randall, *Lincoln's Sons*, 297.

235 "From a son worthy of his illustrious father": Goff, 108.

235 "He is building up a lucrative practice": Ibid.

235 Robert asked President Hayes to name a cousin: Ibid., 109; Harrison County Historical Society (Cynthiana, Kentucky).

236 "I am sorry to say that your mother": Ninian Edwards to RTL, 14 January 1876, Neely and McMurtry, 91.

236 A nurse named Amanda: Neely and McMurtry, 73.

237 "overdressed queen": Baker, 192.

237 "I have no hesitation in pronouncing her sane": Elizabeth Edwards to RTL, 5 November 1875, Neely and McMurty, 75.

238 "I quite agree with her that her dust-soiled veil bonnet and shawl": Elizabeth Edwards to RTL, 12 November 1875, Neely and McMurty, 76.

239 "I merely mention it to you to say that one": RTL to David Davis, 16 November 1875, Neely and McMurtry, 79–80.

240 "She has no conception of your mother's real condition": David Davis to RTL, 20 November 1875, Neely and McMurtry, 82.

240 "order whatever Mr. Swett and I think best": RTL to David Davis, 16 November 1875, Neely and McMurtry, 79.

240 "I write under the influence of motives": John M. Palmer to RTL, 21 December and 25 December 1875, Neely and McMurtry, 89–90.

241 "she had hired two men to take your life": Ninian Edwards to RTL, 14 January 1876, Neely and McMurtry, 91–92.

241 "Elizabeth thinks she could get [the pistol] from her": Ninian Edwards to RTL, 15 January 1876, Neely and McMurtry, 95–96.

241 This "pistol business": Neely and McMurtry, 96.

242 "plainly irrational and the emanation of an insane mind": RTL to Elizabeth Edwards, 12 February and 16 February 1876, Neely and McMurty, 98.

243 "By appointment Mr. Edwards came to see me today": David Davis to RTL, 22 May 1876, Insanity File Collection, The Lincoln Museum, Fort Wayne, Indiana.

243 "I do not believe that any raid on you is contemplated": David Davis to RTL, 4 June 1876, Insanity File Collection, The Lincoln Museum, Fort Wayne, Indiana.

243 "If it pleases the court," Swett began: *Chicago Times*, 16 June 1876; Neely and McMurtry, 101–103.

245 "I regret very much that the verdict stated": Ninian Edwards to RTL, 17 June 1876, Insanity File Collection, The Lincoln Museum, Fort Wayne, Indiana; Baker, 349.

245 Mary's court victory was relegated to a single sentence: Schreiner, 251.

245 "Robert T. Lincoln: Do not fail to send me without *the least* delay": MTL to RTL, 19 June 1876, Turner, *Letters*, 615–616.

246 "monster of mankind": Neely and McMurtry, citing undated letter from MTL to RTL, 107.

246 "Now with such a son bearing patiently for ten years": Leonard Swett to Ninian Edwards, 20 June 1876, Neely and McMurtry, 106.

247 "I cannot endure to meet my former friends": Helm, 298.

14. SECRETARY OF WAR

249 Garfield was looking for geographic balance in his cabinet: Theodore Clarke Smith, *The Life and Letters of James Abram Garfield, Vol. II* (New Haven, Connecticut: Yale University Press, 1925), 1,062.

249 "I quite agree with you that the selection of Robert Lincoln": Joseph Medill to John Logan, 27 January 1881, Goff, 115.

249 "I write to you on the subject of a cabinet position": Ulysses S. Grant to John Logan, 15 February 1881, Ibid., 115.

250 "I am somewhat in doubt": RTL to John Logan, 10 January 1881, Ibid., 116.

251 "Robert Lincoln looks like his mother": Gail Hamilton, *Life in Letters, Vol. II* (Boston: Lee & Shepard, 1901), 814.

252 "You can imagine how elated I felt": MTL to Edward Lewis Baker Jr., 22 June 1879, Turner, *Letters*, 683–684.

253 "Somewhere in Europe": RTL to Henry Darling, 15 November 1877, Barton Collection, University of Chicago, cited by Neely and McMurtry, 121.

254 "Love crowned you at your birth": MTL to Edward Lewis Baker Jr., 22 June 1879, Turner, *Letters*, 682.

254 "I go into exile and alone": Elizabeth Edwards to RTL, 29 October 1876, Insanity File Collection, The Lincoln Museum, Fort Wayne, Indiana.

254 "place an ocean between you and herself": Elizabeth Edwards to RTL, 26

October 1876, Insanity File Collection, The Lincoln Museum, Fort Wayne, Indiana.

255   Mary showed her young companion the graves: Baker, 353.

255   she saw the Howard family production of *Uncle Tom's Cabin*: Ibid., 355.

256   "Such kindness, deference & attention": MTL to Edward Lewis Baker Jr., 17 October 1876, Turner, *Letters*, 618.

256   "It is pleasant to be thus received": Ibid.

256   She boarded the steamer *Columbia*: Baker, 355.

257   "a very expensive place": MTL to Jacob Bunn, 12 December 1876, Turner, *Letters*, 623.

257   "the *most unprincipled, heartless, avaricious*": MTL to Edward Lewis Baker Jr., 12 June 1880, Turner, *Letters*, 699.

258   "That wretched young man, but *old* in sin": MTL to Edward Lewis Baker Jr., 11 April 1877, Ibid., 633.

258   "afraid a letter from me would not be well received": RTL to Elizabeth Edwards, 18 April 1879, cited by Neely and McMurtry, 122.

259   "*waffles, batter cakes*, egg corn bread": MTL to Edward Lewis Baker Jr., 4 October 1879, Turner, *Letters*, 690.

259   she wrapped herself in flannel pajamas: Ibid.

260   Julia let loose a "floodgate" of tears: Julia Dent Grant, *The Personal Memoirs of Julia Dent Grant* (New York: G. P. Putnam's Sons, 1975), 197.

260   The former president and his wife were honored: Baker, 360.

260   "I learned the night before we left that Mrs. Abraham Lincoln": Grant, 260–261.

260   "butcher" during the Civil War and claimed he had "no regard for life": Randall, *Mary Lincoln*, 253.

260   "How dare you be seated until I invite you!": Adam Badeau, an aide to Ulysses S. Grant, recounted the episode in a letter published on 17 January 1887, after Mary Lincoln's death.

261   "broken hearted sorrowing woman": MTL to Edward Lewis Baker Jr., 16 January 1880, Turner, *Letters*, 694.

261   As First Lady, she was attacked for her regal and "queen-like" behavior: National First Ladies' Library, Canton, Ohio.

262   "There are five kinds of actresses: bad actresses": Mark Twain quote cited by Robert Gottlieb, *New York Review of Books*, Vol. 54, No. 8, 10 May 2007.

262   "untuned piano": Ibid.

262   "What a profusion of the letters S. B.!" she exclaimed: Sarah Bernhardt, *Memories of My Life* (New York: D. Appleton & Co., 1907), 369.

263   I had just done this unhappy woman the only service: Ibid., 369–370.

264   "She was dressed plainly; her face was furrowed" and other accounts of MTL's homecoming: *Illinois State Journal*, 10 July 1881; *New York Sun*, 28 October 1880; Baker, 364.

15. DEATHWATCH

265   "How much time have we, Officer?": Kenneth D. Ackerman, *Dark Horse: The Surprise Election and Political Murder of President James A. Garfield* (New York:

Caroll & Graf, 2003), 375–377. Ackerman's book has an excellent account of Garfield's assassination.

266 he had purchased at a gun shop on F Street for ten dollars: Ibid., 355.

267 "I don't think this is serious": Smith, 1,180.

267 "The President wishes me to say to you that he has been seriously hurt": Ibid., 1,181.

268 "Why did that man shoot me?": Ackerman, 392.

268 Harriet Blaine organized the wives: Smith, 1,183.

269 "How many hours of sorrow I have passed in this town": Charles Rosenberg, *The Trial of the Assassin Guiteau* (Chicago: University of Chicago Press, 1968), 4.

269 "I pray to God that the president will recover": Ackerman, 404–405.

270 "The President had a natural movement": Ibid., 416.

270 "I wish I felt better about the President": Goff, 120.

270 Lincoln advised Garfield that the war department was running smoothly: Smith, 1,195. Guiteau was hanged on June 30, 1882.

271 "prostrated by illness, the light of life and joy": Helm, 299.

271 The trunks weighed an estimated four tons: Baker, 365.

271 "shrinking and sensitive": Helm, 299.

272 "Her enjoyment of a darkened room does not accord": Elizabeth Edwards to Emilie Todd Helm, 3 March 1881, Turner, *Letters*, 705.

272 "immediate friends here consider her ailments": *Chicago Tribune*, 24 November 1881.

272 "It was very hard on Cousin Robert": "An Old Lady's Lincoln Memories," *Life* magazine, 9 February 1959.

274 Robert said he was sorry and begged her: W. A. Evans, *Mrs. Abraham Lincoln: A Study of her Personality and Her Influence on Lincoln* (New York: Knopf, 1932), 32; *Illinois State Journal*, 28 May 1881.

274 later that evening Robert dined with the governor of Illinois: *Illinois State Journal*, 28 May 1884; *Chicago Tribune*, 31 May 1884.

274 a grimy room that she facetiously called "choice": MTL to Josephine Remann Edwards (Elizabeth Edwards's daughter-in-law), 23 October 1881, Turner, *Letters*, 709.

275 "Mrs. Lincoln sat propped up with pillows on a sofa": *Illinois State Journal*, 30 November 1881.

275 "Her son Robert was now Secretary of War": *Chicago Tribune*, 24 November 1881.

276 "her son Robert and his wife, Mary, who visit her": *Chicago Tribune*, 24 November 1881; *Illinois State Journal*, 30 November 1881.

276 Mary sat in the room unable to walk, "almost blind": Randall, *Mary Lincoln*, 442.

277 "Leave no one *untalked to*": MTL to Noyes W. Miner, 3 January 1882, Turner, *Letters*, 711.

277 "*Do not* approach Robert T. Lincoln": Ibid., 712.

277 "Until I see the $15,000—I will not believe it": MTL to Noyes W. Miner, 21 February 1882, Ibid., 714–715.

278 "very false" and a "swindle": Ibid.

278 she was stricken with an outbreak of boils: *Chicago Tribune*, 17 July 1882.

279 confined to her house due to "ill-health": *Illinois State Journal*, 19 July 1882.

16. THE MAN WHO COULD BE PRESIDENT

282 "It's mighty lucky I could have this room with so many windows": Florence L. Snow, *Pictures on My Wall: A Lifetime in Kansas* (Lawrence, Kansas: University of Kansas Press, 1945), 66–80.

283 "I long ago came to the conclusion that one could not": Goff, 104–105.

283 longing for the "independence" of Chicago: Goff, 123.

283 Robert usually wrapped up his workday at four: *Chicago Tribune*, 31 May 1884.

284 "considerable friction" between him and Robert Lincoln: *Chicago Tribune*, 21 March 1885.

284 "Me, Tosawi; me good Injun": Dee Brown, *Bury My Heart at Wounded Knee* (New York: Henry Holt & Co., 1970), 170.

284 Lincoln was indifferent to the polar initiative: Alden Todd, *Abandoned: The Story of the Greely Arctic Expedition 1881–1884* (Fairbanks, Alaska: University of Alaska Press, 2001 edition; originally published in 1961 by McGraw-Hill), 16.

285 "did not see any use throwing away more money for dead men": Goff, 136.

286 praised Captain Schley for his "inestimable services": Todd, 279.

000 only the fourth man in U.S. history to be so honored: *Time* magazine, 1 April 1935.

287 "If ever an officer deserved to be court-martialed": *Chicago Tribune*, 8 March 1885.

287 "He is absolutely at the head": *Chicago Tribune*, 31 May 1884.

287 It was an "insinuation which was especially offensive": RTL to Ward Hill Lamon, 10 May 1883, Huntington Library.

288 "I appeal to you in the name of the great dead": David Davis to Ward Hill Lamon, 13 April 1884, David Davis Family Papers.

288 On the first anniversary of Lincoln's assassination: Gene Smith, "The Haunted Major," *American Heritage Magazine*, Feb/March 1994.

290 "I do not think he is overfond of public life": *Chicago Tribune*, 31 May 1884.

290 Robert Lincoln sent word to his old ally Leonard Swett: Ibid.

291 Mary Harlan Lincoln failed to appear: Ibid.

291 The Lincolns became the pioneers of Chicago's Gold Coast: Goff, 150; *Chicago Tribune*, 14 January 1959; 28 April 1889.

292 "I am camping in my new home": Goff, 150.

292 "sentimental considerations": *Harper's Weekly*, 3 September 1887; Goff, 162.

292 "I have seen too much of the wear and tear": *Chicago Tribune*, 11 September 1887.

293 a bowler hat and a Scotch tweed suit from Poole's: *Chicago Tribune*, 20 August 1888.

293 "I am thinking of sending Robert T. Lincoln over there": *Chicago Tribune*, 28 March 1889.

294 Lincoln went to Washington in early May: *Chicago Tribune*, 5 May 1889.

299   presidential yacht USS *Dispatch* and became the sailors' pet: *Chicago Tribune*, 31 May 1884.

300   "He was fond of the history of the late war": *Lincoln Lore*, 16 October 1939, No. 549, Bulletin of the Lincoln National Life Foundation.

300   "Thank you very much," Jessie said: C. J. King, 118.

301   "Is this your ball, and did you break my window?": *Illinois State Journal*, 28 February 1937.

301   "I would like to be as good, as kind": C. J. King, 120.

301   When Jack was fifteen, he was called on: *Journal of the Illinois State Historical Society*, Spring 1958, Vol. 588, No. 1.

302   of "little consequence": *Chicago Tribune*, 3 March 1940. Robert S. McCormick's letters cited in this chapter were published in the *Tribune* fifty years after Jack Lincoln's death.

302   "Jack's carbuncle is running its course": Ibid.

303   "We were very anxious all day yesterday": John Hay to RTL, 30 November 1889, cited by Goff, 195.

303   Jack kept his mind alert reading newspapers and "light" books: Hildene archives.

305   The boy, he said, was "never braver": Hildene archives.

306   "Go upstairs quickly!" she screamed: Allan Nevins, *Henry White: Thirty Years of American Diplomacy* (New York: Harper & Brothers, 1930), 73.

306   "Whether Jack gets well or not I shall always be of the opinion": Hildene archives.

306   but also to the "people of the United States": *Chicago Tribune*, 3 March 1940.

307   "When we got to Kensington Gardens": Nevins, 73.

308   "Gentlemen, I thank you for this kindness": *Illinois State Journal*, 9 November 1890.

310   she seemed ten years older than her age: C. J. King, 131.

310   He attended church every Sunday, went to the theater and the opera: Ibid., 132.

310   "must be pure and brave as Sir Galahad himself": Ibid.

311   the "quietest and most respectful of valets": Lars Anderson, *Letters and Journals of a Diplomat* (London & Edinburgh: Fleming H. Revell Co., 1940), 70. Anderson later served as U.S. ambassador to Japan.

311   "One gave me a printed list of questions to fill out and return": Ibid., 76.

311   The wedding took place Wednesday, September 2, 1891: *New York Times*, 3 September 1891.

312   just before he departed for the Isle of Jersey: Anderson, 79.

312   "I am prepared to say that he is one": Ibid., 69.

312   "Wouldn't it be lovely if I could go home to you": Jessie Lincoln to James Harlan, August 1891, Hildene archives.

313   where it was delayed by a bureaucracic snag: Anderson, 91–92.

313   "I was very glad to know that the most anxious": RTL to Charles Isham, 11 June 1892, Chicago Historical Society.

314   "The papers say he is to be the next President": Mary King Waddington, *Letters of a Diplomat's Wife, 1883–1900* (New York: Charles Scribner's Sons, 1903), 339–340.

314   seen as a rude and ill-mannered snub: Randall, *Lincoln's Sons*, 310.

315   the Lincolns were treated to a special send-off: Hildene archives.

315   Robert Lincoln had endorsed him for president in 1888: Goff, 169.

315   "pleasant and sensible": Goff, 212, citing *The Letters of Queen Victoria*, Vol. II, 238.

315   "I feel about 900 years old": Goff, 216.

315   "I wonder if you are getting to feel so miserably": RTL to John Nicolay, 3 January 1894, cited by Goff, 216.

316   one of the wealthiest men in American history: In a survey of the richest people in American history, *The New York Times* (15 July 2007) ranked Pullman 27th on the list, putting his personal net worth at $34 billion in current dollars.

316   Pullman made a point of hiring "the blackest man": Larry Tye, "The World of a Pullman Porter," *APF Reporter* (Alicia Patterson Foundation), Vol. 21, No. 2; Stanley Turkel, "George Mortimer Pullman: Builder of Hotel Rooms on Wheels," excerpted from *Great Hoteliers: Pioneers of the Hotel Industry* (Jefferson, North Carolina: McFarland & Co., 2006).

317   Ely found that in Pullman, "nothing is free": Richard T. Ely, "Pullman: A Social Study," *Harper's Magazine*, February 1885.

318   Then came the Panic of 1893: Account of the Pullman Strike drawn from R. Conrad Stein, *The Pullman Strike and the Labor Movement in American History* (Berkeley Heights, New Jersey: Enslow Publishers, 2001) and Rosemary Laughlin, *The Pullman Strike of 1894* (Greensboro, North Carolina: Morgan Reynolds, 2006).

319   "absurd stubbornness": *Chicago Tribune*, 11 July 1894.

320   "Shall we take a cab to the Brevort House?" *Chicago Tribune*, 14 July 1894.

320   "The men are hungry": Governor John Altgeld to George Pullman, 21 August 1894, John Altgeld, *Live Questions: Including Our Penal Machinery and Its Victims* (Chicago: Donohue & Hennebery, 1890), 399–400. Altgeld's letters can also be found in Almont Lindsay, *The Pullman Strike: The Story of a Unique Experiment and of a Great Labor Upheaval* (Chicago: University of Chicago Press: 1942), 340.

320   The tycoon died of a heart attack: *New York Times*, 20 October 1897.

321   "in their bereavement was making sure the sonofabitch": quote attributed to Ambrose Bierce, cited in Pullman Virtual Museum and the Pullman State Historic Site.

321   issued the full powers of the presidency: *Chicago Tribune*, 12 November 1897.

321   All two thousand brick houses were sold to the highest bidder: *New York Times*, 8 January 1899.

322   "It is a long way from Abraham Lincoln": undated article, *Fresno Weekly*, Hildene archives.

323 His teammates called him "the dude": *New York Times*, 14 November 1897; *A Century of Baseball* (Austin, Texas: Eakin Press, 1987), cited in *Handbook of Texas Online*.

323 "harum-scarum young fellow": C. J. King, 144, citing *Milwaukee Journal*.

324 the morning of November 10, Jessie told her mother that she was going shopping: Lester W. Olson, "Lincoln's Granddaughter Eloped to Milwaukee," *Historical Messenger* of the Milwaukee County Historical Society, December 1955, Vol. II, No. 4.

326 After dinner, she went up to her room and closed the door: *Chicago Daily News*, 11 November 1897.

326 "The message is more than true": *Chicago Tribune*, 11 November 1897. The front page story was headlined, JESSIE LINCOLN ELOPES.

326 pitch black except for one light: Ibid.

327 "It is said of him that he has never been thrown": Ibid.

327 "About a year ago my daughter and young Beckwith": *Chicago Daily News*, 11 November 1897.

327 "I do not know anything about the details": *Historical Messenger*, 10.

328 "Well, my daughter will remain, I think": *Chicago Daily News*, 11 November 1897.

328 "It is a pity when Abraham Lincoln freed the colored women": C. J. King, 148.

329 Pullman stock was a blue chip favorite: *Chicago Tribune*, 12 November 1897.

329 "I do not care to discuss my affairs in public": *Chicago Journal*, 13 November 1897.

329 "Congratulations and best wishes for a long": Mary Kelly to Jessie Lincoln Beckwith, undated, Hildene archives.

329 "I understand that you do not particularly": Rev. O. P. Christian to RTL, 13 November 1897, Hildene archives.

330 "Keep up the good heart": Warren Beckwith to Jessie Lincoln Beckwith, undated, Hildene archives.

330 "Warren Wallace Beckwith, who eloped": King, 149, citing *Mount Pleasant Daily News*.

331 the Beckwiths came from a distinguished family: information about the Beckwith family courtesy Warren Wallace Beckwith Jr. and Missouri Historical Society.

332 he took the field against the Keokuk College of Physicians and Surgeons: *New York Times*, 17 November 1897.

333 "suitable employment": *New York Times*, 30 March 1989.

334 he had the right of way because he was bringing milk for Abraham Lincoln's great-granddaughter: Iowa History Project, *The Palimpest*, Vol. XII, No. 9, September 1931.

334 "There has been talk that I didn't get along with Robert Lincoln": *Chicago Tribune*, 20 March 1952.

335 He "bade his daughter an affectionate 'good night.'": Brigham, 312–314. James Harlan's wife, Ann Eliza Peck Harlan, died September 4, 1884, after her carriage was involved in a collision with runaway horses.

335 The population was seventy-six million: *Portrait of America, 1899*, from Federal Reserve Bank of San Francisco.

20. PRESIDENTIAL CURSE

336 the train pulled into the station at Dunkirk, outside Buffalo: *Buffalo Evening News*, 4 September 1901.

337 Some called it the greatest speech of McKinley's life: Marshall Everett, *Complete Life of William McKinley and Story of His Assassination* (Whitefish, Montana: Kessinger Publishing Company edition. Originally published in 1901), 34.

337 McKinley shook her hand and fixed a gentle smile: Ibid.

337 "You've shot the president!": *Buffalo Evening News*, 8 September 1884. Czolgosz, an anarchist, died in the electric chair fifty-four days after he shot McKinley. His last words were, "I am not sorry for my crime."

338 Jinxy McDeath: Sarah Vowell, *Assassination Vacation* (New York: Simon & Schuster, 2005), 236.

338 "I do not congratulate you for I have seen": RTL to Theodore Roosevelt, 18 September 1901, RTL Papers, LOC.

339 "If only they knew, they wouldn't want me there": Goff, 234, citing clipping in RTL Papers, LOC.

339 "No, I am not going and they'd better not invite me": *Burlington Free Press*, 27 July 1926.

339 On September 26, 1901, twenty-three people gathered: Dorothy Meserve Kunhardt, *Life* magazine, 15 February 1963.

341 "When I get ready": Hildene archives.

341 "I think [Jessie] would be willing for us to adopt": RTL to Mary Harlan Lincoln, undated, Hildene archives.

342 On New Year's Day 1906: Goff, 235.

342 William Beale, who now represented Field: *New York Times*, 15 January 1906.

342 "Mr. Field's death is a great affliction": RTL to Emily Todd Helm, 20 February 1906, Hildene archives.

342 "ancestral home": RTL to Henry White, 19 March 1905, Henry White Papers, LOC.

343 "I hope you are very well": RTL to John Nicolay, undated, but written sometime in 1898, cited by Randall, *Lincoln's Sons*, 332.

344 Robert Lincoln pulled into Springfield on Friday morning: *Illinois State Register*, 13 February 13, 1909.

345 Robert made an unannounced visit: *Springfield Journal*, 13 February 1909, 3 (for RTL's visit); 5 (for Mary Harlan Lincoln's absence).

346 Reverend L. H. Magee declare, "I would rather": speech quoted in *Abraham Lincoln Centennial Online*.

346 "I hear that Bob Lincoln . . . does not relish": Archibald Butt to Mrs. Lewis Butt, 14 February 1909, Archibald Butt, Lawrence F. Abbott, ed., *The Letters of Archie Butt, Personal Aide to President Roosevelt* (Garden City, New Jersey: Doubleday, Page & Co., 1924), 333–334.

347 "grieved" and "walk over the farm and drink from the spring": Randall, *Lincoln's*

Sons, 335–336. The Lincoln log cabin that is now part of the national historic site in Kentucky is considered a "symbolic" replica of the actual log cabin in which Lincoln was born.

347 "one of the former millions of slaves": *Illinois State Register*, 12 February 1909.

347 Robert Lincoln did appear in the town of Hodgenville: Randall, *Lincoln's Sons*, 334–335.

348 "myth" of Abraham Lincoln's childhood poverty: Michael Beschloss, "The Last of the Lincolns," *The New Yorker*, 28 February 1994.

348 In those days, Kodak cameras were sold with the film already loaded. After one hundred photos were exposed, the film, along with the camera, was sent to the Kodak factory for processing. Then the prints were returned along with the camera, which was then reloaded with fresh photo stock.

348 He also introduced Peggy to golf: C. J. King, 158.

21. FAMILY SECRETS

350 "There was nothing. He was all Todd": Ida Tarbell, *All In a Day's Work: An Autobiography* (New York: Macmillan, 1939), 164–169.

352 "Every line has been written in a spirit of reverence": John Hay to RTL, 27 January 1884, cited by David C. Mearns, *The Lincoln Papers, Vol. I* (Garden City, New York: Doubleday, 1948), 75. Mearns was the director of the Library of Congress' Reference Department and was charged with custody of the Lincoln Papers.

352 "Honest Abe," to be an "epithet": Beschloss, 55.

352 He told Ida Tarbell, "There is nothing of my father's there": Tarbell, 168–169.

353 "I am nearly sixty-nine years old and a year ago": RTL to George H. Thacher, date unknown, reported by *Washington Post*, 16 September 1957.

354 "If my son was still alive, I should probably": Mearns, 91.

354 "fire and accident" that could result in the total loss: Ibid., 92–93.

355 "The collection of original Lincoln letters and documents": Tarbell, cited by Mearns, 98.

355 The library and reception room were turned into a gallery: *Norwich Bulletin*, 26 July 1895.

355 "A stumble meant sudden death": *Washington Post*, 26 November 1916; 13 May 1915; 16 April 1914.

355 "Adonis-like archeologist": undated society column, cited by C. J. King, 205.

356 "Mrs. Beckwith has been so conservative": Ibid.

356 "The man is Frank E. Johnson": undated RTL letter to Katherine Helm, Hildene archives.

356 "He seems inclined to shun the limelight": undated *Cedar Rapids Republican* clip, Hildene archives.

357 "Jessie, he said it was all every bit of it your mother's fault": Anne Dodge to Jessie Lincoln Beckwith, 15 May 1915, Hildene archives.

357 "wedding of wide interest": *Washington Post*, 23 June 1915.

358 a child born with severely crossed eyes: Mark E. Neely Jr. and Harold Holzer, *The Lincoln Family Album* (New York: Doubleday, 1990), 149.

359 "She said there was no point to it, to let the past be": *Chicago Tribune*, 20 March 1952.

359 "desertion from bed and board": Frank "Ned" Johnson to RTL, 18 April 1921, Hildene archives.

359 "What a damned fool that man is": Mary Harlan Lincoln to Jessie Lincoln Beckwith, quoting RTL, 10 June 1921, Hildene archives.

360 "I shall always love Jessie and her children": Alice Johnson to Mary Harlan Lincoln, undated, Hildene archives.

360 "The thought of forgoing this and spending the rest of my life": Jessie Lincoln Beckwith to RTL, 6 July 1920, Hildene archives.

360 "a married daughter of your age having two children": RTL to Jessie Lincoln Beckwith, 18 July 1920, Hildene archives.

361 Lincoln had his Washington lawyers from the firm: Mearns, 103.

361 The Lincoln Papers were locked in compartment 19: Ibid., 104.

000 found his friend "surrounded by a number of large boxes and with many papers": Nicholas Murray Butler, *Across the Busy Years* (New York: Charles Scribner's Sons, 1939), 375–376.

362 "Why, Robert Lincoln, those papers do not belong to you": Ibid.

363 pure of line and flawless: *New York Times*, 31 May 1922.

364 an airplane appeared out of the sky and circled the mall: Ibid.

364 "Isn't it beautiful?": Mearns, 109.

365 "having given considerable thought to the matter": Mary Harlan Lincoln to Lieutenant Colonel Clarence Sherrill, undated, but written in 1925, Hildene archives.

22. THE LINCOLN ISHAM WALTZ

369 "since Papa left us": Mary Harlan Lincoln to Jessie Lincoln Beckwith, undated but probably written in August 1926, Hildene archives.

369 "And it was this: that the beloved one should be interred": Mary Harlan Lincoln to Katherine Helm, undated, Hildene archives.

370 His first wife had been the New York heiress Vera Schuyler Schermerhorn: *New York Times*, 25 March 1927.

371 Mrs. Pritchard had in her possession thirty-seven "lost" letters: Friedman, 72.

371 signed contract with the publishing firm of J. H. Sears & Company: Jason Emerson, *The Madness of Mary Lincoln* (Carbondale, Illinois: Southern Illinois University Press, 2007), 141.

371 "It is better to have Mrs. Pritchard as a friend than to offend her": Ibid., 141.

372 "All I can say is that it sews her up as tight as a drum": Friedman, 75.

372 She fully anticipated that the Lincoln family would set fire to the Mary Todd Lincoln letters: For forty years historians believed the letters had been destroyed. But in 2005 the historian Jason Emerson discovered twenty of the letters inside a steamer trunk once owned by the Lincoln family lawyer Frederic Towers. For an account of the discovery, see Emerson's *The Madness of Mary Lincoln*.

373   She continually wrote checks, marked as "allowances": Hildene archives.

373   "and it was the Lincoln money he was spending": George Ballentyne Jr. interview with author.

373   "It is not fair for her, not fair to her": Frederic Towers to Jessie Lincoln (now Jessie Lincoln Randolph), undated, Hildene archives.

373   "Since your advent you can see me only as occupying a superficial place": Jessie Lincoln to Frederic Towers, undated, Hildene archives.

374   "You know I have no axe to grind": Frederic Towers to Jessie Lincoln, 8 October 1932, Hildene archives.

374   Mrs. Eddy declined to see Abraham Lincoln's youngest granddaughter: C. J. King, 212.

375   He was also a fixture of New York café society: Hildene archives.

375   "Hello Margaret, this is Lincoln": *Washington Post*, 13 February 1959.

376   earning a 74 average grade: Hildene archives.

376   male heirs to the Firestone and Vanderbilt fortunes: *Time* magazine, 5 October 1936.

376   He quoted his mother as forever telling him, "You'll never work, so don't try": interview with Beckwith family friend Tom Grove Jr., 30 September 2006.

377   "I'm a spoiled brat": *Madison* (Wisconsin) *Courier*, 26 December 1985.

377   "After we had gone maybe 70 miles I began": Robert Todd Lincoln Beckwith's "Dearest Granny" letter to MHL, 28 March, year unknown, Hildene archives.

377   The Madeira School was located on Nineteenth Street: *Time* magazine, 31 May 1948; C. J. King, 151; Madeira School Web site.

378   As to the inevitable questions about her sexuality: Beschloss, 56.

378   They both got a kick out of soaring in the sky above Washington: *Washington Post*, 22 December 1929.

379   "That's the only time we knew she wasn't around to be watching us": C. J. King, 181. King's book, *Four Marys and a Jessie*, details life at Hildene in the Peggy Beckwith era.

379   "It was a stunning blow": Jessie Lincoln (Randolph) to Mary Harlan Lincoln, undated, Hildene archives.

380   "I do not feel like writing a long letter": MHL's "Dearest Petticoat" letters to Jessie Lincoln (Randolph), 29 September 1934, Hildene archives.

381   "She was sleeping like a baby": Peggy Beckwith letter to unknown friend, Hildene archives.

381   "shunned publicity on all occasions": *Chicago Tribune*, 1 April 1937.

381   She was buried in Arlington National Cemetery: *Washington Post*, 1 April 1937.

381   a codicil that left Hildene to her daughter Mamie Lincoln Isham: Mary Harlan Lincoln's will on file in District of Manchester Probate Court, Vermont.

382   she died following surgery at a New York City hospital: *New York Times*, 22 November 1938.

23. "I, ROBERT TODD LINCOLN . . ."

383   "I'd like you to meet my sister": Robert Crans Jr. interview, 26 August 2006 and 23 September 2006. Crans Jr. is the son of Doris Beckwith Crans.

384 Twenty-seven other debutantes were presented that night: *Washington Post*, 21 January 1940.

384 "My goodness . . . I didn't even think I would ever have one orchid": Doris Beckwith to Peggy Beckwith, undated, Hildene archives.

384 Crans spent the war years hunting German submarines: Crans Jr. interview.

384 She planted a victory garden, canned vegetables: King, 187.

385 On July 27, 1949, the clock that started ticking: Mearns, 135.

385 "Not since that morning in the Petersen House": Ibid.

385 "There was a hush and then dead silence": Ruth Painter Randall, *I Ruth: Autobiography of a Marriage* (Boston: Little, Brown & Co., 1968), 7. Mrs. Randall married the great Lincoln scholar John G. Randall, and became a Lincoln scholar herself.

386 "Here, for the first time, was Abraham Lincoln": Mearns, 136.

386 The one-time Lincoln wild child died: *Washington Post*, 6 January 1948.

387 "I guess the Lincolns were surprised when Jessie": *Chicago Tribune*, 20 March 1952.

388 Warren Beckwith had left a "large fortune": *The Lincoln Newsletter*, Vol. VI, No. 6, Spring 1986.

388 "As the fellow says, 'Here it is Monday": Peggy Beckwith to Emily Paschal, 11 June 1959. Emily Paschal was Mary Harlan Lincoln's housekeeper in Mount Pleasant, Iowa. Courtesy, Iowa Wesleyan College archives.

388 She found two baby raccoons on the road one night: C. J. King, 195.

389 Peggy's devotion to her three dogs: Ibid., 198.

390 "To be addressed as a member of an organization": Peggy Beckwith to Iowa Wesleyan College, Hildene archives.

390 'There's Lincoln's great-granddaughter': Beschloss, 56.

391 "The aggression of the federal government in forcing integration concerns me": Peggy Beckwith interview with UPI, published in the *Washington Post*, 14 February 1963.

391 "You might as well write me another": Interview with Frank Bareford, Beckwith family friend, 7 October 2006.

391 "Get that one on the way back": Tom Grove Jr. interview.

392 "Why in the world are you letting it stay out here in ruins?": Interview with Beckwith family friend in 2006. The source has requested anonymity due to the sensitive nature of the information.

? He blamed his speech impediment on insecurities: Interview with Lenora Hoverson, Robert Todd Lincoln Beckwith's stepdaughter, 23 August 2006.

395 She was so overweight she could not lift herself out: Barbara Robins interview, 9 August 2007. She attended the services.

395 "I called Maggie and I asked her to divorce me": James Fristoe interview, 2 November 2007.

396 "For many years all of the leading scholars assumed": *Lincoln Newsletter*, Vol. VI, Vol. 6, Spring 1986.

396 "She's a big, fat gal who doesn't give a damn": Beschloss, 56.

396 "I never take part in politics": Ibid.

396 It was said that Disney would well up with tears: New York World's Fair Web site (www.NYWF64.com).

397 "He also inherited the spells of melancholy": *Lincoln Newsletter*, Vol. VI, Vol. 6, Spring 1986.

24. FATHER UNKNOWN

398 "Bar hopping in Picher was an all-day experience": Orville Ray interview, 25 October 2007. Ray is a long-time resident of Picher, Oklahoma.

398 Jack Coffelt grew up destitute in this outlaw town: Byron H. Brown, "The Discovery of D. B. Cooper," *Las Vegan Magazine*, Pt. 1, November 1983. The author is indebted to the work of the late Byron Brown for his investigation into the background of Jack Coffelt.

399 "He was a hard case, which is understandable": E-mail from Robert Hoyt to author, 22 August 2007.

000 considered it spellbinding: Brown, *Las Vegan Magazine*.

400 "I don't like to talk about that part of my life": Brief phone conversation with Annemarie Hoffman, 29 October 2007.

400 "a tall blonde in a stunning blue dress": Hoyt e-mail to author, 30 September 2007.

400 Records at the University of Kansas show that Annemarie was enrolled: E-mail from University of Kansas, 24 October 2007.

400 "I do everything Jack orders": Brown, *Las Vegan Magazine*, Pt. 1, October 1983, 74.

400–401 "I never loved anyone like I loved her": Ibid.

401 "throw a warm and friendly bear hug" around Coffelt: Brown, Pt. II, November 1983, 90.

401 Beckwith opened a joint checking account with Coffelt: Beckwith interrogatory, 12 April 1974, from *Robert T. L. Beckwith v. Annemarie Hoffman Beckwith*, District of Columbia Court of Appeals, Docket No. 9426 (Also filed under Superior Court of the District of Columbia, Family Division, Docket No. 3797-73).

401 "I'm telling you, it was like a soap opera": Lenora Hoverson interview, 23 August, 2006.

403 "He was always coming into the office": John Beck interview, 22 October 2007.

403 "I think Beckwith wanted an heir": Beschloss, 58.

403–404 she "refused" to say who was: *Beckwith v. Beckwith* lawsuit.

404 Beckwith's lawyer drew up a document, entitled "Agreement": Ibid.

404 "fraud and duress": Ibid.

404 Fourteen hours later, at Williamsburg Community Hospital: Records from Williamsburg Community Hospital, on file in *Beckwith v. Beckwith*.

404 "I was practically on the doorsteps of the hospital": John Beck interview.

406 Apartment 108 was filled with historical relics from Beckwith's illustrious family: *Chicago Tribune*, published in *Washington Post*, 16 April 1967.

407 Beckwith had "destroyed her happiness": Annemarie Hoffman Beckwith affidavit, *Beckwith v. Beckwith*.

407 Jack Coffelt told the writer Byron Brown that he was "constantly": Brown, *Las Vegan Magazine*, Pt. II, 91.

407 "Jack gave me these as payment for my legal services": Ibid, 84.

408 "Dad was old school, American pie": Interview with Robert Dobbs's daughter, Debbie Fields, 19 August 2007.

408 *"Burn this letter"*: Brown, *Las Vegan Magazine*, Pt. II, 85.

408 "She was a stranger in a foreign land, and she needed help": Thomas Penfield Jackson interview, 21 July 2007. Jackson is now a retired federal judge.

408 "I felt really sorry for her": Patricia Gurne interview, 24 July 2007.

409 "A trial is a search for truth," Judge Ryan said: Ryan quoted from *Beckwith v. Beckwith*, 19 March 1975.

409 "Socially, it's not done": Elizabeth Young, quoted in *Washington Post*, 26 December 1985.

409 "That's what I'm working on right now": *New York Times*, 20 June 1976.

409 "An acquaintance in Berlin telephoned me to tell me": Annemarie Hoffman Beckwith affidavit, from *Beckwith v. Beckwith*; *Washington Post*, 20 July 1976.

410 found Annemarie in contempt, in abstentia: Ibid.

410 "Subsequent to your marriage to the defendant": Beckwith quotes from interrogatories, 12 April 1974.

411 Beckwith was "sterilized in 1962 and has been sterile since that time": *Washington Post*, 20 July 1976.

411 "Mr. Beckwith was completely sterile: *Washington Post*, 5 August 1976.

411 the product of an "adulterous relationship": Ibid.

411 What if Annemarie had been "forced": Ibid.

411 "more than sufficient to support the trial court's finding of adultery": District of Columbia Court of Appeals. Case argued 13 November 1975; decided 1 April 1976.

25. THE COOPER CONNECTION

413 her ashes spread over the promontory: Donald B. Keelan, *Robert Todd Lincoln's Hildene and How It Was Saved* (Arlington, Vermont. The Keelan Family Foundation, 2001), 1.

413 "Why should anybody be interested in all this old stuff": *The Lincoln Newsletter*, Vol. X, No. 1, Spring 1991.

414 "seriously damaged," went one comment in his report: Keelan, 21.

414 "Their personalities meshed," said Hickey's wife, Betty: Interview with Betty Hickey, 10 August 2006; background on James Hickey, *Lincoln Newsletter*, Vol. 5, No. 3, Winter 1985.

415 "You know, the Lincolns are very private people": Elizabeth Young quoted by Barbara Hughett in *Lincoln Newsletter*, Vol. X, No. 1, Spring 1991.

416 they had never seen anything like this extraordinary cache: Neely and McMurtry, xi.

416 "I believe that because of this file history will treat": Neely and McMurtry, foreword to *The Insanity File*, dated May 1981, written by R. T. L. Beckwith.

417 Coffelt was now sitting in this squalid motel room: Brown, *Las Vegan Magazine*, Part I, 73.

417 on Thanksgiving Eve, November 24, 1971: Ralph P. Himmelsbach and Thomas K. Worcester, *NORJACK: The Investigation of D. B. Cooper* (West Linn, Oregon:

NORJACK Project, 1986), 14–16. Himmelsbach was the FBI agent in charge of the case. The details of the hijacking in this book are drawn from Himmelsbach's account.

418 "magical combination" of initials: Ibid., 53.

419 "A legend was born": Ibid.

419 "I'm D. B. Cooper. I need your help": the quotes attributed to Coffelt are taken from Brown's article in *Las Vegan Magazine*.

421 They felt certain that Coffelt had hired some cronies to eliminate them: Ibid., 79.

421 describing Jack Coffelt's nasty leg injuries: Interview with Beth Brown, 30 August 2007.

421 "He was a walking cripple": Sandra Sue Grafton interview, 16 October 2007. She said Barbara McClean told her about Coffelt's leg injury. Barbara McClean is deceased.

421 that is how the federal agency first linked Coffelt's name to the skyjacking: Ralph Himmelsbach interview, 23 August 2007.

422 Robert Dobbs of Memphis, Tennessee, had received a call from Coffelt from Portland: Brown, *Las Vegan Magazine*, Pt. II, 85. Dobbs is deceased.

422 Coffelt's medical records from the facility were subpoenaed: Himmelsbach, *NORJACK*, 122.

422 "Coffelt did not do it": Himmelsbach interview.

422 three FBI agents came to her house: Louise Brown interview, 9 September 2007.

EPILOGUE: THE LAST LINCOLN

425 "It was painful for Mom": Crans Jr., 23 September 2006.

425 this inscription on the largest bell: *Washington Post*, 29 June 2002.

426 "The house was going to fall down": Lenora Hoverson, 23 August 2006.

426 "They were good friends, and they were both without spouses": Tom Grove Jr., 30 September 2006.

427 Elizabeth Young, was quoted as saying she did not believe Beckwith left any descendants: *Washington Post*, 26 December 1985.

428 "I have yet to have the perfect lawsuit": Beck interview, 22 October 2007.

Bibliography

Ackerman, Kenneth D. *Dark Horse: The Surprise Election and Political Murder of President James A. Garfield*. New York: Caroll & Graf, 2003.

Altgeld, John P. *Live Questions: Including Our Penal Machinery and Its Victims*. Chicago: Donohue & Hennebery, 1890.

Anderson, Lars. *Letters and Journals of a Diplomat*. London & Edinburgh: Fleming H. Revell Co., 1940.

Baker, Jean H. *Mary Todd Lincoln: A Biography*. New York: W. W. Norton & Company, 1987.

Bayne, Julia Taft. *Tad Lincoln's Father*. Lincoln, Nebraska: University of Nebraska Press, 2001.

Bernhardt, Sarah. *Memories of My Life*. New York: D. Appleton & Co., 1907.

Beschloss, Michael. "The Last of the Lincolns," *The New Yorker* (28 February 1994): 54–58.

Birmingham, Stephen. *Our Crowd: The Great Jewish Families of New York*. New York: Harper & Row, 1967.

Bishop, Jim. *The Day Lincoln Was Shot*. New York: Random House, 1955.

Boyden, Anna L. *War Reminiscences: A Record of Mrs. Rebecca R. Pomroy's Experience in War-times*. Boston: D. Lothrop & Co., 1884.

Bremer, Fredrika. *The Homes of the New World: Impressions of America*. New York: Harper & Brothers, 1853.

Brigham, Johnson. *James Harlan*. Iowa City, Iowa: The State Historical Society of Iowa, 1913.

Brown, Byron H. "The Discovery of D. B. Cooper," *Las Vegan Magazine*, Part I (November 1983): 70-79; Part II (December 1983): 66-92.

Brown, Dee. *Bury My Heart at Wounded Knee*. New York: Henry Holt & Co., 1970.

Butler, Nicholas Murray. *Across the Busy Years*. New York: Charles Scribner's Sons, 1939.

Butt, Archibald, Lawrence F. Abbott, ed. *The Letters of Archie Butt, Personal Aide to President Roosevelt*. Garden City: New Jersey: Doubleday, Page & Co., 1924.

Carpenter, Francis B. *The Inner Life of Abraham Lincoln: Six Months at the White House*. Lincoln, Nebraska: University of Nebraska Press, 1995.

Cromie, Robert. *The Great Chicago Fire*. Nashville: Rutledge Hill Press, 1958.

Crook, William H., Margarita Spalding Gerry, ed. *Through Five Administrations: Reminiscences of Colonel William H. Crook, Bodyguard to President Lincoln*. New York: Harper & Brothers, 1907.

Danforth, Isaac Newton. *The Life of Nathan Smith Davis, A.M., M.D., LL.D.* Chicago: Cleveland Press, 1907.

Donald, David Herbert. *Lincoln's Herndon*. New York: Knopf, 1948.

Emerson, Jason. *The Madness of Mary Lincoln*. Carbondale, Illinois: Southern Illinois University Press, 2007.

Evans, W. A. *Mrs. Abraham Lincoln: A Study of her Personality and Her Influence on Lincoln*. New York: Knopf, 1932.

Everett, Marshall. *Complete Life of William McKinley and Story of His Assassination*. Whitefish, Montana: Kessinger Publishing Co., 1901.

Fox, Stephen. *Transatlantic: Samuel Cunard, Isambard Brunel, and the Great Atlantic Steamships*. New York: HarperCollins, 2004.

Friedman, Jane M. *America's First Woman Lawyer: The Biography of Myra Bradwell*. Amherst, New York: Prometheus Books, 1993.

Goff, John S. *Robert Todd Lincoln: A Man in His Own Right*. Norman, Oklahoma: University of Oklahoma Press, 1969.

Goodwin, Doris Kearns. *Team of Rivals: The Political Genius of Abraham Lincoln*. New York: Simon & Schuster, 2005.

Grant, Julia Dent. *The Personal Memoirs of Julia Dent Grant*. New York: G. P. Putnam's Sons, 1875.

Hamilton, Gail. *Life in Letters, Vol. II*. Boston: Lee & Shepard, 1901.

Hanchett, William. *Out of the Wilderness: The Life of Abraham Lincoln*. Champaign, Illinois: University of Illinois Press, 1994.

Helm, Katherine. *Mary, Wife of Lincoln*. New York: Harper & Brothers, 1928.

Herndon, William H. and Jesse W. Weik. *Herndon's Life of Lincoln*. Cleveland: World Publishing Co., 1888.

Himmelsbach, Ralph P., and Thomas K. Worcester. *NORJACK: The Investigation of D. B. Cooper*. West Linn, Oregon: NORJACK Project, 1986.

Keckley, Elizabeth. *Behind the Scenes, or Thirty Years a Slave, and Four Years in the White House*. New York: G. W. Carleton & Co., 1868.

Keelan, Donald B. *Robert Todd Lincoln's Hildene and How It Was Saved*. Arlington, Vermont: The Keelan Family Foundation, 2001.

King, C. J. *Four Marys and a Jessie: The Story of the Lincoln Women*. Manchester, Vermont: Friends of Hildene, Inc., 2005.

King, Willard L. *Lincoln's Manager: David Davis*. Cambridge, Massachusetts: Harvard University Press, 1960.

Lachman, Dr. H. M. *Battle of the Gnomes: The Struggle for Survival in a Microbial World*. Enfield, New Hampshire: Science Publishers, 2006.

Laughlin, Rosemary. *The Pullman Strike of 1894*. Greensboro, North Carolina: Morgan Reynolds, 2006.

Marshall, W. G. *Through America, Or: Nine Months in the United States*. New York: Arno Press, 1881.

Mearns, David C. *The Lincoln Papers, Vol. I*. Garden City, New York: Doubleday, 1948.

Mumler, William H. *Personal Experiences of William H. Mumler in Spirit Photography.* New York: Colby & Rich, 1875.

Neely, Mark E., Jr. and Harold Holzer. *The Lincoln Family Album.* New York: Doubleday, 1990.

Neely, Mark E., Jr., and R. Gerald McMurtry. *The Insanity File: The Case of Mary Todd Lincoln.* Carbondale, Illinois: Southern Illinois University Press, 1986.

Nevins, Allan. *Henry White: Thirty Years of American Diplomacy.* New York: Harper & Brothers, 1930.

Palmer, John McAuley. *The Bench and Bar of Illinois: Historical and Reminiscent.* Chicago: The Lewis Publishing Co., 1899.

Pendel, Thomas F. *Thirty-Six Years in the White House.* Washington, D.C.: Neale Publishing Co., 1901.

Porter, General Horace. *The Surrender at Appomattox Court House*, Battles and Leaders of the Civil War, Vol. 4. New York: The Century Co., 1884.

Pratt, Harry E., ed. *Concerning Mr. Lincoln.* Springfield: The Abraham Lincoln Association, 1944.

Randall, Ruth Painter. *I Ruth: Autobiography of a Marriage.* Boston: Little, Brown and Co., 1968.

Randall, Ruth Painter. *Lincoln's Sons.* Boston: Little, Brown and Company, 1955.

Randall, Ruth Painter. *Mary Lincoln: Biography of a Marriage.* Boston: Little, Brown and Company, 1953.

Rosenberg, Charles. *The Trial of the Assassin Guiteau.* Chicago: University of Chicago Press, 1968.

Ross, Ishbel. *Charmers and Cranks.* New York: Harper & Row, 1965.

Ross, Rodney A. "Mary Todd Lincoln, Patient at Bellevue Place," *Journal of the Illinois State Historical Society* (Spring 1970): 5-34.

Sandburg, Carl. *Abraham Lincoln: The Prairie Years, Vol. II.* New York: Harcourt, Brace & Co., 1926.

Santley, Charles. *Reminiscences of My Life.* London: Isaac Pitman, 1909.

Schreiner, Samuel A., Jr., *The Trials of Mrs. Lincoln.* Lincoln, Nebraska: University of Nebraska Press, 1987.

Segal, Charles M., ed. *Conversations with Lincoln.* New York: G. P. Putnam's Sons, 1961.

Smith, Theodore Clarke. *The Life and Letters of James Abram Garfield, Vol. II.* New Haven, Connecticut: Yale University Press, 1925.

Snow, Florence L. *Pictures on My Wall: A Lifetime in Kansas.* Lawrence, Kansas: University of Kansas Press, 1945.

Sperry, F. M. *A Group of Distinguished Physicians and Surgeons of Chicago.* Chicago: J. H. Beers & Co., 1904.

Steers, Edward Jr. *Blood on the Moon.* Lexington, Kentucky: University Press of Kentucky, 2001.

Stein, R. Conrad. *The Pullman Strike and the Labor Movement in American History.* Berkeley Heights, New Jersey: Enslow Publishers, 2001.

Tarbell, Ida. *All In a Day's Work: An Autobiography.* New York: Macmillan, 1939.

Todd, Alden. *Abandoned: The Story of the Greely Artic Expedition 1881–1884.* Fairbanks, Alaska: University of Alaska Press, 2001.

Trefousse, Hans L. *Andrew Johnson: A Biography.* New York: W. W. Norton, 1989.

Turkel, Stanley. *Great Hoteliers: Pioneers of the Hotel Industry.* Jefferson, North Carolina: McFarland & Co, 2006.

Turner, Justin G., and Linda Levitt Turner, eds. *Mary Todd Lincoln, Her Life and Letters.* New York: Knopf, 1972.

Vowell, Sarah. *Assassination Vacation.* New York: Simon & Schuster, 2005.

Waddington, Mary King. *Letters of a Diplomat's Wife, 1883–1900.* New York: Charles Scribner's Sons, 1903.

Welles, Gideon. *The Diary of Gideon Welles: Secretary of the Navy under Lincoln and Johnson, Vol. II.* Boston and New York: Houghton Mifflin Co., 1911.

Whipple, Wayne. *The Story-Life of Lincoln: A Biography Composed of Five Hundred True Stories.* Philadelphia: The John C. Winston Company, 1908.

Winik, Jay. *April 1865.* New York: HarperPerennial, 2006.

Index

About the Author

CHARLES LACHMAN is the executive producer of the television program *Inside Edition*. *The Last Lincolns* is his second book. He is also the author of *In the Name of the Law*.